COLLAPSE

COLLAPSE

HOW SOCIETIES CHOOSE
TO FAIL OR SUCCEED

JARED DIAMOND

VIKING

VIKING
Published by the Penguin Group
Penguin Group (USA) Inc., 375 Hudson Street,
New York, New York 10014, U.S.A.
Penguin Group (Canada), 10 Alcorn Avenue, Toronto, Ontario, Canada M4V 3B2
(a division of Pearson Penguin Canada Inc.)
Penguin Books Ltd, 80 Strand, London WC2R 0RL, England
Penguin Ireland, 25 St. Stephen's Green, Dublin 2, Ireland
(a division of Penguin Books Ltd)
Penguin Books Australia Ltd, 250 Camberwell Road, Camberwell, Victoria 3124, Australia
(a division of Pearson Australia Group Pty Ltd)
Penguin Books India Pvt Ltd, 11 Community Centre, Panchsheel Park,
New Delhi—110 017, India
Penguin Group (NZ), Cnr Airborne and Rosedale Roads, Albany,
Auckland 1310, New Zealand
(a division of Pearson New Zealand Ltd)
Penguin Books (South Africa) (Pty) Ltd, 24 Sturdee Avenue,
Rosebank, Johannesburg 2196, South Africa

Penguin Books Ltd, Registered Offices: 80 Strand, London WC2R 0RL, England

First published in 2005 by Viking Penguin, a member of Penguin Group (USA) Inc.

9 10 8

Maps by Jeffrey L. Ward

LIBRARY OF CONGRESS CATALOGING IN PUBLICATION DATA
Diamond, Jared M.
Collapse: how societies choose to fail or succeed/Jared Diamond.
p. cm.
Includes index.
ISBN 0-670-03337-5
1. Social history—Case studies. 2. Social change—Case studies. 3. Environmental policy—
Case studies. I. Title.
HN13. D5 2005
304.2'8—dc22   2004057152

This book is printed on acid-free paper. ∞

Printed in the United States of America
Set in Minion
Designed by Francesca Belanger

To
Jack and Ann Hirschy,
Jill Hirschy Eliel and John Eliel,
Joyce Hirschy McDowell,
Dick (1929–2003) and Margy Hirschy,
and their fellow Montanans:
guardians of Montana's big sky

I met a traveler from an antique land
Who said: "Two vast and trunkless legs of stone
Stand in the desert. Near them, on the sand,
Half sunk, a shattered visage lies, whose frown,
And wrinkled lip and sneer of cold command,
Tell that its sculptor well those passions read,
Which yet survive, stampt on these lifeless things,
The hand that mockt them and the heart that fed:
And on the pedestal these words appear:
'My name is Ozymandias, king of kings:
Look on my works, ye Mighty, and despair!'
Nothing beside remains. Round the decay
Of that colossal wreck, boundless and bare
The lone and level sands stretch far away."

"Ozymandias," by Percy Bysshe Shelley (1817)

CONTENTS

LIST OF MAPS

COLLAPSE

A Tale of Two Farms

Two farms ■ Collapses, past and present ■ Vanished Edens? ■
A five-point framework ■ Businesses and the environment ■
The comparative method ■ Plan of the book ■

A few summers ago I visited two dairy farms, Huls Farm and Gardar Farm, which despite being located thousands of miles apart were still remarkably similar in their strengths and vulnerabilities. Both were by far the largest, most prosperous, most technologically advanced farms in their respective districts. In particular, each was centered around a magnificent state-of-the-art barn for sheltering and milking cows. Those structures, both neatly divided into opposite-facing rows of cow stalls, dwarfed all other barns in the district. Both farms let their cows graze outdoors in lush pastures during the summer, produced their own hay to harvest in the late summer for feeding the cows through the winter, and increased their production of summer fodder and winter hay by irrigating their fields. The two farms were similar in area (a few square miles) and in barn size, Huls barn holding somewhat more cows than Gardar barn (200 vs. 165 cows, respectively). The owners of both farms were viewed as leaders of their respective societies. Both owners were deeply religious. Both farms were located in gorgeous natural settings that attract tourists from afar, with backdrops of high snow-capped mountains drained by streams teaming with fish, and sloping down to a famous river (below Huls Farm) or fjord (below Gardar Farm).

Those were the shared strengths of the two farms. As for their shared vulnerabilities, both lay in districts economically marginal for dairying, because their high northern latitudes meant a short summer growing season in which to produce pasture grass and hay. Because the climate was thus suboptimal even in good years, compared to dairy farms at lower latitudes, both farms were susceptible to being harmed by climate change, with drought or cold being the main concerns in the districts of Huls Farm or Gardar Farm respectively. Both districts lay far from population centers to which they could market their products, so that transportation costs and hazards placed them at a competitive disadvantage compared to more centrally located districts. The economies of both farms were hostage to forces beyond their owners' control, such as the changing affluence and tastes of their customers and neighbors. On a larger scale, the economies of the countries in which both farms lay rose and fell with the waxing and waning of threats from distant enemy societies.

The biggest difference between Huls Farm and Gardar Farm is in their current status. Huls Farm, a family enterprise owned by five siblings and their spouses in the Bitterroot Valley of the western U.S. state of Montana, is currently prospering, while Ravalli County in which Huls Farm lies boasts one of the highest population growth rates of any American county. Tim, Trudy, and Dan Huls, who are among Huls Farm's owners, personally took me on a tour of their high-tech new barn, and patiently explained to me the attractions and vicissitudes of dairy farming in Montana. It is inconceivable that the United States in general, and Huls Farm in particular, will collapse in the foreseeable future. But Gardar Farm, the former manor farm of the Norse bishop of southwestern Greenland, was abandoned over 500 years ago. Greenland Norse society collapsed completely: its thousands of inhabitants starved to death, were killed in civil unrest or in war against an enemy, or emigrated, until nobody remained alive. While the strongly built stone walls of Gardar barn and nearby Gardar Cathedral are still standing, so that I was able to count the individual cow stalls, there is no owner to tell me today of Gardar's former attractions and vicissitudes. Yet when Gardar Farm and Norse Greenland were at their peak, their decline seemed as inconceivable as does the decline of Huls Farm and the U.S. today.

Let me make clear: in drawing these parallels between Huls and Gardar Farms, I am not claiming that Huls Farm and American society are doomed to decline. At present, the truth is quite the opposite: Huls Farm is in the process of expanding, its advanced new technology is being studied for adoption by neighboring farms, and the United States is now the most powerful country in the world. Nor am I claiming that farms or societies in general are prone to collapse: while some have indeed collapsed like Gardar, others have survived uninterruptedly for thousands of years. Instead, my trips to Huls and Gardar Farms, thousands of miles apart but visited during the same summer, vividly brought home to me the conclusion that even the richest, technologically most advanced societies today face growing environmental and economic problems that should not be underestimated. Many of our problems are broadly similar to those that undermined Gardar Farm and Norse Greenland, and that many other past societies also struggled to solve. Some of those past societies failed (like the Greenland Norse), and others succeeded (like the Japanese and Tikopians). The past offers us a rich database from which we can learn, in order that we may keep on succeeding.

Norse Greenland is just one of many past societies that collapsed or vanished, leaving behind monumental ruins such as those that Shelley imagined in his poem "Ozymandias." By collapse, I mean a drastic decrease in human population size and/or political/economic/social complexity, over a considerable area, for an extended time. The phenomenon of collapses is thus an extreme form of several milder types of decline, and it becomes arbitrary to decide how drastic the decline of a society must be before it qualifies to be labeled as a collapse. Some of those milder types of decline include the normal minor rises and falls of fortune, and minor political/economic/social restructurings, of any individual society; one society's conquest by a close neighbor, or its decline linked to the neighbor's rise, without change in the total population size or complexity of the whole region; and the replacement or overthrow of one governing elite by another. By those standards, most people would consider the following past societies to have been famous victims of full-fledged collapses rather than of just minor declines: the Anasazi and Cahokia within the boundaries of the modern U.S., the Maya cities in Central America, Moche and Tiwanaku societies in South America, Mycenean Greece and Minoan Crete in Europe, Great Zimbabwe in Africa, Angkor Wat and the Harappan Indus Valley cities in Asia, and Easter Island in the Pacific Ocean (map, pp. 4–5).

The monumental ruins left behind by those past societies hold a romantic fascination for all of us. We marvel at them when as children we first learn of them through pictures. When we grow up, many of us plan vacations in order to experience them at firsthand as tourists. We feel drawn to their often spectacular and haunting beauty, and also to the mysteries that they pose. The scales of the ruins testify to the former wealth and power of their builders—they boast "Look on my works, ye mighty, and despair!" in Shelley's words. Yet the builders vanished, abandoning the great structures that they had created at such effort. How could a society that was once so mighty end up collapsing? What were the fates of its individual citizens?—did they move away, and (if so) why, or did they die there in some unpleasant way? Lurking behind this romantic mystery is the nagging thought: might such a fate eventually befall our own wealthy society? Will tourists

Arctic Ocean

GREENLAN

NORTH AMERICA

MONTANA

CHACO CANYON, NEW MEXICO

CAHOKIA (St. Louis)

Los Angeles
CALIFORNIA
CHANNEL ISLANDS

Atlant

HISPANIOLA

MAYA

Pacific Ocean

TIKOPIA

MOCHE, PERU

MANGAREVA

TIWANAKU, BOLIVIA

SOUTH AMERICA

PITCAIRN ISLAND

EASTER ISLAND

0   Miles   2000   4000

0   Kilometers   4000

Scale at Equator

75°

60°

45°

30°

15°

0°

15°

30°

45°

60°

165°   180°   165°   150°   135°   120°   105°   90°   75°   60°   45°

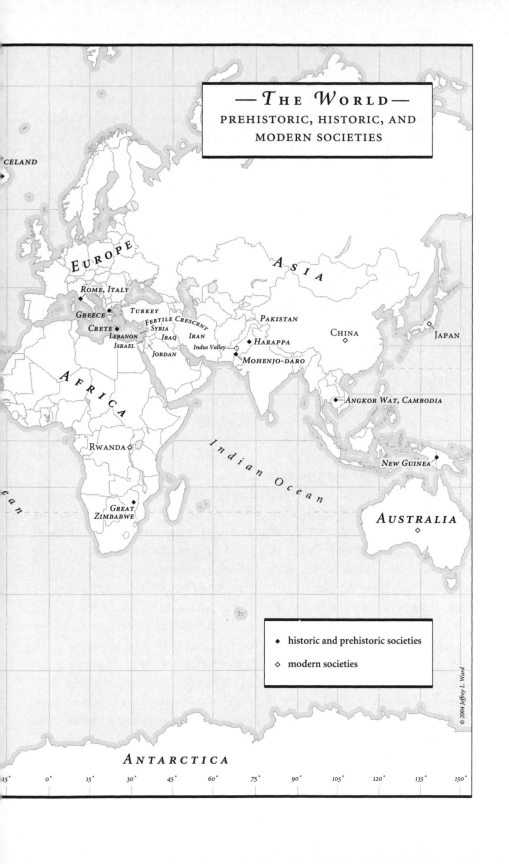

—THE WORLD—
PREHISTORIC, HISTORIC, AND
MODERN SOCIETIES

ICELAND

EUROPE

ASIA

ROME, ITALY

GREECE

TURKEY

CRETE

FERTILE CRESCENT

PAKISTAN

CHINA

JAPAN

LEBANON

SYRIA

IRAN

ISRAEL

IRAQ

Indus Valley

HARAPPA

JORDAN

MOHENJO-DARO

AFRICA

ANGKOR WAT, CAMBODIA

RWANDA

Indian Ocean

NEW GUINEA

GREAT ZIMBABWE

AUSTRALIA

ean

ANTARCTICA

◆ historic and prehistoric societies

◇ modern societies

15°   0°   15°   30°   45°   60°   75°   90°   105°   120°   135°   150°

someday stare mystified at the rusting hulks of New York's skyscrapers, much as we stare today at the jungle-overgrown ruins of Maya cities?

It has long been suspected that many of those mysterious abandonments were at least partly triggered by ecological problems: people inadvertently destroying the environmental resources on which their societies depended. This suspicion of unintended ecological suicide—ecocide—has been confirmed by discoveries made in recent decades by archaeologists, climatologists, historians, paleontologists, and palynologists (pollen scientists). The processes through which past societies have undermined themselves by damaging their environments fall into eight categories, whose relative importance differs from case to case: deforestation and habitat destruction, soil problems (erosion, salinization, and soil fertility losses), water management problems, overhunting, overfishing, effects of introduced species on native species, human population growth, and increased per-capita impact of people.

Those past collapses tended to follow somewhat similar courses constituting variations on a theme. Population growth forced people to adopt intensified means of agricultural production (such as irrigation, double-cropping, or terracing), and to expand farming from the prime lands first chosen onto more marginal land, in order to feed the growing number of hungry mouths. Unsustainable practices led to environmental damage of one or more of the eight types just listed, resulting in agriculturally marginal lands having to be abandoned again. Consequences for society included food shortages, starvation, wars among too many people fighting for too few resources, and overthrows of governing elites by disillusioned masses. Eventually, population decreased through starvation, war, or disease, and society lost some of the political, economic, and cultural complexity that it had developed at its peak. Writers find it tempting to draw analogies between those trajectories of human societies and the trajectories of individual human lives—to talk of a society's birth, growth, peak, senescence, and death—and to assume that the long period of senescence that most of us traverse between our peak years and our deaths also applies to societies. But that metaphor proves erroneous for many past societies (and for the modern Soviet Union): they declined rapidly after reaching peak numbers and power, and those rapid declines must have come as a surprise and shock to their citizens. In the worst cases of complete collapse, everybody in the society emigrated or died. Obviously, though, this grim trajectory is not one that all past societies followed unvaryingly to completion:

different societies collapsed to different degrees and in somewhat different ways, while many societies didn't collapse at all.

The risk of such collapses today is now a matter of increasing concern; indeed, collapses have already materialized for Somalia, Rwanda, and some other Third World countries. Many people fear that ecocide has now come to overshadow nuclear war and emerging diseases as a threat to global civilization. The environmental problems facing us today include the same eight that undermined past societies, plus four new ones: human-caused climate change, buildup of toxic chemicals in the environment, energy shortages, and full human utilization of the Earth's photosynthetic capacity. Most of these 12 threats, it is claimed, will become globally critical within the next few decades: either we solve the problems by then, or the problems will undermine not just Somalia but also First World societies. Much more likely than a doomsday scenario involving human extinction or an apocalyptic collapse of industrial civilization would be "just" a future of significantly lower living standards, chronically higher risks, and the undermining of what we now consider some of our key values. Such a collapse could assume various forms, such as the worldwide spread of diseases or else of wars, triggered ultimately by scarcity of environmental resources. If this reasoning is correct, then our efforts today will determine the state of the world in which the current generation of children and young adults lives out their middle and late years.

But the seriousness of these current environmental problems is vigorously debated. Are the risks greatly exaggerated, or conversely are they underestimated? Does it stand to reason that today's human population of almost seven billion, with our potent modern technology, is causing our environment to crumble globally at a much more rapid rate than a mere few million people with stone and wooden tools already made it crumble locally in the past? Will modern technology solve our problems, or is it creating new problems faster than it solves old ones? When we deplete one resource (e.g., wood, oil, or ocean fish), can we count on being able to substitute some new resource (e.g., plastics, wind and solar energy, or farmed fish)? Isn't the rate of human population growth declining, such that we're already on course for the world's population to level off at some manageable number of people?

All of these questions illustrate why those famous collapses of past civilizations have taken on more meaning than just that of a romantic mystery. Perhaps there are some practical lessons that we could learn from all those past collapses. We know that some past societies collapsed while others didn't: what made certain societies especially vulnerable? What, exactly, were the processes by which past societies committed ecocide? Why did some past societies fail to see the messes that they were getting into, and that (one would think in retrospect) must have been obvious? Which were the solutions that succeeded in the past? If we could answer these questions, we might be able to identify which societies are now most at risk, and what measures could best help them, without waiting for more Somalia-like collapses.

But there are also differences between the modern world and its problems, and those past societies and their problems. We shouldn't be so naïve as to think that study of the past will yield simple solutions, directly transferable to our societies today. We differ from past societies in some respects that put us at lower risk than them; some of those respects often mentioned include our powerful technology (i.e., its beneficial effects), globalization, modern medicine, and greater knowledge of past societies and of distant modern societies. We also differ from past societies in some respects that put us at greater risk than them: mentioned in that connection are, again, our potent technology (i.e., its unintended destructive effects), globalization (such that now a collapse even in remote Somalia affects the U.S. and Europe), the dependence of millions (and, soon, billions) of us on modern medicine for our survival, and our much larger human population. Perhaps we can still learn from the past, but only if we think carefully about its lessons.

Efforts to understand past collapses have had to confront one major controversy and four complications. The controversy involves resistance to the idea that past peoples (some of them known to be ancestral to peoples currently alive and vocal) did things that contributed to their own decline. We are much more conscious of environmental damage now than we were a mere few decades ago. Even signs in hotel rooms now invoke love of the environment to make us feel guilty if we demand fresh towels or let the water run. To damage the environment today is considered morally culpable.

Not surprisingly, Native Hawaiians and Maoris don't like paleontologists telling them that their ancestors exterminated half of the bird species that had evolved on Hawaii and New Zealand, nor do Native Americans like archaeologists telling them that the Anasazi deforested parts of the southwestern U.S. The supposed discoveries by paleontologists and archaeologists sound to some listeners like just one more racist pretext advanced by whites for dispossessing indigenous peoples. It's as if scientists were saying, "Your ancestors were bad stewards of their lands, so they deserved to be dispossessed." Some American and Australian whites, resentful of government payments and land retribution to Native Americans and Aboriginal Australians, do indeed seize on the discoveries to advance that argument today. Not only indigenous peoples, but also some anthropologists and archaeologists who study them and identify with them, view the recent supposed discoveries as racist lies.

Some of the indigenous peoples and the anthropologists identifying with them go to the opposite extreme. They insist that past indigenous peoples were (and modern ones still are) gentle and ecologically wise stewards of their environments, intimately knew and respected Nature, innocently lived in a virtual Garden of Eden, and could never have done all those bad things. As a New Guinea hunter once told me, "If one day I succeed in shooting a big pigeon in one direction from our village, I wait a week before hunting pigeons again, and then I go out in the opposite direction from the village." Only those evil modern First World inhabitants are ignorant of Nature, don't respect the environment, and destroy it.

In fact, both extreme sides in this controversy—the racists and the believers in a past Eden—are committing the error of viewing past indigenous peoples as fundamentally different from (whether inferior to or superior to) modern First World peoples. Managing environmental resources sustainably has *always* been difficult, ever since *Homo sapiens* developed modern inventiveness, efficiency, and hunting skills by around 50,000 years ago. Beginning with the first human colonization of the Australian continent around 46,000 years ago, and the subsequent prompt extinction of most of Australia's former giant marsupials and other large animals, every human colonization of a land mass formerly lacking humans—whether of Australia, North America, South America, Madagascar, the Mediterranean islands, or Hawaii and New Zealand and dozens of other Pacific islands—has been followed by a wave of extinction of large animals that had evolved without fear of humans and were easy to kill, or else succumbed to human-associated habitat changes, introduced pest species, and diseases. Any people can fall into the trap of overexploiting environmental resources, because of ubiquitous problems that we shall consider later in this book: that the resources initially seem inexhaustibly abundant; that signs of their incipient depletion become masked by normal fluctuations in resource levels between years or decades; that it's difficult to get people to agree on exercising restraint in harvesting a shared resource (the so-called tragedy of the commons, to be discussed in later chapters); and that the complexity of ecosystems often makes the consequences of some human-caused perturbation virtually impossible to predict even for a professional ecologist. Environmental problems that are hard to manage today were surely even harder to manage in the past. Especially for past non-literate peoples who couldn't read case studies of societal collapses, ecological damage constituted a tragic, unforeseen, unintended consequence of their best efforts, rather than morally culpable blind or conscious selfishness. The societies that ended up collapsing were (like the Maya) among the most creative and (for a time) advanced and successful of their times, rather than stupid and primitive.

Past peoples were neither ignorant bad managers who deserved to be exterminated or dispossessed, nor all-knowing conscientious environmentalists who solved problems that we can't solve today. They were people like us, facing problems broadly similar to those that we now face. They were prone either to succeed or to fail, depending on circumstances similar to those making us prone to succeed or to fail today. Yes, there are differences between the situation we face today and that faced by past peoples, but there are still enough similarities for us to be able to learn from the past.

Above all, it seems to me wrongheaded and dangerous to invoke historical assumptions about environmental practices of native peoples in order to justify treating them fairly. In many or most cases, historians and archaeologists have been uncovering overwhelming evidence that this assumption (about Eden-like environmentalism) is wrong. By invoking this assumption to justify fair treatment of native peoples, we imply that it would be OK to mistreat them if that assumption could be refuted. In fact, the case against mistreating them isn't based on any historical assumption about their environmental practices: it's based on a moral principle, namely, that it is morally wrong for one people to dispossess, subjugate, or exterminate another people.

That's the controversy about past ecological collapses. As for the complications, of course it's not true that all societies are doomed to collapse because of environmental damage: in the past some societies did while others didn't; the real question is why only some societies proved fragile, and what distinguished those that collapsed from those that didn't. Some societies that I shall discuss, such as the Icelanders and Tikopians, succeeded in solving extremely difficult environmental problems, have thereby been able to persist for a long time, and are still going strong today. For example, when Norwegian colonists of Iceland first encountered an environment superficially similar to that of Norway but in reality very different, they inadvertently destroyed much of Iceland's topsoil and most of its forests. Iceland for a long time was Europe's poorest and most ecologically ravaged country. However, Icelanders eventually learned from experience, adopted rigorous measures of environmental protection, and now enjoy one of the highest per-capita national average incomes in the world. Tikopia Islanders inhabit a tiny island so far from any neighbors that they were forced to become self-sufficient in almost everything, but they micromanaged their resources and regulated their population size so carefully that their island is still productive after 3,000 years of human occupation. Thus, this book is not an uninterrupted series of depressing stories of failure, but also includes success stories inspiring imitation and optimism.

In addition, I don't know of any case in which a society's collapse can be attributed solely to environmental damage: there are always other contributing factors. When I began to plan this book, I didn't appreciate those complications, and I naïvely thought that the book would just be about environmental damage. Eventually, I arrived at a five-point framework of possible contributing factors that I now consider in trying to understand any putative environmental collapse. Four of those sets of factors—environmental damage, climate change, hostile neighbors, and friendly trade partners—may or may not prove significant for a particular society. The fifth set of factors—the society's responses to its environmental problems—always proves significant. Let's consider these five sets of factors one by one, in a sequence not implying any primacy of cause but just convenience of presentation.

A first set of factors involves damage that people inadvertently inflict on their environment, as already discussed. The extent and reversibility of that damage depend partly on properties of people (e.g., how many trees they cut down per acre per year), and partly on properties of the environment (e.g., properties determining how many seedlings germinate per acre, and how rapidly saplings grow, per year). Those environmental properties are referred to either as fragility (susceptibility to damage) or as resilience (potential for recovery from damage), and one can talk separately of the fragility or resilience of an area's forests, its soils, its fish populations, and so on. Hence the reasons why only certain societies suffered environmental collapses might in principle involve either exceptional imprudence of their people, exceptional fragility of some aspects of their environment, or both.

A next consideration in my five-point framework is climate change, a term that today we tend to associate with global warming caused by humans. In fact, climate may become hotter or colder, wetter or drier, or more or less variable between months or between years, because of changes in natural forces that drive climate and that have nothing to do with humans. Examples of such forces include changes in the heat put out by the sun, volcanic eruptions that inject dust into the atmosphere, changes in the orientation of the Earth's axis with respect to its orbit, and changes in the distribution of land and ocean over the face of the Earth. Frequently discussed cases of natural climate change include the advance and retreat of continental ice sheets during the Ice Ages beginning over two million years ago, the so-called Little Ice Age from about A.D. 1400 to 1800, and the global cooling following the enormous volcanic eruption of Indonesia's Mt. Tambora on April 5, 1815. That eruption injected so much dust into the upper atmosphere that the amount of sunlight reaching the ground decreased until the dust settled out, causing widespread famines even in North America and Europe due to cold temperatures and reduced crop yields in the summer of 1816 ("the year without a summer").

Climate change was even more of a problem for past societies with short human lifespans and without writing than it is today, because climate in many parts of the world tends to vary not just from year to year but also on a multi-decade time scale; e.g., several wet decades followed by a dry half-century. In many prehistoric societies the mean human generation time—average number of years between births of parents and of their children—was only a few decades. Hence towards the end of a string of wet decades, most people alive could have had no firsthand memory of the previous period of dry climate. Even today, there is a human tendency to increase production and population during good decades, forgetting (or, in the past, never realizing) that such decades were unlikely to last. When the good decades then do end, the society finds itself with more population than can be supported, or with ingrained habits unsuitable to the new climate conditions. (Just think today of the dry U.S. West and its urban or rural policies of profligate water use, often drawn up in wet decades on the tacit assumption that they were typical.) Compounding these problems of climate change, many past societies didn't have "disaster relief" mechanisms to import food surpluses from other areas with a different climate into areas developing food shortages. All of those considerations exposed past societies to increased risk from climate change.

Natural climate changes may make conditions either better or worse for any particular human society, and may benefit one society while hurting another society. (For example, we shall see that the Little Ice Age was bad for the Greenland Norse but good for the Greenland Inuit.) In many historical cases, a society that was depleting its environmental resources could absorb the losses as long as the climate was benign, but was then driven over the brink of collapse when the climate became drier, colder, hotter, wetter, or more variable. Should one then say that the collapse was caused by human environmental impact, or by climate change? Neither of those simple alternatives is correct. Instead, if the society hadn't already partly depleted its environmental resources, it might have survived the resource depletion caused by climate change. Conversely, it was able to survive its self-inflicted resource depletion until climate change produced further resource depletion. It was neither factor taken alone, but the combination of environmental impact and climate change, that proved fatal.

A third consideration is hostile neighbors. All but a few historical societies have been geographically close enough to some other societies to have had at least some contact with them. Relations with neighboring societies may be intermittently or chronically hostile. A society may be able to hold off its enemies as long as it is strong, only to succumb when it becomes weakened for any reason, including environmental damage. The proximate cause of the collapse will then be military conquest, but the ultimate cause—the factor whose change led to the collapse—will have been the factor that caused the weakening. Hence collapses for ecological or other reasons often masquerade as military defeats.

The most familiar debate about such possible masquerading involves the fall of the Western Roman Empire. Rome became increasingly beset by barbarian invasions, with the conventional date for the Empire's fall being taken somewhat arbitrarily as A.D. 476, the year in which the last emperor of the West was deposed. However, even before the rise of the Roman Empire, there had been "barbarian" tribes who lived in northern Europe and Central Asia beyond the borders of "civilized" Mediterranean Europe, and who periodically attacked civilized Europe (as well as civilized China and India). For over a thousand years, Rome successfully held off the barbarians, for instance slaughtering a large invading force of Cimbri and Teutones bent on conquering northern Italy at the Battle of Campi Raudii in 101 B.C.

Eventually, it was the barbarians rather than Romans who won the battles: what was the fundamental reason for that shift in fortune? Was it because of changes in the barbarians themselves, such that they became more numerous or better organized, acquired better weapons or more horses, or profited from climate change in the Central Asian steppes? In that case, we would say that barbarians really could be identified as the fundamental cause of Rome's fall. Or was it instead that the same old unchanged barbarians were always waiting on the Roman Empire's frontiers, and that they couldn't prevail until Rome became weakened by some combination of economic, political, environmental, and other problems? In that case we would blame Rome's fall on its own problems, with the barbarians just providing the coup de grâce. This question continues to be debated. Essentially the same question has been debated for the fall of the Khmer Empire centered on Angkor Wat in relation to invasions by Thai neighbors, for the decline in Harappan Indus Valley civilization in relation to Aryan invasions, and for the fall of Mycenean Greece and other Bronze Age Mediterranean societies in relation to invasions by Sea Peoples.

The fourth set of factors is the converse of the third set: decreased support by friendly neighbors, as opposed to increased attacks by hostile neighbors. All but a few historical societies have had friendly trade partners as well as neighboring enemies. Often, the partner and the enemy are one and the same neighbor, whose behavior shifts back and forth between friendly and hostile. Most societies depend to some extent on friendly neighbors, either for imports of essential trade goods (like U.S. imports of oil, and Japanese imports of oil, wood, and seafood, today), or else for cultural ties that lend cohesion to the society (such as Australia's cultural identity imported from Britain until recently). Hence the risk arises that, if your trade partner becomes weakened for any reason (including environmental damage) and can no longer supply the essential import or the cultural tie, your own society may become weakened as a result. This is a familiar problem today because of the First World's dependence on oil from ecologically fragile and politically troubled Third World countries that imposed an oil embargo in 1973. Similar problems arose in the past for the Greenland Norse, Pitcairn Islanders, and other societies.

The last set of factors in my five-point framework involves the ubiquitous question of the society's responses to its problems, whether those problems are environmental or not. Different societies respond differently to similar problems. For instance, problems of deforestation arose for many past societies, among which Highland New Guinea, Japan, Tikopia, and Tonga developed successful forest management and continued to prosper, while Easter Island, Mangareva, and Norse Greenland failed to develop successful forest management and collapsed as a result. How can we understand such differing outcomes? A society's responses depend on its political, economic, and social institutions and on its cultural values. Those institutions and values affect whether the society solves (or even tries to solve) its problems. In this book we shall consider this five-point framework for each past society whose collapse or persistence is discussed.

I should add, of course, that just as climate change, hostile neighbors, and trade partners may or may not contribute to a particular society's collapse, environmental damage as well may or may not contribute. It would be absurd to claim that environmental damage must be a major factor in all collapses: the collapse of the Soviet Union is a modern counter-example, and the destruction of Carthage by Rome in 146 B.C. is an ancient one. It's obviously true that military or economic factors alone may suffice. Hence a full title for this book would be "Societal collapses involving an environmental component, and in some cases also contributions of climate change, hostile neighbors, and trade partners, plus questions of societal responses." That restriction still leaves us ample modern and ancient material to consider.

Issues of human environmental impacts today tend to be controversial, and opinions about them tend to fall on a spectrum between two opposite camps. One camp, usually referred to as "environmentalist" or "pro-environment," holds that our current environmental problems are serious and in urgent need of addressing, and that current rates of economic and population growth cannot be sustained. The other camp holds that environmentalists' concerns are exaggerated and unwarranted, and that continued economic and population growth is both possible and desirable. The latter camp isn't associated with an accepted short label, and so I shall refer to it simply as "non-environmentalist." Its adherents come especially from the world of big business and economics, but the equation "non-environmentalist" = "pro-business" is imperfect; many businesspeople consider themselves environmentalists, and many people skeptical of environmentalists' claims are not in the world of big business. In writing this book, where do I stand myself with the respect to these two camps?

On the one hand, I have been a bird-watcher since I was seven years old. I trained professionally as a biologist, and I have been doing research on New Guinea rainforest birds for the past 40 years. I love birds, enjoy watching them, and enjoy being in rainforest. I also like other plants, animals, and habitats and value them for their own sakes. I've been active in many efforts to preserve species and natural environments in New Guinea and elsewhere.

For the past dozen years I've been a director of the U.S. affiliate of World Wildlife Fund, one of the largest international environmentalist organizations and the one with the most cosmopolitan interests. All of those things have earned me criticism from non-environmentalists, who use phrases such as "fearmonger," "Diamond preaches gloom and doom," "exaggerates risks," and "favors endangered purple louseworts over the needs of people." But while I do love New Guinea birds, I love much more my sons, my wife, my friends, New Guineans, and other people. I'm more interested in environmental issues because of what I see as their consequences for people than because of their consequences for birds.

On the other hand, I have much experience, interest, and ongoing involvement with big businesses and other forces in our society that exploit environmental resources and are often viewed as anti-environmentalist. As a teenager, I worked on large cattle ranches in Montana, to which, as an adult and father, I now regularly take my wife and my sons for summer vacations. I had a job on a crew of Montana copper miners for one summer. I love Montana and my rancher friends, I understand and admire and sympathize with their agribusinesses and their lifestyles, and I've dedicated this book to them. In recent years I've also had much opportunity to observe and become familiar with other large extractive companies in the mining, logging, fishing, oil, and natural gas industries. For the last seven years I've been monitoring environmental impacts in Papua New Guinea's largest producing oil and natural gas field, where oil companies have engaged World Wildlife Fund to provide independent assessments of the environment. I have often been a guest of extractive businesses on their properties, I've talked a lot with their directors and employees, and I've come to understand their own perspectives and problems.

While these relationships with big businesses have given me close-up views of the devastating environmental damage that they often cause, I've also had close-up views of situations where big businesses found it in their interests to adopt environmental safeguards more draconian and effective than I've encountered even in national parks. I'm interested in what motivates these differing environmental policies of different businesses. My involvement with large oil companies in particular has brought me condemnation from some environmentalists, who use phrases such as "Diamond has sold out to big business," "He's in bed with big businesses," or "He prostitutes himself to the oil companies."

In fact, I am not hired by big businesses, and I describe frankly what I see happening on their properties even though I am visiting as their guest.

On some properties I have seen oil companies and logging companies being destructive, and I have said so; on other properties I have seen them being careful, and that was what I said. My view is that, if environmentalists aren't willing to engage with big businesses, which are among the most powerful forces in the modern world, it won't be possible to solve the world's environmental problems. Thus, I am writing this book from a middle-of-the-road perspective, with experience of both environmental problems and of business realities.

How can one study the collapses of societies "scientifically"? Science is often misrepresented as "the body of knowledge acquired by performing replicated controlled experiments in the laboratory." Actually, science is something much broader: the acquisition of reliable knowledge about the world. In some fields, such as chemistry and molecular biology, replicated controlled experiments in the laboratory are feasible and provide by far the most reliable means to acquire knowledge. My formal training was in two such fields of laboratory biology, biochemistry for my undergraduate degree and physiology for my Ph.D. From 1955 to 2002 I conducted experimental laboratory research in physiology, at Harvard University and then at the University of California in Los Angeles.

When I began studying birds in New Guinea rainforest in 1964, I was immediately confronted with the problem of acquiring reliable knowledge without being able to resort to replicated controlled experiments, whether in the laboratory or outdoors. It's usually neither feasible, legal, nor ethical to gain knowledge about birds by experimentally exterminating or manipulating their populations at one site while maintaining their populations at another site as unmanipulated controls. I had to use different methods. Similar methodological problems arise in many other areas of population biology, as well as in astronomy, epidemiology, geology, and paleontology.

A frequent solution is to apply what is termed the "comparative method" or the "natural experiment"—i.e., to compare natural situations differing with respect to the variable of interest. For instance, when I as an ornithologist am interested in effects of New Guinea's Cinnamon-browed Melidectes Honeyeater on populations of other honeyeater species, I compare bird communities on mountains that are fairly similar except that some do and others don't happen to support populations of Cinnamon-browed Melidectes Honeyeaters. Similarly, my books *The Third Chimpanzee: The Evolution and Future of the Human Animal* and *Why Is Sex Fun?*

The Evolution of Human Sexuality compared different animal species, especially different species of primates, in an effort to figure out why women (unlike females of most other animal species) undergo menopause and lack obvious signs of ovulation, why men have a relatively large penis (by animal standards), and why humans usually have sex in private (rather than in the open, as almost all other animal species do). There is a large scientific literature on the obvious pitfalls of that comparative method, and on how best to overcome those pitfalls. Especially in historical sciences (like evolutionary biology and historical geology), where it's impossible to manipulate the past experimentally, one has no choice except to renounce laboratory experiments in favor of natural ones.

This book employs the comparative method to understand societal collapses to which environmental problems contribute. My previous book (*Guns, Germs, and Steel: The Fates of Human Societies*) had applied the comparative method to the opposite problem: the differing rates of buildup of human societies on different continents over the last 13,000 years. In the present book focusing instead on collapses rather than on buildups, I compare many past and present societies that differed with respect to environmental fragility, relations with neighbors, political institutions, and other "input" variables postulated to influence a society's stability. The "output" variables that I examine are collapse or survival, and form of the collapse if a collapse does occur. By relating output variables to input variables, I aim to tease out the influence of possible input variables on collapses.

A rigorous, comprehensive, and quantitative application of this method was possible for the problem of deforestation-induced collapses on Pacific islands. Prehistoric Pacific peoples deforested their islands to varying degrees, ranging from only slight to complete deforestation, and with societal outcomes ranging from long-term persistence to complete collapses that left everybody dead. For 81 Pacific islands my colleague Barry Rolett and I graded the extent of deforestation on a numerical scale, and we also graded values of nine input variables (such as rainfall, isolation, and restoration of soil fertility) postulated to influence deforestation. By a statistical analysis we were able to calculate the relative strengths with which each input variable predisposed the outcome to deforestation. Another comparative experiment was possible in the North Atlantic, where medieval Vikings from Norway colonized six islands or land masses differing in suitability for agriculture, ease of trade contact with Norway, and other input variables, and also differing in outcome (from quick abandonment, to everybody dead after 500 years, to still thriving after 1,200 years). Still other comparisons are possible between societies from different parts of the world.

All of these comparisons rest on detailed information about individual societies, patiently accumulated by archaeologists, historians, and other scholars. At the end of this book I provide references to the many excellent books and papers on the ancient Maya and Anasazi, the modern Rwandans and Chinese, and the other past and present societies that I compare. Those individual studies constitute the indispensable database for my book. But there are additional conclusions that can be drawn from comparisons among those many societies, and that could not have been drawn from detailed study of just a single society. For example, to understand the famous Maya collapse requires not only accurate knowledge of Maya history and the Maya environment; we can place the Maya in a broader context and gain further insights by comparing them with other societies that did or didn't collapse, and that resembled the Maya in some respects and differed from them in other respects. Those further insights require the comparative method.

I have belabored this necessity for both good individual studies and good comparisons, because scholars practicing one approach too often belittle the contributions of the other approach. Specialists in the history of one society tend to dismiss comparisons as superficial, while those who compare tend to dismiss studies of single societies as hopelessly myopic and of limited value for understanding other societies. But we need both types of studies if we are to acquire reliable knowledge. In particular, it would be dangerous to generalize from one society, or even just to be confident about interpreting a single collapse. Only from the weight of evidence provided by a comparative study of many societies with different outcomes can one hope to reach convincing conclusions.

So that readers will have some advance idea where they are heading, here is how this book is organized. Its plan resembles a boa constrictor that has swallowed two very large sheep. That is, my discussions of the modern world and also of the past both consist of a disproportionately long account of one society, plus briefer accounts of four other societies.

We shall begin with the first large sheep. Part One comprises a single lengthy chapter (Chapter 1), on the environmental problems of southwestern Montana, where Huls Farm and the ranches of my friends the Hirschys (to whom this book is dedicated) are located. Montana has the advantage of being a modern First World society whose environmental and population problems are real but still relatively mild compared to those of most of the rest of the First World. Above all, I know many Montanans well, so that I can connect the policies of Montana society to the often-conflicting motivations of individual people. From that familiar perspective of Montana, we can more easily imagine what was happening in the remote past societies that initially strike us as exotic, and where we can only guess what motivated individual people.

Part Two begins with four briefer chapters on past societies that did collapse, arranged in a sequence of increasing complexity according to my five-point framework. Most of the past societies that I shall discuss in detail were small and peripherally located, and some were geographically bounded, or socially isolated, or in fragile environments. Lest the reader thereby be misled into concluding that they are poor models for familiar big modern societies, I should explain that I selected them for close consideration precisely because processes unfolded faster and reached more extreme outcomes in such small societies, making them especially clear illustrations. It is not the case that large central societies trading with neighbors and located in robust environments didn't collapse in the past and can't collapse today. One of the past societies that I do discuss in detail, the Maya, had a population of many millions or tens of millions, was located within one of the two most advanced cultural areas of the New World before European arrival (Mesoamerica), and traded with and was decisively influenced by other advanced societies in that area. I briefly summarize in the Further Readings section for Chapter 9 some of the many other famous past societies— Fertile Crescent societies, Angkor Wat, Harappan Indus Valley society, and others—that resembled the Maya in those respects, and to whose declines environmental factors contributed heavily.

Our first case study from the past, the history of Easter Island (Chapter 2), is as close as we can get to a "pure" ecological collapse, in this case due to total deforestation that led to war, overthrow of the elite and of the famous stone statues, and a massive population die-off. As far as we know, Easter's Polynesian society remained isolated after its initial founding, so that Easter's trajectory was uninfluenced by either enemies or friends. Nor do we have evidence of a role of climate change on Easter, though that could still emerge from future studies. Barry Rolett's and my comparative analysis helps us understand why Easter, of all Pacific islands, suffered such a severe collapse.

Pitcairn Island and Henderson Island (Chapter 3), also settled by Polynesians, offer examples of the effect of item four of my five-point framework: loss of support from neighboring friendly societies. Both Pitcairn and Henderson islands suffered local environmental damage, but the fatal blow came from the environmentally triggered collapse of their major trade partner. There were no known complicating effects of hostile neighbors or of climate change.

Thanks to an exceptionally detailed climate record reconstructed from tree rings, the Native American society of the Anasazi in the U.S. Southwest (Chapter 4) clearly illustrates the intersection of environmental damage and population growth with climate change (in this case, drought). Neither friendly or hostile neighbors, nor (except towards the end) warfare, appear to have been major factors in the Anasazi collapse.

No book on societal collapses would be complete without an account (Chapter 5) of the Maya, the most advanced Native American society and the quintessential romantic mystery of cities covered by jungle. As in the case of the Anasazi, the Maya illustrate the combined effects of environmental damage, population growth, and climate change without an essential role of friendly neighbors. Unlike the case with the Anasazi collapse, hostile neighbors were a major preoccupation of Maya cities already from an early stage. Among the societies discussed in Chapters 2 through 5, only the Maya offer us the advantage of a deciphered written record.

Norse Greenland (Chapters 6–8) offers us our most complex case of a prehistoric collapse, the one for which we have the most information (because it was a well-understood literate European society), and the one warranting the most extended discussion: the second sheep inside the boa constrictor. All five items in my five-point framework are well documented: environmental damage, climate change, loss of friendly contacts with Norway, rise of hostile contacts with the Inuit, and the political, economic, social, and cultural setting of the Greenland Norse. Greenland provides us with our closest approximation to a controlled experiment in collapses: two societies (Norse and Inuit) sharing the same island, but with very different cultures, such that one of those societies survived while the other was dying. Thus, Greenland history conveys the message that, even in a harsh environment, collapse isn't inevitable but depends on a society's choices. Comparisons are also possible between Norse Greenland and five other North Atlantic societies founded by Norse colonists, to help us understand why the Orkney Norse thrived while their Greenland cousins were succumbing.

One of those five other Norse societies, Iceland, ranks as an outstanding success story of triumph over a fragile environment to achieve a high level of modern prosperity.

Part Two concludes (Chapter 9) with three more societies that (like Iceland) succeeded, as contrast cases for understanding societies that failed. While those three faced less severe environmental problems than Iceland or than most of those that failed, we shall see that there are two different paths to success: a bottom-up approach exemplified by Tikopia and the New Guinea highlands, and a top-down approach exemplified by Japan of the Tokugawa Era.

Part Three then returns to the modern world. Having already considered modern Montana in Chapter 2, we now take up four markedly different modern countries, the first two small and the latter two large or huge: a Third World disaster (Rwanda), a Third World survivor-so-far (the Dominican Republic), a Third World giant racing to catch up with the First World (China), and a First World society (Australia). Rwanda (Chapter 10) represents a Malthusian catastrophe happening under our eyes, an overpopulated land that collapsed in horrible bloodshed, as the Maya did in the past. Rwanda and neighboring Burundi are notorious for their Hutu/Tutsi ethnic violence, but we shall see that population growth, environmental damage, and climate change provided the dynamite for which ethnic violence was the fuse.

The Dominican Republic and Haiti (Chapter 11), sharing the island of Hispaniola, offer us a grim contrast, as did Norse and Inuit societies in Greenland. From decades of equally vile dictatorships, Haiti emerged as the modern New World's saddest basket case, while there are signs of hope in the Dominican Republic. Lest one suppose that this book preaches environmental determinism, the latter country illustrates what a big difference one person can make, especially if he or she is the country's leader.

China (Chapter 12) suffers from heavy doses of all 12 modern types of environmental problems. Because China is so huge in its economy, population, and area, China's environmental and economic impact is important not only for China's own people but also for the whole world.

Australia (Chapter 13) is at the opposite extreme from Montana, as the First World society occupying the most fragile environment and experiencing the most severe environmental problems. As a result, it is also among the countries now considering the most radical restructuring of its society, in order to solve those problems.

This book's concluding section (Part Four) extracts practical lessons for us today. Chapter 14 asks the perplexing question arising for every past society that ended up destroying itself, and that will perplex future earthlings if we too end up destroying ourselves: how could a society fail to have seen the dangers that seem so clear to us in retrospect? Can we say that their end was the inhabitants' own fault, or that they were instead tragic victims of insoluble problems? How much past environmental damage was unintentional and imperceptible, and how much was perversely wrought by people acting in full awareness of the consequences? For instance, what were Easter Islanders saying as they cut down the last tree on their island? It turns out that group decision-making can be undone by a whole series of factors, beginning with failure to anticipate or perceive a problem, and proceeding through conflicts of interest that leave some members of the group to pursue goals good for themselves but bad for the rest of the group.

Chapter 15 considers the role of modern businesses, some of which are among the most environmentally destructive forces today, while others provide some of the most effective environmental protection. We shall examine why some (but only some) businesses find it in their interests to be protective, and what changes would be necessary before other businesses would find it in their interests to emulate them.

Finally, Chapter 16 summarizes the types of environmental dangers facing the modern world, the commonest objections raised against claims of their seriousness, and differences between environmental dangers today and those faced by past societies. A major difference has to do with globalization, which lies at the heart of the strongest reasons both for pessimism and for optimism about our ability to solve our current environmental problems. Globalization makes it impossible for modern societies to collapse in isolation, as did Easter Island and the Greenland Norse in the past. Any society in turmoil today, no matter how remote—think of Somalia and Afghanistan as examples—can cause trouble for prosperous societies on other continents, and is also subject to their influence (whether helpful or destabilizing). For the first time in history, we face the risk of a global decline. But we also are the first to enjoy the opportunity of learning quickly from developments in societies anywhere else in the world today, and from what has unfolded in societies at any time in the past. That's why I wrote this book.

PART ONE

MODERN MONTANA

■ ■ ■

CHAPTER 1

Under Montana's Big Sky

Stan Falkow's story ■ Montana and me ■ Why begin with Montana? ■
Montana's economic history ■ Mining ■ Forests ■ Soil ■ Water ■
Native and non-native species ■ Differing visions ■
Attitudes towards regulation ■ Rick Laible's story ■
Chip Pigman's story ■ Tim Huls's story ■ John Cook's story ■
Montana, model of the world ■

When I asked my friend Stan Falkow, a 70-year-old professor of microbiology at Stanford University near San Francisco, why he had bought a second home in Montana's Bitterroot Valley, he told me how it had fitted into the story of his life:

"I was born in New York State and then moved to Rhode Island. That meant that, as a child, I knew nothing about mountains. While I was in my early 20s, just after graduating college, I took off a couple of years from my education to work on the night shift in a hospital autopsy room. For a young person like myself without previous experience of death, it was very stressful. A friend who had just returned from the Korean War and had seen a lot of stress there took one look at me and said, 'Stan, you look nervous; you need to reduce your stress level. Try fly-fishing!'

"So I started fly-fishing to catch bass. I learned how to tie my own flies, really got into it, and went fishing every day after work. My friend was right: it did reduce stress. But then I entered graduate school in Rhode Island and got into another stressful work situation. A fellow graduate student told me that bass weren't the only fish that one could catch by fly-fishing: I could also fly-fish for trout nearby in Massachusetts. So I took up trout-fishing. My thesis supervisor loved to eat fish, and he encouraged me to go fishing: those were the only occasions when he didn't frown at my taking time off from work in the laboratory.

"Around the time that I turned 50, it was another stressful period of my life, because of a difficult divorce and other things. By then, I was taking off time to go fly-fishing only three times a year. Fiftieth birthdays make many of us reflect on what we want to do with what's left of our lives. I reflected on my own father's life, and I remembered that he had died at age 58. I realized with a jolt that, if I were to live only as long as he did, I could count on only 24 more fly-fishing trips before I died. That felt like very few times to do something that I enjoyed so much. The realization made me start thinking about how I could spend more of my time doing what I really liked during the years that I had left, including fly-fishing.

"At that point, I happened to be asked to go evaluate a research laboratory in the Bitterroot Valley of southwestern Montana. I had never been to Montana before; in fact, I had never even been west of the Mississippi River until I was 40 years old. I flew into Missoula airport, picked up a rental car, and began to drive south to the town of Hamilton where the lab was located. A dozen miles south of Missoula is a long straight stretch of road where the valley floor is flat and covered with farmland, and where the snowcapped Bitterroot Mountains on the west and the Sapphire Mountains on the east rise abruptly from the valley. I was overwhelmed by the beauty and scale of it; I had never seen anything like it before. It filled me with a sense of peace, and with an extraordinary perspective on my place in the world.

"When I arrived at the lab, I ran into a former student of mine who was working there and knew about my interest in fly-fishing. He suggested that I come back the next year to do some experiments at the lab, and also to go fly-fishing for trout, for which the Bitterroot River is famous. So I returned the next summer with the intention of spending two weeks, and I ended up staying a month. The summer after that, I came intending to stay a month and ended up staying for the whole summer, at the end of which my wife and I bought a house in the valley. We have been coming back ever since, spending a large part of each year in Montana. Every time I return to the Bitterroot, when I enter it on that stretch of road south of Missoula, that first sight of the valley fills me again with that same feeling of tranquility and grandeur, and that same perspective on my relation to the universe. It's easier to preserve that sense in Montana than anywhere else."

That's what the beauty of Montana does to people: both to those who had grown up in places completely unlike it, like Stan Falkow and me; to other friends, like John Cook, who grew up in other mountainous areas of the American West but still found themselves drawn to Montana; and to still other friends, like the Hirschy family, who did grow up in Montana and chose to stay there.

Like Stan Falkow, I was born in the northeastern U.S. (Boston) and had never been west of the Mississippi until the age of 15, when my parents took me to spend a few weeks of the summer in the Big Hole Basin just south of the Bitterroot Valley (map, p. 31). My father was a pediatrician who had taken care of a ranchers' child, Johnny Eliel, afflicted by a rare disease for which his family pediatrician in Montana had recommended that he go to Boston for specialty treatment. Johnny was a great-grandson of Fred Hirschy Sr., a Swiss immigrant who became one of the pioneer ranchers in the Big Hole in the 1890s. His son Fred Jr., by the time of my visit 69 years old, was still running the family ranch, along with his grown sons Dick and Jack Hirschy and his daughters Jill Hirschy Eliel (Johnny's mother) and Joyce Hirschy McDowell. Johnny did well under my father's treatment, and so his parents and grandparents invited our family to come visit them.

Also like Stan Falkow, I was immediately overwhelmed by the Big Hole's setting: a broad flat valley floor covered with meadows and meandering creeks, but surrounded by a wall of seasonally snow-covered mountains rising abruptly on every horizon. Montana calls itself the "Big Sky State." It's really true. In most other places where I've lived, either one's view of the lower parts of the sky is obscured by buildings, as in cities; or else there are mountains but the terrain is rugged and the valleys are narrow, so one sees only a slice of the sky, as in New Guinea and the Alps; or else there is a broad expanse of sky but it's less interesting, because there is no ring of distinctive mountains on the horizon—as on the plains of Iowa and Nebraska. Three years later, while I was a student in college, I came back for the summer to Dick Hirschy's ranch with two college friends and my sister, and we all worked for the Hirschys on the hay harvest, I driving a scatterrake, my sister a buckrake, and my two friends stacking hay.

After that summer of 1956, it was a long time before I returned to Montana. I spent my summers in other places that were beautiful in other ways, such as New Guinea and the Andes, but I couldn't forget Montana or the Hirschys. Finally, in 1998 I happened to receive an invitation from a private non-profit foundation called the Teller Wildlife Refuge in the Bitterroot Valley. It was an opportunity to bring my own twin sons to Montana, at an age only a few years younger than the age at which I had first visited the state, and to introduce them to fly-fishing for trout. My boys took to it; one of them is now learning to be a fishing guide. I reconnected to Montana and revisited my rancher boss Dick Hirschy and his brother and sisters, who were now in their 70s and 80s, still working hard all year round, just as when I had first met them 45 years previously. Since that reconnection, my wife and sons and I have been visiting Montana every year—drawn to it ultimately by the same unforgettable beauty of its big sky that drew or kept my other friends there (Plates 1–3).

That big sky grew on me. After living for so many years elsewhere, I found that it took me several visits to Montana to get used to the panorama of the sky above, the mountain ring around, and the valley floor below—to appreciate that I really could enjoy that panorama as a daily setting for part of my life—and to discover that I could open myself up to it, pull myself away from it, and still know that I could return to it. Los Angeles has its own practical advantages for me and my family as a year-round base of work, school, and residence, but Montana is infinitely more beautiful and (as Stan Falkow said) peaceful. To me, the most beautiful view in the world is the view down to the Big Hole's meadows and up to the snowcapped peaks of the Continental Divide, as seen from the porch of Jill and John Eliel's ranch house.

Montana in general, and the Bitterroot Valley in its southwest, are a land of paradoxes. Among the lower 48 states, Montana is the third largest in area, yet the sixth smallest in population, hence the second lowest in population density. Today the Bitterroot Valley looks lush, belying its original natural vegetation of just sagebrush. Ravalli County in which the valley is located is so beautiful and attracts so many immigrants from elsewhere in the U.S. (including even from elsewhere in Montana) that it is one of our nation's fastest growing counties, yet 70% of its own high school graduates leave the valley, and most of those leave Montana. Although population is increasing in the Bitterroot, it is falling in eastern Montana, so that for the state of Montana as a whole the population trend is flat. Within the past decade the number of Ravalli County residents in their 50s has increased steeply, but the number in their 30s has actually decreased. Some of the people recently establishing homes in the valley are extremely wealthy, such as the brokerage house founder Charles Schwab and the Intel president Craig Barrett, but Ravalli County is nevertheless one of the poorest counties in the state of Montana, which in turn is nearly the poorest state in the U.S. Many of the county's residents find that they have to hold two or three jobs even to earn an income at U.S. poverty levels.

We associate Montana with natural beauty. Indeed, environmentally Montana is perhaps the least damaged of the lower 48 states; ultimately, that's the main reason why so many people are moving to Ravalli County.

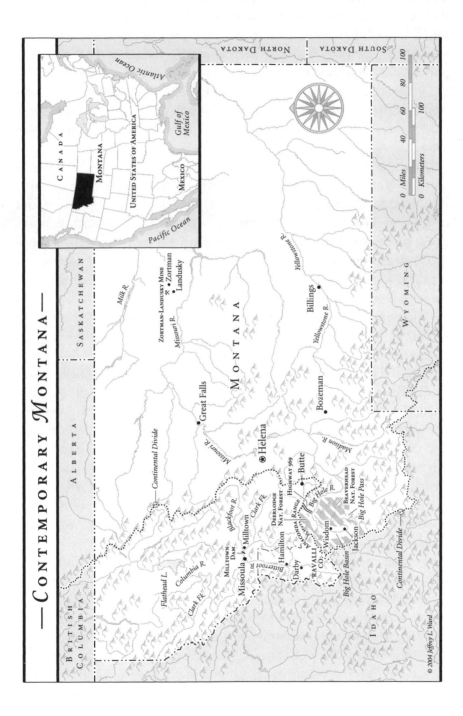

— CONTEMPORARY MONTANA —

BRITISH COLUMBIA

ALBERTA

SASKATCHEWAN

Milk R.

Missouri R.

ZORTMAN-LANDUSKY MINE
Zortman
Landusky

MONTANA

Great Falls

Continental Divide

Helena

Missouri R.

Butte

Highway 569

DEERLODGE
NAT. FOREST

ANACONDA RANGE

Big Hole R.

BEAVERHEAD
NAT. FOREST

Big Hole Pass

Madison R.

Bozeman

Yellowstone R.

Yellowstone R.

Billings

Flathead L.

Columbia R.

Clark Fk.

Blackfoot R.

Clark Fk.

MILLTOWN
DAM

Milltown

Missoula

Bitterroot R.

Hamilton

Darby

RAVALLI
CO.

Wisdom

Big Hole Basin

Jackson

Continental Divide

IDAHO

WYOMING

NORTH DAKOTA

SOUTH DAKOTA

© 2004 Jeffrey L. Ward

0   Miles   100

0   Kilometers   100

20   40   60   80   100

CANADA

MONTANA

UNITED STATES OF AMERICA

MEXICO

Pacific Ocean

Atlantic Ocean

Gulf of
Mexico

The federal government owns over one-quarter of the land in the state and three-quarters of the land in the county, mostly under the title of national forest. Nevertheless, the Bitterroot Valley presents a microcosm of the environmental problems plaguing the rest of the United States: increasing population, immigration, increasing scarcity and decreasing quality of water, locally and seasonally poor air quality, toxic wastes, heightened risks from wildfires, forest deterioration, losses of soil or of its nutrients, losses of biodiversity, damage from introduced pest species, and effects of climate change.

Montana provides an ideal case study with which to begin this book on past and present environmental problems. In the case of the past societies that I shall discuss—Polynesian, Anasazi, Maya, Greenland Norse, and others—we know the eventual outcomes of their inhabitants' decisions about managing their environment, but for the most part we don't know their names or personal stories, and we can only guess at the motives that led them to act as they did. In contrast, in modern Montana we do know names, life histories, and motives. Some of the people involved have been my friends for over 50 years. From understanding Montanans' motives, we can better imagine motives operating in the past. This chapter will put a personal face on a subject that could otherwise seem abstract.

In addition, Montana provides a salutory balance to the following chapters' discussions of small, poor, peripheral, past societies in fragile environments. I intentionally chose to discuss those societies because they were the ones suffering the biggest consequences of their environmental damage, and they thus powerfully illustrate the processes that form the subject of this book. But they are not the only types of societies exposed to serious environmental problems, as illustrated by the contrast case of Montana. It is part of the richest country in the modern world, and it is one of the most pristine and least populated parts of that country, seemingly with fewer problems of environment and population than the rest of the U.S. Certainly, Montana's problems are far less acute than those of crowding, traffic, smog, water quality and quantity, and toxic wastes that beset Americans in Los Angeles, where I live, and in the other urban areas where most Americans live. If, despite that, even Montana has environmental and population problems, it becomes easier to understand how much more serious those problems are elsewhere in the U.S. Montana will illustrate the five main themes of this book: human impacts on the environment; climate change; a society's relations with neighboring friendly societies (in the case of Montana, those in other U.S. states); a society's exposure to acts of other potentially hostile societies (such as overseas terrorists and oil producers today); and the importance of a society's responses to its problems.

The same environmental disadvantages that penalize food production throughout the whole of the American Intermontane West also limit Montana's suitability for growing crops and raising livestock. They are: Montana's relatively low rainfall, resulting in low rates of plant growth; its high latitude and high altitude, both resulting in a short growing season and limiting crops to one a year rather than the two a year possible in areas with a longer summer; and its distance from markets in the more densely populated areas of the U.S. that might buy its products. What those disadvantages mean is that anything grown in Montana can be grown more cheaply and with higher productivity, and transported faster and more cheaply to population centers, elsewhere in North America. Hence Montana's history consists of attempts to answer the fundamental question of how to make a living in this beautiful but agriculturally non-competitive land.

Human occupation of Montana falls into several economic phases. The first phase was of Native Americans, who arrived at least 13,000 years ago. In contrast to the agricultural societies that they developed in eastern and southern North America, Montana's Native Americans before European arrival remained hunter-gatherers, even in areas where agriculture and herding are practiced today. One reason is that Montana lacked native wild plant and animal species lending themselves to domestication, so there were no independent origins of agriculture in Montana, in contrast to the situation in eastern North America and Mexico. Another reason is that Montana lay far from those two Native American centers of independent agricultural origins, so that crops originating there had not spread to Montana by the time of European arrival. Today, about three-quarters of Montana's remaining Native Americans live on seven reservations, most of which are poor in natural resources except for pasture.

The first recorded Europeans to visit Montana were the members of the transcontinental Lewis and Clark Expedition of 1804–1806, which spent more time in what was later to become Montana than in any other state. They were followed by Montana's second economic phase involving the "mountain men," fur trappers and traders coming down from Canada and also from the U.S. The next phase began in the 1860s and was based on three foundations of Montana's economy that have continued (albeit with diminishing importance) until the present: mining, especially of copper and gold; logging; and food production, involving raising cattle and sheep and growing grains, fruits, and vegetables. The influx of miners to Montana's big copper mine at Butte stimulated other sectors of the economy to meet the needs of that internal market within the state. In particular, much timber was taken out of the nearby Bitterroot Valley to provide power for the mines, to construct miners' houses, and to shore up the mine shafts; and much food for the miners was grown in the valley, whose southerly location and mild climate (by Montana standards) give it the nickname of "Montana's Banana Belt." Although the valley's rainfall is low (13 inches per year) and the natural vegetation is sagebrush, the first European settlers in the 1860s already began overcoming that disadvantage by building small irrigation ditches fed by streams draining the Bitterroot Mountains on the valley's west side; and later, by engineering two sets of large-scale and expensive irrigation systems, one (the so-called Big Ditch) built in 1908–1910 to take water from Lake Como on the west side of the valley, and the other consisting of several large irrigation canals drawing water from the Bitterroot River itself. Among other things, irrigation permitted a boom in apple orchards that began in the Bitterroot Valley in the 1880s and peaked in the early decades of the 20th century, but today few of those orchards remain in commercial operation.

Of those former bases of Montana's economy, hunting and fishing have shifted from a subsistence activity to a recreation; the fur trade is extinct; and mines, logging, and agriculture are declining in importance, because of economic and environmental factors to be discussed below. Instead, the sectors of the economy that are growing nowadays are tourism, recreation, retirement living, and health care. A symbolic landmark in the Bitterroot Valley's recent economic transformation took place in 1996, when a 2,600-acre farm called the Bitterroot Stock Farm, formerly the estate of the Montana copper baron Marcus Daly, was acquired by the wealthy brokerage house owner Charles Schwab. He began to develop Daly's estate for very rich out-of-staters who wanted a second (or even a third or fourth) home in the beautiful valley to visit for fishing, hunting, horseback riding, and golfing a couple of times each year. The Stock Farm includes an 18-hole championship golf course and about 125 sites for what are called either houses or cabins, "cabin" being a euphemism for a structure of up to six bedrooms and 6,000 square feet selling for $800,000 or more. Buyers of Stock Farm lots must be able to prove that they meet high standards of net worth and income, the least of which is the ability to afford a club membership initiation fee of $125,000, which is more than seven times the average annual income of Ravalli County residents. The whole Stock Farm is fenced, and the entrance gate bears a sign, MEMBERS AND GUESTS ONLY. Many of the owners arrive by private jet and rarely shop or set foot in Hamilton, but prefer to eat at the Stock Farm club or else have their groceries picked up from Hamilton by club employees. As one local Hamilton resident explained to me bitterly, "You can spot coveys of the aristocracy when they decide to go slumming downtown in tight packs like foreign tourists."

The announcement of the Stock Farm's development plan came as a shock to some Bitterroot Valley long-timers, who predicted that no one would pay so much money for valley land, and that the lots would never sell. As it turned out, the long-timers were wrong. While rich out-of-staters had already been visiting and buying in the valley as individuals, the Stock Farm's opening was a symbolic milestone because it involved so many very rich people buying Bitterroot land at once. Above all, the Stock Farm drove home how much more valuable the valley's land had become for recreation than for its traditional uses of growing cows and apples.

Montana's environmental problems today include almost all of the dozen types of problems that have undermined pre-industrial societies in the past, or that now threaten societies elsewhere in the world as well. Particularly conspicuous in Montana are problems of toxic wastes, forests, soils, water (and sometimes air), climate change, biodiversity losses, and introduced pests. Let's begin with seemingly the most transparent problem, that of toxic wastes.

While concern is mounting in Montana about runoff of fertilizer, manure, septic tank contents, and herbicides, by far the biggest toxic waste issue is posed by residues from metal mining, some of it from the last century and some of it recent or ongoing. Metal mining—especially of copper, but also of lead, molybdenum, palladium, platinum, zinc, gold, and silver—stood as one of the traditional pillars of Montana's economy. No one disagrees that mining is essential, somewhere and somehow: modern civilization and its chemical, construction, electric, and electronic industries run on metals. Instead, the question is where and how best to mine metal-bearing ores.

Unfortunately, the ore concentrate that is eventually carried away from a Montana mine in order to extract the metals represents only a fraction of the earth that must first be dug up. The remainder is waste rock and tailings still containing copper, arsenic, cadmium, and zinc, which are toxic to people (as well as to fish, wildlife, and our livestock) and hence are bad news when they get into groundwater, rivers, and soil. In addition, Montana ores are rich in iron sulfide, which yields sulfuric acid. In Montana there are about 20,000 abandoned mines, some of them recent but many of them a century or more old, that will be leaking acid and those toxic metals essentially forever. The vast majority of those mines have no surviving owners to bear financial responsibility, or else the known owners aren't rich enough to reclaim the mine and treat its acid drainage in perpetuity.

Toxicity problems associated with mining were already recognized at Butte's giant copper mine and nearby smelter a century ago, when neighboring ranchers saw their cows dying and sued the mine's owner, Anaconda Copper Mining Company. Anaconda denied responsibility and won the resulting lawsuit, but in 1907 it nevertheless built the first of several settling ponds to contain the toxic wastes. Thus, we have known for a long time that mine wastes can be sequestered so as to minimize problems; some new mines around the world now do so with state-of-the-art technology, while others continue to ignore the problem. In the U.S. today, a company opening a new mine is required by law to buy a bond by which a separate bond-holding company pledges to pay for the mine's cleanup costs in case the mining company itself goes bankrupt. But many mines have been "under-bonded" (i.e., the eventual cleanup costs have proved to exceed the value of the bond), and older mines were not required to buy such bonds at all.

In Montana as elsewhere, companies that have acquired older mines respond to demands to pay for cleanup in either of two ways. Especially if the company is small, its owners may declare the company bankrupt, in some cases conceal its assets, and transfer their business efforts to other companies or to new companies that do not bear responsibility for cleanup at the old mine. If the company is so large that it cannot claim that it would be bankrupted by cleanup costs (as in the case of ARCO that I shall discuss below), the company instead denies its responsibility or else seeks to minimize the costs. In either case, either the mine site and areas downstream of it remain toxic, thereby endangering people, or else the U.S. federal government and the Montana state government (hence ultimately all taxpayers) pay for the cleanup through the federal Superfund and a corresponding Montana state fund.

These two alternative responses by mining companies pose a question that will recur throughout this book, as we try to understand why any person or group in any society would knowingly do something harmful to the society as a whole. While denial or minimization of responsibility may be in the short-term financial interests of the mining company, it is bad for society as a whole, and it may also be bad for the long-term interests of the company itself, or of the entire mining industry. Despite Montanans' long-standing embrace of mining as a traditional value defining their state's identity, they have recently become increasingly disillusioned with mining and have contributed to the industry's near-demise within Montana. For instance, in 1998, to the shock of the industry, and to politicians supporting and supported by the industry, Montana voters passed a ballot initiative banning a problem-plagued method of gold mining termed cyanide heap-leach mining and discussed further below. Some of my Montana friends now say: in retrospect, when we compare the multi-billion-dollar mine cleanup costs borne by us taxpayers with Montana's own meager past earnings from its mines, most of whose profits went to shareholders in the eastern U.S. or in Europe, we realize that Montana would have been better off in the long run if it had never mined copper at all but had just imported it from Chile, leaving the resulting problems to the Chileans!

It is easy for us non-miners to become indignant at mining companies and to view their behavior as morally culpable. Didn't they knowingly do things that harmed us, and aren't they now shirking their responsibility? A sign posted over the toilet of one Montanan friend of mine reads, "Do not flush. Be like the mining industry and let someone else clean up your waste!"

In fact, the moral issue is more complex. Here is one explanation that I quote from a recent book: ". . . ASARCO [American Smelting and Refining Company, a giant mining and smelting company] can hardly be blamed [for not cleaning up an especially toxic mine that it owned]. American businesses exist to make money for their owners; it is the modus operandi of American capitalism. A corollary to the money-making process is not spending it needlessly . . . Such a tight-fisted philosophy is not limited to the mining industry. Successful businesses differentiate between those expenses necessary to stay in business and those more pensively characterized as 'moral obligations.' Difficulties or reluctance to understand and accept this distinction underscores much of the tension between advocates of broadly mandated environmental programs and the business community. Business leaders are more likely to be accountants or attorneys than members of the clergy." That explanation does not come from the CEO of ASARCO, but from environmental consultant David Stiller, who sought in his book

Wounding the West: Montana, Mining, and the Environment to understand
how Montana's toxic mine waste problem arose, and what society really has
to do to fix it.

It's a cruel fact that no simple cheap way exists to clean up old mines.
Early miners behaved as they did because the government required almost
nothing of them, and because they were businessmen operating according
to the principles that David Stiller explained. Not until 1971 did the state of
Montana pass a law requiring mining companies to clean up their property
when their mine closed. Even rich companies (like ARCO and ASARCO)
that may be inclined to clean up become reluctant to do so when they realize that they may then be asked to do the impossible, or that the costs will be
excessive, or that the achievable results will be less than the public expected.
When the mine owner can't or won't pay, taxpayers don't want to step in
and pay billions of dollars of cleanup costs either. Instead, taxpayers feel
that the problem has existed for a long time, out of sight and out of their
backyards, so it must be tolerable; most taxpayers balk at spending money if
there isn't an immediate crisis; and not enough taxpayers complain about
toxic wastes or support high taxes. In this sense, the American public is as
responsible for inaction as are miners and the government; we the public
bear the ultimate responsibility. Only when the public pressures its politicians into passing laws demanding different behavior from mining companies will the companies behave differently: otherwise, the companies would
be operating as charities and would be violating their responsibility to their
shareholders. Three cases will serve to illustrate some of the various outcomes of these dilemmas to date: the cases of the Clark Fork, Milltown
Dam, and Pegasus Zortman-Landusky Mine.

In 1882 the mining companies that later became the Anaconda Copper
Mining Company began operations at Butte near the headwaters of the
Clark Fork of the Columbia River. By 1900, Butte accounted for half of the
U.S.'s copper output. Until 1955 most mining at Butte involved underground tunnels, but in 1955 Anaconda began excavating an open-pit mine
called the Berkeley Pit, now an enormous hole over a mile in diameter and
1,800 feet deep. Huge quantities of acidic mine tailings with toxic metals
ended up in the Clark Fork River. But Anaconda's fortunes then declined
because of cheaper foreign competition, expropriation of its mines in Chile,
and growing environmental concerns in the U.S. In 1976 Anaconda was
bought by the big oil company ARCO (more recently bought in turn by the
bigger oil company BP), which closed the smelter in 1980 and the mine it-

self in 1983, thereby eliminating thousands of jobs and three-quarters of the economic base for the Butte area.

The Clark Fork River, including the Berkeley Pit, is now the largest and most expensive Superfund cleanup site in the U.S. In ARCO's view, it is unfair to hold ARCO responsible for damage done by the mine's previous owner, before the Superfund law even existed. In the view of the federal and state governments, ARCO acquired Anaconda's assets, including Anaconda's liabilities. At least, ARCO and BP are not declaring bankruptcy. As one environmentalist friend told me, "They are trying to get away with paying as little as possible, but there are worse companies to deal with than ARCO." The acidic water seeping into the Berkeley Pit will be pumped out and treated forever. ARCO has already paid several hundred million dollars to the state of Montana for restoration of the Clark Fork, and its total eventual liability is estimated at one billion dollars, but that estimate is uncertain because the cleanup treatment consumes much power: who knows what power will cost 40 years from now?

The second case involves Milltown Dam, built in 1907 across the Clark Fork River downstream of Butte to generate power for a nearby sawmill. Since then, 6,600,000 cubic yards of sediments contaminated with arsenic, cadmium, copper, lead, and zinc have been washed down from Butte's mines and accumulated in the reservoir behind the dam. A resulting "minor" problem is that the dam prevents fish from migrating along the Clark Fork and Blackfoot Rivers (the latter is the trout stream made famous by Norman Maclean's novella and Robert Redford's film *A River Runs Through It*). The major problem, discovered in 1981 when local people noticed a bad taste in drinking water from their wells, is that a huge plume of groundwater with dangerous arsenic levels 42 times higher than federal water standards is spreading from the reservoir. The dam is decrepit, in need of repair, poorly anchored, located in an earthquake zone, was nearly broken by an ice jam in 1996, and is expected to break sooner or later. No one would think of constructing such a flimsy dam today. If the dam did break and release its toxic sediments, the water supply of Missoula, southwestern Montana's largest city located just seven miles downstream of the dam, would become undrinkable, and the lower Clark Fork River would be ruined for fishing.

ARCO acquired the liability for the toxic sediments behind the dam when it bought Anaconda Copper Mining Company, whose activities created the sediments. The near-disaster in the ice jam of 1996, and fish deaths

downstream resulting from releases of water with toxic copper levels from
the dam then and again in 1998, triggered recognition that something had
to be done about the dam. Federal and state scientists recommended removing it and its accumulated toxic sediments, at a cost to ARCO of about
$100,000,000. For a long time, ARCO denied that the toxic sediments caused
the fish deaths, denied its liability for the arsenic in Milltown groundwater
or for cancer in the Milltown area, funded a "grass-roots" movement in the
nearby town of Bonner to oppose removing the dam, and proposed instead
just strengthening it, at the much lower cost of $20,000,000. But Missoula
politicians, businesspeople, and the public, who initially considered the
proposal to remove the dam crazy, switched to being strongly in favor of it.
In 2003 the federal Environmental Protection Agency adopted the proposal,
making it almost certain that the dam will be removed.

The remaining case is that of the Zortman-Landusky Mine owned by
Pegasus Gold, a small company founded by people from other mining companies. That mine employed a method known as cyanide heap-leaching, developed for extracting very low-grade gold ores requiring 50 tons of ores to
yield one ounce of gold. The ore is excavated from an open pit, piled in a
big heap (approximating a small mountain) inside a lined leach pad, and
sprayed with a solution of cyanide, best known as the poison used to generate the hydrogen cyanide gas used both in Nazi gas chambers and in American prison gas chambers, but with the virtue of binding to gold. Hence as
the cyanide-containing solution seeps through the ore heap, it picks up the
gold and is drained off to a nearby pond, whence it is pumped to a processing plant for extracting the gold. The leftover cyanide solution containing
toxic metals is disposed of by spraying it on nearby forests or rangeland, or
else is enriched with more cyanide and sprayed back on the heap.

Obviously, in this heap-leach process several things can go wrong, all of
which did go wrong at the Zortman-Landusky Mine (Plate 4). The leach pad's
liner is as thin as a nickel and inevitably develops leaks under the weight
of millions of tons of ore being pushed around by heavy machinery. The
pond with its noxious brew may overflow; that happened at the Zortman-
Landusky Mine during a rainstorm. Finally, the cyanide itself is dangerous:
in a flooding emergency at the mine, when the owners received permission
to dispose of excess solution by spraying it nearby to prevent the pads from
bursting, mishandling of the spraying operation led to the formation of
cyanide gas that nearly killed some of the workers. Pegasus Gold eventually
declared bankruptcy, abandoning its huge open pits, heaps, and ponds from

which acid and cyanide will leak out forever. Pegasus' bond proved insufficient to cover the cleanup cost, leaving taxpayers to pay the remaining bills, estimated at $40,000,000 or more. These three case studies of toxic mine waste problems that I have described, and thousands of others, illustrate why visitors from Germany, South Africa, Mongolia, and other countries contemplating mining investments have recently been coming to Montana to inform themselves at first hand about bad mining practices and their consequences.

A second set of environmental problems in Montana involves the logging and burning of its forests. Just as no one denies that metal mining is essential, somewhere and somehow, no one would dispute that logging is also necessary to obtain wood for timber and for making paper. The question that my Montana friends sympathetic to logging raise is: if you object to logging in Montana, where do you propose to get wood instead? Rick Laible defended to me a controversial recent Montana logging proposal by noting, "It beats cutting down the rainforest!" Jack Ward Thomas's defense was similar: "By refusing to harvest our own dead trees and instead importing live trees from Canada, we have exported both the environmental effects of logging, and the economic benefits of it, to Canada." Dick Hirschy sarcastically commented, "There's a saying, 'Don't rape the land by logging'—so we are raping Canada instead."

Commercial logging began in the Bitterroot Valley in 1886, to provide Ponderosa Pine logs for the mining community at Butte. The post–World War II housing boom in the U.S., and the resulting surge in demand for wood, caused timber sales on U.S. National Forest land to peak around 1972 at over six times their 1945 levels. DDT was released over forests from airplanes to control insect tree pests. In order to be able to reestablish uniform even-aged trees of chosen tree species, and thereby to maximize timber yields and increase logging efficiency, logging was carried out by clear-cutting all trees rather than by selective logging of marked individual trees. Set against those big advantages of clear-cutting were some disadvantages: water temperatures in streams no longer shaded by trees rose above values optimal for fish spawning and survival; snow on unshaded bare ground melted in a quick pulse in the spring, instead of the shaded forest's snow-pack gradually melting and releasing water for irrigating ranches throughout the summer; and, in some cases, sediment runoff increased, and water quality decreased. But the most visible evil of clear-cutting, for citizens of a state who considered their land's most valuable resource to be its beauty, was that clear-cut hillsides looked ugly, really ugly.

The resulting debate became known as the Clearcut Controversy. Outraged Montana ranchers, landowners, and the general public protested. U.S. Forest Service managers made the mistake of insisting that they were the professionals who knew all about logging, and that the public was ignorant and should keep quiet. The 1970 Bolle Report, prepared by forestry professionals outside the Forest Service, criticized Forest Service policies and, fanned by similar disputes over clear-cutting of West Virginia national forests, led to national changes, including restrictions on clear-cutting and a return to emphasis on managing forests for multiple purposes other than timber production (as already envisioned when the Forest Service was established in 1905).

In the decades since the Clearcut Controversy, Forest Service annual timber sales have decreased by more than 80%—in part because of environmental regulations mandated in the Endangered Species Act, the Clean Water Act, and requirements for national forests to maintain habitats for all species, and in part because of the decline in easily accessible big trees due to logging itself. When the Forest Service now proposes a timber sale, environmental organizations file protests and appeals that take up to 10 years to resolve and that make logging less economic even if the appeals are ultimately denied. Virtually all my Montana friends, even those who consider themselves dedicated environmentalists, told me that they consider the pendulum to have swung too far in the direction away from logging. They feel frustrated that logging proposals appearing well justified to them (such as for the purpose of reducing the forest fire fuel loads discussed below) encounter long delays in the courts. But the environmental organizations filing the protests have concluded that they should suspect the usual disguised pro-logging agenda behind any seemingly reasonable government proposal involving logging. All of the Bitterroot Valley's former timber mills have now closed, because so little timber is available from Montana publicly owned timberland, and because the valley's privately owned timberland has already been logged twice. The mills' closing has meant the loss of many high-paying unionized jobs, as well as of traditional Montanan self-image.

Elsewhere in Montana, outside the Bitterroot Valley, much private timberland remains, most of it originating from government land grants made in the 1860s to the Great Northern Railroad as an inducement for building a transcontinental railroad. In 1989 that land was spun off from the rail-

roads to a Seattle-based entity called Plum Creek Timber Company, organized for tax purposes as a real estate investment trust (so that its earnings
will be taxed at lower rates as capital gains), and now the largest owner of
private timberland in Montana and the second-largest one in the U.S. I've
read Plum Creek's publications and talked with their director of corporate
affairs, Bob Jirsa, who defends Plum Creek's environmental policies and
sustainable forestry practices. I've also heard numerous Montana friends
vent unfavorable opinions about Plum Creek. Typical of their complaints
are the following: "Plum Creek cares only about the bottom line"; "they are
not interested in sustainable forestry"; "they have a corporate culture,
and their goal is 'Get out more logs!' "; "Plum Creek earns money in whatever way it can from the land"; "they do weed control only if someone
complains."

Should these polarized views remind you of the views that I already
quoted about mining companies, you're right. Plum Creek is organized as a
profit-making business, not as a charity. If Montana citizens want Plum
Creek to do things that would diminish its profits, it's their responsibility to
get their politicians to pass and enforce laws demanding those things, or to
buy out the lands and manage them differently. Looming over this dispute
is a basic hard fact: Montana's cold dry climate and high elevation place
most of its land at a relative disadvantage for forestry. Trees grow several
times faster in the U.S. Southeast and Northeast than in Montana. While
Plum Creek's largest land holdings are in Montana, four other states (Ar-
kansas, Georgia, Maine, and Mississippi) each produce more timber for
Plum Creek on only 60 to 64% of its Montana acreage. Plum Creek cannot
get a high rate of return from its Montana logging operations: it has to pay
taxes and fire protection on the land while sitting on it for 60 to 80 years before harvesting trees, whereas trees reach a harvestable size in 30 years on its
southeastern U.S. lands. When Plum Creek faces economic realities and sees
more value in developing its Montana lands, especially those along rivers
and lakes, for real estate than for timber, that's because prospective buyers
who seek beautiful waterfront property hold the same opinion. Those buyers are often representatives of conservation interests, including the government. For all these reasons, the future of logging in Montana even more
than elsewhere in the U.S. is uncertain, as is that of mining.

Related to these issues of forest logging are issues of forest fires, which
have recently increased in intensity and extent in some forest types in Montana and throughout the western U.S., with the summers of 1988, 1996,
2000, 2002, and 2003 being especially severe fire years. In the summer of

2000, one-fifth of the Bitterroot Valley's remaining area of forest burned. Whenever I fly back to the Bitterroot nowadays, my first thought on looking out my airplane's window is to count the number of fires or to gauge the amount of smoke on this particular day. (On August 19, 2003, as I was flying to Missoula airport, I counted a dozen fires whose smoke reduced visibility to a few miles.) Each time that John Cook took my sons out fly-fishing in 2000, his choice of which stream to fish depended partly on where the fires were burning that day. Some of my friends in the Bitterroot have had to be evacuated repeatedly from their homes because of approaching fires.

This recent increase in fires has resulted partly from climate change (the recent trend towards hot dry summers) and partly from human activities, for complicated reasons that foresters came increasingly to understand about 30 years ago but whose relative importance is still debated. One factor is the direct effects of logging, which often turns a forest into something approximating a huge pile of kindling: the ground in a logged forest may remain covered with lopped-off branches and treetops, left behind when the valuable trunks are carted away; a dense growth of new vegetation springs up, further increasing the forest's fuel loads; and the trees logged and removed are of course the biggest and most fire-resistant individuals, leaving behind smaller and more flammable trees. Another factor is that the U.S. Forest Service in the first decade of the 1900s adopted a policy of fire suppression (attempting to put out forest fires) for the obvious reasons that it didn't want valuable timber to go up in smoke, nor people's homes and lives to be threatened. The Forest Service's announced goal became, "Put out every forest fire by 10:00 A.M. on the morning after the day when it is first reported." Firefighters became much more successful at achieving that goal after World War II, thanks to the availability of firefighting planes, an expanded road system for sending in fire trucks, and improved firefighting technology. For a few decades after World War II, the annual acreage burnt decreased by 80%.

That happy situation began to change in the 1980s, due to the increasing frequency of large forest fires that were essentially impossible to extinguish unless rain and low winds combined to help. People began to realize that the U.S. federal government's fire suppression policy was contributing to those big fires, and that natural fires caused by lightning had previously played an important role in maintaining forest structure. That natural role of fire varies with altitude, tree species, and forest type. To take the Bitterroot's low-altitude Ponderosa Pine forest as an example, historical records, plus counts of annual tree rings and datable fire scars on tree stumps, demonstrated that a Ponderosa Pine forest experiences a lightning-lit fire about once a decade under natural conditions (i.e., before fire suppression began around 1910 and became effective after 1945). The mature Ponderosa trees have bark two inches thick and are relatively resistant to fire, which instead burns out the understory of fire-sensitive Douglas Fir seedlings that have grown up since the last fire. But after only a decade's growth until the next fire, those seedlings are still too low for fire to spread from them into the crowns. Hence the fire remains confined to the ground and understory. As a result, many natural Ponderosa Pine forests have a park-like appearance, with low fuel loads, big trees well spaced apart, and a relatively clear understory.

Of course, though, loggers concentrated on removing those big, old, valuable, fire-resistant Ponderosa Pines, while fire suppression for decades let the understory fill up with Douglas Fir saplings that would in turn become valuable when full-grown. Tree densities increased from 30 to 200 trees per acre, the forest's fuel load increased by a factor of 6, and Congress repeatedly failed to appropriate money to thin out the saplings. Another human-related factor, sheep grazing in national forests, may also have played a major role by reducing understory grasses that would otherwise have fueled frequent low-intensity fires. When a fire finally does start in a sapling-choked forest, whether due to lightning or human carelessness or (regrettably often) intentional arson, the dense tall saplings may become a ladder that allows the fire to jump into the crowns. The outcome is sometimes an unstoppable inferno in which flames shoot 400 feet into the air, leap from crown to crown across wide gaps, reach temperatures of 2,000 degrees Fahrenheit, kill the tree seed bank in the soil, and may be followed by mudslides and mass erosion.

Foresters now identify the biggest problem in managing western forests as what to do with those increased fuel loads that built up during the previous half-century of effective fire suppression. In the wetter eastern U.S., dead trees rot away more quickly than in the drier West, where more dead trees persist like giant matchsticks. In an ideal world, the Forest Service would manage and restore the forests, thin them out, and remove the dense understory by cutting or by controlled small fires. But that would cost over a thousand dollars per acre for the one hundred million acres of western U.S. forests, or a total of about $100 billion. No politician or voter wants to spend that kind of money. Even if the cost were lower, much of the public would be suspicious of such a proposal as just an excuse for resuming logging of their beautiful forest. Instead of a regular program of expenditures for main-

taining our western forests in a less fire-susceptible condition, the federal
government tolerates flammable forests and is forced to spend money unpredictably whenever a firefighting emergency arises: e.g., about $1.6 billion
to fight the summer 2000 forest fires that burned 10,000 square miles.

Montanans themselves hold diverse and often self-contradictory views
about forest management and forest fires. On the one hand, the public fears
and instinctively dislikes the "let it burn" response that the Forest Service is
forced to take towards huge fires that would be dangerous or impossible to
try to extinguish. When the 1988 fires in much of Yellowstone National Park
were allowed to burn, the public was especially loud in its protests, not understanding that in fact there was nothing that could be done except to pray
for rain or snow. On the other hand, the public also dislikes proposals for
forest thinning programs that could make the forests less flammable, because people prefer beautiful views of dense forests, they object to "unnatural" interference with nature, they want to leave the forest in a "natural"
condition, and they certainly don't want to pay for thinning by increased
taxes. They (like most foresters until recently) fail to understand that western forests are already in a highly unnatural condition, as the result of a century of fire suppression, logging, and sheep grazing.

Within the Bitterroot, people build trophy homes next to or surrounded
by flammable forests at the urban/wildland interface and then expect the
government to protect those homes against fires. In July 2001, when my
wife and I went for a hike west of the town of Hamilton through what had
been the Blodgett forest, we found ourselves in a landscape of fire-charred
dead trees killed in one of the big forest fires whose smoke had filled the valley during our summer 2000 visit. Blodgett-area residents who had previously blocked Forest Service proposals to thin the forest demanded then
that the Service hire 12 big firefighting helicopters at a cost of $2,000 per
hour to save their homes by dropping water on them, while the Forest Service, obeying a government-imposed mandate to protect lives, people's
property, and then the forest in that order, was simultaneously allowing expanses of public timberlands far more valuable than those homes to burn.
The Forest Service subsequently announced that it will no longer spend so
much money and endanger firefighters' lives just to protect private property. Many homeowners sue the Forest Service if their house burns in a forest fire, or if it burns in a backfire lit by the Forest Service to control a much
bigger fire, or if it doesn't burn but if a forest providing a pretty view from
the deck of their house does burn. Yet some Montana homeowners are afflicted with such a rabidly anti-government attitude that they don't want to

pay taxes towards the costs of firefighting, nor to allow government employees onto their land to carry out fire prevention measures.

The next set of environmental problems in Montana involves its soils. One "minor" and specific soil problem is that the Bitterroot Valley's boom in commercial apple orchards, which were initially very profitable, collapsed, due in part to apple trees exhausting the soil's nitrogen. A more widespread soil problem is erosion, resulting from any of several changes that remove the plant cover normally protecting the soil: overgrazing, noxious weed infestation, logging, or excessively hot forest fires that sterilize the topsoil. Long-timer ranching families know better than to overgraze their pastures: as Dick and Jack Hirschy expressed it to me, "We must take good care of our land, or we will be ruined." However, one of the Hirschys' neighbors is an outsider who paid more for his property than it could sustainably support by ranching, and who is now overstocking his pastures in the short-sighted hope of recouping his investment. Other neighbors made the mistake of renting grazing rights on their land to tenants, who overgrazed for a quick profit during their three-year lease and didn't care about the resulting long-term damage. The net result of these various causes of soil erosion is that about one-third of the Bitterroot's watersheds are considered to be in good shape and not eroded, one-third are at risk of erosion, and one-third are already eroded and in need of restoration.

The remaining soil problem in Montana, besides nitrogen exhaustion and erosion, is salinization, a process involving salt accumulation in soil and groundwater. While such accumulation has always occurred naturally in some areas, a more recent concern is the ruining of large areas of farmland by salinization resulting from some human agricultural practices that I'll explain in the next few paragraphs and in Chapter 13—particularly from clearing of natural vegetation, and from irrigation. In parts of Montana, salt concentrations in soil water have reached levels double those of seawater.

Besides certain salts having specific toxic effects on crops, high salt concentrations exert a general harmful effect on crops similar to the effect of a drought, by raising the osmotic pressure of soil water and thereby making it harder for roots to absorb water by osmosis. The salty groundwater may also end up in wells and streams and may evaporate on the surface to leave a caked layer of salt. If you imagine yourself drinking a glass of "water" more concentrated than the ocean, you will appreciate that not only does it taste horrible and prevent farmers from growing crops, but that its dissolved boron, selenium, and other toxic ingredients may be bad for your health (and for that of wildlife and your livestock). Salinization is a problem today in many parts of the world besides the U.S., including India, Turkey, and especially Australia (see Chapter 13). In the past it contributed to the decline of the world's oldest civilizations, those of Mesopotamia: salinization provides a large part of the explanation for why applying the term "Fertile Crescent" today to Iraq and Syria, formerly the leading center of world agriculture, would be a cruel joke.

Montana's main form of salinization is one that has ruined several million acres of cropland in the northern Great Plains as a whole, including several hundred thousand acres in northern, eastern, and central Montana. The form is called "saline seep," because salty water building up in the ground in an uphill area percolates through the soil to emerge as a seep in a downhill area up to half a mile or farther distant. Saline seeps frequently become bad for neighborly friendship when the agricultural practices of one farmer uphill cause a saline seep on a downhill neighbor's property.

Here is how a saline seep arises. Eastern Montana has lots of water-soluble salts (especially sodium, calcium, and magnesium sulfates) present as components of the rocks and soils themselves, and also trapped in marine deposits (because much of the region used to be ocean). Below the soil zone is a layer of bedrock (shale, sandstone, or coal) that has low permeability to water. In dry eastern Montana environments covered with native vegetation, almost all rain that falls is promptly taken up by the vegetation's roots and transpired back into the atmosphere, leaving the soil below the root layer dry. However, when a farmer clears the native vegetation to practice crop-and-fallow agriculture, in which an annual crop like wheat is grown during one year and the land is left fallow the next year, there are no plant roots to take up rainwater falling in the fallow year. That rainwater accumulates in the soil, waterlogs it below the root layer, and dissolves salts that then rise into the root zone as the water table rises. Because of the impermeable underlying bedrock, the salty water doesn't drain deeply into the ground but emerges somewhere downhill nearby as a saline seep. The result is that crops grow more poorly or not at all, both in the uphill area where the problem arises and in the downhill area where the seep emerges.

Saline seeps became widespread in much of Montana after 1940 as a consequence of changes in agricultural practices—especially the increasing use of tractors and more efficient soil tilling devices, weed-killers to kill weed plant cover during the fallow period, and more land under fallow each year. The problem must be combatted by various intensive types of farm management, such as sowing salt-tolerant plants in the downhill seep areas to start reclaiming them, decreasing the length of fallow time in the uphill area by a crop schedule known as flexible cropping, and planting alfalfa and other perennial water-demanding crops with deep roots to take up excess water from the soil.

In the areas of Montana where agriculture depends directly on rainfall, saline seeps are the main salt-related form of land damage. But they are not the only form. Several million acres of agricultural land that depend for their water on irrigation rather than on rainfall are distributed patchily throughout the whole state, including in my summering areas of the Bitterroot Valley and Big Hole Basin. Salinization is starting to appear in some of those areas where the irrigation water contains salt. Another form arises from an industrial method to extract methane for natural gas from coal beds by drilling into the coal and pumping in water to carry the methane up to the surface. Unfortunately, water dissolves not only methane but also salt. Since 1988, the adjacent state of Wyoming, which is almost as poor as Montana, has been seeking to boost its economy by embarking on a big program of methane extraction by this method, yielding salty water that drains from Wyoming into southeastern Montana's Powder River Basin.

To start to understand the apparently intractable water problems that bedevil Montana along with other dry areas of the American West, think of the Bitterroot Valley as having two largely separate water supplies: irrigation from ditches fed by mountain streams, lakes, or the Bitterroot River itself, to water fields for agriculture; and wells drilled into underground aquifers, which provide most of the water for domestic use. The valley's larger towns provide municipal water supplies, but houses outside those few towns all get their water from individual private wells. Both the irrigation water supply and the well water supply are facing the same fundamental dilemma: an increasing number of users for decreasing amounts of water. As the Bitterroot's water commissioner, Vern Woolsey, explained it succinctly to me, "Whenever you have a source of water and more than two people using it, there will be a problem. But why fight about water? Fighting won't make more water!"

The ultimate reason for decreasing amounts of water is climate change: Montana is becoming warmer and drier. While global warming will produce winners as well as losers in different places around the world, Montana will be among the big losers because its rainfall was already marginally adequate for agriculture. Drought has now forced abandonment of large areas of farmland in eastern Montana, as well as in adjacent areas of Alberta and Saskatchewan. Visible effects of global warming in my summering areas in western Montana are that snow in the mountains is becoming confined to higher altitudes and often now no longer remains throughout the summer on the mountains surrounding the Big Hole Basin, as it did when I first visited in 1953.

The most visible effect of global warming in Montana, and perhaps anywhere in the world, is in Glacier National Park. While glaciers all over the world are in retreat—on Mt. Kilimanjaro, in the Andes and Alps, on the mountains of New Guinea, and around Mt. Everest—the phenomenon has been especially well studied in Montana because its glaciers are so accessible to climatologists and tourists. When the area of Glacier National Park was first visited by naturalists in the late 1800s, it contained over 150 glaciers; now, there are only about 35 left, mostly at just a small fraction of their first-reported size. At present rates of melting, Glacier National Park will have no glaciers at all by the year 2030. Such declines in the mountain snowpack are bad for irrigation systems, whose summer water comes from melting of the snow that remains up in the mountains. It's also bad for well systems tapping the Bitterroot River's aquifer, whose volume has decreased because of recent drought.

As in other dry areas of the American West, agriculture would be impossible in the Bittterroot Valley without irrigation, because annual rainfall in the valley bottom is only about 13 inches per year. Without irrigation, the valley's vegetation would be sagebrush, which is what Lewis and Clark reported on their visit in 1805–1806, and which one still sees today as soon as one crosses the last irrigation ditch on the valley's eastern side. Construction of irrigation systems fed by snowmelt water from the high mountains forming the valley's western side began already in the late 1800s and peaked in 1908–1910. Within each irrigation system or district, each landowner or group of landowners has the right to take for his or her land a specified quantity of water from the system.

Unfortunately, in most Bitterroot irrigation districts the water is "overallocated." That is—incredibly to a naïve outsider like me—the sum of the water rights allocated to all landowners exceeds the flow of water available in most years, at least later in the summer when snowmelt is decreasing. Part of the reason is that allocations are calculated on the assumption of a fixed water supply, but in fact water supplies vary from year to year with climate, and the assumed fixed water supply is the value for a relatively wet year. The solution is to assign priorities among landowners according to the historical date on which the water right was claimed for that property, and to cut off water deliveries first to the most junior right-owner and then to earlier right-owners as water flows in the ditches decrease. That's already a recipe for conflict, because the oldest farms with the earliest rights claimed are often downhill, and it's hard for uphill farmers with lower-ranking rights to see water that they desperately need flowing merrily downhill past their property and yet to refrain from taking the water. But if they did take it, their downhill neighbors could sue them.

A further problem results from land subdivision: originally the land was owned in large blocks whose single owner of course took water from the ditch for his different fields in sequence, and who wouldn't have been so silly as to try to water all his fields simultaneously and thus run out of water. But as those original 160-acre blocks have become subdivided each into 40 four-acre house lots, there isn't enough water when each of those 40 house-owners tries to water and keep the house's garden green without realizing that the other 39 neighbors are irrigating simultaneously. Still another problem is that irrigation rights apply only to so-called "beneficial" use of water benefitting the piece of land holding the right. Leaving water in the river for the fish and for the tourists trying to float down the river on rafts is not considered a "beneficial" right. Sections of the Big Hole River have actually dried up in some recent dry summers. Until 2003, many of those potential conflicts in the Bitterroot Valley were amicably adjudicated for several decades by Vern Woolsey, the 82-year-old water commissioner whom everyone respected, but my Bitterroot friends are terrified at the potential for conflict now that Vern has finally stepped down.

Bitterroot irrigation systems include 28 small privately owned dams constructed across mountain streams, in order to store snowmelt water in the spring and to release it for irrigating fields in the summer. These dams constitute ticking time bombs. They were all built a century ago, to weak designs now considered primitive and dangerous. They have been maintained poorly or not at all. Many are at risk of collapses that would flood houses and property lying below them. Devastating floods resulting from failures of two such dams several decades ago convinced the Forest Service to declare that a dam's owners, and also any contractor that has ever worked on the dam, bear the liability for damages caused by a dam failure. Owners are responsible for either fixing or removing their dam. While this principle may seem reasonable, three facts often make it financially onerous: most of the present owners bearing the liability get little financial benefit from their dam and no longer care to fix it (e.g., because the land has been subdivided into house lots, and they now use the dam just to water their lawns rather than to earn a living as farmers); the federal and state governments offer money on a cost-sharing basis to fix a dam, but not to remove one; and half of the dams are on lands now designated as wilderness areas, where roads are forbidden and repair machinery must be flown in by expensive helicopter charters.

One example of such a time bomb is Tin Cup Dam, whose collapse would inundate Darby, the largest town in the southern Bitterroot Valley. Leaks and the dam's poor condition triggered lengthy arguments and lawsuits between the dam's owners, the Forest Service, and environmental groups about whether and how to repair the dam, climaxing in an emergency when a serious leak was noted in 1998. Unfortunately, the contractor whom the owners hired to drain the dam's reservoir soon encountered heavy rocks whose removal would require big excavation equipment to be flown in by helicopter. At that point the owners declared that they had run out of money, and both the state of Montana and Ravalli County also decided against spending money on the dam, but the situation remained a potentially life-threatening emergency for Darby. Hence the Forest Service itself hired the helicopters and equipment to work on the dam and billed the owners, who have not paid; the U.S. Department of Justice is now preparing to sue them in order to collect the costs.

The Bitterroot's other water supply besides snowmelt-fed irrigation consists of wells for domestic water use, tapping into underground aquifers. They, too, face the problem of increasing demand for decreasing water. While mountain snowpack and underground aquifers may seem to be separate, they are in fact coupled: some runoff of used irrigation water may percolate down through the ground to the aquifers, and some aquifer water may originate ultimately from snowmelt. Hence the ongoing decrease in Montana's snowpack forebodes a decrease in the aquifers as well.

There is no doubt about increasing demand for aquifer water: the Bitterroot's continuing population explosion means more people drinking more water and flushing more toilets. Roxa French, coordinator for the local Bitter Root Water Forum, advises people building new houses to drill their wells deep, because there are going to be "more straws in the milkshake"— i.e., more wells drilled into the same aquifer and lowering its level. Montana law and county regulations about domestic water are currently weak. The well that one new house-owner drills may lower the water level of a neighbor's well, but it is difficult for the latter person to collect damages. In order to calculate how much domestic water use an aquifer could support, one would have to map the aquifer and to measure how rapidly water is flowing into it, but—astonishingly—those two elementary steps have not been accomplished for any Bitterroot Valley aquifer. The county itself lacks the resources to monitor its aquifers and does not carry out independent assessments of water availability when it is considering a developer's application to build a new house. Instead, the county relies on the developer's assurance that enough well water will be available for the house.

Everything that I have said about water so far concerns water quantity. However, there are also issues of water quality, which rivals western Montana's scenery as its most valuable natural resource because the rivers and irrigation systems originate from relatively pure snowmelt. Despite that advantage, the Bitterroot River is already on Montana's list of "impaired streams," for several reasons. The most important of those reasons is buildup of sediments released by erosion, road construction, forest fires, logging, and falling water levels in ditches and streams due to use for irrigation. Most of the Bitterroot's watersheds are now already eroded or at risk. A second problem is fertilizer runoff: every farmer growing hay adds at least 200 pounds of fertilizer to each acre of land, but it is unknown how much of that fertilizer ends up in the river. Waste nutrients from septic tanks are yet another increasing hazard to water quality. Finally, as I already explained, toxic minerals draining out of mines are the most serious water quality problem in some other parts of Montana, though not in the Bitterroot.

Air quality also deserves brief mention. It may at first seem shameless for me, as a resident of the American city (Los Angeles) with the worst air quality, to say anything negative about Montana in this regard. In fact, some areas of Montana do suffer seasonally from poor air quality, worst of all in Missoula, whose air (despite improvements since the 1980s) is sometimes as bad as in Los Angeles. Missoula's air problems, exacerbated by winter temperature inversions and by its location in a valley that traps air, stem from a combination of vehicle emissions throughout the year, wood-burning stoves in the winter, and forest fires and logging in the summer.

Montana's remaining major sets of environmental problems are the linked ones of introductions of harmful non-native species and losses of valuable native species. These problems especially involve fish, deer and elk, and weeds.

Montana originally supported valuable fisheries based on native Cut-throat Trout (Montana's state fish), Bull Trout, Arctic Grayling, and White-fish. All of those species except Whitefish have now declined in Montana from a combination of causes whose relative impact varies among the species: less water in the mountain streams where they spawn and develop, because of water removal for irrigation; warmer temperatures and more sediment in those streams, because of logging; overfishing; competition from, and in some cases hybridization with, introduced Rainbow Trout, Brook Trout, and Brown Trout; predation by introduced Northern Pike and Lake Trout; and infection by an introduced parasite causing whirling dis-ease. For example, Northern Pike, which are voracious fish-eaters, have been illegally introduced into some western Montana lakes and rivers by fisher-men fond of catching pike, and have virtually eliminated from those lakes and rivers the populations of Bull Trout and Cutthroat on which they prey. Similarly, Flathead Lake's formerly robust fishery based on several native fish species has been destroyed by introduced Lake Trout.

Whirling disease was accidentally introduced into the U.S from its na-tive Europe in 1958 when a Pennsylvania fish hatchery imported some Dan-ish fish that proved to be infected with the disease. It has now spread throughout most of the western U.S., partly through transport by birds, but especially as a result of people (including government agencies and private fish hatcheries) stocking lakes and rivers with infected fish. Once the para-site gets into a body of water, it is impossible to eradicate. By 1994 whirling disease had reduced the Rainbow Trout population of the Madison River, Montana's most famous trout stream, by more than 90%.

At least whirling disease is not transmissible to humans; it is merely bad for fishing-based tourism. Another introduced disease, chronic wasting dis-ease (CWD) of deer and elk, is of more concern because it might cause an incurably fatal human illness. CWD is the deer/elk equivalent of prion dis-eases in other animals, of which the most notorious are Creutzfeldt-Jakob disease in humans, mad cow disease or bovine spongiform encephalopathy (BSE) of cattle (transmissible to humans), and scrapie of sheep. These in-fections cause an untreatable degeneration of the nervous system; no hu-man infected with Creutzfeldt-Jakob disease has ever recovered. CWD was first detected in western North American deer and elk in the 1970s, possibly (some people suggest) because deer housed for studies at a western univer-sity in a pen near scrapie-infected sheep were released into the wild after completion of the studies. (Today, such a release would be considered a criminal act.) Further spread from state to state was accelerated by transfers of exposed deer and elk from one commercial game farm to another. We do not know yet whether CWD can be transmitted from deer or elk to people, as can mad cow disease, but the recent deaths of some elk hunters from Creutzfeldt-Jakob disease have raised alarms in some quarters. The state of Wisconsin, concerned that fear of transmission could cripple the state's one-billion-dollar-per-year deer hunting industry, is in the process of killing 25,000 deer (a desperate solution that sickens everybody involved) in an infected area in hopes of controlling the CWD epidemic there.

While CWD is potentially Montana's most frightening problem caused by an introduced pest, introduced weeds are already Montana's most expensive such problem. About 30 noxious weed species, mostly of Eurasian origin, have become established in Montana after arriving accidentally in hay or as wind-blown seeds, or in one case being introduced intentionally as an attractive ornamental plant whose dangers weren't anticipated. They cause damage in several ways: they are inedible or poorly edible to livestock and wild animals, but they crowd out edible plant species, so they reduce the amount of livestock fodder by up to 90%; some of them are toxic to animals; and they may triple rates of erosion because their roots hold the soil less well than do roots of native grasses.

Economically, the two most important of these weeds are Spotted Knapweed and Leafy Spurge, both now widespread throughout Montana. Spotted Knapweed takes over from native grasses by secreting chemicals that quickly kill them, and by producing vast numbers of seeds. While it can be pulled out by hand from selected small fields, it has now infested 566,000 acres in the Bitterroot Valley alone and 5,000,000 acres in all of Montana, an area far too large for hand-pulling to be feasible. Spotted Knapweed can also be controlled by herbicides, but the cheaper herbicides that kill it also kill many other plant species, and the herbicide specific for Spotted Knapweed is very expensive ($800 per gallon). In addition, it is uncertain whether the breakdown products of those herbicides end up in the Bitterroot River or in the aquifers used for human drinking water, and whether those products themselves have harmful effects. Because Spotted Knapweed has become established on large areas of national forest as well as of pastureland, it reduces the fodder production not only for domestic animals but also for wild herbivores in the forest, so that it may have the effect of driving deer and elk from forest down into pastures by reducing the amount of food available in the forest. Leafy Spurge is at present less widespread than knapweed but much harder to control and impossible to pull out by hand, because it establishes underground roots 20 feet long.

Estimates of the direct economic damage that these and other weeds cause in Montana are over $100,000,000 per year. Their presence also reduces real estate values and farm productivity. Above all, they are a huge pain in the neck for farmers, because they cannot be controlled by any single measure alone but require complex integrated management systems. They force farmers to change many practices simultaneously: pulling out weeds, applying herbicides, changing fertilizer use, releasing insect and fungus enemies of weeds, lighting controlled fires, changing mowing schedules, and altering crop rotations and annual grazing practices. All that because of a few small plants whose dangers were mostly unappreciated at the time, and some of whose seeds arrived unnoticed!

Thus, seemingly pristine Montana actually suffers from serious environmental problems involving toxic wastes, forests, soils, water, climate change, biodiversity losses, and introduced pests. All of these problems translate into economic problems. They provide much of the explanation for why Montana's economy has been declining in recent decades to the point where what was formerly one of our richest states is now one of the poorest.

Whether or how these problems become resolved will depend on the attitudes and values that Montanans hold. But Montana's population is becoming increasingly heterogeneous and cannot agree on a vision for their state's environment and future. Many of my friends commented on the growing polarization of opinion. For instance, banker Emil Erhardt explained to me, "There is too much raucous debate here. The prosperity of the 1950s meant that all of us were poor then, or we felt poor. There were no extremes of wealth; at least, wealth wasn't visible. Now, we have a two-tiered society with lower-income families struggling to survive at the bottom, and the wealthier newcomers at the top able to acquire enough property that they can isolate themselves. In essence, we are zoning by money, not by land use!"

The polarization that my friends mention is along many axes: rich versus poor, old-timers versus newcomers, those clinging to a traditional lifestyle versus others welcoming change, pro-growth versus anti-growth voices, those for and against governmental planning, and those with and without school-age children. Fueling these disagreements are Montana's paradoxes that I mentioned near the beginning of this chapter: a state with poor residents but attracting rich newcomers, even while the state's own children are deserting Montana upon graduating high school.

I initially wondered whether Montana's environmental problems and polarizing disputes might involve selfish behavior on the part of individuals who advanced their own interests in full knowledge that they were simultaneously damaging the rest of Montana society. This may be true in some cases, such as the proposals of some mining executives to carry out cyanide heap-leach gold extraction despite the abundant evidence of resulting toxicity problems; the transfers of deer and elk between game farms by some farm owners despite the known resulting risk of spreading chronic wasting disease; and the illegal introductions of pike into lakes and rivers by some fishermen for their own fishing pleasure, despite the history of such transfers having destroyed many other fisheries. Even in these cases, though, I haven't interviewed individuals involved and don't know whether they could honestly claim that they thought they had been acting safely. Whenever I have actually been able to talk with Montanans, I have found their actions to be consistent with their values, even if those values clash with my own or those of other Montanans. That is, for the most part Montana's difficulties cannot be simplistically attributed to selfish evil people knowingly and reprehensibly profiting at the expense of neighbors. Instead, they involve clashes between people whose own particular backgrounds and values cause them to favor policies differing from those favored by people with different backgrounds and values. Here are some of the points of view currently competing to shape Montana's future.

One clash is between "old-timers" and "newcomers": i.e., people born in Montana, of families resident in the state for many generations, respecting a lifestyle and economy traditionally built on the three pillars of mining, logging, and agriculture, versus recent arrivals or seasonal visitors. All three of those economic pillars are now in steep decline in Montana. All but a few Montana mines are already closed, due to toxic waste problems plus competition from overseas mines with lower costs. Timber sales are now more than 80% below former peak levels, and most mills and timber businesses other than specialty firms (notably, log cabin home builders) have closed because of a combination of factors: increasing public preference for maintaining intact forests, huge costs of forest management and fire suppression, and competition from logging operations in warmer and wetter climates with inherent advantages over logging operations in cold dry Montana. Agriculture, the third pillar, is also dwindling: for instance, of the 400 dairies operating in the Bitterroot Valley in 1964, only nine still exist. The reasons behind Montana agriculture's decline are more complex than those behind the decline in mining and logging, though in the background looms the fundamental competitive disadvantage of Montana's cold dry climate for growing crops and cows as well as trees.

Montana farmers today who continue to farm into their old age do it in part because they love the lifestyle and take great pride in it. As Tim Huls told me, "It's a wonderful lifestyle to get up before dawn and see the sunrise, to watch hawks fly overhead, and to see deer jump through your hay field to avoid your haying equipment." Jack Hirschy, a rancher whom I met in 1950 when he was 29 years old, is still working on his ranch today at the age of 83, while his father Fred rode a horse on his 91st birthday. But "ranching and farming are hazardous hard work," in the words of Jack's rancher sister Jill. Jack suffered internal injuries and broken ribs from a tractor accident at age 77, while Fred was almost killed by a falling tree at age 58. Tim Huls added to his proud comment about the wonderful lifestyle, "Occasionally I get up at 3 A.M. and work until 10 P.M. This isn't a 9 to 5 job. But none of our children will sign up for being a farmer if it is 3 A.M. to 10 P.M. every day."

That remark by Tim illustrates one reason for the rise and fall of Montana farming: the lifestyle was highly valued by older generations, but many farmers' children today have different values. They want jobs that involve sitting indoors in front of computer screens rather than heaving hay bales, and taking off evenings and weekends rather than having to milk cows and harvest hay that don't take evenings and weekends off. They don't want a life forcing them to do literally back-breaking physical work into their 80s, as all three surviving Hirschy brothers and sisters are still doing.

Steve Powell explained to me, "People used to expect no more of a farm than to produce enough to feed themselves; today, they want more out of life than just getting fed; they want to earn enough to send their kids to college." When John Cook was growing up on a farm with his parents, "At dinnertime, my mother was satisfied to go to the orchard and gather asparagus, and as a boy I was satisfied for fun to go hunting and fishing. Now, kids expect fast food and HBO; if their parents don't provide that, they feel deprived compared to their peers. In my day a young adult expected to be poor for the next 20 years, and only thereafter, if you were lucky, might you hope to end up more comfortably. Now, young adults expect to be comfortable early; a kid's first questions about a job are 'What are the pay, the hours, and the vacations?'" Every Montana farmer whom I know, and who loves being a farmer, is either very concerned whether any of his/her children will want to carry on the family farm, or already knows that none of them will.

Economic considerations now make it difficult for farmers to earn a living at farming, because farm costs have been rising much faster than farm income. The price that a farmer receives for milk and beef today is virtually the same as 20 years ago, but costs of fuel, farm machinery, fertilizers, and other farm necessities are higher. Rick Laible gave me an example: "Fifty years ago, a farmer who wanted to buy a new truck paid for it by selling two cows. Nowadays, a new truck costs around $15,000, but a cow still sells for only $600, so the farmer would have to sell 25 cows to pay for the truck." That's the logic underlying the following joke that I was told by a Montana farmer. Question: "What would you do if you were given a million dollars?" Answer: "I love farming, and I would stay here on my money-losing farm until I had used up the million dollars!"

Those shrinking profit margins, and increasing competition, have made the Bitterroot Valley's hundreds of formerly self-supporting small farms uneconomic. First, the farmers found that they needed additional income from outside jobs to survive, and then they had to give up the farm because it required too much work on evenings and weekends after the outside job. For instance, 60 years ago Kathy Vaughn's grandparents supported themselves on a 40-acre farm, and so Kathy and Pat Vaughn bought their own 40-acre farm in 1977. With six cows, six sheep, a few pigs, hay, Kathy working as a schoolteacher, and Pat as an irrigation system builder, they fed and raised three children on the farm, but it provided no security or retirement income. After eight years, they sold the farm, moved into town, and all of their children have now left Montana.

Throughout the U.S., small farms are being squeezed out by large farms, the only ones able to survive on shrinking profit margins by economies of scale. But in southwestern Montana it is now impossible for small farmers to become large farmers by buying more land, for reasons succinctly explained by Allen Bjergo: "Agriculture in the U.S. is shifting to areas like Iowa and Nebraska, where no one would live for the fun of it because it isn't beautiful as in Montana! Here in Montana, people do want to live for the fun of it, and so they are willing to pay much more for land than agriculture on the land would support. The Bitterroot is becoming a horse valley. Horses are economic because, whereas prices for agricultural products depend on the value of the food itself and are not unlimited, many people are willing to spend anything for horses that yield no economic benefit."

Land prices in the Bitterroot are now 10 or 20 times higher than a few decades ago. At those prices, carrying costs for a mortgage are far higher than could be paid by use of the land as a farm. That's the immediate reason why small farmers in the Bitterroot can't survive by expanding, and why the farms eventually become sold for non-farm use. If old farmers are still living on their farm when they die, their heirs are forced to sell the land to a developer for much more than it would fetch by sale to another farmer, in order to pay the estate taxes on the great increase in land value during the deceased farmer's lifetime. More often, the farm is sold by the old farmers themselves. Much as they cringe at seeing the land that they have farmed and loved for 60 years subdivided into 5-acre lots of suburban sprawl, the rise in land prices lets them sell even a small formerly self-supporting farm to a developer for a million dollars. They have no other choice to obtain the money necessary to support themselves after retirement, because they have not been able to save money as farmers, and because their children don't want to continue farming anyway. In Rick Laible's words, "For a farmer, his land is his only pension fund."

What accounts for the enormous jump in land prices? Basically, it's because the Bitterroot's gorgeous environment attracts wealthy newcomers. The people who buy out old farmers are either those new arrivals themselves, or else land speculators who will subdivide the farm into lots to sell to newcomers or to wealthy people already living in the valley. Almost all of the valley's recent 4%-per-year population growth represents newcomers moving in from outside the valley, not an excess of births over deaths within the valley. Seasonal recreational tourism is also on the increase, thanks to out-of-staters (like Stan Falkow, Lucy Tompkins, and my sons) visiting to fly-fish, golf, or hunt. As a recent economic analysis commissioned by Ravalli County explains it, "There should be no mystery as to why so many residents are coming to the Bitterroot Valley. Simply put, it is a very attractive place to live with its mountains, forests, streams, wildlife, views and vistas, and relatively mild climate."

The largest group of immigrants consists of "half-retirees" or early retirees in the age bracket 45–59, supporting themselves by real estate equity from their out-of-state homes that they sold, and often also by income that they continue to earn from their out-of-state businesses or Internet businesses. That is, their sources of support are immune to the economic problems associated with Montana's environment. For example, a Californian who sells a tiny house in California for $500,000 can use that money in Montana to buy five acres of land with a large house and horses, go fishing, and support herself in her early retirement with savings and with what remains of her cashed-out California house equity. Hence nearly half of the recent immigrants to the Bitterroot have been Californians. Because they are buying Bitterroot land for its beauty and not for the value of the cows or apples that it could produce, the price that they are willing to offer for

Bitterroot land bears no relation to what the land would be worth if used for agriculture.

But that huge jump in house prices has created a housing problem for Bitterroot Valley residents who have to support themselves by working. Many end up unable to afford houses, having to live in mobile homes or recreational vehicles or with their parents, and having to hold two or three jobs simultaneously to support even that spartan lifestyle.

Naturally, these cruel economic facts create antagonism between the old-time residents and the new arrivals from out-of-state, especially rich out-of-staters who maintain a second, third, or even fourth home in Montana (in addition to their homes in San Francisco, Palm Springs, and Florida), and who visit for just short periods each year in order to fish, hunt, golf, or ski. The old-timers complain about the noisy private jet planes flying rich visitors in and out of Hamilton Airport within a single day from their home in San Francisco, just to spend a few hours playing golf at their fourth home on the Stock Farm. Old-timers resent outsiders buying up large former farms that local residents would also like to buy but can no longer afford, and on which the locals could formerly get permission to hunt or fish, but now the new landowners want to hunt or fish there exclusively with their rich friends and keep out the locals. Misunderstandings arise from the clash of values and expectations: for instance, newcomers want elk to come down from the mountains to ranch areas, because they look pretty or in order to hunt them, but old-timers don't want elk to come down and eat their hay.

Rich out-of-state homeowners are careful to stay in Montana for less than 180 days per year, in order to avoid having to pay Montana income tax and thereby to contribute to the cost of local government and schools. One local told me, "Those outsiders have different priorities from us here: what they want is privacy and expensive isolation, and they don't want to be involved locally except when they take their out-of-state friends to the local bar to show their friends the rural lifestyle and the quaint local people. They like wildlife, fishing, hunting, and the scenery, but they're not part of the local community." Or, as Emil Erhardt said, "Their attitude is, 'I came here to ride my horse, enjoy the mountains, and go fishing: don't bother me with issues I moved here to get away from.' "

But there's another side to the rich out-of-staters. Emil Erhardt added, "The Stock Farm provides employment with high-paying jobs, it pays a high fraction of the property taxes for the whole Bitterroot Valley, it pays for its own security staff, and it doesn't make many demands on the community or on local government services. Our sheriff doesn't get called to the Stock Farm to break up bar fights, and Stock Farm owners don't send their children to the schools here." John Cook acknowledged, "The plus side of those rich owners is that if Charles Schwab hadn't bought up all that land, it wouldn't still be providing wildlife habitat and green open space, because that land would otherwise have been subdivided by some developer."

Because the rich out-of-staters were attracted to Montana by its beautiful environment, some of them take good care of their property and become leaders in defending the environment and instituting land planning. For example, my summer home for the last seven years has been a rented house situated on the Bitterroot River south of Hamilton, and belonging to a private entity called the Teller Wildlife Refuge. Otto Teller was a rich Californian who liked to come to Montana to fish for trout. One day, he was infuriated to encounter large construction machinery dumping dirt into one of his favorite fishing holes on the Gallatin River. He became further enraged when he saw how massive clear-cutting carried out by logging companies in the 1950s was devastating his beloved trout streams and damaging their water quality. In 1984 Otto began buying up prime riverside land along the Bitterroot River and incorporated it into a private wildlife refugee, which he nevertheless let local people continue to visit in order to hunt and fish. He ultimately donated conservation easements on his land to a nonprofit organization called the Montana Land Reliance, in order to ensure that the land would be managed in perpetuity so as to preserve its environmental qualities. Had Otto Teller, that wealthy Californian, not bought that 1,600 acres of land, it would have been subdivided for small house lots.

The influx of newcomers, the resulting rise in land prices and property taxes, the poverty of Montana old-timer residents, and their conservative attitude towards government and taxes (see below) all contribute to the plight of Montana schools, which are funded largely by property taxes. Because Ravalli County has so little industrial or commercial property, the main source of property taxes there is residential property taxes, and those have been rising with the increase in land values. To old-timers and less affluent newcomers already on a tight budget, every increase in property taxes is a big deal. Not surprisingly, they often react by voting against proposed school bonds and supplemental local property tax levies for their schools.

As a result, while public schools account for two-thirds of Ravalli County local government spending, that spending as a percentage of personal income stands last among 24 rural western U.S. counties comparable to Ravalli County, and personal income itself is low in Ravalli County. Even by the low school-funding standards of the state of Montana, Ravalli County school funding stands out as low. Most Ravalli County school districts keep their spending down to the absolute minimum required by Montana state law. The average salaries of Montana schoolteachers rank among the lowest in the U.S., and especially in Ravalli County those low salaries plus soaring land prices make it hard for teachers to afford housing.

Montana-born children are leaving the state because many of them aspire to non-Montana lifestyles, and because those who do aspire to Montana lifestyles can't find jobs within the state. For instance, in the years since Steve Powell graduated from Hamilton High School, 70% of his classmates have left the Bitterroot Valley. Without exception, all of my friends who chose to live in Montana discussed, as a painful subject, whether their children had remained or would come back. All eight of Allen and Jackie Bjergo's children, and six of Jill and John Eliel's eight children, are now living outside Montana.

To quote Emil Erhardt again, "We in the Bitterroot Valley export children. Outside influences, like TV, have now made our children aware of what's available outside the valley, and what's unavailable inside it. People bring their children here because of the outdoors, and because it's a great place to bring up kids, but then their children don't want the outdoors." I recall my own sons, who love coming to Montana to fish for two weeks in the summer but are accustomed to the urban life of Los Angeles for the rest of the year, expressing shock as they came out of a Hamilton fast-food restaurant and realized how few urban recreational opportunities were available to the local teenagers who had just waited on them. Hamilton has the grand total of two movie theatres, and the nearest mall is 50 miles away in Missoula. A similar shock grows on many of those Hamilton teenagers themselves, when they travel outside Montana and realize what they are missing back at home.

Like rural western Americans in general, Montanans tend to be conservative, and suspicious of governmental regulation. That attitude arose historically because early settlers were living at low population density on a frontier far from government centers, had to be self-sufficient, and couldn't look to government to solve their problems. Montanans especially bristle at the geographically and psychologically remote federal government in

Washington, D.C., telling them what to do. (But they don't bristle at the federal government's money, of which Montana receives and accepts about a dollar-and-a-half for every dollar sent from Montana to Washington.) In the view of Montanans, the American urban majority that runs the federal government has no comprehension of conditions in Montana. In the view of federal government managers, Montana's environment is a treasure belonging to all Americans and is not there just for the private benefit of Montanans.

Even by Montana standards, the Bitterroot Valley is especially conservative and anti-government. That may be due to many early Bitterroot settlers having come from Confederate states, and to a further influx of bitter right-wing conservatives from Los Angeles after that city's race riots. As Chris Miller said, "Liberals and Democrats living here weep as they read the results after each election, because the outcomes are so conservative." Extreme proponents of right-wing conservativism in the Bitterroot are members of the so-called militias, groups of landowners who hoard weapons, refuse to pay taxes, keep all others off their property, and are variously tolerated or else regarded as paranoid by other valley residents.

One consequence of those political attitudes in the Bitterroot is opposition to governmental zoning or planning, and a feeling that landowners should enjoy the right to do whatever they want with their private property. Ravalli County has neither a county building code nor county-wide zoning. Outside of two towns plus voluntary zoning districts formed by local voters in some rural areas outside towns, there aren't even any restrictions on the use to which land can be put. For instance, one evening when I was visiting the Bitterroot with my teenaged son Joshua, he read in the newspaper that a movie he had wanted to see was playing in one of Hamilton's two movie theatres. I asked for directions to that theatre, drove him there, and discovered to my astonishment that it had been built recently in an area otherwise consisting entirely of farmland, except for an adjacent large biotechnology laboratory. There were no zoning regulations about that changed use of farmland. In contrast, in many other parts of the U.S. there is sufficient public concern about loss of farmland that zoning regulations restrict or prohibit its conversion to commercial property, and voters would be especially horrified at the prospect of a theatre with lots of traffic next to a potentially sensitive biotechnology facility.

Montanans are beginning to realize that two of their most cherished attitudes are in direct opposition: their pro-individual-rights anti-government-regulation attitude, and their pride in their quality of life. That phrase "quality of life" has come up in virtually every conversation that I have had with Montanans about their future. The phrase refers to Montanans' being able to enjoy, every day of their lives, that beautiful environment which out-of-state tourists like me consider it a privilege to be able to visit for a week or two each year. The phrase also refers to Montanans' pride in their traditional lifestyle as a rural, low-density, egalitarian population descended from old-timer settlers. Emil Erhardt told me, "In the Bitterroot people want to maintain the essence of a rural quiet little community in which everyone is in the same condition, poor and proud of it." Or, as Stan Falkow said, "Formerly, when you drove down the road in the Bitterroot, you waved at any car that passed, because you knew everyone."

Unfortunately, by permitting unrestricted land use and thereby making possible an influx of new residents, Montanans' long-standing and continuing opposition to government regulation is responsible for degradation of the beautiful natural environment and quality of life that they cherish. This was best explained to me by Steve Powell: "I tell my real estate agent and developer friends, 'You have to protect the beauty of the landscape, the wildlife, and the agricultural land.' Those are the things that create property value. The longer we wait to do planning, the less landscape beauty there will be. Undeveloped land is valuable to the community as a whole: it's an important part of that 'quality of life' that attracts people here. With increasing growth pressure, the same people who used to be anti-government are now concerned about growth. They say that their favorite recreation area is becoming crowded, and they now admit that there have to be rules." When Steve was a Ravalli County commissioner in 1993, he sponsored public meetings just to start discussion of land use planning and to stimulate the public to think about it. Tough-looking members of the militias came to those meetings to disrupt them, openly carrying holsters with guns in order to intimidate other people. Steve lost his subsequent bid for reelection.

It's still unclear how the clash between this resistance to government planning and that need for government planning will be resolved. To quote Steve Powell again, "People are trying to preserve the Bitterroot as a rural community, but they can't figure out how to preserve it in a way that would let them survive economically." Land Lindbergh and Hank Goetz made essentially the same point: "The fundamental problem here is how we hang on to these attractions that brought us to Montana, while still dealing with the change that can't be avoided."

■ ■ ■

To conclude this chapter about Montana, largely related in my words, I'll now let four of my Montanan friends relate in their own words how they came to be Montanans, and their concerns for Montana's future. Rick Laible is a newcomer, now a state senator; Chip Pigman, an old-timer and a land developer; Tim Huls, an old-timer and a dairy farmer; and John Cook, a newcomer and a fishing guide.

Here is Rick Laible's story: "I was born and brought up in the area around Berkeley, California, where I have a business manufacturing wooden store fixtures. My wife Frankie and I were both working hard. One day, Frankie looked at me and said, 'You're working 10 to 12 hours a day, seven days a week.' We decided to semi-retire, drove 4,600 miles around the West to find a place to settle, bought our first house in a remote part of the Bitterroots in 1993, and moved to a ranch that we bought near the town of Victor in 1994. My wife raises Egyptian Arabian horses on the ranch, and I go back to California once a month for my business that I still own there. We have five children. Our oldest son always wanted to move to Montana, and he manages our ranch. The other four of our kids don't understand the Montana quality of life, don't understand that Montanans are nicer people, and don't understand why their parents moved here.

"Nowadays, after each of my monthly four-day visits to California, I want to get out of there: I feel, 'They're like rats in a cage!' Frankie goes back to California only twice a year to see her grandchildren, and that's enough of California for her. As an example of what I don't like about California, I was recently back there for a meeting, and I had a little free time, so I took a walk on the town street. I noticed that people coming in the other direction lowered their eyes and avoided eye contact with me. When I say 'good morning' to people that I don't know in California, they're taken aback. Here, in the Bitterroot, it's the rule that when you pass someone that you don't know, you make eye contact.

"As for how I got into politics, I've always had many political opinions. The state assembly legislator for my district here in the Bitterroots decided not to run and suggested to me that I run instead. He tried to convince me, and so did Frankie. Why did I decide to run? It was 'to put something back'—I felt that life has been good to me, and I wanted to make life better for local people.

"The legislative issue in which I'm particularly interested is forest management, because my district is forested and many of my constituents are woodworkers. The town of Darby, which lies in my district, used to be a rich lumber town, and forest management would create jobs for the valley. Originally, there were about seven lumber mills in the valley, but now there are none, so the valley has lost those jobs and infrastructure. The decisions about forest management here are currently made by environmental groups and the federal government, with the county and state being excluded. I'm working on forest management legislation that would involve collaboration between the three lead parties within the state: federal, state, and county agencies.

"Several decades ago Montana was among the top 10 U.S. states in its per-capita income; now, it stands 49 out of 50, because of the decline of the extraction industries (logging, coal, mines, oil, and gas). Those lost jobs were high-paying union jobs. Of course, we should not go back to over-extraction, of which there was some in the old days. Here in the Bitterroot, both a husband and wife have to work, and often they each have to hold two jobs, in order to make ends meet, yet here we are surrounded by this over-fueled forest. Everybody here, environmentalists or not, agrees that we need some fuel reduction in our forests. Forest restoration would eliminate over-fueling of the forests, especially of the low small trees. Now, that overfueling is eliminated just by burning it. The federal government's National Fire Plan would do it by mechanical extraction of the logs, the purpose being to re-duce the biomass of fuel. Most of our American timber comes from Canada! Yet the original mandate of our national forests was to provide a steady stream of timber, and to provide watershed protection. It used to be that 25% of the revenue from national forests went to schools, but that national forest revenue has decreased greatly recently. More logging would mean more money for our schools.

"At present, there is no growth policy for all of Ravalli County! The val-ley's population has grown by 40% in the last decade, and it may grow by 40% in the next decade: where will that next 40% go? Can we lock the door to more people moving in? Do we have the *right* to lock the door? Should a farmer be forbidden to subdivide and develop his property, and should he be sentenced to a life of farming? A farmer's money for his retirement is all in his land. If the farmer is forbidden to sell his land for development or to build a house, what are you doing to him?

"As for the long-term effects of growth, there will be cycles here in the future, as there have been in the past, and in one of the cycles the newcom-ers will go back home. Montana will never overdevelop, but Ravalli County will continue to develop. There is a huge amount of publicly owned land here in the county. The price of land here will rise until it gets too high, at which point prospective buyers will start a land boom somewhere else with cheaper land. Ultimately, all of the farmland in the valley will be developed."

Now, this is Chip Pigman's story: "My mother's grandfather moved here from Oklahoma around 1925 and had an apple orchard. My mother grew up here on a dairy and sheep farm, and she now owns a real estate agency in town. My father moved here as a child, was in mining and sugarbeets, and held a second job in construction; that's how I got into construction. I was born and went to school here, and I got my B.A. in accounting at the University of Montana nearby in Missoula.

"For three years I moved to Denver, but I disliked city living and I was determined to move back here, in part because the Bitterroot is a great place to raise children. My bicycle was stolen within my first two weeks in Denver. I didn't like the city's traffic and large groups of people. My needs are satisfied here. I was raised without 'culture' and I don't need it. I waited just until my stock in the Denver company that employed me was vested, and then I moved back here. That meant leaving a Denver job paying $35,000 a year plus fringe benefits, and coming back here to earn $17,000 per year without any benefits. I was willing to give up the secure Denver job in order to be able to live in the valley, where I can hike. My wife had never experienced that insecurity, but I had always lived with that insecurity in the Bitterroot. Here in the Bitterroot, you have to be a two-income household in order to survive, and my parents always had to hold multiple odd jobs. I was prepared if necessary to take a nighttime job stocking groceries to earn money for my family. After we returned here, it took five years before I again had an income at my Denver level, and it was another year or two after that until I had health insurance.

"My business is mainly house construction, plus development of the less expensive parcels of raw land—I can't afford to buy and develop high-end parcels. Originally, the lots that I developed used to be ranches, but most of them are no longer operating ranches by the time that I acquire them; they have already been sold, resold, and possibly subdivided several times since they were last farmed. They're already out of production, and they carry knapweed rather than pasture.

"An exception is my current Hamilton Heights project, a 40-acre former ranch that I acquired and that I'm now trying to subdivide for the first time. I submitted to the county a detailed development plan requiring three sets of approvals, of which I succeeded in getting the first two. But the third and last step was a public hearing, at which 80 people living nearby appeared and protested on the grounds that subdivision would mean a loss of agricultural land. Yes, the lot has good soil and used to be good agricultural land, but it was no longer in agricultural production when I bought it. I paid $225,000 for those 40 acres; it would be impossible to support that high cost by agriculture. But public opinion doesn't look at the economics. Instead, neighbors say, 'We like to see open space of farmland or forest around us.' But how is one to maintain that open space if the lot's seller is someone in their sixties who needs the money to retire? If the neighbors had wanted to preserve that lot as open land, they should have bought it themselves. They could have bought it, but they didn't. They want still to control it, even though they don't own it.

"I was turned down at that public hearing because the county planners didn't want to oppose 80 voters shortly before an election. I hadn't negotiated with the neighbors before submitting my plan, because I am bullheaded, I want to do what I think I have the right to do, and I don't like being told what to do. Also, people don't realize that, on a small project like this one, negotiations are very expensive of my time and money. On a similar project next time, I would talk first with the neighbors, but I would also bring 50 of my own workers to the hearing, so that the county commissioners would see that there's also public demand in favor of the project. I've been stuck with the carrying cost of the land during this fight. The neighbors would like the land to sit with nothing done to it!

"People talk about there being too much development here and the valley eventually becoming overpopulated, and they try to blame me. My answer is: there's demand for my product, the demand isn't something that I'm creating. Every year there are more buildings and traffic in the valley. But I like to hike, and when you hike or fly over the valley, you see lots of open space here. The media say that there was 44% growth in the valley in the last 10 years, but that just meant a population increase from 25,000 to still only 35,000 people. Young people are leaving the valley. I have 30 employees, to whom my company gives employment and provides a pension plan, health insurance, paid vacation, and a profit-sharing plan. No competitor offers that package, so I have only low turnover of my workforce. I'm frequently seen by environmentalists as a cause of the problems in the valley, but I can't create demand; someone else will put up the buildings if I don't.

"I intend to stay here in the valley for the rest of my life. I belong to this community, and I support many community projects: for example, I support the local baseball, swim, and football teams. Because I'm from here and I want to stay here, I don't have a get-rich-and-get-out mentality. I expect still to be here in 20 years, driving by my old projects. I don't want to look out then and have to admit to myself, 'That was a bad project that I did!' "

Tim Huls is a dairy farmer from an old-timer family: "My great-grandparents were the first ones in our family to come here in 1912. They bought 40 acres when land was still very cheap, and they kept a dozen dairy cows which they milked by hand for two hours every morning and then again for two hours every evening. My grandparents bought 110 more acres for just pennies per acre, sold cream from their cows' milk to make cheese, and raised apples and hay. However, it was a struggle. There were difficult times, and they hung on by their fingernails, while some other farmers weren't able to. My father considered going to college but decided instead to stay on the farm. He was the innovative visionary who made the crucial business decision to commit himself to specialized dairy farming and to build a 150-cow milking barn, as a way to increase the value obtained from the land.

"My brothers and I bought the farm from our parents. They didn't give it to us. Instead, they sold it to us, because they wanted us to decide who really wanted badly enough to do farming to be willing to pay for the farm. Each brother and spouse own their own land and lease it to our family corporation. Most of the work of running the farm is done by us brothers, our wives, and our children; we have only a small number of non-family employees. There are very few family farm corporations like ours. One thing that lets us succeed is that we all share a common religious faith; most of us go to the same community church in Corvallis. Sure, we do have family conflicts. But we can have a good fight and still be best friends at night; our parents fought too, but they always talked about it before sundown. We have figured out which hills are worth dying on, and which are not.

"Somehow, that family spirit got passed on to my two sons. The two of them learned cooperation as children: when the youngest was still only seven years old, they began shifting 40-foot sections of aluminum sprinkler pipe, 16 sections in a line, one boy at each end of a 40-foot section. After leaving home, they became roommates, and now they are best friends and neighbors. Other families try to raise their children to maintain family ties as did our children, but the children of those other families didn't stay together, even though they seemed to be doing the same things that our family did.

"Farm economics are tough, because the highest value to which land can be put here in the Bitterroot is for homes and development. Farmers in our area face the decision: should we continue farming, or should we sell our land for home sites and retire? There's no legal crop that would let us compete with the house development value of our land, so we can't afford to buy more land. Instead, what determines our survival is whether we can be as efficient as possible on the 760 acres that we already own or lease. Our costs, like the price of pickup trucks, have increased, but we still get the same money today for 100 pounds of milk as we did 20 years ago. How can we make a profit on a tighter profit margin? We have to adopt new technology, which takes capital, and we have to continue to educate ourselves on applying the technology to our circumstances. We have to be willing to abandon old ways.

"For instance, this year we spent substantial capital to build a new computerized 200-cow dairy parlor. It will have automatic manure collection, and a moving fence to push cows towards an automatic milking machine through which they'll be moved automatically. Each cow is recognized by computer, is milked with a computer at her stall, the conductivity of her milk is measured at once to detect an infection early, each milking is weighed to track her health and nutritional needs, and the computer's sorting criteria let us group cows together into different pens. Our farm is now serving as a model for the whole state of Montana. Other farmers are watching us to see if this will work.

"We have some doubts ourselves whether it will work, because of two risks beyond our control. But if we're to have any hope of staying in agriculture, we had to do this modernization, or else we would have no alternative to becoming developers: here one either has to grow cows or to grow houses on one's land. One of the two risks beyond our control is price fluctuations in the farm machinery and services that we have to buy, and in the price we get for our milk. Dairy farmers have no control over the price of milk. Our milk is perishable; once the cow is milked, we have only two days to get that milk off the ranch to market, so we have no bargaining power. We sell the milk, and buyers *tell* us what price it will fetch.

"The other risk beyond our control is the public's environmental concerns, which include our treatment of animals, their wastes, and associated odor. We try to control these impacts to the best of our ability, but our efforts will probably not please everyone. The newcomers to the Bitterroot come for the view. At first, they like to see the cows and hayfields in the distance, but sometimes they don't comprehend all that comes with agricultural operations, especially dairies. In other areas where dairies and development coexist, the objections to dairies are associated with their odor, the sound of running equipment too late at night, truck traffic on 'our quiet rural road,' and more. We even had a complaint once when a neighbor got cow manure on her white jogging shoes. One of our concerns is that people unsympathetic with animal agriculture could propose an initiative to restrict or ban dairy farming in our area. For example, two years ago an initiative banning hunting on game farms put a Bitterroot elk ranch out of business. We never thought that that would happen, and we can't help but feel that there is a possibility that, if we are not vigilant, it could happen to us. In a society that espouses tolerance, it's amazing how intolerant some folks are to animal agriculture and what comes with producing food."

The last of these four life stories that I'll quote is that of John Cook, the fishing guide who with infinite patience introduced my then-10-year-old sons to fly-fishing and has been taking them out on the Bitterroot River for the last seven summers: "I grew up on an apple orchard in Washington's Wenatchee Valley. At the end of high school I had a wild hippie phase and set off for India on a motorcycle. I only got as far as the U.S. East Coast, but by then I had traveled all over the U.S. After I met my wife Pat, we moved to Washington's Olympic Peninsula and then to Kodiak Island in Alaska, where I worked for 16 years as a wildlife and fisheries ranger. We next moved down to Portland, so that Pat could take care of her sick grandmother and grandfather. The grandmother died soon, and then one week after the grandfather's death we got out of Portland and came to Montana.

"I had first visited Montana in the 1970s, when Pat's father was a wilderness outfitter working in Idaho's Selway-Bitterroot Wilderness just over the Montana border. Pat and I used to work for him part-time, with Pat doing the cooking and me doing the guiding. Already then, Pat loved the Bitterroot River and wanted to live on it, but land there already cost a thousand dollars per acre, much too expensive to support the cost of a mortgage by farming. Then in 1994, when we were looking to leave Portland, the opportunity arose to buy a 10-acre farm near the Bitterroot River at an affordable price. The farmhouse needed some attention, so we spent a few years fixing it up, and I took out a license as an outfitter and fishing guide.

"There are only two places in the world to which I feel a deep spiritual bond: one of them is the Oregon coast, and the other is here in the Bitterroot Valley. When we bought this farm, we thought of it as 'dying property':

that is, a house where we wanted to live for the rest of our lives. Right here, on our property, we have great horned owls, pheasants, quail, wood ducks, and a pasture big enough for our two horses.

"People may be born into a time in which they feel that they can live, and they may not want to live in another time. We love this valley as it was 30 years ago. Since then, it has been filling up with people. I wouldn't want to be living here if the valley became a strip mall, with a million people living on the valley floor between Missoula and Darby. A view of open space is important to me. The land across the road from my house is an old farm two miles long and half a mile wide, consisting entirely of pastureland, with a couple of barns as the only buildings. It's owned by an out-of-state rock singer and actor called Huey Lewis, who comes here for just a month or so each year to hunt and fish, and for the rest of the year has a caretaker who runs cows, grows hay, and leases some of the land to farmers. If Huey Lewis's land across the street got subdivided into house lots, I couldn't stand the sight facing me every day, and I would move.

"I often think about how I would want to die. My own father recently died a slow death of lung disease. He lost control over his own life, and his last year was painful. I don't want to die that way. It may seem cold-blooded, but here is my fantasy of how I would die if I had my choice. In my fantasy, Pat would die before me. That's because, when we got married, I promised to love, honor, and take care of her, and if she died first, I would know that I had fulfilled my promise. Also, I have no life insurance to support her, so it would be hard if she outlived me. After Pat died—my fantasy continues—I would turn over the deed of the house to my son Cody, then I would go trout-fishing every day as long as I was physically in condition to do it. When I became no longer capable of fishing, I would get hold of a large supply of morphine and go off a long way into the woods. I would pick some remote place where nobody would ever find my body, and from which I could enjoy an especially beautiful view. I'd lie down facing that view and—take my morphine. That would be the best way to die: dying in the way that I chose, with the last sight I see being a view of Montana as I want to remember it."

In short, the life stories of these four Montanans, and my own comments preceding them, illustrate that Montanans differ among themselves in their values and goals. They want more or less population growth, more or less government regulation, more or less development and subdivision of agricultural land, more or less retention of agricultural uses of land, more or less mining, and more or less outdoor-based tourism. Some of these goals are obviously incompatible with others of them.

We have previously seen in this chapter how Montana is experiencing many environmental problems that translate into economic problems. Application of these different values and goals that we have just seen illustrated would result in different approaches to these environmental problems, presumably associated with different probabilities of succeeding or failing at solving them. At present, there is honest and wide difference of opinion about the best approaches. We don't know which approaches the citizens of Montana will ultimately choose, and we don't know whether Montana's environmental and economic problems will get better or worse.

It may initially have seemed absurd to select Montana as the subject of this first chapter of a book on societal collapses. Neither Montana in particular, nor the U.S. in general, is in imminent danger of collapse. But: please reflect that half of the income of Montana residents doesn't come from their work within Montana, but instead consists of money flowing into Montana from other U.S. states: federal government transfer payments (such as Social Security, Medicare, Medicaid, and poverty programs) and private out-of-state funds (out-of-state pensions, earnings on real estate equity, and business income). That is, Montana's own economy already falls far short of supporting the Montana lifestyle, which is instead supported by and dependent on the rest of the U.S. If Montana were an isolated island, as Easter Island in the Pacific Ocean was in Polynesian times before European arrival, its present First World economy would already have collapsed, nor could it have developed that economy in the first place.

Then reflect that Montana's environmental problems that we have been discussing, although serious, are still much less severe than those in most of the rest of the U.S., almost all of which has much denser human populations and heavier human impacts, and much of which is environmentally more fragile than Montana. The U.S. in turn depends for essential resources on, and is economically, politically, and militarily involved with, other parts of the world, some of which have even more severe environmental problems and are in much steeper decline than is the U.S.

In the remainder of this book we shall be considering environmental problems, similar to Montana's, in various past and modern societies. For the past societies that I shall discuss, half of which lack writing, we know far less about individual people's values and goals than we do for Montana. For the modern societies, information about values and goals is available, but I myself have more experience of them in Montana than elsewhere in the modern world. Hence as you read this book, and as you consider environmental problems posed mostly in impersonal terms, please think of the problems of those other societies as viewed by individual people like Stan Falkow, Rick Laible, Chip Pigman, Tim Huls, John Cook, and the Hirschy brothers and sisters. When we discuss Easter Island's apparently homogeneous society in the next chapter, imagine an Easter Island chief, farmer, stone carver, and porpoise fisherman each relating his or her particular life story, values, and goals, just as my Montana friends did for me.

PART TWO

PAST SOCIETIES

■ ■ ■

CHAPTER 2

Twilight at Easter

The quarry's mysteries ▪ Easter's geography and history ▪ People and
food ▪ Chiefs, clans, and commoners ▪ Platforms and statues ▪
Carving, transporting, erecting ▪ The vanished forest ▪
Consequences for society ▪ Europeans and explanations ▪
Why was Easter fragile? ▪ Easter as metaphor ▪

No other site that I have visited made such a ghostly impression on me as Rano Raraku, the quarry on Easter Island where its famous gigantic stone statues were carved (Plate 5). To begin with, the island is the most remote habitable scrap of land in the world. The nearest lands are the coast of Chile 2,300 miles to the east and Polynesia's Pitcairn Islands 1,300 miles to the west (map, pp. 84–85). When I arrived in 2002 by jet plane from Chile, my flight took more than five hours, all spent over the Pacific Ocean stretching endlessly between the horizons, with nothing to see below us except water. By the time, towards sunset, that the small low speck that was Easter Island finally did become dimly visible ahead in the twilight, I had become concerned whether we would succeed in finding the island before nightfall, and whether our plane had enough fuel to return to Chile if we overshot and missed Easter. It is hardly an island that one would expect to have been discovered and settled by any humans before the large swift European sailing ships of recent centuries.

Rano Raraku is an approximately circular volcanic crater about 600 yards in diameter, which I entered by a trail rising steeply up to the crater rim from the low plain outside, and then dropping steeply down again toward the marshy lake on the crater floor. No one lives in the vicinity today. Scattered over both the crater's outer and inner walls are 397 stone statues, representing in a stylized way a long-eared legless human male torso, mostly 15 to 20 feet tall but the largest of them 70 feet tall (taller than the average modern 5-story building), and weighing from 10 up to 270 tons. The remains of a transport road can be discerned passing out of the crater through a notch cut into a low point in its rim, from which three more transport roads about 25 feet wide radiate north, south, and west for up to

9 miles towards Easter's coasts. Scattered along the roads are 97 more statues, as if abandoned in transport from the quarry. Along the coast and occasionally inland are about 300 stone platforms, a third of them formerly supporting or associated with 393 more statues, all of which until a few decades ago were not erect but thrown down, many of them toppled so as to break them deliberately at the neck.

From the crater rim, I could see the nearest and largest platform (called Ahu Tongariki), whose 15 toppled statues the archaeologist Claudio Cristino described to me re-erecting in 1994 by means of a crane capable of lifting 55 tons. Even with that modern machinery, the task proved challenging for Claudio, because Ahu Tongariki's largest statue weighed 88 tons. Yet Easter Island's prehistoric Polynesian population had owned no cranes, no wheels, no machines, no metal tools, no draft animals, and no means other than human muscle power to transport and raise the statues.

The statues remaining at the quarry are in all stages of completion. Some are still attached to the bedrock out of which they were being carved, roughed out but with details of the ears or hands missing. Others are finished, detached, and lying on the crater slopes below the niche where they had been carved, and still others had been erected in the crater. The ghostly impression that the quarry made on me came from my sense of being in a factory, all of whose workers had suddenly quit for mysterious reasons, thrown down their tools, and stomped out, leaving each statue in whatever stage it happened to be at the moment. Littering the ground at the quarry are the stone picks, drills, and hammers with which the statues were being carved. Around each statue still attached to rock is the trench in which the carvers stood. Chipped in the rock wall are stone notches on which the carvers may have hung the gourds that served as their water bottles. Some statues in the crater show signs of having been deliberately broken or defaced, as if by rival groups of carvers vandalizing one another's products. Under one statue was found a human finger bone, possibly the result of carelessness by a member of that statue's transport crew. Who carved the statues, why did they carve them at such effort, how did the carvers transport and raise such huge stone masses, and why did they eventually throw them all down?

Easter's many mysteries were already apparent to its European discoverer, the Dutch explorer Jacob Roggeveen, who spotted the island on Easter Day (April 5, 1722), hence the name that he bestowed and that has remained. As a sailor who had just spent 17 days crossing the Pacific from

Chile in three large European ships without any sight of land, Roggeveen asked himself: how had the Polynesians greeting him when he landed on Easter's coast reached such a remote island? We know now that the voyage to Easter from the nearest Polynesian island to the west would have taken at least as many days. Hence Roggeveen and subsequent European visitors were surprised to find that the islanders' only watercraft were small and leaky canoes, no more than 10 feet long, capable of holding only one or at most two people. In Roggeveen's words: "As concerns their vessels, these are bad and frail as regards use, for their canoes are put together with manifold small planks and light inner timbers, which they cleverly stitched together with very fine twisted threads, made from the above-named field-plant. But as they lacked the knowledge and particularly the materials for caulking and making tight the great number of seams of the canoes, these are accordingly very leaky, for which reason they are compelled to spend half the time in bailing." How could a band of human colonists plus their crops, chickens, and drinking water have survived a two-and-a-half-week sea journey in such watercraft?

Like all subsequent visitors, including me, Roggeveen was puzzled to understand how the islanders had erected their statues. To quote his journal again, "The stone images at first caused us to be struck with astonishment, because we could not comprehend how it was possible that these people, who are devoid of heavy thick timber for making any machines, as well as strong ropes, nevertheless had been able to erect such images, which were fully 30 feet high and thick in proportion." No matter what had been the exact method by which the islanders raised the statues, they needed heavy timber and strong ropes made from big trees, as Roggeveen realized. Yet the Easter Island that he viewed was a wasteland with not a single tree or bush over 10 feet tall (Plates 6, 7): "We originally, from a further distance, have considered the said Easter Island as sandy, the reason for that is this, that we counted as sand the withered grass, hay, or other scorched and burnt vegetation, because its wasted appearance could give no other impression than of a singular poverty and barrenness." What had happened to all the former trees that must have stood there?

Organizing the carving, transport, and erection of the statues required a complex populous society living in an environment rich enough to support it. The statues' sheer number and size suggest a population much larger than the estimated one of just a few thousand people encountered by European visitors in the 18th and early 19th centuries: what had happened to the former large population? Carving, transporting, and erecting statues would have called for many specialized workers: how were they all fed, when the Easter Island seen by Roggeveen had no native land animals larger than insects, and no domestic animals except chickens? A complex society is also implied by the scattered distribution of Easter's resources, with its stone quarry near the eastern end, the best stone for making tools in the southwest, the best beach for going out fishing in the northwest, and the best farmland in the south. Extracting and redistributing all of those products would have required a system capable of integrating the island's economy: how could it ever have arisen in that poor barren landscape, and what happened to it?

All those mysteries have spawned volumes of speculation for almost three centuries. Many Europeans were incredulous that Polynesians, "mere savages," could have created the statues or the beautifully constructed stone platforms. The Norwegian explorer Thor Heyerdahl, unwilling to attribute such abilities to Polynesians spreading out of Asia across the western Pacific, argued that Easter Island had instead been settled across the eastern Pacific by advanced societies of South American Indians, who in turn must have received civilization across the Atlantic from more advanced societies of the Old World. Heyerdahl's famous *Kon-Tiki* expedition and his other raft voyages aimed to prove the feasibility of such prehistoric transoceanic contacts, and to support connections between ancient Egypt's pyramids, the giant stone architecture of South America's Inca Empire, and Easter's giant stone statues. My own interest in Easter was kindled over 40 years ago by reading Heyerdahl's *Kon-Tiki* account and his romantic interpretation of Easter's history; I thought then that nothing could top that interpretation for excitement. Going further, the Swiss writer Erich von Däniken, a believer in visits to Earth by extraterrestrial astronauts, claimed that Easter's statues were the work of intelligent spacelings who owned ultramodern tools, became stranded on Easter, and were finally rescued.

The explanation of these mysteries that has now emerged attributes statue-carving to the stone picks and other tools demonstrably littering Rano Raraku rather than to hypothetical space implements, and to Easter's known Polynesian inhabitants rather than to Incas or Egyptians. This history is as romantic and exciting as postulated visits by *Kon-Tiki* rafts or extraterrestrials—and much more relevant to events now going on in the modern world. It is also a history well suited to leading off this series of chapters on past societies, because it proves to be the closest approximation that we have to an ecological disaster unfolding in complete isolation.

■   ■   ■

Easter is a triangular island consisting entirely of three volcanoes that arose from the sea, in close proximity to each other, at different times within the last million or several million years, and that have been dormant throughout the island's history of human occupation. The oldest volcano, Poike, erupted about 600,000 years ago (perhaps as much as 3,000,000 years ago) and now forms the triangle's southeast corner, while the subsequent eruption of Rano Kau formed the southwest corner. Around 200,000 years ago, the eruption of Terevaka, the youngest volcano centered near the triangle's north corner, released lavas now covering 95% of the island's surface.

Easter's area of 66 square miles and its elevation of 1,670 feet are both modest by Polynesian standards. The island's topography is mostly gentle, without the deep valleys familiar to visitors to the Hawaiian Islands. Except at the steep-sided craters and cinder cones, I found it possible almost anywhere on Easter to walk safely in a straight line to anywhere else nearby, whereas in Hawaii or the Marquesas such a walking path would have quickly taken me over a cliff.

The subtropical location at latitude 27 degrees south—approximately as far south of the equator as Miami and Taipei lie north of the equator—gives Easter a mild climate, while its recent volcanic origins give it fertile soils. By themselves, this combination of blessings should have endowed the island with the makings of a miniature paradise, free from the problems besetting much of the rest of the world. Nevertheless, Easter's geography did pose several challenges to its human colonists. While a subtropical climate is warm by the standards of European and North American winters, it is cool by the standards of mostly tropical Polynesia. All other Polynesian-settled islands except New Zealand, the Chathams, Norfolk, and Rapa lie closer to the equator than does Easter. Hence some tropical crops that are important elsewhere in Polynesia, such as coconuts (introduced to Easter only in modern times), grow poorly on Easter, and the surrounding ocean is too cold for coral reefs that could rise to the surface and their associated fish and shellfish. As Barry Rolett and I found while tramping around on Teravaka and Poike, Easter is a windy place, and that caused problems for ancient farmers and still does today; the wind makes recently introduced breadfruits drop before they are ripe. Easter's isolation meant, among other things, that it is deficient not just in coral-reef fish but in fish generally, of which it has only 127 species compared to more than a thousand fish species on Fiji. All of those geographic factors resulted in fewer food sources for Easter Islanders than for most other Pacific Islanders.

The remaining problem associated with Easter's geography is its rainfall,

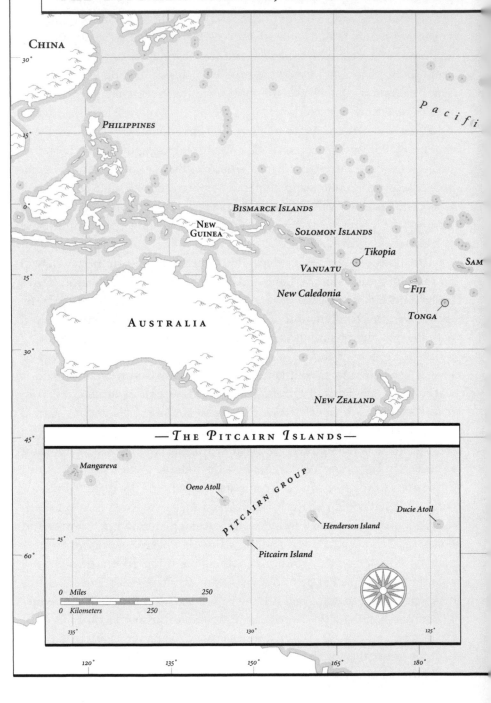

THE PACIFIC OCEAN,
THE PITCAIRN ISLANDS, AND EASTER ISLAND

CHINA

45°

30°

15°

0°

15°

30°

45°

60°

PHILIPPINES

Pacifi

BISMARCK ISLANDS

NEW
GUINEA

SOLOMON ISLANDS

Tikopia

SAM

VANUATU

New Caledonia

FIJI

TONGA

AUSTRALIA

NEW ZEALAND

—THE PITCAIRN ISLANDS—

Mangareva

Oeno Atoll

PITCAIRN GROUP

Ducie Atoll

Henderson Island

25°

Pitcairn Island

60°

| 0 | Miles | | 250 |
| 0 | Kilometers | 250 | |

135°

130°

125°

120°   135°   150°   165°   180°

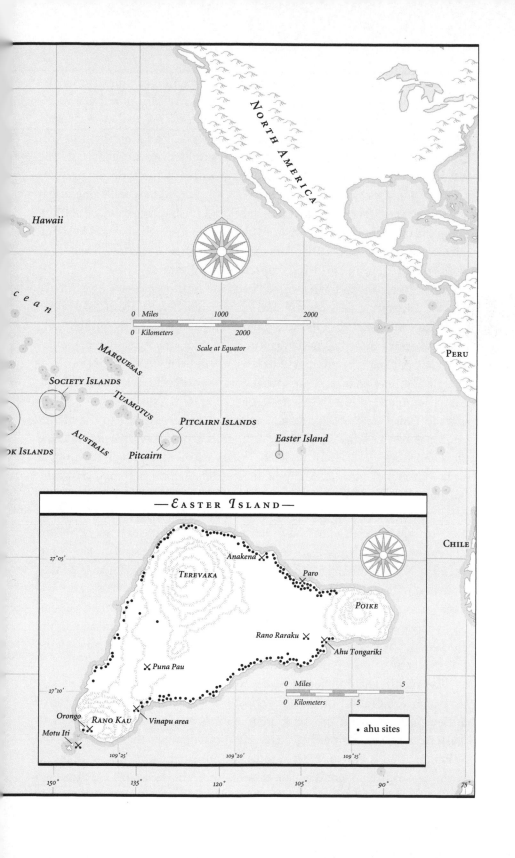

NORTH AMERICA

Hawaii

Ocean

PERU

Marquesas

Society Islands

Tuamotus

Pitcairn Islands

Easter Island

Australs

Cook Islands

Pitcairn

Chile

0 Miles 1000 2000

0 Kilometers 2000

Scale at Equator

—Easter Island—

27°05′

Terevaka

Anakena

Paro

Poike

Rano Raraku

Ahu Tongariki

Puna Pau

27°10′

Orongo

Rano Kau

Vinapu area

Motu Iti

0 Miles 5

0 Kilometers 5

• ahu sites

109°25′ 109°20′ 109°15′

150° 135° 120° 105° 90° 75°

on the average only about 50 inches per year: seemingly abundant by the standards of Mediterranean Europe and Southern California, but low by Polynesian standards. Compounding the limitations imposed by that modest rainfall, the rain that does fall percolates quickly into Easter's porous volcanic soils. As a consequence, freshwater supplies are limited: just one intermittent stream on Mt. Teravaka's slopes, dry at the time of my visit; ponds or marshes at the bottoms of three volcanic craters; wells dug down where the water table is near the surface; and freshwater springs bubbling up on the ocean bottom just offshore or between the high-tide and low-tide lines. Nevertheless, Easter Islanders did succeed in getting enough water for drinking, cooking, and growing crops, but it took effort.

Both Heyerdahl and von Däniken brushed aside overwhelming evidence that the Easter Islanders were typical Polynesians derived from Asia rather than from the Americas, and that their culture (including even their statues) also grew out of Polynesian culture. Their language was Polynesian, as Captain Cook had already concluded during his brief visit to Easter in 1774, when a Tahitian man accompanying him was able to converse with the Easter Islanders. Specifically, they spoke an eastern Polynesian dialect related to Hawaiian and Marquesan, and most closely related to the dialect known as Early Mangarevan. Their fishhooks, stone adzes, harpoons, coral files, and other tools were typically Polynesian and especially resembled early Marquesan models. Many of their skulls exhibit a characteristically Polynesian feature known as a "rocker jaw." When DNA extracted from 12 skeletons found buried in Easter's stone platforms was analyzed, all 12 samples proved to exhibit a nine-base-pair deletion and three base substitutions present in most Polynesians. Two of those three base substitutions do not occur in Native Americans and thus argue against Heyerdahl's claim that Native Americans contributed to Easter's gene pool. Easter's crops were bananas, taro, sweet potato, sugarcane, and paper mulberry, typical Polynesian crops mostly of Southeast Asian origin. Easter's sole domestic animal, the chicken, was also typically Polynesian and ultimately Asian, as were even the rats that arrived as stowaways in the canoes of the first settlers.

The prehistoric Polynesian expansion was the most dramatic burst of overwater exploration in human prehistory. Until 1200 B.C., the spread of ancient humans from the Asian mainland through Indonesia's islands to Australia and New Guinea had advanced no farther into the Pacific than the Solomon Islands east of New Guinea. Around that time, a seafaring and farming people, apparently originating from the Bismarck Archipelago northeast of New Guinea, and producing ceramics known as Lapita-style pottery, swept nearly a thousand miles across the open oceans east of the Solomons to reach Fiji, Samoa, and Tonga, and to become the ancestors of the Polynesians. While Polynesians lacked compasses and writing and metal tools, they were masters of navigational arts and of sailing canoe technology. Abundant archaeological evidence at radiocarbon-dated sites—such as pottery and stone tools, remains of houses and temples, food debris, and human skeletons—testifies to the approximate dates and routes of their expansion. By around A.D. 1200, Polynesians had reached every habitable scrap of land in the vast watery triangle of ocean whose apexes are Hawaii, New Zealand, and Easter Island.

Historians used to assume that all those Polynesian islands were discovered and settled by chance, as a result of canoes full of fishermen happening to get blown off course. It is now clear, however, that both the discoveries and the settlements were meticulously planned. Contrary to what one would expect for accidental drift voyages, much of Polynesia was settled in a west-to-east direction opposite to that of the prevailing winds and currents, which are from east to west. New islands could have been discovered by voyagers sailing upwind on a predetermined bearing into the unknown, or waiting for a temporary reversal of the prevailing winds. Transfers of many species of crops and livestock, from taro to bananas and from pigs to dogs and chickens, prove beyond question that settlement was by well-prepared colonists, carrying products of their homelands deemed essential to the survival of the new colony.

The first expansion wave of Lapita potters ancestral to Polynesians spread eastwards across the Pacific only as far as Fiji, Samoa, and Tonga, which lie within just a few days' sail of each other. A much wider gap of ocean separates those West Polynesian islands from the islands of East Polynesia: the Cooks, Societies, Marquesas, Australs, Tuamotus, Hawaii, New Zealand, Pitcairn group, and Easter. Only after a "Long Pause" of about 1,500 years was that gap finally breached—whether because of improvements in Polynesian canoes and navigation, changes in ocean currents, emergence of stepping-stone islets due to a drop in sea level, or just one lucky voyage. Some time around A.D. 600–800 (the exact dates are debated), the Cooks, Societies, and Marquesas, which are the East Polynesian islands most accessible from West Polynesia, were colonized and became in turn the sources of colonists for the remaining islands. With New Zealand's occupation around A.D. 1200, across a huge water gap of at least 2,000 miles, the settlement of the Pacific's habitable islands was at last complete.

By what route was Easter itself, the Polynesian island farthest east, occupied? Winds and currents would probably have ruled out a direct voyage to Easter from the Marquesas, which supported a large population and do seem to have been the immediate source for Hawaii's settlement. Instead, the jumping-off points for the colonization of Easter are more likely to have been Mangareva, Pitcairn, and Henderson, which lie about halfway between the Marquesas and Easter, and the fates of whose populations will be the story of our next chapter (Chapter 3). The similarity between Easter's language and Early Mangarevan, the similarity between a Pitcairn statue and some Easter statues, the resemblances of Easter tool styles to Mangarevan and Pitcairn tool styles, and the correspondence of Easter Island skulls to two Henderson Island skulls even more closely than to Marquesan skulls all suggest use of Mangareva, Pitcairn, and Henderson as stepping-stones. In 1999 the reconstructed Polynesian sailing canoe *Hokule'a* succeeded in reaching Easter from Mangareva after a voyage of 17 days. To us modern landlubbers, it is literally incredible that canoe voyagers sailing east from Mangareva could have had the good luck to hit an island only nine miles wide from north to south after such a long voyage. However, Polynesians knew how to anticipate an island long before land became visible, from the flocks of nesting seabirds that fly out over a radius of a hundred miles from land to forage. Thus, the effective diameter of Easter (originally home to some of the largest seabird colonies in the whole Pacific) would have been a respectable 200 miles to Polynesian canoe-voyagers, rather than a mere nine.

Easter Islanders themselves have a tradition that the leader of the expedition to settle their island was a chief named Hotu Matu'a ("the Great Parent") sailing in one or two large canoes with his wife, six sons, and extended family. (European visitors in the late 1800s and early 1900s recorded many oral traditions from surviving islanders, and those traditions contain much evidently reliable information about life on Easter in the century or so before European arrival, but it is uncertain whether the traditions accurately preserve details about events a thousand years earlier.) We shall see (Chapter 3) that the populations of many other Polynesian islands remained in contact with each other through regular interisland two-way voyaging after their initial discovery and settlement. Might that also have been true of Easter, and might other canoes have arrived after Hotu Matu'a? Archaeologist Roger Green has suggested that possibility for Easter, on the basis of similarities between some Easter tool styles and the styles of Mangarevan tools at a time several centuries after Easter's settlement. Against that possibility, however, stands Easter's traditional lack of dogs, pigs, and some typical Polynesian crops that one might have expected subsequent voyagers to have brought if those animals and crops had by chance failed to survive in Hotu Matu'a's canoe or had died out soon after his arrival. In addition, we shall see in the next chapter that finds of numerous tools made of stone whose chemical composition is distinctive for one island, turning up on another island, unequivocally prove interisland voyaging between the Marquesas, Pitcairn, Henderson, Mangareva, and Societies, but no stone of Easter origin has been found on any other island or vice versa. Thus, Easter Islanders may have remained effectively completely isolated at the end of the world, with no contact with outsiders for the thousand years or so separating Hotu Matu'a's arrival from Roggeveen's.

Given that East Polynesia's main islands may have been settled around A.D. 600–800, when was Easter itself occupied? There is considerable uncertainty about the date, as there is for the settlement of the main islands. The published literature on Easter Island often mentions possible evidence for settlement at A.D. 300–400, based especially on calculations of language divergence times by the technique known as glottochronology, and on three radiocarbon dates from charcoal in Ahu Te Peu, in the Poike ditch, and in lake sediments indicative of forest clearance. However, specialists on Easter Island history increasingly question these early dates. Glottochronological calculations are considered suspect, especially when applied to languages with as complicated histories as Easter's (known to us mainly through, and possibly contaminated by, Tahitian and Marquesan informants) and Mangareva's (apparently secondarily modified by later Marquesan arrivals). All three of the early radiocarbon dates were obtained on single samples dated by older methods now superseded, and there is no proof that the charcoal objects dated were actually associated with humans.

Instead, what appear to be the most reliable dates for early occupation of Easter are the radiocarbon dates of A.D. 900 that paleontologist David Steadman and archaeologists Claudio Cristino and Patricia Vargas obtained on wood charcoal and on bones of porpoises eaten by people, from the oldest archaeological layers offering evidence of human presence at Easter's Anakena Beach. Anakena is by far the best canoe landing beach on the island, the obvious site at which the first settlers would have based themselves. The dating of the porpoise bones was done by the modern state-of-the-art radiocarbon method known as AMS (accelerator mass spectrometry), and a so-called marine reservoir correction for radiocarbon dating of bones of marine creatures like porpoises was roughly estimated. These dates are likely to be close to the time of first settlement, because they came from archaeological layers containing bones of native land birds that were exterminated very quickly on Easter and many other Pacific islands, and because canoes to hunt porpoises soon became unavailable. Hence the current best estimate of Easter's settlement is somewhat before A.D. 900.

What did the islanders eat, and how many of them were there?

At the time of European arrival, they subsisted mainly as farmers, growing sweet potatoes, yams, taro, bananas, and sugarcane, plus chickens as their sole domestic animal. Easter's lack of coral reefs or of a lagoon meant that fish and shellfish made a smaller contribution to the diet than on most other Polynesian islands. Seabirds, land birds, and porpoises were available to the first settlers, but we shall see that they declined or disappeared later. The result was a high-carbohydrate diet, exacerbated by the islanders' compensating for Easter's limited sources of fresh water by copiously drinking sugarcane juice. No dentist would be surprised to learn that the islanders ended up with the highest incidence of cavities and tooth decay of any known prehistoric people: many children already had cavities by age 14, and everyone did by their 20s.

Easter's population at its peak has been estimated by methods such as counting the number of house foundations, assuming 5 to 15 people per house, and assuming one-third of identified houses to have been occupied simultaneously, or by estimating the numbers of chiefs and their followers from the numbers of platforms or erected statues. The resulting estimates range from a low of 6,000 to a high of 30,000 people, which works out to an average of 90 to 450 people per square mile. Some of the island's area, such as the Poike Peninsula and the highest elevations, was less suitable for agriculture, so that population densities on the better land would have been somewhat higher, but not much higher because archaeological surveys show that a large fraction of the land surface was utilized.

As usual anywhere in the world when archaeologists debate rival estimates for prehistoric population densities, those preferring the lower estimates refer to the higher estimates as absurdly high, and vice versa. My own opinion is that the higher estimates are more likely to be correct, in part because those estimates are by the archaeologists with the most extensive recent experience of surveying Easter: Claudio Cristino, Patricia Vargas, Edmundo Edwards, Chris Stevenson, and Jo Anne Van Tilburg. In addition, the earliest reliable estimate of Easter's population, 2,000 people, was made by missionaries who took up residence in 1864 just after an epidemic of smallpox had killed off most of the population. And that was after the kidnapping of about 1,500 islanders by Peruvian slave ships in 1862–63, after two previous documented smallpox epidemics dating back to 1836, after the virtual certainty of other undocumented epidemics introduced by regular European visitors from 1770 onwards, and after a steep population crash that began in the 1600s and that we shall discuss below. The same ship that brought the third smallpox epidemic to Easter went on to the Marquesas, where the resulting epidemic is known to have killed seven-eighths of the population. For these reasons it seems to me impossible that the 1864 post-smallpox population of 2,000 people represented the residue of a pre-smallpox, pre-kidnapping, pre-other-epidemic, pre-17th-century-crash population of only 6,000 to 8,000 people. Having seen the evidence for intensive prehistoric agriculture on Easter, I find Claudio's and Edmundo's "high" estimates of 15,000 or more people unsurprising.

That evidence for agricultural intensification is of several types. One type consists of stone-lined pits 5 to 8 feet in diameter and up to 4 feet deep that were used as composting pits in which to grow crops, and possibly also as vegetable fermentation pits. Another type of evidence is a pair of stone dams built across the bed of the intermittent stream draining the southeastern slope of Mt. Terevaka, in order to divert water onto broad stone platforms. That water diversion system resembles systems for irrigated taro production elsewhere in Polynesia. Still further evidence for agricultural intensification is numerous stone chicken houses (called *hare moa*), mostly up to 20 feet long (plus a few 70-foot monsters), 10 feet wide, and 6 feet high, with a small entrance near the ground for chickens to run in and out, and with an adjacent yard ringed by a stone wall to prevent the precious chickens from running away or being stolen. If it were not for the fact that Easter's abundant big stone *hare moa* are overshadowed by its even bigger stone platforms and statues, tourists would remember Easter as the island of stone chicken houses. They dominate much of the landscape near the coast, because today the prehistoric stone chicken houses—all 1,233 of them—are much more conspicuous than the prehistoric human houses, which had only stone foundations or patios and no stone walls.

But the most widespread method adopted to increase agricultural output involved various uses of lava rocks studied by archaeologist Chris Stevenson. Large boulders were stacked as windbreaks to protect plants from being dried out by Easter's frequent strong winds. Smaller boulders were piled to create protected aboveground or sunken gardens, for growing bananas and also for starting seedlings to be transplanted after they had grown larger. Extensive areas of ground were partly covered by rocks placed at close intervals on the surface, such that plants could come up between the rocks. Other large areas were modified by so-called "lithic mulches," which means partly filling the soil with rocks down to a depth of a foot, either by carrying rocks from nearby outcrops or else by digging down to and breaking up bedrock. Depressions for planting taro were excavated into natural gravel fields. All of these rock windbreaks and gardens involved a huge effort to construct, because they required moving millions or even billions of rocks. As archaeologist Barry Rolett, who has worked in other parts of Polynesia, commented to me when he and I made our first visit to Easter together, "I have never been to a Polynesian island where people were so desperate, as they were on Easter, that they piled small stones together in a circle to plant a few lousy small taro and protect them against the wind! On the Cook Islands, where they have irrigated taro, people will never stoop to that effort!"

Indeed, why did farmers go to all that effort on Easter? On farms in the northeastern U.S. where I spent my boyhood summers, farmers exerted themselves to carry stones *out* of fields, and would have been horrified at the thought of intentionally bringing stones *into* the fields. What good does it do to have a rocky field?

The answer has to do with Easter's windy, dry, cool climate that I already described. Rock garden or lithic mulch agriculture was invented independently by farmers in many other dry parts of the world, such as Israel's Negev desert, southwestern U.S. deserts, and dry parts of Peru, China, Roman Italy, and Maori New Zealand. Rocks make the soil moister by covering it, reducing evaporative water loss due to sun and wind, and replacing a hard surface crust of soil that would otherwise promote rain runoff. Rocks damp out diurnal fluctuations in soil temperature by absorbing solar heat during the day and releasing it at night; they protect soil against being eroded by splashing rain droplets; dark rocks on lighter soil warm up the soil by absorbing more solar heat; and rocks may also serve as slow-time-release fertilizer pills (analogous to the slow-time-release vitamin pills that some of us take with breakfast), by containing needed minerals that gradually become leached out into the soil. In modern agricultural experiments in the U.S. Southwest designed to understand why the ancient Anasazi (Chapter 4) used lithic mulches, it turned out that the mulches yielded big advantages to farmers. Mulched soils ended up with double the soil moisture content, lower maximum soil temperatures during the day, higher minimum soil temperatures at night, and higher yields for every one of 16 plant species grown—four times higher yields averaged over the 16 species, and 50 times higher yields of the species most benefited by the mulch. Those are enormous advantages.

Chris Stevenson interprets his surveys as documenting the spread of rock-assisted intensive agriculture on Easter. For about the first 500 years of Polynesian occupation, in his view, farmers remained in the lowlands within a few miles of the coast, in order to be closer to freshwater sources and fishing and shellfishing opportunities. The first evidence for rock gardens that he can discern appears around A.D. 1300, in higher-elevation inland areas that have the advantage of higher rainfall than coastal areas but cooler temperatures (mitigated by the use of dark rocks to raise soil temperatures). Much of Easter's interior was converted into rock gardens. Interestingly, it seems clear that farmers themselves didn't live in the interior, because there are remains of only small numbers of commoners' houses there, lacking chicken houses and with only small ovens and garbage piles. Instead, there are scattered elite-type houses, evidently for resident upper-class managers who ran the extensive rock gardens as large-scale plantations (not as individual family gardens) to produce surplus food for the chiefs' labor force, while all the peasants continued to live near the coast and walked back and forth several miles inland each day. Roads five yards wide with stone edges, running between the uplands and the coast, may mark the routes of those daily commutes. Probably the upland plantations did not require year-round effort: the peasants just had to march up and plant taro and other root crops in the spring, then return later in the year for the harvest.

As elsewhere in Polynesia, traditional Easter Island society was divided into chiefs and commoners. To archaeologists today, the difference is obvious from remains of the different houses of the two groups. Chiefs and members of the elite lived in houses termed *hare paenga*, in the shape of a long and slender upside-down canoe, typically around 40 feet long (in one case, 310 feet), not more than 10 feet wide, and curved at the ends. The house's walls and roof (corresponding to the canoe's inverted hull) were of three layers of thatch, but the floor was outlined by neatly cut and fitted foundation stones of basalt. Especially the curved and beveled stones at each end were difficult to make, prized, and stolen back and forth between rival clans. In front of many *hare paenga* was a stone-paved terrace. *Hare paenga* were built in the 200-yard-broad coastal strip, 6 to 10 of them at each major site, immediately inland of the site's platform bearing the statues. In contrast, houses of commoners were relegated to locations farther inland, were smaller, and were associated each with its own chicken house, oven, stone garden circle, and garbage pit—utilitarian structures banned by religious *tapu* from the coastal zone containing the platforms and the beautiful *hare paenga*.

Both oral traditions preserved by the islanders, and archaeological surveys, suggest that Easter's land surface was divided into about a dozen (either 11 or 12) territories, each belonging to one clan or lineage group, and each starting from the seacoast and extending inland—as if Easter were a pie cut into a dozen radial wedges. Each territory had its own chief and its own major ceremonial platforms supporting statues. The clans competed peacefully by seeking to outdo each other in building platforms and statues, but eventually their competition took the form of ferocious fighting. That division into radially sliced territories is typical for Polynesian islands elsewhere in the Pacific. What is unusual in that respect about Easter is that, again according to both oral traditions and archaeological surveys, those competing clan territories were also integrated religiously, and to some extent economically and politically, under the leadership of one paramount chief. In contrast, on both Mangareva and the larger Marquesan islands each major valley was an independent chiefdom locked in chronic fierce warfare against other chiefdoms.

What might account for Easter's integration, and how was it detectable archaeologically? It turns out that Easter's pie does not consist of a dozen identical slices, but that different territories were endowed with different valuable resources. The most obvious example is that Tongariki territory (called Hotu Iti) contained Rano Raraku crater, the island's only source of the best stone for carving statues, and also a source of moss for caulking canoes. The red stone cylinders on top of some statues all came from Puna Pau quarry in Hanga Poukura territory. Vinapu and Hanga Poukura territories controlled the three major quarries of obsidian, the fine-grained volcanic stone used for making sharp tools, while Vinapu and Tongariki had the best basalt for *hare paenga* slabs. Anakena on the north coast had the two best beaches for launching canoes, while Heki'i, its neighbor on the same coast, had the third best beach. As a result, artifacts associated with fishing have been found mainly on that coast. But those same north-coast territories have the poorest land for agriculture, the best land being along the south and west coasts. Only five of the dozen territories had extensive areas of interior uplands used for rock-garden plantations. Nesting seabirds eventually became virtually confined to a few offshore islets along the south coast, especially in Vinapu territory. Other resources such as timber, coral for making files, red ochre, and paper mulberry trees (the source of bark pounded into tapa cloth) were also unevenly distributed.

The clearest archaeological evidence for some degree of integration among the competing clan territories is that stone statues and their red cylinders, from quarries in the territories of the Tongariki and Hanga Poukura clans respectively, ended up on platforms in all 11 or 12 territories distributed all over the island. Hence the roads to transport the statues and crowns out of those quarries over the island also had to traverse many territories, and a clan living at a distance from the quarries would have needed permission from several intervening clans to transport statues and cylinders across the latter's territories. Obsidian, the best basalt, fish, and other localized resources similarly became distributed all over Easter. At first, that seems only natural to us moderns living in large politically unified countries like the U.S.: we take it for granted that resources from one coast are routinely transported long distances to other coasts, traversing many other states or provinces en route. But we forget how complicated it has usually been throughout history for one territory to negotiate access to another territory's resources. A reason why Easter may thus have become integrated, while large Marquesan islands never did, is Easter's gentle terrain, contrasting with Marquesan valleys so steep-sided that people in adjacent valleys communicated with (or raided) each other mainly by sea rather than overland.

We now return to the subject that everyone thinks of first at the mention of Easter Island: its giant stone statues (termed *moai*), and the stone platforms (termed *ahu*) on which they stood. About 300 ahu have been identified, of which many were small and lacked moai, but about 113 did bear moai, and 25 of them were especially large and elaborate. Each of the island's dozen territories had between one and five of those large ahu. Most of the statue-bearing ahu are on the coast, oriented so that the ahu and its statues faced inland over the clan's territory; the statues do not look out to sea.

The ahu is a rectangular platform, made not of solid stone but of rubble fill held in place by four stone retaining walls of gray basalt. Some of those walls, especially those of Ahu Vinapu, have beautifully fitted stones reminiscent of Inca architecture and prompting Thor Heyerdahl to seek connections with South America. However, the fitted walls of Easter ahu just have stone facing, not big stone blocks as do Inca walls. Nevertheless, one of Easter's facing slabs still weighs 10 tons, which sounds impressive to us until we compare it with the blocks of up to 361 tons at the Inca fortress of Sacsahuaman. The ahu are up to 13 feet high, and many are extended by lateral wings to a width of up to 500 feet. Hence an ahu's total weight—from about 300 tons for a small ahu, up to more than 9,000 tons for Ahu Tongariki— dwarfs that of the statues that it supports. We shall return to the significance of this point when we estimate the total effort involved in building Easter's ahu and moai.

An ahu's rear (seaward) retaining wall is approximately vertical, but the front wall slopes down to a flat rectangular plaza about 160 feet on each side. In back of an ahu are crematoria containing the remains of thousands of bodies. In that practice of cremation, Easter was unique in Polynesia, where bodies were otherwise just buried. Today the ahu are dark gray, but originally they were a much more colorful white, yellow, and red: the facing slabs were encrusted with white coral, the stone of a freshly cut moai was yellow, and the moai's crown and a horizontal band of stone coursing on the front wall of some ahu were red.

As for the moai, which represent high-ranking ancestors, Jo Anne Van Tilburg has inventoried a total of 887 carved, of which nearly half still remain in Rano Raraku quarry, while most of those transported out of the quarry were erected on ahu (between 1 and 15 per ahu). All statues on ahu were of Rano Raraku tuff, but a few dozen statues elsewhere (the current count is 53) were carved from other types of volcanic stone occurring on the island (variously known as basalt, red scoria, gray scoria, and trachyte). The "average" erected statue was 13 feet tall and weighed about 10 tons. The tallest ever erected successfully, known as Paro, was 32 feet tall but was slender and weighed "only" about 75 tons, and was thus exceeded in weight by the 87-ton slightly shorter but bulkier statue on Ahu Tongariki that taxed Claudio Cristino in his efforts to reerect it with a crane. While islanders successfully transported a statue a few inches taller than Paro to its intended site on Ahu Hanga Te Tenga, it unfortunately fell over during the attempt to erect it. Rano Raraku quarry contains even bigger unfinished statues, including one 70 feet long and weighing about 270 tons. Knowing what we do about Easter Island technology, it seems impossible that the islanders could ever have transported and erected it, and we have to wonder what megalomania possessed its carvers.

To extraterrestrial-enthusiast Erich von Däniken and others, Easter Island's statues and platforms seemed unique and in need of special explanation. Actually, they have many precedents in Polynesia, especially in East Polynesia. Stone platforms called *marae,* used as shrines and often supporting temples, were widespread; three were formerly present on Pitcairn Island, from which the colonists of Easter might have set out. Easter's ahu differ from marae mainly in being larger and not supporting a temple. The Marquesas and Australs had large stone statues; the Marquesas, Australs, and Pitcairn had statues carved of red scoria, similar to the material used for some Easter statues, while another type of volcanic stone called a tuff (related to Rano Raraku stone) was also used in the Marquesas; Mangareva and Tonga had other stone structures, including on Tonga a well-known big trilithon (a pair of vertical stone pillars supporting a horizontal crosspiece, each pillar weighing about 40 tons); and there were wooden statues on Tahiti and elsewhere. Thus, Easter Island architecture grew out of an existing Polynesian tradition.

We would of course love to know exactly when Easter Islanders erected their first statues, and how styles and dimensions changed with time. Unfortunately, because stone cannot be radiocarbon-dated, we are forced to rely on indirect dating methods, such as radiocarbon-dated charcoal found in ahu, a method known as obsidian-hydration dating of cleaved obsidian surfaces, styles of discarded statues (assumed to be early ones), and successive stages of reconstruction deduced for some ahu, including those that have been excavated by archaeologists. It seems clear, however, that later statues tended to be taller (though not necessarily heavier), and that the biggest ahu underwent multiple rebuildings with time to become larger and more elaborate. The ahu-building period seems to have fallen mainly in the years A.D. 1000–1600. These indirectly derived dates have recently gained support from a clever study by J. Warren Beck and his colleagues, who applied radiocarbon dating to the carbon contained in the coral used for files and for the statues' eyes, and contained in the algae whose white nodules decorated the plaza. That direct dating suggests three phases of construction and reconstruction of Ahu Nau Nau at Anakena, the first phase around A.D. 1100 and the last phase ending around 1600. The earliest ahu were probably platforms without any statues, like Polynesian marae elsewhere. Statues inferred to be early were reused in the walls of later ahu and other structures. They tend to be smaller, rounder, and more human than late ones, and to be made of various types of volcanic stone other than Rano Raraku tuff.

Eventually, Easter Islanders settled on the volcanic tuff from Rano Raraku, for the simple reason that it was infinitely superior for carving. The tuff has a hard surface but an ashlike consistency inside and is thus easier to carve than very hard basalt. As compared to red scoria, the tuff is less breakable and lends itself better to polishing and to carving of details. With time, insofar as we can infer relative dates, Rano Raraku statues became larger, more rectangular, more stylized, and almost mass-produced, although each statue is slightly different from others. Paro, the tallest statue ever erected, was also one of the latest.

The increase in statue size with time suggests competition between rival chiefs commissioning the statues to outdo each other. That conclusion also screams from an apparently late feature called a *pukao:* a cylinder of red scoria, weighing up to 12 tons (the weight of Paro's pukao), mounted as a separate piece to rest on top of a moai's flat head (Plate 8). (When you read that, just ask yourself: how did islanders without cranes manipulate a 12-ton block so that it balanced on the head of a statue up to 32 feet tall? That is one of the mysteries that drove Erich von Däniken to invoke extraterrestrials. The mundane answer suggested by recent experiments is that the pukao and statue were probably erected together.) We don't know for sure what the pukao represented; our best guess is a headdress of red birds' feathers prized throughout Polynesia and reserved for chiefs, or else a hat of feathers and tapa cloth. For instance, when a Spanish exploring expedition reached the Pacific island of Santa Cruz, what really impressed the local people was not Spanish ships, swords, guns, or mirrors, but their red cloth. All pukao are of red scoria from a single quarry, Puna Pau, where (just as is true of moai at the moai workshop on Rano Raraku) I observed unfinished pukao, plus finished ones awaiting transport.

We know of not more than a hundred pukao, reserved for statues on the biggest and richest ahu built late in Easter prehistory. I cannot resist the thought that they were produced as a show of one-upsmanship. They seem to proclaim: "All right, so *you* can erect a statue 30 feet high, but look at me: I can put this 12-ton pukao on top of *my* statue; you try to top that, you wimp!" The pukao that I saw reminded me of the activities of Hollywood moguls living near my home in Los Angeles, similarly displaying their wealth and power by building ever larger, more elaborate, more ostentatious houses. Tycoon Marvin Davis topped previous moguls with his house of 50,000 square feet, so Aaron Spelling had to top that with a house of 56,000 square feet. All that those moguls' houses lack to make explicit their message of power is a 12-ton red pukao on the house's highest tower, raised into position without resort to cranes.

Given the widespread distribution over Polynesia of platforms and statues, why were Easter Islanders the only ones to go overboard, to make by far the largest investment of societal resources in building them, and to erect the biggest ones? At least four different factors cooperated to produce that outcome. First, Rano Raraku tuff is the best stone in the Pacific for carving: to a sculptor used to struggling with basalt and red scoria, it almost cries out, "Carve me!" Second, other Pacific island societies on islands within a few days' sail of other islands devoted their energy, resources, and labor to interisland trading, raiding, exploration, colonization, and emigration, but those competing outlets were foreclosed for Easter Islanders by their isolation. While chiefs on other Pacific islands could compete for prestige and status by seeking to outdo each other in those interisland activities, "The boys on Easter Island didn't have those usual games to play," as one of my students put it. Third, Easter's gentle terrain and complementary resources in different territories led as we have seen to some integration of the island, thereby letting clans all over the island obtain Rano Raraku stone and go overboard in carving it. If Easter had remained politically fragmented, like the Marquesas, the Tongariki clan in whose territory Rano Raraku lay could have monopolized its stone, or neighboring clans could have barred transport of statues across their territories—as in fact eventually happened. Finally, as we shall see, building platforms and statues required feeding lots of people, a feat made possible by the food surpluses produced by the elite-controlled upland plantations.

How did all those Easter Islanders, lacking cranes, succeed in carving, transporting, and erecting those statues? Of course we don't know for sure, because no European ever saw it being done to write about it. But we can make informed guesses from oral traditions of the islanders themselves (especially about erecting statues), from statues in the quarries at successive stages of completion, and from recent experimental tests of different transport methods.

In Rano Raraku quarry one can see incomplete statues still in the rock face and surrounded by narrow carving canals only about two feet wide. The hand-held basalt picks with which the carvers worked are still at the quarry. The most incomplete statues are nothing more than a block of stone roughly carved out of the rock with the eventual face upwards, and with the back still attached to the underlying cliff below by a long keel of rock. Next to be carved were the head, nose, and ears, followed by the arms, hands, and loincloth. At that stage the keel connecting the statue's back to the cliff was chipped through, and transport of the statue out of its niche began. All statues in the process of being transported still lack the eye sockets, which were evidently not carved until the statue had been transported to the ahu and erected there. One of the most remarkable recent discoveries about the statues was made in 1979 by Sonia Haoa and Sergio Rapu Haoa, who found buried near an ahu a separate complete eye of white coral with a pupil of red scoria. Subsequently, fragments of other similar eyes were unearthed. When such eyes are inserted into a statue, they create a penetrating, blinding gaze that is awesome to look at. The fact that so few eyes have been recovered suggests that few actually were made, to remain under guard by priests, and to be placed in the sockets only at times of ceremonies.

The still-visible transport roads on which statues were moved from quarries follow contour lines to avoid the extra work of carrying statues up and down hills, and are up to nine miles long for the west-coast ahu farthest from Rano Raraku. While the task may strike us as daunting, we know that many other prehistoric peoples transported very heavy stones at Stonehenge, Egypt's pyramids, Teotihuacán, and centers of the Incas and Olmecs, and something can be deduced of the methods in each case. Modern scholars have experimentally tested their various theories of statue transport on Easter by actually moving statues, beginning with Thor Heyerdahl, whose theory was probably wrong because he damaged the tested statue in the process. Subsequent experimenters have variously tried hauling statues either standing or prone, with or without a wooden sled, and on or not on a prepared track of lubricated or unlubricated rollers or else with fixed crossbars. The method most convincing to me is Jo Anne Van Tilburg's suggestion that Easter Islanders modified the so-called canoe ladders that were widespread on Pacific islands for transporting heavy wooden logs, which had to be cut in the forest and shaped there into dugout canoes and then transported to the coast. The "ladders" consist of a pair of parallel wooden rails joined by fixed wooden crosspieces (not movable rollers) over which the log is dragged. In the New Guinea region I have seen such ladders more than a mile long, extending from the coast hundreds of feet uphill to a forest clearing at which a huge tree was being felled and then hollowed out to make a canoe hull. We know that some of the biggest canoes that the Hawaiians moved over canoe ladders weighed more than an average-size Easter Island moai, so the proposed method is plausible.

Jo Anne enlisted modern Easter Islanders to put her theory to a test by building such a canoe ladder, mounting a statue prone on a wooden sled, attaching ropes to the sled, and hauling it over the ladder. She found that 50 to 70 people, working five hours per day and dragging the sled five yards at each pull, could transport an average-sized 12-ton statue nine miles in a week. The key, Jo Anne and the islanders discovered, was for all of those people to synchronize their pulling effort, just as canoe paddlers synchronize their paddling strokes. By extrapolation, transport of even big statues like Paro could have been accomplished by a team of 500 adults, which would have been just within the manpower capabilities of an Easter Island clan of one or two thousand people.

Easter Islanders told Thor Heyerdahl how their ancestors had erected statues on ahu. They were indignant that archaeologists had never deigned to ask them, and they erected a statue for him without a crane to prove their point. Much more information has emerged in the course of subsequent experiments on transporting and erecting statues by William Mulloy, Jo Anne Van Tilburg, Claudio Cristino, and others. The islanders began by building a gently sloping ramp of stones from the plaza up to the top of the front of the platform, and pulling the prone statue with its base end forwards up the ramp. Once the base had reached the platform, they levered the statue's head an inch or two upwards with logs, slipped stones under the head to support it in the new position, and continued to lever up the head and thereby to tilt the statue increasingly towards the vertical. That left the ahu's owners with a long ramp of stones, which may then have been dismantled and recycled to create the ahu's lateral wings. The pukao was probably erected at the same time as the statue itself, both being mounted together in the same supporting frame.

The most dangerous part of the operation was the final tilting of the statue from a very steep angle to the vertical position, because of the risk that the statue's momentum in that final tilt might carry it beyond the vertical and tip it off the rear of the platform. Evidently to reduce that risk, the carvers designed the statue so that it was not strictly perpendicular to its flat base but just short of perpendicular (e.g., at an angle of about 87 degrees to the base, rather than 90 degrees). In that way, when they had raised the statue to a stable position with the base flat on the platform, the body was still leaning slightly forwards and at no risk of tipping over backwards. They could then slowly and carefully lever up the front edge of the base that final few degrees, slipping stones under the front of the base to stabilize it, until the body was vertical. But tragic accidents could still occur at that last stage, as evidently happened in the attempt to erect at Ahu Hanga Te Tenga a statue even taller than Paro, which ended with its tipping over and breaking.

The whole operation of constructing statues and platforms must have been enormously expensive of food resources for whose accumulation, transport, and delivery the chiefs commissioning the statues must have arranged. Twenty carvers had to be fed for a month, they may also have been paid in food, then a transport crew of 50 to 500 people and a similar erecting crew had to be fed while doing hard physical work and thus requiring more food than usual. There must also have been much feasting for the whole clan owning the ahu, and for the clans across whose territories the statue was transported. Archaeologists who first tried to calculate the work performed, the calories burned, and hence the food consumed overlooked the fact that the statue itself was the smaller part of the operation: an ahu outweighed its statues by a factor of about 20 times, and all that stone for the ahu also had to be transported. Jo Anne Van Tilburg and her architect husband Jan, whose business it is to erect large modern buildings in Los Angeles and to calculate the work involved for cranes and elevators, did a rough calculation of the corresponding work on Easter. They concluded that, given the number and size of Easter's ahu and moai, the work of constructing them added about 25% to the food requirements of Easter's population over the 300 peak years of construction. Those calculations explain Chris Stevenson's recognition that those 300 peak years coincided with the centuries of plantation agriculture in Easter's interior uplands, producing a large food surplus over that available previously.

However, we have glossed over another problem. The statue operation required not only lots of food, but also lots of thick long ropes (made in Polynesia from fibrous tree bark) by which 50 to 500 people could drag statues weighing 10 to 90 tons, and also lots of big strong trees to obtain all the timber needed for the sleds, canoe ladders, and levers. But the Easter Island seen by Roggeveen and subsequent European visitors had very few trees, all of them small and less than 10 feet tall: the most nearly treeless island in all of Polynesia. Where were the trees that provided the required rope and timber?

Botanical surveys of plants living on Easter within the 20th century have identified only 48 native species, even the biggest of them (the toromiro, up to seven feet tall) hardly worthy of being called a tree, and the rest of them low ferns, grasses, sedges, and shrubs. However, several methods for recovering remains of vanished plants have shown within the last few decades that, for hundreds of thousands of years before human arrival and still during the early days of human settlement, Easter was not at all a barren waste-land but a subtropical forest of tall trees and woody bushes.

The first such method to yield results was the technique of pollen analysis (palynology), which involves boring out a column of sediment deposited in a swamp or pond. In such a column, provided that it has not been shaken or disturbed, the surface mud must have been deposited most recently, while more deeply buried mud represents more ancient deposits. The actual age of each layer in the deposit can be dated by radiocarbon methods. There remains the incredibly tedious task of examining tens of thousands of pollen grains in the column under a microscope, counting them, and then identifying the plant species producing each grain by comparison with modern pollen from known plant species. For Easter Island the first bleary-eyed scientist to perform that task was the Swedish palynologist Olof Selling, who examined cores collected from the swamps in Rano Raraku's and Rano Kau's craters by Heyerdahl's 1955 expedition. He detected abundant pollen of an unidentified species of palm tree, of which Easter today has no native species.

In 1977 and 1983 John Flenley collected many more sediment cores and again noticed abundant palm pollen, but by good luck Flenley in 1983 also obtained from Sergio Rapu Haoa some fossil palm nuts that visiting French cave explorers had discovered that year in a lava cave, and he sent them to the world's leading palm expert for identification. The nuts turned out to be very similar to, but slightly larger than, those of the world's largest existing palm tree, the Chilean wine palm, which grows up to 65 feet tall and 3 feet in diameter. Subsequent visitors to Easter have found more evidence of the palm, in the form of casts of its trunks buried in Mt. Terevaka's lava flows a few hundred thousand years ago, and casts of its root bundles proving that the Easter palm's trunk reached diameters exceeding seven feet. It thus dwarfed even the Chilean palm and was (while it existed) the biggest palm in the world.

Chileans prize their palm today for several reasons, and Easter Islanders would have done so as well. As the name implies, the trunk yields a sweet sap that can be fermented to make wine or boiled down to make honey or sugar. The nuts' oily kernels are rated a delicacy. The fronds are ideal for fabricating into house thatching, baskets, mats, and boat sails. And of course the stout trunks would have served to transport and erect moai, and perhaps to make rafts.

Flenley and Sarah King recognized pollen of five other now-extinct trees in the sediment cores. More recently, the French archaeologist Catherine Orliac has been sieving out 30,000 fragments of wood burned to charcoal from cores dug into Easter Island ovens and garbage heaps. With a heroism matching that of Selling, Flenley, and King, she has compared 2,300 of those carbonized wood fragments to wood samples of plants still existing today elsewhere in Polynesia. In that way she has identified about 16 other plant species, most of them trees related to or the same as tree species still widespread in East Polynesia, that formerly grew on Easter Island as well. Thus, Easter used to support a diverse forest.

Many of those 21 vanished species besides the palm would have been valuable to the islanders. Two of the tallest trees, *Alphitonia* cf. *zizyphoides* and *Elaeocarpus* cf. *rarotongensis* (up to 100 and 50 feet tall respectively), are used elsewhere in Polynesia for making canoes and would have been much better suited to that purpose than was the palm. Polynesians everywhere make rope from the bark of the hauhau *Triumfetta semitriloba,* and that was presumably how Easter Islanders dragged their statues. Bark of the paper mulberry *Broussonetia papyrifera* is beaten into tapa cloth; *Psydrax odorata* has a flexible straight trunk suited for making harpoons and outriggers; the Malay apple *Syzygium malaccense* bears an edible fruit; the oceanic rosewood *Thespesia populanea* and at least eight other species have hardwood suitable for carving and construction; toromiro yields an excellent wood for fires, like acacia and mesquite; and the fact that Orliac recovered all of those species as burnt fragments from fires proves that they too were used for firewood.

The person who pored through 6,433 bones of birds and other vertebrates from early middens at Anakena Beach, probably the site of the first human landing and first settlement on Easter, was zooarchaeologist David Steadman. As an ornithologist myself, I bow in awe before Dave's identification skills and tolerance of eye strain: whereas I wouldn't know how to tell a robin's bone from a dove's or even from a rat's, Dave has learned how to distinguish even the bones of a dozen closely related petrel species from each other. He thereby proved that Easter, which today supports not a single species of native land bird, was formerly home to at least six of them, including one species of heron, two chicken-like rails, two parrots, and a barn owl. More impressive was Easter's prodigious total of at least 25 nesting seabird species, making it formerly the richest breeding site in all of Polynesia and probably in the whole Pacific. They included albatross, boobies, frigatebirds, fulmars, petrels, prions, shearwaters, storm-petrels, terns, and tropicbirds, attracted by Easter's remote location and complete lack of predators that made it an ideal safe haven as a breeding site—until humans arrived. Dave also recovered a few bones of seals, which breed today on the Galápagos Islands and the Juan Fernández Islands to the east of Easter, but it is uncertain whether those few seal bones on Easter similarly came from former breeding colonies or just vagrant individuals.

The Anakena excavations that yielded those bird and seal bones tell us much about the diet and lifestyle of Easter's first human settlers. Out of those 6,433 vertebrate bones identified in their middens, the most frequent ones, accounting for more than one-third of the total, proved to belong to the largest animal available to Easter Islanders: the Common Dolphin, a porpoise weighing up to 165 pounds. That's astonishing: nowhere else in Polynesia do porpoises account for even as much as 1% of the bones in middens. The Common Dolphin generally lives out to sea, hence it could not have been hunted by line-fishing or spear-fishing from shore. Instead, it must have been harpooned far offshore, in big seaworthy canoes built from the tall trees identified by Catherine Orliac.

Fish bones also occur in the middens but account there for only 23% of all bones, whereas elsewhere in Polynesia they were the main food (90% or more of all the bones). That low contribution of fish to Easter diets was because of its rugged coastline and steep drop-offs of the ocean bottom, so that there are few places to catch fish by net or handline in shallow water. For the same reason the Easter diet was low in molluscs and sea urchins. To compensate, there were those abundant seabirds plus the land birds. Bird stew would have been seasoned with meat from large numbers of rats, which reached Easter as stowaways in the canoes of the Polynesian colonists. Easter is the sole known Polynesian island at whose archaeological sites rat bones outnumber fish bones. In case you're squeamish and consider rats inedible, I still recall, from my years of living in England in the late 1950s, recipes for creamed laboratory rat that my British biologist friends who kept them for experiments also used to supplement their diet during their years of wartime food rationing.

Porpoises, fish, shellfish, birds, and rats did not exhaust the list of meat sources available to Easter's first settlers. I already mentioned a few seal records, and other bones testify to the occasional availability of sea turtles and perhaps of large lizards. All those delicacies were cooked over firewood that can be identified as having come from Easter's subsequently vanished forests.

Comparison of those early garbage deposits with late prehistoric ones or with conditions on modern Easter reveals big changes in those initially bountiful food sources. Porpoises, and open-ocean fish like tuna, virtually disappeared from the islanders' diet, for reasons to be mentioned below. The fish that continued to be caught were mainly inshore species. Land birds disappeared completely from the diet, for the simple reason that every species became extinct from some combination of overhunting, deforestation, and predation by rats. It was the worst catastrophe to befall Pacific island birds, surpassing even the record on New Zealand and Hawaii, where to be sure the moas and flightless geese and other species became extinct but many other species managed to survive. No Pacific island other than Easter ended up without any native land birds. Of the 25 or more formerly breeding seabirds, overharvesting and rat predation brought the result that 24 no longer breed on Easter itself, about 9 are now confined to breeding in modest numbers on a few rocky islets off Easter's coasts, and 15 have been eliminated on those islets as well. Even shellfish were overexploited, so that people ended up eating fewer of the esteemed large cowries and more of the second-choice smaller black snails, and the sizes of both cowry and snail shells in the middens decreased with time because of preferential overharvesting of larger individuals.

The giant palm, and all the other now-extinct trees identified by Catherine Orliac, John Flenley, and Sarah King, disappeared for half a dozen reasons that we can document or infer. Orliac's charcoal samples from ovens prove directly that trees were being burned for firewood. They were also being burned to cremate bodies: Easter crematoria contain remains of thousands of bodies and huge amounts of human bone ash, implying massive fuel consumption for the purposes of cremation. Trees were being cleared for gardens, because most of Easter's land surface except at the highest elevations ended up being used to grow crops. From the early midden abundance of bones of open-ocean porpoises and tuna, we infer that big trees like *Alphitonia* and *Elaeocarpus* were being felled to make seaworthy canoes; the frail, leaky little watercraft seen by Roggeveen would not have served for harpooning platforms or venturing far out to sea. We infer that trees furnished timber and rope for transporting and erecting statues, and undoubtedly for a multitude of other purposes. The rats introduced accidentally as stowaways "used" the palm tree and doubtless other trees for their own purposes: every Easter palm nut that has been recovered shows tooth marks from rats gnawing on it and would have been incapable of germinating.

Deforestation must have begun some time after human arrival by A.D. 900, and must have been completed by 1722, when Roggeveen arrived and saw no trees over 10 feet tall. Can we specify more closely when, be-tween those dates of 900 and 1722, deforestation occurred? There are five types of evidence to guide us. Most radiocarbon dates on the palm nuts themselves are before 1500, suggesting that the palm became rare or extinct thereafter. On the Poike Peninsula, which has Easter's most infertile soils and hence was probably deforested first, the palms disappeared by around 1400, and charcoal from forest clearance disappeared around 1440 although later signs of agriculture attest to continued human presence there. Orliac's radiocarbon-dated charcoal samples from ovens and garbage pits show wood charcoal being replaced by herb and grass fuels after 1640, even at elite houses that might have claimed the last precious trees after none was left for the peasants. Flenley's pollen cores show the disappearance of palm, tree daisy, toromiro, and shrub pollen, and their replacement by grass and herb pollen, between 900 and 1300, but radiocarbon dates on sediment cores are a less direct clock for deforestation than are direct dates on the palms and their nuts. Finally, the upland plantations that Chris Stevenson studied, and whose operation may have paralleled the period of maximum timber and rope use for statues, were maintained from the early 1400s to the 1600s. All this suggests that forest clearance began soon after human ar-rival, reached its peak around 1400, and was virtually complete by dates that varied locally between the early 1400s and the 1600s.

The overall picture for Easter is the most extreme example of forest destruc-tion in the Pacific, and among the most extreme in the world: the whole for-est gone, and all of its tree species extinct. Immediate consequences for the islanders were losses of raw materials, losses of wild-caught foods, and de-creased crop yields.

Raw materials lost or else available only in greatly decreased amounts consisted of everything made from native plants and birds, including wood, rope, bark to manufacture bark cloth, and feathers. Lack of large timber and rope brought an end to the transport and erection of statues, and also to the construction of seagoing canoes. When five of Easter's little two-man leaky canoes paddled out to trade with a French ship anchored off Easter in 1838, its captain reported, "All the natives repeated often and excitedly the word *miru* and became impatient because they saw that we did not understand it: this word is the name of the timber used by Polynesians to make their ca-noes. This was what they wanted most, and they used every means to make us understand this . . ." The name "Terevaka" for Easter's largest and highest mountain means "place to get canoes": before its slopes were stripped of their trees to convert them to plantations, they were used for timber, and they are still littered with the stone drills, scrapers, knives, chisels, and other woodworking and canoe-building tools from that period. Lack of large timber also meant that people were without wood for fuel to keep themselves warm during Easter's winter nights of wind and driving rain at a temperature of 50 degrees Fahrenheit. Instead, after 1650 Easter's inhabitants were reduced to burning herbs, grasses, and sugarcane scraps and other crop wastes for fuel. There would have been fierce competition for the remaining woody shrubs, among people trying to obtain thatching and small pieces of wood for houses, wood for implements, and bark cloth. Even funeral practices had to be changed: cremation, which had required burning much wood per body, became impractical and yielded to mummification and bone burials.

Most sources of wild food were lost. Without seagoing canoes, bones of porpoises, which had been the islanders' principal meat during the first centuries, virtually disappeared from middens by 1500, as did tuna and pelagic fish. Midden numbers of fishhooks and fish bones in general also declined, leaving mainly just fish species that could be caught in shallow water or from the shore. Land birds disappeared completely, and seabirds were reduced to relict populations of one-third of Easter's original species, confined to breeding on a few offshore islets. Palm nuts, Malay apples, and all other wild fruits dropped out of the diet. The shellfish consumed became smaller species and smaller and many fewer individuals. The only wild food source whose availability remained unchanged was rats.

In addition to those drastic decreases in wild food sources, crop yields also decreased, for several reasons. Deforestation led locally to soil erosion by rain and wind, as shown by huge increases in the quantities of soil-derived metal ions carried into Flenley's swamp sediment cores. For example, excavations on the Poike Peninsula show that crops were initially grown there interspersed with palm trees left standing, so that their crowns could shade and protect the soil and crops against hot sun, evaporation, wind, and direct rain impacts. Clearance of the palms led to massive erosion that buried ahu and buildings downhill with soil, and that forced the abandonment of Poike's fields around 1400. Once grassland had established itself on Poike, farming was resumed there around 1500, to be abandoned again a century later in a second wave of erosion. Other damages to soil that resulted from deforestation and reduced crop yields included desiccation and nutrient leaching. Farmers found themselves without most of the wild plant leaves, fruit, and twigs that they had been using as compost.

Those were the immediate consequences of deforestation and other human environmental impacts. The further consequences start with starvation, a population crash, and a descent into cannibalism. Surviving islanders' accounts of starvation are graphically confirmed by the proliferation of little statues called *moai kavakava,* depicting starving people with hollow cheeks and protruding ribs. Captain Cook in 1774 described the islanders as "small, lean, timid, and miserable." Numbers of house sites in the coastal lowlands, where almost everybody lived, declined by 70% from peak values around 1400–1600 to the 1700s, suggesting a corresponding decline in numbers of people. In place of their former sources of wild meat, islanders turned to the largest hitherto unused source available to them: humans, whose bones became common not only in proper burials but also (cracked to extract the marrow) in late Easter Island garbage heaps. Oral traditions of the islanders are obsessed with cannibalism; the most inflammatory taunt that could be snarled at an enemy was "The flesh of your mother sticks between my teeth."

Easter's chiefs and priests had previously justified their elite status by claiming relationship to the gods, and by promising to deliver prosperity and bountiful harvests. They buttressed that ideology by monumental architecture and ceremonies designed to impress the masses, and made possible by food surpluses extracted from the masses. As their promises were being proved increasingly hollow, the power of the chiefs and priests was overthrown around 1680 by military leaders called *matatoa,* and Easter's formerly complexly integrated society collapsed in an epidemic of civil war. The obsidian spear-points (termed *mata'a*) from that era of fighting still littered Easter in modern times. Commoners now built their huts in the coastal zone, which had been previously reserved for the residences *(hare paenga)* of the elite. For safety, many people turned to living in caves that were enlarged by excavation and whose entrances were partly sealed to create a narrow tunnel for easier defense. Food remains, bone sewing needles, woodworking implements, and tools for repairing tapa cloth make clear that the caves were being occupied on a long-term basis, not just as temporary hiding places.

What had failed, in the twilight of Easter's Polynesian society, was not only the old political ideology but also the old religion, which became discarded along with the chiefs' power. Oral traditions record that the last ahu and moai were erected around 1620, and that Paro (the tallest statue) was among the last. The upland plantations whose elite-commandeered production fed the statue teams were progressively abandoned between 1600 and 1680. That the sizes of statues had been increasing may reflect not only rival chiefs vying to outdo each other, but also more urgent appeals to ancestors necessitated by the growing environmental crisis. Around 1680, at the time of the military coup, rival clans switched from erecting increasingly large statues to throwing down one another's statues by toppling a statue forwards onto a slab placed so that the statue would fall on the slab and break. Thus, as we shall also see for the Anasazi and Maya in Chapters 4 and 5, the collapse of Easter society followed swiftly upon the society's reaching its peak of population, monument construction, and environmental impact.

We don't know how far the toppling had proceeded at the time of the first European visits, because Roggeveen in 1722 landed only briefly at a single site, and González's Spanish expedition of 1770 wrote nothing about their visit except in the ship's log. The first semi-adequate European description was by Captain Cook in 1774, who remained for four days, sent a detachment to reconnoiter inland, and had the advantage of bringing a Tahitian whose Polynesian language was sufficiently similar to that of Easter Islanders that he could converse with them. Cook commented on seeing statues that had been thrown down, as well as others still erect. The last European mention of an erect statue was in 1838; none was reported as standing in 1868. Traditions relate that the final statue to be toppled (around 1840) was Paro, supposedly erected by a woman in honor of her husband, and thrown down by enemies of her family so as to break Paro at mid-body.

Ahu themselves were desecrated by pulling out some of the fine slabs in order to construct garden walls (*manavai*) next to the ahu, and by using other slabs to create burial chambers in which to place dead bodies. As a result, today the ahu that have not been restored (i.e., most of them) look at first sight like mere piles of boulders. As Jo Anne Van Tilburg, Claudio Cristino, Sonia Haoa, Barry Rolett, and I drove around Easter, saw ahu after ahu as a rubble pile with its broken statues, reflected on the enormous effort that had been devoted for centuries to constructing the ahu and to carving and transporting and erecting the moai, and then remembered that it was the islanders themselves who had destroyed their own ancestors' work, we were filled with an overwhelming sense of tragedy.

Easter Islanders' toppling of their ancestral moai reminds me of Russians and Romanians toppling the statues of Stalin and Ceauşescu when the

Communist governments of those countries collapsed. The islanders must have been filled with pent-up anger at their leaders for a long time, as we know that Russians and Romanians were. I wonder how many of the statues were thrown down one by one at intervals, by particular enemies of a statue's owner, as described for Paro; and how many were instead destroyed in a quickly spreading paroxysm of anger and disillusionment, as took place at the end of communism. I'm also reminded of a cultural tragedy and rejection of religion described to me in 1965 at a New Guinea highland village called Bomai, where the Christian missionary assigned to Bomai boasted to me with pride how one day he had called upon his new converts to collect their "pagan artifacts" (i.e., their cultural and artistic heritage) at the airstrip and burn them—and how they obeyed. Perhaps Easter Island's matatoa issued a similar summons to their own followers.

I don't want to portray social developments on Easter after 1680 as wholly negative and destructive. The survivors adapted as best they could, both in their subsistence and in their religion. Not only cannibalism but also chicken houses underwent explosive growth after 1650; chickens had accounted for less than 0.1% of the animal bones in the oldest middens that David Steadman, Patricia Vargas, and Claudio Cristino excavated at Anakena. The matatoa justified their military coup by adopting a religious cult, based on the creator god Makemake, who had previously been just one of Easter's pantheon of gods. The cult was centered at Orongo village on the rim of Rano Kau caldera, overlooking the three largest offshore islets to which nesting seabirds had become confined. The new religion developed its own new art styles, expressed especially in petroglyphs (rock carvings) of women's genitals, birdmen, and birds (in order of decreasing frequency), carved not only on Orongo monuments but also on toppled moai and pukao elsewhere. Each year the Orongo cult organized a competition between men to swim across the cold, shark-infested, one-mile-wide strait separating the islets from Easter itself, to collect the first egg laid in that season by Sooty Terns, to swim back to Easter with the unbroken egg, and to be anointed "Birdman of the year" for the following year. The last Orongo ceremony took place in 1867 and was witnessed by Catholic missionaries, just as the residue of Easter Island society not already destroyed by the islanders themselves was being destroyed by the outside world.

The sad story of European impacts on Easter Islanders may be quickly summarized. After Captain Cook's brief sojourn in 1774, there was a steady trickle of European visitors. As documented for Hawaii, Fiji, and many other Pacific islands, they must be assumed to have introduced European diseases and thereby to have killed many previously unexposed islanders, though our first specific mention of such an epidemic is of smallpox around 1836. Again as on other Pacific islands, "black-birding," the kidnapping of islanders to become laborers, began on Easter around 1805 and climaxed in 1862–63, the grimmest year of Easter's history, when two dozen Peruvian ships abducted about 1,500 people (half of the surviving population) and sold them at auction to work in Peru's guano mines and other menial jobs. Most of those kidnapped died in captivity. Under international pressure, Peru repatriated a dozen surviving captives, who brought another smallpox epidemic to the island. Catholic missionaries took up residence in 1864. By 1872 there were only 111 islanders left on Easter.

European traders introduced sheep to Easter in the 1870s and claimed land ownership. In 1888 the Chilean government annexed Easter, which effectively became a sheep ranch managed by a Chile-based Scottish company. All islanders were confined to living in one village and to working for the company, being paid in goods at the company store rather than in cash. A revolt by the islanders in 1914 was ended by the arrival of a Chilean warship. Grazing by the company's sheep, goats, and horses caused soil erosion and eliminated most of what had remained of the native vegetation, including the last surviving hauhau and toromiro individuals on Easter around 1934. Not until 1966 did islanders become Chilean citizens. Today, islanders are undergoing a resurgence of cultural pride, and the economy is being stimulated by the arrival of several airplane flights each week from Santiago and Tahiti by Chile's national airline, carrying visitors (like Barry Rolett and me) attracted by the famous statues. However, even a brief visit makes obvious that tensions remain between islanders and mainland-born Chileans, who are now represented in roughly equal numbers on Easter.

Easter Island's famous rongo-rongo writing system was undoubtedly invented by the islanders, but there is no evidence for its existence until its first mention by the resident Catholic missionary in 1864. All 25 surviving objects with writing appear to postdate European contact; some of them are pieces of foreign wood or a European oar, and some may have been manufactured by islanders specifically to sell to representatives of Tahiti's Catholic bishop, who became interested in the writing and sought examples. In 1995 linguist Steven Fischer announced a decipherment of rongo-rongo texts as procreation chants, but his interpretation is debated by other scholars. Most Easter Island specialists, including Fischer, now conclude that the invention

of rongo-rongo was inspired by the islanders' first contact with writing during the Spanish landing of 1770, or else by the trauma of the 1862–63 Peruvian slave raid that killed so many carriers of oral knowledge.

In part because of this history of exploitation and oppression, there has
been resistance among both islanders and scholars to acknowledging the
reality of self-inflicted environmental damage before Roggeveen's arrival in
1722, despite all the detailed evidence that I have summarized. In essence,
the islanders are saying, "Our ancestors would never have done that," while
visiting scientists are saying, "Those nice people whom we have come to
love would never have done that." For example, Michel Orliac wrote about
similar questions of environmental change in Tahiti, ". . . it is at least as
likely—if not more so—that environmental modifications originated in
natural causes rather than in human activities. This is a much-debated
question (McFadgen 1985; Grant 1985; McGlone 1989) to which I do not
claim to bring a definitive solution, even if my affection for the Polynesians
incites me to choose natural actions [e.g., cyclones] to explain the damages
suffered by the environment." Three specific objections or alternative theories have been raised.

First, it has been suggested that Easter's deforested condition seen by
Roggeveen in 1722 was not caused by the islanders in isolation but resulted
in some unspecified way from disruption caused by unrecorded European
visitors before Roggeveen. It is perfectly possible that there were indeed one
or more such unrecorded visits: many Spanish galleons were sailing across
the Pacific in the 1500s and 1600s, and the islanders' nonchalant, unafraid,
curious reaction to Roggeveen does suggest prior experience of Europeans,
rather than the shocked reaction expected for people who had been living
in total isolation and had assumed themselves to be the only humans in the
world. However, we have no specific knowledge of any pre-1722 visit, nor is
it obvious how it would have triggered deforestation. Even before Magellan
became the first European to cross the Pacific in 1521, abundant evidence
attests to massive human impacts on Easter: extinctions of all the land bird
species, disappearance of porpoises and tuna from the diet, declines of forest tree pollen in Flenley's sediment cores before 1300, deforestation of the
Poike Peninsula by around 1400, lack of radiocarbon-dated palm nuts after
1500, and so on.

A second objection is that deforestation might instead have been due
to natural climate changes, such as droughts or El Niño episodes. It would
not surprise me at all if a contributing role of climate change does eventually emerge for Easter, because we shall see that climatic downturns did

exacerbate human environmental impacts by the Anasazi (Chapter 4), Maya (Chapter 5), Greenland Norse (Chapters 7 and 8), and probably many other societies. At present, we lack information about climate changes on Easter in the relevant period of A.D. 900–1700: we don't know whether the climate got drier and stormier and less favorable to forest survival (as postulated by critics), or wetter and less stormy and more favorable to forest survival. But there seems to me to be compelling evidence against climate change by itself having caused the deforestation and bird extinctions: the palm trunk casts in Mt. Terevaka's lava flows prove that the giant palm had already survived on Easter for several hundred thousand years; and Flenley's sediment cores demonstrate pollen of the palm, tree daisies, toromiro, and half-a-dozen other tree species on Easter between 38,000 and 21,000 years ago. Hence Easter's plants had already survived innumerable droughts and El Niño events, making it unlikely that all those native tree species finally chose a time coincidentally just after the arrival of those innocent humans to drop dead simultaneously in response to yet another drought or El Niño event. In fact, Flenley's records show that a cool dry period on Easter between 26,000 and 12,000 years ago, more severe than any worldwide cool dry period in the last thousand years, merely caused Easter's trees at higher elevation to undergo a retreat to the lowlands, from which they subsequently recovered.

A third objection is that Easter Islanders surely wouldn't have been so foolish as to cut down all their trees, when the consequences would have been so obvious to them. As Catherine Orliac expressed it, " Why destroy a forest that one needs for his [i.e., the Easter Islanders'] material and spiritual survival?" This is indeed a key question, one that has nagged not only Catherine Orliac but also my University of California students, me, and everyone else who has wondered about self-inflicted environmental damage. I have often asked myself, "What did the Easter Islander who cut down the last palm tree say while he was doing it?" Like modern loggers, did he shout "Jobs, not trees!"? Or: "Technology will solve our problems, never fear, we'll find a substitute for wood"? Or: "We don't have proof that there aren't palms somewhere else on Easter, we need more research, your proposed ban on logging is premature and driven by fear-mongering"? Similar questions arise for every society that has inadvertently damaged its environment. When we return to this question in Chapter 14, we shall see that there is a whole series of reasons why societies nevertheless do make such mistakes.

■ ■ ■

We still have not faced the question why Easter Island ranks as such an extreme example of deforestation. After all, the Pacific encompasses thousands of inhabited islands, almost all of whose inhabitants were chopping down trees, clearing gardens, burning firewood, building canoes, and using wood and rope for houses and other things. Yet, among all those islands, only three in the Hawaiian Archipelago, all of them much drier than Easter—the two islets of Necker and Nihoa, and the larger island of Niihau—even approach Easter in degree of deforestation. Nihoa still supports one species of large palm tree, and it is uncertain whether tiny Necker, with an area of barely forty acres, ever had trees. Why were Easter Islanders unique, or nearly so, in destroying every tree? The answer sometimes given, "because Easter's palm and toromiro were very slow-growing," fails to explain why at least 19 other tree or plant species related to or the same as species still widespread on East Polynesian islands were eliminated on Easter but not on other islands. I suspect that this question lies behind the reluctance of Easter Islanders themselves and of some scientists to accept that the islanders caused the deforestation, because that conclusion seems to imply that they were uniquely bad or improvident among Pacific peoples.

Barry Rolett and I were puzzled by that apparent uniqueness of Easter. Actually, it's just part of a broader puzzling question: why degree of deforestation varies among Pacific islands in general. For example, Mangareva (to be discussed in the next chapter), most of the Cook and Austral Islands, and the leeward sides of the main Hawaiian and Fijian Islands were largely deforested, though not completely as in the case of Easter. The Societies and Marquesas, and the windward sides of the main Hawaiian and Fijian Islands, supported primary forests at higher elevation and a mixture of secondary forests, fernlands, and grasslands at low elevation. Tonga, Samoa, most of the Bismarcks and Solomons, and Makatea (the largest of the Tuamotus) remained largely forested. How can all that variation be explained?

Barry began by combing through the journals of early European explorers of the Pacific, to locate descriptions of what the islands looked like then. That enabled him to extract the degree of deforestation on 81 islands as first seen by Europeans—i.e., after centuries or millennia of impacts by native Pacific Islanders but before European impacts. For those same 81 islands, we then tabulated values of nine physical factors whose interisland variation we thought might contribute to explaining those different outcomes of de-forestation. Some trends immediately became obvious to us when we just eyeballed the data, but we ground the data through many statistical analyses in order to be able to put numbers on the trends.

What Affects Deforestation on Pacific Islands?

Deforestation is more severe on:
>   dry islands than wet islands;
>   cold high-latitude islands than warm equatorial islands;
>   old volcanic islands than young volcanic islands;
>   islands without aerial ash fallout than islands with it;
>   islands far from Central Asia's dust plume than islands near it;
>   islands without makatea than islands with it;
>   low islands than high islands;
>   remote islands than islands with near neighbors; and
>   small islands than big islands.

It turned out that all nine of the physical variables did contribute to the outcome (see the table above). Most important were variations in rainfall and latitude: dry islands, and cooler islands farther from the equator (at higher latitude), ended up more deforested than did wetter equatorial islands. That was as we had expected: the rate of plant growth and of seedling establishment increases with rainfall and with temperature. When one chops trees down in a wet hot place like the New Guinea lowlands, within a year new trees 20 feet tall have sprung up on the site, but tree growth is much slower in a cold dry desert. Hence regrowth can keep pace with moderate rates of cutting trees on wet hot islands, leaving the island in a steady state of being largely tree-covered.

Three other variables—island age, ash fallout, and dust fallout—had effects that we hadn't anticipated, because we hadn't been familiar with the scientific literature on the maintenance of soil fertility. Old islands that hadn't experienced any volcanic activity for over a million years ended up more deforested than young, recently active volcanic islands. That's because soil derived from fresh lava and ash contains nutrients that are necessary for plant growth, and that gradually become leached out by rain on older islands. One of the two main ways that those nutrients then become renewed on Pacific islands is by fallout of ash carried in the air from volcanic explosions. But the Pacific Ocean is divided by a line famous to geologists and known as the Andesite Line. In the Southwest Pacific on the Asian side of that line, volcanoes blow out ash that may be wind-carried for hundreds of miles and that maintains the fertility even of islands (like New Caledonia) that have no volcanoes of their own. In the central and eastern Pacific beyond the Andesite Line, the main aerial input of nutrients to renew soil fertility is instead in dust carried high in the atmosphere by winds from the steppes of Central Asia. Hence islands east of the Andesite Line, and far from Asia's dust plume, ended up more deforested than islands within the Andesite Line or nearer to Asia.

Another variable required consideration only for half a dozen islands that consist of the rock known as makatea—basically, a coral reef thrust into the air by geological uplift. The name arises from the Tuamotu island of Makatea, which consists largely of that rock. Makatea terrain is absolute hell to walk over; the deeply fissured, razor-sharp coral cuts one's boots, feet, and hands to shreds. When I first encountered makatea on Rennell Island in the Solomons, it took me 10 minutes to walk a hundred yards, and I was in constant terror of macerating my hands on a coral boulder if I touched it while thoughtlessly extending my hands to maintain my balance. Makatea can slice up stout modern boots within a few days of walking. While Pacific Islanders somehow managed to get around on it in bare feet, even they had problems. No one who has endured the agony of walking on makatea will be surprised that Pacific islands with makatea ended up less deforested than those without it.

That leaves three variables with more complex effects: elevation, distance, and area. High islands tended to become less deforested (even in their lowlands) than low islands, because mountains generate clouds and rain, which descends to the lowlands as streams stimulating lowland plant growth by their water, by their transport of eroded nutrients, and by transport of atmospheric dust. The mountains themselves may remain forest-covered if they are too high or too steep for gardening. Remote islands became more deforested than islands near neighbors—possibly because islanders were more likely to stay home and do things impacting their own environment than to spend time and energy visiting other islands to trade, raid, or settle. Big islands tended to become less deforested than small islands, for numerous reasons including lower perimeter/area ratios, hence fewer marine resources per person and lower population densities, more centuries required to chop down the forest, and more areas unsuitable for gardening remaining.

How does Easter rate according to these nine variables predisposing to deforestation? It has the third highest latitude, among the lowest rainfalls, the lowest volcanic ash fallout, the lowest Asian dust fallout, no makatea, and the second greatest distance from neighboring islands. It is among the lower and smaller of the 81 islands that Barry Rolett and I studied. All eight of those variables make Easter susceptible to deforestation. Easter's volcanoes are of moderate age (probably 200,000 to 600,000 years); Easter's Poike Peninsula, its oldest volcano, was the first part of Easter to become deforested and exhibits the worst soil erosion today. Combining the effects of all those variables, Barry's and my statistical model predicted that Easter, Nihoa, and Necker should be the worst deforested Pacific islands. That agrees with what actually happened: Nihoa and Necker ended up with no human left alive and with only one tree species standing (Nihoa's palm), while Easter ended up with no tree species standing and with about 90% of its former population gone.

In short, the reason for Easter's unusually severe degree of deforestation isn't that those seemingly nice people really were unusually bad or improvident. Instead, they had the misfortune to be living in one of the most fragile environments, at the highest risk for deforestation, of any Pacific people. For Easter Island, more than for any other society discussed in this book, we can specify in detail the factors underlying environmental fragility.

Easter's isolation makes it the clearest example of a society that destroyed itself by overexploiting its own resources. If we return to our five-point checklist of factors to be considered in connection with environmental collapses, two of those factors—attacks by neighboring enemy societies, and loss of support from neighboring friendly societies—played no role in Easter's collapse, because there is no evidence that there were any enemies or friends in contact with Easter Island society after its founding. Even if it turns out that some canoes did arrive subsequently, such contacts could not have been on a large enough scale to constitute either dangerous attacks or important support. For a role of a third factor, climate change, we also have no evidence at present, though it may emerge in the future. That leaves us with just two main sets of factors behind Easter's collapse: human environmental impacts, especially deforestation and destruction of bird populations; and the political, social, and religious factors behind the impacts, such as the impossibility of emigration as an escape valve because of Easter's isolation, a focus on statue construction for reasons already discussed, and competition between clans and chiefs driving the erection of bigger statues requiring more wood, rope, and food.

The Easter Islanders' isolation probably also explains why I have found that their collapse, more than the collapse of any other pre-industrial society, haunts my readers and students. The parallels between Easter Island and the whole modern world are chillingly obvious. Thanks to globalization, international trade, jet planes, and the Internet, all countries on Earth today share resources and affect each other, just as did Easter's dozen clans. Polynesian Easter Island was as isolated in the Pacific Ocean as the Earth is today in space. When the Easter Islanders got into difficulties, there was nowhere to which they could flee, nor to which they could turn for help; nor shall we modern Earthlings have recourse elsewhere if our troubles increase. Those are the reasons why people see the collapse of Easter Island society as a metaphor, a worst-case scenario, for what may lie ahead of us in our own future.

Of course, the metaphor is imperfect. Our situation today differs in important respects from that of Easter Islanders in the 17th century. Some of those differences increase the danger for us: for instance, if mere thousands of Easter Islanders with just stone tools and their own muscle power sufficed to destroy their environment and thereby destroyed their society, how can billions of people with metal tools and machine power now fail to do worse? But there are also differences in our favor, differences to which we shall return in the last chapter of this book.

CHAPTER 3

The Last People Alive:
Pitcairn and Henderson Islands

Pitcairn before the *Bounty* ■ Three dissimilar islands ■ Trade ■
The movie's ending ■

M any centuries ago, immigrants came to a fertile land blessed with apparently inexhaustible natural resources. While the land lacked a few raw materials useful for industry, those materials were readily obtained by overseas trade with poorer lands that happened to have deposits of them. For a time, all the lands prospered, and their populations multiplied.

But the population of the rich land eventually multiplied beyond the numbers that even its abundant resources could support. As its forests were felled and its soils eroded, its agricultural productivity was no longer sufficient to generate export surpluses, build ships, or even to nourish its own population. With that decline of trade, shortages of the imported raw materials developed. Civil war spread, as established political institutions were overthrown by a kaleidoscopically changing succession of local military leaders. The starving populace of the rich land survived by turning to cannibalism. Their former overseas trade partners met an even worse fate: deprived of the imports on which they had depended, they in turn ravaged their own environments until no one was left alive.

Does this grim scenario represent the future of the United States and our trade partners? We don't know yet, but the scenario has already played itself out on three tropical Pacific islands. One of them, Pitcairn Island, is famous as the "uninhabited" island to which the mutineers from the H.M.S. *Bounty* fled in 1790. They chose Pitcairn because it was indeed uninhabited at that time, remote, and hence offered a hiding place from the vengeful British navy searching for them. But the mutineers did find temple platforms, petroglyphs, and stone tools giving mute evidence that Pitcairn had formerly supported an ancient Polynesian population. East of Pitcairn, an even more remote island named Henderson remains uninhabited to this

day. Even now, Pitcairn and Henderson are among the most inaccessible islands in the world, without any air or scheduled sea traffic, and visited only
by the occasional yacht or cruise ship. Yet Henderson, too, bears abundant
marks of a former Polynesian population. What happened to those original
Pitcairn Islanders, and to their vanished cousins on Henderson?

The romance and mystery of the H.M.S. *Bounty* mutineers on Pitcairn,
retold in many books and films, are matched by the mysterious earlier ends
of these two populations. Basic information about them has at last emerged
from recent excavations by Marshall Weisler, an archaeologist at the University of Otago in New Zealand, who spent eight months on those lonely out-
posts. The fates of the first Pitcairners and the Henderson Islanders prove to
have been linked to a slowly unfolding environmental catastrophe hundreds
of miles overseas on their more populous island trading partner, Mangareva, whose population survived at the cost of a drastically lowered standard of living. Thus, just as Easter Island offered us our clearest example of
a collapse due to human environmental impacts with a minimum of other
complicating factors, Pitcairn and Henderson Islands furnish our clearest
examples of collapses triggered by the breakdown of an environmentally
damaged trade partner: a preview of risks already developing today in association with modern globalization. Environmental damage on Pitcairn and
Henderson themselves also contributed to the collapses there, but there is
no evidence for roles of climate change or of enemies.

Mangareva, Pitcairn, and Henderson are the sole habitable islands in the
area known as Southeast Polynesia, which otherwise includes just a few low
atolls supporting only temporary populations or visitors but no permanent
populations. These three habitable islands were settled sometime around
A.D. 800, as part of the eastwards Polynesian expansion explained in the
preceding chapter. Even Mangareva, the westernmost of the three islands
and hence the one closest to previously settled parts of Polynesia, lies about
a thousand miles beyond the nearest large high islands, such as the Societies
(including Tahiti) to the west and the Marquesas to the northwest. The Societies and Marquesas in turn, which are the largest and most populous islands in East Polynesia, lie more than a thousand miles east of the nearest
high islands of West Polynesia and may not have been colonized until perhaps nearly 2,000 years after West Polynesia's settlement. Thus, Mangareva
and its neighbors were isolated outliers even within Polynesia's more remote eastern half. They were probably occupied from the Marquesas or

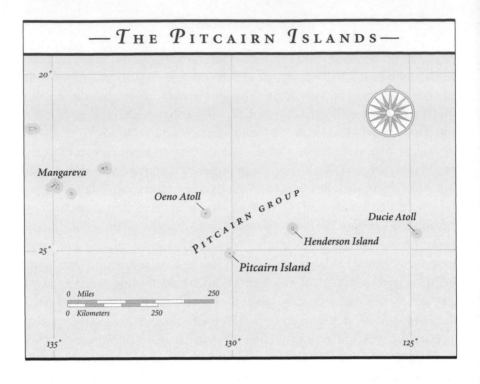

20°

Mangareva

Oeno Atoll

PITCAIRN GROUP

Ducie Atoll

Henderson Island

25°

Pitcairn Island

0   Miles   250

0   Kilometers   250

135°   130°   125°

Societies during the same colonizing push that reached the even more remote Hawaiian Islands and Easter, and that completed the settlement of
Polynesia (maps, pp. 84–85 and this page).

Of those three habitable islands of Southeast Polynesia, the one capable
of supporting by far the largest human population, and most abundantly
endowed with natural resources important to humans, was Mangareva. It
consists of a large lagoon 15 miles in diameter, sheltered by an outer reef,
and containing two dozen extinct volcanic islands and a few coral atolls
with a total land area of 10 square miles. The lagoon, its reefs, and the ocean
outside the lagoon teem with fish and shellfish. Especially valuable among
the species of shellfish is the black-lipped pearl oyster, a very large oyster of
which the lagoon offered virtually inexhaustible quantities to Polynesian
settlers, and which is the species used today to raise the famous black cultured pearls. In addition to the oyster itself being edible, its thick shell, up to
eight inches long, was an ideal raw material that Polynesians carved into
fishhooks, vegetable peelers and graters, and ornaments.

The higher islands of Mangareva's lagoon received enough rain to have
springs and intermittent streams, and were originally forested. In the narrow band of flat land around the coasts, the Polynesian colonists built their

settlements. On the slopes behind the villages they grew crops such as sweet potato and yams; terraced slopes and flats below the springs were planted in taro, irrigated by spring water; and higher elevations were planted in tree crops such as breadfruit and bananas. In this way, farming and fishing and gathering of shellfish would have been able to support a human population of several thousand on Mangareva, more than 10 times the likely combined populations of Pitcairn and Henderson in ancient Polynesian times.

From a Polynesian perspective, Mangareva's most significant drawback was its lack of high-quality stone for making adzes and other stone tools. (That's as if the United States contained all important natural resources except high-grade iron deposits.) The coral atolls in Mangareva lagoon had no good raw stone at all, and even the volcanic islands offered only relatively coarse-grained basalt. That was adequate for building houses and garden walls, using as oven stones, and fashioning into canoe anchors and food pounders and other crude tools, but coarse-grained basalt yielded only inferior adzes.

Fortunately, that deficiency was spectacularly remedied on Pitcairn, the much smaller (2^1/$_2$ square miles) and steeper extinct volcanic island lying 300 miles southeast of Mangareva. Imagine the excitement when the first canoeload of Mangarevans discovered Pitcairn after several days' travel on open ocean, landed at its only feasible beach, scrambled up the steep slopes, and came upon Down Rope Quarry, Southeast Polynesia's sole useable lode of volcanic glass, whose flakes could serve as sharp tools for fine cutting tasks—the Polynesian equivalent of scissors and scalpels. Their excitement would have turned to ecstasy when, barely a mile farther west along the coast, they discovered the Tautama lode of fine-grained basalt, which became Southeast Polynesia's biggest quarry for making adzes.

In other respects, Pitcairn offered much more limited opportunities than did Mangareva. It did have intermittent streams, and its forests included trees large enough to fashion into hulls of outrigger canoes. But Pitcairn's steepness and small total area meant that the area of level plateau suitable for agriculture was very small. An equally serious drawback is that Pitcairn's coastline lacks a reef, and the surrounding sea bottom falls off steeply, with the result that fishing and the search for shellfish are much less rewarding than on Mangareva. In particular, Pitcairn has no beds of those black-lipped pearl oysters so useful for eating and tool-making. Hence the total population of Pitcairn in Polynesian times was probably not much greater than a hundred people. The descendants of the *Bounty* mutineers and their Polynesian companions living on Pitcairn today number only 52.

When their number climbed from the original band of 27 settlers in 1790 to 194 descendants in the year 1856, that population overtaxed Pitcairn's agricultural potential, and much of the population had to be evacuated by the British government to distant Norfolk Island.

The remaining habitable island of Southeast Polynesia, Henderson, is the largest (14 square miles) but is also the most remote (100 miles northeast of Pitcairn, 400 miles east of Mangareva) and the most marginal for human existence. Unlike Mangareva or Pitcairn, Henderson is not volcanic but is in effect a coral reef that geological processes thrust up 100 feet above sea level. Hence Henderson is devoid of basalt or other rocks suitable for tool-making. That's a severe limitation for a society of stone tool makers. An additional severe limitation for any humans is that Henderson has no streams or reliable freshwater sources, because the island consists of porous limestone. At best, for a few days after the unpredictable arrivals of rain, water drips from the roofs of caves, and puddles of water can be found on the ground. There is also a freshwater spring that bubbles up in the ocean about 20 feet offshore. During Marshall Weisler's months on Henderson, he found obtaining drinking water even with modern tarpaulins to catch the rain a constant effort, and most of his cooking and all of his washing and bathing had to be carried out with saltwater.

Even soil on Henderson is confined to small pockets between the limestone. The island's tallest trees are only about 50 feet high and not big enough to fashion into canoe hulls. The resulting stunted forest and thick undergrowth are so dense that they require a machete to penetrate them. Henderson's beaches are narrow and confined to the north end; its south coast consists of vertical cliffs where it is impossible to land a boat; and the south end of the island is a makatea landscape thrown into alternating rows of razor-sharp limestone ridges and fissures. That south end has been reached only three times by groups of Europeans, one of them Weisler's group. It took Weisler, wearing hiking boots, five hours to cover the five miles from Henderson's north coast to its south coast—where he promptly discovered a rock shelter formerly occupied by barefoot Polynesians.

Offsetting these fearsome disadvantages, Henderson does have attractions. In the reef and shallow waters nearby live lobsters, crabs, octopus, and a limited variety of fish and shellfish—unfortunately, not including black-lipped pearl oyster. On Henderson is Southeast Polynesia's sole known turtle nesting beach, where green turtles come ashore to lay eggs between January and March of each year. Henderson formerly supported at least 17 species of breeding seabirds, including petrel colonies possibly as large as millions of birds, whose adults and chicks would have been easy to catch on the nest—enough for a population of a hundred people each to eat one bird every day of the year without endangering the colonies' survival. The island was also home to nine species of resident land birds, five of them flightless or weak fliers and hence easy to catch, including three species of large pigeons that would have been especially delectable.

All those features would have made Henderson a great place for an afternoon picnic ashore, or for a short vacation to glut yourself on seafood and birds and turtles—but a risky and marginal home in which to try to eke out a permanent existence. Weisler's excavations nevertheless showed, to the surprise of anyone who has seen or heard of Henderson, that the island did evidently support a permanent tiny population, possibly comprising a few dozen people who went to extreme effort in order to survive. Proof of their former presence is provided by 98 human bones and teeth representing at least 10 adults (both men and women, some of them over 40 years old), six teenaged boys and girls, and four children in the age range of 5 to 10 years. The children's bones in particular suggest a resident population; modern Pitcairn Islanders usually don't take young children when they visit Henderson to collect wood or seafood.

Further evidence of human use is a huge buried midden, one of the largest known from Southeast Polynesia, running for 300 yards in length and 30 yards in width along the north-coast beach facing the only passage through Henderson's fringing reef. Among the midden's garbage left behind from generations of people feasting, and identified in small test pits excavated by Weisler and his colleagues, are enormous quantities of fish bones (14,751 fish bones in just two-thirds of a cubic yard of sand tested!), plus 42,213 bird bones comprising tens of thousands of bones of seabirds (especially petrels, terns, and tropicbirds) and thousands of bones of land birds (especially the flightless pigeons, rail, and sandpiper). When one extrapolates from the number of bones in Weisler's small test pits to the likely number in the whole midden, one calculates that Henderson Islanders must have disposed of the remains of tens of millions of fish and birds over the centuries. The oldest human-associated radiocarbon date on Henderson is from that midden, and the next-oldest date is from the turtle nesting beach on the northeast coast, implying that people settled first in those areas where they could glut themselves on wild-caught food.

Where could people live on an island that is nothing more than an uplifted coral reef covered with low trees? Henderson is unique among islands inhabited or formerly inhabited by Polynesians in its almost-complete lack of evidence for buildings, such as the usual houses and temples. There are only three signs of any construction: a stone pavement and post holes in the midden, suggesting the foundations of a house or shelter; one small low wall for protection against the wind; and a few slabs of beach rock for a burial vault. Instead, literally every cave and rock shelter near the coast and with a flat floor and accessible opening—even small recesses only three yards wide and two yards deep, barely large enough for a few people to seek protection from the sun—contained debris testifying to former human habitation. Weisler found 18 such shelters, of which 15 were on the heavily used north, northeast, and northwest coasts near the only beaches, and the other three (all of them very cramped) were on the eastern or southern cliffs. Because Henderson is small enough that Weisler was able to survey essentially the entire coast, the 18 caves and rock shelters, plus one shelter on the north beach, probably constitute all the "dwellings" of Henderson's population.

Charcoal, piles of stones, and relict stands of crop plants showed that the northeast part of the island had been burned and laboriously converted to garden patches where crops could be planted in natural pockets of soil, extended by piling surface stones into mounds. Among the Polynesian crops and useful plants that were introduced intentionally by the settlers, and that have been identified in Henderson archaeological sites or that still grow wild on Henderson today, are coconuts, bananas, swamp taro, possibly taro itself, several species of timber trees, candlenut trees whose nut husks are burned for illumination, hibiscus trees yielding fiber for making rope, and the ti shrub. The latter's sugary roots serve usually just as an emergency food supply elsewhere in Polynesia but were evidently a staple vegetable food on Henderson. Ti leaves could be used to make clothing, house thatching, and food wrappings. All of those sugary and starchy crops add up to a high-carbohydrate diet, which may explain why the teeth and jaws of Henderson Islanders that Weisler found exhibit enough signs of periodontal disease, tooth wear, and tooth loss to give nightmares to a dentist. Most of the islanders' protein would have come from the wild birds and seafood, but finds of a couple of pig bones show that they kept or brought pigs at least occasionally.

Thus, Southeast Polynesia presented colonists with only a few potentially habitable islands. Mangareva, the one capable of supporting the largest population, was largely self-sufficient in the necessities for Polynesian life, except for lacking high-quality stone. Of the other two islands, Pitcairn was so small, Henderson so ecologically marginal, that each could support only a tiny population unable to constitute a viable human society in the long run. Both were also deficient in important resources—Henderson so much so that we moderns, who wouldn't dream of going there even for a weekend without a full tool chest, drinking water, and food other than seafood, find it mind-boggling that Polynesians managed to survive there as residents. But both Pitcairn and Henderson offered compensating attractions to Polynesians: high-quality stone on the former, abundant seafood and birds on the latter.

Weisler's archaeological excavations uncovered extensive evidence of trade among all three islands, whereby each island's deficiencies were filled by the other islands' surpluses. Trade objects, even those (such as ones of stone) lacking organic carbon suitable for radiocarbon dating, can still be dated by radiocarbon measurements on charcoal excavated from the same archaeological layer. In that way, Weisler established that trade began at least by the year A.D. 1000, probably simultaneously with the first settlement by humans, and continued for many centuries. Numerous objects excavated at Weisler's sites on Henderson could immediately be identified as imports because they were made from materials foreign to Henderson: oyster shell fishhooks and vegetable peelers, volcanic glass cutting tools, and basalt adzes and oven stones.

Where did those imports come from? A reasonable guess is that the oyster shell for fishhooks came from Mangareva, because oysters are abundant there but absent on Pitcairn as well as on Henderson, and other islands with oyster beds are much more distant than Mangareva. A few oyster shell artifacts have also been found on Pitcairn and are similarly presumed to have come from Mangareva. But it is a much more difficult problem to identify origins of the volcanic stone artifacts found on Henderson, because both Mangareva and Pitcairn, as well as many other distant Polynesian islands, have volcanic sources.

Hence Weisler developed or adapted techniques for discriminating among volcanic stones from different sources. Volcanoes spew out many different types of lava, of which basalt (the category of volcanic stone occurring on Mangareva and Pitcairn) is defined by its chemical composition and color. However, basalts from different islands, and often even from different quarries on the same island, differ from each other in finer details of chemical composition, such as their relative content of major elements (like silicon and aluminum) and minor elements (like niobium and zirconium).

An even finer discriminating detail is that the element lead occurs naturally as several isotopes (i.e., several forms differing slightly in atomic weight), whose proportions also differ from one basalt source to another. To a geologist, all these details of composition constitute a fingerprint that may allow one to identify a stone tool as coming from one particular island or quarry.

Weisler analyzed the chemical composition and, with a colleague, the lead isotope ratios in dozens of stone tools and stone fragments (possibly broken off in the course of preparing or repairing stone tools) that he had excavated from dated layers of archaeological sites on Henderson. For comparison, he analyzed volcanic rocks from quarries and rock outcroppings on Mangareva and Pitcairn, the most likely sources of rock imported to Henderson. Just to be sure, he also analyzed volcanic rocks from Polynesian islands that were much more distant and hence less likely to have served as sources of Henderson imports, including Hawaii, Easter, Marquesas, Societies, and Samoa.

The conclusions emerging from these analyses were unequivocal. All analyzed pieces of volcanic glass found on Henderson originated at the Down Rope quarry on Pitcairn. That conclusion had already been suggested by visual inspection of the pieces, even before chemical analysis, because Pitcairn volcanic glass is colored so distinctively with black and gray patches. Most of Henderson's basalt adzes, and its basalt flakes likely to have resulted from adze-making, also originated from Pitcairn, but some came from Mangareva. On Mangareva itself, although far fewer searches have been made for stone artifacts than on Henderson, some adzes were also evidently made from Pitcairn basalt, imported presumably because of its superiority to Mangareva's own basalt. Conversely, of the vesicular basalt stones excavated on Henderson, most came from Mangareva, but a minority were from Pitcairn. Such stones were regularly used throughout Polynesia as oven stones, to be heated in a fire for cooking, much like the charcoal bricks used in modern barbecues. Many of those putative oven stones were found in cooking pits on Henderson and showed signs of having been heated, confirming their surmised function.

In short, archaeological studies have now documented a former flourishing trade in raw materials and possibly also in finished tools: in oyster shell, from Mangareva to Pitcairn and Henderson; in volcanic glass, from Pitcairn to Henderson; and in basalt, from Pitcairn to Mangareva and Henderson, and from Mangareva to Henderson. In addition, Polynesia's pigs and its bananas, taro, and other main crops are species that did not occur on Polynesian islands before humans arrived. If Mangareva was settled be-

fore Pitcairn and Henderson, as seems likely because Mangareva is the closest of the three to other Polynesian islands, then trade from Mangareva
probably also brought the indispensable crops and pigs to Pitcairn and
Henderson. Especially at the time when Mangareva's colonies on Pitcairn
and Henderson were being founded, the canoes bringing imports from
Mangareva represented an umbilical cord essential for populating and
stocking the new colonies, in addition to their later role as a permanent
lifeline.

As for what products Henderson exported to Pitcairn and Mangareva in
return, we can only guess. They must have been perishable items unlikely to
survive in Pitcairn and Mangareva archaeological sites, since Henderson
lacks stones or shells worth exporting. One plausible candidate is live sea
turtles, which today breed in Southeast Polynesia only on Henderson, and
which throughout Polynesia were prized as a prestigious luxury food consumed mainly by chiefs—like truffles and caviar nowadays. A second candidate is red feathers from Henderson's parrot, fruit dove, and red-tailed
tropicbird, red feathers being another prestigious luxury item used for ornaments and feather cloaks in Polynesia, analogous to gold and sable fur
today.

However, then as now, exchanges of raw materials, manufactured items,
and luxuries would not have been the sole motive for transoceanic trade
and travel. Even after Pitcairn's and Henderson's populations had grown to
their maximum possible size, their numbers—about a hundred and a few
dozen individuals respectively—were so low that people of marriageable
age would have found few potential partners on the island, and most of
those partners would have been close relatives subject to incest taboos.
Hence exchanges of marriage partners would have been an additional important function of the trade with Mangareva. It would also have served
to bring skilled craftspeople with technical skills from Mangareva's large
population to Pitcairn and Henderson, and to reimport crops that by
chance had died out in Pitcairn's and Henderson's small cultivable areas. In
the same way, more recently the supply fleets from Europe were essential
not only for populating and stocking but also maintaining Europe's overseas colonies in America and Australia, which required a long time to develop even rudiments of self-sufficiency.

From the perspective of Mangarevans and Pitcairn Islanders, there
would have been still another likely function of the trade with Henderson.
The journey from Mangareva to Henderson would take four or five days by
Polynesian sailing canoes; from Pitcairn to Henderson, about one day. My

own perspective on sea journeys in Pacific native canoes is based on much briefer voyages, which left me constantly terrified of the canoe's capsizing or breaking up and in one case nearly cost me my life. That makes the thought of a several-day canoe voyage across open ocean intolerable to me, something that only a desperate need to save my life could induce me to undertake. But to modern Pacific seafaring peoples, who sail their canoes five days just to buy cigarettes, the journeys are part of normal life. For the former Polynesian inhabitants of Mangareva or Pitcairn, a visit to Henderson for a week would have been a wonderful picnic, a chance to feast on nesting turtles and their eggs and on Henderson's millions of nesting seabirds. To Pitcairn Islanders in particular, living on an island without reefs or calm inshore waters or rich shellfish beds, Henderson would also have been attractive for fish, shellfish, and just for the chance to hang out on the beach. For the same reason, the descendants of the *Bounty* mutineers today, bored with their tiny island prison, jump at the chance of a "vacation" on the beach of a coral atoll a few hundred miles distant.

Mangareva, it turns out, was the geographic hub of a much larger trade network, of which the ocean journey to Pitcairn and Henderson a few hundred miles to the southeast was the shortest spoke. The longer spokes, of about a thousand miles each, connected Mangareva to the Marquesas to the north–northwest, to the Societies to the west–northwest, and possibly to the Australs due west. The dozens of low coral atolls of the Tuamotu Archipelago offered small intermediate stepping-stones for breaking up these journeys. Just as Mangareva's population of several thousand people dwarfed that of Pitcairn and Henderson, the populations of the Societies and Marquesas (around a hundred thousand people each) dwarfed that of Mangareva.

Hard evidence for this larger trade network emerged in the course of Weisler's chemical studies of basalt, when he had the good fortune to identify two adzes of basalt originating from a Marquesas quarry and one adze from a Societies quarry among 19 analyzed adzes collected on Mangareva. Other evidence comes from tools whose styles vary from island to island, such as adzes, axes, fishhooks, octopus lures, harpoons, and files. Similarities of styles between islands, and appearances of examples of one island's type of tool on another island, attest to trade especially between the Marquesas and Mangareva, with an accumulation of Marquesas-style tools on Mangareva around A.D. 1100–1300 suggesting a peak in interisland voyaging then. Still further evidence comes from studies by the linguist Steven Fischer, who concludes that the Mangarevan language as known in recent times is descended from the language originally brought to Mangareva by its first settlers and then heavily modified by subsequent contact with the language of the southeastern Marquesas (the portion of the Marquesas Archipelago closest to Mangareva).

As for the functions of all that trade and contact in the larger network, one was certainly economic, just as in the smaller Mangareva/Pitcairn/Henderson network, because the networks' archipelagoes complemented one another in resources. The Marquesas were the "motherland," with a big land area and human population and one good basalt quarry, but poor marine resources because there were no lagoons or fringing reefs. Mangareva, a "second motherland," boasted a huge and rich lagoon, offset by a small land area and population and inferior stone. Mangareva's daughter colonies on Pitcairn and Henderson had the drawbacks of a tiny land area and population but great stone on Pitcairn and great feasting on Henderson. Finally, the Tuamotu Archipelago offered only a small land area and no stone at all, but good seafood and a convenient stepping-stone location.

Trade within Southeast Polynesia continued from about A.D.1000 to 1450, as gauged by artifacts in radiocarbon-dated archaeological layers on Henderson. But by A.D. 1500, the trade had stopped, both in Southeast Polynesia and along the other spokes radiating from Mangareva's hub. Those later archaeological layers on Henderson contain no more imported Mangareva oyster shell, no more Pitcairn volcanic glass, no more Pitcairn fine-grained basalt for cutting tools, and no more Mangareva or Pitcairn basalt oven stone. Apparently the canoes were no longer arriving from either Mangareva or Pitcairn. Because trees on Henderson itself are too small to make canoes, Henderson's population of a few dozen was now trapped on one of the most remote, most daunting islands in the world. Henderson Islanders confronted a problem that seems insoluble to us: how to survive on a raised limestone reef without any metal, without stones other than limestone, and without imports of any type.

They survived in ways that strike me as a mixture of ingenious, desperate, and pathetic. For the raw material of adzes, in place of stone, they turned to shells of giant clams. For awls to punch holes, they fell back on bird bones. For oven stones, they turned to limestone or coral or giant clamshell, all of which are inferior to basalt because they retain heat for less time, tend to crack after heating, and cannot be reused as often. They now made their fishhooks out of purse shell, which is much smaller than black-lipped pearl oyster shell, so that it yields only one hook per shell (instead of a dozen hooks from an oyster shell) and restricts the types of hooks that can be fashioned.

Radiocarbon dates suggest that, struggling on in this way, Henderson's population of originally a few dozen people survived for several generations, possibly a century or more, after all contact with Mangareva and Pitcairn was cut. But by A.D. 1606, the year of Henderson's "discovery" by Europeans, when a boat from a passing Spanish ship landed on the island and saw no one, Henderson's population had ceased to exist. Pitcairn's own population had disappeared at least by 1790 (the year when the *Bounty* mutineers arrived to find the island uninhabited), and probably disappeared much earlier.

Why did Henderson's contact with the outside world come to a halt? That outcome stemmed from disastrous environmental changes on Mangareva and Pitcairn. All over Polynesia, human settlement on islands that had developed for millions of years in the absence of humans led to habitat damage and mass extinctions of plants and animals. Mangareva was especially susceptible to deforestation for most of the reasons that I identified for Easter Island in the preceding chapter: high latitude, low ash and dust fallout, and so on. Habitat damage was extreme in Mangareva's hilly interior, most of which the islanders proceeded to deforest in order to plant their gardens. As a result, rain carried topsoil down the steep slopes, and the forest became replaced by a savannah of ferns, which were among the few plants able to grow on the now-denuded ground. That soil erosion in the hills removed much of the area formerly available on Mangareva for gardening and tree crops. Deforestation indirectly reduced yields from fishing as well, because no trees large enough to build canoes remained: when Europeans "discovered" Mangareva in 1797, the islanders had no canoes, only rafts.

With too many people and too little food, Mangareva society slid into a nightmare of civil war and chronic hunger, whose consequences are recalled in detail by modern islanders. For protein, people turned to cannibalism, in the form not only of eating freshly dead people but also of digging up and eating buried corpses. Chronic fighting broke out over the precious remaining cultivable land; the winning side redistributed the land of the losers. Instead of an orderly political system based on hereditary chiefs, nonhereditary warriors took over. The thought of Lilliputian military dictatorships on eastern and western Mangareva, battling for control of an island only five miles long, could seem funny if it were not so tragic. All that political chaos alone would have made it difficult to muster the manpower and supplies necessary for oceangoing canoe travel, and to go off for a month and leave one's garden undefended, even if trees for canoes themselves had not become unavailable. With the collapse of Mangareva at its hub, the whole East Polynesia trade network that had joined Mangareva to the Marquesas, Societies, Tuamotus, Pitcairn, and Henderson disintegrated, as documented by Weisler's sourcing studies of basalt adzes.

While much less is known about environmental changes on Pitcairn, limited archaeological excavations there by Weisler indicate massive deforestation and soil erosion on that island as well. Henderson itself also suffered environmental damage that reduced its human carrying capacity. Five out of its nine species of land birds (including all three large pigeons), and colonies of about six of its species of breeding seabirds, were exterminated. Those extinctions probably resulted from a combination of hunting for food, habitat destruction due to parts of the island being burned for gardens, and depredations of rats that arrived as stowaways in Polynesian canoes. Today, those rats continue to prey on chicks and adults of the remaining species of seabirds, which are unable to defend themselves because they evolved in the absence of rats. Archaeological evidence for gardening appears on Henderson only after those bird disappearances, suggesting that people were being forced into reliance on gardens by the dwindling of their original food sources. The disappearance of edible horn shells and decline in turban shells in later layers of archaeological sites on Henderson's northeast coast also suggest the possibility of overexploitation of shellfish.

Thus, environmental damage, leading to social and political chaos and to loss of timber for canoes, ended Southeast Polynesia's interisland trade. That end of trade would have exacerbated problems for Mangarevans, now cut off from Pitcairn, Marquesas, and Societies sources of high-quality stone for making tools. For the inhabitants of Pitcairn and Henderson, the results were even worse: eventually, no one was left alive on those islands.

Those disappearances of Pitcairn's and Henderson's populations must have resulted somehow from the severing of the Mangarevan umbilical cord. Life on Henderson, always difficult, would have become more so with the loss of all imported volcanic stone. Did everyone die simultaneously in a mass calamity, or did the populations gradually dwindle down to a single survivor, who lived on alone with his or her memories for many years? That actually happened to the Indian population of San Nicolas Island off Los Angeles, reduced finally to one woman who survived in complete isolation for 18 years. Did the last Henderson Islanders spend much time on the beaches, for generation after generation, staring out to sea in the hopes of sighting the canoes that had stopped coming, until even the memory of what a canoe looked like grew dim?

While the details of how human life flickered out on Pitcairn and Henderson remain unknown, I can't tear myself free of the mysterious drama. In my head, I run through alternative endings of the movie, guiding my speculation by what I know actually did happen to some other isolated societies. When people are trapped together with no possibility of emigration, enemies can no longer resolve tensions merely by moving apart. Those tensions may have exploded in mass murder, which later nearly did destroy the colony of *Bounty* mutineers on Pitcairn itself. Murder could also have been driven by food shortage and cannibalism, as happened to the Mangarevans, Easter Islanders, and—closer to home for Americans—the Donner Party in California. Perhaps people grown desperate turned to mass suicide, which was recently the choice of 39 members of the Heaven's Gate cult near San Diego, California. Desperation might instead have led to insanity, the fate of some members of the Belgian Antarctic Expedition, whose ship was trapped by ice for over a year in 1898–1899. Still another catastrophic ending could have been starvation, the fate of Japan's garrison stranded on Wake Island during World War II, and perhaps exacerbated by a drought, typhoon, tsunami, or other environmental disaster.

Then my mind turns to gentler possible endings of the movie. After a few generations of isolation on Pitcairn or Henderson, everyone in their microsociety of a hundred or a few dozen people would have been everyone else's cousin, and it would have become impossible to contract a marriage not in violation of incest taboos. Hence people may just have grown old together and stopped having children, as happened to California's last surviving Yahi Indians, the famous Ishi and his three companions. If the small population did ignore incest taboos, the resulting inbreeding may have caused congenital physical anomalies to proliferate, as exemplified by deafness on Martha's Vineyard Island off Massachusetts or on the remote Atlantic island of Tristan da Cunha.

We may never know which way the movies of Pitcairn and Henderson actually ended. Regardless of the final details, though, the main outline of the story is clear. The populations of Mangareva, Pitcairn, and Henderson all inflicted heavy damage on their environments and destroyed many of the resources necessary for their own lives. Mangareva Islanders were numerous enough to survive, albeit under chronically terrifying conditions and with a drastically reduced standard of living. But from the very beginning, even before the accumulation of environmental damage, the inhabitants of Pitcairn and Henderson had remained dependent on imports of agricultural products, technology, stone, oyster shell, and people from their mother population on Mangareva. With Mangareva's decline and its inability to sustain exports, not even the most heroic efforts to adapt could save the last people alive on Pitcairn and Henderson. Lest those islands still seem to you too remote in space and time to be relevant to our modern societies, just think about the risks (as well as the benefits) of our increasing globalization and increasing worldwide economic interdependence. Many economically important but ecologically fragile areas (think of oil) already affect the rest of us, just as Mangareva affected Pitcairn and Henderson.

CHAPTER 4

The Ancient Ones:
The Anasazi and Their Neighbors

Desert farmers ■ Tree rings ■ Agricultural strategies ■
Chaco's problems and packrats ■ Regional integration ■
Chaco's decline and end ■ Chaco's message ■

O f the sites of societal collapses considered in this book, the most
remote are Pitcairn and Henderson Islands discussed in the last
chapter. At the opposite extreme, the ones closest to home for
Americans are the Anasazi sites of Chaco Culture National Historical Park
(Plates 9, 10) and Mesa Verde National Park, lying in the U.S. Southwest on
New Mexico state highway 57 and near U.S. highway 666, respectively, less
than 600 miles from my home in Los Angeles. Like the Maya cities that will
be the subject of the next chapter, they and other ancient Native American
ruins are popular tourist attractions that thousands of modern First World
citizens visit each year. One of those former southwestern cultures, Mimbres, is also a favorite of art collectors because of its beautiful pottery decorated with geometrical patterns and realistic figures: a unique tradition
created by a society numbering barely 4,000 people, and sustained at its
peak for just a few generations before abruptly disappearing.

I concede that U.S. southwestern societies operated on a much smaller
scale than did Maya cities, with populations of thousands rather than millions. As a result, Maya cities are far more extensive in area, have more lavish
monuments and art, were products of more steeply stratified societies
headed by kings, and possessed writing. But the Anasazi did manage to construct in stone the largest and tallest buildings erected in North America
until the Chicago steel girder skyscrapers of the 1880s. Even though the
Anasazi lacked a writing system such as the one that allows us to date Maya
inscriptions to the exact day, we shall see that many U.S. southwestern
structures can still be dated to within a year, thereby enabling archaeologists
to understand the societies' history with much finer time resolution than is
possible for Easter, Pitcairn, and Henderson Islands.

In the U.S. Southwest we are dealing with not just a single culture and collapse, but with a whole series of them (map, p. 142). Southwestern cultures that underwent regional collapses, drastic reorganizations, or abandonments at different locations and different times include Mimbres around A.D. 1130; Chaco Canyon, North Black Mesa, and the Virgin Anasazi in the middle or late 12th century; around 1300, Mesa Verde and the Kayenta Anasazi; Mogollon around 1400; and possibly as late as the 15th century, Hohokam, well known for its elaborate system of irrigation agriculture. While all of those sharp transitions occurred before Columbus's arrival in the New World in 1492, the Anasazi did not vanish as people: other southwestern Native American societies incorporating some of their descendants persist to this day, such as the Hopi and Zuni pueblos. What accounts for all those declines or abrupt changes in so many neighboring societies?

Favorite single-factor explanations invoke environmental damage, drought, or warfare and cannibalism. Actually, the field of U.S. southwestern prehistory is a graveyard for single-factor explanations. Multiple factors have operated, but they all go back to the fundamental problem that the U.S. Southwest is a fragile and marginal environment for agriculture—as is also much of the world today. It has low and unpredictable rainfall, quickly exhausted soils, and very low rates of forest regrowth. Environmental problems, especially major droughts and episodes of streambed erosion, tend to recur at intervals much longer than a human lifetime or oral memory span. Given those severe difficulties, it's impressive that Native Americans in the Southwest developed such complex farming societies as they did. Testimony to their success is that most of this area today supports a much sparser population growing their own food than it did in Anasazi times. It was a moving and unforgettable experience for me, while I was driving through areas of desert dotted with the remains of former Anasazi stone houses, dams, and irrigation systems, to see a now virtually empty landscape with just the occasional occupied house. The Anasazi collapse and other southwestern collapses offer us not only a gripping story but also an instructive one for the purposes of this book, illustrating well our themes of human environmental impact and climate change intersecting, environmental and population problems spilling over into warfare, the strengths but also the dangers of complex non-self-sufficient societies dependent on imports and exports, and societies collapsing swiftly after attaining peak population numbers and power.

■ ■ ■

Our understanding of southwestern prehistory is detailed because of two advantages that archaeologists in this area enjoy. One is the packrat midden method that I'll discuss below, which provides us with a virtual time capsule of the plants growing within a few dozen yards of a midden within a few decades of a calculated date. That advantage has allowed paleobotanists to reconstruct changes in local vegetation. The other advantage allows archaeologists to date building sites to the nearest year by the tree rings of the site's wood construction beams, instead of having to rely on the radiocarbon method used by archaeologists elsewhere, with its inevitable errors of 50 to 100 years.

The tree ring method depends on the fact that rainfall and temperature vary seasonally in the Southwest, so that tree growth rates also vary seasonally, as true at other sites in the temperate zones as well. Hence temperate zone trees lay down new wood in annual growth rings, unlike tropical rainforest trees whose growth is more nearly continuous. But the Southwest is better for tree ring studies than most other temperate zone sites, because the dry climate results in excellent preservation of wooden beams from trees felled over a thousand years ago.

Here's how tree ring dating, known to scientists as *dendrochronology* (from the Greek roots *dendron* = tree, and *chronos* = time), works. If you cut down a tree today, it's straightforward to count the rings inwards, starting from the tree's outside (corresponding to this year's growth ring), and thereby to state that the 177th ring from the outermost one towards the center was laid down in the year 2005 minus 177, or 1828. But it's less straightforward to attach a date to a particular ring in an ancient Anasazi wooden beam, because at first you don't know in what year the beam was cut. However, the widths of tree growth rings vary from year to year, depending on rain or drought conditions in each year. Hence the sequence of rings in a tree cross-section is like a message in the Morse code formerly used for sending telegraph messages; dot-dot-dash-dot-dash in the Morse code, wide-wide-narrow-wide-narrow in a tree ring sequence. Actually, the ring sequence is even more diagnostic and richer in information than the Morse code, because trees actually contain rings spanning many different widths, rather than the Morse code's choice between only a dot or a dash.

Tree ring specialists (known as dendrochronologists) proceed by noting the sequence of wider and narrower rings in a tree cut down in a known recent year, and also noting the sequence in beams from trees cut down at various unknown times in the past. They then match up and align ring sequences with the same diagnostic wide/narrow patterns from different beams. For instance, suppose that this year (2005) you cut down a tree that proves to be 400 years old (400 rings), and that has an especially distinctive sequence of five wide rings, two narrow rings, and six wide rings for the 13 years from 1643 back to 1631. If you find that same distinctive sequence starting seven years from the outermost ring in an old beam of unknown felling date with 332 rings, then you can conclude that the old beam came from a tree cut down in 1650 (seven years after 1643), and that the tree began to grow in the year 1318 (332 years before 1650). You then go on to align that beam, from the tree living between 1318 and 1650, with even older beams, and you similarly try to match up tree ring patterns and find a beam whose pattern shows that it comes from a tree that was cut down after 1318 but began growing before 1318, thereby extending your tree ring record farther back into the past. In that way, dendrochronologists have constructed tree ring records extending back for thousands of years in some parts of the world. Each such record is valid for a geographic area whose extent depends on local weather patterns, because weather and hence tree growth patterns vary with location. For instance, the basic tree ring chronology of the American Southwest applies (with some variation) to the area from northern Mexico to Wyoming.

A bonus of dendrochronology is that the width and substructure of each ring reflect the amount of rain and the season at which the rain fell during that particular year. Thus, tree ring studies also allow one to reconstruct past climate; e.g., a series of wide rings means a wet period, and a series of narrow rings means a drought. Tree rings thereby provide southwestern archaeologists with uniquely exact dating and uniquely detailed year-to-year environmental information.

The first humans to reach the Americas, living as hunter-gatherers, arrived in the U.S. Southwest by 11,000 B.C. but possibly earlier, as part of the colonization of the New World from Asia by peoples ancestral to modern Native Americans. Agriculture did not develop indigenously in the U.S. Southwest, because of a paucity of domesticable wild plant and animal species. Instead, it arrived from Mexico, where corn, squash, beans, and many other crops were domesticated—corn arriving by 2000 B.C., squash around 800 B.C., beans somewhat later, and cotton not until A.D. 400. People also kept domestic turkeys, about which there is some debate whether they were first domesticated in Mexico and spread to the Southwest, or vice versa, or whether they were domesticated independently in both areas. Originally, southwestern Native Americans just incorporated some agriculture as part of their hunter-gatherer lifestyle, as did the modern Apache in the 18th and 19th centuries: the Apache settled down to plant and harvest crops during the growing season, then moved around as hunter-gatherers during the rest of the year. By A.D. 1, some southwestern Native Americans had already taken up residence in villages and become primarily dependent on agriculture with ditch irrigation. Thereafter, their populations exploded in numbers and spread over the landscape until the retrenchments beginning around A.D. 1117.

At least three alternative types of agriculture emerged, all involving different solutions to the Southwest's fundamental problem: how to obtain enough water to grow crops in an environment most of which has rainfall so low and unpredictable that little or no farming is practiced there today. One of the three solutions consisted of so-called dryland agriculture, which meant relying on rainfall at the higher elevations where there really was enough rain to promote growth of crops in the fields on which the rain fell. A second solution did not depend on rain falling directly on the field, but instead was adopted in areas where the water table in the ground reached close enough to the surface that plant roots could extend down into the water table. That method was employed in canyon bottoms with intermittent or permanent streams and a shallow alluvial groundwater table, such as in Chaco Canyon. The third solution, practiced especially by the Hohokam and also at Chaco Canyon, consisted of collecting water runoff in ditches or canals to irrigate fields.

While the methods used in the Southwest to obtain enough water to grow crops were variants on those three types, people experimented in different locations with alternative strategies for applying those methods. The experiments lasted for almost a thousand years, and many of them succeeded for centuries, but eventually all except one succumbed to environmental problems caused by human impact or climate change. Each alternative involved different risks.

One strategy was to live at higher elevations where rainfall was higher, as did the Mogollon, the people at Mesa Verde, and the people of the early agricultural phase known as the Pueblo I phase. But that carried the risk that it is cooler at high than at low elevations, and in an especially cool year it might be too cold to grow crops at all. An opposite extreme was to farm at the warmer low elevations, but there the rainfall is insufficient for dryland agriculture. The Hohokam got around that problem by constructing the most extensive irrigation system in the Americas outside Peru, with hundreds of miles of secondary canals branching off a main canal 12 miles long, 16 feet deep, and 80 feet wide. But irrigation entailed the risk that human cutting of ditches and canals could lead to sudden heavy water runoff from rainstorms digging further down into the ditches and canals and incising deep channels called arroyos, in which the water level would drop below the field level, making irrigation impossible for people without pumps. Also, irrigation poses the danger that especially heavy rains or floods could wash away the dams and channels, as may indeed eventually have happened to the Hohokam.

Another, more conservative, strategy was to plant crops only in areas with reliable springs and groundwater tables. That was the solution initially adopted by the Mimbres, and by people in the farming phase known as Pueblo II at Chaco Canyon. However, it then became dangerously tempting to expand agriculture, in wet decades with favorable growing conditions, into marginal areas with less reliable springs or groundwater. The population multiplying in those marginal areas might then find itself unable to grow crops and starving when the unpredictable climate turned dry again. That fate actually befell the Mimbres, who started by safely farming the floodplain and then began to farm adjacent land above the floodplain as their population came to saturate the floodplain's capacity to support it. They got away with their gamble during a wet climate phase, when they were able to obtain half of their food requirements outside the floodplain. However, when drought conditions returned, that gamble left them with a population double what the floodplain could support, and Mimbres society collapsed suddenly under the stress.

Still another solution was to occupy an area for only a few decades, until the area's soil and game became exhausted, then to move on to another area. That method worked when people were living at low population densities, so that there were lots of unoccupied areas to which to move, and so that each occupied area could be left unoccupied again for sufficiently long after occupation that its vegetation and soil nutrients had time to recover. Most southwestern archaeological sites were indeed inhabited for only a few decades, even though our attention today is drawn to a few big sites that were inhabited continuously for several centuries, such as Pueblo Bonito in Chaco Canyon. However, the method of shifting sites after a short occupation became impossible at high population densities, when people filled up the whole landscape and there was nowhere left empty to move to.

One more strategy was to plant crops at many sites even though rainfall is locally unpredictable, and then to harvest crops at whichever sites did get

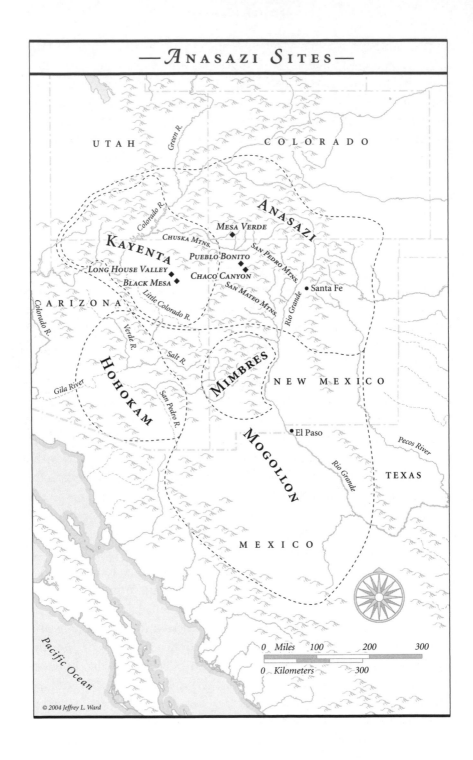

—ANASAZI SITES—

UTAH
COLORADO

Green R.

ANASAZI

Colorado R.

MESA VERDE

CHUSKA MTNS.
KAYENTA
PUEBLO BONITO
San Pedro Mtns.

LONG HOUSE VALLEY
CHACO CANYON
BLACK MESA
Little Colorado R.
SAN MATEO MTNS.
• Santa Fe

ARIZONA

Colorado R.

Verde R.

Salt R.

MIMBRES

HOHOKAM

Gila River

San Pedro R.

NEW MEXICO

• El Paso

MOGOLLON

Rio Grande

Pecos River

TEXAS

Rio Grande

MEXICO

Pacific Ocean

0 Miles 100   200   300

0 Kilometers   300

© 2004 Jeffrey L. Ward

enough rain to produce a good harvest, and to redistribute some of that harvest to the people still living at all the sites that didn't happen to receive enough rain that year. That was one of the solutions eventually adopted at Chaco Canyon. But it involved the risk that redistribution required a complex political and social system to integrate activities between different sites, and that lots of people then ended up starving when that complex system collapsed.

The remaining strategy was to plant crops and live near permanent or dependable sources of water, but on landscape benches above the main floodways, so as to avoid the risk of a heavy flood washing out fields and villages; and to practice a diverse economy, exploiting ecologically diverse zones, so that each settlement would be self-sufficient. That solution, adopted by people whose descendants live today in the Southwest's Hopi and Zuni Pueblos, has succeeded for more than a thousand years. Some modern Hopis and Zunis, looking at the extravagance of American society around them, shake their heads and say, "We were here long before you came, and we expect still to be here long after you too are gone."

All of these alternative solutions face a similar overarching risk: that a series of good years, with adequate rainfall or with sufficiently shallow groundwater tables, may result in population growth, resulting in turn in society becoming increasingly complex and interdependent and no longer locally self-sufficient. Such a society then cannot cope with, and rebuild itself after, a series of bad years that a less populous, less interdependent, more self-sufficient society had previously been able to cope with. As we shall see, precisely that dilemma ended Anasazi settlement of Long House Valley, and perhaps other areas as well.

The most intensively studied abandonment was of the most spectacular and largest set of sites, the Anasazi sites in Chaco Canyon of northwestern New Mexico. Chaco Anasazi society flourished from about A.D. 600 for more than five centuries, until it disappeared some time between 1150 and 1200. It was a complexly organized, geographically extensive, regionally integrated society that erected the largest buildings in pre-Columbian North America. Even more than the barren treeless landscape of Easter Island, the barren treeless landscape of Chaco Canyon today, with its deep-cut arroyos and sparse low vegetation of salt-tolerant bushes, astonishes us, because the canyon is now completely uninhabited except for a few National Park Service rangers' houses. Why would anyone have built an advanced city in that wasteland, and why, having gone to all that work of building it, did they then abandon it?

When Native American farmers moved into the Chaco Canyon area around A.D. 600, they initially lived in underground pit houses, as did other contemporary Native Americans in the Southwest. Around A.D. 700 the Chaco Anasazi, out of contact with Native American societies building structures of stone a thousand miles to the south in Mexico, independently invented techniques of stone construction and eventually adopted rubble cores with veneers of cut stone facing (Plate 11). Initially, those structures were only one story high, but around A.D. 920 what eventually became the largest Chacoan site of Pueblo Bonito went up to two stories, then over the next two centuries rose to five or six stories with 600 rooms whose roof supports were logs up to 16 feet long and weighing up to 700 pounds.

Why, out of all the Anasazi sites, was it at Chaco Canyon that construction techniques and political and societal complexity reached their apogee? Likely reasons are some environmental advantages of Chaco Canyon, which initially represented a favorable environmental oasis within northwestern New Mexico. The narrow canyon caught rain runoff from many side-channels and a large upland area, which resulted in high alluvial ground-water levels permitting farming independent of local rainfall in some areas, and also high rates of soil renewal from the runoff. The large habitable area in the canyon and within 50 miles of it could support a relatively high population for such a dry environment. The Chaco region has a high diversity of useful wild plant and animal species, and a relatively low elevation that provides a long growing season for crops. At first, nearby pinyon and juniper woodlands provided the construction logs and firewood. The earliest roof beams identified by their tree rings, and still well preserved in the Southwest's dry climate, are of locally available pinyon pines, and firewood remains in early hearths are of locally available pinyon and juniper. Anasazi diets depended heavily on growing corn, plus some squash and beans, but early archaeological levels also show much consumption of wild plants such as pinyon nuts (75% protein), and much hunting of deer.

All those natural advantages of Chaco Canyon were balanced by two major disadvantages resulting from the Southwest's environmental fragility. One involved problems of water management. Initially, rain runoff would have been as a broad sheet over the flat canyon bottom, permitting flood-plain agriculture watered both by the runoff and by the high alluvial groundwater table. When the Anasazi began diverting water into channels for irrigation, the concentration of water runoff in the channels and the

clearing of vegetation for agriculture, combined with natural processes, resulted around A.D. 900 in the cutting of deep arroyos in which the water
level was below field levels, thereby making irrigation agriculture and also
agriculture based on groundwater impossible until the arroyos filled up
again. Such arroyo-cutting can develop surprisingly suddenly. For example,
at the Arizona city of Tucson in the late 1880s, American settlers excavated a
so-called intercept ditch to intercept the shallow groundwater table and divert its water downstream onto the floodplain. Unfortunately, floods from
heavy rains in the summer of 1890 cut into the head of that ditch, starting an arroyo that within a mere three days extended itself for a distance
of six miles upstream, leaving an incised and agriculturally useless floodplain near Tucson. Early Southwest Native American societies probably attempted similar intercept ditches, with similar results. The Chaco Anasazi
dealt with that problem of arroyos in the canyon in several ways: by building dams inside side-canyons above the elevation of the main canyon to
store rainwater; by laying out field systems that that rainwater could irrigate; by storing rainwater coming down over the tops of the cliffs rimming
the canyon's north wall between each pair of side-canyons; and by building
a rock dam across the main canyon.

The other major environmental problem besides water management involved deforestation, as revealed by the method of packrat midden analysis.
For those of you who (like me until some years ago) have never seen packrats, don't know what their middens are, and can't possibly imagine their
relevance to Anasazi prehistory, here is a quick crash course in midden
analysis. In 1849, hungry gold miners crossing the Nevada desert noticed
some glistening balls of a candy-like substance on a cliff, licked or ate the
balls, and discovered them to be sweet-tasting, but then they developed
nausea. Eventually it was realized that the balls were hardened deposits
made by small rodents, called packrats, that protect themselves by building
nests of sticks, plant fragments, and mammal dung gathered in the vicinity,
plus food remains, discarded bones, and their own feces. Not being toilet-
trained, the rats urinate in their nests, and sugar and other substances crys-
tallize from their urine as it dries out, cementing the midden to a brick-like
consistency. In effect, the hungry gold miners were eating dried rat urine
laced with rat feces and rat garbage.

Naturally, to save themselves work and to minimize their risk of being
grabbed by a predator while out of the nest, packrats gather vegetation
within just a few dozen yards of the nest. After a few decades the rats'
progeny abandon their midden and move on to build a new nest, while the

crystallized urine prevents the material in the old midden from decaying. By identifying the remains of the dozens of urine-encrusted plant species in a midden, paleobotanists can reconstruct a snapshot of the vegetation growing near the midden at the time that the rats were accumulating it, while zoologists can reconstruct something of the fauna from the insect and vertebrate remains. In effect, a packrat midden is a paleontologist's dream: a time capsule preserving a sample of the local vegetation, gathered within a few dozen yards of the spot within a period of a few decades, at a date fixed by radiocarbon-dating the midden.

In 1975 paleoecologist Julio Betancourt happened to visit Chaco Canyon while driving through New Mexico as a tourist. Looking down on the treeless landscape around Pueblo Bonito, he thought to himself, "This place looks like beat-up Mongolian steppe; where did those people get their timber and firewood?" Archaeologists studying the ruins had been asking themselves the same question. In a moment of inspiration three years later, when a friend asked him for completely unrelated reasons to write a grant proposal to study packrat middens, Julio recalled his first impression of Pueblo Bonito. A quick phone call to midden expert Tom Van Devender established that Tom had already collected a few middens at the National Park Service campground near Pueblo Bonito. Almost all of them had proved to contain needles of pinyon pines, which don't grow anywhere within miles today but which had nevertheless somehow furnished the roof beams for early phases of Pueblo Bonito's construction, as well as furnishing much of the charcoal found in hearths and trash middens. Julio and Tom realized that those must be old middens from a time when pines did grow nearby, but they had no idea how old: they thought perhaps just a century or so. Hence they submitted samples of those middens for radiocarbon dating. When the dates came back from the radiocarbon laboratory, Julio and Tom were astonished to learn that many of the middens were over a thousand years old.

That serendipitous observation triggered an explosion of packrat midden studies. Today we know that middens decay extremely slowly in the Southwest's dry climate. If protected from the elements under an overhang or inside a cave, middens can last 40,000 years, far longer than anyone would have dared to guess. As Julio showed me my first packrat midden near the Chaco Anasazi site of Kin Kletso, I stood in awe at the thought that that apparently fresh-looking nest might have been built at a time when mammoths, giant ground sloths, American lions, and other extinct Ice Age mammals were still living in the territory of the modern U.S.

In the Chaco Canyon area Julio went on to collect and radiocarbon-date 50 middens, whose dates turned out to encompass the entire period of the rise and fall of Anasazi civilization, from A.D. 600 to 1200. In this way Julio was able to reconstruct vegetational changes in Chaco Canyon throughout the history of Anasazi occupation. Those midden studies identified deforestation as the other one (besides water management) of the two major environmental problems caused by the growing population that had developed in Chaco Canyon by around A.D. 1000. Middens before that date still incorporated pinyon pine and juniper needles, like the first midden that Julio had analyzed, and like the midden that he showed me. Hence Chaco Anasazi settlements were initially constructed in a pinyon/juniper woodland unlike the present treeless landscape but convenient for obtaining firewood and construction timber nearby. However, middens dated after A.D. 1000 lacked pinyon and juniper, showing that the woodland had then become completely destroyed and the site had achieved its present treeless appearance. The reason why Chaco Canyon became deforested so quickly is the same as the reason that I discussed in Chapter 2 to explain why Easter Island and other dry Pacific islands settled by people were more likely to end up deforested than were wet islands: in a dry climate, the rate of tree regrowth on logged land may be too slow to keep up with the rate of logging.

The loss of the woodland not only eliminated pinyon nuts as a local food supply but also forced Chaco residents to find a different timber source for their construction needs, as shown by the complete disappearance of pinyon beams from Chaco architecture. Chacoans coped by going far afield to forests of ponderosa pine, spruce, and fir trees, growing in mountains up to 50 miles away at elevations several thousand feet higher than Chaco Canyon. With no draft animals available, about 200,000 logs weighing each up to 700 pounds were carried down the mountains and over that distance to Chaco Canyon by human muscle power alone.

A recent study by Julio's student Nathan English, working in collaboration with Julio, Jeff Dean, and Jay Quade, identified more exactly where the big spruce and fir logs came from. There are three potential sources of them in the Chaco area, growing at high elevations on three mountain ranges nearly equidistant from the canyon: the Chuska, San Mateo, and San Pedro Mountains. From which of those mountains did the Chaco Anasazi actually get their conifers? Trees from the three mountain ranges belong to the same species and look identical to each other. As a diagnostic signature, Nathan used isotopes of strontium, an element chemically very similar to calcium and hence incorporated along with calcium into plants and animals. Strontium exists as alternative forms (isotopes) differing slightly in atomic weight, of which strontium-87 and strontium-86 are commonest in nature. But the strontium-87/strontium 86 ratio varies with rock age and rock rubidium content, because strontium is produced by radioactive decay of a rubidium isotope. It turned out that living conifers from the three mountain ranges proved to be clearly separated by their strontium-87/strontium-86 ratios, with no overlap at all. From six Chaco ruins, Nathan sampled 52 conifer logs selected on the basis of their tree rings to have been felled at dates ranging from A.D. 974 to 1104. The result he obtained was that two-thirds of the logs could be traced by their strontium ratios to the Chuska Mountains, one-third to the San Mateo Mountains, and none at all to the San Pedro Mountains. In some cases a given Chaco building incorporated logs from both mountain ranges in the same year, or used logs from one mountain in one year and from the other mountain in another year, while the same mountain furnished logs to several different buildings in the same year. Thus, we have here unequivocal evidence of a well-organized, long-distance supply network for the Anasazi capital of Chaco Canyon.

Despite the development of these two environmental problems that reduced crop production and virtually eliminated timber supplies within Chaco Canyon itself, or because of the solutions that the Anasazi found to these problems, the canyon's population continued to increase, particularly during a big spurt of construction that began in A.D. 1029. Such spurts went on especially during wet decades, when more rain meant more food, more people, and more need for buildings. A dense population is attested not only by the famous Great Houses (such as Pueblo Bonito) spaced about a mile apart on the north side of Chaco Canyon, but also by holes drilled into the northern cliff face to support roof beams, indicating a continuous line of residences at the base of the cliffs between the Great Houses, and by the remains of hundreds of small settlements on the south side of the canyon. The size of the canyon's total population is unknown and much debated. Many archaeologists think that it was less than 5,000, and that those enormous buildings had few permanent occupants except priests and were just visited seasonally by peasants at the time of rituals. Other archaeologists note that Pueblo Bonito, which is just one of the large houses at Chaco Canyon, by itself was a building of 600 rooms, and that all those post holes suggest dwellings for much of the length of the canyon, thus implying a population much greater than 5,000. Such debates about estimated population sizes arise frequently in archaeology, as discussed for Easter Island and the Maya in other chapters of this book.

Whatever the number, this dense population could no longer support it- self but was subsidized by outlying satellite settlements constructed in simi- lar architectural styles and joined to Chaco Canyon by a radiating regional network of hundreds of miles of roads that are still visible today. Those out- liers had dams to catch rain, which fell unpredictably and very patchily: a thunderstorm might produce abundant rain in one desert wash and no rain in another wash just a mile away. The dams meant that when a particular wash was fortunate enough to receive a rainstorm, much of the rainwater became stored behind the dam, and people living there could quickly plant crops, irrigate, and grow a huge surplus of food at that wash in that year. The surplus could then feed people living at all the other outliers that didn't happen to receive rain then.

Chaco Canyon became a black hole into which goods were imported but from which nothing tangible was exported. Into Chaco Canyon came: those tens of thousands of big trees for construction; pottery (all late-period pot- tery in Chaco Canyon was imported, probably because exhaustion of local firewood supplies precluded firing pots within the canyon itself); stone of good quality for making stone tools; turquoise for making ornaments, from other areas of New Mexico; and macaws, shell jewelry, and copper bells from the Hohokam and from Mexico, as luxury goods. Even food had to be imported, as shown by a recent study tracing the origins of corncobs exca- vated from Pueblo Bonito by means of the same strontium isotope method used by Nathan English to trace the origins of Pueblo Bonito's wooden beams. It turns out that, already in the 9th century, corn was being im- ported from the Chuska Mountains 50 miles to the west (also one of the two sources of roof beams), while a corncob from the last years of Pueblo Bonito in the 12th century came from the San Juan River system 60 miles to the north.

Chaco society turned into a mini-empire, divided between a well-fed elite living in luxury and a less well-fed peasantry doing the work and rais- ing the food. The road system and the regional extent of standardized archi- tecture testify to the large size of the area over which the economy and culture of Chaco and its outliers were regionally integrated. Styles of build- ings indicate a three-step pecking order: the largest buildings, so-called Great Houses, in Chaco Canyon itself (residences of the governing chiefs?); outlier Great Houses beyond the canyon ("provincial capitals" of junior chiefs?); and small homesteads of just a few rooms (peasants' houses?).

Compared to smaller buildings, the Great Houses were distinguished by finer construction with veneer masonry, large structures called Great Kivas used for religious rituals (similar to ones still used today in modern Pueblos), and a higher ratio of storage space to total space. Great Houses far exceeded homesteads in their contents of imported luxury goods, such as the turquoise, macaws, shell jewelry, and copper bells mentioned above, plus imported Mimbres and Hohokam pottery. The highest concentration of luxury items located to date comes from Pueblo Bonito's room number 33, which held burials of 14 individuals accompanied by 56,000 pieces of turquoise and thousands of shell decorations, including one necklace of 2,000 turquoise beads and a basket covered with a turquoise mosaic and filled with turquoise and shell beads. As for evidence that the chiefs ate better than did the peasants, garbage excavated near Great Houses contained a higher proportion of deer and antelope bones than did garbage from homesteads, with the result that human burials indicate taller, better-nourished, less anemic people and lower infant mortality at Great Houses.

Why would outlying settlements have supported the Chaco center, dutifully delivering timber, pottery, stone, turquoise, and food without receiving anything material in return? The answer is probably the same as the reason why outlying areas of Italy and Britain today support our cities such as Rome and London, which also produce no timber or food but serve as political and religious centers. Like the modern Italians and British, Chacoans were now irreversibly committed to living in a complex, interdependent society. They could no longer revert to their original condition of self-supporting mobile little groups, because the trees in the canyon were gone, the arroyos were cut below field levels, and the growing population had filled up the region and left no unoccupied suitable areas to which to move. When the pinyon and juniper trees were cut down, the nutrients in the litter underneath the trees were flushed out. Today, more than 800 years later, there is still no pinyon/juniper woodland growing anywhere near the pack-rat middens containing twigs of the woodland that had grown there before A.D. 1000. Food remains in rubbish at archaeological sites attest to the growing problems of the canyon's inhabitants in nourishing themselves: deer declined in their diets, to be replaced by smaller game, especially rabbits and mice. Remains of complete headless mice in human coprolites (preserved dry feces) suggest that people were catching mice in the fields, beheading them, and popping them in whole.

■   ■   ■

The last identified construction at Pueblo Bonito, dating from the decade after 1110, was from a wall of rooms enclosing the south side of the plaza, which had formerly been open to the outside. That suggests strife: people were evidently now visiting Pueblo Bonito not just to participate in its religious ceremonies and to receive orders, but also to make trouble. The last tree-ring-dated roof beam at Pueblo Bonito and at the nearby Great House of Chetro Ketl was cut in A.D. 1117, and the last beam anywhere in Chaco Canyon in A.D. 1170. Other Anasazi sites show more abundant evidence of strife, including signs of cannibalism, plus Kayenta Anasazi settlements at the tops of steep cliffs far from fields and water and understandable only as easily defended locations. At those southwestern sites that outlasted Chaco and survived until after A.D. 1250, warfare evidently became intense, as reflected in a proliferation of defensive walls and moats and towers, clustering of scattered small hamlets into larger hilltop fortresses, apparently deliberately burned villages containing unburied bodies, skulls with cut marks caused by scalping, and skeletons with arrowheads inside the body cavity. That explosion of environmental and population problems in the form of civil unrest and warfare is a frequent theme in this book, both for past societies (the Easter Islanders, Mangarevans, Maya, and Tikopians) and for modern societies (Rwanda, Haiti, and others).

The signs of warfare-related cannibalism among the Anasazi are an interesting story in themselves. While everyone acknowledges that cannibalism may be practiced in emergencies by desperate people, such as the Donner Party trapped by snow at Donner Pass en route to California in the winter of 1846–47, or by starving Russians during the siege of Leningrad during World War II, the existence of non-emergency cannibalism is controversial. In fact, it was reported in hundreds of non-European societies at the times when they were first contacted by Europeans within recent centuries. The practice took two forms: eating either the bodies of enemies killed in war, or else eating one's own relatives who had died of natural causes. New Guineans with whom I have worked over the past 40 years have matter-of-factly described their cannibalistic practices, have expressed disgust at our own Western burial customs of burying relatives without doing them the honor of eating them, and one of my best New Guinean workers quit his job with me in 1965 in order to partake in the consumption of his recently deceased prospective son-in-law. There have also been many archaeological finds of ancient human bones in contexts suggestive of cannibalism.

Nevertheless, many or most European and American anthropologists, brought up to regard cannibalism with horror in their own societies, are also horrified at the thought of it being practiced by peoples that they admire and study, and so they deny its occurrence and consider claims of it as racist slander. They dismiss all the descriptions of cannibalism by non-European peoples themselves or by early European explorers as unreliable hearsay, and they would evidently be convinced only by a videotape taken by a government official or, most convincing of all, by an anthropologist. However, no such tape exists, for the obvious reason that the first Europeans to encounter people reported to be cannibals routinely expressed their disgust at the practice and threatened its practitioners with arrest.

Such objections have created controversy around the many reports of human remains, with evidence consistent with cannibalism, found at Anasazi sites. The strongest evidence comes from an Anasazi site at which a house and its contents had been smashed, and the scattered bones of seven people were left inside the house, consistent with their having been killed in a war raid rather than properly buried. Some of the bones had been cracked in the same way that bones of animals consumed for food were cracked to extract the marrow. Other bones showed smooth ends, a hallmark of animal bones boiled in pots, but not of ones not boiled in pots. Broken pots themselves from that Anasazi site had residues of the human muscle protein myoglobin on the pots' inside, consistent with human flesh having been cooked in the pots. But skeptics might still object that boiling human meat in pots, and cracking open human bones, does not prove that other humans actually consumed the meat of the former owners of those bones (though why else would they go to all that trouble of boiling and cracking bones to be left scattered on the floor?). The most direct sign of cannibalism at the site is that dried human feces, found in the house's hearth and still well preserved after nearly a thousand years in that dry climate, proved to contain human muscle protein, which is absent from normal human feces, even from the feces of people with injured and bleeding intestines. This makes it probable that whoever attacked that site, killed the inhabitants, cracked open their bones, boiled their flesh in pots, scattered the bones, and relieved himself or herself by depositing feces in that hearth had actually consumed the flesh of his or her victims.

The final blow for Chacoans was a drought that tree rings show to have begun around A.D. 1130. There had been similar droughts previously, around A.D. 1090 and 1040, but the difference this time was that Chaco Canyon now held more people, more dependent on outlying settlements, and with no land left unoccupied. A drought would have caused the groundwater table to drop below the level where it could be tapped by plant roots and could support agriculture; a drought would also make rainfall-supported dryland agriculture and irrigation agriculture impossible. A drought that lasted more than three years would have been fatal, because modern Puebloans can store corn for only two or three years, after which it is too rotten or infested to eat. Probably the outlying settlements that had formerly supplied the Chaco political and religious centers with food lost faith in the Chacoan priests whose prayers for rain remained unanswered, and they refused to make more food deliveries. A model for the end of Anasazi settlement at Chaco Canyon, which Europeans did not observe, is what happened in the Pueblo Indian revolt of 1680 against the Spaniards, a revolt that Europeans did observe. As in Chaco Anasazi centers, the Spaniards had extracted food from local farmers by taxing them, and those food taxes were tolerated until a drought left the farmers themselves short of food, provoking them to revolt.

Some time between A.D. 1150 and 1200, Chaco Canyon was virtually abandoned and remained largely empty until Navajo sheepherders reoccupied it 600 years later. Because the Navajo did not know who had built the great ruins that they found there, they referred to those vanished former inhabitants as the Anasazi, meaning "the Ancient Ones." What actually happened to the thousands of Chacoan inhabitants? By analogy with historically witnessed abandonments of other pueblos during a drought in the 1670s, probably many people starved to death, some people killed each other, and the survivors fled to other settled areas in the Southwest. It must have been a planned evacuation, because most rooms at Anasazi sites lack the pottery and other useful objects that people would be expected to take with them in a planned evacuation, in contrast to the pottery still in the rooms of the above-mentioned site whose unfortunate occupants were killed and eaten. The settlements to which Chaco survivors managed to flee include some pueblos in the area of the modern Zuni pueblos, where rooms built in a style similar to Chaco Canyon houses and containing Chaco styles of pottery have been found at dates around the time of Chaco's abandonment.

Jeff Dean and his colleagues Rob Axtell, Josh Epstein, George Gumerman, Steve McCarroll, Miles Parker, and Alan Swedlund have carried out an especially detailed reconstruction of what happened to a group of about a thousand Kayenta Anasazi in Long House Valley in northeastern Arizona. They calculated the valley's actual population at various times from

A.D. 800 to 1350, based on numbers of house sites containing pottery that changed in style with time, thereby permitting dating of the house sites. They also calculated the valley's annual corn harvests as a function of time, from annual tree rings that provide a measure of rainfall, and from soil studies that provide information about the rise and fall of groundwater levels. It turned out that the rises and falls of the actual population after A.D. 800 closely mirrored the rises and falls of calculated annual corn harvests, except that the Anasazi completely abandoned the valley by A.D. 1300, at a time when some reduced corn harvests sufficient to support one-third of the valley's peak population (400 out of the peak of 1,070 people) could still have been extracted.

Why did those last 400 Kayenta Anasazi of Long House Valley not remain when most of their relatives were leaving? Perhaps the valley in A.D. 1300 had deteriorated for human occupation in other ways besides its reduced agricultural potential calculated in the authors' model. For instance, perhaps soil fertility had been exhausted, or else the former forests may have been felled, leaving no nearby timber for buildings and firewood, as we know to have been the case in Chaco Canyon. Alternatively, perhaps the explanation was that complex human societies require a certain minimum population size to maintain institutions that its citizens consider to be essential. How many New Yorkers would choose to remain in New York City if two-thirds of their family and friends had just starved to death there or fled, if the subway trains and taxis were no longer running, and if offices and stores had closed?

Along with those Chaco Canyon Anasazi and Long House Valley Anasazi whose fates we have followed, I mentioned at the start of this chapter that many other southwestern societies—the Mimbres, Mesa Verdeans, Hohokam, Mogollon, and others—also underwent collapses, reorganizations, or abandonments at various times within the period A.D. 1100–1500. It turns out that quite a few different environmental problems and cultural responses contributed to these collapses and transitions, and that different factors operated in different areas. For example, deforestation was a problem for the Anasazi, who required trees to supply the roof beams of their houses, but it wasn't as much of a problem for the Hohokam, who did not use beams in their houses. Salinization resulting from irrigation agriculture hurt the Hohokam, who had to irrigate their fields, but not the Mesa Verdeans, who did not have to irrigate. Cold affected the Mogollon and

Mesa Verdeans, living at high altitudes and at temperatures somewhat marginal for agriculture. Other southwestern peoples were done in by dropping water tables (e.g., the Anasazi) or by soil nutrient exhaustion (possibly the Mogollon). Arroyo cutting was a problem for the Chaco Anasazi, but not for the Mesa Verdeans.

Despite these varying proximate causes of abandonments, all were ultimately due to the same fundamental challenge: people living in fragile and difficult environments, adopting solutions that were brilliantly successful and understandable "in the short run," but that failed or else created fatal problems in the long run, when people became confronted with external environmental changes or human-caused environmental changes that societies without written histories and without archaeologists could not have anticipated. I put "in the short run" in quotation marks, because the Anasazi did survive in Chaco Canyon for about 600 years, considerably longer than the duration of European occupation anywhere in the New World since Columbus's arrival in A.D. 1492. During their existence, those various southwestern Native Americans experimented with half-a-dozen alternative types of economies (pp. 140–143). It took many centuries to discover that, among those economies, only the Pueblo economy was sustainable "in the long run," i.e., for at least a thousand years. That should make us modern Americans hesitate to be too confident yet about the sustainability of our First World economy, especially when we reflect how quickly Chaco society collapsed after its peak in the decade A.D. 1110–1120, and how implausible the risk of collapse would have seemed to Chacoans of that decade.

Within our five-factor framework for understanding societal collapses, four of those factors played a role in the Anasazi collapse. There were indeed human environmental impacts of several types, especially deforestation and arroyo cutting. There was also climate change in rainfall and temperature, and its effects interacted with the effects of human environmental impacts. Internal trade with friendly trade partners did play a crucial role in the collapse: different Anasazi groups supplied food, timber, pottery, stone, and luxury goods to each other, supporting each other in an interdependent complex society, but putting the whole society at risk of collapsing. Religious and political factors apparently played an essential role in sustaining the complex society, by coordinating the exchanges of materials, and by motivating people in outlying areas to supply food, timber, and pottery to the political and religious centers. The only factor in our five-factor list for whose operation there is not convincing evidence in the case of the Anasazi collapse is external enemies. While the Anasazi did indeed attack each other as their population grew and as the climate deteriorated, the civilizations of the U.S. Southwest were too distant from other populous societies to have been seriously threatened by any external enemies.

From that perspective, we can propose a simple answer to the long-standing either/or debate: was Chaco Canyon abandoned because of human impact on the environment, or because of drought? The answer is: it was abandoned for both reasons. Over the course of six centuries the human population of Chaco Canyon grew, its demands on the environment grew, its environmental resources declined, and people came to be living increasingly close to the margin of what the environment could support. That was the *ultimate* cause of abandonment. The *proximate* cause, the proverbial last straw that broke the camel's back, was the drought that finally pushed Chacoans over the edge, a drought that a society living at a lower population density could have survived. When Chaco society did collapse, its inhabitants could no longer reconstruct their society in the way that the first farmers of the Chaco area had built up their society. The reason is that the initial conditions of abundant nearby trees, high groundwater levels, and a smooth floodplain without arroyos had disappeared.

That type of conclusion is likely to apply to many other collapses of past societies (including the Maya to be considered in the next chapter), and to our own destiny today. All of us moderns—house-owners, investors, politicians, university administrators, and others—can get away with a lot of waste when the economy is good. We forget that conditions fluctuate, and we may not be able to anticipate when conditions will change. By that time, we may already have become attached to an expensive lifestyle, leaving an enforced diminished lifestyle or bankruptcy as the sole outs.

CHAPTER 5

The Maya Collapses

Mysteries of lost cities ■ The Maya environment ■ Maya agriculture ■ Maya history ■ Copán ■ Complexities of collapses ■ Wars and droughts ■ Collapse in the southern lowlands ■ The Maya message ■

B y now, millions of modern tourists have visited ruins of the ancient Maya civilization that collapsed over a thousand years ago in Mexico's Yucatán Peninsula and adjacent parts of Central America. All of us love a romantic mystery, and the Maya offer us one at our doorstep, almost as close for Americans as the Anasazi ruins. To visit a former Maya city, we need only board a direct flight from the U.S. to the modern Mexican state capital city of Mérida, jump into a rental car or minibus, and drive an hour on a paved highway (map, p. 161).

Today, many Maya ruins, with their great temples and monuments, still lie surrounded by jungle, far from current human settlement (Plate 12). Yet they were once the sites of the New World's most advanced Native American civilization before European arrival, and the only one with extensive deciphered written texts. How could ancient peoples have supported urban societies in areas where few farmers eke out a living today? The Maya cities impress us not only with that mystery and with their beauty, but also because they are "pure" archaeological sites. That is, their locations became depopulated, so they were not covered up by later buildings as were so many other ancient cities, like the Aztec capital of Tenochtitlán (now buried under modern Mexico City) and Rome.

Maya cities remained deserted, hidden by trees, and virtually unknown to the outside world until rediscovered in 1839 by a rich American lawyer named John Stephens, together with the English draftsman Frederick Catherwood. Having heard rumors of ruins in the jungle, Stephens got President Martin Van Buren to appoint him ambassador to the Confederation of Central American Republics, an amorphous political entity then extending from modern Guatemala to Nicaragua, as a front for his archaeological explorations. Stephens and Catherwood ended up exploring 44 sites and cities. From the extraordinary quality of the buildings and the art, they realized that these were not the work of savages (in their words) but of a vanished high civilization. They recognized that some of the carvings on the stone monuments constituted writing, and they correctly guessed that it related historical events and the names of people. On his return, Stephens wrote two travel books, illustrated by Catherwood and describing the ruins, that became best sellers.

A few quotes from Stephens's writings will give a sense of the romantic appeal of the Maya: "The city was desolate. No remnant of this race hangs round the ruins, with traditions handed down from father to son and from generation to generation. It lay before us like a shattered bark in the midst of the ocean, her mast gone, her name effaced, her crew perished, and none to tell whence she came, to whom she belonged, how long on her journey, or what caused her destruction. . . . Architecture, sculpture, and painting, all the arts which embellish life, had flourished in this overgrown forest; orators, warriors, and statesmen, beauty, ambition, and glory had lived and passed away, and none knew that such things had been, or could tell of their past existence. . . . Here were the remains of a cultivated, polished, and peculiar people, who had passed through all the stages incident to the rise and fall of nations; reached their golden age, and perished. . . . We went up to their desolate temples and fallen altars; and wherever we moved we saw the evidence of their taste, their skill in arts. . . . We called back into life the strange people who gazed in sadness from the wall; pictured them, in fanciful costumes and adorned with plumes of feather, ascending the terraces of the palace and the steps leading to the temples. . . . In the romance of the world's history nothing ever impressed me more forcibly than the spectacle of this once great and lovely city, overturned, desolate, and lost, . . . overgrown with trees for miles around, and without even a name to distinguish it." Those sensations are what tourists drawn to Maya ruins still feel today, and why we find the Maya collapse so fascinating.

The Maya story has several advantages for all of us interested in prehistoric collapses. First, the Maya written records that have survived, although frustratingly incomplete, are still useful for reconstructing Maya history in much greater detail than we can reconstruct Easter Island, or even Anasazi history with its tree rings and packrat middens. The great art and architecture of Maya cities have resulted in far more archaeologists studying the Maya than would have been the case if they had just been illiterate hunter-gatherers living in archaeologically invisible hovels. Climatologists and paleoecologists have recently been able to recognize several signals of ancient climate and environmental changes that contributed to the Maya collapse.

Finally, today there are still Maya people living in their ancient homeland and speaking Maya languages. Because much ancient Maya culture survived the collapse, early European visitors to the homeland recorded information about contemporary Maya society that played a vital role in our understanding ancient Maya society. The first Maya contact with Europeans came already in 1502, just 10 years after Christopher Columbus's "discovery" of the New World, when Columbus on the last of his four voyages captured a trading canoe that may have been Maya. In 1527 the Spanish began in earnest to conquer the Maya, but it was not until 1697 that they subdued the last principality. Thus, the Spanish had opportunities to observe independent Maya societies for a period of nearly two centuries. Especially important, both for bad and for good, was the bishop Diego de Landa, who resided in the Yucatán Peninsula for most of the years from 1549 to 1578. On the one hand, in one of history's worst acts of cultural vandalism, he burned all Maya manuscripts that he could locate in his effort to eliminate "paganism," so that only four survive today. On the other hand, he wrote a detailed account of Maya society, and he obtained from an informant a garbled explanation of Maya writing that eventually, nearly four centuries later, turned out to offer clues to its decipherment.

A further reason for our devoting a chapter to the Maya is to provide an antidote to our other chapters on past societies, which consist disproportionately of small societies in somewhat fragile and geographically isolated environments, and behind the cutting edge of contemporary technology and culture. The Maya were none of those things. Instead, they were culturally the most advanced society (or among the most advanced ones) in the pre-Columbian New World, the only one with extensive preserved writing, and located within one of the two heartlands of New World civilization (Mesoamerica). While their environment did present some problems associated with its karst terrain and unpredictably fluctuating rainfall, it does not rank as notably fragile by world standards, and it was certainly less fragile than the environments of ancient Easter Island, the Anasazi area, Greenland, or modern Australia. Lest one be misled into thinking that crashes are a risk only for small peripheral societies in fragile areas, the Maya warn us that crashes can also befall the most advanced and creative societies.

From the perspective of our five-point framework for understanding societal collapses, the Maya illustrate four of our points. They did damage their environment, especially by deforestation and erosion. Climate changes (droughts) did contribute to the Maya collapse, probably repeatedly. Hostilities among the Maya themselves did play a large role. Finally, political/

cultural factors, especially the competition among kings and nobles that led to a chronic emphasis on war and erecting monuments rather than on solving underlying problems, also contributed. The remaining item on our five-point list, trade or cessation of trade with external friendly societies, does not appear to have been essential in sustaining the Maya or in causing their downfall. While obsidian (their preferred raw material for making into stone tools), jade, gold, and shells were imported into the Maya area, the latter three items were non-essential luxuries. Obsidian tools remained widely distributed in the Maya area long after the political collapse, so obsidian was evidently never in short supply.

To understand the Maya, let's begin by considering their environment, which we think of as "jungle" or "tropical rainforest." That's not true, and the reason why not proves to be important. Properly speaking, tropical rainforests grow in high-rainfall equatorial areas that remain wet or humid all year round. But the Maya homeland lies more than a thousand miles from the equator, at latitudes 17° to 22°N, in a habitat termed a "seasonal tropical forest." That is, while there does tend to be a rainy season from May to October, there is also a dry season from January through April. If one focuses on the wet months, one calls the Maya homeland a "seasonal tropical forest"; if one focuses on the dry months, one could instead describe it as a "seasonal desert."

From north to south in the Yucatán Peninsula, rainfall increases from 18 to 100 inches per year, and the soils become thicker, so that the southern peninsula was agriculturally more productive and supported denser populations. But rainfall in the Maya homeland is unpredictably variable between years; some recent years have had three or four times more rain than other years. Also, the timing of rainfall within the year is somewhat unpredictable, so it can easily happen that farmers plant their crops in anticipation of rain and then the rains do not come when expected. As a result, modern farmers attempting to grow corn in the ancient Maya homelands have faced frequent crop failures, especially in the north. The ancient Maya were presumably more experienced and did better, but nevertheless they too must have faced risks of crop failures from droughts and hurricanes.

Although southern Maya areas received more rainfall than northern areas, problems of water were paradoxically more severe in the wet south. While that made things hard for ancient Maya living in the south, it has also made things hard for modern archaeologists who have difficulty under-

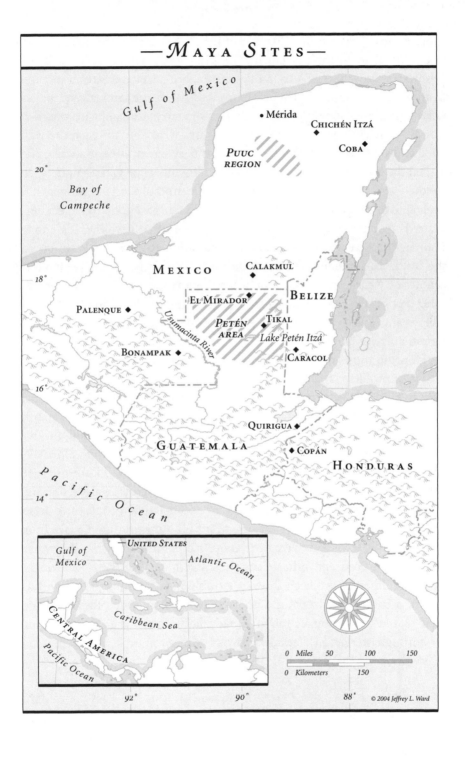

—Maya Sites—

Gulf of Mexico

• Mérida

CHICHÉN ITZÁ ◆

PUUC
REGION

COBA ◆

20°

Bay of
Campeche

18°

MEXICO

CALAKMUL ◆

EL MIRADOR ◆

BELIZE

PALENQUE ◆

Usumacinta River

PETÉN
AREA

TIKAL ◆

Lake Petén Itzá

BONAMPAK ◆

CARACOL ◆

16°

QUIRIGUA ◆

GUATEMALA

◆ COPÁN

HONDURAS

Pacific Ocean

14°

UNITED STATES

Gulf of
Mexico

Atlantic Ocean

CENTRAL AMERICA

Caribbean Sea

Pacific Ocean

0 Miles 50 100 150

0 Kilometers 150

92°

90°

88° © 2004 Jeffrey L. Ward

standing why ancient droughts would have caused bigger problems in the wet south than in the dry north. The likely explanation is that a lens of freshwater underlies the Yucatán Peninsula, but surface elevation increases from north to south, so that as one moves south the land surface lies increasingly higher above the water table. In the northern peninsula the elevation is sufficiently low that the ancient Maya were able to reach the water table at deep sinkholes called cenotes, or at deep caves; all tourists who have visited the Maya city of Chichén Itzá will remember the great cenotes there. In low-elevation north coastal areas without sinkholes, the Maya may have been able to get down to the water table by digging wells up to 75 feet deep. Water is readily available in many parts of Belize that have rivers, along the Usumacinta River in the west, and around a few lakes in the Petén area of the south. But much of the south lies too high above the water table for cenotes or wells to reach down to it. Making matters worse, most of the Yucatán Peninsula consists of karst, a porous sponge-like limestone terrain where rain runs straight into the ground and where little or no surface water remains available.

How did those dense southern Maya populations deal with their resulting water problem? It initially surprises us that many of their cities were not built next to the few rivers but instead on promontories in rolling uplands. The explanation is that the Maya excavated depressions, modified natural depressions, and then plugged up leaks in the karst by plastering the bottoms of the depressions in order to create cisterns and reservoirs, which collected rain from large plastered catchment basins and stored it for use in the dry season. For example, reservoirs at the Maya city of Tikal held enough water to meet the drinking water needs of about 10,000 people for a period of 18 months. At the city of Coba the Maya built dikes around a lake in order to raise its level and make their water supply more reliable. But the inhabitants of Tikal and other cities dependent on reservoirs for drinking water would still have been in deep trouble if 18 months passed without rain in a prolonged drought. A shorter drought in which they exhausted their stored food supplies might already have gotten them in deep trouble through starvation, because growing crops required rain rather than reservoirs.

Of particular importance for our purposes are the details of Maya agriculture, which was based on crops domesticated in Mexico—especially corn, with beans being second in importance. For the elite as well as commoners, corn constituted at least 70% of the Maya diet, as deduced from isotope analyses of ancient Maya skeletons. Their sole domestic animals were the dog, turkey, Muscovy duck, and a stingless bee yielding honey, while their most important wild meat source was deer that they hunted, plus fish at some sites. However, the few animal bones at Maya archaeological sites suggest that the quantity of meat available to the Maya was low. Venison was mainly a luxury food for the elite.

It was formerly believed that Maya farming was based on slash-and-burn agriculture (so-called swidden agriculture) in which forest is cleared and burned, crops are grown in the resulting field for a year or a few years until the soil is exhausted, and then the field is abandoned for a long fallow period of 15 or 20 years until regrowth of wild vegetation restores fertility to the soil. Because most of the landscape under a swidden agricultural system is fallow at any given time, it can support only modest population densities. Thus, it was a surprise for archaeologists to discover that ancient Maya population densities, estimated from numbers of stone foundations of farmhouses, were often far higher than what swidden agriculture could support. The actual values are the subject of much dispute and evidently varied among areas, but frequently cited estimates reach 250 to 750, possibly even 1,500, people per square mile. (For comparison, even today the two most densely populated countries in Africa, Rwanda and Burundi, have population densities of only about 750 and 540 people per square mile, respectively.) Hence the ancient Maya must have had some means of increasing agricultural production beyond what was possible through swidden alone.

Many Maya areas do show remains of agricultural structures designed to increase production, such as terracing of hill slopes to retain soil and moisture, irrigation systems, and arrays of canals and drained or raised fields. The latter systems, which are well attested elsewhere in the world and which require a lot of labor to construct, but which reward the labor with increased food production, involve digging canals to drain a waterlogged area, fertilizing and raising the level of the fields between the canals by dumping muck and water hyacinths dredged out of canals onto the fields, and thereby keeping the fields themselves from being inundated. Besides harvesting crops grown over the fields, farmers with raised fields also "grow" wild fish and turtles in the canals (actually, let them grow themselves) as an additional food source. However, other Maya areas, such as the well-studied cities of Copán and Tikal, show little archaeological evidence of terracing, irrigation, or raised- or drained-field systems. Instead, their inhabitants must have used archaeologically invisible means to increase food production, by mulching, floodwater farming, shortening the time that a field is left fallow, and tilling the soil to restore soil fertility, or in the extreme omitting the fallow period entirely and growing crops every year, or in especially moist areas growing two crops per year.

Socially stratified societies, including modern American and European society, consist of farmers who produce food, plus non-farmers such as bureaucrats and soldiers who do not produce food but merely consume the food grown by the farmers and are in effect parasites on farmers. Hence in any stratified society the farmers must grow enough surplus food to meet not only their own needs but also those of the other consumers. The number of non-producing consumers that can be supported depends on the society's agricultural productivity. In the United States today, with its highly efficient agriculture, farmers make up only 2% of our population, and each farmer can feed on the average 125 other people (American non-farmers plus people in export markets overseas). Ancient Egyptian agriculture, although much less efficient than modern mechanized agriculture, was still efficient enough for an Egyptian peasant to produce five times the food required for himself and his family. But a Maya peasant could produce only twice the needs of himself and his family. At least 70% of Maya society consisted of peasants. That's because Maya agriculture suffered from several limitations.

First, it yielded little protein. Corn, by far the dominant crop, has a lower protein content than the Old World staples of wheat and barley. The few edible domestic animals already mentioned included no large ones and yielded much less meat than did Old World cows, sheep, pigs, and goats. The Maya depended on a narrower range of crops than did Andean farmers (who in addition to corn also had potatoes, high-protein quinoa, and many other plants, plus llamas for meat), and much narrower again than the variety of crops in China and in western Eurasia.

Another limitation was that Maya corn agriculture was less intensive and productive than the Aztecs' *chinampas* (a very productive type of raised-field agriculture), the raised fields of the Tiwanaku civilization of the Andes, Moche irrigation on the coast of Peru, or fields tilled by animal-drawn plows over much of Eurasia.

Still a further limitation arose from the humid climate of the Maya area, which made it difficult to store corn beyond a year, whereas the Anasazi living in the dry climate of the U.S. Southwest could store it for three years.

Finally, unlike Andean Indians with their llamas, and unlike Old World peoples with their horses, oxen, donkeys, and camels, the Maya had no animal-powered transport or plows. All overland transport for the Maya went on the backs of human porters. But if you send out a porter carrying a load of corn to accompany an army into the field, some of that load of corn is required to feed the porter himself on the trip out, and some more to feed him on the trip back, leaving only a fraction of the load available to feed the army. The longer the trip, the less of the load is left over from the porter's own requirements. Beyond a march of a few days to a week, it becomes un-economical to send porters carrying corn to provision armies or markets. Thus, the modest productivity of Maya agriculture, and their lack of draft animals, severely limited the duration and distance possible for their mili-tary campaigns.

We are accustomed to thinking of military success as determined by quality of weaponry, rather than by food supply. But a clear example of how improvements in food supply may decisively increase military success comes from the history of Maori New Zealand. The Maori are the Polyne-sian people who were the first to settle New Zealand. Traditionally, they fought frequent fierce wars against each other, but only against closely neighboring tribes. Those wars were limited by the modest productivity of their agriculture, whose staple crop was sweet potatoes. It was not possible to grow enough sweet potatoes to feed an army in the field for a long time or on distant marches. When Europeans arrived in New Zealand, they brought potatoes, which beginning around 1815 considerably increased Maori crop yields. Maori could now grow enough food to supply armies in the field for many weeks. The result was a 15-year period in Maori history, from 1818 until 1833, when Maori tribes that had acquired potatoes and guns from the English sent armies out on raids to attack tribes hundreds of miles away that had not yet acquired potatoes and guns. Thus, the potato's productivity relieved previous limitations on Maori warfare, similar to the limitations that low-productivity corn agriculture imposed on Maya warfare.

Those food supply considerations may contribute to explaining why Maya society remained politically divided among small kingdoms that were perpetually at war with each other, and that never became unified into large empires like the Aztec Empire of the Valley of Mexico (fed with the help of their *chinampa* agriculture and other forms of intensification) or the Inca Empire of the Andes (fed by more diverse crops carried by llamas over well-built roads). Maya armies and bureaucracies remained small and unable to mount lengthy campaigns over long distances. (Even much later, in 1848, when the Maya revolted against their Mexican overlords and a Maya army seemed to be on the verge of victory, the army had to break off fighting and go home to harvest another crop of corn.) Many Maya kingdoms held populations of only up to 25,000 to 50,000 people, none over half a million, within a radius of two or three days' walk from the king's palace. (The actual numbers are again highly controversial among archaeologists.) From the tops of the temples of some Maya kingdoms, it was possible to see the temples of the nearest kingdom. Maya cities remained small (mostly less than one square mile in area), without the large populations and big markets of Teotihuacán and Tenochtitlán in the Valley of Mexico, or of Chan-Chan and Cuzco in Peru, and without archaeological evidence of the royally managed food storage and trade that characterized ancient Greece and Mesopotamia.

Now for a quick crash-course in Maya history. The Maya area is part of the larger ancient Native American cultural region known as Mesoamerica, which extended approximately from Central Mexico to Honduras and constituted (along with the Andes of South America) one of the two New World centers of innovation before European arrival. The Maya shared much in common with other Mesoamerican societies not only in what they possessed, but also in what they lacked. For example, surprisingly to modern Westerners with expectations based on Old World civilizations, Mesoamerican societies lacked metal tools, pulleys and other machines, wheels (except locally as toys), boats with sails, and domestic animals large enough to carry loads or pull a plow. All of those great Maya temples were constructed by stone and wooden tools and by human muscle power alone.

Of the ingredients of Maya civilization, many were acquired by the Maya from elsewhere in Mesoamerica. For instance, Mesoamerican agriculture, cities, and writing first arose outside the Maya area itself, in valleys and coastal lowlands to the west and southwest, where corn and beans and squash were domesticated and became important dietary components by 3000 B.C., pottery arose around 2500 B.C., villages by 1500 B.C., cities among the Olmecs by 1200 B.C., writing appeared among the Zapotecs in Oaxaca around or after 600 B.C., and the first states arose around 300 B.C. Two complementary calendars, a solar calendar of 365 days and a ritual calendar of 260 days, also arose outside the Maya area. Other elements of Maya civilization were either invented, perfected, or modified by the Maya themselves.

Within the Maya area, villages and pottery appeared around or after 1000 B.C., substantial buildings around 500 B.C., and writing around

400 B.C. All preserved ancient Maya writing, constituting a total of about 15,000 inscriptions, is on stone and pottery and deals only with kings, nobles, and their conquests (Plate 13). There is not a single mention of commoners. When Spaniards arrived, the Maya were still using bark paper coated with plaster to write books, of which the sole four that escaped Bishop Landa's fires turned out to be treatises on astronomy and the calendar. The ancient Maya also had had such bark-paper books, often depicted on their pottery, but only decayed remains of them have survived in tombs.

The famous Maya Long Count calendar begins on August 11, 3114 B.C.— just as our own calendar begins on January 1 of the first year of the Christian era. We know the significance to us of that day-zero of our calendar: it's the supposed beginning of the year in which Christ was born. Presumably the Maya also attached some significance to their own day zero, but we don't know what it was. The first preserved Long Count date is only A.D. 197 for a monument in the Maya area and 36 B.C. outside the Maya area, indicating that the Long Count calendar's day-zero was backdated to August 11, 3114 B.C. long after the facts; there was no writing anywhere in the New World then, nor would there be for 2,500 years after that date.

Our calendar is divided into units of days, weeks, months, years, decades, centuries, and millennia: for example, the date of February 19, 2003, on which I wrote the first draft of this paragraph, means the 19th day of the second month in the third year of the first decade of the first century of the third millennium beginning with the birth of Christ. Similarly, the Maya Long Count calendar named dates in units of days *(kin)*, 20 days *(uinal)*, 360 days *(tun)*, 7,200 days or approximately 20 years *(katunn)*, and 144,000 days or approximately 400 years *(baktun)*. All of Maya history falls into baktuns 8, 9, and 10.

The so-called Classic period of Maya civilization begins in baktun 8, around A.D. 250, when evidence for the first kings and dynasties appears. Among the glyphs (written signs) on Maya monuments, students of Maya writing recognized a few dozen, each of which was concentrated in its own geographic area, and which are now considered to have had the approximate meaning of dynasties or kingdoms. In addition to Maya kings having their own name glyphs and palaces, many nobles also had their own inscriptions and palaces. In Maya society the king also functioned as high priest carrying the responsibility to attend to astronomical and calendrical rituals, and thereby to bring rain and prosperity, which the king claimed to have the supernatural power to deliver because of his asserted family relationship to the gods. That is, there was a tacitly understood quid pro quo:

the reason why the peasants supported the luxurious lifestyle of the king and his court, fed him corn and venison, and built his palaces was because he had made implicit big promises to the peasants. As we shall see, kings got into trouble with their peasants if a drought came, because that was tantamount to the breaking of a royal promise.

From A.D. 250 onwards, the Maya population (as judged from the number of archaeologically attested house sites), the number of monuments and buildings, and the number of Long Count dates on monuments and pottery increased almost exponentially, to reach peak numbers in the 8th century A.D. The largest monuments were erected towards the end of that Classic period. Numbers of all three of those indicators of a complex society declined throughout the 9th century, until the last known Long Count date on any monument fell in baktun 10, in the year A.D. 909. That decline of Maya population, architecture, and the Long Count calendar constitutes what is known as the Classic Maya collapse.

As an example of the collapse, let's consider in more detail a small but densely built city whose ruins now lie in western Honduras at a site known as Copán, and described in two recent books by archaeologist David Webster. For agricultural purposes the best land in the Copán area consists of five pockets of flat land with fertile alluvial soil along a river valley, with a tiny total area of only 10 square miles; the largest of those five pockets, known as the Copán pocket, has an area of only 5 square miles. Much of the land around Copán consists of steep hills, and nearly half of the hill area has a slope above 16% (approximately double the slope of the steepest grade that you are likely to encounter on an American highway). Soil in the hills is less fertile, more acidic, and poorer in phosphate than valley soil. Today, corn yields from valley-bottom fields are two or three times those of fields on hill slopes, which suffer rapid erosion and lose three-quarters of their productivity within a decade of farming.

As judged by numbers of house sites, population growth in the Copán Valley rose steeply from the 5th century up to a peak estimated at around 27,000 people at A.D. 750–900. Maya written history at Copán begins in the year with a Long Count date corresponding to A.D. 426, when later monuments record retrospectively that some person related to nobles at Tikal and Teotihuacán arrived. Construction of royal monuments glorifying kings was especially massive between A.D. 650 and 750. After A.D. 700, nobles other than kings also got into the act and began erecting their own palaces, of which there were about twenty by the year A.D. 800, when one of those palaces is known to have consisted of 50 buildings with room for about 250 people. All of those nobles and their courts would have increased the burden that the king and his own court imposed on the peasants. The last big buildings at Copán were put up around A.D. 800, and the last Long Count date on an incomplete altar possibly bearing a king's name has the date of A.D. 822.

Archaeological surveys of different types of habitats in the Copán Valley show that they were occupied in a regular sequence. The first area farmed was the large Copán pocket of valley bottomland, followed by occupation of the other four bottomland pockets. During that time the human population was growing, but there was not yet occupation of the hills. Hence that increased population must have been accommodated by intensifying production in the bottomland pockets by some combination of shorter fallow periods, double-cropping, and possibly some irrigation.

By the year A.D. 650, people started to occupy the hill slopes, but those hill sites were cultivated only for about a century. The percentage of Copán's total population that was in the hills, rather than in the valleys, reached a maximum of 41%, then declined until the population again became concentrated in the valley pockets. What caused that pullback of population from the hills? Excavation of the foundations of buildings in the valley floor showed that they became covered with sediment during the 8th century, meaning that the hill slopes were getting eroded and probably also leached of nutrients. Those acidic infertile hill soils were being carried down into the valley and blanketing the more fertile valley soils, where they would have reduced agricultural yields. This ancient quick abandonment of hillsides coincides with modern Maya experience that fields in the hills have low fertility and that their soils become rapidly exhausted.

The reason for that erosion of the hillsides is clear: the forests that formerly covered them and protected their soils were being cut down. Dated pollen samples show that the pine forests originally covering the upper elevations of the hill slopes were eventually all cleared. Calculation suggests that most of those felled pine trees were being burned for fuel, while the rest were used for construction or for making plaster. At other Maya sites from the pre-Classic era, where the Maya went overboard in lavish use of thick plaster on buildings, plaster production may have been a major cause of deforestation. Besides causing sediment accumulation in the valleys and depriving valley inhabitants of wood supplies, that deforestation may have begun to cause a "man-made drought" in the valley bottom, because forests play a major role in water cycling, such that massive deforestation tends to result in lowered rainfall.

Hundreds of skeletons recovered from Copán archaeological sites have been studied for signs of disease and malnutrition, such as porous bones and stress lines in the teeth. These skeletal signs show that the health of Copán's inhabitants deteriorated from A.D. 650 to 850, both among the elite and among the commoners, although the health of commoners was worse.

Recall that Copán's population was increasing steeply while the hills were being occupied. The subsequent abandonment of all of those fields in the hills meant that the burden of feeding the extra population formerly dependent on the hills now fell increasingly on the valley floor, and that more and more people were competing for the food grown on those 10 square miles of valley bottomland. That would have led to fighting among the farmers themselves for the best land, or for any land, just as in modern Rwanda (Chapter 10). Because Copán's king was failing to deliver on his promises of rain and prosperity in return for the power and luxuries that he claimed, he would have been the scapegoat for this agricultural failure. That may explain why the last that we hear from any Copán king is A.D. 822 (that last Long Count date at Copán), and why the royal palace was burned around A.D. 850. However, the continued production of some luxury goods suggest that some nobles managed to carry on with their lifestyle after the king's downfall, until around A.D. 975.

To judge from datable pieces of obsidian, Copán's total population decreased more gradually than did its signs of kings and nobles. The estimated population in the year A.D. 950 was still around 15,000, or 54% of the peak population of 27,000. That population continued to dwindle, until there are no more signs of anyone in the Copán Valley by around A.D. 1250. The reappearance of pollen from forest trees thereafter provides independent evidence that the valley became virtually empty of people, and that the forests could at last begin to recover.

The general outline of Maya history that I have just related, and the example of Copán's history in particular, illustrates why we talk about "the Maya collapse." But the story grows more complicated, for at least five reasons.

First, there was not only that enormous Classic collapse, but at least two previous smaller collapses at some sites, one around the year A.D. 150 when El Mirador and some other Maya cities collapsed (the so-called pre-Classic collapse), the other (the so-called Maya hiatus) in the late 6th century and early 7th century, a period when no monuments were erected at the well-studied site of Tikal. There were also some post-Classic collapses in areas whose populations survived the Classic collapse or increased after it—such as the fall of Chichén Itzá around 1250 and of Mayapán around 1450.

Second, the Classic collapse was obviously not complete, because there were hundreds of thousands of Maya who met and fought the Spaniards—far fewer Maya than during the Classic peak, but still far more people than in the other ancient societies discussed in detail in this book. Those survivors were concentrated in areas with stable water supplies, especially in the north with its cenotes, the coastal lowlands with their wells, near a southern lake, and along rivers and lagoons at lower elevations. However, population otherwise disappeared almost completely in what previously had been the Maya heartland in the south.

Third, the collapse of population (as gauged by numbers of house sites and of obsidian tools) was in some cases much slower than the decline in numbers of Long Count dates, as I already mentioned for Copán. What collapsed quickly during the Classic collapse was the institution of kingship and the Long Count calendar.

Fourth, many apparent collapses of cities were really nothing more than "power cycling": i.e., particular cities becoming more powerful, then declining or getting conquered, and then rising again and conquering their neighbors, without changes in the whole population. For example, in the year 562 Tikal was defeated by its rivals Caracol and Calakmul, and its king was captured and killed. However, Tikal then gradually gained strength again and finally conquered its rivals in 695, long before Tikal joined many other Maya cities in the Classic collapse (last dated Tikal monuments A.D. 869). Similarly, Copán grew in power until the year 738, when its king Waxak-lahuun Ub'aah K'awil (a name better known to Maya enthusiasts today by its unforgettable translation of "18 Rabbit") was captured and put to death by the rival city of Quirigua, but then Copán thrived during the following half-century under more fortunate kings.

Finally, cities in different parts of the Maya area rose and fell on different trajectories. For example, the Puuc region in the northwest Yucatán Peninsula, after being almost empty of people in the year 700, exploded in population after 750 while the southern cities were collapsing, peaked in population between 900 and 925, and then collapsed in turn between 950 and 1000. El Mirador, a huge site in the center of the Maya area with one of the world's largest pyramids, was settled in 200 B.C. and abandoned around A.D. 150, long before the rise of Copán. Chichén Itzá in the northern peninsula grew after A.D. 850 and was the main northern center around 1000, only to be destroyed in a civil war around 1250.

Some archaeologists focus on these five types of complications and don't want to recognize a Classic Maya collapse at all. But this overlooks the obvious facts that cry out for explanation: the disappearance of between 90 and 99% of the Maya population after A.D. 800, especially in the formerly most densely populated area of the southern lowlands, and the disappearance of kings, Long Count calendars, and other complex political and cultural institutions. That's why we talk about a Classic Maya collapse, a collapse both of population and of culture that needs explaining.

Two other phenomena that I have mentioned briefly as contributing to Maya collapses require more discussion: the roles of warfare and of drought.

Archaeologists for a long time believed the ancient Maya to be gentle and peaceful people. We now know that Maya warfare was intense, chronic, and unresolvable, because limitations of food supply and transportation made it impossible for any Maya principality to unite the whole region in an empire, in the way that the Aztecs and Incas united Central Mexico and the Andes, respectively. The archaeological record shows that wars became more intense and frequent towards the time of the Classic collapse. That evidence comes from discoveries of several types over the last 55 years: archaeological excavations of massive fortifications surrounding many Maya sites, vivid depictions of warfare and captives on stone monuments, vases (Plate 14), and on the famous painted murals discovered in 1946 at Bonampak; and the decipherment of Maya writing, much of which proved to consist of royal inscriptions boasting of conquests. Maya kings fought to take one another captive, one of the unfortunate losers being Copán's King 18 Rabbit. Captives were tortured in unpleasant ways depicted clearly on the monuments and murals (such as yanking fingers out of sockets, pulling out teeth, cutting off the lower jaw, trimming off the lips and fingertips, pulling out the fingernails, and driving a pin through the lips), culminating (sometimes several years later) in the sacrifice of the captive in other equally unpleasant ways (such as tying the captive up into a ball by binding the arms and legs together, then rolling the balled-up captive down the steep stone staircase of a temple).

Maya warfare involved several well-documented types of violence: wars between separate kingdoms; attempts of cities within a kingdom to secede by revolting against the capital; and civil wars resulting from frequent violent attempts by would-be kings to usurp the throne. All of these types were described or depicted on monuments, because they involved kings and nobles. Not considered worthy of description, but probably even more frequent, were fights between commoners over land, as overpopulation became excessive and as land became scarce.

The other phenomenon important to understanding Maya collapses is the repeated occurrence of droughts, studied especially by Mark Brenner, David Hodell, the late Edward Deevey, and their colleagues at the University of Florida, and discussed in a recent book by Richardson Gill. Cores bored into layers of sediments at the bottoms of Maya lakes yield many measurements that let us infer droughts and environmental changes. For example, gypsum (a.k.a. calcium sulfate) precipitates out of solution in a lake into sediments when lake water becomes concentrated by evaporation during a drought. Water containing the heavy form of oxygen known as the isotope oxygen-18 also becomes concentrated during droughts, while water containing the lighter isotope oxygen-16 evaporates away. Molluscs and crustacea living in the lake take up oxygen to lay down in their shells, which remain preserved in the lake sediments, waiting for climatologists to analyze for those oxygen isotopes long after the little animals have died. Radiocarbon dating of a sediment layer identifies the approximate year when the drought or rainfall conditions inferred from those gypsum and oxygen isotope measurements were prevailing. The same lake sediment cores provide palynologists with information about deforestation (which shows up as a decrease in pollen from forest trees at the expense of an increase in grass pollen), and also soil erosion (which shows up as a thick clay deposit and minerals from the washed-down soil).

Based on these studies of radiocarbon-dated layers from lake sediment cores, climatologists and paleoecologists conclude that the Maya area was relatively wet from about 5500 B.C. until 500 B.C. The following period from 475 to 250 B.C., just before the rise of pre–Classic Maya civilization, was dry. The pre-Classic rise may have been facilitated by the return of wetter conditions after 250 B.C., but then a drought from A.D. 125 until A.D. 250 was associated with the pre-Classic collapse at El Mirador and other sites. That collapse was followed by the resumption of wetter conditions and of the buildup of Classic Maya cities, temporarily interrupted by a drought around A.D. 600 corresponding to a decline at Tikal and some other sites. Finally, around A.D. 760 there began the worst drought in the last 7,000 years, peaking around the year A.D. 800, and suspiciously associated with the Classic collapse.

Careful analysis of the frequency of droughts in the Maya area shows a tendency for them to recur at intervals of about 208 years. Those drought cycles may result from small variations in the sun's radiation, possibly made more severe in the Maya area as a result of the rainfall gradient in the Yucatán (drier in the north, wetter in the south) shifting southwards. One might expect those changes in the sun's radiation to affect not just the Maya region but, to varying degrees, the whole world. In fact, climatologists have noted that some other famous collapses of prehistoric civilizations far from the Maya realm appear to coincide with the peaks of those drought cycles, such as the collapse of the world's first empire (the Akkadian Empire of Mesopotamia) around 2170 B.C., the collapse of Moche IV civilization on the Peruvian coast around A.D. 600, and the collapse of Tiwanaku civilization in the Andes around A.D. 1100.

In the most naïve form of the hypothesis that drought contributed to causing the Classic collapse, one could imagine a single drought around A.D. 800 uniformly affecting the whole realm and triggering the fall of all Maya centers simultaneously. Actually, as we have seen, the Classic collapse hit different centers at slightly different times in the period A.D. 760–910, while sparing other centers. That fact makes many Maya specialists skeptical of a role of drought.

But a properly cautious climatologist would not state the drought hypothesis in that implausibly oversimplied form. Finer-resolution variation in rainfall from one year to the next can be calculated from annually banded sediments that rivers wash into ocean basins near the coast. These yield the conclusion that "The Drought" around A.D. 800 actually had four peaks, the first of them less severe: two dry years around A.D. 760, then an even drier decade around A.D. 810–820, three drier years around A.D. 860, and six drier years around A.D. 910. Interestingly, Richardson Gill concluded, from the latest dates on stone monuments at various large Maya centers, that collapse dates vary among sites and fall into three clusters: around A.D. 810, 860, and 910, in agreement with the dates for the three most severe droughts. It would not be at all surprising if a drought in any given year varied locally in its severity, hence if a series of droughts caused different Maya centers to collapse in different years, while sparing centers with reliable water supplies such as cenotes, wells, and lakes.

■   ■   ■

The area most affected by the Classic collapse was the southern lowlands, probably for the two reasons already mentioned: it was the area with the densest population, and it may also have had the most severe water problems because it lay too high above the water table for water to be obtained from cenotes or wells when the rains failed. The southern lowlands lost more than 99% of their population in the course of the Classic collapse. For example, the population of the Central Petén at the peak of the Classic Maya period is variously estimated at between 3,000,000 and 14,000,000 people, but there were only about 30,000 people there at the time that the Spanish arrived. When Cortés and his Spanish army passed through the Central Petén in 1524 and 1525, they nearly starved because they encountered so few villages from which to acquire corn. Cortés passed within a few miles of the ruins of the great Classic cities of Tikal and Palenque, but he heard or saw nothing of them because they were covered by jungle and almost nobody was living in the vicinity.

How did such a huge population of millions of people disappear? We asked ourselves that same question about the disappearance of Chaco Canyon's (admittedly smaller) Anasazi population in Chapter 4. By analogy with the cases of the Anasazi and of subsequent Pueblo Indian societies during droughts in the U.S. Southwest, we infer that some people from the southern Maya lowlands survived by fleeing to areas of the northern Yucatán endowed with cenotes or wells, where a rapid population increase took place around the time of the Maya collapse. But there is no sign of all those millions of southern lowland inhabitants surviving to be accommodated as immigrants in the north, just as there is no sign of thousands of Anasazi refugees being received as immigrants into surviving pueblos. As in the U.S. Southwest during droughts, some of that Maya population decrease surely involved people dying of starvation or thirst, or killing each other in struggles over increasingly scarce resources. The other part of the decrease may reflect a slower decrease in the birthrate or child survival rate over the course of many decades. That is, depopulation probably involved both a higher death rate and a lower birth rate.

In the Maya area as elsewhere, the past is a lesson for the present. From the time of Spanish arrival, the Central Petén's population declined further to about 3,000 in A.D. 1714, as a result of deaths from diseases and other causes associated with Spanish occupation. By the 1960s, the Central Petén's population had risen back only to 25,000, still less than 1% of what it had been at the Classic Maya peak. Thereafter, however, immigrants flooded into the Central Petén, building up its population to about 300,000 in the 1980s, and ushering in a new era of deforestation and erosion. Today, half of the Petén is once again deforested and ecologically degraded. One-quarter of all the forests of Honduras were destroyed between 1964 and 1989.

To summarize the Classic Maya collapse, we can tentatively identify five strands. I acknowledge, however, that Maya archaeologists still disagree vigorously among themselves—in part, because the different strands evidently varied in importance among different parts of the Maya realm; because detailed archaeological studies are available for only some Maya sites; and because it remains puzzling why most of the Maya heartland remained nearly empty of population and failed to recover after the collapse and after regrowth of forests.

With those caveats, it appears to me that one strand consisted of population growth outstripping available resources: a dilemma similar to the one foreseen by Thomas Malthus in 1798 and being played out today in Rwanda (Chapter 10), Haiti (Chapter 11), and elsewhere. As the archaeologist David Webster succinctly puts it, "Too many farmers grew too many crops on too much of the landscape." Compounding that mismatch between population and resources was the second strand: the effects of deforestation and hillside erosion, which caused a decrease in the amount of useable farmland at a time when more rather than less farmland was needed, and possibly exacerbated by an anthropogenic drought resulting from deforestation, by soil nutrient depletion and other soil problems, and by the struggle to prevent bracken ferns from overrunning the fields.

The third strand consisted of increased fighting, as more and more people fought over fewer resources. Maya warfare, already endemic, peaked just before the collapse. That is not surprising when one reflects that at least 5,000,000 people, perhaps many more, were crammed into an area smaller than the state of Colorado (104,000 square miles). That warfare would have decreased further the amount of land available for agriculture, by creating no-man's lands between principalities where it was now unsafe to farm. Bringing matters to a head was the strand of climate change. The drought at the time of the Classic collapse was not the first drought that the Maya had lived through, but it was the most severe. At the time of previous droughts, there were still uninhabited parts of the Maya landscape, and people at a site affected by drought could save themselves by moving to another site. However, by the time of the Classic collapse the landscape was now full, there was no useful unoccupied land in the vicinity on which to begin anew, and the whole population could not be accommodated in the few areas that continued to have reliable water supplies.

As our fifth strand, we have to wonder why the kings and nobles failed to recognize and solve these seemingly obvious problems undermining their society. Their attention was evidently focused on their short-term concerns of enriching themselves, waging wars, erecting monuments, competing with each other, and extracting enough food from the peasants to support all those activities. Like most leaders throughout human history, the Maya kings and nobles did not heed long-term problems, insofar as they perceived them. We shall return to this theme in Chapter 14.

Finally, while we still have some other past societies to consider in this book before we switch our attention to the modern world, we must already be struck by some parallels between the Maya and the past societies discussed in Chapters 2–4. As on Easter Island, Mangareva, and among the Anasazi, Maya environmental and population problems led to increasing warfare and civil strife. As on Easter Island and at Chaco Canyon, Maya peak population numbers were followed swiftly by political and social collapse. Paralleling the eventual extension of agriculture from Easter Island's coastal lowlands to its uplands, and from the Mimbres floodplain to the hills, Copán's inhabitants also expanded from the floodplain to the more fragile hill slopes, leaving them with a larger population to feed when the agricultural boom in the hills went bust. Like Easter Island chiefs erecting ever larger statues, eventually crowned by pukao, and like Anasazi elite treating themselves to necklaces of 2,000 turquoise beads, Maya kings sought to outdo each other with more and more impressive temples, covered with thicker and thicker plaster—reminiscent in turn of the extravagant conspicuous consumption by modern American CEOs. The passivity of Easter chiefs and Maya kings in the face of the real big threats to their societies completes our list of disquieting parallels.

CHAPTER 6

The Viking Prelude and Fugues

Experiments in the Atlantic ■ The Viking explosion ■ Autocatalysis ■
Viking agriculture ■ Iron ■ Viking chiefs ■ Viking religion ■
Orkneys, Shetlands, Faeroes ■ Iceland's environment ■
Iceland's history ■ Iceland in context ■ Vinland ■

W hen moviegoers of my generation hear the word "Vikings," we picture chieftain Kirk Douglas, star of the unforgettable 1958 epic film *The Vikings,* clad in his nail-studded leather shirt as he leads his bearded barbarians on voyages of raiding, raping, and killing. Nearly half a century after watching that film on a date with a college girlfriend, I can still replay in my imagination the opening scene in which Viking warriors batter down a castle gate while its unsuspecting occupants carouse inside, the occupants scream as the Vikings burst in and slaughter them, and Kirk Douglas begs his beautiful captive Janet Leigh to heighten his pleasure by vainly attempting to resist him. There is much truth to those gory images: the Vikings did indeed terrorize medieval Europe for several centuries. In their own language (Old Norse), even the word *víkingar* meant "raiders."

But other parts of the Viking story are equally romantic and more relevant to this book. Besides being feared pirates, the Vikings were farmers, traders, colonizers, and the first European explorers of the North Atlantic. The settlements that they founded met very different fates. Viking settlers of Continental Europe and the British Isles eventually merged with local populations and played a role in forming several nation-states, notably Russia, England, and France. The Vinland colony, representing Europeans' first attempt to settle North America, was quickly abandoned; the Greenland colony, for 450 years the most remote outpost of European society, finally vanished; the Iceland colony struggled for many centuries through poverty and political difficulties, to emerge in recent times as one of the world's most affluent societies; and the Orkney, Shetland, and Faeroe colonies survived with little difficulty. All of those Viking colonies were derived from the same ancestral society: their differing fates were transparently related to the different environments in which the colonists found themselves.

Thus, the Viking expansion westwards across the North Atlantic offers us an instructive natural experiment, just as does the Polynesian expansion eastwards across the Pacific (map, pp. 182–183). Nested within this large natural experiment, Greenland offers us a smaller one: the Vikings met another people there, the Inuit, whose solutions to Greenland's environmental problems were very different from those of the Vikings. When that smaller experiment ended five centuries later, Greenland's Vikings had all perished, leaving Greenland uncontested in the hands of the Inuit. The tragedy of the Greenland Norse (Greenland Scandinavians) thus carries a hopeful message: even in difficult environments, collapses of human societies are not inevitable; it depends on how people respond.

The environmentally triggered collapse of Viking Greenland and the struggles of Iceland have parallels with the environmentally triggered collapses of Easter Island, Mangareva, the Anasazi, the Maya, and many other pre-industrial societies. However, we enjoy advantages in understanding Greenland's collapse and Iceland's troubles. For Greenland's and especially Iceland's history, we possess contemporary written accounts from those societies as well as from their trade partners—accounts that are frustratingly fragmentary, but still much better than our complete lack of written eyewitness records for those other pre-industrial societies. The Anasazi died or scattered, and the society of the few surviving Easter Islanders became transformed by outsiders, but most modern Icelanders are still the direct descendants of the Viking men and their Celtic wives who were Iceland's first settlers. In particular, medieval European Christian societies, such as those of Iceland and Norse Greenland, that evolved directly into modern European Christian societies. Hence we know what the church ruins, preserved art, and archaeologically excavated tools meant, whereas much guesswork is required to interpret archaeological remains of those other societies. For instance, when I stood within an opening in the west wall of the well-preserved stone building erected around A.D. 1300 at Hvalsey in Greenland, I knew by comparison with Christian churches elsewhere that this building too was a Christian church, that this particular one was an almost exact replica of a church at Eidfjord in Norway, and that the opening in the west wall was the main entrance as in other Christian churches (Plate 15). In contrast, we can't hope to understand the significance of Easter Island's stone statues in such detail.

The fates of Viking Iceland and Greenland tell an even more complex, hence more richly instructive, story than do the fates of Easter Island, Mangareva's neighbors, the Anasazi, and the Maya. All five sets of factors that I discussed in the Prologue played a role. The Vikings did damage their environment, they did suffer from climate changes, and their own responses and cultural values did affect the outcome. The first and third of those three factors also operated in the histories of Easter and Mangareva's neighbors, and all three operated for the Anasazi and the Maya, but in addition trade with friendly outsiders played an essential role in the histories of Iceland and Greenland as of Mangareva's neighbors and the Anasazi, although not in Easter Island and Maya history. Finally, among these societies, only in Viking Greenland did hostile outsiders (the Inuit) intervene crucially. Thus, if the histories of Easter Island and Mangareva's neighbors are fugues weaving together two and three themes respectively, as do some fugues by Johann Sebastian Bach, Iceland's troubles are a quadruple fugue, like the mighty unfinished fugue with which the dying Bach meant to complete his last great composition, the *Art of the Fugue.* Only Greenland's demise gives us what Bach himself never attempted, a full quintuple fugue. For all these reasons, Viking societies will be presented in this chapter and the next two as the most detailed example in this book: the second and larger of the two sheep inside our boa constrictor.

The prelude to the Iceland and Greenland fugues was the Viking explosion that burst upon medieval Europe after A.D. 793, from Ireland and the Baltic to the Mediterranean and Constantinople. Recall that all the basic elements of medieval European civilization arose over the previous 10,000 years in or near the Fertile Crescent, that crescent-shaped area of Southwest Asia from Jordan north to southeastern Turkey and then east to Iran. From that region came the world's first crops and domestic animals and wheeled transport, the mastery of copper and then of bronze and iron, and the rise of towns and cities, chiefdoms and kingdoms, and organized religions. All of those elements gradually spread to and transformed Europe from southeast to northwest, beginning with the arrival of agriculture in Greece from Anatolia around 7000 B.C. Scandinavia, the corner of Europe farthest from the Fertile Crescent, was the last part of Europe to be so transformed, being reached by agriculture only around 2500 B.C. It was also the corner farthest from the influence of Roman civilization: unlike the area of modern Germany, Roman traders never reached it, nor did it share any boundary with the Roman Empire. Hence, until the Middle Ages, Scandinavia remained Europe's backwater.

Yet Scandinavia possessed two sets of natural advantages awaiting exploitation: the furs of northern forest animals, seal skins, and beeswax prized as luxury imports in the rest of Europe; and (in Norway as in Greece) a highly indented coastline, making travel by sea potentially faster than travel by land, and offering rewards to those who could develop seafaring techniques. Until the Middle Ages, Scandinavians had only oar-propelled rowboats without sails. Sailboat technology from the Mediterranean finally reached Scandinavia around A.D. 600, at a time when climatic warming and the arrival of improved plows happened to be stimulating food production and a human population explosion in Scandinavia. Because most of Norway is steep and mountainous, only 3% of its land area can be used for agriculture, and that arable land was coming under increasing population pressure by A.D. 700, especially in western Norway. With decreasing opportunities to establish new farms back at home, Scandinavia's growing population began expanding overseas. Upon the arrival of sails, Scandinavians quickly developed fast, shallow-draft, highly maneuverable, sailed-and-rowed ships that were ideal for carrying their luxury exports to eager buyers in Europe and Britain. Those ships let them cross the ocean but then also pull up on any shallow beach or row far up rivers, without being confined to the few deepwater harbors.

But for medieval Scandinavians, as for other seafarers throughout history, trading paved the way for raiding. Once some Scandinavian traders had discovered sea routes to rich peoples who could pay for furs with silver and gold, ambitious younger brothers of those traders realized that they could acquire that same silver and gold without paying for it. Those ships used for trade could also be sailed and rowed over those same sea routes to arrive by surprise at coastal and riverside towns, including ones far inland on rivers. Scandinavians became Vikings, i.e., raiders. Viking ships and sailors were fast enough compared to those elsewhere in Europe that they could escape before being overtaken by the locals' slower ships, and Europeans never attempted counterraids on the Viking homelands to destroy their bases. The lands that are now Norway and Sweden were then not yet united under single kings, but were still fragmented among chiefs or pettykings eager to compete for overseas booty with which to attract and reward followers. Chiefs who lost in the struggle against other chiefs at home were especially motivated to try their luck overseas.

The Viking raids began abruptly on June 8, A.D. 793, with an attack on the rich but defenseless monastery of Lindisfarne Island off the northeast English coast. Thereafter, the raids continued each summer, when the seas were calmer and more conducive to sailing, until after some years the

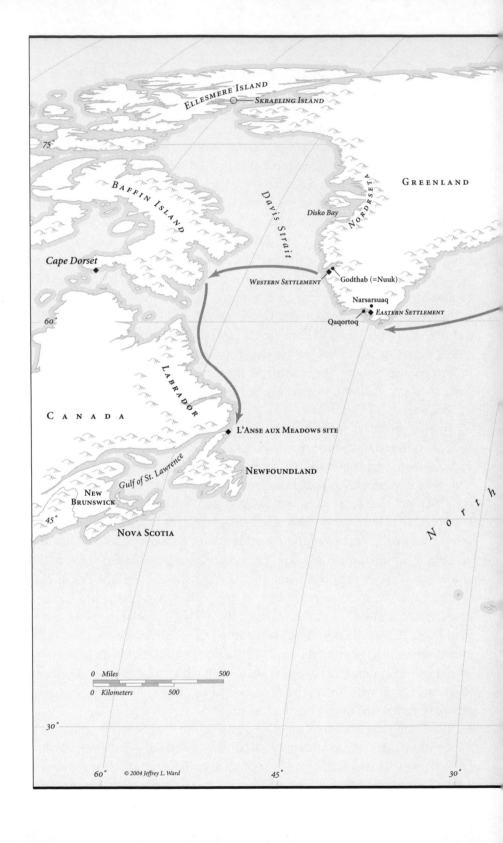

ELLESMERE ISLAND — SKRAELING ISLAND

75°

BAFFIN ISLAND

GREENLAND

Davis Strait

NORDRSETA

Disko Bay

Cape Dorset

WESTERN SETTLEMENT

Godthab (=Nuuk)

60°

Narsarsuaq

EASTERN SETTLEMENT

Qaqortoq

LABRADOR

CANADA

L'ANSE AUX MEADOWS SITE

NEWFOUNDLAND

Gulf of St. Lawrence

NEW
BRUNSWICK

45°

North

NOVA SCOTIA

| 0   Miles | | 500 |
| 0   Kilometers | 500 | |

30°

60°   © 2004 Jeffrey L. Ward   45°   30°

THE VIKING EXPANSION

ICELAND

FAEROE
ISLANDS

Trondheim

SHETLAND
ISLANDS

Bergen

NORWAY

VIKING EXPANSION

ORKNEY
ISLANDS

SWEDEN

LINDISFARNE
ISLAND

DENMARK

Baltic Sea

A t l a n t i c

IRELAND

BRITAIN

BRITTANY

NORMANDY

Seine R.

EUROPE

Loire R.

M e d i t e r r a n e a n S e a

AFRICA

15°

0°

15°

Vikings stopped bothering to return home in the autumn but instead made winter settlements on the targeted coast so that they could begin raiding earlier in the next spring. From those beginnings arose a flexible mixed strategy of alternative methods to acquire wealth, depending on the relative strengths of the Viking fleets and the targeted peoples. As the strength or number of Vikings relative to locals increased, the methods progressed from peaceful trading, through extorting tribute in return for a promise not to raid, to plundering and retreating, and culminated in conquest and the establishment of overseas Viking states.

Vikings from different parts of Scandinavia went raiding in different directions. Those from the area of modern Sweden, termed Varangians, sailed east into the Baltic Sea, navigated up rivers flowing from Russia into the Baltic, continued south to reach the heads of the Volga and other rivers flowing into the Black Sea and Caspian Sea, traded with the rich Byzantine Empire, and founded the principality of Kiev that became the forerunner of the modern Russian state. Vikings from modern Denmark sailed west to the coast of northwest Europe and the east coast of England, found their way up the Rhine and Loire rivers, settled at their mouths and in Normandy and Brittany, established the Danelaw state in eastern England and the Duchy of Normandy in France, and rounded the Atlantic coast of Spain to enter the Mediterranean at the Straits of Gibraltar and raid Italy. Vikings from modern Norway sailed to Ireland and the north and west coast of Britain and set up a major trading center at Dublin. In each area of Europe the Vikings settled, intermarried, and gradually became assimilated into the local population, with the result that Scandinavian languages and distinct Scandinavian settlements eventually disappeared outside of Scandinavia. Swedish Vikings merged into the Russian population, Danish Vikings into the English population, while the Vikings who settled in Normandy eventually abandoned their Norse language and began speaking French. In that process of assimilation, Scandinavian words as well as genes were absorbed. For instance, the modern English language owes "awkward," "die," "egg," "skirt," and dozens of other everyday words to the Scandinavian invaders.

In the course of these voyages to inhabited European lands, many Viking ships were blown off-course into the North Atlantic Ocean, which at those times of warm climate was free of the sea ice that later became a barrier to ship navigation, contributing to the fate of the Norse Greenland colony and of the *Titanic*. Those off-course ships thereby discovered and settled other lands previously unknown either to Europeans or to any peoples: the uninhabited Faeroe Islands some time after A.D. 800 and Iceland around 870;

around A.D. 980 Greenland, at that time occupied only in the far north by Native American predecessors of the Inuit known as the Dorset people; and in A.D. 1000 Vinland, an exploration zone encompassing Newfoundland, the Gulf of St. Lawrence, and possibly some other coastal areas of north-eastern North America teeming with Native Americans whose presence forced the Vikings to depart after only a decade.

The Viking raids on Europe declined as their European targets gradually came to expect them and to defend themselves, as the power of the English and French kings and the German emperor grew, and as the rising power of the Norwegian king began to harness his uncontrolled hotbed of plundering chiefs and to channel their efforts into those of a respectable trading state. On the continent, the Franks drove the Vikings from the River Seine in A.D. 857, won a major victory at the Battle of Louvain in modern Belgium in 891, and expelled them from Brittany in 939. In the British Isles the Vikings were thrown out of Dublin in A.D. 902, and their Danelaw kingdom in England disintegrated in 954, although it was then reconstituted by further raids between 980 and 1016. The year 1066, famous for the Battle of Hastings at which William the Conqueror (William of Normandy) led French-speaking descendants of former Viking raiders to conquer England, can also be taken to mark the end of the Viking raids. The reason why William was able to defeat the English king Harold at Hastings on England's southeast coast on October 14 was that Harold and his soldiers were exhausted. They had marched 220 miles south in less than three weeks after defeating the last Viking invading army and killing their king at Stamford Bridge in central England on September 25. Thereafter, the Scandinavian kingdoms evolved into normal states trading with other European states and only occasionally indulging in wars, rather than constantly raiding. Medieval Norway became known not for its feared raiders but for its exports of dried codfish.

In light of this history that I have related, how can we explain why the Vikings left their homelands to risk their lives in battle or in such difficult environments as that of Greenland? After millennia of their remaining in Scandinavia and leaving the rest of Europe alone, why did their expansion build up so quickly to a peak after 793, and then grind to a complete halt less than three centuries later? With any historical expansion, one can ask whether it was triggered by "push" (population pressure and lack of opportunities at home), "pull" (good opportunities and empty areas to colonize overseas), or both. Many expansion waves have been driven by a combination of push and pull, and that was also true of the Vikings: they were pushed by population growth and consolidation of royal power at home, and pulled by uninhabited new lands to settle and inhabited but defenseless rich lands to plunder overseas. Similarly, European immigration to North America reached its peak in the 1800s and early 1900s through a combination of push and pull: population growth, famines, and political oppression in Europe pushed immigrants from their homelands, while the availability of almost unlimited fertile farmland and economic opportunities in the United States and Canada pulled them.

As for why the sum of push/pull forces switched so abruptly from unattractive to attractive after A.D. 793, and then subsided so quickly towards 1066, the Viking expansion is a good example of what is termed an *autocatalytic process*. In chemistry the term *catalysis* means the speeding-up of a chemical reaction by an added ingredient, such as an enzyme. Some chemical reactions produce a product that also acts as a catalyst, so that the speed of the reaction starts from nothing and then runs away as some product is formed, catalyzing and driving the reaction faster and producing more product which drives the reaction still faster. Such a chain reaction is termed *autocatalytic,* the prime example being the explosion of an atomic bomb when neutrons in a critical mass of uranium split uranium nuclei to release energy plus more neutrons, which split still more nuclei.

Similarly, in an autocatalytic expansion of a human population, some initial advantages that a people gains (such as technological advantages) bring them profits or discoveries, which in turn stimulate more people to seek profits and discoveries, which result in even more profits and discoveries stimulating even more people to set out, until that people has filled up all the areas available to them with those advantages, at which point the autocatalytic expansion ceases to catalyze itself and runs out of steam. Two specific events set off the Viking chain reaction: the A.D. 793 raid on Lindisfarne Monastery, yielding a rich haul of booty that in the following year stimulated raids yielding more booty; and the discovery of the unpopulated Faeroe Islands suitable for raising sheep, leading to the discovery of larger and more distant Iceland and then of still larger and more distant Greenland. Vikings returning home with booty or with reports of islands ripe for settlement fired the imagination of more Vikings to set out in search of more booty and more empty islands. Other examples of autocatalytic expansions besides the Viking expansion include the expansion of ancestral Polynesians eastwards over the Pacific Ocean beginning around 1200 B.C., and of Portuguese and Spaniards over the world beginning in the 1400s and especially with Columbus's "discovery" of the New World in 1492.

Like those Polynesian and Portuguese/Spanish expansions, the Viking expansion began to fizzle out when all areas readily accessible to their ships had already been raided or colonized, and when Vikings returning home ceased to bring stories of uninhabited or easily raided lands overseas. Just as two specific events set off the Viking chain reaction, two other events symbolize what throttled it. One was the Battle of Stamford Bridge in 1066, capping a long series of Viking defeats and demonstrating the futility of further raids. The other was the forced abandonment of the Vikings' most remote colony of Vinland around A.D. 1000, after only a decade. The two preserved Norse sagas describing Vinland say explicitly that it was abandoned because of fighting with a dense population of Native Americans far too numerous to be defeated by the few Vikings able to cross the Atlantic in ships of those times. With the Faeroes, Iceland, and Greenland already full of Viking settlers, Vinland impossibly dangerous, and no more discoveries of uninhabited Atlantic islands being made, the Vikings got the point that there were no longer any rewards to greet pioneers risking their lives in the stormy North Atlantic.

When immigrants from overseas colonize a new homeland, the lifestyle that they establish usually incorporates features of the lifestyle that they had practiced in their land of origin—a "cultural capital" of knowledge, beliefs, subsistence methods, and social organization accumulated in their homeland. That is especially the case when, as true of the Vikings, they occupy a land that is originally either uninhabited, or else inhabited by people with whom the colonists have little contact. Even in the United States today, where new immigrants must deal with a vastly more numerous established American population, each immigrant group still retains many of its own distinctive characteristics. For instance, within my city of Los Angeles there are big differences between the cultural values, educational levels, jobs, and wealth of recent immigrant groups such as Vietnamese, Iranians, Mexicans, and Ethiopians. Different groups here have adapted with different ease to American society, depending in part on the lifestyle that they brought with them.

In the case of the Vikings, too, the societies that they created on the North Atlantic islands were modeled on the continental Viking societies that the immigrants had left behind. That legacy of cultural history was especially important in the areas of agriculture, iron production, class structure, and religion.

While we think of Vikings as raiders and seafarers, they thought of themselves as farmers. The particular animals and crops that grew well in southern Norway became an important consideration in overseas Viking history, not only because those were the animal and plant species available for Viking colonists to carry with them to Iceland and Greenland, but also because those species were involved in the Vikings' social values. Different foods and lifestyles have different status among different peoples: for instance, cattle ranked high but goats ranked low in the values of ranchers in the western United States. Problems arise when the agricultural practices of immigrants in their land of origin prove ill-matched to their new homeland. Australians, for example, are struggling today with the question of whether the sheep that they brought with them from Britain have really done more harm than good in Australian environments. As we shall see, a similar mismatch between what was suitable in old and new landscapes had heavy consequences for the Greenland Norse.

Livestock grew better than crops in Norway's cool climate. The livestock were the same five species that had provided the basis of Fertile Crescent and European food production for thousands of years: cows, sheep, goats, pigs, and horses. Of those species, the ones considered of highest status by Vikings were pigs bred for meat, cows for milk products such as cheese, and horses used for transport and prestige. In Old Norse sagas, pork was the meat on which warriors of the Norse war god Odin feasted daily in Valhalla after their deaths. Much lower in prestige, but still useful economically, were sheep and goats, kept more for milk products and wool or hair than for meat.

Counts of bones in an archaeologically excavated garbage heap at a 9th-century chieftain's farm in southern Norway revealed the relative numbers of different animal species that the chieftain's household consumed. Nearly half of all livestock bones in the midden were of cows, and one-third were of the prized pigs, while only one-fifth belonged to sheep and goats. Presumably an ambitious Viking chief setting up a farm overseas would have aspired to that same mix of species. Indeed, a similar mix is found in garbage heaps from the earliest Viking farms in Greenland and Iceland. However, the bone proportions differed on later farms there, because some of those species proved less well adapted than others to Greenland and Iceland conditions: cow numbers decreased with time, and pigs almost vanished, but the numbers of sheep and goats increased.

The farther north that one lives in Norway, the more essential it becomes in the winter to bring livestock indoors into stalls and to provide them with food there, instead of leaving them outdoors to forage for themselves. Hence those heroic Viking warriors actually had to spend much of their time during the summer and fall at the homely tasks of cutting, drying, and gathering hay for winter livestock feed, rather than fighting the battles for which they were more famous.

In areas where the climate was mild enough to permit gardening, Vikings also grew cold-tolerant crops, especially barley. Other crops less important than barley (because they are less hardy) were the cereals oats, wheat, and rye; the vegetables cabbage, onions, peas, and beans; flax, to make linen cloth; and hops, to brew beer. At sites progressively farther north in Norway, crops receded in importance compared to livestock. Wild meat was a major supplement to domestic livestock as a source of protein—especially fish, which account for half or more of the animal bones in Norwegian Viking middens. Hunted animals included seals and other marine mammals, reindeer and moose and small land mammals, seabirds taken on their breeding colonies, and ducks and other waterfowl.

Iron implements discovered at Viking sites by archaeologists tell us that Vikings used iron for many purposes: for heavy agricultural tools such as plows, shovels, axes, and sickles; small household tools, including knives, scissors, and sewing needles; nails, rivets, and other construction hardware; and, of course, military tools, especially swords, spears, battle-axes, and armor. The remains of slag heaps and charcoal-producing pits at iron-processing sites let us reconstruct how Vikings obtained their iron. It was not mined on an industrial scale at centralized factories, but at small-scale mom-and-pop operations on each individual farm. The starting material was so-called bog iron widespread in Scandinavia: i.e., iron oxide that has become dissolved in water and then precipitated by acidic conditions or bacteria in bogs and lake sediments. Whereas modern iron-mining companies select ores containing between 30 and 95% iron oxide, Viking smiths accepted far poorer ores, with as little as 1% iron oxide. Once such an "iron-rich" sediment had been identified, the ore was dried, heated to melting temperature in a furnace in order to separate the iron from impurities (the slag), hammered to remove more impurities, and then forged into the desired shape.

Burning wood itself does not yield a temperature high enough for working with iron. Instead, the wood must first be burned to form charcoal, which does sustain a sufficiently hot fire. Measurements in several countries show that it takes on the average about four pounds of wood to make one pound of charcoal. Because of that requirement, plus the low iron content of bog iron, Viking iron extraction and tool production and even the repair of iron tools consumed enormous quantities of wood, which became a limiting factor in the history of Viking Greenland, where trees were in short supply.

As for the social system that Vikings brought overseas with them from the Scandinavian mainland, it was hierarchical, with classes ranging at the lowest level from slaves captured in raids, through free men, up to chiefs. Large unified kingdoms (as opposed to small local chiefdoms under chiefs who might assume a title of "king") were just emerging in Scandinavia during the Viking expansion, and overseas Viking settlers eventually had to deal with kings of Norway and (later) of Denmark. However, the settlers had emigrated in part to escape the emerging power of would-be Norwegian kings, so that neither Iceland nor Greenland societies ever developed kings of their own. Instead, the power there remained in the hands of a military aristocracy of chiefs. Only they could afford their own boat and a full set of livestock, including the prized and hard-to-maintain cows as well as the less esteemed low-maintenance sheep and goats. The chief's dependents, retainers, and supporters included slaves, free laborers, tenant farmers, and independent free farmers.

Chiefs constantly competed with one another both by peaceful means and by war. The peaceful competition involved chiefs seeking to outdo each other in giving gifts and holding feasts, so as to gain prestige, reward followers, and attract allies. Chiefs accumulated the necessary wealth through trading, raiding, and the production of their own farms. But Viking society was also a violent one, in which chiefs and their retainers fought each other at home as well as fighting other peoples overseas. The losers in those internecine struggles were the ones who had the most to gain by trying their luck overseas. For instance, in the A.D. 980s, when an Icelander named Erik the Red was defeated and exiled, he explored Greenland and led a band of followers to settle the best farm sites there.

Key decisions of Viking society were made by the chiefs, who were motivated to increase their own prestige, even in cases where that might conflict with the good of the current society as a whole and of the next generation.

We already encountered those same conflicts of interest for Easter Island chiefs and Maya kings (Chapters 2 and 5), and they also had heavy consequences for the fate of Greenland Norse society (Chapter 8).

When the Vikings began their overseas expansion in the A.D. 800s, they still were "pagans" worshipping gods traditional in Germanic religion, such as the fertility god Frey, the sky god Thor, and the war god Odin. What most horrified European societies targeted by Viking raiders was that Vikings were not Christians and did not observe the taboos of a Christian society. Quite the opposite: they seemed to take sadistic pleasure in targeting churches and monasteries for attack. For instance, when in A.D. 843 a large Viking fleet went plundering up the Loire River in France, the raiders began by capturing the cathedral of Nantes at the river's mouth and killing the bishop and all the priests. Actually, though, the Vikings had no sadistic special fondness for plundering churches, nor any prejudice against secular sources of booty. While the undefended wealth of churches and monasteries was an obvious source of easy rich pickings, the Vikings were also pleased to attack rich trading centers whenever the opportunity presented itself.

Once established overseas in Christian lands, Vikings were quite prepared to intermarry and adapt to local customs, and that included embracing Christianity. Conversions of Vikings overseas contributed to the emergence of Christianity at home in Scandinavia, as overseas Vikings returning on visits brought information about the new religion, and as chiefs and kings in Scandinavia began to recognize the political advantages that Christianity could bring them. Some Scandinavian chiefs adopted Christianity informally, even before their kings did. Decisive events in Christianity's establishment in Scandinavia were the "official" conversion of Denmark under its king Harald Bluetooth around A.D. 960, of Norway beginning around A.D. 995, and of Sweden during the following century.

When Norway began to convert, the overseas Viking colonies of Orkney, Shetland, Faeroe, Iceland, and Greenland followed suit. That was partly because the colonies had few ships of their own, depended on Norwegian shipping for trade, and had to recognize the impossibility of remaining pagan after Norway became Christian. For instance, when Norway's King Olaf I converted, he banned pagan Icelanders from trading with Norway, captured Icelanders visiting Norway (including relatives of leading Iceland pagans), and threatened to mutilate or kill those hostages unless Iceland renounced paganism. At the meeting of Iceland's national assembly in the summer of A.D. 999, Icelanders accepted the inevitable and declared themselves Christian. Around that same year, Leif Eriksson, the son of that Erik the Red who founded the Greenland colony, supposedly introduced Christianity to Greenland.

The Christian churches that were created in Iceland and Greenland after A.D. 1000 were not independent entities owning their own land and buildings, as are modern churches. Instead, they were built and owned by a leading local farmer/chief on his own land, and the farmer was entitled to a share of the taxes collected as tithes by that church from other local people. It was as if the chief negotiated a franchise agreement with McDonald's, under which he was granted a local monopoly by McDonald's, erected a church building and supplied merchandise according to uniform McDonald's standards, and kept a part of the proceeds for himself while sending the rest of the proceeds to central management—in this case, the pope in Rome via the archbishop in Nidaros (modern Trondheim). Naturally, the Catholic Church struggled to make its churches independent of the farmers/owners. In 1297 the Church finally succeeded in forcing Iceland church owners to transfer ownership of many church farms to the bishop. No records have been preserved to show whether something similar also happened in Greenland, but Greenland's acceptance (at least nominally) of Norwegian rule in 1261 probably put some pressure on Greenland church owners. We do know that in 1341 the bishop of Bergen sent to Greenland an overseer named Ivar Bardarson, who eventually returned to Norway with a detailed list and description of all Greenland churches, suggesting that the bishopric was trying to tighten its grip on its Greenland "franchises" as it did in Iceland.

The conversion to Christianity constituted a dramatic cultural break for the Viking overseas colonies. Christianity's claims of exclusivity, as the sole true religion, meant abandoning pagan traditions. Art and architecture became Christian, based on continental models. Overseas Vikings built big churches and even cathedrals equal in size to those of much more populous mainland Scandinavia, and thus huge in relation to the size of the much smaller overseas populations supporting them. The colonies took Christianity seriously enough that they paid tithes to Rome: we have records of the crusade tithe that the Greenland bishop sent to the pope in 1282 (paid in walrus tusks and polar bear hides rather than in money), and also an official papal receipt in 1327 acknowledging the delivery of the six-years' tithe from Greenland. The Church became a major vehicle for introducing the latest European ideas to Greenland, especially because every bishop appointed to Greenland was a mainland Scandinavian rather than a native Greenlander.

Perhaps the most important consequence of the colonists' conversion to Christianity involved how they viewed themselves. The outcome reminds me of how Australians, long after the founding of Britain's Australian colonies in 1788, continued to think of themselves not as an Asian and Pacific people but as overseas British, still prepared to die in 1915 at far-off Gallipoli fighting with the British against Turks irrelevant to Australia's national interests. In the same way, Viking colonists on the North Atlantic islands thought of themselves as European Christians. They kept in step with mainland changes in church architecture, burial customs, and units of measurement. That shared identity enabled a few thousand Greenlanders to cooperate with each other, withstand hardships, and maintain their existence in a harsh environment for four centuries. As we shall see, it also prevented them from learning from the Inuit, and from modifying their identity in ways that might have permitted them to survive beyond four centuries.

The six Viking colonies on North Atlantic islands constitute six parallel experiments in establishing societies derived from the same ancestral source. As I mentioned at the beginning of this chapter, those six experiments resulted in different outcomes: the Orkney, Shetland, and Faeroe colonies have continued to exist for more than a thousand years without their survival ever being in serious doubt; the Iceland colony also persisted but had to overcome poverty and serious political difficulties; the Greenland Norse died out after about 450 years; and the Vinland colony was abandoned within the first decade. Those differing outcomes are clearly related to environmental differences among the colonies. The four main environmental variables responsible for the different outcomes appear to be: ocean distances or sailing times by ship from Norway and Britain; resistance offered by non-Viking inhabitants, if there were any; suitability for agriculture, depending especially on latitude and local climate; and environmental fragility, especially susceptibility to soil erosion and deforestation.

With only six experimental outcomes but four variables that might explain those outcomes, we cannot hope to proceed in our search for explanations as we did in the Pacific, where we had 81 outcomes (81 islands) compared to only nine explanatory variables. For statistical correlational analysis to have any chance of succeeding, one needs many more separate experimental outcomes than there are variables to be tested. Hence, in the

Pacific, with so many islands available, statistical analysis alone sufficed to determine the relative importance of those independent variables. In the North Atlantic, there are not nearly enough separate natural experiments to achieve that aim. A statistician, presented only with that information, would declare the Viking problem to be insoluble. This will be a frequent dilemma for historians trying to apply the comparative method to problems of human history: apparently too many potentially independent variables, and far too few separate outcomes to establish those variables' importance statistically.

But historians know much more about human societies than just the initial environmental conditions and the final outcomes: they also have huge quantities of information about the sequence of steps connecting initial conditions to outcomes. Specifically, Viking scholars can test the importance of ocean sailing times by counting recorded numbers of ship sailings and reported cargos of the ships; they can test effects of indigenous resistance by historical accounts of fighting between Viking invaders and the locals; they can test suitability for agriculture by records of what plant and livestock species were actually grown; and they can test environmental fragility by historical signs of deforestation and soil erosion (such as pollen counts and fossilized pieces of plants), and by identification of wood and other building materials. Drawing on this knowledge of intervening steps as well as of outcomes, let us now briefly examine five of the six North Atlantic colonies in sequence of increasing isolation and decreasing wealth: Orkney, Shetland, Faeroe, Iceland, and Vinland. The next two chapters will discuss in detail the fate of Viking Greenland.

The Orkneys are an island archipelago just off the northern tip of Britain, wrapped around the large sheltered harbor of Scapa Flow that served as the main base for the British navy in both world wars. From John O'Groats, the northernmost point of the Scottish mainland, to the nearest Orkney Island is only 11 miles, and from the Orkneys to Norway barely a 24-hour sail in Viking ships. That made it easy for Norwegian Vikings to invade the Orkneys, to import whatever they needed from Norway or the British Isles, and to ship out their own exports cheaply. The Orkneys are so-called continental islands, really just a piece of the British mainland that became separated only when sea levels rose around the world with glacial melting at the end of the Ice Ages 14,000 years ago. Over that land bridge, many species of land mammals, including elk (alias red deer in Britain), otters, and hares, immigrated and provided good hunting. Viking invaders quickly subdued the indigenous population, known as the Picts.

As the southernmost of the Viking North Atlantic colonies except for Vinland, and lying in the Gulf Stream, the Orkneys enjoy a mild climate. Their fertile, heavy soils have been renewed by glaciation and are not at serious risk of erosion. Hence farming in the Orkneys was already being practiced by the Picts before the Vikings arrived, was continued under the Vikings, and remains highly productive to this day. Modern Orkney agricultural exports include beef and eggs, plus pork, cheese, and some crops.

The Vikings conquered the Orkneys around A.D. 800, proceeded to use the islands as a base for raiding the nearby British and Irish mainlands, and built up a rich, powerful society that remained for some time an independent Norse kingdom. One manifestation of the Orkney Vikings' wealth is a 17-pound cache of silver buried around A.D. 950, unmatched on any other North Atlantic island and equal in size to the largest silver caches of mainland Scandinavia. Another manifestation is St. Magnus Cathedral, erected in the 12th century and inspired by Britain's mighty Durham Cathedral. In A.D. 1472 ownership of the Orkneys passed without conquest from Norway (then subject to Denmark) to Scotland, for a trivial reason of dynastic politics (Scotland's King James demanded compensation for Denmark's failure to pay the dowry promised to accompany the Danish princess whom he married). Under Scottish rule, the Orkney islanders continued to speak a Norse dialect until the 1700s. Today, the Orkney descendants of indigenous Picts and Norse invaders remain prosperous farmers enriched by a terminal for North Sea oil.

Some of what I have just said about the Orkneys also applies to the next North Atlantic colony, the Shetland Islands. They too were originally occupied by Pict farmers, conquered by Vikings in the ninth century, ceded to Scotland in 1472, spoke Norse for some time thereafter, and have recently profited from North Sea oil. Differences are that they are slightly more remote and northerly (50 miles north of Orkney and 130 miles north of Scotland), windier, have poorer soils, and are less productive agriculturally. Raising sheep for wool has been an economic mainstay in the Shetlands as in the Orkneys, but raising cattle failed in the Shetlands and was replaced by increased emphasis on fishing.

Next in isolation after the Orkneys and Shetlands were the Faeroe Islands, 200 miles north of the Orkneys and 400 miles west of Norway. That made the Faeroes still readily accessible to Viking ships carrying settlers and trade goods, but beyond reach of earlier ships. Hence the Vikings found the Faeroes uninhabited except perhaps for a few Irish hermits, about whose existence there are vague stories but no firm archaeological evidence.

Lying 300 miles south of the Arctic Circle, at a latitude intermediate between that of the two largest towns on Norway's west coast (Bergen and Trondheim), the Faeroes enjoy a mild oceanic climate. However, their more northerly location than that of the Orkneys and Shetlands meant a shorter growing season for would-be farmers and herders. Salt spray from the ocean, blown onto all parts of the islands because of their small area, combined with strong winds to prevent the development of forests. The original vegetation consisted of nothing taller than low willows, birches, aspen, and junipers, which were quickly cleared by the first settlers and prevented from regenerating by browsing sheep. In a drier climate that would have been a recipe for soil erosion, but the Faeroes are very wet and foggy and "enjoy" rain on an average of 280 days each year, including several rain showers on most days. The settlers themselves also adopted policies to minimize erosion, such as building walls and terraces to prevent soil loss. Viking settlers in Greenland and especially in Iceland were much less successful in controlling erosion, not because they were more imprudent than Faeroe Islanders but because Iceland soils and Greenland climate made the risk of erosion greater.

Vikings settled the Faeroes during the ninth century. They managed to grow some barley but few or no other crops; even today, only about 6% of the land area of the Faeroes is devoted to growing potatoes and other vegetables. The cows and pigs prized in Norway, and even the low-status goats, were abandoned by the settlers within the first 200 years to prevent overgrazing. Instead, the Faeroe economy became focused on raising sheep to export wool, supplemented later by export of salt fish, and today of dried cod, halibut, and farmed salmon. In return for those wool and fish exports, the islanders imported from Norway and Britain the bulk necessities that were lacking or deficient in the Faeroe environment: especially, huge quantities of wood, because no construction timber was locally available except for driftwood; iron for tools, also completely lacking locally; and other stones and minerals, such as grindstones, whetstones, and soft soapstone out of which to carve kitchenware to replace pottery.

As for the Faeroes' history after settlement, the islanders converted to Christianity around A.D. 1000, i.e., around the same time as the other Viking North Atlantic colonies, and later they constructed a Gothic cathedral. The islands became a tributary to Norway in the 11th century, passed with Norway to Denmark in 1380 when Norway itself came under the Danish crown, and achieved self-government under Denmark in 1948. The 47,000 inhabitants today still speak a Faeroese language, directly derived from Old Norse and very similar to modern Icelandic; Faeroese and Icelanders can understand each other's speech and Old Norse texts.

In short, the Faeroes were spared the problems that beset Norse Iceland and Greenland: the erosion-prone soils and active volcanoes of Iceland, and the shorter growing season, drier climate, much greater sailing distances, and hostile local population of Greenland. While more isolated than the Orkneys or Shetlands, and poorer in local resources compared especially to the Orkneys, Faeroe islanders survived without difficulty by importing large quantities of necessities—an option not open to the Greenlanders.

The purpose of my first visit to Iceland was to attend a NATO-sponsored conference on restoring ecologically damaged environments. It was especially appropriate that NATO had chosen Iceland as the conference's site, because Iceland is ecologically the most heavily damaged country in Europe. Since human settlement began, most of the country's original trees and vegetation have been destroyed, and about half of the original soils have eroded into the ocean. As a result of that damage, large areas of Iceland that were green at the time that Vikings landed are now lifeless brown desert without buildings, roads, or any current signs of people. When the American space agency NASA wanted to find some place on Earth resembling the surface of the moon, so that our astronauts preparing for the first moon landing could practice in an environment similar to what they would encounter, NASA picked a formerly green area of Iceland that is now utterly barren.

The four elements that form Iceland's environment are volcanic fire, ice, water, and wind. Iceland lies in the North Atlantic Ocean about 600 miles west of Norway, on what is called the Mid-Atlantic Ridge, where the American and Eurasian continental plates collide and where volcanoes periodically rise from the ocean to build up chunks of new land, of which Iceland is the largest. On the average, at least one of Iceland's many volcanoes undergoes a major eruption every decade or two. Besides the volcanoes themselves, Iceland's hot springs and geothermal areas are so numerous that much of the country (including the entire capital of Reykjavík) heats its houses not by burning fossil fuels but just by tapping volcanic heat.

The second element in Iceland's landscape is ice, which forms and remains as ice caps on much of Iceland's interior plateau because it is at high elevation (up to 6,952 feet high), just below the Arctic Circle, and hence cold. Water falling as rain and snow reaches the ocean in glaciers, in rivers that periodically flood, and in occasional spectacular superfloods when a natural dam of lava or ice across a lake gives way, or when a volcanic eruption under an ice cap suddenly melts a lot of ice. Finally, Iceland is also a very windy place. It is the interaction between these four elements of volcanoes, cold, water, and wind that has made Iceland so susceptible to erosion.

When the first Viking settlers reached Iceland, its volcanoes and hot springs were strange sights, unlike anything known to them in Norway or the British Isles, but otherwise the landscape looked familiar and encouraging. Almost all of the plants and birds belonged to familiar European species. The lowlands were mostly covered by low birch and willow forest that was easily cleared for pastures. In those cleared locations, in natural low-lying treeless areas such as bogs, and at higher elevations above timberline the settlers found lush pasture grass, herbs, and moss ideal for raising the livestock that they had already been raising in Norway and the British Isles. The soil was fertile, in some places up to 50 feet deep. Despite the high-altitude ice caps and the location near the Arctic Circle, the nearby Gulf Stream made the climate in the lowlands mild enough in some years to grow barley in the south. The lakes, rivers, and surrounding seas teemed with fish and with never-before-hunted and hence unafraid seabirds and ducks, while equally unafraid seals and walruses lived along the coast.

But Iceland's apparent similarity to southwestern Norway and Britain was deceptive in three crucial respects. First, Iceland's more northerly location, hundreds of miles north of southwestern Norway's main farmlands, meant a cooler climate and shorter growing season, making agriculture more marginal. Eventually, as the climate became colder in the late Middle Ages, the settlers gave up on crops to become solely herders. Second, the ash that volcanic eruptions periodically ejected over wide areas poisoned fodder for livestock. Repeatedly throughout Iceland's history, such eruptions have caused animals and people to starve, the worst such disaster being the 1783 Laki eruption after which about one-fifth of the human population starved to death.

The biggest set of problems that deceived the settlers involved differences between Iceland's fragile, unfamiliar soils and Norway's and Britain's robust, familiar soils. The settlers could not appreciate those differences partly because some of them are subtle and still not well understood by professional soil scientists, but also because one of those differences was invisible at first sight and would take years to appreciate: namely, that Iceland's soils form more slowly and erode much more quickly than those of Norway and Britain. In effect, when the settlers saw Iceland's fertile and locally thick soils, they reacted with delight, as any of us would react to inheriting a bank account with a large positive balance, for which we would assume familiar interest rates and would expect the account to throw off large interest payments each year. Unfortunately, while Iceland's soils and dense woodlands were impressive to the eye—corresponding to the large balance of the bank account—that balance had accumulated very slowly (as if with low interest rates) since the end of the last Ice Age. The settlers eventually discovered that they were not living off of Iceland's ecological annual interest, but that they were drawing down its accumulated capital of soil and vegetation that had taken ten thousand years to build up, and much of which the settlers exhausted in a few decades or even within a year. Inadvertently, the settlers were not using the soil and vegetation sustainably, as resources that can persist indefinitely (like a well-managed fishery or forest) if harvested no faster than the resources can renew themselves. They were instead exploiting the soil and vegetation in the way that miners exploit oil and mineral deposits, which renew themselves only infinitely slowly and are mined until they are all gone.

What is it that makes Iceland's soils so fragile and slow to form? A major reason has to do with their origin. In Norway, northern Britain, and Greenland, which lack recently active volcanoes and were completely glaciated during the Ice Ages, heavy soils were generated either as uplifted marine clays or else by glaciers grinding the underlying rock and carrying the particles, which were later deposited as sediment when the glaciers melted. In Iceland, though, frequent eruptions of volcanoes throw clouds of fine ash into the air. That ash includes light particles that strong winds proceed to carry over much of the country, resulting in the formation of an ash layer (tephra) that can be as light as talcum powder. On that rich fertile ash, vegetation eventually grows up, covering the ash and protecting it from erosion. But when that vegetation is removed (by sheep grazing it or farmers burning it), the ash becomes exposed again, making it susceptible to erosion. Because the ash was light enough to be carried in by the wind in the first place, it is also light enough to be carried out by the wind again. In addition to that wind erosion, Iceland's locally heavy rains and frequent floods also remove the exposed ash by water erosion, especially on steep slopes.

The other reasons for the fragility of Iceland's soils have to do with the fragility of its vegetation. Growth of vegetation tends to protect soil against erosion by covering it, and by adding organic matter that cements it and increases its bulk. But vegetation grows slowly in Iceland because of its northerly location, cool climate, and short growing season. Iceland's combination of fragile soils and slow plant growth creates a positive feedback cycle to erosion: after the protective cover of vegetation is stripped off by sheep or farmers, and soil erosion has then begun, it is difficult for plants to reestablish themselves and to protect the soil again, so the erosion tends to spread.

Iceland's colonization began in earnest around the year 870 and virtually ended by the year 930, when almost all land suitable for farming had been settled or claimed. Most settlers came directly from western Norway, the remainder being Vikings who had already emigrated to the British Isles and married Celtic wives. Those settlers tried to re-create a herding economy similar to the lifestyle that they had known in Norway and the British Isles, and based on the same five barnyard animals, among which sheep eventually became by far the most numerous. Sheep milk was made into and stored as butter, cheese, and an Icelandic specialty called *skyr,* which to my taste is like a delicious thick yogurt. To make up the rest of their diet, Icelanders relied on wild game and fish, as revealed again by the patient efforts of zooarchaeologists identifying 47,000 bones in garbage heaps. The breeding walrus colonies were quickly exterminated, and the breeding seabirds became depleted, leaving hunters to shift attention to seals. Eventually, the main source of wild protein became fish—both the abundant trout, salmon, and char in lakes and rivers, and the abundant cod and haddock along the coast. Those cod and haddock were crucial in enabling Icelanders to survive the hard centuries of the Little Ice Age and in driving Iceland's economy today.

At the time that settlement of Iceland began, one-quarter of the island's area was forested. The settlers proceeded to clear the trees for pastures, and for using the trees themselves as firewood, timber, and charcoal. About 80% of that original woodland was cleared within the first few decades, and 96% as of modern times, thus leaving only 1% of Iceland's area still forested (Plate 16). Big chunks of scorched wood found in the earliest archaeological sites show that—incredible as it seems today—much of the wood from that land clearance was wasted or just burned, until Icelanders realized that they would be short of wood for the indefinite future. Once the original trees had been removed, grazing by sheep, and rooting by the pigs initially present, prevented seedlings from regenerating. As one drives across Iceland today, it is striking to notice how the occasional clumps of trees still standing are mostly ones enclosed by fences to protect them from sheep.

Iceland's highlands above tree line, supporting natural grassland on fertile shallow soil, were particularly attractive to the settlers, who didn't even have to clear trees there in order to create pastures. But the highlands were more fragile than the lowlands, because they were colder and drier, hence had lower rates of plant regrowth, and were not protected by woodland cover. Once the natural carpet of grassland had been cleared or browsed off, the soil originating as windblown ash was now exposed to wind erosion. In addition, water running downhill, either as rain or as snowmelt runoff, could start to erode gullies into the now-bare soil. But as a gully developed and as the water table dropped from the level of the top of the gully to the bottom, the soil dried out and became even more subject to wind erosion. Within a short time after settlement, Iceland's soils began to be carried from the highlands down to the lowlands and out to sea. The highlands became stripped of soil as well as of vegetation, the former grasslands of Iceland's interior became the man-made (or sheep-made) desert that one sees today, and then large eroded areas started to develop in the lowlands as well.

Today we have to ask ourselves: why on Earth did those foolish settlers manage their land in ways that caused such obvious damage? Didn't they realize what would happen? Yes, they eventually did, but they couldn't at first, because they were faced with an unfamiliar and difficult problem of land management. Except for its volcanoes and hot springs, Iceland looked rather similar to areas of Norway and Britain whence the settlers had emigrated. Viking settlers had no way of knowing that Iceland's soils and vegetation were much more fragile than what they were used to. It seemed natural to the settlers to occupy the highlands and to stock many sheep there, just as they had in the Scottish highlands: how would they know that Iceland's highlands couldn't support sheep indefinitely, and that even the lowlands were being overstocked? In short, the explanation of why Iceland became the European country with the most serious ecological damage is not that cautious Norwegian and British immigrants suddenly threw caution to the winds when they landed in Iceland, but that they found themselves in an apparently lush but actually fragile environment for which their Norwegian and British experience had failed to prepare them.

When the settlers finally realized what was happening, they did take corrective action. They stopped throwing away big pieces of wood, stopped keeping ecologically destructive pigs and goats, and abandoned much of the highlands. Groups of neighboring farms cooperated in jointly making decisions critical for preventing erosion, such as the decision about when in the late spring the grass growth warranted taking the sheep up to communally owned high-altitude mountain pastures for the summer, and when in the fall to bring the sheep back down. Farmers sought to reach agreement on the maximum number of sheep that each communal pasture could support, and how that number was to be divided among sheep quotas for the individual farmers.

That decision-making is flexible and sensitive, but it is also conservative. Even my Icelandic friends describe their society to me as conservative and rigid. The Danish government that ruled Iceland after 1397 was regularly frustrated by that attitude whenever it made genuine efforts to improve the Icelanders' condition. Among the long list of improvements that Danes tried to introduce were: growing grain; improved fishing nets; fishing from decked rather than open boats; processing fish for export with salt, rather than just drying them; a rope-making industry; a hide-tanning industry; and mining sulfur for export. To these and any other proposals involving change, the Danes (as well as innovative Icelanders themselves) found that Icelanders' routine response was "no," regardless of the potential benefits for the Icelanders.

My Icelandic friends explained to me that this conservative outlook is understandable when one reflects on Iceland's environmental fragility. Icelanders became conditioned by their long history of experience to conclude that, whatever change they tried to make, it was much more likely to make things worse than better. In the first years of experimentation during Iceland's early history, its settlers managed to devise an economic and social system that worked, more or less. Granted, that system left most people poor, and from time to time many people starved to death, but at least the society persisted. Other experiments that Icelanders had tried during their history had tended to end disastrously. The evidence of those disasters lay everywhere around them, in the form of the moonscape highlands, the abandoned former farms, and the eroded areas of farms that survived. From all that experience, Icelanders took away the conclusion: This is not a country in which we can enjoy the luxury of experimenting. We live in a fragile land; we know that our ways will allow at least some of us to survive; don't ask us to change.

Iceland's political history from 870 onwards can be quickly summarized. For several centuries Iceland was self-governing, until fighting between chiefs belonging to the five leading families resulted in many killings of people and burnings of farms in the first half of the 13th century. In 1262 Icelanders invited Norway's king to govern them, reasoning that a distant king was less of a danger to them, would leave them more freedom, and could not possibly plunge their land into such disorder as their own nearby chiefs. Marriages among Scandinavian royal houses resulted in the thrones of Denmark, Sweden, and Norway becoming unified in the year 1397 under one king, who was most interested in Denmark because it was his richest province, and less interested in Norway and Iceland, which were poorer. In 1874 Iceland achieved some self-government, home rule in 1904, and full independence from Denmark in 1944.

Beginning in the late Middle Ages, Iceland's economy was stimulated by the rise of trade in stockfish (dried cod) caught in Iceland waters and exported to the European mainland's growing cities whose urban populations required food. Because Iceland itself lacked big trees for good shipbuilding, those fish were caught and exported by ships belonging to an assortment of foreigners that included especially Norwegians, English, and Germans, joined by French and Dutch. In the early 1900s Iceland at last began to develop a fleet of its own and underwent an explosion of industrial-scale fishing. By 1950, more than 90% of Iceland's total exports were marine products, dwarfing the importance of the formerly dominant agricultural sector. Already in 1923, Iceland's urban population overtook its rural population in numbers. Iceland is now the most urbanized Scandinavian country, with half its population in the capital of Reykjavík alone. The flow of population from rural to urban areas continues today, as Iceland's farmers abandon their farms or convert them to summer houses and move to the towns to find jobs, Coca-Cola, and global culture.

Today, thanks to its abundance of fish, geothermal power, and hydro-electric power from all its rivers, and relieved of the necessity to scrape up timber for making ships (now constructed of metal), Europe's former poorest country has become one of the world's richest countries on a per-capita basis, a great success story to balance the stories of societal collapse in Chapters 2–5. Iceland's Nobel Prize–winning novelist Halldór Laxness put into the mouth of the heroine of his novel *Salka Valka* the immortal sentence that only an Icelander could utter: "When all is said and done, life is first and foremost salt fish." But fish stocks pose difficult management problems, just as do forests and soil. Icelanders are working hard now to repair past damage to their forests and soils, and to prevent similar damage to their fisheries.

With this tour of Iceland history in mind, let's see where Iceland stands with respect to the other five Norse North Atlantic colonies. I had mentioned that the differing fates of those colonies depended especially on differences in four factors: sailing distance from Europe, resistance offered by pre-Viking inhabitants, suitability for agriculture, and environmental fragility. In Iceland's case two of those factors were favorable, and the other two caused trouble. Good news for Iceland's settlers was that the island had no (or virtually no) prior inhabitants, and that its distance from Europe (much less than that of Greenland or Vinland, though greater than that of the Orkneys, Shetlands, and Faeroes) was close enough to permit bulk trade even in medieval ships. Unlike the Greenlanders, the Icelanders remained in ship contact with Norway and/or Britain every year, could receive bulk imports of essentials (especially timber, iron, and eventually pottery), and could send out bulk exports. In particular, the export of dried fish proved decisive in saving Iceland economically after 1300 but was impractical for the more remote Greenland colony, whose shipping lanes to Europe were often blocked by sea ice.

On the negative side, Iceland's northerly location gave it the second most unfavorable potential for food production, after Greenland. Barley agriculture, marginal even in the mild early years of settlement, was abandoned when the climate became cooler in the late Middle Ages. Even pastoralism based on sheep and cows was marginal on poorer farms in poorer years. Nevertheless, in most years sheep thrived sufficiently well in Iceland that wool export dominated the economy for several centuries after settlement. Iceland's biggest problem was environmental fragility: by far the most fragile soils among the Norse colonies, and the second most fragile vegetation after Greenland.

What about Icelandic history from the perpective of the five factors that provide the framework for this book: self-inflicted environmental damage, climate change, hostilities with other societies, friendly trading relations with other societies, and cultural attitudes? Four of these factors play a role in Icelandic history; only the factor of hostile outsiders was minor, except for a period of pirate raids. Iceland illustrates clearly the interaction among the other four factors. Icelanders had the misfortune to inherit an especially difficult set of environmental problems, which became exacerbated by climatic cooling in the Little Ice Age. Trade with Europe was important in enabling Iceland to survive despite those environmental problems. Icelanders' response to their environment was framed by their cultural attitudes. Some of those attitudes were ones that they imported with them from Norway: especially, their pastoral economy, their initial overfondness for cows and pigs, and their initial environmental practices appropriate to Norwegian and British soils but inappropriate in Iceland. Attitudes that they then developed in Iceland included learning to eliminate pigs and goats and to downplay cows, learning how to take better care of the fragile Iceland environment, and adopting a conservative outlook. That outlook frustrated their Danish governors and in some cases may have harmed the Icelanders themselves, but ultimately helped them survive by not taking risks.

Iceland's government today is very concerned about Iceland's historical curses of soil erosion and sheep overgrazing, which played such a large role in their country's long impoverishment. An entire government department has as its charge to attempt to retain soil, regrow the woodlands, revegetate the interior, and regulate sheep stocking rates. In Iceland's highlands I saw lines of grass planted by this department on otherwise bare moonscapes, in an effort to establish some protective plant cover and to halt the spread of erosion. Often these replanting efforts—thin green lines on a brown panorama—struck me as a pathetic attempt to cope with an overwhelming problem. But Icelanders are making some progress.

Almost everywhere else in the world, my archaeologist friends have an uphill struggle to convince governments that what archaeologists do has any conceivable practical value. They try to get funding agencies to understand that studies of the fates of past societies may help us understand what could happen to societies living in that same area today. In particular, they reason, environmental damage that developed in the past could develop again in the present, so one might use knowledge of the past to avoid repeating the same mistakes.

Most governments ignore these pleas of archaeologists. That is not the case in Iceland, where the effects of erosion that began 1,130 years ago are obvious, where most of the vegetation and half of the soil have already been lost, and where the past is so stark and omnipresent. Many studies of medieval Icelandic settlements and erosion patterns are now under way. When one of my archaeologist friends approached the Icelandic government and began to deliver the usual lengthy justification required in other countries, the government's response was: "Yes, of course we realize that understanding medieval soil erosion will help us understand our present problem. We already know that, you don't have to spend time convincing us. Here is the money, go do your study."

The brief existence of the most remote Viking North Atlantic colony, Vinland, is a separate story fascinating in its own right. As the first European effort to colonize the Americas, nearly 500 years before Columbus, it has been the subject of romantic speculation and many books. For our purposes in this book, the most important lessons to be drawn from the Vinland venture are the reasons for its failure.

The coast of northeastern North America reached by the Vikings lies thousands of miles from Norway, across the North Atlantic, far beyond direct reach of Viking ships. Instead, all Viking ships destined for North America sailed from the westernmost established colony, Greenland. Even Greenland, though, was far from North America by Viking sailing standards. The Vikings' main camp on Newfoundland lay nearly 1,000 miles from the Greenland settlements by a direct voyage, but required a voyage of 2,000 miles and up to six weeks by the actual coast-hugging route that Vikings took for safety, given their rudimentary navigational abilities. To sail from Greenland to Vinland and then return within the summer sailing season of favorable weather would have left little time for exploring Vinland before setting sail again. Hence the Vikings established a base camp on Newfoundland, where they could remain for the winter, so as to be able to spend the entire subsequent summer exploring.

The known Vinland voyages were organized in Greenland by two sons, a daughter, and a daughter-in-law of that same Erik the Red who had founded the Greenland colony in 984. Their motive was to reconnoiter the land, in order to see what products it offered and to gauge its suitability for settlement. According to the sagas, those initial voyagers took along livestock in their boats, so that they would have the option of making a permanent settlement if the land seemed good to them. Subsequently, after the Vikings had given up on that hope of settling, they continued to visit the coast of North America for more than 300 years in order to fetch lumber (always in short supply in Greenland), and possibly in order to extract iron at sites where plenty of wood was available to make charcoal (also in short supply in Greenland) for iron-smithing.

We have two sources of information about the Vikings' attempt to settle North America: written accounts and archaeological excavations. The written accounts consist mainly of two sagas describing the initial Vinland voyages of discovery and exploration, transmitted orally for several centuries and finally written down in Iceland during the 1200s. In the absence of independent confirming evidence, scholars tended to dismiss the sagas as fiction and to doubt that the Vikings ever reached the New World, until the debate was finally settled when archaeologists located the Vikings' Newfoundland base camp in 1961. The saga accounts of Vinland are now recognized to be the oldest written descriptions of North America, although scholars still debate the accuracy of their details. They are contained in two separate manuscripts, termed the *Greenlanders' Saga* and *Erik the Red's Saga,* which are in broad agreement but have many differences of finer points. They describe up to five separate voyages from Greenland to Vinland, within the short span of barely a decade, each voyage involving only a single ship, except that the last voyage used either two or three ships.

In those two Vinland sagas, the main North American sites visited by the Vikings are described briefly and given the Norse names of Helluland, Markland, Vinland, Leifsbudir, Straumfjord, and Hop. Much effort has been poured by scholars into identifying these names and brief descriptions (e.g., "This land [Markland] was flat and forested, sloping gently seaward, and they came across many beaches of white sand. . . . This land will be named for what it has to offer and called Markland [Forest Land]"). It seems clear that Helluland means the east coast of Baffin Island in the Canadian Arctic, and that Markland is the Labrador coast south of Baffin Island, both Baffin Island and Labrador lying due west of Greenland across the narrow Davis Strait separating Greenland from North America. In order to remain within sight of land as much as possible, the Greenland Vikings didn't sail straight across the open North Atlantic to Newfoundland but instead crossed Davis Strait to Baffin Island and then headed south, following the coast. The remaining place names in the sagas evidently refer to coastal areas of Canada south of Labrador, including surely Newfoundland, probably the Gulf of St. Lawrence and New Brunswick and Nova Scotia (which collectively were termed Vinland), and possibly some of the New England coast. Vikings in the New World would initially have explored widely in order to find the most useful areas, just as we know that they did in Greenland before picking the two fjords with the best pastureland to settle.

Our other source of information about Vikings in the New World is archaeological. Despite much searching by archaeologists, only a single Viking camp has been identified and excavated, at L'Anse aux Meadows on the northwest coast of Newfoundland. Radiocarbon dating indicated that the camp was occupied around A.D. 1000, in agreement with saga accounts that the Vinland voyages were led by grown children of Erik the Red, who organized the settlement of Greenland around 984, and whom the sagas describe as still alive at the time of the voyages. The L'Anse aux Meadows site, whose location seems to agree with the sagas' description of a camp known as Leifsbudir, consists of the remains of eight buildings, including three residential halls large enough to hold 80 people, an iron smithy to extract bog iron and make iron nails for boats, a carpenter's shop, and boat repair shops, but no farm buildings or farm implements.

According to the sagas, Leifsbudir was just a base camp at a location convenient for overwintering and going out on summer explorations; the resources of interest to the Vikings were instead to be found in those exploration areas termed Vinland. This is confirmed by a tiny but important discovery made during the archaeological excavation of the L'Anse aux Meadows camp: two wild walnuts known as butternuts, which do not grow in Newfoundland. Even during the centuries of warmer climate prevailing around A.D. 1000, the walnut trees closest to Newfoundland occurred south of the St. Lawrence River Valley. That was also the closest area where the wild grapes described in the sagas grew. It was probably for those grapes that the Vikings named the area Vinland, meaning "wine land."

The sagas describe Vinland as rich in prized resources lacking in Greenland. High on Vinland's list of advantages were a relatively mild climate, much lower latitude and hence longer summer growing season than Greenland, tall grass, and mild winters, making it possible for Norse cattle to graze outdoors for themselves throughout the winter, and thus sparing the Norse the effort of having to make hay in the summer for feeding their cattle in barns during the winter. Forests with good timber were everywhere. Other natural resources included lake and river salmon larger than any salmon seen in Greenland, one of the world's richest ocean fishing grounds in the seas surrounding Newfoundland, and game, including deer, caribou, and nesting birds and their eggs.

Despite the valuable shiploads of timber, grapes, and animal furs that the Vinland voyagers brought back to Greenland, the voyages were discontinued and the L'Anse aux Meadows camp was abandoned. Although the archaeological excavations of the camp were exciting in finally proving that Vikings had indeed reached the New World before Columbus, the excavations were disappointing as well, because the Norse left nothing of value. Objects recovered were confined to small items that had probably been discarded or else dropped and lost, such as 99 broken iron nails, a single whole nail, a bronze pin, a whetstone, a spindle, one glass bead, and a knitting needle. Evidently, the site was not abandoned hastily, but as part of a planned permanent evacuation in which all tools and possessions of value were taken back to Greenland. Today we know that North America was by far the largest and most valuable North Atlantic land discovered by the Norse; even the tiny fraction of it that the Norse surveyed impressed them. Why, then, did the Norse give up on Vinland, land of plenty?

The sagas offer a simple answer to that question: the large population of hostile Indians, with whom the Vikings failed to establish good relations. According to the sagas, the first Indians that the Vikings met were a group of nine, of whom they killed eight, while the ninth fled. That was not a promising start to establishing friendship. Not surprisingly, the Indians came back in a fleet of small boats, shot arrows at the Norse, and killed their leader, Erik the Red's son Thorvald. Pulling the arrow out of his intestines, the dying Thorvald is said to have lamented, "This is a rich country we have found; there is plenty of fat around my belly. We've found a land of fine resources, though we'll hardly enjoy much of them."

The next group of Norse voyagers did manage to establish a trade with local Indians (Norse cloth and cow's milk in exchange for animal furs brought by Indians), until one Viking killed an Indian trying to steal weapons. In the ensuing battle many Indians were killed before fleeing, but that was enough to convince the Norse of the chronic problems that they would face. As the unknown author of *Erik the Red's Saga* put it, "The [Viking] party then realized that, despite everything that the land had to offer there, they would be under constant threat of attack from its former inhabitants. They made ready to depart for their own country [i.e., Greenland]."

After thus abandoning Vinland to the Indians, the Greenland Norse continued to make visits farther north on the Labrador coast, where there were many fewer Indians, in order to fetch timber and iron. Tangible evidence of such visits are a handful of Norse objects (bits of smelted copper, smelted iron, and spun goat's wool) found at Native American archaeological sites scattered over the Canadian Arctic. The most notable such find is a silver penny minted in Norway between 1065 and 1080 during the reign of King Olav the Quiet, found at an Indian site on the coast of Maine hundreds of miles south of Labrador, and pierced for use as a pendant. The Maine site had been a big trading village at which archaeologists excavated stone and tools originating in Labrador as well as over much of Nova Scotia, New England, New York, and Pennsylvania. Probably the penny had been dropped or traded by a Norse visitor to Labrador, and had then reached Maine by an Indian trade network.

Other evidence of continuing Norse visits to Labrador is the mention, in Iceland's chronicle for the year 1347, of a Greenland ship with a crew of 18 that had reached Iceland after losing its anchor and being blown off course on the return voyage from "Markland." The chronicle mention is brief and matter-of-fact, as if there were nothing unusual requiring explanation—as if the chronicler were instead to have written equally matter-of-factly, "So, the news this year is that one of those ships that visit Markland each summer lost its anchor, and also Thorunn Ketilsdóttir spilled a big pitcher of milk at her Djupadalur farm, and one of Bjarni Bollason's sheep died, and that's all the news for this year, just the usual stuff."

In short, the Vinland colony failed because the Greenland colony itself was too small and poor in timber and iron to support it, too far from both Europe and from Vinland, owned too few oceangoing ships, and could not finance big fleets of exploration; and that one or two shiploads of Greenlanders were no match for hordes of Nova Scotia and Gulf of St. Lawrence Indians when they were provoked. In A.D. 1000 the Greenland colony probably numbered no more than 500 people, so that the 80 adults at the L'Anse camp would have represented a huge drain on Greenland's available manpower. When European colonizers finally returned to North America after 1500, the history of European attempts to settle then shows how long were the odds that those attempts faced, even for colonies backed by Europe's wealthiest and most populous nations, sending annual supply fleets of ships far larger than medieval Viking vessels, and equipped with guns and abundant iron tools. At the first English and French colonies in Massachusetts, Virginia, and Canada, about half of the settlers died of starvation and disease within the first year. It's no surprise, then, that 500 Greenlanders, from the most remote colonial outpost of Norway, one of Europe's poorer nations, could not succeed at conquering and colonizing North America.

For our purposes in this book, the most important thing about the failure of the Vinland colony within 10 years is that it was in part a greatly speeded-up preview of the failure that overtook the Greenland colony after 450 years. Norse Greenland survived much longer than Norse Vinland because it was closer to Norway and because hostile natives did not make their appearance for the first few centuries. But Greenland shared, albeit in less extreme form, Vinland's twin problems of isolation and Norse inability to establish good relations with Native Americans. If it had not been for Native Americans, the Greenlanders might have survived their ecological problems, and the Vinland settlers might have persisted. In that case, Vinland might have undergone a population explosion, the Norse might have spread over North America after A.D. 1000, and I as a twentieth-century American might now be writing this book in an Old Norse–based language like modern Icelandic or Faeroese, rather than in English.

CHAPTER 7

Norse Greenland's Flowering

Europe's outpost ▪ Greenland's climate today ▪ Climate in the past ▪
Native plants and animals ▪ Norse settlement ▪ Farming ▪
Hunting and fishing ▪ An integrated economy ▪ Society ▪
Trade with Europe ▪ Self-image ▪

My initial impression of Greenland was that its name was a cruel misnomer, because I saw only a three-colored landscape: white, black, and blue, with white overwhelmingly predominant. Some historians think that the name really was coined with deceitful intent by Erik the Red, founder of Greenland's Viking settlement, so as to induce other Vikings to join him. As my airplane from Copenhagen approached Greenland's east coast, the first thing visible after the dark blue ocean was a vast area of brilliant white stretching out of sight, the world's largest ice cap outside Antarctica. Greenland's shores rise steeply to an ice-covered high plateau covering most of the island and drained by enormous glaciers flowing into the sea. For hundreds of miles our plane flew over this white expanse, where the sole other color visible was the black of bare stone mountains rising out of that ocean of ice, and scattered over it like black islands. Only as our plane descended from the plateau towards the west coast did I spot two other colors in a thin border outlining the ice sheet, combining brown areas of bare gravel with faint green areas of moss or lichens.

But when I landed at southern Greenland's main airport of Narsarsuaq and crossed the iceberg-strewn fjord to Brattahlid, the site that Erik the Red chose for his own farm, I discovered to my surprise that the name Greenland might have been bestowed honestly, not as false PR. Exhausted by my long plane flight from Los Angeles to Copenhagen and back to Greenland, involving shifts of 13 time zones, I set out to stroll among the Norse ruins but was soon ready for a nap, too sleepy even to return the few hundred yards to the youth hostel where I had left my rucksack. Fortunately, the ruins lay amidst lush meadows of soft grass over a foot high, growing up out of thick moss and dotted with abundant yellow buttercups, yellow dandelions, blue bluebells, white asters, and pink willow-herbs. There was no need for an air mattress or pillow here: I fell into a deep sleep in the softest and most beautiful natural bed imaginable.

As my Norwegian archaeologist friend Christian Keller expressed it, "Life in Greenland is all about finding the good patches of useful resources." While 99% of the island is indeed uninhabitable white or black, there are green areas deep inside two fjord systems on the southwest coast. There, long narrow fjords penetrate far inland, such that their heads are remote from the cold ocean currents, icebergs, salt spray, and wind that suppress growth of vegetation along Greenland's outer coast. Here and there along the mostly steep-sided fjords are patches of flatter terrain with luxuriant pastures, including the one in which I took a nap, and good for maintaining livestock (Plate 17). For nearly 500 years between A.D. 984 and sometime in the 1400s, those two fjord systems supported European civilization's most remote outpost, where Scandinavians 1,500 miles from Norway built a cathedral and churches, wrote in Latin and Old Norse, wielded iron tools, herded farm animals, followed the latest European fashions in clothing—and finally vanished.

The mystery of their disappearance is symbolized by the stone church at Hvalsey, Norse Greenland's most famous building, whose photograph will be found in any travel brochure promoting Greenland tourism. Lying in meadows at the head of the long, broad, mountain-rimmed fjord, the church commands a gorgeous view over a panorama of dozens of square miles. Its walls, west doorway, niches, and gables of stone are still intact: only the original roof of turf is missing. Around the church lie the remains of the residential halls, barns, storehouses, boathouse, and pastures that sustained the people who erected those buildings. Among all medieval European societies, Norse Greenland is the one whose ruins are best preserved, precisely because its sites were abandoned while intact, whereas almost all major medieval sites of Britain and continental Europe continued to be occupied and became submerged by post-medieval construction. Visiting Hvalsey today, one almost expects to see Vikings walking out of those buildings, but in fact all is silent: practically no one now lives within twenty miles of there (Plate 15). Whoever built that church knew enough to re-create a European community, and to maintain it for centuries—but not enough to maintain it for longer.

Compounding the mystery, the Vikings shared Greenland with another people, the Inuit (Eskimos), whereas the Iceland Norse had Iceland to themselves and faced no such additional problem to compound their own difficulties. The Vikings disappeared, but the Inuit survived, proving that human survival in Greenland was not impossible and the Vikings' disappearance not inevitable. As one walks around modern Greenland farms, one sees again those same two populations that shared the island in the Middle Ages: Inuits and Scandinavians. In 1721, three hundred years after the medieval Vikings died out, other Scandinavians (Danes) came back to take control of Greenland, and it was not until 1979 that Native Greenlanders gained home rule. I found it disconcerting throughout my Greenland visit to look at the many blue-eyed blond-haired Scandinavians working there, and to reflect that it was people like them who built Hvalsey Church and the other ruins that I was studying, and who died out there. Why did those medieval Scandinavians ultimately fail to master Greenland's problems while the Inuits succeeded?

Like the fate of the Anasazi, the fate of the Greenland Norse has often been laid to various single-factor explanations, without agreement being reached as to which of those explanations is correct. A favorite theory has been climatic cooling, invoked in overschematic formulations approximating (in the words of archaeologist Thomas McGovern) "It got too cold, and they died." Other single-factor theories have included extermination of the Norse by the Inuit, abandonment of the Norse by mainland Europeans, environmental damage, and a hopelessly conservative outlook. In fact, the Greenland Norse extinction is a richly instructive case precisely because it involves major contributions of all five of the explanatory factors that I discussed in the introduction to this book. It is a rich case not only in reality, but also in our available information about it, because the Norse left written accounts of Greenland (whereas the Easter Islanders and Anasazi were not literate), and because we understand medieval European society much better than we understand Polynesian or Anasazi society. Nevertheless, major questions remain about even this most richly documented pre-industrial collapse.

What was the environment in which the Greenland Norse colonies arose, thrived, and fell? The Norse lived in two settlements on Greenland's west coast somewhat below the Arctic Circle, around latitudes 61 and 64 degrees north. That's south of most of Iceland, and comparable to the latitudes of Bergen and Trondheim on Norway's west coast. But Greenland is colder than either Iceland or Norway, because the latter are bathed by the warm Gulf Stream flowing up from the south, whereas Greenland's west coast is bathed by the cold West Greenland Current flowing down from the Arctic.

As a result, even at the sites of the former Norse settlements, which enjoy the most benign climate in Greenland, the weather can be summed up in four words: cold, variable, windy, and foggy.

Mean summer temperatures today at the settlements are around 42 degrees Fahrenheit (5–6 degrees Celsius) on the outer coast, 50°F (10°C) in the interiors of the fjords. While that doesn't sound so cold, remember that that's only for the warmest months of the year. In addition, strong dry winds frequently blow down from Greenland's ice cap, bringing drift ice from the north, blocking the fjords with icebergs even during the summer, and causing dense fogs. I was told that the large short-term climate fluctuations that I encountered during my summer visit to Greenland, including heavy rain, strong winds, and fog, were common and often made it impossible to travel by boat. But boats are the main means of transport in Greenland, because the coast is so deeply indented with branching fjords. (Even today, there are no roads connecting Greenland's main population centers, and the sole communities joined by road are either located on the same side of the same fjord or else on adjacent different fjords separated by just a low spine of hills.) Such a storm aborted my first attempt to reach Hvalsey Church: I arrived by boat at Qaqortoq in nice weather on July 25, to find ship traffic out of Qaqortoq on July 26 immobilized by wind, rain, fog, and icebergs. On July 27 the weather turned mild again and we reached Hvalsey, and on the following day we steamed back out of Qaqortoq Fjord to Brattahlid under blue skies.

I experienced Greenland weather at its best, at the site of the southernmost Norse settlement in peak summer. As a Southern Californian accustomed to warm sunny days, I would describe the temperatures that I encountered then as "variably cool to cold." I always needed to wear a windbreaker over my T-shirt, long-sleeved shirt, and sweatshirt, and often added as well the thick down parka that I had acquired on my first trip to the Arctic. The temperature seemed to change quickly and in wide swings, repeatedly within each hour. It sometimes felt as if my main occupation while out walking in Greenland consisted of taking my parka on and off to adjust to those frequent changes in temperature.

Complicating this picture I have just drawn of modern Greenland's average climate, the weather can change over short distances and from year to year. The changes over short distances partly account for Christian Keller's comment to me about the importance of finding the good patches of resources in Greenland. The changes from year to year affect each year's growth of pasture hay on which the Norse economy depended, and also af-

fect the quantities of sea ice that in turn affect seal hunting plus the possibility of ship travel for trade, both of which were important to the Vikings.
Both the weather changes over short distances and from year to year were
critical, as Greenland was at best marginally suitable for Norse hay production, so being at a slightly worse site or in a slightly colder-than-usual year
could translate into not having enough hay to feed one's livestock through
the winter.

As for the changes with location, an important difference is that one of
the two Viking settlements lay 300 miles north of the other, but they were
confusingly called Western and Eastern Settlement instead of Northern and
Southern Settlement. (Those names had unfortunate consequences centuries later, when the name "Eastern Settlement" misled Europeans looking
for the long-lost Greenland Norse to hunt for them in the wrong place, on
Greenland's east coast, instead of on the west coast where the Norse had
actually lived.) Summer temperatures are as warm at the more northerly
Western Settlement as at the Eastern Settlement. However, the summer
growing season is shorter at Western Settlement (just five months with average temperatures above freezing, instead of seven months as at Eastern
Settlement), because there are fewer summer days of sunlight and warm
temperatures as one gets further north. Another change in weather with location is that it is colder, wetter, and foggier on the seacoast at the mouths of
fjords, directly exposed to the cold West Greenland Current, than in the
sheltered interiors of the fjords far from the sea.

Still another change with location that I couldn't help noticing during
my travels in Greenland is that some fjords have glaciers dumping into
them, while others don't. Those fjords with glaciers constantly receive icebergs of local origin, while those without glaciers only receive whatever icebergs drift in from the ocean. For example, in July I found Igaliku Fjord (on
which lay Viking Greenland's cathedral) free of icebergs, because no glacier
flows into it; Eirik's Fjord (on which lay Brattahlid) had scattered icebergs,
because one glacier enters that fjord; and the next fjord north of Brattahlid, Sermilik Fjord, has many big glaciers and was solidly clogged with ice.
(Those differences, and the great variations of size and shape among the
icebergs, were one of the reasons why I found Greenland such a constantly
interesting landscape, despite its few colors.) While Christian Keller was
studying an isolated archaeological site on Eirik's Fjord, he used to walk
over the hill to visit some Swedish archaeologists excavating a site on Sermilik Fjord. The Swedes' campsite was considerably colder than Christian's
campsite, and correspondingly the Viking farm that the unfortunate Swedes

had chosen to study had been poorer than the farm that Christian was studying (because the Swedes' site was colder and yielded less hay).

Weather changes from year to year are illustrated by recent experience of hay yields on sheep farms that resumed operation in Greenland beginning in the 1920s. Wetter years yield more growth of vegetation, which generally is good news to pastoralists because it means more hay to feed their sheep, and more grass to nourish the wild caribou (hence more caribou to hunt). However, if too much rain falls during the hay harvest season in August and September, hay yields decrease because the hay is hard to dry. A cold summer is bad because it decreases hay growth; a long winter is bad because it means that animals have to be kept indoors in barns for more months and require more hay; and a summer with much drift ice coming down from the north is bad because it results in dense summer fogs that are bad for hay growth. Year-to-year weather differences like those making life dicey for modern Greenland sheep farmers must have made it dicey for the medieval Norse as well.

Those are the climate changes that one can observe from year to year, or from decade to decade, in Greenland today. What about climate changes in the past? For instance, what was the weather like at the time that the Norse arrived in Greenland, and how did it change over the five centuries that they survived? How can one learn about past climate in Greenland? We have three main sources of information: written records, pollen, and ice cores.

First, because the Greenland Norse were literate and were visited by literate Icelanders and Norwegians, it would have been nice for those of us interested today in the Greenland Vikings' fate if they had bothered to leave some accounts of Greenland's weather then. Unfortunately for us, they didn't. For Iceland, though, we have many accounts of weather in different years—including mentions of cold weather, rainfall, and sea ice—from incidental comments in diaries, letters, annals, and reports. That information about the climate in Iceland is of some use for understanding the climate in Greenland, because a cold decade in Iceland tends to be cold in Greenland as well, though the agreement isn't perfect. We are on more secure ground in interpreting the significance for Greenland of comments about sea ice around Iceland, because that was the ice that made it difficult to sail to Greenland from Iceland or Norway.

Our second source of information about past Greenland climates consists of pollen samples from sediment cores drilled into Greenland lakes and bogs by palynologists, the scientists who study pollen and whose insights into the vegetational history of Easter Island and the Maya area we already encountered (Chapters 2 and 5). Drilling down into the mud at the bottom of a lake or bog may not strike the rest of us as exciting, but it's nirvana for a palynologist, because the deeper mud layers were deposited longer ago in the past. Radiocarbon dating of organic materials in a mud sample establishes when that particular layer of mud settled out. Pollen grains from different plant species look different under the microscope, so that the pollen grains in your (you the palynologist's) mud sample tell you what plants were growing near your lake or bog and were releasing pollen that fell into it in that year. As past climates became colder in Greenland, palynologists find pollen shifting from that of warmth-demanding trees to that of cold-tolerant grasses and sedges. But that same shift in pollen may also mean that the Norse were cutting down trees, and palynologists have found other ways to distinguish those two interpretations of declining tree pollen.

Finally, by far our most detailed information about Greenland climates in the past comes from ice cores. In Greenland's cold and intermittently wet climate, trees are small, grow only locally, and their timber deteriorates quickly, so we don't have for Greenland the logs with beautifully preserved tree rings that have enabled archaeologists to reconstruct year-to-year climate changes in the dry U.S. southwestern deserts inhabited by the Anasazi. Instead of tree rings, Greenland archaeologists have the good fortune of being able to study ice rings—or, actually, ice layers. Snow that falls each year on Greenland's ice cap becomes compressed by the weight of later years of snow into ice. The oxygen in the water that constitutes snow or ice consists of three different isotopes, i.e., three different types of oxygen atoms differing just in atomic weight because of different numbers of uncharged neutrons in the oxygen nucleus. The overwhelmingly prevalent form of natural oxygen (99.8% of the total) is the isotope oxygen-16 (meaning oxygen of atomic weight 16), but there is also a small proportion (0.2%) of oxygen-18, and an even smaller amount of oxygen-17. All three of those isotopes are stable, not radioactive, but they can still be distinguished by an instrument called a mass spectrometer. The warmer the temperature at which snow forms, the higher is the proportion of oxygen-18 in the snow's oxygen. Hence each year's summer snow is higher in its proportion of oxygen-18 than the same year's winter snow. For the same reason, snow oxygen-18 in a given month of a warm year is higher than in the same month of a cold year.

Thus, as you drill down through the Greenland ice cap (something that

Greenland-ice-cap-drilling scientists have now done down to a depth of almost two miles) and measure the oxygen-18 proportion as a function of depth, you see the oxygen-18 proportion wiggling up and down as you bore through one year's summer ice into the preceding winter's ice and then into the preceding summer's ice, because of the predictable seasonal changes in temperature. You also find oxygen-18 values to differ among different summers or different winters, because of unpredictable year-to-year fluctuations in temperature. Hence the Greenland ice core yields information similar to what archaeologists studying the Anasazi deduce from tree rings: it tells us each year's summer temperature and each year's winter temperature, and as a bonus the thickness of the ice layer between consecutive summers (or between consecutive winters) tells us the amount of precipitation that fell during that year.

There is one other feature of weather about which we can learn from ice cores, but not from tree rings, and that is storminess. Storm winds pick up salt spray from the ocean around Greenland, may blow it far inland over the ice cap, and drop there some of the spray frozen as snow, including the sodium ions in seawater. Onto the ice cap, storm winds also blow atmospheric dust, which originates far away in dry dusty areas of the continents, and that dust is high in calcium ions. Snow formed from pure water lacks those two ions. When one finds high concentrations of sodium and calcium in an ice layer of the ice cap, it may mean that that was a stormy year.

In short, we can reconstruct past Greenland climates from Icelandic records, pollen, and ice cores, and the latter let us reconstruct climate on a year-to-year basis. What have we thereby learned?

As expected, we've learned that the climate warmed up after the end of the last Ice Age around 14,000 years ago; the fjords of Greenland became merely "cool," not "bitterly cold," and they developed low forests. But Greenland's climate hasn't remained boringly steady for the last 14,000 years: it has gotten colder for some periods, then reverted to being milder again. Those climate fluctuations were important to the settling of Greenland by Native American peoples before the Norse. While the Arctic has few prey species—notably reindeer, seals, whales, and fish—those few species are often abundant. But if the usual prey species die out or move away, there may be no alternative prey for hunters to fall back on, as they can at lower latitudes where species are so diverse. Hence the history of the Arctic, including that of Greenland, is a history of people arriving, occupying large areas for many centuries, and then declining or disappearing or having to change their lifestyle over large areas when climate changes bring changes in prey abundance.

Such consequences of climate changes for native hunters have been observed firsthand in Greenland during the 20th century. A warming of sea temperatures early in that century caused seals almost to disappear from southern Greenland. Good seal hunting returned when the weather got cooler again. Then, when the weather got very cold between 1959 and 1974, populations of migratory seal species plummeted because of all the sea ice, and total sea catches by native Greenland seal hunters declined, but the Greenlanders avoided starvation by concentrating on ringed seals, a species that remained common because it makes holes in the ice through which to breathe. Similar climate fluctuations with consequent changes in prey abundance may have contributed to the first settlement by Native Americans around 2500 B.C., their decline or disappearance around 1500 B.C., their subsequent return, their decline again, and then their complete abandonment of southern Greenland some time before the Norse arrived around A.D. 980. Hence the Norse settlers initially encountered no Native Americans, though they did find ruins left by former populations. Unfortunately for the Norse, the warm climate at the time of their arrival was simultaneously allowing the Inuit people (alias Eskimos) to expand quickly eastwards from Bering Strait across the Canadian Arctic, because the ice that had permanently closed the channels between northern Canadian islands during cold centuries began to melt in the summer, permitting bowhead whales, the mainstay of Inuit subsistence, to penetrate those Canadian Arctic waterways. That climate change allowed the Inuit to enter northwestern Greenland from Canada around A.D. 1200—with big consequences for the Norse.

Between A.D. 800 and 1300, ice cores tell us that the climate in Greenland was relatively mild, similar to Greenland's weather today or even slightly warmer. Those mild centuries are termed the Medieval Warm Period. Thus, the Norse reached Greenland during a period good for growing hay and pasturing animals—good by the standards of Greenland's average climate over the last 14,000 years. Around 1300, though, the climate in the North Atlantic began to get cooler and more variable from year to year, ushering in a cold period termed the Little Ice Age that lasted into the 1800s. By around 1420, the Little Ice Age was in full swing, and the increased summer drift ice between Greenland, Iceland, and Norway ended ship communication between the Greenland Norse and the outside world. Those cold conditions were tolerable or even beneficial for the Inuit, who could hunt ringed seals, but were bad news for the Norse, who depended on growing hay. As we shall see, the onset of the Little Ice Age was a factor behind the demise of the Greenland Norse. But the climate shift from the Medieval Warm Period to the Little Ice Age was complex, and not a simple matter that "it got steadily colder and killed off the Norse." There had been sprinklings of cold periods before 1300 that the Norse survived, and sprinklings of warm periods after A.D. 1400 that failed to save them. Above all, there remains the nagging question: why didn't the Norse learn to cope with the Little Ice Age's cold weather by watching how the Inuit were meeting the same challenges?

To complete our consideration of Greenland's environment, let's mention its native plants and animals. The best-developed vegetation is confined to areas of mild climate sheltered from salt spray in the long inner fjords of the Western and Eastern Settlements on Greenland's southwest coast. There, vegetation in areas not grazed by livestock varies by location. At higher elevations where it is cold, and in the outer fjords near the sea where plant growth is inhibited by cold, fog, and salt spray, the vegetation is dominated by sedges, which are shorter than grasses and have lower nutritional value to grazing animals. Sedges can grow in these poor locations because they are more resistant to drying out than are grasses, and they can thus establish themselves in gravel containing little water-retaining soil. Inland in areas protected from salt spray, the steep slopes and cold windy sites near glaciers are virtually bare rock without vegetation. Less hostile inland sites mostly support a heath vegetation of dwarf shrubs. The best inland sites—i.e., ones at low elevation, with good soil, protected from the wind, well watered, and with a south-facing exposure that lets them receive much sunlight—carry an open woodland of dwarf birch and willows with some junipers and alders, mostly less than 16 feet tall, in the very best sites with birches up to 30 feet tall.

In areas grazed today by sheep and horses, the vegetation presents a different picture, and would have in Norse times as well (Plate 17). Moist meadows on gentle slopes, such as those around Gardar and Brattahlid, have lush grass up to one foot high, with many flowers. Patches of dwarf willow and birch grazed down by sheep reach only a foot-and-a-half in height. Drier, more sloping and exposed fields carry grasses or dwarf willow up to only a few inches high. Only where grazing sheep and horses have been excluded, such as within the perimeter fence around Narsarsuaq Airport, did I see dwarf willows and birches up to seven feet tall, stunted by cold wind coming off a nearby glacier.

As for Greenland's wild animals, the ones potentially most important to the Norse and Inuit were land and sea mammals and birds, fish, and marine invertebrates. Greenland's sole native large terrestrial herbivore in the former Norse areas (i.e., not considering the musk ox in the far north) is the caribou, which Lapps and other native peoples of the Eurasian continent domesticated as reindeer but which the Norse and Inuit never did. Polar bears and wolves were virtually confined in Greenland to areas north of the Norse settlements. Smaller game animals included hares, foxes, land birds (of which the largest were grouse relatives called ptarmigans), freshwater birds (the largest being swans and geese), and seabirds (especially eider ducks and auks, a.k.a. alcids). The most important marine mammals were seals of six different species, differing in significance to the Norse and Inuit, related to differences in their distribution and behavior that I shall explain below. The largest of these six species is the walrus. Various species of whales occur along the coast, and were successfully hunted by the Inuit but not by the Norse. Fish abounded in rivers, lakes, and oceans, while shrimp and mussels were the most valuable edible marine invertebrates.

According to sagas and medieval histories, around the year 980 a hot-blooded Norwegian known as Erik the Red was charged with murder and forced to leave for Iceland, where he soon killed a few more people and was chased out to another part of Iceland. Having ended up, there too, in a quarrel and killed still more people, he was this time exiled entirely from Iceland for three years beginning around 982.

Erik remembered that, many decades earlier, one Gunnbjörn Ulfsson had been blown westwards far off course while sailing for Iceland and had spotted some barren small islands, which we now know lay just off Greenland's southeast coast. Those islands had been revisited around 978 by Erik's distant relative Snaebjörn Galti, who of course got into a quarrel of his own there with his shipmates and was duly murdered. Erik sailed for those islands to try his luck, spent the next three years exploring much of the Greenland coast, and discovered good pastureland inside the deep fjords. On his return to Iceland he lost yet another fight, impelling him to lead a fleet of 25 ships to settle the newly explored land that he shrewdly named Greenland. News brought back to Iceland of the fine homesteads available for the asking in Greenland motivated three more fleets of settlers to sail from Iceland during the next decade. As a result, by A.D. 1000 virtually all the land suitable for farms in both Western and Eastern Settlements had been occupied, yielding an eventual total Norse population estimated at around 5,000: about 1,000 people at Western Settlement, 4,000 at Eastern Settlement.

From their settlements the Norse undertook explorations and annual hunting trips northwards along the west coast, far north of the Arctic Circle. One of those trips may have gotten as far north as latitude 79°N, only 700 miles from the North Pole, where numerous Norse artifacts including pieces of chain mail armor, a carpenter's plane, and ships' rivets were discovered in an Inuit archaeological site. More certain evidence of northwards exploration is a cairn at latitude 73°N containing a runestone (a stone with writing in the Norse runic alphabet), which states that Erling Sighvatsson, Bjarni Thordarson, and Eindridi Oddson erected that cairn on the Saturday before Minor Rogation Day (April 25), probably in some year around 1300.

Greenland Norse subsistence was based on a combination of pastoralism (growing domestic livestock) and hunting wild animals for meat. After Erik the Red brought livestock with him from Iceland, the Greenland Norse proceeded to develop a dependence on additional wild food to a degree much greater than in Norway and Iceland, whose milder climate permitted people to obtain most of their food requirements from pastoralism and (in Norway) gardening alone.

Greenland's settlers started out with aspirations based on the mix of livestock maintained by prosperous Norwegian chiefs: lots of cows and pigs, fewer sheep and still fewer goats, plus some horses, ducks, and geese. As gauged by counts of animal bones identified in radiocarbon-dated Greenland garbage middens from different centuries of Norse occupation, it quickly turned out that that ideal mix was not well suited to Greenland's colder conditions. Barnyard ducks and geese dropped out immediately, perhaps even on the voyage to Greenland: there is no archaeological evidence of their ever having been kept there. Although pigs found abundant nuts to eat in Norway's forests, and although Vikings prized pork above all other meats, pigs proved terribly destructive and unprofitable in lightly wooded Greenland, where they rooted up the fragile vegetation and soil. Within a short time they were reduced to low numbers or virtually eliminated. Archaeological finds of packsaddles and sledges show that horses were kept as work animals, but there was a Christian religious ban against eating them, so their bones rarely ended up in the garbage. Cows required far more effort than sheep or goats to rear in Greenland's climate, because they could find grass in pastures only during the three snow-free summer months. For the rest of the year they had to be kept indoors in barns and fed on hay and other fodder whose acquisition became the main summer chore of Greenland farmers. The Greenlanders might have been better off to discard their labor-intensive cows, whose numbers did become reduced through the centuries, but they were too prized as status symbols to be eliminated entirely.

Instead, the staple food-producing animals in Greenland became hardy breeds of sheep and goats much better adapted to cold climates than were the cattle. They had the additional advantage that, unlike cows, they can dig down under snow to find grass for themselves in the winter. In Greenland today, sheep can be kept outdoors for nine months per year (three times as long as cows) and have to be brought into shelter and fed for only the three months of heaviest snow cover. Numbers of sheep plus goats started off barely equal to cow numbers at early Greenland sites, and then rose with time to as many as eight sheep or goats for every cow. As between sheep and goats, Icelanders kept six or more of the former for every one of the latter, and that was also the ratio at the best Greenland farms during early years of settlement, but relative numbers shifted with time until goat numbers rivaled those of sheep. That's because goats but not sheep can digest the tough twigs, shrubs, and dwarf trees prevalent in poor Greenland pastures. Thus, while the Norse arrived in Greenland with a preference for cows over sheep over goats, the suitability of those animals under Greenland conditions was in the opposite sequence. Most farms (especially those in the more northerly and hence more marginal Western Settlement) had to content themselves eventually with more of the despised goats and few of the honored cows; only the most productive Eastern Settlement farms succeeded in indulging their cow preference and goat scorn.

The ruins of the barns in which the Greenland Norse kept their cows for nine months per year are still visible. They consisted of long narrow buildings with stone and turf walls several yards thick to keep the barn warm inside during the winter, because cows could not stand cold as could the Greenland breeds of sheep and goats. Each cow was kept in its own rectangular stall, marked off from adjacent stalls by stone dividing slabs that are still standing in many of the ruined barns. From the size of the stalls, from the height of the doors through which cows were led in and out of the barn, and of course from excavated skeletons of the cows themselves, one can calculate that Greenland cows were the smallest known in the modern world, not more than four feet high at the shoulder. During the winter they re-mained all the time in their stalls, where the dung that they dropped accu-mulated as a rising tide around them until the spring, when the sea of dung was shoveled outside. During the winter the cows were fed on harvested hay, but if its quantities weren't sufficient, it had to be supplemented with seaweed brought inland. The cows evidently didn't like the seaweed, so that farm laborers had to live in the barn with the cows and their rising sea of dung during the winter, and perhaps to force-feed the cows, which gradu-ally became smaller and weaker. Around May, when the snow started to melt and new grass came up, the cows could at last be brought out of doors to start grazing themselves, but by then they were so weak that they could no longer walk and had to be carried outside. In extreme winters, when hay and seaweed stores ran out before the new growth of summer grass, farmers collected the first willow and birch twigs of the spring as a starvation diet to feed their animals.

Greenland cows, sheep, and goats were used mainly for milking rather than for meat. After the animals gave birth in May or June, they yielded milk just during the few summer months. The Norse then turned the milk into cheese, butter, and the yogurt-like product called *skyr,* which they stored in huge barrels kept cold by being placed either in mountain streams or in turf houses, and they ate those dairy products throughout the winter. The goats were also kept for their hair, and the sheep for their wool, which was of exceptionally high quality because sheep in those cold climates produce fatty wool that is naturally waterproof. Meat was available from the live-stock just at times of culling, especially in the autumn, when farmers calcu-lated how many animals they would be able to feed through the winter on the hay that they had brought in that fall. They slaughtered any remaining animals for which they estimated that they would not have enough winter fodder. Because meat of barnyard animals was thus in short supply, almost all bones of slaughtered animals in Greenland were split and broken to ex-tract the last bits of marrow, far more so than in other Viking countries. At archaeological sites of Greenland Inuit, who were skilled hunters bringing in more wild meat than the Norse, the preserved larvae of flies that feed on rotting marrow and fat are abundant, but those flies found slim pickings at Norse sites.

It took several tons of hay to maintain a cow, much less to maintain a sheep, throughout an average Greenland winter. Hence the main occupa-tion of most Greenland Norse during the late summer had to be cutting, drying, and storing hay. The hay quantities accumulated then were critical because they determined how many animals could be fed throughout the following winter, but that depended on the duration of that winter, which could not be predicted exactly in advance. Hence each September the Norse had to make the agonizing decision how many of their precious livestock to cull, basing that decision on the amount of fodder available and on their guess as to the length of the coming winter. If they killed too many animals in September, they would end up in May with uneaten hay and just a small herd, and they might kick themselves for not having gambled on being able to feed more animals. But if they killed too few animals in September, they might find themselves running out of hay before May and risk the whole herd starving.

Hay was produced in three types of fields. Most productive would be so-called infields near the main house, fenced to keep livestock out, manured to increase grass growth, and used just for hay production. At the cathedral farm of Gardar and a few other Norse farm ruins, one can see the remains of irrigation systems of dams and channels that spread mountain stream water over the infields to further increase productivity. The second zone of hay production was the so-called outfields, somewhat farther from the main house and outside the fenced-off area. Finally, the Greenland Norse carried over from Norway and Iceland a system called *shielings* or *saeters*, consisting of buildings in more remote upland areas suitable for producing hay and grazing animals during the summer but too cold for keeping live-stock during the winter. The most complex shielings were virtually minia-ture farms, complete with houses where laborers lived during the summer to tend animals and make hay but returned to live on the main farm during the winter. Each year the snow melted off and the grass began to grow first at low altitude and then at increasingly higher altitudes, but new grass is es-pecially high in nutrients and low in less-digestible fiber. Shielings were thus a sophisticated method to help Norse farmers solve the problem of Green-land's patchy and limited resources, by exploiting even temporarily useful patches in the mountains, and by moving livestock gradually uphill to take advantage of the new grass appearing at progressively higher altitudes as the summer went on.

As I mentioned earlier, Christian Keller had told me before we visited Greenland together that "life in Greenland was about finding the best patches." What Christian meant was that, even in those two fjord systems that were the sole areas of Greenland with good potential for pastures, the best areas along those fjords were few and scattered. As I cruised or walked up and down Greenland's fjords, even as a naïve city-dweller I felt myself gradually learning to recognize the criteria by which the Norse would have recognized patches good for being turned into farms. While Greenland's actual settlers from Iceland and Norway had a huge advantage over me as experienced farmers, I had the advantage of hindsight: I knew, and they couldn't know, at which patches Norse farms were actually tried or proved poor or became abandoned. It would have taken years or even generations for the Norse themselves to have weeded out deceptively good-looking patches that eventually proved unsuitable. Jared Diamond's city-dweller criteria for a good medieval Norse farm site are as follows:

1. The site should have a large area of flat or gently sloping lowlands (at elevations below 700 feet above sea level) to develop as a productive infield, because lowlands have the warmest climate and longest snow-free growing season, and because grass growth is poorer on steeper slopes. Among Greenland Norse farms, the cathedral farm of Gardar was preeminent in its expanse of flat lowlands, followed by some of the Vatnahverfi farms.

2. Complementary to this requirement for a large lowland infield is a large area of outfield at mid-elevations (up to 1,300 feet above sea level) for producing additional hay. Calculations show that the area of lowlands alone at most Norse farms would not have yielded enough hay to feed the farm's number of livestock, estimated by counting stalls or measuring areas of ruined barns. Erik the Red's farm at Brattahlid was preeminent in its large area of usable upland.

3. In the northern hemisphere, south-facing slopes receive the most sunlight. That's important so that the winter's snow will melt off earlier in the spring, the growing season for hay production will last more months, and the daily hours of sunlight will be longer. All of the best Norse Greenland farms—Gardar, Brattahlid, Hvalsey, and Sandnes—had south-facing exposures.

4. A good supply of streams is important for watering pastures by natural stream flow or by irrigation systems, to increase hay production.

5. It's a recipe for poverty to place your farm in, near, or facing a glacial valley off of which come cold strong winds that decrease grass growth and increase soil erosion on heavily grazed pastures. Glacial winds were a curse that ensured the poverty of farms at Narssaq and in Sermilik Fjord, and that eventually forced the abandonment of farms at the head of Qoroq Valley and at higher elevations in the Vatnahverfi district.

6. If possible, place your farm directly on a fjord with a good harbor for transporting supplies in and out by boat.

■ ■ ■

Dairy products alone were not enough to feed the 5,000 Norse inhabitants of Greenland. Gardening was of little use in making up that resulting deficit, because growing crops was so marginal in Greenland's cold climate and short growing season. Contemporary Norwegian documents mentioned that most Greenland Norse never saw wheat, a piece of bread, or beer (brewed from barley) during their entire lives. Today, when Greenland's climate is similar to what it was at the time that the Norse arrived, I saw at the former best Norse farm site of Gardar two small gardens in which modern Greenlanders were growing a few cold-resistant crops: cabbage, beets, rhubarb, and lettuce, which grew in medieval Norway, plus potatoes, which arrived in Europe only after the demise of the Norse Greenland colony. Presumably the Norse, too, could have grown those same crops (other than potatoes) in a few gardens, plus perhaps a little barley in especially mild years. At Gardar and two other Eastern Settlement farms I saw small fields at sites that might have served as Norse gardens, at the base of cliffs that would have retained the sun's heat, and with walls to keep sheep and winds out. But our only direct evidence for gardening by the Greenland Norse is some pollen and seeds of flax, a medieval European crop plant that was not native to Greenland, hence that must have been introduced by the Norse, and that was useful for making linen textiles and linseed oil. If the Norse did grow any other crops, they would have made only an extremely minor contribution to the diet, probably just as an occasional luxury food for a few chiefs and clergy.

Instead, the main other component of the Greenland Norse diet was meat of wild animals, especially caribou and seals, consumed to a far greater extent than in Norway or Iceland. Caribou live in large herds that spend the summer in the mountains and descend to lower elevations during the winter. Caribou teeth found in Norse garbage middens show that the animals were hunted in the fall, probably by bow and arrow in communal drives with dogs (the middens also had bones of big elkhounds). The three main seal species hunted were the common seal (alias harbor seal), which is resident all year round in Greenland and comes out on beaches in inner fjords to bear its pups in the spring, at which time it would have been easy to net from boats or to kill by clubbing; and the migratory harp seal and hooded seal, both of which breed in Newfoundland but arrive in Greenland around May in large herds along the seacoast, rather than in the inner fjords where most Norse farms were located. To hunt those migratory seals, the Norse established seasonal bases on the outer fjords, dozens of miles from any farm.

The May arrival of harp and hooded seals was critical to Norse survival, because at that time of year the stocks of stored dairy products from the previous summer and of caribou meat hunted in the previous fall would be
running out, but the snow had not yet disappeared from the Norse farms so
that livestock could not yet be put out to pasture, and consequently the livestock had not yet given birth and were not yet producing milk. As we shall
see, that made the Norse vulnerable to starvation from a failure of the seal
migration, or from any obstacle (such as ice in the fjords and along the
coast, or else hostile Inuit) that impeded their access to the migratory seals.
Such ice conditions may have been especially likely in cold years when the
Norse were already vulnerable because of cold summers and hence low hay
production.

By means of measurements of bone composition (so-called carbon isotope analyses), one can calculate the ratio of seafood to land-grown food
that the human or animal owner of those bones had consumed over the
course of a lifetime. As applied to Norse skeletons recovered from Greenland cemeteries, this method shows that the percentage of seafood (mostly
seals) consumed in Eastern Settlement at the time of its founding was
only 20% but rose to 80% during the later years of Norse survival: presumably because their ability to produce hay to feed wintering livestock had declined, and also because the increased human population needed more food
than their livestock could provide. At any given time, seafood consumption
was higher in Western Settlement than in Eastern Settlement, because hay
production was lower at Western Settlement's more northerly location. Seal
consumption by the Norse population may have been even higher than
these measurements indicate, since archaeologists would understandably
rather excavate big rich farms than small poor farms, but available bone
studies show that people at small poor farms with just a single cow ate more
seal meat than did rich farmers. At one poor Western Settlement farm, an
astonishing 70% of all animal bones in garbage middens were of seals.

Apart from that heavy reliance on seals and caribou, the Norse obtained
minor amounts of wild meat from small mammals (especially hares), seabirds, ptarmigans, swans, eider ducks, beds of mussels, and whales. The latter probably just consisted of the occasional stranded animal; Norse sites
contain no harpoons or other whale-hunting equipment. All meat not consumed immediately, whether from livestock or wild animals, would have
been dried in storage buildings called *skemmur*, built of uncemented stones
for the wind to whistle through and dry out the meat, and located on windy
sites like tops of ridges.

Conspicuously nearly absent from Norse archaeological sites are fish, even though the Greenland Norse were descended from Norwegians and Icelanders who spent much time fishing and happily ate fish. Fish bones account for much less than 0.1% of animal bones recovered at Greenland Norse archaeological sites, compared to between 50 and 95% at most contemporary Iceland, northern Norway, and Shetland sites. For instance, the archaeologist Thomas McGovern found the grand total of three fish bones in Norse garbage from Vatnahverfi farms next to lakes teeming with fish, while Georg Nygaard recovered only two fish bones from a total of 35,000 animal bones in the garbage of the Norse farm Ö34. Even at the GUS site, which yielded the largest number of fish bones—166, representing a mere 0.7% of all animal bones recovered from the site—26 of those bones come from the tail of a single cod, and bones of all fish species are still outnumbered 3 to 1 by bones of one bird species (the ptarmigan) and outnumbered 144 to 1 by mammal bones.

This paucity of fish bones is incredible when one considers how abundant fish are in Greenland, and how saltwater fish (especially haddock and cod) are by far the largest export of modern Greenland. Trout and salmon-like char are so numerous in Greenland's rivers and lakes that, on my first night in the youth hostel at Brattahlid, I shared the kitchen with a Danish tourist cooking two large char, each weighing two pounds and about 20 inches long, that she had caught with her bare hands in a small pool where they had become trapped. The Norse were surely as adept with their hands as that tourist, and they could also have caught fish in fjords with nets while they were netting seals. Even if the Norse didn't want to eat those easily caught fish themselves, they could at least have fed them to their dogs, thereby reducing the amount of seal and other meat that their dogs required, and sparing more meat for themselves.

Every archaeologist who comes to excavate in Greenland refuses initially to believe the incredible claim that the Greenland Norse didn't eat fish, and starts out with his or her own idea about where all those missing fish bones might be hiding. Could the Norse have strictly confined their munching on fish to within a few feet of the shoreline, at sites now underwater because of land subsidence? Could they have faithfully saved all their fish bones for fertilizer, fuel, or feeding to cows? Could their dogs have run off with those fish carcasses, dropped the fish bones in fields chosen with foresight to be ones where future archaeologists would rarely bother to dig, and carefully avoided carrying the carcasses back to the house or midden lest archaeologists subsequently find them? Might the Norse have had so much meat that they didn't need to eat fish?—but why, then, did they break bones to get out the last bit of marrow? Might all of those little fish bones have rotted away in the ground?—but preservation conditions in Greenland middens are good enough to preserve even sheep lice and sheep fecal pellets. The trouble with all those excuses for the lack of fish bones at Greenland Norse sites is that they would apply equally well to Greenland Inuit and Icelandic and Norwegian Norse sites, where fish bones prove instead to be abundant. Nor do these excuses explain why Greenland Norse sites contain almost no fish-hooks, fish line sinkers, or net sinkers, which are common in Norse sites elsewhere.

I prefer instead to take the facts at face value: even though Greenland's Norse originated from a fish-eating society, they may have developed a taboo against eating fish. Every society has its own arbitrary food taboos, as one of the many ways to distinguish itself from other societies: we virtuous clean people don't eat those disgusting things that those other gross weirdos seem to savor. By far the highest proportion of those taboos involves meat and fish. For instance, the French eat snails and frogs and horses, New Guineans eat rats and spiders and beetle larvae, Mexicans eat goat, and Polynesians eat marine annelid worms, all of which are nutritious and (if you let yourself taste them) delicious, but most Americans would recoil at the thought of eating any of those things.

As for the ultimate reasons why meat and fish so often get tabooed, they are much more likely than plant foods to develop bacteria or protozoa that give us food poisoning or parasites if we eat them. That's especially likely to happen in Iceland and Scandinavia, whose people employ many fermentation methods for long-term preservation of smelly (non-Scandinavians would say "rotting") fish, including methods using deadly botulism-causing bacteria. The most painful illness of my life, worse even than malaria, arose when I contracted food poisoning from eating shrimp that I had bought in a market in Cambridge, England, and that were evidently not fresh. I was confined to bed for several days with awful retching, intense muscle pain, headaches, and diarrhea. That suggests to me a scenario for the Greenland Norse: perhaps Erik the Red, in the first years of the Greenland settlement, got an equally awful case of food poisoning from eating fish. On his recovery, he would have told everybody who would listen to him how bad fish is for you, and how we Greenlanders are a clean, proud people who would never stoop to the unhealthy habits of those desperate grubby ichthyophagous Icelanders and Norwegians.

■　■　■

Greenland's marginality for raising livestock meant that the Greenland Norse had to develop a complex, integrated economy in order to make ends meet. That integration involved both time and space: different activities were scheduled at different seasons, and different farms specialized in producing different things to share with other farms.

To understand the seasonal schedule, let's begin in the spring. In late May and early June came the brief but crucial season of seal hunting, when the migratory harp and hooded seals moved in herds along the outer fjords, and the resident common seals came out on beaches to give birth and were easiest to catch. The summer months of June through August were an especially busy season, when the livestock were brought out to pastures to graze, livestock were yielding milk to turn into storable dairy products, some men set out in boats for Labrador to cut timber, other boats headed north to hunt walruses, and cargo boats arrived from Iceland or Europe for trading. August and early September were hectic weeks of cutting, drying, and storing hay, just before the weeks in September when the cows were led back to barns from pastures and the sheep and goats were brought nearer to shelter. September and October were the season of the caribou hunt, while the winter months from November to April were a time to tend the animals in barns and shelters, to weave, to build and repair with wood, to process the tusks of walrus killed during the summer—and to pray that the stores of dairy products and dried meat for human food, the hay for animal fodder, and the fuel for heating and cooking didn't run out before the winter's end.

Besides that economic integration over time, integration over space was also necessary, because not even the richest Greenland farm was self-sufficient in everything required to survive through the year. That integration involved transfers between outer and inner fjords, between upland and lowland farms, between Western and Eastern Settlement, and between rich and poor farms. For instance, while the best pastures were in the lowlands at the heads of the inner fjords, the caribou hunt took place at upland farms suboptimal for pasturing because of cooler temperatures and a shorter growing season, while the seal hunt was concentrated in outer fjords where salt spray, fog, and cold weather meant poor farming. Those outer fjord hunting sites were beyond reach of inner-fjord farms whenever the fjords froze or filled up with icebergs. The Norse solved these spatial problems by transporting seal and seabird carcasses from outer to inner fjords, and caribou joints downhill from upland to lowland farms. For instance, seal bones remain abundant in the garbage of the highest-elevation inland farms, to which the carcasses must have been carried dozens of miles from the fjord mouths. At Vatnahverfi farms far inland, seal bones are as common in the garbage as are the bones of sheep and goats. Conversely, caribou bones are even commoner at big rich lowland farms than at the poorer uphill farms where the animals must have been killed.

Because Western Settlement lies 300 miles north of Eastern Settlement, its hay production per acre of pasture was barely one-third that of Eastern Settlement. However, Western Settlement was closer to the hunting grounds for walruses and polar bears that were Greenland's chief export to Europe, as I shall explain. Yet walrus ivory has been found at most Eastern Settlement archaeological sites, where it was evidently being processed during the winter, and ship trade (including ivory export) with Europe took place mainly at Gardar and other big Eastern Settlement farms. Thus, Western Settlement, although much smaller than Eastern Settlement, was crucial to the Norse economy.

Integration of poorer with richer farms was necessary because hay production and grass growth depend especially on a combination of two factors: temperature, and hours of sunlight. Warmer temperatures, and more hours or days of sunlight during the summer growing season, meant that a farm could produce more grass or hay and hence feed more livestock, both because the livestock could graze the grass for themselves during the summer and had more hay to eat during the winter. Hence in a good year the best farms at low elevation, on the inner fjords, or with south-facing exposures produced big surpluses of hay and livestock over and above the amounts required for the farm's human inhabitants to survive, while small poor farms at higher elevations, near the outer fjords, or without south-facing exposures produced smaller surpluses. In a bad year (colder and/or foggier), when hay production was depressed everywhere, the best farms might still have been left with some surplus, albeit a small one. But poorer farms might have found themselves with not even enough hay to feed all their animals through the winter. Hence they would have had to cull some animals in the fall and might at worst have had no animals left alive in the spring. At best, they might have had to divert their herd's entire milk production to rearing calves, lambs, and kids, and the farmers themselves would have had to depend on seal or caribou meat rather than dairy products for their own food.

One can recognize that pecking order of farm quality by the pecking order of space for cows in the ruins of Norse barns. By far the best farm, as reflected in the space for the most cows, was Gardar, unique in having two huge barns capable of holding the grand total of about 160 cows. The barns at several second-rank farms, such as Brattahlid and Sandnes, could have held 30 to 50 cows each. But poor farms had room for only a few cows, perhaps just a single one. The result was that the best farms subsidized poor farms in bad years by lending them livestock in the spring so that the poor farms could rebuild their herds.

Thus, Greenland society was characterized by much interdependence and sharing, with seals and seabirds being transported inland, caribou downhill, walrus tusks south, and livestock from richer to poorer farms. But in Greenland, as elsewhere in the world where rich and poor people are interdependent, rich and poor people didn't all end up with the same average wealth. Instead, different people ended up with different proportions of high-status and low-status foods in their diets, as reflected in counts of bones of different animal species in their garbage. The ratio of high-status cow to lower-status sheep bones, and of sheep to bottom-status goat bones, tends to be higher on good than on poorer farms, and higher on Eastern than on Western Settlement farms. Caribou bones, and especially seal bones, are more frequent at Western than at Eastern Settlement sites because Western Settlement was more marginal for raising livestock and was also near larger areas of caribou habitat. Among those two wild foods, caribou is better represented at the richest farms (especially Gardar), while people at poor farms ate much more seal. Having forced myself out of curiosity to taste seal while I was in Greenland, and not gotten beyond the second bite, I can understand why people from a European dietary background might prefer venison over seal if given the choice.

As an illustration of these trends with some actual numbers, the garbage of the poor Western Settlement farm known as W48 or Niaquusat tells us that the meat consumed by its unfortunate inhabitants came to the horrifying extent of 85% from seals, with 6% from goats, only 5% from caribou, 3% from sheep, and 1% (O rare blessed day!) from beef. At the same time, the gentry at Sandnes, the richest Western Settlement farm, was enjoying a diet of 32% caribou venison, 17% beef, 6% sheep, and 6% goat, leaving only 39% to be made up by seal. Happiest of all was the Eastern Settlement elite at Erik the Red's farm of Brattahlid, who succeeded in elevating beef consumption above either caribou or sheep, and suppressing goat to insignificant levels.

Two poignant anecdotes further illustrate how high-status people got to eat preferred foods much less available to low-status people even on the same farm. First, when archaeologists excavated the ruins of the Cathedral of St. Nicholas at Gardar, they found under the stone floor the skeleton of a man holding a bishop's staff and ring, probably John Arnason Smyrill, who served as Greenland's bishop from 1189 to 1209. Carbon isotope analysis of his bones shows that his diet had consisted 75% of land-based foods (probably mostly beef and cheese) and only 25% of marine foods (mostly seal). A contemporary man and woman whose skeletons were buried immediately beneath the bishop's, and who thus were presumably also of high status, had consumed a diet somewhat higher (45%) in marine food, but that percentage ranged up to 78% for other skeletons from Eastern Settlement, and 81% from Western Settlement. Second, at Sandnes, the richest farm in Western Settlement, the animal bones in the garbage outside the manor house proved that its occupants were eating plenty of caribou and livestock and not much seal. Only fifty yards away was a barn in which animals would have been kept for the winter, and in which farm workers would have lived then along with the animals and the manure. The garbage dump outside that barn showed that those workers had to content themselves with seal and had little caribou, beef, or mutton to enjoy.

The complexly integrated economy that I have described, based on raising livestock, hunting on land, and hunting in the fjords, enabled the Greenland Norse to survive in an environment where no one of those components alone was sufficient for survival. But that economy also hints at a possible reason for the Greenlanders' eventual demise, because it was vulnerable to failure of any of those components. Many possible climatic events could raise the specter of starvation: a short, cool, foggy summer, or a wet August, that decreased hay production; a long snowy winter that was hard on both the livestock and the caribou, and that increased the winter hay requirements of the livestock; ice pile-up in the fjords, impeding access to the outer fjords during the May–June sealing season; a change in ocean temperatures, affecting fish populations and hence the populations of fish-eating seals; or a climate change far away in Newfoundland, affecting harp and hooded seals on their breeding grounds. Several of these events have been documented in modern Greenland: for instance, the cold winter and heavy snows of 1966–1967 killed 22,000 sheep, while migratory harp seals during the cold years of 1959–1974 fell to a mere 2% of their former numbers. Even in the best years, Western Settlement was closer to the margin for hay production than was Eastern Settlement, and a drop in summer temperature by a mere 1°C would suffice to cause failure of the hay crop at the former location.

The Norse could cope with livestock losses from one bad summer or bad winter, provided that it was followed by a series of good years enabling them to rebuild their herds, and provided that they could hunt enough seal and caribou to eat during those years. More dangerous was a decade with several bad years, or a summer of low hay production followed by a long snowy winter necessitating much hay for feeding livestock indoors, in combination with a crash in seal numbers or else anything impeding spring access to the outer fjords. As we shall see, that was what actually happened eventually at Western Settlement.

Five adjectives, mutually somewhat contradictory, characterize Greenland Norse society: communal, violent, hierarchical, conservative, and Eurocentric. All of those features were carried over from the ancestral Icelandic and Norwegian societies, but became expressed to an extreme degree in Greenland.

To begin with, Greenland's Norse population of about 5,000 lived on 250 farms, with an average of 20 people per farm, organized in turn into communities centered on 14 main churches, with an average of about 20 farms per church. Norse Greenland was a strongly communal society, in which one person could not go off, make a living by himself or herself, and hope to survive. On the one hand, cooperation among people of the same farm or community was essential for the spring seal hunt, summer Nordrseta hunt (described below), late-summer hay harvest, and autumn caribou hunt and for building, each of which activities required many people working together and would have been inefficient or impossible for a single person alone. (Imagine trying to round up a herd of wild caribou or seals, or lifting a 4-ton stone of a cathedral into place, by yourself.) On the other hand, cooperation was also necessary for economic integration between farms and especially between communities, because different Greenland locations produced different things, such that people at different locations depended on each other for the things that they did not produce. I already mentioned the transfers of seals hunted at the outer fjords to the inner fjords, of caribou meat hunted at upland sites to lowland sites, and of livestock from rich to poor farms when the latter lost their animals in a harsh winter. The 160 cattle for which the Gardar barns contained stalls far exceeded any conceivable local needs at Gardar. As we shall see below, walrus tusks, Greenland's most valuable export, were acquired by a few Western Settlement hunters in the Nordrseta hunting grounds but were then distributed widely among Western and Eastern Settlement farms for the laborious task of processing before export.

Belonging to a farm was essential both to survival and to social identity. Every piece of the few useful patches of land in the Western and Eastern Settlements was owned either by some individual farm or else communally by a group of farms, which thereby held the rights to all of that land's resources, including not only its pastures and hay but also its caribou, turf, berries, and even its driftwood. Hence a Greenlander wanting to go it alone couldn't just go off hunting and foraging for himself. In Iceland, if you lost your farm or got ostracized, you could try living somewhere else—on an island, an abandoned farm, or the interior highlands. You didn't have that option in Greenland, where there wasn't any "somewhere else" to which to go.

The result was a tightly controlled society, in which the few chiefs of the richest farms could prevent anyone else from doing something that seemed to threaten their interests—including anyone experimenting with innovations that did not promise to help the chiefs. At the top, Western Settlement was controlled by Sandnes, its richest farm and its sole one with access to the outer fjords, while Eastern Settlement was controlled by Gardar, its richest farm and the seat of its bishop. We shall see that this consideration may help us understand the eventual fate of Greenland Norse society.

Also carried to Greenland from Iceland and Norway along with this communality was a strong violent streak. Some of our evidence is written: when Norway's King Sigurd Jorsalfar proposed in 1124 to a priest named Arnald that Arnald go to Greenland as its first resident bishop, Arnald's excuses for not wanting to accept included that the Greenlanders were such cantankerous people. To which the shrewd king replied, "The greater the trials that you suffer at the hands of men, the greater will be your own merits and rewards." Arnald accepted on condition that a highly respected Greenland chief's son named Einar Sokkason swear to defend him and the Greenland church properties, and to smite his enemies. As related in Einar Sokkason's saga (see synopsis following), Arnald did get involved in the usual violent quarrels when he reached Greenland, but he handled them so skillfully that all the main litigants (including even Einar Sokkason) ended up killing each other while Arnald retained his life and authority.

The other evidence for violence in Greenland is more concrete. The church cemetery at Brattahlid includes, in addition to many individual graves with neatly placed whole skeletons, a mass grave dating from the earliest phase of the Greenland colony, and containing the disarticulated bones of 13 adult men and one nine-year-old child, probably a clan party that lost a feud. Five of those skeletons bear skull wounds inflicted by a sharp instrument, presumably an axe or sword. While two of the skull wounds show

A Typical Week in the Life of a Greenland Bishop: The Saga of Einar Sokkason

While off hunting with 14 friends, Sigurd Njalsson found a beached ship full of valuable cargo. In a nearby hut were the stinking corpses of the ship's crew and its captain Arnbjorn, who had died of starvation. Sigurd brought the bones of the crew back to Gardar Cathedral for burial, and donated the ship itself to Bishop Arnald for the benefit of the corpses of the souls. As for the cargo, he asserted finders/keepers rights and divided it among his friends and himself.

When Arnbjorn's nephew Ozur heard the news, he came to Gardar, together with the relatives of others of the dead crew. They told the Bishop that they felt entitled to inherit the cargo. But the Bishop answered that Greenland law specified finders/keepers, that the cargo and ship should now belong to the church to pay for masses for the souls of the dead men who had owned the cargo, and that it was shabby of Ozur and his friends to claim the cargo now. So Ozur filed a suit in the Greenland Assembly, attended by Ozur and all his men and also by Bishop Arnald and his friend Einar Sokkason and many of their men. The court ruled against Ozur, who didn't like the ruling at all and felt humiliated, so he ruined Sigurd's ship (now belonging to Bishop Arnald) by cutting out planks along the full length of each side. That made the Bishop so angry that he declared Ozur's life forfeit.

While the Bishop was saying holiday mass in church, Ozur was in the congregation and complained to the Bishop's servant about how badly the Bishop had treated him. Einar seized an axe from the hand of another worshipper and struck Ozur a death-blow. The Bishop asked Einar, "Einar, did you cause Ozur's death?" "Very true," said Einar, "I have." The Bishop's response was: "Such acts of murder are not right. But this particular one is not without justification." The Bishop didn't want to give Ozur a church burial, but Einar warned that big trouble was on its way.

In fact, Ozur's relative Simon, a big strong man, said that this was not the time for merely big talk. He gathered his friends Kolbein Thorljotsson, Keitel Kalfsson, and many men from Western Settle-

ment. An old man named Sokki Thorisson offered to mediate between Simon and Einar. As compensation for having murdered Ozur,
Einar offered some articles including an ancient suit of armor, which
Simon rejected as rubbish. Kolbein slipped around behind Einar and
hit him between the shoulders with his axe, just at the moment when
Einar was bringing down his own axe on Simon's head. As both Simon
and Einar fell dying, Einar commented, "It is only what I expected."
Einar's foster-brother Thord rushed at Kolbein, who managed to kill
him at once by jabbing an axe into his throat.

Einar's men and Kolbein's men then started a battle against each
other. A man called Steingrim told them all to please stop fighting, but
both sides were so mad that they thrust a sword through Steingrim.
On Kolbein's side, Krak, Thorir, and Vighvat ended up dead, as well as
Simon. On Einar's side, Bjorn, Thorarin, Thord, and Thorfinn ended
up dead as well as Einar, plus Steingrim counted as a member of
Einar's side. Many men were badly wounded. At a peace meeting organized by a level-headed farmer called Hall, Kolbein's side was ordered
to pay compensation because Einar's side had lost more men. Even so,
Einar's side was bitterly disappointed in the verdict. Kolbein sailed off
to Norway with a polar bear that he gave as a present to King Harald
Gilli, still complaining about how cruelly he had been treated. King
Harald considered Kolbein's story a pack of lies and refused to pay a
bounty for the polar bear. So Kolbein attacked and wounded the king
and sailed off to Denmark but drowned en route. And that is the end
of this saga.

signs of bone healing, implying that the victims survived the blow to die
much later, the wounds of three others exhibit little or no healing, implying
a quick death. That outcome isn't surprising when one sees photos of the
skulls, one of which had a piece of bone three inches long by two inches
wide sliced out of it. The skull wounds were all on either the left side of the
front of the skull or the right side of the back, as expected for a right-
handed assailant striking from in front or behind, respectively. (Most sword
combat wounds fit this pattern, because most people are right-handed.)

Another male skeleton at the same churchyard has a knife blade between
the ribs. Two female skeletons from Sandnes cemetery with similar cut
wounds of the skull testify that women as well as men could die in feuds.

Dating from later years of the Greenland colony, at a time when axes and swords had become vanishingly rare because of scarcity of iron, are skulls of four adult women and one eight-year-old child, each with one or two sharp-edged holes between half an inch and one inch in diameter and evidently made by a crossbow bolt or arrow. Domestic violence is suggested by the skeleton of a 50-year-old woman at Gardar Cathedral with a fractured throat bone called the hyoid; forensic pathologists have learned to interpret a fractured hyoid as evidence that the victim was strangled by a hand choke hold.

Along with that violent streak coexisting uneasily with an emphasis on communal cooperation, the Greenland Norse also carried over from Iceland and Norway a sharply stratified, hierarchically organized social organization, such that a small number of chiefs dominated owners of small farms, tenants who didn't even own their own farms, and (initially) slaves. Again like Iceland, Greenland politically was not organized as a state but as a loose federation of chiefdoms operating under feudal conditions, with neither money nor a market economy. Within the first century or two of the Greenland colony, slavery disappeared, and the slaves became freedmen. However, the number of independent farmers probably decreased with time as they were forced into becoming tenants of the chiefs, a process that is well documented in Iceland. We don't have corresponding records for the process in Greenland, but it seems likely there too, because the forces promoting it were even more marked in Greenland than in Iceland. Those forces consisted of climate fluctuations driving poorer farmers in bad years into debt to richer farmers who lent them hay and livestock, and who could eventually foreclose on them. Evidence of those farm hierarchies is still visible today among Greenland farm ruins: compared to poor farms, the best-located farms had a larger area of good pasture, larger cow and sheep barns with stalls for more animals, bigger hay barns, larger houses, larger churches, and smithies. The hierarchies are also visible today as the higher ratios of cow and caribou bones to sheep and seal bones in garbage middens at rich farms compared to those at poor farms.

Still like Iceland, Viking Greenland was a conservative society resistant to change and sticking to old ways, compared to the society of the Vikings who remained behind in Norway. Over the centuries, there was little change in styles of tools and of carvings. Fishing was abandoned in the earliest years of the colony, and Greenlanders did not reconsider that decision during the four-and-a-half centuries of their society's existence. They did not learn from the Inuit how to hunt ringed seals or whales, even though that meant not eating locally common foods, and starving as a result. The ultimate reason behind that conservative outlook of the Greenlanders may have been the same as the reason to which my Icelandic friends attribute their own society's conservatism. That is, even more than the Icelanders, the Greenlanders found themselves in a very difficult environment. While they succeeded in developing an economy that let them survive there for many generations, they found that variations on that economy were much more likely to prove disastrous than advantageous. That was good reason to be conservative.

The remaining adjective that characterizes Greenland Norse society is "Eurocentric." From Europe, the Greenlanders received material trade goods, but even more important were non-material imports: identities as Christians, and as Europeans. Let us consider first the material trade. What trade items were imported into Greenland, and with what exports did the Greenlanders pay for those imports?

For medieval sailing ships, the voyage to Greenland from Norway took a week or more and was dangerous; annals often mention shipwrecks, or ships that sailed and were never heard from again. Hence the Greenlanders were visited by at most a couple of European ships a year, and sometimes only one every few years. In addition, the capacities of European cargo ships in those days were small. Estimates of the frequency of ship visits, ship capacities, and Greenland's population let one calculate that imports worked out to about seven pounds of cargo per person per year—on the average. Most Greenlanders received much less than that average, because much of that arriving cargo capacity was devoted to materials for churches and luxuries for the elite. Hence imports could only be valuable items occupying little space. In particular, Greenland had to be self-sufficient in food and could not depend on bulk imports of cereals and other food staples.

Our two sources of information about Greenland's imports are lists in Norwegian records, and items of European origin found in Greenland archaeological sites. They included especially three necessities: iron that the Greenlanders were hard-pressed to produce for themselves; good lumber for buildings and furniture, of which they were equally short; and tar as a lubricant and wood preservative. As for non-economic imports, many were for the church, including church bells, stained glass windows, bronze candlesticks, communion wine, linen, silk, silver, and churchmen's robes and jewelry. Among secular luxuries found in archaeological sites at farmhouses were pewter, pottery, and glass beads and buttons. Small-volume luxury food imports probably included honey to ferment into mead, plus salt as a preservative.

In exchange for those imports, the same consideration of limited ship cargo capacity would have prevented Greenlanders from exporting bulk fish, as did medieval Iceland and as does modern Greenland, even if Greenlanders had been willing to fish. Instead, Greenland's exports, too, had to be things of low volume and high value. They included skins of goats, cattle, and seals, which Europeans could also obtain from other countries but of which medieval Europe required large quantities to make leather clothes, shoes, and belts. Like Iceland, Greenland exported wool cloth that was valued for being water-repellent. But Greenland's most prized exports mentioned in Norwegian records were five products derived from Arctic animals rare or absent in most of Europe: walrus ivory from walrus tusks, walrus hide (valued because it yielded the strongest rope for ships), live polar bears or their hides as a spectacular status symbol, tusks of the narwhal (a small whale) known then in Europe as unicorn horns, and live gyrfalcons (the world's largest falcon). Walrus tusks became the only ivory available in medieval Europe for carving after Moslems gained control of the Mediterranean, thereby cutting off supplies of elephant ivory to Christian Europe. As an example of the value placed on Greenland gyrfalcons, 12 of those birds sufficed in 1396 to ransom the Duke of Burgundy's son after he was captured by the Saracens.

Walruses and polar bears were virtually confined to latitudes far to the north of the two Norse settlements, in an area called the Nordrseta (the northern hunting ground), which began several hundred miles beyond Western Settlement and stretched farther north along Greenland's west coast. Hence each summer the Greenlanders sent out hunting parties in small, open, six-oared rowboats with sails, which could cover about 20 miles per day and could hold up to a ton-and-a-half of cargo. Hunters set off in June after the peak of the harp seal hunt, taking two weeks to reach the Nordrseta from Western Settlement or four weeks from Eastern Settlement, and returning again at the end of August. In such small boats they obviously could not carry the carcasses of hundreds of walruses and polar bears, each of which weighs about a ton or half-a-ton respectively. Instead, the animals were butchered on the spot, and only the walrus jaws with the tusks, and the bear skins with the paws (plus the occasional live captive bear), were brought home, for the tusks to be extracted and the skin to be cleaned at leisure back in the settlements during the long winter. Also brought home was the baculum of male walruses, a bone like a straight rod about one foot long that forms the core of the walrus penis, because it proved to be of just the right size and shape (and, one suspects, conversation value) to make into an axe handle or a hook.

The Nordrseta hunt was dangerous and expensive in many ways. To begin with, hunting walruses and polar bears without a gun must have been very dangerous. Please imagine yourself, equipped with just a lance, spear, bow and arrow, or club (take your choice) trying to kill a huge enraged walrus or bear before it could kill you. Please also imagine yourself spending several weeks in a small rowboat shared with a live, trussed-up polar bear or its cubs. Even without a live bear as companion, the boat journey itself along the cold stormy coast of West Greenland exposed hunters to risk of death from shipwreck or exposure for several weeks. Apart from those dangers, the trip constituted expensive use of boats, manpower, and summer time for people short of all three. Because of Greenland's scarcity of lumber, few Greenlanders owned boats, and using those precious boats to hunt walruses came at the expense of other possible uses of the boats, such as going to Labrador to acquire more lumber. The hunt took place in the summer, when men were needed to harvest the hay required to feed livestock through the winter. Much of what the Greenlanders obtained materially by trade with Europe in return for those walrus tusks and bearskins was just luxury goods for churches and chiefs. From our perspective today, we can't help thinking of seemingly more important uses that the Greenlanders could have made of those boats and man-time. From the Greenlanders' perspective, though, the hunt must have brought great prestige to the individual hunters, and it maintained for the whole society the psychologically vital contact with Europe.

Greenland's trade with Europe was mainly through the Norwegian ports of Bergen and Trondheim. While at first some cargo was carried in ocean-going ships belonging to Icelanders and to the Greenlanders themselves, those ships as they aged could not be replaced due to the islands' lack of timber, leaving the trade to Norwegian ships. By the mid 1200s, there were often periods of several years in which no ship at all visited Greenland. In 1257 Norway's King Haakon Haakonsson, as part of his effort to assert his authority over all of the Norse Atlantic island societies, sent three commissioners to Greenland to persuade the hitherto-independent Greenlanders to acknowledge his sovereignty and pay tribute. Although the details of the resulting agreement have not been preserved, some documents suggest that Greenland's acceptance of Norwegian sovereignty in 1261 was in return for the king's promise to dispatch two ships each year, similar to his simultaneous agreement with Iceland which we know stipulated six ships each year. Thereafter, Greenland's trade became a Norwegian royal monopoly. But Greenland's association with Norway remained loose, and Norwegian authority difficult to enforce because of Greenland's distance. We know for sure only that a royal agent resided in Greenland at various times during the 1300s.

At least as important as Europe's material exports to Greenland were its psychological exports of Christian identity and European identity. Those two identities may explain why the Greenlanders acted in ways that—we today would say with the value of hindsight—were maladaptive and ultimately cost them their lives, but that for many centuries enabled them to maintain a functioning society under the most difficult conditions faced by any medieval Europeans.

Greenland converted to Christianity around A.D. 1000, at the same time as the conversions of Iceland and the other Viking Atlantic colonies, and of Norway itself. For more than a century the Greenland churches remained small structures built of turf on some farmer's land, mainly on the largest farms. Most likely, as in Iceland, they were so-called proprietary churches, built and owned by the landowning farmer, who received part of the tithes paid to that church by its local members.

But Greenland still had no resident bishop, whose presence was required for performing confirmations and for a church to be considered consecrated. Hence around 1118 that very same Einar Sokkason whom we have already encountered as a saga hero killed by an axe blow from behind was sent by the Greenlanders to Norway in order to persuade its king to provide Greenland with a bishop. As inducements, Einar took along to give the king a large supply of ivory, walrus hides, and—best of all—a live polar bear. That did the trick. The king, in turn, persuaded that Arnald whom we already met in Einar Sokkason's saga to become Greenland's first resident bishop, to be followed by about nine others over the succeeding centuries. Without exception, all were born and educated in Europe and came to Greenland only upon their appointment as bishop. Not surprisingly, they looked to Europe for their models, preferred beef over seal meat, and directed resources of Greenland society to the Nordrseta hunt that enabled them to buy wine and vestments for themselves, and stained glass windows for their churches.

A big construction program of churches modeled on European churches followed Arnald's appointment, and continued to around 1300, when the lovely church at Hvalsey was erected as one of the last. Greenland's ecclesiastical establishment came to consist of one cathedral, about 13 large parish churches, many smaller churches, and even a monastery and a nunnery. While most of the churches were built with stone lower walls and turf upper walls, Hvalsey Church and at least three others had walls entirely of stone. These big churches were all out of proportion to the size of the tiny society that erected and supported them.

For instance, St. Nicholas's Cathedral at Gardar, measuring 105 feet long by 53 feet wide, was as large as either of the two cathedrals of Iceland, whose population was ten times that of Greenland. I estimated the largest of the stone blocks of its lower walls, carefully carved to fit each other and transported from sandstone quarries at least a mile distant, to weigh about three tons. Even larger was a flagstone of about 10 tons in front of the bishop's house. Adjacent structures included a bell tower 80 feet high, and a ceremonial hall with a floor area of 1,400 square feet, the largest hall in Greenland and nearly three-quarters the size of the hall of the archbishop of Trondheim in Norway. On an equally lavish scale were the cathedrals' two cow barns, one of them 208 feet long (the largest barn in Greenland) and fitted with a stone lintel weighing about four tons. As a splendid welcome to visitors, the cathedral's grounds were decorated with about 25 complete walrus skulls and five narwhal skulls, which may be the only ones preserved at any Greenland Norse site: otherwise, archaeologists have found only chips of ivory, because it was so valuable and was almost all exported to Europe.

Gardar Cathedral and the other Greenland churches must have consumed horrifyingly large amounts of scarce timber to support their walls and roofs. Imported church paraphernalia, such as bronze bells and communion wine, were also expensive to Greenlanders because they were ultimately bought with the sweat and blood of Nordrseta hunters and competed against essential iron for the limited cargo space on arriving ships. Recurrent expenses that their churches cost the Greenlanders were an annual tithe paid to Rome, and additional Crusade tithes levied on all Christians. These tithes were paid with Greenland exports shipped to Bergen and converted to silver there. A surviving receipt for one such shipment, the six-year Crusade Tithe of 1274–1280, shows that it consisted of 1,470 pounds of ivory from the tusks of 191 walruses, which Norway's archbishop managed to sell for 26 pounds of pure silver. That the Church was able to extract such tithes and complete such building programs testifies to the authority it commanded in Greenland.

Church-associated land ultimately came to comprise much of the best land in Greenland, including about one-third of the land of Eastern Settlement. Greenland's church tithes, and possibly its other exports to Europe, went through Gardar, where one can still see the ruins of a large storage shed standing immediately next to the cathedral's southeast corner. With Gardar thus boasting Greenland's largest storage building, as well as by far its largest cattle herd and richest land, whoever controlled Gardar controlled Greenland. What remains unclear is whether Gardar and the other church farms in Greenland were owned by the Church itself or else by the farmers on whose land the churches stood. But whether authority and ownership rested with the bishop or with the chiefs doesn't alter the main conclusion: Greenland was a hierarchical society, with great differences of wealth justified by the Church, and with disproportionate investment in churches. Again, we moderns have to wonder if the Greenlanders wouldn't have been better off had they imported fewer bronze bells, and more iron with which to make tools, weapons to defend themselves against the Inuit, or goods to trade with the Inuit for meat in times of stress. But we ask our question with the gift of hindsight, and without regard to the cultural heritage that led the Greenlanders to make their choices.

Besides that specific identity as Christians, Greenlanders maintained their European identity in many other ways, including their importation of European bronze candlesticks, glass buttons, and gold rings. Over the centuries of their colony's existence, the Greenlanders followed and adopted changing European customs in detail. One well-documented set of examples involves burial customs, as revealed by excavations of bodies in Scandinavian and Greenland churchyards. Medieval Norwegians buried infants and stillborns around a church's east gable; so did the Greenlanders. Early medieval Norwegians buried bodies in coffins, with women on the south side of churchyards and men on the north side; later Norwegians dispensed with coffins, just wrapped bodies in clothing or a shroud, and mingled the sexes in the churchyard. Greenlanders made those same shifts with time. In continental European cemeteries throughout the Middle Ages, bodies were laid out on their backs with the head towards the west and the feet towards the east (so that the deceased could "face" east), but the position of the arms changed with time: until 1250 the arms were arranged to extend parallel to the sides, then around 1250 they were bent slightly over the pelvis, later bent further to rest over the stomach, and finally in the late Middle Ages folded tightly over the chest. Even those shifts in arm positions are observed in Greenland cemeteries.

Greenland church construction similarly followed Norwegian European models and their changes with time. Any tourist accustomed to European cathedrals, with their long nave, west-facing main entrance, chancel, and north and south transepts, will immediately recognize all those features in the stone ruins of Gardar Cathedral today. Hvalsey Church so closely resembles Eidfjord Church in Norway that we can conclude that Greenlanders must either have brought over the same architect or else copied the blueprints. Between 1200 and 1225, Norwegian builders abandoned their previous unit of linear measurement (the so-called international Roman foot) and adopted the shorter Greek foot; Greenland builders followed suit.

Imitation of European models extended to homely details like combs and clothes. Norwegian combs were single-sided, with the tines on just one side of the shaft, until around 1200, when those combs went out of fashion and were replaced by two-sided models with sets of tines projecting in opposite directions; Greenlanders followed that switch in comb styles. (That calls to mind Henry Thoreau's comment, in his book *Walden*, about people who slavishly adopt the latest style of fashion designers in a distant land: "The head monkey at Paris puts on a traveler's cap, and all the monkeys in America do the same.") The excellent preservation of garments wrapped around the corpses buried in the permafrost at Herjolfsnes Churchyard from the final decades of the Greenland colony's existence shows us that Greenland clothes followed smart European fashions, even though they seem far less appropriate to Greenland's cold climate than the Inuit one-piece tailored parka with fitted sleeves and attached hood. Those clothes of the last Greenland Norse included: for women, a long, low-necked gown with a narrow waist; for men, a sporty coat called a *houpelande,* which was a long loose outer garment held in by a belt at the waist and with loose sleeves up which the wind could whistle; jackets buttoned up the front; and tall cylindrical caps.

All these adoptions of European styles make it obvious that the Greenlanders paid very close attention to European fashions and followed them in detail. The adoptions carry the unconscious message, "We are Europeans, we are Christians, God forbid that anyone could confuse us with the Inuit." Just as Australia, when I began visiting it in the 1960s, was more British than Britain itself, Europe's most remote outpost of Greenland remained emotionally tied to Europe. That would have been innocent if the ties had expressed themselves only in two-sided combs and in the position in which the arms were folded over a corpse. But the insistence on "We are Europeans" becomes more serious when it leads to stubbornly maintaining cows in Greenland's climate, diverting manpower from the summer hay harvest to the Nordrseta hunt, refusing to adopt useful features of Inuit technology, and starving to death as a result. To us in our secular modern society, the predicament in which the Greenlanders found themselves is difficult to fathom. To them, however, concerned with their social survival as much as with their biological survival, it was out of the question to invest less in churches, to imitate or intermarry with the Inuit, and thereby to face an eternity in Hell just in order to survive another winter on Earth. The Greenlanders' clinging to their European Christian image may have been a factor in their conservatism that I mentioned above: more European than Europeans themselves, and thereby culturally hampered in making the drastic lifestyle changes that could have helped them survive.

CHAPTER 8

Norse Greenland's End

Introduction to the end ▪ Deforestation ▪ Soil and turf damage ▪
The Inuit's predecessors ▪ Inuit subsistence ▪ Inuit/Norse relations ▪
The end ▪ Ultimate causes of the end ▪

In the previous chapter we saw how the Norse initially prospered in Greenland, due to a fortunate set of circumstances surrounding their arrival.
They had the good luck to discover a virgin landscape that had never
been logged or grazed, and that was suitable for use as pasture. They arrived
at a time of relatively mild climate, when hay production was sufficient
in most years, when the sea lanes to Europe were free of ice, when there
was European demand for their exports of walrus ivory, and when there
were no Native Americans anywhere near the Norse settlements or hunting
grounds.

All of those initial advantages gradually turned against the Norse, in
ways for which they bore some responsibility. While climate change, Europe's changing demand for ivory, and the arrival of the Inuit were beyond
their control, how the Norse dealt with those changes was up to them. Their
impact on the landscape was a factor entirely of their own making. In this
chapter we shall see how the shifts in those advantages, and the Norse reactions to them, combined to bring an end to the Norse Greenland colony.

The Greenland Norse damaged their environment in at least three ways: by
destroying the natural vegetation, by causing soil erosion, and by cutting
turf. As soon as they arrived, they burned woodlands to clear land for pasture, then cut down some of the remaining trees for purposes such as lumber and firewood. Trees were prevented from regenerating by livestock
grazing and trampling, especially in the winter, when plants were most vulnerable because of not growing then.

The effects of those impacts on the natural vegetation have been gauged
by our friends the palynologists examining radiocarbon-dated slices of sediments collected from the bottoms of lakes and bogs. In those sediments oc-

cur at least five environmental indicators: whole plant parts such as leaves, and plant pollen, both of which serve to identify the plant species growing near the lake at that time; charcoal particles, proof of fires nearby; magnetic susceptibility measurements, which in Greenland reflect mainly the amounts of magnetic iron minerals in the sediment, arising from topsoil washed or blown into the lake's basin; and sand similarly washed or blown in.

These studies of lake sediments yield the following picture of vegetational history around the Norse farms. As temperatures warmed up at the end of the last Ice Age, pollen counts show that grasses and sedges became replaced by trees. For the next 8,000 years there were few further changes in the vegetation, and few or no signs of deforestation and erosion—until the Vikings arrived. That event was signaled by a layer of charcoal from Viking fires to clear pastures for their livestock. Pollen of willow and birch trees decreased, while pollen of grasses, sedges, weeds, and pasture plants introduced by the Norse for animal feed rose. Increased magnetic susceptibility values show that topsoil was carried into lakes, the topsoil having lost the plant cover that had previously protected it from erosion by wind and water. Finally, sand underlying the topsoil also was carried in when whole valleys had been denuded of their plant cover and soil. All of these changes became reversed, indicating recovery of the landscape, after the Viking settlements went extinct in the 1400s. Finally, the same set of changes that accompanied Norse arrival appeared all over again after 1924, when the Danish government of Greenland reintroduced sheep five centuries after their demise along with their Viking caretakers.

So what?—an environmental skeptic might ask. That's sad for willow trees, but what about people? It turned out that deforestation, soil erosion, and turf cutting all had serious consequences for the Norse. The most obvious consequence of deforestation was that the Norse quickly became short of lumber, as did the Icelanders and Mangarevans. The low and thin trunks of the willow, birch, and juniper trees remaining were suitable for making only small household wooden objects. For large pieces of wood to fashion into beams of houses, boats, sledges, barrels, wall panels, and beds, the Norse came to depend on three sources of timber: Siberian driftwood washed up on the beaches, imported logs from Norway, and trees felled by the Greenlanders themselves on voyages to the Labrador coast ("Markland") discovered in the course of the Vinland explorations. Lumber evidently remained so scarce that wooden objects were recycled rather than discarded. This can be deduced from the absence of large wooden panels and furniture at most Greenland Norse ruins except for the last houses in which the Norse of

Western Settlement died. At a famous Western Settlement archaeological site called "Farm Beneath the Sands," which became almost perfectly preserved under frozen river sands, most timber found was in the upper layers rather than in the lower layers, again suggesting that timber of old rooms and buildings was too precious to discard and was scavenged as rooms were remodeled or added. The Norse also dealt with their poverty in timber by resorting to turf for walls of buildings, but we shall see that that solution posed its own set of problems.

Another answer to the "so what?" response to deforestation is: poverty in firewood. Unlike the Inuit, who learned to use blubber for heating and lighting their dwellings, remains in Norse hearths show that the Norse continued to burn willow and alder wood in their houses. A major additional demand for firewood that most of us modern city-dwellers would never think of was in the dairy. Milk is an ephemeral, potentially dangerous food source: it is so nourishing, not only to us but also to bacteria, that it quickly spoils if left to stand without the pasteurization and refrigeration that we take for granted and that the Norse, like everyone else before modern times, didn't practice. Hence the vessels in which the Norse collected and stored milk and made cheese had to be washed frequently with boiled water, twice a day in the case of milk buckets. Milking animals at saeters (those summer farm buildings in the hills) was consequently confined to elevations below 1,300 feet, above which firewood was unavailable, even though pasture grasses good for feeding livestock grew up to much higher elevations of about 2,500 feet. In both Iceland and Norway we know that saeters had to be closed down when local firewood became exhausted, and the same presumably held for Greenland as well. Just as was true for scarce lumber, the Norse substituted other materials for scarce firewood, by burning animal bones, manure, and turf. But those solutions too had disadvantages: the bones and manure could otherwise have been used to fertilize fields for increased hay production, and burning turf was tantamount to destroying pasture.

The remaining heavy consequences of deforestation, besides shortages of lumber and firewood, involved shortages of iron. Scandinavians obtained most of their iron as bog iron—i.e., by extracting the metal from bog sediments with low iron content. Bog iron itself is locally available in Greenland, as in Iceland and Scandinavia: Christian Keller and I saw an iron-colored bog at Gardar in the Eastern Settlement, and Thomas McGovern saw other such bogs in the Western Settlement. The problem lay not with finding bog iron in Greenland but with extracting it, because the extraction required huge quantities of wood to make the charcoal with which to produce the necessary very high temperature of fire. Even when the Greenlanders skipped that step by importing iron ingots from Norway, they still needed charcoal to work the iron into tools, and to sharpen, repair, and remake iron tools, which they had to do frequently.

We know that the Greenlanders possessed iron tools and worked with iron. Many of the larger Norse Greenland farms have remains of iron smithies and iron slag, though that doesn't tell us whether the smithies were used just to rework imported iron or to extract bog iron. At Greenland Viking archaeological sites have been found examples of the usual iron objects expected for a medieval Scandinavian society, including axe heads, scythes, knives, sheep shears, ships' rivets, carpenters' planes, awls to punch holes, and gimlets to bore holes.

But those same sites make clear that the Greenlanders were desperately short of iron, even by the standards of medieval Scandinavia, where iron wasn't plentiful. For example, far more nails and other iron objects are found at British and Shetland Viking sites, and even at Iceland sites and at the Vinland site of L'Anse aux Meadows, than at Greenland sites. Discarded iron nails are the commonest iron item at L'Anse aux Meadows, and many are also found at sites in Iceland, despite Iceland's own shortage of wood and iron. But iron poverty was extreme in Greenland. A few iron nails have been found in the lowest archaeological layers there, almost none in later layers, because iron became too precious to discard. Not a single sword, helmet, or even a piece of one has been found in Greenland, and just a couple of pieces of chain mail armor, possibly all from a single suit. Iron tools were reused and resharpened until worn down to stubs. For example, from excavations in Qorlortoq Valley I was struck by the pathos of a knife whose blade had been worn down to almost nothing, still mounted on a handle whose length was all out of proportion to that stub, and evidently still valuable enough to have been resharpened.

The Greenlanders' iron poverty is also clear from the many objects, recovered at their archaeological sites, that in Europe were routinely made of iron but that the Greenlanders made of other, often unexpected, materials. Those objects included wooden nails and caribou-antler arrowheads. Iceland's annals for the year 1189 describe with surprise how a Greenland ship that had drifted off course to Iceland was nailed not with iron nails but with wooden pegs, and then lashed together with whale baleen. However, for

Vikings whose self-image focused on terrifying opponents by swinging a mighty battleaxe, to be reduced to making that weapon out of whalebone must have been the ultimate humiliation.

A result of the Greenlanders' iron poverty was reduced efficiency of essential processes of their economy. With few iron scythes, cleavers, and shears available, or with those tools having to be made of bone or stone, it would have taken more time to harvest hay, butcher a carcass, and shear sheep, respectively. But a more immediately fatal consequence was that, by losing iron, the Norse lost their military advantage over the Inuit. Elsewhere around the world, in innumerable battles between European colonizers and the native peoples whom they encountered, steel swords and armor gave Europeans enormous advantages. For instance, during the Spanish conquest of Peru's Inca Empire in 1532–1533, there were five battles in which respectively 169, 80, 30, 110, and 40 Spaniards slaughtered armies of thousands to tens of thousands of Incas, with not a single Spaniard killed and only a few injured—because Spanish steel swords cut through Indian cotton armor, and the Spaniards' steel armor protected them against blows from Indian stone or wooden weapons. But there is no evidence that the Greenland Norse after the first few generations had steel weapons or steel armor anymore, except for that one suit of chain mail whose pieces have been discovered, and which may have belonged to a visiting European on a European ship rather than to a Greenlander. Instead, they fought with bows, arrows, and lances, just as did the Inuit. Nor is there any evidence that the Greenland Norse used their horses in battle as cavalry steeds, which again gave decisive advantages to Spanish conquistadors battling the Incas and Aztecs; their Icelandic relatives certainly didn't. The Greenland Norse also lacked professional military training. They thereby ended up with no military advantage whatsoever over the Inuit—with probable consequences for their fate that we shall see.

Thus, the impact of the Norse on the natural vegetation left them short of lumber, fuel, and iron. Their other two main types of impact, on soil and on turf, left them short of useful land. In Chapter 6 we saw how the fragility of Iceland's light volcanic soils opened the door there to big problems of soil erosion. While Greenland's soils are not as supersensitive as Iceland's, they still rank as relatively fragile by world standards, because Greenland's short cool growing season results in slow rates of plant growth, slow soil formation, and thin topsoil layers. Slow plant growth also translates into low soil content of organic humus and clay, soil constituents that serve to bind water and keep the soil moist. Hence Greenland soils are easily dried out by the frequent strong winds.

The sequence of soil erosion in Greenland begins with cutting or burning the cover of trees and shrubs, which are more effective at holding soil than is grass. With the trees and shrubs gone, livestock, especially sheep and goats, graze down the grass, which regenerates only slowly in Greenland's climate. Once the grass cover is broken and the soil is exposed, soil is carried away especially by the strong winds, and also by pounding from occasionally heavy rains, to the point where the topsoil can be removed for a distance of miles from an entire valley. In areas where sand becomes exposed, as for example in river valleys, sand is picked up by the wind and dumped downwind.

Lake cores and soil profiles document the development of serious soil erosion in Greenland after the Norse arrived, and the dumping of topsoil and then sand by wind and running water into lakes. For instance, at the site of an abandoned Norse farm that I passed at the mouth of the Qoroq Fjord, downwind of a glacier, so much soil was blown away by high-velocity winds that only stones remained. Wind-blown sand is very common at Norse farms: some abandoned ones in the Vatnahverfi area are covered by sand ten feet deep.

The other means besides soil erosion by which the Norse inadvertently made land useless was that they cut turf for buildings and to burn as fuel, because of their shortage of timber and firewood. Almost all Greenland buildings were constructed mostly of turf, with at best only a stone foundation plus some wooden beams to support the roof. Even St. Nicholas's Cathedral at Gardar had only the lowest six feet of its walls made of stone, above which the walls were of turf, with a roof supported by wooden beams and with a wood-paneled front. Although Hvalsey Church was exceptional in having walls entirely of stone up to their full height, it was still roofed with turf. Greenland turf walls tended to be thick (up to six feet thick!) in order to provide insulation against the cold.

A large Greenland residential house is estimated to have consumed about 10 acres of turf. Furthermore, that amount of turf was needed more than once, because turf gradually disintegrates, so that a building must be "returfed" every few decades. The Norse referred to that process of acquiring turf for construction as "flaying the outfield," a good description of the damage done to what would otherwise be pastureland. The slow regeneration of turf in Greenland meant that that damage was long-lasting.

Again, a skeptic, on being told about soil erosion and turf cutting, might answer: "So what?" The answer is simple. Remember that, among the Norse Atlantic islands, Greenland even before human impact was the coldest island, hence the one most marginal for hay and pasture growth and most susceptible to loss of vegetation cover by overgrazing, trampling, soil erosion, and turf-cutting. A farm had to have sufficient pasture area to support at least the minimum number of animals required to breed back herd numbers after a long cold winter had reduced them, before the next long cold winter. Estimates suggest that the loss of only one-quarter of the total pasture area at Eastern Settlement or Western Settlement would have sufficed to drop the herd size below that minimum critical threshold. That's what actually appears to have happened at Western Settlement, and possibly at Eastern Settlement as well.

Just as in Iceland, the environmental problems that beset the medieval Norse remain concerns in modern Greenland. For five centuries after Greenland's medieval Norse died out, the island was without livestock under Inuit occupation and then under Danish colonial rule. Finally, in 1915, before the recent studies of medieval environmental impacts had been carried out, the Danes introduced Icelandic sheep on a trial basis, and the first full-time sheep breeder reestablished the farm at Brattahlid in 1924. Cows were also tried but were abandoned because they took too much work.

Today, about 65 Greenland families raise sheep as their main occupation, with the result that overgrazing and soil erosion have reemerged. Greenland lake cores show the same changes after 1924 as occurred after A.D. 984: a decrease in tree pollen, increase in grass and weed pollen, and increase of topsoil carried into lakes. Initially after 1924, sheep were left outdoors in the winter to forage for themselves whenever the winter was sufficiently mild. That caused grazing damage at the time when the vegetation was least capable of regenerating. Juniper trees are especially sensitive, because both sheep and horses browse them in the winter when there is nothing else available to eat. When Christian Keller arrived at Brattahlid in 1976, juniper was still growing there, but during my visit in 2002 I saw only dead juniper.

After more than half of Greenland's sheep starved to death in the cold winter of 1966–67, the government founded a Greenland Experimental Station to study the environmental effects of sheep by comparing vegetation and soil in heavily grazed pastures, lightly grazed ones, and fields fenced to keep sheep out. A component of that research involved enlisting archaeologists to study pasture changes during Viking times. As a result of the appreciation thereby gained about Greenland's fragility, Greenlanders have fenced off their most vulnerable pastures and brought sheep indoors for barn feeding throughout the entire winter. Efforts are being made to increase the supplies of winter hay by fertilizing natural pastures, and by cultivating oats, rye, timothy, and other non-native grasses.

Despite these efforts, soil erosion is a big problem in Greenland today. Along Eastern Settlement fjords, I saw areas of bare stone and gravel, largely devoid of vegetation as a result of recent sheep grazing. Within the last 25 years, high-velocity winds have eroded the modern farm at the site of the old Norse farm at the mouth of the Qorlortoq Valley, thereby furnishing us with a model for what happened at that farm seven centuries ago. While both the Greenland government and the sheep farmers themselves understand the long-term damage caused by sheep, they also feel under pressure to generate jobs in a society with high unemployment. Ironically, raising sheep in Greenland doesn't pay even in the short run: the government has to give each sheep-farming family about $14,000 each year to cover their losses, provide them with an income, and induce them to carry on with the sheep.

The Inuit play a major role in the story of the demise of Viking Greenland. They constituted the biggest difference between the histories of the Greenland and Iceland Norse: while the Icelanders did enjoy the advantages of a less daunting climate and shorter trade routes to Norway compared to their Greenland brethren, the Icelanders' clearest advantage lay in not being threatened by the Inuit. At minimum, the Inuit represent a missed opportunity: the Greenland Vikings would have had a better chance of surviving if they had learned from or traded with the Inuit, but they didn't. At maximum, Inuit attacks on or threats to the Vikings may have played a direct role in the Vikings' extinction. The Inuit are also significant in proving to us that persistence of human societies wasn't impossible in medieval Greenland. Why did the Vikings eventually fail where the Inuit succeeded?

Today we think of the Inuit as *the* native inhabitants of Greenland and the Canadian Arctic. In reality, they were just the most recent in a series of at least four archaeologically recognized peoples who expanded eastward across Canada and entered Northwest Greenland over the course of nearly 4,000 years before Norse arrival. Successive waves of them spread, remained in Greenland for centuries, and then vanished, raising their own questions of societal collapses similar to the questions that we are considering for the

Norse, Anasazi, and Easter Islanders. However, we know too little about those earlier disappearances to discuss them in this book except as background to the Vikings' fate. While archaeologists have given to these earlier cultures names like Point Independence I, Point Independence II, and Saqqaq, depending on the sites where their artifacts became recognized, the languages of those people, and their names for themselves, all are lost to us forever.

The Inuits' immediate predecessors were a culture referred to by archaeologists as the Dorset people, from their habitations identified at Cape Dorset on Canada's Baffin Island. After occupying most of the Canadian Arctic, they entered Greenland around 800 B.C. and inhabited many parts of the island for about a thousand years, including the areas of the later Viking settlements in the southwest. For unknown reasons, they then abandoned all of Greenland and much of the Canadian Arctic by around A.D. 300 and contracted their distribution back to some core areas of Canada. Around A.D. 700, though, they expanded again to reoccupy Labrador and northwestern Greenland, though on this migration they did not spread south to the later Viking sites. At Western and Eastern Settlements, the initial Viking colonists described seeing only uninhabited house ruins, fragments of skin boats, and stone tools that they guessed were left by vanished natives similar to the ones that they had encountered in North America during the Vinland voyages.

From bones recovered at archaeological sites, we know that Dorset people hunted a wide range of prey species varying among sites and time periods: walrus, seals, caribou, polar bears, foxes, ducks, geese, and seabirds. There was long-distance trade between the Dorset populations of Arctic Canada, Labrador, and Greenland, as proven by discoveries of tools of stone types quarried from one of these sites appearing at other sites a thousand kilometers distant. Unlike their successors the Inuit or some of their Arctic predecessors, though, Dorset people lacked dogs (hence also dogsleds) and didn't use bows and arrows. Unlike the Inuit, they also lacked boats of skin stretched over a framework and hence could not go to sea to hunt whales. Without dogsleds, they were poorly mobile, and without whale-hunting, they were unable to feed large populations. Instead, they lived in small settlements of just one or two houses, big enough for no more than 10 people and just a few adult men. That made them the least formidable of the three Native American groups that the Norse encountered: Dorset people, Inuit, and Canadian Indians. And that, surely, is why the Greenland Norse felt safe enough to continue for more than three centuries to visit the Dorset-occupied coast of Labrador to fetch timber, long after they had given up on visiting "Vinland" farther south in Canada because of the dense hostile Indian populations there.

Did Vikings and Dorset people meet each other in Northwest Greenland? We have no firm proof, but it seems likely, because Dorset people survived there for about 300 years after the Norse settled the southwest, and because the Norse were making annual visits to the Nordrseta hunting grounds only a few hundred miles south of Dorset-occupied areas and made exploratory trips farther north. Below, I shall mention one Norse account of an encounter with natives who might have been Dorset people. Other evidence consists of some objects clearly originating with Vikings—especially pieces of smelted metal that would have been prized for making tools—discovered at Dorset sites scattered over Northwest Greenland and the Canadian Arctic. Of course, we don't know whether Dorset people acquired those objects by face-to-face contacts, peaceful or otherwise, with Norse, or whether they were merely scavenged from abandoned Norse sites. Whichever was the case, we can be confident that Norse relations with the Inuit had the potential for becoming much more dangerous than those relatively harmless relations with Dorset people.

Inuit culture and technology, including mastery of whale-hunting in open waters, arose in the Bering Strait region somewhat before A.D. 1000. Dogsleds on land, and large boats at sea, enabled the Inuit to travel and transport supplies much more rapidly than could Dorset people. As the Arctic became warmer in the Middle Ages and the frozen waterways separating Canadian Arctic islands thawed, the Inuit followed their bowhead whale prey through those waterways eastwards across Canada, entering Northwest Greenland by A.D. 1200, and thereafter moving south along Greenland's west coast to reach the Nordrseta, then the vicinity of Western Settlement around A.D. 1300, and the vicinity of Eastern Settlement around 1400.

The Inuit hunted all of the same prey species that Dorset people had targeted, and probably did so more effectively because they (unlike their Dorset predecessors) possessed bows and arrows. But the hunting of whales as well gave them an additional major food supply unavailable to either Dorset people or the Norse. Hence Inuit hunters could feed lots of wives and children and lived in large settlements, typically housing dozens of people, including 10 or 20 adult male hunters and fighters. In the prime hunting grounds of the Nordrseta itself, the Inuit established, at a site called Sermermiut, a huge settlement that gradually accumulated hundreds of dwellings. Just imagine the problems it must have created for the success of the Norse Nordrseta hunt if a group of Norse hunters, who could hardly have numbered more than a few dozen, were detected by such a big group of Inuit and failed to establish good relations.

Unlike the Norse, the Inuit represented the climax of thousands of years of cultural developments by Arctic peoples learning to master Arctic conditions. So, Greenland has little wood available for building, heating, or illuminating houses during the months of Arctic winter darkness? That was no problem for the Inuit: they built igloos for winter housing out of snow, and they burned whale and seal blubber both for fuel and for lighting lamps. Little wood available to build boats? Again, that was no problem for the Inuit: they stretched sealskins over frameworks to build kayaks (Plate 18), as well as to make their boats called *umiaqs* big enough to take out into unprotected waters for hunting whales.

Despite having read about what exquisite watercraft Inuit kayaks were, and despite having used the modern recreational kayaks now made of plastic and widely available in the First World, I was still astonished when I first saw a traditional Inuit kayak in Greenland. It reminded me of a miniature version of the long, narrow, fast battleships of the U.S.S. *Iowa* class built by the American navy during World War II, with all of their available deck space bristling with bombardment guns, anti-aircraft guns, and other weaponry. Nineteen feet long, tiny compared to a battleship, but still much longer than I had ever imagined, the deck of the slim kayak was packed with its own weaponry: a harpoon shaft, with a spear-thrower extension at the grip end; a separate harpoon head about six inches long, attachable to the shaft by a toggle connection; a dart to throw at birds, with not only an arrow point at the tip but three forward-facing sharp barbs lower on the dart shaft to hit the bird in case the tip just missed; several sealskin bladders to act as drags on harpooned whales or seals; and a lance for delivering the death blow to the harpooned animal. Unlike a battleship or any other watercraft known to me, the kayak was individually tailored to its paddler's size, weight, and arm strength. It was actually "worn" by its owner, and its seat was a sewn garment joined to the owner's parka and guaranteeing a waterproof seal so that ice-cold water splashing over the decks could not wet him. Christian Keller tried in vain to "wear" modern kayaks tailored to his Greenlander friends, only to discover that his feet couldn't fit under the deck and that his upper legs were too big to enter the manhole.

In their range of hunting strategies, the Inuit were the most flexible and sophisticated hunters in Arctic history. Besides killing caribou, walruses, and land birds in ways not unlike those of the Norse, the Inuit differed from the Norse in using their fast kayaks to harpoon seals and to run down seabirds on the ocean, and in using umiaqs and harpoons to kill whales in open waters. Not even an Inuit can stab to death at one blow a healthy whale, so the whale hunt began with a hunter harpooning the whale from an umiaq rowed by other men. That is not an easy task, as all you devotees of Sherlock Holmes stories may remember from the "Adventure of Black Peter," in which an evil retired ship's captain is found dead in his house, with a harpoon that had been decorating his wall thrust clean through him. After spending a morning at a butcher's shop, vainly attempting himself to drive a harpoon through a pig's carcass, Sherlock Holmes deduces correctly that the murderer must have been a professional harpooner, because an untrained man no matter how strong cannot drive in a harpoon deeply. Two things made that possible for the Inuit: the harpoon's spear-thrower grip that extended the throwing arc and hence increased the hunter's throwing force and the impact; and, as in the case of Black Peter's murderer, long practice. For the Inuit, though, that practice began already in childhood, resulting in Inuit men developing a condition called hyperextension of the throwing arm: in effect, an additional built-in spear-thrower.

Once the harpoon head became embedded in the whale, the cleverly designed toggle connection released, allowing the hunters to retrieve the harpoon shaft now separated from the harpoon head embedded in the whale. Otherwise, if the harpooner had continued to hold a rope tied to the harpoon head and shaft, the angry whale would have dragged underwater the umiaq and all its Inuit occupants. Left attached to the harpoon head was an air-filled bladder of sealskin, whose buoyancy forced the whale to work harder against the bladder's resistance and to grow tired as it dived. When the whale surfaced to breathe, the Inuit launched another harpoon with yet another bladder attached, to tire the whale even more. Only when the whale had thus become exhausted did the hunters dare bring the umiaq alongside the beast to lance it to death.

The Inuit also devised a specialized technique for hunting ringed seal, the most abundant seal species in Greenland waters but one whose habits made it difficult to capture. Unlike other Greenland seal species, the ringed seal winters off the Greenland coast under the ice, by opening breathing holes through the ice just large enough for its head (but not for its body). The holes are difficult to spot because the seal leaves them covered with a cone of snow. Each seal has several breathing holes, just as a fox makes an underground burrow with several foxholes as alternate entrances. A hunter could not knock the snow cone off the hole, else the seal would realize that someone was waiting for it. Hence the hunter stood patiently next to a cone in the cold darkness of the Arctic winter, waited motionless for as many hours as necessary to hear a seal arrive to catch a quick breath, and then tried to harpoon the animal *through* the snow cone, without being able to see it. As the impaled seal swam off, the harpoon head then detached from the shaft but remained attached to a rope, which the hunter played out and pulled until the seal became exhausted and could be dragged in and lanced. That whole operation is difficult to learn and execute successfully; the Norse never did. As a result, in the occasional years when other seal species declined in numbers, the Inuit switched to hunting ringed seals, but the Norse did not have that option, and so they were at risk of starving.

Thus, the Inuit enjoyed those and other advantages over the Norse and the Dorset people. Within a few centuries of the Inuit expansion across Canada into Northwest Greenland, the Dorset culture, which had previously occupied both areas, disappeared. Hence we have not one but two Inuit-related mysteries: the disappearance first of the Dorset people, then of the Norse, both of them soon after Inuit arrival in their territories. In Northwest Greenland some Dorset settlements survived for a century or two after the Inuit appeared, and it would have been impossible for two such peoples to be unaware of each other's presence, yet there is no direct archaeological evidence of contact between them, such as Inuit objects at contemporary Dorset sites or vice versa. But there is indirect evidence of contact: the Greenland Inuit ended up with several Dorset cultural traits that they had lacked before arriving in Greenland, including a bone knife for cutting snow blocks, domed snow houses, soapstone technology, and the so-called Thule 5 harpoon head. Clearly, the Inuit not only had some opportunities to learn from Dorset people but also must have had *something* to do with their disappearance after the latter had lived in the Arctic for 2,000 years. Each of us can imagine our own scenario for the end of Dorset culture. One guess of mine is that, among groups of Dorset people starving in a difficult winter, the women just deserted their men and walked over to Inuit camps where they knew that people were feasting on bowhead whales and ringed seals.

■   ■   ■

What about relations between the Inuit and the Norse? Incredibly, during the centuries that those two peoples shared Greenland, Norse annals include only two or three brief references to the Inuit.

The first of those three annal passages may refer to either the Inuit or else Dorset people because it describes an incident from the 11th or 12th century, when a Dorset population still survived in Northwest Greenland, and when the Inuit were just arriving. A *History of Norway* preserved in a 15th-century manuscript explains how the Norse first encountered Greenland natives: "Farther to the north beyond the Norse settlements, hunters have come across small people, whom they call skraelings. When they are stabbed with a nonfatal wound, their wounds turn white and they don't bleed, but when they are mortally wounded, they bleed incessantly. They have no iron, but they use walrus tusks as missiles and sharp stones as tools."

Brief and matter-of-fact as this account is, it suggests that the Norse had a "bad attitude" that got them off to a dreadful start with the people with whom they were about to share Greenland. "Skraelings," the Old Norse word that the Norse applied to all three groups of New World natives that they encountered in Vinland or Greenland (Inuit, Dorset, and Indians), translates approximately as "wretches." It also bodes poorly for peaceful relations if you take the first Inuit or Dorset person whom you see, and you try stabbing him as an experiment to figure out how much he bleeds. Recall also, from Chapter 6, that when the Norse first encountered a group of Indians in Vinland, they initiated friendship by killing eight of the nine. These first contacts go a long way towards explaining why the Norse did not establish a good trading relationship with the Inuit.

The second of the three mentions is equally brief and imputes to the "skraelings" a role in destroying the Western Settlement around A.D. 1360; we shall consider that role below. The skraelings in question could only have been Inuit, as by then the Dorset population had vanished from Greenland. The remaining mention is a single sentence in Iceland's annals for the year 1379: "The skraelings assaulted the Greenlanders, killing 18 men, and captured two boys and one bondswoman and made them slaves." Unless the annals were mistakenly attributing to Greenland an attack actually carried out in Norway by Saami people, this incident would presumably have taken place near Eastern Settlement, because Western Settlement no longer existed in 1379 and a Norse hunting party in the Nordrseta would have been unlikely to include a woman. How should we construe this laconic story? To us today, 18 Norse killed doesn't seem like a big deal, in this century of world wars in which tens of millions of people were slaughtered. But consider that the entire population of Eastern Settlement was probably not more than 4,000, and that 18 men would have constituted about 2% of the adult males. If an enemy today were to attack the U.S., with its population of 280,000,000, and killed adult males in the same proportion, the result would be 1,260,000 American men dead. That is, that single documented attack of 1379 represented a disaster to Eastern Settlement, regardless of how many more men died in the attacks of 1380, 1381, and so on.

Those three brief texts are our sole written sources of information about Norse/Inuit relations. Archaeological sources of information consist of Norse artifacts or copies of Norse artifacts found at Inuit sites, and vice versa. A total of 170 objects of Norse origin are known from Inuit sites, including a few complete tools (a knife, a shears, and a fire-starter), but mostly just pieces of metal (iron, copper, bronze, or tin) that the Inuit would have prized for making their own tools. Such Norse objects occur not only at Inuit sites in locations where the Vikings lived (Eastern and Western Settlements) or often visited (Nordrseta), but also in locations that the Norse never visited, such as East Greenland and Ellesmere Island. Hence Norse material must have been of sufficient interest to the Inuit that it passed by trade between Inuit groups hundreds of miles apart. For most of the objects it is impossible for us to know whether the Inuit acquired them from the Norse themselves by trade, by killing or robbing Norse, or by scavenging Norse settlements after the Norse had abandoned them. However, 10 of the pieces of metal come from bells of Eastern Settlement churches, which the Norse surely wouldn't have traded. Those bells were presumably obtained by the Inuit after the demise of the Norse, for instance when Inuit were living in houses of their own that they built within Norse ruins.

Firmer evidence of face-to-face contact between the two peoples comes from nine Inuit carvings of human figures that are unmistakably Norse, as judged by depictions of a characteristically Viking hairdo, clothing, or a crucifix decoration. The Inuit also learned some useful technologies from the Norse. While Inuit tools in the shape of a European knife or saw could just have been copied from plundered Norse objects without any friendly contact with a live Norseman, Inuit-made barrel staves and screw-threaded arrowheads suggest that the Inuit actually saw Norse men making or using barrels and screws.

On the other hand, corresponding evidence of Inuit objects at Norse sites is almost non-existent. One Inuit antler comb, two bird darts, one ivory towline handle, and one piece of meteoric iron: those five items are the grand total known to me for all of Norse Greenland throughout the centuries of Inuit/Norse coexistence. Even those five items would seem not to be valuable trade items but just discarded curiosities that some Norse person picked up. Astounding by their complete absence are all the useful pieces of Inuit technology that the Norse could have copied with profit but didn't. For instance, there is not a single harpoon, spear-thrower, or kayak or umiaq piece from any Norse site.

If trade did develop between the Inuit and Norse, it would probably have involved walrus ivory, which the Inuit were skilled at hunting and which the Norse sought as their most valuable export to Europe. Unfortunately, direct evidence of such trade would be hard for us to recognize, because there is no way to determine whether the pieces of ivory found on many Norse farms came from walruses killed by the Norse themselves or by Inuit. But we certainly don't find at Norse sites the bones of what I think would have been the most precious things that the Inuit could have traded to the Norse: ringed seals, Greenland's most abundant seal species during the winter, hunted successfully by the Inuit but not by the Norse, and available at a time of year when the Norse were chronically at risk of exhausting their stored winter food supply and starving. That suggests to me that there really was very little, if any, trade between the two peoples. As far as archaeological evidence for contact is concerned, the Inuit might as well have been living on a different planet from the Norse, rather than sharing the same island and hunting grounds. Nor do we have any skeletal or genetic evidence of Inuit/Norse intermarriage. Careful study of the skulls of skeletons buried in Greenland Norse churchyards showed them to resemble continental Scandinavian skulls and failed to detect any Inuit/Norse hybrid.

Both the failure to develop trade with the Inuit, and the failure to learn from them, represented from our perspective huge losses to the Norse, although they themselves evidently didn't see it that way. Those failures were not for lack of opportunity. Norse hunters must have seen Inuit hunters in the Nordrseta, and then at the Western Settlement outer fjords when the Inuit arrived there. Norsemen with their own heavy wooden rowboats and their own techniques for hunting walruses and seals must have recognized the superior sophistication of Inuit light skin boats and hunting methods: the Inuit were succeeding at doing exactly what the Norse hunters were trying to do. When later European explorers began visiting Greenland in the late 1500s, they were immediately amazed at the speed and maneuverability of kayaks and commented on the Inuit appearing to be half-fish, darting around in the water much faster than any European boat could travel. They were equally impressed by Inuit umiaqs, marksmanship, sewn skin clothing and boats and mittens, harpoons, bladder floats, dogsleds, and seal-hunting methods. The Danes who began colonizing Greenland in 1721 promptly embraced Inuit technology, used Inuit umiaqs to travel along the Greenland coast, and traded with the Inuit. Within a few years, the Danes had learned more about harpoons and ringed seals than the Norse had in a few centuries. Yet some of the Danish colonists were racist Christians who despised the pagan Inuit just as had the medieval Norse.

If one tried to guess without prejudice what form Norse/Inuit relations might have taken, there are many possibilities that were actually realized in later centuries when Europeans such as the Spanish, Portuguese, French, English, Russians, Belgians, Dutch, Germans, and Italians, as well as the Danes and Swedes themselves, encountered native peoples elsewhere in the world. Many of those European colonists became middlemen and developed integrated trade economies: European traders settled down or visited areas with native peoples, brought European goods coveted by the natives, and in exchange obtained native products coveted in Europe. For instance, the Inuit craved metal so much that they went to the effort of making cold-forged iron tools from iron in the Cape York meteor that had fallen in Northern Greenland. Hence one could have imagined the development of a trade in which the Norse obtained walrus tusks, narwhal tusks, sealskins, and polar bears from the Inuit and sent those goods to Europe in exchange for the iron prized by the Inuit. The Norse could also have supplied the Inuit with cloth and with milk products: even if lactose intolerance would have prevented the Inuit from drinking milk itself, they would still have consumed lactose-free milk products such as cheese and butter, which Denmark exports to Greenland today. Not only the Norse but also the Inuit were at frequent risk of starvation in Greenland, and the Inuit could have reduced that risk and diversified their diet by trading for Norse milk products. Such trade between Scandinavians and Inuit promptly developed in Greenland after 1721: why didn't it develop already in medieval times?

One answer is the cultural obstacles to intermarriage or just to learning between the Norse and the Inuit. An Inuit wife would not have been nearly as useful to a Norseman as was a Norse wife: what a Norseman wanted from a wife was the ability to weave and spin wool, to tend and milk cattle and sheep, and to make *skyr* and butter and cheese, which Norse but not Inuit girls learned from childhood. Even if a Norse hunter did befriend an Inuit hunter, the Norseman couldn't just borrow his friend's kayak and learn how to use it, because the kayak was in effect a very complicated and individually tailored piece of clothing connected to a boat, made to fit that particular Inuit hunter, and fabricated by the Inuit's wife who (unlike Norse girls) had learned from childhood to sew skins. Hence a Norse hunter who had seen an Inuit kayak couldn't just come home and tell his wife to "sew me one of those things."

If you hope to persuade an Inuit woman to make you a kayak to your own measurements, or to let you marry her daughter, you have to establish a friendly relationship in the first place. But we have seen that the Norse had a "bad attitude" from the beginning, referring to both North American Indians in Vinland and Inuit in Greenland as "wretches," and killing the first natives they encountered in both places. As church-oriented Christians, the Norse shared the scorn of pagans widespread among medieval Europeans.

Still another factor behind their bad attitude is that the Norse would have thought of themselves as the natives in the Nordrseta, and the Inuit as the interlopers. The Norse arrived in the Nordrseta and hunted there for several centuries before the Inuit arrived. When the Inuit finally appeared from northwestern Greenland, the Norse would have been understandably reluctant to pay the Inuit for walrus tusks that they, the Norse, regarded as their own privilege to hunt. By the time that they encountered the Inuit, the Norse themselves were desperately starved for iron, the most coveted trade item that they could have offered to the Inuit.

To us moderns, living in a world in which all "native peoples" have already been contacted by Europeans except for a few tribes in the most remote parts of the Amazon and New Guinea, the difficulties in establishing contact are not obvious. What do you really expect the first Norseman spotting a group of Inuit in the Nordrseta to have done?—shout out "Hello!", walk over to them, smile, start using sign language, point to a walrus tusk, and hold out a lump of iron? Over the course of my biological fieldwork in New Guinea I have lived through such "first-contact situations," as they are called, and I found them dangerous and utterly terrifying. In such situations the "natives" initially regard the Europeans as trespassers and correctly perceive that any intruder may bring threats to their health, lives, and land ownership. Neither side knows what the other will do, both sides are tense and frightened, both are uncertain whether to flee or to start shooting, and both are scrutinizing the other side for a gesture that could hint that the others might panic and shoot first. To turn a first-contact situation into a friendly relationship, let alone to survive the situation, requires extreme caution and patience. Later European colonialists eventually developed some experience at dealing with such situations, but the Norse evidently shot first.

In short, the 18th-century Danes in Greenland, and other Europeans meeting native peoples elsewhere, encountered the same range of problems that the Norse did: their own prejudices against "primitive pagans," the question of whether to kill them or rob them or trade with them or marry them or take their land, and the problem of how to convince them not to flee or shoot. Later Europeans dealt with those problems by cultivating that whole range of options and choosing whichever option worked best under the particular circumstances, depending on whether the Europeans were or were not outnumbered, whether the European colonist men did or did not have enough European women along as wives, whether the native people had trade goods coveted in Europe, and whether the natives' land was attractive to Europeans to settle. But the medieval Norse had not developed that range of options. Refusing or unable to learn from the Inuit, and lacking any military advantage over them, the Norse rather than the Inuit became the ones who eventually disappeared.

The end of the Greenland Norse colony is often described as a "mystery." That's true, but only partly so, because we need to distinguish ultimate reasons (i.e., underlying long-term factors behind the slow decline of Greenland Norse society) from proximate reasons (i.e., the final blow to the weakened society, killing the last individuals or forcing them to abandon their settlements). Only the proximate reasons remain partly mysterious; the ultimate reasons are clear. They consist of the five sets of factors that we have already discussed in detail: Norse impact on the environment, climate change, decline in friendly contact with Norway, increase in hostile contact with the Inuit, and the conservative outlook of the Norse.

Briefly, the Norse inadvertently depleted the environmental resources on which they depended, by cutting trees, stripping turf, overgrazing, and causing soil erosion. Already at the outset of Norse settlement, Greenland's natural resources were only marginally sufficient to support a European pastoral society of viable size, but hay production in Greenland fluctuates markedly from year to year. Hence that depletion of environmental resources threatened the society's survival in poor years. Second, calculations of climate from Greenland ice cores show that it was relatively mild (i.e., as "mild" as it is today) when the Norse arrived, went through several runs of cold years in the 1300s, and then plunged in the early 1400s into the cold period called the Little Ice Age that lasted until the 1800s. That lowered hay production further, as well as clogging the ship lanes between Greenland and Norway with sea ice. Third, those obstacles to shipping were only one reason for the decline and eventual end of trade with Norway on which the Greenlanders depended for their iron, some timber, and their cultural identity. About half of Norway's population died when the Black Death (a plague epidemic) struck in 1349–1350. Norway, Sweden, and Denmark became joined in 1397 under one king, who proceeded to neglect Norway as the poorest of his three provinces. The demand by European carvers for walrus ivory, Greenland's principal export, declined when the Crusades gave Christian Europe access again to Asia's and East Africa's elephant ivory, whose deliveries to Europe had been cut off by the Arab conquest of the Mediterranean shores. By the 1400s, carving with ivory of any sort, whether from walruses or elephants, was out of fashion in Europe. All those changes undermined Norway's resources and motivation for sending ships to Greenland. Other peoples besides the Greenland Norse have similarly discovered their economies (or even their survival) to be at risk when their major trading partners encountered problems; they include us oil-importing Americans at the time of the 1973 Gulf oil embargo, Pitcairn and Henderson Islanders at the time of Mangareva's deforestation, and many others. Modern globalization will surely multiply the examples. Finally, the arrival of the Inuit, and the inability or unwillingness of the Norse to make drastic changes, completed the quintet of ultimate factors behind the Greenland colony's demise.

These five factors all developed gradually or operated over long times. Hence we should not be surprised to discover that various Norse farms were abandoned at different times before the final catastrophes. On the floor of a large house on the largest farm of the Vatnahverfi district of Eastern Settlement was found a skull of a 25-year-old man with a radiocarbon date around A.D. 1275. That suggests that the whole Vatnahverfi district was abandoned then, and that the skull was of one of the last inhabitants, because any survivors would surely have buried the dead man rather than just leave his body on the floor. The last radiocarbon dates from farms of Qorlortoq Valley of Eastern Settlement cluster around A.D. 1300. Western Settlement's "Farm Beneath the Sands" was abandoned and buried under glacial outwash sand around A.D. 1350.

Of the two Norse settlements, the first to vanish completely was the smaller Western Settlement. It was more marginal for raising livestock than was Eastern Settlement, because its more northerly location meant a shorter growing season, considerably less hay production even in a good year, and hence greater likelihood that a cold or wet summer would result in too little hay to feed the animals through the following winter. A further cause of vulnerability at Western Settlement was that its only access to the sea was by a single fjord, so that a hostile group of Inuit at the mouth of that one fjord could cut off all access to the crucial seal migration along the coast on which the Norse depended for food in the late spring.

We have two sources of information about the end of Western Settlement: written and archaeological. The written account is by a priest named Ivar Bardarson, who was sent to Greenland from Norway by the bishop of Bergen to act as ombudsman and royal tax collector, and to report on the condition of the Church in Greenland. Some time after his return to Norway around 1362, Bardarson wrote an account called *Description of Greenland*, of which the original text is lost and which we know only through later copies. Most of the preserved description consists of lists of Greenland churches and properties, buried among which is an exasperatingly brief account of the end of Western Settlement: "In the Western Settlement stands a large church, named Stensnes [Sandnes] Church. That church was for a time the cathedral and bishop's seat. Now the skraelings [= wretches, i.e., the Inuit] have the entire Western Settlement. . . . All the foregoing was told us by Ivar Bardarson Greenlander, who was the superintendent of the bishop's establishment at Gardar in Greenland for many years, that he had seen all this, and he was one of those that the lawman [a high-ranking official] had appointed to go to the Western Settlement to fight against the skraelings, in order to drive the skraelings out of the Western Settlement. On their arrival they found no men, either Christian or heathen . . ."

I feel like shaking Ivar Bardarson's corpse in frustration at all the questions that he left unanswered. Which year did he go there, and in which month? Did he find any stored hay or cheese left? How could a thousand people have vanished, down to the last individual? Were there any signs of fighting, burned buildings, or dead bodies? But Bardarson tells us nothing more.

Instead, we have to turn to the findings of archaeologists who excavated the uppermost layer of debris at several Western Settlement farms, corresponding to the remains left in the settlement's final months by the last Norse to occupy it. In the ruins of those farms are doors, posts, roof timbers, furniture, bowls, crucifixes, and other big wooden objects. That's unusual: when a farm building is abandoned intentionally in northern Scandinavia, such precious wooden objects are typically scavenged and carried away to reuse wherever the farm owners are resettling, because wood is at such a premium. Recall that the Norse camp at L'Anse aux Meadows on Newfoundland, which was abandoned after such a planned evacuation, contained little of value except 99 broken nails, one whole nail, and a knitting needle. Evidently, Western Settlement was either abandoned hastily, or else its last occupants couldn't carry away their furniture because they died there.

The animal bones in those topmost layers tell a grim story. They include: foot bones of small wild birds and rabbits, which would normally have been considered too small to be worth hunting and usable only as last-ditch famine food; bones of a newborn calf and lamb, which would have been born in the late spring; the toe bones of a number of cows approximately equal to the number of spaces in that farm's cow barn, suggesting that all cows had been slaughtered and were eaten down to the hoofs; and partial skeletons of big hunting dogs with knife marks on the bones. Dog bones are otherwise virtually absent in Norse houses, because the Norse were no more willing to eat their dogs than we are today. By killing the dogs on which they depended to hunt caribou in the autumn, and by killing the newborn livestock needed to rebuild their herds, the last inhabitants were in effect saying that they were too desperately hungry to care about the future. In lower debris layers of the houses, the carrion-eating flies associated with human feces belong to warmth-loving fly species, but the top layer had only cold-tolerant fly species, suggesting that the inhabitants had run out of fuel as well as food.

All of these archaeological details tell us that the last inhabitants of those Western Settlement farms starved and froze to death in the spring. Either it was a cold year in which the migratory seals failed to arrive; or else heavy ice in the fjords, or perhaps a band of Inuit who remembered their relatives having been stabbed by the Norse as an experiment to see how much blood ran out of them, blocked access to the seal herds in the outer fjords. A cold summer had probably caused the farmers to run out of enough hay to feed their livestock through the winter. The farmers were reduced to killing their last cows, eating even the hoofs, killing and eating their dogs, and scrounging for birds and rabbits. If so, one has to wonder why archaeologists did not also find the skeletons of the last Norse themselves in those collapsed houses. I suspect that Ivar Bardarson failed to mention that his group from Eastern Settlement performed a cleanup of Western Settlement and gave a Christian burial to the bodies of their kinsmen—or else that the copyist who copied and shortened Bardarson's lost original omitted his account of the cleanup.

As for the end of Eastern Settlement, the last Greenland voyage of the royal trading ship promised by the king of Norway was in 1368; that ship sank in the following year. Thereafter, we have records of only four other sailings to Greenland (in 1381, 1382, 1385, and 1406), all by private ships whose captains alleged that their destination had really been Iceland and that they had reached Greenland unintentionally as a result of being blown off course. When we recall that the Norwegian king asserted exclusive rights to the Greenland trade as a royal monopoly, and that it was illegal for private ships to visit Greenland, we must consider four such "unintentional" voyages as an astonishing coincidence. Much more likely, the captains' claims that to their deep regret they had been caught in dense fog and ended up by mistake in Greenland were just alibis to cover their real intentions. As the captains undoubtedly knew, so few ships by then were visiting Greenland that the Greenlanders were desperate for trade goods, and Norwegian imports could be sold to Greenlanders at a big profit. Thorstein Olafsson, captain of the 1406 ship, could not have been too sad at his navigational error, because he spent nearly four years in Greenland before returning to Norway in 1410.

Captain Olafsson brought back three pieces of recent news from Greenland. First, a man named Kolgrim was burned at the stake in 1407 for having used witchcraft to seduce a woman named Steinunn, the daughter of the lawman Ravn and the wife of Thorgrim Sölvason. Second, poor Steinunn then went insane and died. Finally, Olafsson himself and a local girl named Sigrid Bjornsdotter were married in Hvalsey Church on September 14, 1408, with Brand Halldorsson, Thord Jorundarson, Thorbjorn Bardarson, and Jon Jonsson as witnesses, after the banns had been read for the happy couple on three previous Sundays and no one had objected. Those laconic accounts of burning at the stake, insanity, and marriage are just the usual goings-on for any medieval European Christian society and give no hint of trouble. They are our last definite written notices of Norse Greenland.

We don't know exactly when Eastern Settlement vanished. Between 1400 and 1420 the climate in the North Atlantic became colder and stormier, and mentions of ship traffic to Greenland ceased. A radiocarbon date of 1435 for a woman's dress excavated from Herjolfsnes churchyard suggests that some Norse may have survived for a few decades after that last ship returned from Greenland in 1410, but we should not lay too much stress on that date of 1435 because of the statistical uncertainties of several decades associated with the radiocarbon determination. It was not until 1576–1587 that we know definitely of further European visitors, when the English explorers Martin Frobisher and John Davis sighted and landed in Greenland, met Inuit, were very impressed by their skills and technology, traded with them, and kidnapped several to bring back to exhibit in England. In 1607 a Danish-Norwegian expedition set out specifically to visit Eastern Settlement, but was deceived by the name into supposing that it lay on Greenland's east coast and hence found no evidence of the Norse. From then on, throughout the 17th century, more Danish-Norwegian expeditions and Dutch and English whalers stopped in Greenland and kidnapped more Inuit, who (incomprehensibly to us today) were assumed to be nothing more than descendants of blue-eyed blond-haired Vikings, despite their completely different physical appearance and language.

Finally, in 1721 the Norwegian Lutheran missionary Hans Egede sailed for Greenland, in the conviction that the kidnapped Inuit really were Norse Catholics who had been abandoned by Europe before the Reformation, had reverted to paganism, and must by now be eager for a Christian missionary to convert them to Lutheranism. He happened first to land in the fjords of Western Settlement, where to his surprise he found only people who were clearly Inuit and not Norse, and who showed him ruins of former Norse farms. Still convinced that the Eastern Settlement lay on Greenland's east coast, Egede looked there and found no signs of the Norse. In 1723 the Inuit showed him more extensive Norse ruins, including Hvalsey Church, on the southwest coast at the site of what we now know to be Eastern Settlement. That forced him to admit to himself that the Norse colony really had vanished, and his search for an answer to the mystery began. From the Inuit, Egede gathered orally transmitted memories of alternating periods of fighting and friendly relations with the former Norse population, and he wondered whether the Norse had been exterminated by the Inuit. Ever since then, generations of visitors and archaeologists have been trying to find out the answer.

Let's be clear about exactly what the mystery involves. The ultimate causes of the Norse decline are not in doubt, and the archaeological investigations of the top layers at Western Settlement tell us something about the proximate causes of the collapse in the final year there. But we have no corresponding information about what happened in the last year of Eastern Settlement, because its top layers have not been investigated. Having taken the story this far, I can't resist fleshing out the end with some speculation.

It seems to me that the collapse of Eastern Settlement must have been sudden rather than gentle, like the sudden collapse of the Soviet Union and of Western Settlement. Greenland Norse society was a delicately balanced deck of cards whose ability to remain standing depended ultimately on the authority of the Church and of the chiefs. Respect for both of those authorities would have declined when the promised ships stopped coming from Norway, and when the climate got colder. The last bishop of Greenland died around 1378, and no new bishop arrived from Norway to replace him. But social legitimacy in Norse society depended on proper functioning of the Church: priests had to be ordained by a bishop, and without an ordained priest one couldn't be baptized, married, or receive a Christian burial. How could that society have continued to function when the last priest ordained by the last bishop eventually died? Similarly, the authority of a chief depended on the chief's having resources to redistribute to his followers in hard times. If people on poor farms were starving to death while the chief survived on an adjacent richer farm, would the poor farmers have continued to obey their chief up to their last breath?

Compared to Western Settlement, Eastern Settlement lay farther south, was less marginal for Norse hay production, supported more people (4,000 instead of just 1,000), and was thus less at risk of collapse. Of course, colder climate was in the long run bad for Eastern as well as Western Settlement: it would just take a longer string of cold years to reduce the herds and drive people to starvation at Eastern Settlement. One can imagine the smaller and more marginal farms of the Eastern Settlement getting starved out. But what could have happened at Gardar, whose two cattle barns had space for 160 cows, and which had uncounted herds of sheep?

I would guess that, at the end, Gardar was like an overcrowded lifeboat. When hay production was failing and the livestock had all died or been eaten at the poorer farms of Eastern Settlement, their settlers would have tried to push their way onto the best farms that still had some animals: Brattahlid, Hvalsey, Herjolfsnes, and last of all Gardar. The authority of the church officials at Gardar Cathedral, or of the landowning chief there, would have been acknowledged as long as they and the power of God were visibly protecting their parishioners and followers. But famine and associated disease would have caused a breakdown of respect for authority, much as the Greek historian Thucydides described in his terrifying account of the plague of Athens 2,000 years earlier. Starving people would have poured into Gardar, and the outnumbered chiefs and church officials could no longer prevent them from slaughtering the last cattle and sheep. Gardar's

Plate 1. The Bitterroot River, Montana.
Plate 2. An irrigated hayfield in the Bitterroot Valley.

Plate 3. Mountains and forests in the Bitterroot Valley.

Plate 4. The now abandoned Zortman-Landusky Mine, in Montana, which was the first mine in the U.S. to attempt large-scale cyanide heap-leach extraction of low-grade gold ores.

Plate 5. A stone platform (ahu) and its re-erected stereotypical stone statues (moai), on Easter Island.

Plate 6. Easter Island's now completely deforested landscape and its volcanic cinder cones, formerly covered by forests. The large crater is Rano Raraku, site of the main stone quarry. The small square patch of forest at its base is a recent plantation of non-native trees.

Plate 7. Another view of the formerly forested, now completely deforested landscape and its volcanic cinder cones.

Plate 8. Statues (moai) whose heads bear a re-erected pukao, a separate cylinder of red stone weighing up to 12 tons and possibly representing a head-dress of red feathers.

Plate 9. Aerial view of now deforested Chaco Canyon, with the ruins of Pueblo Bonito, the canyon's largest former Anasazi site whose buildings rose five or six stories.

ABOVE: Plate 10. Close-up of the ruins of an Anasazi site in the now deforested landscape of Chaco Canyon.

LEFT: Plate 11. An Anasazi doorway, illustrating construction techniques of dry-fitted (i.e., not cemented) stone facing over a concealed rubble core.

Plate 12. A steep-sided temple at the Maya city of Tikal, which was abandoned over a thousand years ago and over-grown by forests, and from which the forest has now been partly cleared.

RIGHT: Plate 13. At the site of Tikal, a stele (carved stone slab) covered with writing. The sole pre-Columbian writing systems to develop in the New World were in Mesoamerica, the area including the Maya homeland.

BELOW: Plate 14. Roll-out of a painted Maya vase with a scene of warriors.

Plate 15. Hvalsey stone church, built in Eastern Settlement by the Greenland Norse around A.D. 1300.

Plate 16. Eroded Icelandic landscape, as a legacy of deforestation and sheep grazing.

Plate 17. Eriks Fjord, in Greenland, a deeply indented iceberg-strewn fjord on which lay Brattahlid, one of the richest Norse farms of Eastern Settlement.

Plate 18. An Inuit hunter with kayak and harpoon, two potent and ingenious hunting technologies that the Greenland Norse must have observed in use by Inuit but never adopted themselves.

Plate 19. A densely populated agricultural landscape in the Wahgi Valley, in the New Guinea Highlands. It had become largely deforested, but 1200 years ago people began growing native casuarina trees in villages and gardens here to maintain timber and fuel supplies.

Plate 20. The forested surroundings of Mt. Fujiyama. As a result of rigorous top-down forest management beginning four centuries ago, Japan is the First World country with the highest percentage (74%) of its land area forested, despite supporting one of the highest human population densities.

Plate 21. Several dozen of the nearly one million victims of the 1994 genocidal killings in Rwanda.

Plate 22. Nine of the two million Rwandan refugees displaced by the 1994 genocidal killings.

Plate 23. A partly wooded agricultural landscape of the Dominican Republic, occupying the eastern part of the island of Hispaniola, and many times richer than Haiti.

Plate 24. The almost completely deforested landscape of the New World's poorest country, Haiti, which occupies the western part of the island of Hispaniola.

Plate 25. City dwellers in China protecting their faces against the world's worst urban air pollution.

Plate 26. Massive erosion that has ruined large areas of the Loess Plateau, in China.

Plate 27. Imported electronic garbage in China represents a direct transfer of pollution from the First World to the Third World.

Plate 28. Surface salt deposits, a form of salinization, along Australia's largest river, the Murray River.

Plate 29. The plague of sheep that consume vegetation and contribute to erosion in Australia.

Plate 30. The plague of introduced rabbits that consume vegetation and contribute to erosion in Australia.

Plate 31. Kudzu, a rapidly growing introduced plant species that smothers native vegetation in a North American forest.

Plate 32. President John F. Kennedy and his advisors deliberating during the Cuban Missile Crisis, when they learned from their mistakes during the Bay of Pigs Crisis and adopted more productive methods of group decision-making.

Plate 33. One of the best-publicized and most expensive industrial disasters of the last 20 years: the 1988 fire on Occidental Petroleum's Piper Alpha oil platform in the North Sea that killed 167 workers and cost the company huge financial losses.

Plate 34. Another of the best-publicized and most expensive industrial disasters of the last 20 years: two of the victims of the 1984 chemical spill at a chemical manufacturing plant in Bhopal, India, that killed 4,000 people and ultimately cost Union Carbide its existence as an independent company.

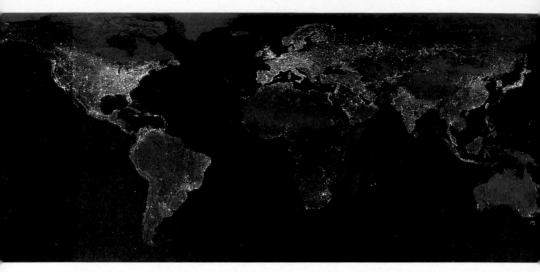

Plate 35. A composite of satellite photos at night over each area. Some areas (especially the U.S., Europe, and Japan) are much more brightly lit at night than are other areas (e.g., most of Africa, South America, and Australia). These differences in night illumination and electric power consumption are directly proportional to the differences in resource consumption in general, waste production, and standard of living between the First and Third Worlds. Will it really be possible to maintain such differences?

Plate 36. An affluent gated community whose residents are able to insulate themselves from some of the problems of the rest of my city, Los Angeles.

Plate 37. The freeways and urban sprawl that cover the landscape of much of my city.

Plate 38. The smog for which my city is notorious.

Plate 39. Unsuccessful water management of Dutch coastal lowlands in the floods of February 1953 that killed nearly 2,000 Dutch people.

Plate 40. Successful water management of a drained and reclaimed Dutch polder landscape lying below sea level.

Plate 41. Mohenjo Daro, ruins of an urban civilization that declined after 2000 B.C. in the Indus Valley of what is now Pakistan, due perhaps to climate change, river shifts, and water management problems.

Plate 42. Angkor Wat, temples of the Khmer Empire, at a city abandoned after A.D. 1400 in what is now Cambodia, due perhaps to water management problems that reduced the empire's military ability to resist enemies.

supplies, which might have sufficed to keep Gardar's own inhabitants alive if all the neighbors could have been kept out, would have been used up in the last winter when everybody tried to climb into the overcrowded lifeboat, eating the dogs and newborn livestock and the cows' hoofs as they had at the end of Western Settlement.

I picture the scene at Gardar as like that in my home city of Los Angeles in 1992 at the time of the so-called Rodney King riots, when the acquittal of policemen on trial for brutally beating a poor person provoked thousands of outraged people from poor neighborhoods to spread out to loot businesses and rich neighborhoods. The greatly outnumbered police could do nothing more than put up pieces of yellow plastic warning tape across roads entering rich neighborhoods, in a futile gesture aimed at keeping the looters out. We are increasingly seeing a similar phenomenon on a global scale today, as illegal immigrants from poor countries pour into the overcrowded lifeboats represented by rich countries, and as our border controls prove no more able to stop that influx than were Gardar's chiefs and Los Angeles's yellow tape. That parallel gives us another reason not to dismiss the fate of the Greenland Norse as just a problem of a small peripheral society in a fragile environment, irrelevant to our own larger society. Eastern Settlement was also larger than Western Settlement, but the outcome was the same; it merely took longer.

Were the Greenland Norse doomed from the outset, trying to practice a lifestyle that could not possibly succeed, so that it was only a matter of time before they would starve to death? Were they at a hopeless disadvantage compared to all the Native American hunter-gatherer peoples who had occupied Greenland on and off for thousands of years before the Norse arrived?

I don't think so. Remember that, before the Inuit, there had been at least four previous waves of Native American hunter-gatherers who had arrived in Greenland from the Canadian Arctic, and who had died out one after another. That's because climate fluctuations in the Arctic cause the large prey species essential for sustaining human hunters—caribou, seals, and whales—to migrate, fluctuate widely in numbers, or periodically abandon whole areas. While the Inuit have persisted in Greenland for eight centuries since their arrival, they too were subject to those fluctuations in prey numbers. Archaeologists have discovered many Inuit houses, sealed up like time capsules, containing the bodies of Inuit families that starved to death in that house during a harsh winter. In Danish colonial times it happened often that an Inuit would stagger into a Danish settlement, saying that he or she was the last survivor of some Inuit settlement all of whose other members had died of starvation.

Compared to the Inuit and all previous hunter-gatherer societies in Greenland, the Norse enjoyed the big advantage of an additional food source: livestock. In effect, the sole use that Native American hunters could make of the biological productivity of Greenland's land plant communities was by hunting the caribou (plus hares, as a minor food item) that fed on the plants. The Norse also ate caribou and hares, but in addition they allowed their cows, sheep, and goats to convert the plants into milk and meat. In that respect the Norse potentially had a much broader food base, and a better chance of surviving, than any previous occupants of Greenland. If only the Norse, besides eating many of the wild foods used by Native American societies in Greenland (especially caribou, migratory seals, and harbor seals), had also taken advantage of the other wild foods that Native Americans used but that the Norse did not (especially fish, ringed seals, and whales other than beached whales), the Norse might have survived. That they did not hunt the ringed seals, fish, and whales which they must have seen the Inuit hunting was their own decision. The Norse starved in the presence of abundant unutilized food resources. Why did they make that decision, which from our perspective of hindsight seems suicidal?

Actually, from the perspective of their own observations, values, and previous experience, Norse decision-making was no more suicidal than is ours today. Four sets of considerations stamped their outlook. First, it is difficult to make a living in Greenland's fluctuating environment, even for modern ecologists and agricultural scientists. The Norse had the fortune or misfortune to arrive in Greenland at a period when its climate was relatively mild. Not having lived there for the previous thousand years, they had not experienced a series of cold and warm cycles, and had no way to foresee the later difficulties of maintaining livestock when Greenland's climate would go into a cold cycle. After 20th-century Danes reintroduced sheep and cows to Greenland, they too proceeded to make mistakes, caused soil erosion by overstocking sheep, and quickly gave up on cows. Modern Greenland is not self-sufficient but depends heavily on Danish foreign aid and on fishing license payments from the European Union. Thus, even by today's standards, the achievement of the medieval Norse in developing a complex mix of activities that permitted them to feed themselves for 450 years is impressive and not at all suicidal.

Second, the Norse did not enter Greenland with their minds a blank slate, open to considering any solution to Greenland's problems. Instead, like all colonizing peoples throughout history, they arrived with their own knowledge, cultural values, and preferred lifestyle, based on generations of Norse experience in Norway and Iceland. They thought of themselves as dairy farmers, Christians, Europeans, and specifically Norse. Their Norwegian forebears had successfully practiced dairy farming for 3,000 years. Shared language, religion, and culture bound them to Norway, just as those shared attributes bound Americans and Australians to Britain for centuries. All of Greenland's bishops were Norwegians sent out to Greenland, rather than Norse who had grown up in Greenland. Without those shared Norwegian values, the Norse could not have cooperated to survive in Greenland. In that light their investments in cows, the Nordrseta hunt, and churches are understandable, even though on purely economic grounds those may not have been the best use of Norse energy. The Norse were undone by the same social glue that had enabled them to master Greenland's difficulties. That proves to be a common theme throughout history and also in the modern world, as we already saw in connection with Montana (Chapter 1): the values to which people cling most stubbornly under inappropriate conditions are those values that were previously the source of their greatest triumphs over adversity. We shall return to this dilemma in Chapters 14 and 16, when we consider societies that succeeded by figuring out which of their core values they could hold on to.

Third, the Norse, like other medieval European Christians, scorned pagan non-European peoples and lacked experience of how best to deal with them. Only after the age of exploration that began with Columbus's voyage in 1492 did Europeans learn Machiavellian ways of exploiting native peoples to their own advantage, even while continuing to despise them. Hence the Norse refused to learn from the Inuit and probably behaved towards them in ways ensuring their enmity. Many later groups of Europeans in the Arctic similarly perished as a result of ignoring or antagonizing the Inuit, most notably the 138 British members of the well-financed 1845 Franklin Expedition, every single one of whom died while trying to cross areas of the Canadian Arctic populated by Inuit. The European explorers and settlers who succeeded best in the Arctic were those most extensively adopting Inuit ways, like Robert Peary and Roald Amundsen.

Finally, power in Norse Greenland was concentrated at the top, in the hands of the chiefs and clergy. They owned most of the land (including all the best farms), owned the boats, and controlled the trade with Europe. They chose to devote much of that trade to importing goods that brought prestige to them: luxury goods for the wealthiest households, vestments and jewelry for the clergy, and bells and stained glass for the churches. Among the uses to which they allocated their few boats were the Nordrseta hunt, in order to acquire the luxury exports (such as ivory and polar bear hides) with which to pay for those imports. Chiefs had two motives for running large sheep herds that could damage the land by overgrazing: wool was Greenland's other principal export with which to pay for imports; and independent farmers on overgrazed land were more likely to be forced into tenancy, and thereby to become a chief's followers in his competition with other chiefs. There were many innovations that might have improved the material conditions of the Norse, such as importing more iron and fewer luxuries, allocating more boat time to Markland journeys for obtaining iron and timber, and copying (from the Inuit) or inventing different boats and different hunting techniques. But those innovations could have threatened the power, prestige, and narrow interests of the chiefs. In the tightly controlled, interdependent society of Norse Greenland, the chiefs were in a position to prevent others from trying out such innovations.

Thus, Norse society's structure created a conflict between the short-term interests of those in power, and the long-term interests of the society as a whole. Much of what the chiefs and clergy valued proved eventually harmful to the society. Yet the society's values were at the root of its strengths as well as of its weaknesses. The Greenland Norse did succeed in creating a unique form of European society, and in surviving for 450 years as Europe's most remote outpost. We modern Americans should not be too quick to brand them as failures, when their society survived in Greenland for longer than our English-speaking society has survived so far in North America. Ultimately, though, the chiefs found themselves without followers. The last right that they obtained for themselves was the privilege of being the last to starve.

CHAPTER 9

Opposite Paths to Success

Bottom up, top down ■ New Guinea highlands ■ Tikopia ■
Tokugawa problems ■ Tokugawa solutions ■ Why Japan succeeded ■
Other successes ■

The preceding chapters have described six past societies whose failure to solve the environmental problems that they created or encountered contributed to their eventual collapse: Easter Island, Pitcairn Island, Henderson Island, the Anasazi, the Classic Lowland Maya, and the Greenland Norse. I dwelt on their failures because they offer us many lessons. However, it's certainly not the case that all past societies were doomed to environmental disaster: the Icelanders have survived in a difficult environment for over 1,100 years, and many other societies have persisted for thousands of years. Those success stories also hold lessons for us, as well as hope and inspiration. They suggest that there are two contrasting types of approaches to solving environmental problems, which we may term the bottom-up and the top-down approach.

This recognition stems especially from the work of archaeologist Patrick Kirch on Pacific islands of different sizes, with different societal outcomes. The occupation of tiny Tikopia Island (1.8 square miles) was still sustainable after 3,000 years; medium-size Mangaia (27 square miles) underwent a deforestation-triggered collapse, similar to that of Easter Island; and the largest of the three islands, Tonga (288 square miles), has been operating more or less sustainably for 3,200 years. Why did the small island and the large island ultimately succeed in mastering their environmental problems, while the medium-sized island failed? Kirch argues that the small island and the large island adopted opposite approaches to success, and that neither approach was feasible on the medium-sized island.

Small societies occupying a small island or homeland can adopt a bottom-up approach to environmental management. Because the homeland is small, all of its inhabitants are familiar with the entire island, know that they are affected by developments throughout the island, and share a sense of identity and common interests with other inhabitants. Hence everybody realizes that they will benefit from sound environmental measures that they and their neighbors adopt. That's bottom-up management, in which people work together to solve their own problems.

Most of us have experience of such bottom-up management in our neighborhoods where we live or work. For instance, all homeowners on the Los Angeles street where I live belong to a neighborhood homeowners' association, whose purpose is to keep the neighborhood safe, harmonious, and attractive for our own benefit. All of us elect the association's directors each year, discuss policy at an annual meeting, and provide the association's budget by means of an annual dues payment. With that money, the association maintains flower gardens at road intersections, requires homeowners not to cut down trees without good cause, reviews building plans to ensure that ugly or oversized houses aren't built, resolves disputes between neighbors, and lobbies city officials on matters affecting the whole neighborhood. As another example, I mentioned in Chapter 1 that landowners living near Hamilton in Montana's Bitterroot Valley have banded together to operate the Teller Wildlife Refuge, and have thereby contributed to improving their own land values, lifestyle, and fishing and hunting opportunities, even though that in itself does not solve the problems of the United States or of the world.

The opposite approach is the top-down approach suited to a large society with centralized political organization, like Polynesian Tonga. Tonga is much too large for any individual peasant farmer to be familiar with the whole archipelago or even just with any single one of its large islands. Some problem might be going on in a distant part of the archipelago that could ultimately prove fatal to the farmer's lifestyle, but of which he initially has no knowledge. Even if he did know about it, he might dismiss it with the standard ISEP excuse ("It's someone else's problem"), because he might think that it made no difference to him or else its effects would just lie far off in the future. Conversely, a farmer might be inclined to gloss over problems in his own area (e.g., deforestation) because he assumes that there are plenty of trees somewhere else, but in fact he doesn't know.

Yet Tonga is still large enough for a centralized government under a paramount chief or king to have arisen. That king does have an overview over the whole archipelago, unlike local farmers. Also unlike the farmers, the king may be motivated to attend to the long-term interests of the whole archipelago, because the king derives his wealth from the whole archipelago, he is the latest in a line of rulers that has been there for a long time, and he expects his descendants to rule Tonga forever. Thus, the king or central authority may practice top-down management of environmental resources, and may give all of his subjects orders that are good for them in the long run but that they don't know enough to have formulated themselves.

This top-down approach is as familiar to citizens of modern First World countries as is the bottom-up approach. We're accustomed to the fact that governmental entities, especially (in the U.S.) state and federal governments, pursue environmental and other policies affecting the whole state or country, supposedly because the government leaders can have an overview of the state or country beyond the capacity of most individual citizens. For example, while the citizens of Montana's Bitterroot Valley do have their own Teller Wildlife Refuge, half of the valley's acreage is owned or managed by the federal government, as national forest or under the Bureau of Land Management.

Traditional middle-sized societies, occupying medium-sized islands or homelands, may not be well suited for either of these two approaches. The island is too large for a local farmer to have an overview of, or stake in, all parts of the island. Hostility between chiefs in neighboring valleys prevents agreement or coordinated action, and even contributes to environmental destruction: each chief leads raids to cut down trees and wreak havoc on rivals' land. The island may be too small for a central government to have arisen, capable of controlling the entire island. That appears to have been the fate of Mangaia, and may have affected other middle-sized societies in the past. Today, when the whole world is organized into states, fewer middle-sized societies may be facing this dilemma, but it may still arise in countries where state control is weak.

To illustrate these contrasting approaches to success, I shall now relate briefly the story of two small-scale societies where bottom-up approaches worked (the New Guinea highlands and Tikopia Island), and one large-scale society where top-down measures worked (Japan of the Tokugawa era, now the eighth most populous country in the world). In all three cases the environmental problems addressed were deforestation, erosion, and soil fertility. However, many other past societies have adopted similar approaches for solving problems of water resources, fishing, and hunting. It should also be understood that bottom-up and top-down approaches can coexist within a large-scale society that is organized as a pyramidal hierarchy of units. For example, in the United States and other democracies we have bottom-up management by local neighborhood and citizens' groups coexisting with top-down management by many levels of government (city, county, state, and national).

■ ■ ■

The first example is the highlands of New Guinea, one of the world's great success stories of bottom-up management. People have been living self-sustainably in New Guinea for about 46,000 years, until recent times without economically significant inputs from societies outside the highlands, and without inputs of any sort except trade items prized just for status (such as cowry shells and bird-of-paradise plumes). New Guinea is the large island just north of Australia (map, p. 84), lying almost on the equator and hence with hot tropical rainforest in the lowlands, but whose rugged interior consists of alternating ridges and valleys culminating in glacier-covered mountains up to 16,500 feet high. The terrain ruggedness confined European explorers to the coast and lowland rivers for 400 years, during which it became assumed that the interior was forest-covered and uninhabited.

It was therefore a shock, when airplanes chartered by biologists and miners first flew over the interior in the 1930s, for the pilots to see below them a landscape transformed by millions of people previously unknown to the outside world. The scene looked like the most densely populated areas of Holland (Plate 19): broad open valleys with few clumps of trees, divided as far as the eye could see into neatly laid-out gardens separated by ditches for irrigation and drainage, terraced steep hillsides reminiscent of Java or Japan, and villages surrounded by defensive stockades. When more Europeans followed up the pilots' discoveries overland, they found that the inhabitants were farmers who grew taro, bananas, yams, sugarcane, sweet potatoes, pigs, and chickens. We now know that the first four of those major crops (plus other minor ones) were domesticated in New Guinea itself, that the New Guinea highlands were one of only nine independent centers of plant domestication in the world, and that agriculture has been going on there for about 7,000 years—one of the world's longest-running experiments in sustainable food production.

To European explorers and colonizers, New Guinea highlanders seemed "primitive." They lived in thatched huts, were chronically at war with each other, had no kings or even chiefs, lacked writing, and wore little or no clothing even under cold conditions with heavy rain. They lacked metal and made their tools instead of stone, wood, and bone. For instance, they felled trees with stone axes, dug gardens and ditches with wooden sticks, and fought each other with wooden spears and arrows and bamboo knives.

That "primitive" appearance proved deceptive, because their farming methods are sophisticated, so much so that European agronomists still don't understand today in some cases the reasons why New Guineans' methods work and why well-intentioned European farming innovations failed there. For instance, one European agricultural advisor was horrified to notice that a New Guinean sweet potato garden on a steep slope in a wet area had vertical drainage ditches running straight down the slope. He convinced the villagers to correct their awful mistake, and instead to put in drains running horizontally along contours, according to good European practices. Awed by him, the villagers reoriented their drains, with the result that water built up behind the drains, and in the next heavy rains a landslide carried the entire garden down the slope into the river below. To avoid exactly that outcome, New Guinea farmers long before the arrival of Europeans learned the virtues of vertical drains under highland rain and soil conditions.

That's only one of the techniques that New Guineans worked out by trial and error, over the course of thousands of years, for growing crops in areas receiving up to 400 inches of rain per year, with frequent earthquakes, landslides, and (at higher elevations) frost. To maintain soil fertility, especially in areas of high population density where short fallow periods or even continuous growing of crops were essential to produce enough food, they resorted to a whole suite of techniques besides the silviculture that I'll explain in a moment. They added weeds, grass, old vines, and other organic matter to the soil as compost at up to 16 tons per acre. They applied garbage, ash from fires, vegetation cut from fields resting in fallow, rotten logs, and chicken manure as mulches and fertilizers to the soil surface. They dug ditches around fields to lower the watertable and prevent waterlogging, and transferred the organic muck dug out of those ditches onto the soil surface. Legume food crops that fix atmospheric nitrogen, such as beans, were rotated with other crops—in effect, an independent New Guinean invention of a crop rotation principle now widespread in First World agriculture for maintaining soil nitrogen levels. On steep slopes New Guineans constructed terraces, erected soil retention barriers, and of course removed excess water by the vertical drains that aroused the agronomist's ire. A consequence of their relying on all these specialized methods is that it takes years of growing up in a village to learn how to farm successfully in the New Guinea highlands. My highland friends who spent their childhood years away from their village to pursue an education found, on returning to the village, that they were incompetent at farming their family gardens because they had missed out on mastering a large body of complex knowledge.

Sustainable agriculture in the New Guinea highlands poses difficult problems not only of soil fertility but also of wood supplies, as a result of

forests having to be cleared for gardens and villages. The traditional highland lifestyle relied on trees for many purposes, such as for timber to build
houses and fences, wood for making tools and utensils and weapons, and
fuel for cooking and for heating the hut during the cold nights. Originally,
the highlands were covered with oak and beech forests, but thousands of
years of gardening have left the most densely populated areas (especially the
Wahgi Valley of Papua New Guinea and the Baliem Valley of Indonesian
New Guinea) completely deforested up to an elevation of 8,000 feet. Where
do highlanders obtain all the wood that they need?

Already on the first day of my visit to the highlands in 1964, I saw groves
of a species of casuarina tree in villages and gardens. Also known as she-
oaks or ironwood, casuarinas are a group of several dozen tree species with
leaves resembling pine needles, native to Pacific islands, Australia, Southeast
Asia, and tropical East Africa, but now widely introduced elsewhere because
of their easily split but very hard wood (hence that name "ironwood"). A
species native to the New Guinea highlands, *Casuarina oligodon*, is the one
that several million highlanders grow on a massive scale by transplanting
seedlings that have sprouted naturally along stream banks. Highlanders
similarly plant several other tree species, but casuarina is the most prevalent. So extensive is the scale of transplanting casuarinas in the highlands
that the practice is now referred to as "silviculture," the growing of trees instead of field crops as in conventional agriculture (*silva*, *ager*, and *cultura*
are the Latin words for woodland, field, and cultivation, respectively).

Only gradually have European foresters come to appreciate the particular advantages of *Casuarina oligodon*, and the benefits that highlanders obtain from its groves. The species is fast-growing. Its wood is excellent for
timber and fuel. Its root nodules that fix nitrogen, and its copious leaf-fall,
add both nitrogen and carbon to the soil. Hence casuarinas grown interspersed in active gardens increase the soil's fertility, while casuarinas grown
in abandoned gardens shorten the length of time that the site must be left
fallow to recover its fertility before a new crop can be planted. The roots
hold soil on steep slopes and thereby reduce erosion. New Guinea farmers
claim that the trees somehow reduce garden infestation with a taro beetle,
and experience suggests that they are right about that claim as they are
about many others, though agronomists still haven't figured out the basis of
the tree's claimed anti-beetle potency. Highlanders also say that they appreciate their casuarina groves for esthetic reasons, because they like the sound
of the wind blowing through the branches, and because the trees provide
shade to the village. Thus, even in broad valleys from which the original for-

est has been completely cleared, casuarina silviculture permits a wood-dependent society to continue to thrive.

How long have New Guinea highlanders been practicing silviculture? The clues used by paleobotanists to reconstruct the vegetational history of the highlands have been basically similar to those I already discussed for Easter Island, the Maya area, Iceland, and Greenland in Chapters 2–8: analysis of swamp and lake cores for pollen identified down to the level of the plant species producing the pollen; presence of charcoal or carbonized particles resulting from fires (either natural or else lit by humans to clear forests); sediment accumulation suggesting erosion following forest clearance; and radiocarbon dating.

It turns out that New Guinea and Australia were first settled around 46,000 years ago by humans moving eastwards from Asia through Indonesia's islands on rafts or canoes. At that time, New Guinea was still joined in a single landmass to Australia, where early human arrival is well attested at numerous sites. By 32,000 years ago, the appearance of charcoal from frequent fires and an increase in pollen of non-forest tree species compared to forest tree species at New Guinea highland sites hint that people were already visiting the sites, presumably to hunt and to gather forest pandanus nuts as they still do today. Signs of sustained forest clearance and the appearance of artificial drains within valley swamps by around 7,000 years ago suggest the origins of highland agriculture then. Forest pollen continues to decrease at the expense of non-forest pollen until around 1,200 years ago, when the first big surge in quantities of casuarina pollen appears almost simultaneously in two valleys 500 miles apart, the Baliem Valley in the west and the Wahgi Valley in the east. Today those are the broadest, most extensively deforested highland valleys, supporting the largest and densest human populations, and those same features were probably true of those two valleys 1,200 years ago.

If we take that casuarina pollen surge as a sign of the beginning of casuarina silviculture, why should it have arisen then, apparently independently in two separate areas of the highlands? Two or three factors were working together at that time to produce a wood crisis. One was the advance of deforestation, as the highland's farming population increased from 7,000 years ago onwards. A second factor is associated with a thick layer of volcanic ashfall, termed the Ogowila tephra, which at just that time blanketed eastern New Guinea (including the Wahgi Valley) but wasn't blown as far west as the Baliem Valley. That Ogowila tephra originated from an enormous eruption on Long Island off the coast of eastern New Guinea. When I visited Long Island in 1972, the island consisted of a ring of mountains 16 miles in diameter surrounding a huge hole filled by a crater lake, one of the largest lakes on any Pacific island. As discussed in Chapter 2, the nutrients carried in such an ashfall would have stimulated crop growth and thereby stimulated human population growth, in turn creating increased need for wood for timber and fuel, and increased rewards for discovering the virtues of casuarina silviculture. Finally, if one can extrapolate to New Guinea from the time record of El Niño events demonstrated for Peru, droughts and frost might have stressed highland societies then as a third factor.

To judge by an even bigger surge in casuarina pollen between 300 and 600 years ago, highlanders may then have expanded silviculture further under the stimulus of two other events: the Tibito tephra, an even bigger volcanic ashfall and boost to soil fertility and human population than the Ogowila tephra, also originating from Long Island and directly responsible for the hole filled by the modern lake that I saw; and possibly the arrival then of the Andean sweet potato in the New Guinea highlands, permitting crop yields several times those previously available with just New Guinean crops. After its initial appearance in the Wahgi and Baliem Valleys, casuarina silviculture (as attested by pollen cores) reached other highland areas at various later times, and was adopted in some outlying areas only within the 20th century. That spread of silviculture probably involved diffusion of knowledge of the technique from its first two sites of invention, plus perhaps some later independent inventions in other areas.

I have presented New Guinea highland casuarina silviculture as an example of bottom-up problem-solving, even though there are no written records from the highlands to tell us exactly how the technique was adopted. But it could hardly have been by any other type of problem-solving, because New Guinea highland societies represent an ultra-democratic extreme of bottom-up decision-making. Until the arrival of Dutch and Australian colonial government in the 1930s, there had not been even any beginnings of political unification in any part of the highlands: merely individual villages alternating between fighting each other and joining in temporary alliances with each other against other nearby villages. Within each village, instead of hereditary leaders or chiefs, there were just individuals, called "big-men," who by force of personality were more influential than other individuals but still lived in a hut like everybody else's and tilled a garden like anybody else's. Decisions were (and often still are today) reached by means of everybody in the village sitting down together and talking, and talking, and talking. The big-men couldn't give orders, and they might or might not succeed in persuading others to adopt their proposals. To outsiders today (including not just me but often New Guinea government officials themselves), that bottom-up approach to decision-making can be frustrating, because you can't go to some designated village leader and get a quick answer to your request; you have to have the patience to endure talk-talk-talk for hours or days with every villager who has some opinion to offer.

That must have been the context in which casuarina silviculture and all those other useful agricultural practices were adopted in the New Guinea highlands. People in any village could see the deforestation going on around them, could recognize the lower growth rates of their crops as gardens lost fertility after being initially cleared, and experienced the consequences of timber and fuel scarcity. New Guineans are more curious and experimental than any other people that I have encountered. When in my early years in New Guinea I saw someone who had acquired a pencil, which was still an unfamiliar object then, the pencil would be tried out for myriad purposes other than writing: a hair decoration? a stabbing tool? something to chew on? a long earring? a plug through the pierced nasal septum? Whenever I take New Guineans to work with me in areas away from their own village, they are constantly picking up local plants, asking local people about the plants' uses, and selecting some of the plants to bring back with them and try growing at home. In that way, someone 1,200 years ago would have noticed the casuarina seedlings growing beside a stream, brought them home as yet another plant to try out, noticed the beneficial effects in a garden— and then some other people would have observed those garden casuarinas and tried the seedlings for themselves.

Besides thereby solving their problems of wood supply and soil fertility, New Guinea highlanders also faced a population problem as their numbers increased. That population increase became checked by practices that continued into the childhoods of many of my New Guinea friends—especially by war, infanticide, use of forest plants for contraception and abortion, and sexual abstinence and natural lactational amenorrhea for several years while a baby was being nursed. New Guinea societies thereby avoided the fates that Easter Island, Mangareva, the Maya, the Anasazi, and many other societies suffered through deforestation and population growth. Highlanders managed to operate sustainably for tens of thousands of years before the origins of agriculture, and then for another 7,000 years after the origins of agriculture, despite climate changes and human environmental impacts constantly creating altered conditions.

Today, New Guineans are facing a new population explosion because of the success of public health measures, introduction of new crops, and the end or decrease of intertribal warfare. Population control by infanticide is no longer socially acceptable as a solution. But New Guineans already adapted in the past to such big changes as the extinction of the Pleistocene megafauna, glacial melting and warming temperatures at the end of the Ice Ages, the development of agriculture, massive deforestation, volcanic tephra fallouts, El Niño events, the arrival of the sweet potato, and the arrival of Europeans. Will they now also be able to adapt to the changed conditions producing their current population explosion?

Tikopia, a tiny, isolated, tropical island in the Southwest Pacific Ocean, is another success story of bottom-up management (map, p. 84). With a total area of just 1.8 square miles, it supports 1,200 people, which works out to a population density of 800 people per square mile of farmable land. That's a dense population for a traditional society without modern agricultural techniques. Nevertheless, the island has been occupied continuously for almost 3,000 years.

The nearest land of any sort to Tikopia is the even-tinier (one-seventh of a square mile) island of Anuta 85 miles distant, inhabited by only 170 people. The nearest larger islands, Vanua Lava and Vanikoro in the Vanuatu and Solomon Archipelagoes respectively, are 140 miles distant and still only 100 square miles each in area. In the words of the anthropologist Raymond Firth, who lived on Tikopia for a year in 1928–29 and returned for subsequent visits, "It's hard for anyone who has not actually lived on the island to realize its isolation from the rest of the world. It is so small that one is rarely out of sight or sound of the sea. [The maximum distance from the center of the island to the coast is three-quarters of a mile.] The native concept of space bears a distinct relation to this. They find it almost impossible to conceive of any really large land mass. . . . I was once asked seriously by a group of them, 'Friend, is there any land where the sound of the sea is not heard?' Their confinement has another less obvious result. For all kinds of spatial reference they use the expressions *inland* and *to seawards.* Thus an axe lying on the floor of a house is localized in this way, and I have even heard a man direct the attention of another in saying: 'There is a spot of mud on your seaward cheek.' Day by day, month after month, nothing breaks the level line of a clear horizon, and there is no faint haze to tell of the existence of any other land."

In Tikopia's traditional small canoes, the open-ocean voyage over the cyclone-prone Southwest Pacific to any of those nearest-neighbor islands was dangerous, although Tikopians considered it a great adventure. The canoes' small sizes and the infrequency of the voyages severely limited the quantity of goods that could be imported, so that in practice the only economically significant imports were stone for making tools, and unmarried young people from Anuta as marriage partners. Because Tikopia rock is of poor quality for making tools (just as we saw for Mangareva and Henderson Islands in Chapter 3), obsidian, volcanic glass, basalt, and chert were imported from Vanua Lava and Vanikoro, with some of that imported stone in turn originating from much more distant islands in the Bismarck, Solomon, and Samoan Archipelagoes. Other imports consisted of luxury goods: shells for ornaments, bows and arrows, and (formerly) pottery.

There could be no question of importing staple foods in amounts sufficient to contribute meaningfully to Tikopian subsistence. In particular, Tikopians had to produce and store enough surplus food to be able to avoid starvation during the annual dry season of May and June, and after cyclones that at unpredictable intervals destroy gardens. (Tikopia lies in the Pacific's main cyclone belt, with on the average 20 cyclones per decade.) Hence surviving on Tikopia required solving two problems for 3,000 years: How could a food supply sufficient for 1,200 people be produced reliably? And how could the population be prevented from increasing to a higher level that would be impossible to sustain?

Our main source of information about the traditional Tikopian lifestyle comes from Firth's observations, one of the classic studies of anthropology. While Tikopia had been "discovered" by Europeans already in 1606, its isolation ensured that European influence remained negligible until the 1800s, the first visit by missionaries did not take place until 1857, and the first conversions of islanders to Christianity did not begin until after 1900. Hence Firth in 1928–29 had a better opportunity than subsequent visiting anthropologists to observe a culture that still contained many of its traditional elements, although already then in the process of change.

Sustainability of food production on Tikopia is promoted by some of the environmental factors discussed in Chapter 2 as tending to make societies on some Pacific islands more sustainable, and less susceptible to environmental degradation, than societies on other islands. Working in favor of sustainability on Tikopia are its high rainfall, moderate latitude, and location in the zone of high volcanic ash fallout (from volcanoes on other islands) and high fallout of Asian dust. Those factors constitute a geographical stroke of good luck for the Tikopians: favorable conditions for which they personally could claim no credit. The remainder of their good fortune must be credited to what they have done for themselves. Virtually the whole island is micromanaged for continuous and sustainable food production, instead of the slash-and-burn agriculture prevalent on many other Pacific islands. Almost every plant species on Tikopia is used by people in one way or another: even grass is used as a mulch in gardens, and wild trees are used as food sources in times of famine.

As you approach Tikopia from the sea, the island appears to be covered with tall, multi-storied, original rainforest, like that mantling uninhabited Pacific islands. Only when you land and go among the trees do you realize that true rainforest is confined to a few patches on the steepest cliffs, and that the rest of the island is devoted to food production. Most of the island's area is covered with an orchard whose tallest trees are native or introduced tree species producing edible nuts or fruit or other useful products, of which the most important are coconuts, breadfruit, and sago palms yielding a starchy pith. Less numerous but still valuable canopy trees are the native almond (*Canarium harveyi*), the nut-bearing *Burckella ovovata,* the Tahitian chestnut *Inocarpus fagiferus,* the cut-nut *Barringtonia procera,* and the tropical almond *Terminalia catappa.* Smaller useful trees in the middle story include the betelnut palm with narcotic-containing nuts, the vi-apple *Spondias dulcis,* and the medium-sized mami tree *Antiaris toxicara,* which fits well into this orchard and whose bark was used for cloth, instead of the paper mulberry used on other Polynesian islands. The understory below these tree layers is in effect a garden for growing yams, bananas, and the giant swamp taro *Cyrtosperma chamissonis,* most of whose varieties require swampy conditions but of which Tikopians grow a genetic clone specifically adapted to dry conditions in their well-drained hillside orchards. This whole multi-story orchard in unique in the Pacific in its structural mimicry of a rainforest, except that its plants are all edible whereas most rainforest trees are inedible.

In addition to these extensive orchards, there are two other types of small areas that are open and treeless but also used for food production. One is a small freshwater swamp, devoted to growing the usual moisture-adapted form of giant swamp taro instead of the distinctive dry-adapted clone grown on hillsides. The other consists of fields devoted to short-fallow, labor-intensive, nearly continuous production of three root crops: taro, yams, and now the South American–introduced crop manioc, which has largely replaced native yams. These fields require almost constant labor input for weeding, plus mulching with grass and brushwood to prevent crop plants from drying out.

The main food products of these orchards, swamps, and fields are starchy plant foods. For their protein, in the absence of domestic animals larger than chickens and dogs, traditional Tikopians relied to a minor extent on ducks and fish obtained from the island's one brackish lake, and to a major extent on fish and shellfish from the sea. Sustainable exploitation of seafood resulted from taboos administered by chiefs, whose permission was required to catch or eat fish; the taboos therefore had the effect of preventing overfishing.

Tikopians still had to fall back on two types of emergency food supply to get them over the annual dry season when crop production was low, and the occasional cyclone that could destroy gardens and orchard crops. One type consisted of fermenting surplus breadfruit in pits to produce a starchy paste that can be stored for two or three years. The other type consisted of exploiting the small remaining stands of original rainforest to harvest fruits, nuts, and other edible plant parts that were not preferred foods but could save people from otherwise starving. In 1976, while I was visiting another Polynesian island called Rennell, I asked Rennell Islanders about the edibility of fruit from each of the dozens of Rennell species of forest trees. There proved to be three answers: some trees were said to have "edible" fruit; some trees were said to have "inedible" fruit; and other trees had fruit "eaten only at the time of the *hungi kenge*." Never having heard of a *hungi kenge*, I inquired about it. I was told that it was the biggest cyclone in living memory, which had destroyed Rennell's gardens around 1910 and reduced people to the point of starvation, from which they saved themselves by eating forest fruits that they didn't especially like and normally wouldn't eat. On Tikopia, with its two cyclones in the average year, such fruits must be even more important than on Rennell.

Those are the ways in which Tikopians assure themselves of a sustainable food supply. The other prerequisite for sustainable occupation of Tikopia is a stable, non-increasing population. During Firth's visit in 1928–29 he counted the island's population to be 1,278 people. From 1929 to 1952 the population increased at 1.4% per year, which is a modest rate of increase that would surely have been exceeded during the generations following the first settlement of Tikopia around 3,000 years ago. Even supposing, however, that Tikopia's initial population growth rate was also only 1.4% per year, and that the initial settlement had been by a canoe holding

25 people, then the population of the 1.8-square-mile island would have built up to the absurd total of 25 million people after a thousand years, or to 25 million trillion people by 1929. Obviously that's impossible: the population could not have continued to grow at that rate, because it would already have reached its modern level of 1,278 people within only 283 years after human arrival. How was Tikopia's population held constant after 283 years?

Firth learned of six methods of population regulation still operating on the island in 1929, and a seventh that had operated in the past. Most readers of this book will also have practiced one or more of those methods, such as contraception or abortion, and our decisions to do so may have been implicitly influenced by considerations of human population pressure or family resources. On Tikopia, however, people are explicit in saying that their motive for contraception and other regulatory behaviors is to prevent the island from becoming overpopulated, and to prevent the family from having more children than the family's land could support. For instance, Tikopia chiefs each year carry out a ritual in which they preach an ideal of Zero Population Growth for the island, unaware that an organization founded with that name (but subsequently renamed) and devoted to that goal has also arisen in the First World. Tikopia parents feel that it is wrong for them to continue to give birth to children of their own once their eldest son has reached marriageable age, or to have more children than a number variously given as four children, or one boy and a girl, or one boy and one or two girls.

Of traditional Tikopia's seven methods of population regulation, the simplest was contraception by coitus interruptus. Another method was abortion, induced by pressing on the belly, or placing hot stones on the belly, of a pregnant woman near term. Alternatively, infanticide was carried out by burying alive, smothering, or turning a newborn infant on its face. Younger sons of families poor in land remained celibate, and many among the resulting surplus of marriageable women also remained celibate rather than enter into polygamous marriages. (Celibacy on Tikopia means not having children, and does not preclude having sex by coitus interruptus and then resorting to abortion or infanticide if necessary.) Still another method was suicide, of which there were seven known cases by hanging (six men and one woman) and 12 (all of them women) by swimming out to sea between 1929 and 1952. Much commoner than such explicit suicide was "virtual suicide" by setting out on dangerous overseas voyages, which claimed the lives of 81 men and three women between 1929 and 1952. Such sea voyaging accounted for more than one-third of all deaths of young bachelors.

Whether sea voyaging constituted virtual suicide or just reckless behavior on the part of young men undoubtedly varied from case to case, but the bleak prospects of younger sons in poor families on a crowded island during a famine were probably often a consideration. For instance, Firth learned in 1929 that a Tikopian man named Pa Nukumara, the younger brother of a chief still alive then, had gone to sea with two of his own sons during a severe drought and famine, with the express intent of dying quickly, instead of slowly starving to death on shore.

The seventh method of population regulation was not operating during Firth's visits but was reported to him by oral traditions. Sometime in the 1600s or early 1700s, to judge by accounts of the number of elapsed generations since the events, Tikopia's former large saltwater bay became converted into the current brackish lake by the closing-off of a sandbar across its mouth. That resulted in the death of the bay's former rich shellfish beds and a drastic decrease in its fish populations, hence in starvation for the Nga Ariki clan living on that part of Tikopia at that time. The clan reacted to acquire more land and coastline for itself by attacking and exterminating the Nga Ravenga clan. A generation or two later, the Nga Ariki also attacked the remaining Nga Faea clan, who fled the island in canoes (thereby committing virtual suicide) rather than await their deaths by murder on land. These oral memories are confirmed by archaeological evidence of the bay's closing and of the village sites.

Most of these seven methods for keeping Tikopia's population constant have disappeared or declined under European influence during the 20th century. The British colonial government of the Solomons forbade sea voyaging and warfare, while Christian missions preached against abortion, infanticide, and suicide. As a result, Tikopia's population grew from its 1929 level of 1,278 people to 1,753 people by 1952, when two destructive cyclones within the span of 13 months destroyed half of Tikopia's crops and caused widespread famine. The British Solomon Islands' colonial government responded to the immediate crisis by sending food, and then dealt with the long-term problem by permitting or encouraging Tikopians to relieve their overpopulation by resettling onto less populated Solomon islands. Today, Tikopia's chiefs limit the number of Tikopians who are permitted to reside on their island to 1,115 people, close to the population size that was traditionally maintained by infanticide, suicide, and other now-unacceptable means.

How and when did Tikopia's remarkable sustainable economy arise? Archaeological excavations by Patrick Kirch and Douglas Yen show that it was not invented all at once but developed over the course of nearly 3,000 years. The island was first settled around 900 B.C. by Lapita people ancestral to the modern Polynesians, as described in Chapter 2. Those first settlers made a heavy impact on the island's environment. Remains of charcoal at archaeological sites show that they cleared forest by burning it. They feasted on breeding colonies of seabirds, land birds, and fruit bats, and on fish, shellfish, and sea turtles. Within a thousand years, the Tikopian populations of five bird species (Abbott's Booby, Audubon's Shearwater, Banded Rail, Common Megapode, and Sooty Tern) were extirpated, to be followed later by the Red-footed Booby. Also in that first millennium, archaeological middens reveal the virtual elimination of fruit bats, a three-fold decrease in fish and bird bones, a 10-fold decrease in shellfish, and a decrease in the maximum size of giant clams and turban shells (presumably because people were preferentially harvesting the largest individuals).

Around 100 B.C., the economy began to change as those initial food sources disappeared or were depleted. Over the course of the next thousand years, charcoal accumulation ceased, and remains of native almonds (*Canarium harveyi*) appeared, in archaeological sites, indicating that Tikopians were abandoning slash-and-burn agriculture in favor of maintaining orchards with nut trees. To compensate for the drastic declines in birds and seafood, people shifted to intensive husbandry of pigs, which came to account for nearly half of all protein consumed. An abrupt change in economy and artifacts around A.D. 1200 marks the arrival of Polynesians from the east, whose distinctive cultural features had been forming in the area of Fiji, Samoa, and Tonga among descendants of the Lapita migration that had initially also colonized Tikopia. It was those Polynesians who brought with them the technique of fermenting and storing breadfruit in pits.

A momentous decision taken consciously around A.D. 1600, and recorded in oral traditions but also attested archaeologically, was the killing of every pig on the island, to be replaced as protein sources by an increase in consumption of fish, shellfish, and turtles. According to Tikopians' accounts, their ancestors had made that decision because pigs raided and rooted up gardens, competed with humans for food, were an inefficient means to feed humans (it takes about 10 pounds of vegetables edible to humans to produce just one pound of pork), and had become a luxury food for the chiefs. With that elimination of pigs, and the transformation of Tikopia's bay into a brackish lake around the same time, Tikopia's economy achieved essentially the form in which it existed when Europeans first began to take up residence in the 1800s. Thus, until colonial government and

Christian mission influence became important in the 20th century, Tikopians had been virtually self-supporting on their micromanaged remote little speck of land for three millennia.

Tikopians today are divided among four clans each headed by a hereditary chief, who holds more power than does a non-hereditary big-man of the New Guinea highlands. Nevertheless, the evolution of Tikopian subsistence is better described by the bottom-up metaphor than by the top-down metaphor. One can walk all the way around the coastline of Tikopia in under half a day, so that every Tikopian is familiar with the entire island. The population is small enough that every Tikopian resident on the island can also know all other residents individually. While every piece of land has a name and is owned by some patrilineal kinship group, each house owns pieces of land in different parts of the island. If a garden is not being used at the moment, anyone can temporarily plant crops in that garden without asking the owner's permission. Anyone can fish on any reef, regardless of whether it happens to be in front of someone else's house. When a cyclone or drought arrives, it affects the entire island. Thus, despite differences among Tikopians in their clan affiliation and in how much land their kinship group owns, they all face the same problems and are at the mercy of the same dangers. Tikopia's isolation and small size have demanded collective decision-making ever since the island was settled. Anthropologist Raymond Firth entitled his first book *We, the Tikopia* because he often heard that phrase *("Matou nga Tikopia")* from Tikopians explaining their society to him.

Tikopia's chiefs do serve as the overlords of clan lands and canoes, and they redistribute resources. By Polynesian standards, however, Tikopia is among the least stratified chiefdoms with the weakest chiefs. Chiefs and their families produce their own food and dig in their own gardens and orchards, as do commoners. In Firth's words, "Ultimately the mode of production is inherent in the social tradition, of which the chief is merely the prime agent and interpreter. He and his people share the same values: an ideology of kinship, ritual, and morality reinforced by legend and mythology. The chief is to a considerable extent a custodian of this tradition, but he is not alone in this. His elders, his fellow chiefs, the people of his clan, and even the members of his family are all imbued with the same values, and advise and criticize his actions." Thus, that role of Tikopian chiefs represents much less top-down management than does the role of the leaders of the remaining society that we shall now discuss.

■ ■ ■

Our other success story resembles Tikopia in that it too involves a densely populated island society isolated from the outside world, with few economically significant imports, and with a long history of a self-sufficient and sustainable lifestyle. But the resemblance ends there, because this island has a population 100,000 times larger than Tikopia's, a powerful central government, an industrial First World economy, a highly stratified society presided over by a rich powerful elite, and a big role of top-down initiatives in solving environmental problems. Our case study is of Japan before 1868.

Japan's long history of scientific forest management is not well known to Europeans and Americans. Instead, professional foresters think of the techniques of forest management widespread today as having begun to develop in German principalities in the 1500s, and having spread from there to much of the rest of Europe in the 1700s and 1800s. As a result, Europe's total area of forest, after declining steadily ever since the origins of European agriculture 9,000 years ago, has actually been increasing since around 1800. When I first visited Germany in 1959, I was astonished to discover the extent of neatly laid-out forest plantations covering much of the country, because I had thought of Germany as industrialized, populous, and urban.

But it turns out that Japan, independently of and simultaneously with Germany, also developed top-down forest management. That too is surprising, because Japan, like Germany, is industrialized, populous, and urban. It has the highest population density of any large First World country, with nearly 1,000 people per square mile of total area, or 5,000 people per square mile of farmland. Despite that high population, almost 80% of Japan's area consists of sparsely populated forested mountains (Plate 20), while most people and agriculture are crammed into the plains that make up only one-fifth of the country. Those forests are so well protected and managed that their extent is still increasing, even though they are being utilized as valuable sources of timber. Because of that forest mantle, the Japanese often refer to their island nation as "the green archipelago." While the mantle superficially resembles a primeval forest, in fact most of Japan's accessible original forests were cut by 300 years ago and became replaced with regrowth forest and plantations as tightly micromanaged as those of Germany and Tikopia.

Japanese forest policies arose as a response to an environmental and population crisis paradoxically brought on by peace and prosperity. For almost 150 years beginning in 1467, Japan was convulsed by civil wars as the ruling coalition of powerful houses that had emerged from the earlier disintegration of the emperor's power in turn collapsed, and as control passed instead to dozens of autonomous warrior barons (called *daimyo*), who fought each other. The wars were finally ended by the military victories of a warrior named Toyotomi Hideyoshi and his successor Tokugawa Ieyasu. In 1615 Ieyasu's storming of the Toyotomi family stronghold at Osaka, and the deaths by suicide of the remaining Toyotomis, marked the wars' end.

Already in 1603, the emperor had invested Ieyasu with the hereditary title of *shogun*, the chief of the warrior estate. From then on, the shogun based at his capital city of Edo (modern Tokyo) exercised the real power, while the emperor at the old capital of Kyoto remained a figurehead. A quarter of Japan's area was directly administered by the shogun, the remaining three-quarters being administered by the 250 daimyo whom the shogun ruled with a firm hand. Military force became the shogun's monopoly. Daimyo could no longer fight each other, and they even needed the shogun's permission to marry, to modify their castles, or to pass on their property in inheritance to a son. The years from 1603 to 1867 in Japan are called the Tokugawa era, during which a series of Tokugawa shoguns kept Japan free of war and foreign influence.

Peace and prosperity allowed Japan's population and economy to explode. Within a century of the wars' end, population doubled because of a fortunate combination of factors: peaceful conditions, relative freedom from the disease epidemics afflicting Europe at the time (due to Japan's ban on foreign travel or visitors: see below), and increased agricultural productivity as the result of the arrival of two productive new crops (potatoes and sweet potatoes), marsh reclamation, improved flood control, and increased production of irrigated rice. While the population as a whole thus grew, cities grew even faster, to the point where Edo became the world's most populous city by 1720. Throughout Japan, peace and a strong centralized government brought a uniform currency and uniform system of weights and measures, the end of toll and customs barriers, road construction, and improved coastal shipping, all of which contributed to a trade boom within Japan.

But Japan's trade with the rest of the world was cut to almost nothing. Portuguese navigators bent on trade and conquest, having rounded Africa to reach India in 1498, advanced to the Moluccas in 1512, China in 1514, and Japan in 1543. Those first European visitors to Japan were just a pair of shipwrecked sailors, but they caused unsettling changes by introducing guns, and even bigger changes when they were followed by Catholic missionaries six years later. Hundreds of thousands of Japanese, including some daimyo, became converted to Christianity. Unfortunately, rival Jesuit and Franciscan missionaries began competing with each other, and stories spread that friars were trying to Christianize Japan as a prelude to a European takeover.

In 1597 Toyotomi Hideyoshi crucified Japan's first group of 26 Christian martyrs. When Christian daimyo then tried to bribe or assassinate government officials, the shogun Tokugawa Ieyasu concluded that Europeans and Christianity posed a threat to the stability of the shogunate and Japan. (In retrospect, when one considers how European military intervention followed the arrival of apparently innocent traders and missionaries in China, India, and many other countries, the threat foreseen by Ieyasu was real.) In 1614 Ieyasu prohibited Christianity and began to torture and execute missionaries and those of their converts who refused to disavow their religion. In 1635 a later shogun went even further by forbidding Japanese to travel overseas and forbidding Japanese ships to leave Japan's coastal waters. Four years later, he expelled all the remaining Portuguese from Japan.

Japan thereupon entered a period, lasting over two centuries, in which it cordoned itself off from the rest of the world, for reasons reflecting even more its agendas related to China and Korea than to Europe. The sole foreign traders admitted were a few Dutch merchants (considered less dangerous than Portuguese because they were anti-Catholic), kept isolated like dangerous germs on an island in Nagasaki harbor, and a similar Chinese enclave. The only other foreign trade permitted was with Koreans on Tsushima Island lying between Korea and Japan, with the Ryukyu Islands (including Okinawa) to the south, and with the aboriginal Ainu population on Hokkaido Island to the north (then not yet part of Japan, as it is today). Apart from those contacts, Japan did not even maintain overseas diplomatic relations, not even with China. Nor did Japan attempt foreign conquests after Hideyoshi's two unsuccessful invasions of Korea in the 1590s.

During those centuries of relative isolation, Japan was able to meet most of its needs domestically, and in particular was virtually self-sufficient in food, timber, and most metals. Imports were largely restricted to sugar and spices, ginseng and medicines and mercury, 160 tons per year of luxury woods, Chinese silk, deer skin and other hides to make leather (because Japan maintained few cattle), and lead and saltpeter to make gunpowder. Even the amounts of some of those imports decreased with time as domestic silk and sugar production rose, and as guns became restricted and then virtually abolished. This remarkable state of self-sufficiency and self-imposed isolation lasted until an American fleet under Commodore Perry arrived in 1853 to demand that Japan open its ports to supply fuel and provisions to American whaling and merchant ships. When it then became clear that the Tokugawa shogunate could no longer protect Japan from bar-barians armed with guns, the shogunate collapsed in 1868, and Japan began its remarkably rapid transformation from an isolated semi-feudal society to a modern state.

Deforestation was a major factor in the environmental and population crisis brought on by the peace and prosperity of the 1600s, as Japan's timber consumption (almost entirely consisting of domestic timber) soared. Until the late 19th century, most Japanese buildings were made of wood, rather than of stone, brick, cement, mud, or tiles as in many other countries. That tradition of timber construction stemmed partly from a Japanese esthetic preference for wood, and partly from the ready availability of trees through-out Japan's early history. With the onset of peace, prosperity, and a popula-tion boom, timber use for construction took off to supply the needs of the growing rural and urban population. Beginning around 1570, Hideyoshi, his successor the shogun Ieyasu, and many of the daimyo led the way, in-dulging their egos and seeking to impress each other by constructing huge castles and temples. Just the three biggest castles built by Ieyasu required clear-cutting about 10 square miles of forests. About 200 castle towns and cities arose under Hideyoshi, Ieyasu, and the next shogun. After Ieyasu's death, urban construction outstripped elite monument construction in its demand for timber, especially because cities of thatch-roofed wooden buildings set closely together and with winter heating by fireplaces were prone to burn, so cities needed to be rebuilt repeatedly. The biggest of those urban fires was the Meireki fire that burned half of the capital at Edo and killed 100,000 people in 1657. Much of that timber was transported to cities by coastal ships, in turn built of wood and hence consuming more wood. Still more wooden ships were required to transport Hideyoshi's armies across the Korea Strait in his unsuccessful attempts to conquer Korea.

Timber for construction was not the only need driving deforestation. Wood was also the fuel used for heating houses, for cooking, and for indus-trial uses such as making salt, tiles, and ceramics. Wood was burned to char-coal to sustain the hotter fires required for smelting iron. Japan's expanding population needed more food, and hence more forested land cleared for agriculture. Peasants fertilized their fields with "green fertilizer" (i.e., leaves, bark, and twigs), and fed their oxen and horses with fodder (brush and grass), obtained from the forests. Each acre of cropland required 5 to 10 acres of forest to provide the necessary green fertilizer. Until the civil wars ended in 1615, the warring armies under daimyo and the shogun took fod-der for their horses, and bamboo for their weapons and defensive palisades, from the forests. Daimyo in forested areas fulfilled their annual obligation to the shogun in the form of timber.

The years from about 1570 to 1650 marked the peak of the construction boom and of deforestation, which slowed down as timber became scarce. At first, wood was cut either under the direct order of the shogun or daimyo, or else by peasants themselves for their local needs, but by 1660 logging by private entrepreneurs overtook government-ordered logging. For instance, when yet another fire broke out in Edo, one of the most famous of those private lumbermen, a merchant named Kinokuniya Bunzaemon, shrewdly recognized that the result would be more demand for timber. Even before the fire had been put out, he sailed off on a ship to buy up huge quantities of timber in the Kiso district, for resale at a big profit in Edo.

The first part of Japan to become deforested, already by A.D. 800, was the Kinai Basin on the largest Japanese island of Honshu, site of early Japan's main cities such as Osaka and Kyoto. By the year 1000, deforestation was spreading to the nearby smaller island of Shikoku. By 1550 about one-quarter of Japan's area (still mainly just central Honshu and eastern Shikoku) had been logged, but other parts of Japan still held much lowland forest and old-growth forest.

In 1582 Hideyoshi became the first ruler to demand timber from all over Japan, because timber needs for his lavish monumental construction exceeded the timber available on his own domains. He took control of some of Japan's most valuable forests and requisitioned a specified amount of timber each year from each daimyo. In addition to forests, which the shogun and daimyo claimed for themselves, they also claimed all valuable species of timber trees on village or private land. To transport all that timber from increasingly distant logging areas to the cities or castles where the timber was needed, the government cleared obstacles from rivers so that logs could be floated or rafted down them to the coast, whence they were then transported by ships to port cities. Logging spread over Japan's three main islands, from the southern end of the southernmost island of Kyushu through Shikoku to the northern end of Honshu. In 1678 loggers had to turn to the southern end of Hokkaido, the island north of Honshu and at that time not yet part of the Japanese state. By 1710, most accessible forest had been cut on the three main islands (Kyushu, Shikoku, and Honshu) and on southern Hokkaido, leaving old-growth forests just on steep slopes, in inaccessible areas, and at sites too difficult or costly to log with Tokugawa-era technology.

Deforestation hurt Tokugawa Japan in other ways besides the obvious one of wood shortages for timber, fuel, and fodder and the forced end to monumental construction. Disputes over timber and fuel became increasingly frequent between and within villages, and between villages and the daimyo or shogun, all of whom competed for Japan's forests. There were also disputes between those who wanted to use rivers for floating or rafting logs, and those who instead wanted to use them for fishing or for irrigating cropland. Just as we saw for Montana in Chapter 1, wildfires increased, because the second-growth woods springing up on logged land were more flammable than were old-growth forests. Once the forest cover protecting steep slopes had been removed, the rate of soil erosion increased as a consequence of Japan's heavy rainfall, snowmelt, and frequent earthquakes. Flooding in the lowlands due to increased water runoff from the denuded slopes, higher water levels in lowland irrigation systems due to soil erosion and river siltation, increased storm damage, and shortages of forest-derived fertilizer and fodder acted together to decrease crop yields at a time of increasing population, and thus to contribute to major famines that beset Tokugawa Japan from the late 1600s onwards.

The 1657 Meireki fire, and the resulting demand for timber to rebuild Japan's capital, served as a wake-up call exposing the country's growing scarcity of timber and other resources at a time when its population, especially its urban population, had been growing rapidly. That might have led to an Easter Island–like catastrophe. Instead, over the course of the next two centuries Japan gradually achieved a stable population and much more nearly sustainable resource consumption rates. The shift was led from the top by successive shoguns, who invoked Confucian principles to promulgate an official ideology that encouraged limiting consumption and accumulating reserve supplies in order to protect the country against disaster.

Part of the shift involved increased reliance on seafood and on trade with the Ainu for food, in order to relieve the pressure on farming. Expanded fishing efforts incorporated new fishing techniques, such as very large nets and deepwater fishing. The territories claimed by individual daimyo and villages now included the sea adjacent to their land, in recognition of the sense that fish and shellfish stocks were limited and might become exhausted if anyone else could freely fish in one's territory. Pressure on forests as a source of green fertilizer for cropland was reduced by making much more use of fish meal fertilizers. Hunting of sea mammals (whales, seals, and sea otters) increased, and syndicates were formed to finance the necessary boats, equipment, and large workforces. The greatly expanded trade with the Ainu on Hokkaido Island brought smoked salmon, dried sea cucumber, abalone, kelp, deer skins, and sea otter pelts to Japan, in exchange for rice, sake (rice wine), tobacco, and cotton delivered to the Ainu. Among the results were the depletion of salmon and deer on Hokkaido, the weaning of the Ainu away from self-sufficiency as hunters to dependence on Japanese imports, and eventually the destruction of the Ainu through economic disruption, disease epidemics, and military conquests. Thus, part of the Tokugawa solution for the problem of resource depletion in Japan itself was to conserve Japanese resources by causing resource depletion elsewhere, just as part of the solution of Japan and other First World countries to problems of resource depletion today is to cause resource depletion elsewhere. (Remember that Hokkaido was not incorporated politically into Japan until the 19th century.)

Another part of the shift consisted of the near-achievement of Zero Population Growth. Between 1721 and 1828, Japan's population barely increased at all, from 26,100,000 to only 27,200,000. Compared to earlier centuries, Japanese in the 18th and 19th century married later, nursed their babies for longer, and spaced their children at longer intervals through the resulting lactational amenorrhea as well as through contraception, abortion, and infanticide. Those decreased birth rates represented responses of individual couples to perceived shortages of food and other resources, as shown by rises and falls in Tokugawa Japanese birth rates in phase with falls and rises in rice prices.

Still other aspects of the shift served to reduce wood consumption. Beginning in the late 17th century, Japan's use of coal instead of wood as a fuel rose. Lighter construction replaced heavy-timbered houses, fuel-efficient cooking stoves replaced open-hearth fireplaces, small portable charcoal heaters replaced the practice of heating the whole house, and reliance on the sun to heat houses during the winter increased.

Many top-down measures were aimed at curing the imbalance between cutting trees and producing trees, initially mainly by negative measures (reducing the cutting), then increasingly by positive measures as well (producing more trees). One of the first signs of awareness at the top was a proclamation by the shogun in 1666, just nine years after the Meireki fire, warning of the dangers of erosion, stream siltation, and flooding caused by deforestation, and urging people to plant seedlings. Beginning in that same decade, Japan launched a nationwide effort at all levels of society to regulate use of its forest, and by 1700 an elaborate system of woodland management was in place. In the words of historian Conrad Totman, the system focused on "specifying who could do what, where, when, how, how much, and at what price." That is, the first phase of the Tokugawa-era response to Japan's forest problem emphasized negative measures that didn't restore lumber production to previous levels, but that at least bought time, prevented the situation from getting worse until positive measures could take effect, and set ground rules for the competition within Japanese society over increasingly scarce forest products.

The negative responses aimed at three stages in the wood supply chain: woodland management, wood transport, and wood consumption in towns. At the first stage, the shogun, who directly controlled about a quarter of Japan's forests, designated a senior magistrate in the finance ministry to be responsible for his forests, and almost all of the 250 daimyo followed suit by each appointing his own forest magistrate for his land. Those magistrates closed off logged lands to permit forest regeneration, issued licenses specifying the peasants' rights to cut timber or graze animals on government forest land, and banned the practice of burning forests to clear land for shifting cultivation. In those forests controlled not by the shogun or daimyo but by villages, the village headman managed the forest as common property for the use of all villagers, developed rules about the harvesting of forest products, forbade "foreign" peasants of other villages to use his own village's forest, and hired armed guards to enforce all these rules.

Both the shogun and the daimyo paid for very detailed inventories of their forests. Just as one example of the managers' obsessiveness, an inventory of a forest near Karuizawa 80 miles northwest of Edo in 1773 recorded that the forest measured 2.986 square miles in area and contained 4,114 trees, of which 573 were crooked or knotty and 3,541 were good. Of those 4,114 trees, 78 were big conifers (66 of them good) with trunks 24–36 feet long and 6–7 feet in circumference, 293 were medium-sized conifers (253 of them good) 4–5 feet in circumference, 255 good small conifers 6–18 feet long and 1–3 feet in circumference to be harvested in the year 1778, and 1,474 small conifers (1,344 of them good) to harvest in later years. There were also 120 medium-sized ridgeline conifers (104 of them good) 15–18 feet long and 3–4 feet in circumference, 15 small ridgeline conifers 12–24 feet long and 8 inches to 1 foot in circumference to be harvested in 1778, and 320 small ridgeline conifers (241 of them good) to harvest in later years, not to mention 448 oaks (412 of them good) 12–24 feet long and

3–5½ feet in circumference, and 1,126 other trees whose properties were similarly enumerated. Such counting represents an extreme of top-down management that left nothing to the judgment of individual peasants.

The second stage of negative responses involved the shogun and daimyo establishing guard posts on highways and rivers to inspect wood shipments and make sure that all those rules about woodland management were actually being obeyed. The last stage consisted of a host of government rules specifying, once a tree had been felled and had passed inspection at a guard post, who could use it for what purpose. Valuable cedars and oaks were reserved for government uses and were off limits to peasants. The amount of timber that you could use in building your house varied with your social status: 30 *ken* (one ken is a beam 6 feet long) for a headman presiding over several villages, 18 ken for such a headman's heir, 12 ken for a headman of a single village, 8 ken for a local chief, 6 ken for a taxable peasant, and a mere 4 ken for an ordinary peasant or fisherman. The shogun also issued rules about permissible wood use for objects smaller than houses. For instance, in 1663 an edict forbade any woodworker in Edo to fabricate a small box out of cypress or sugi wood, or household utensils out of sugi wood, but permitted large boxes to be made of either cypress or sugi. In 1668 the shogun went on to ban use of cypress, sugi, or any other good tree for public signboards, and 38 years later large pines were removed from the list of trees approved for making New Year decorations.

All of these negative measures aimed at solving Japan's forestry crisis by ensuring that wood be used only for purposes authorized by the shogun or daimyo. However, a big role in Japan's crisis had been played by wood use by the shogun and daimyo themselves. Hence a full solution to the crisis required positive measures to produce more trees, as well as to protect land from erosion. Those measures began already in the 1600s with Japan's development of a detailed body of scientific knowledge about silviculture. Foresters employed both by the government and by private merchants observed, experimented, and published their findings in an outpouring of silvicultural journals and manuals, exemplified by the first of Japan's great silvicultural treatises, the *Nōgyō zensho* of 1697 by Miyazaki Antei. There, you will find instructions for how best to gather, extract, dry, store, and prepare seeds; how to prepare a seedbed by cleaning, fertilizing, pulverizing, and stirring it; how to soak seeds before sowing them; how to protect sown seeds by spreading straw over them; how to weed the seedbed; how to transplant and space seedlings; how to replace failed seedlings over the next four years; how to thin out the resulting saplings; and how to trim branches from the growing trunk in order that it yield a log of the desired shape. As an alternative to thus growing trees from seed, some tree species were instead grown by planting cuttings or shoots, and others by the technique known as coppicing (leaving live stumps or roots in the ground to sprout).

Gradually, Japan independently of Germany developed the idea of plantation forestry: that trees should be viewed as a slow-growing crop. Both governments and private entrepreneurs began planting forests on land that they either bought or leased, especially in areas where it would be economically favorable, such as near cities where wood was in demand. On the one hand, plantation forestry is expensive, risky, and demanding of capital. There are big costs up front to pay workers to plant the trees, then more labor costs for several decades to tend the plantation, and no recovery of all that investment until the trees are big enough to harvest. At any time during those decades, one may lose one's tree crop to disease or a fire, and the price that the lumber will eventually fetch is subject to market fluctuations unpredictable decades in advance when the seeds are planted. On the other hand, plantation forestry offers several compensating advantages compared to cutting naturally sown forests. You can plant just preferred valuable tree species, instead of having to accept whatever sprouts in the forest. You can maximize the quality of your trees and the price received for them, for instance by trimming them as they grow to obtain eventually straight and well-shaped logs. You can pick a convenient site with low transport costs near a city and near a river suitable for floating logs out, instead of having to haul logs down a remote mountainside. You can space out your trees at equal intervals, thereby reducing the costs of eventual cutting. Some Japanese plantation foresters specialized in wood for particular uses and were thereby able to command top prices for an established "brand name." For instance, Yoshino plantations became known for producing the best staves for cedar barrels to hold sake (rice wine).

The rise of silviculture in Japan was facilitated by the fairly uniform institutions and methods over the whole country. Unlike the situation in Europe, divided at that time among hundreds of principalities or states, Tokugawa Japan was a single country governed uniformly. While southwestern Japan is subtropical and northern Japan is temperate, the whole country is alike in being wet, steep, erodable, of volcanic origins, and divided between steep forested mountains and flat cropland, thus providing some ecological uniformity in conditions for silviculture. In place of Japan's tradition of multiple use of forests, under which the elite claimed the timber and the peasants gathered fertilizer, fodder, and fuel, plantation forest became specified as being for the primary purpose of timber production, other uses being allowed only insofar as they did not harm timber production. Forest patrols guarded against illegal logging activity. Plantation forestry thereby became widespread in Japan between 1750 and 1800, and by 1800 Japan's long decline in timber production had been reversed.

An outside observer who visited Japan in 1650 might have predicted that Japanese society was on the verge of a societal collapse triggered by catastrophic deforestation, as more and more people competed for fewer resources. Why did Tokugawa Japan succeed in developing top-down solutions and thereby averting deforestation, while the ancient Easter Islanders, Maya, and Anasazi, and modern Rwanda (Chapter 10) and Haiti (Chapter 11) failed? This question is one example of the broader problem, to be explored in Chapter 14, why and at what stages people succeed or fail at group decision-making.

The usual answers advanced for Middle and Late Tokugawa Japan's success—a supposed love for Nature, Buddhist respect for life, or a Confucian outlook—can be quickly dismissed. In addition to those simple phrases not being accurate descriptions of the complex reality of Japanese attitudes, they did not prevent Early Tokugawa Japan from depleting Japan's resources, nor are they preventing modern Japan from depleting the resources of the ocean and of other countries today. Instead, part of the answer involves Japan's environmental advantages: some of the same environmental factors already discussed in Chapter 2 to explain why Easter and several other Polynesian and Melanesian islands ended up deforested, while Tikopia, Tonga, and others did not. People of the latter islands have the good fortune to be living in ecologically robust landscapes where trees regrow rapidly on logged soils. Like robust Polynesian and Melanesian islands, Japan has rapid tree regrowth because of high rainfall, high fallout of volcanic ash and Asian dust restoring soil fertility, and young soils. Another part of the answer has to do with Japan's social advantages: some features of Japanese society that already existed before the deforestation crisis and did not have to arise as a response to it. Those features included Japan's lack of goats and sheep, whose grazing and browsing activities elsewhere have devastated forests of many lands; the decline in number of horses in Early Tokugawa Japan, due to the end of warfare eliminating the need for cavalry; and the abundance of seafood, relieving pressure on forests as sources of protein and fertilizer. Japanese society did make use of oxen and horses as draft animals, but their numbers were allowed to decrease in response to deforestation and loss of forest fodder, to be replaced by people using spades, hoes, and other devices.

The remaining explanations constitute a suite of factors that caused both the elite and the masses in Japan to recognize their long-term stake in preserving their own forests, to a degree greater than for most other people. As for the elite, the Tokugawa shoguns, having imposed peace and eliminated rival armies at home, correctly anticipated that they were at little risk of a revolt at home or an invasion from overseas. They expected their own Tokugawa family to remain in control of Japan, which in fact it did for 250 years. Hence peace, political stability, and well-justified confidence in their own future encouraged Tokugawa shoguns to invest in and to plan for the long-term future of their domain: in contrast to Maya kings and to Haitian and Rwandan presidents, who could not or cannot expect to be succeeded by their sons or even to fill out their own term in office. Japanese society as a whole was (and still is) relatively homogeneous ethnically and religiously, without the differences destabilizing Rwandan society and possibly also Maya and Anasazi societies. Tokugawa Japan's isolated location, negligible foreign trade, and renunciation of foreign expansion made it obvious that it had to depend on its own resources and wouldn't solve its needs by pillaging another country's resources. By the same token, the shogun's enforcement of peace within Japan meant that people knew that they couldn't meet their timber needs by seizing a Japanese neighbor's timber. Living in a stable society without input of foreign ideas, Japan's elite and peasants alike expected the future to be like the present, and future problems to have to be solved with present resources.

The usual assumption of Tokugawa well-to-do peasants, and the hope of poorer villagers, were that their land would pass eventually to their own heirs. For that and other reasons, the real control of Japan's forests fell increasingly into the hands of people with a vested long-term interest in their forest: either because they thus expected or hoped their children would inherit the rights to its use, or because of various long-term lease or contract arrangements. For instance, much village common land became divided into separate leases for individual households, thereby minimizing the tragedies of the common to be discussed in Chapter 14. Other village forests were managed under timber sale agreements drawn up long in advance of logging. The government negotiated long-term contracts on government forest land, dividing eventual timber proceeds with a village or merchant in return for the latter managing the forests. All these political and social factors made it in the interests of the shogun, daimyo, and peasants to manage their forests sustainably. Equally obviously after the Meireki fire, those factors made short-term overexploitation of forests foolish.

Of course, though, people with long-term stakes don't always act wisely. Often they still prefer short-term goals, and often again they do things that are foolish in both the short term and the long term. That's what makes biography and history infinitely more complicated and less predictable than the courses of chemical reactions, and that's why this book doesn't preach environmental determinism. Leaders who don't just react passively, who have the courage to anticipate crises or to act early, and who make strong insightful decisions of top-down management really can make a huge difference to their societies. So can similarly courageous, active citizens practicing bottom-up management. The Tokugawa shoguns, and my Montana landowner friends committed to the Teller Wildlife Refuge, exemplify the best of each type of management, in pursuit of their own long-term goals and of the interests of many others.

In thus devoting one chapter to these three success stories of the New Guinea highlands, Tikopia, and Tokugawa Japan, after seven chapters mostly on societies brought down by deforestation and other environmental problems plus a few other success stories (Orkney, Shetland, Faeroes, Iceland), I'm not implying that success stories constitute rare exceptions. Within the last few centuries Germany, Denmark, Switzerland, France, and other western European countries stabilized and then expanded their forested area by top-down measures, as did Japan. Similarly, about 600 years earlier, the largest and most tightly organized Native American society, the Inca Empire of the Central Andes with tens of millions of subjects under an absolute ruler, carried out massive reafforestation and terracing to halt soil erosion, increase crop yields, and secure its wood supplies.

Examples of successful bottom-up management of small-scale farming, pastoral, hunting, or fishing economies also abound. One example that I briefly mentioned in Chapter 4 comes from the U.S. Southwest, where Native American societies far smaller than the Inca Empire attempted many different solutions to the problem of developing a long-lasting economy in a difficult environment. The Anasazi, Hohokam, and Mimbres solutions eventually came to an end, but the somewhat different Pueblo solution has now been operating in the same region for over a thousand years. While the Greenland Norse disappeared, the Greenland Inuit maintained a self-sufficient hunter-gatherer economy for at least 500 years, from their arrival by A.D. 1200 until the disruptions caused by Danish colonization beginning in A.D. 1721. After the extinction of Australia's Pleistocene megafauna around 46,000 years ago, Aboriginal Australians maintained hunter-gatherer economies until European settlement in A.D. 1788. Among the numerous, self-sustaining, small-scale rural societies in modern times, especially well-studied ones include communities in Spain and in the Philippines maintaining irrigation systems, and Swiss alpine villages operating mixed farming and pastoral economies, in both cases for many centuries and with detailed local agreements about managing communal resources.

Each of these cases of bottom-up management that I have just mentioned involves a small society holding exclusive rights to all economic activities on its lands. Interesting and more complex cases exist (or traditionally existed) on the Indian subcontinent, where the caste system instead operates to permit dozens of economically specialized sub-societies to share the same geographic area by carrying out different economic activities. Castes trade extensively with each other and often live in the same village but are endogamous—i.e., people generally marry within their caste. Castes coexist by exploiting different environmental resources and lifestyles, such as by fishing, farming, herding, and hunting/gathering. There is even finer specialization, e.g., with multiple castes of fishermen fishing by different methods in different types of waters. As in the case of Tikopians and of the Tokugawa Japanese, members of the specialized Indian castes know that they can count on only a circumscribed resource base to maintain themselves, but they expect to pass those resources on to their children. Those conditions have fostered the acceptance of very detailed societal norms by which members of a given caste ensure that they are exploiting their resources sustainably.

The question remains why these societies of Chapter 9 succeeded while most of the societies selected for discussion in Chapters 2–8 failed. Part of the explanation lies in environmental differences: some environments are more fragile and pose more challenging problems than do others. We already saw in Chapter 2 the multitude of reasons causing Pacific island environments to be more or less fragile, and explaining in part why Easter and Mangareva societies collapsed while Tikopia society didn't. Similarly, the success stories of the New Guinea highlands and Tokugawa Japan recounted in this chapter involved societies that enjoyed the good fortune to be occupying relatively robust environments. But environmental differences aren't the whole explanation, as proved by the cases, such as those of Greenland

and the U.S. Southwest, in which one society succeeded while one or more societies practicing different economies in the same environment failed. That is, not only the environment, but also the proper choice of an economy to fit the environment, is important. The remaining large piece of the puzzle involves whether, even for a particular type of economy, a society practices it sustainably. Regardless of the resources on which the economy rests—farmed soil, grazed or browsed vegetation, a fishery, hunted game, or gathered plants or small animals—some societies evolve practices to avoid overexploitation, and other societies fail at that challenge. Chapter 14 will consider the types of mistakes that must be avoided. First, however, the next four chapters will examine four modern societies, for comparison with the past societies that we have been discussing since Chapter 2.

PART THREE

MODERN SOCIETIES

■ ■ ■

CHAPTER 10

Malthus in Africa:
Rwanda's Genocide

A dilemma ▪ Events in Rwanda ▪ More than ethnic hatred ▪
Buildup in Kanama ▪ Explosion in Kanama ▪ Why it happened ▪

When my twin sons were 10 years old and again when they were 15, my wife and I took them on family vacations to East Africa. Like many other tourists, the four of us were overwhelmed by our firsthand experience of Africa's famous large animals, landscapes, and people. No matter how often we had already seen wildebeest moving across the TV screen of *National Geographic* specials viewed in the comfort of our living rooms, we were unprepared for the sight, sound, and smell of millions of them on the Serengeti Plains, as we sat in a Land Rover surrounded by a herd stretching from our vehicle to the horizon in all directions. Nor had television prepared us for the immense size of Ngorongoro Crater's flat and treeless floor, and for the steepness and height of its inner walls down which one drives from a tourist hotel perched on the rim to reach that floor.

East Africa's people also overwhelmed us, with their friendliness, warmth to our children, colorful clothes—and their sheer numbers. To read in the abstract about "the population explosion" is one thing; it is quite another thing to encounter, day after day, lines of African children along the roadside, many of them about the same size and age as my sons, calling out to passing tourist vehicles for a pencil that they could use in school. The impact of those numbers of people on the landscape is visible even along stretches of road where the people are off doing something else. In pastures the grass is sparse and grazed closely by herds of cattle, sheep, and goats. One sees fresh erosion gullies, in whose bottoms run streams brown with mud washed down from the denuded pastures.

All of those children add up to rates of human population growth in East Africa that are among the highest in the world: recently, 4.1% per year in Kenya, resulting in the population doubling every 17 years. That population explosion has arisen despite Africa's being the continent inhabited by humans much longer than any other, so that one might naïvely have expected Africa's population to have leveled off long ago. In fact, it has been exploding recently for many reasons: the adoption of crops native to the New World (especially corn, beans, sweet potatoes, and manioc, alias cassava), broadening the agricultural base and increasing food production beyond that previously possible with native African crops alone; improved hygiene, preventive medicine, vaccinations of mothers and children, antibiotics, and some control of malaria and other endemic African diseases; and national unification and the fixing of national boundaries, thereby opening to settlement some areas that were formerly no-man's lands fought over by adjacent smaller polities.

Population problems such as those of East Africa are often referred to as "Malthusian," because in 1798 the English economist and demographer Thomas Malthus published a famous book in which he argued that human population growth would tend to outrun the growth of food production. That's because (Malthus reasoned) population growth proceeds exponentially, while food production increases only arithmetically. For instance, if a population's doubling time is 35 years, then a population of 100 people in the year 2000, if it continues to grow with that same doubling time, will have doubled in the year 2035 to 200 people, who will in turn double to 400 people in 2070, who will double to 800 people in the year 2105, and so on. But improvements in food production add rather than multiply: this breakthrough increases wheat yields by 25%, that breakthrough increases yields by an additional 20%, etc. That is, there is a basic difference between how population grows and how food production grows. When population grows, the extra people added to the population also themselves reproduce—as in compound interest, where the interest itself draws interest. That allows exponential growth. In contrast, an increase in food yield does not then further increase yields, but instead leads only to arithmetic growth in food production. Hence a population will tend to expand to consume all available food and never leave a surplus, unless population growth itself is halted by famine, war, or disease, or else by people making preventive choices (e.g., contraception or postponing marriage). The notion, still widespread today, that we can promote human happiness *merely* by increasing food production, without a simultaneous reining-in of population growth, is doomed to end in frustration—or so said Malthus.

The validity of his pessimistic argument has been much debated. Indeed, there are modern countries that have drastically reduced their population growth by means of voluntary (e.g., Italy and Japan) or government-ordered (China) birth control. But modern Rwanda illustrates a case where Malthus's worst-case scenario does seem to have been right. More generally, both Malthus's supporters and his detractors could agree that population and environmental problems created by non-sustainable resource use will ultimately get solved in one way or another: if not by pleasant means of our own choice, then by unpleasant and unchosen means, such as the ones that Malthus initially envisioned.

A few months ago, while I was teaching a course to UCLA undergraduates on environmental problems of societies, I came to discuss the difficulties that regularly confront societies trying to reach agreements about environmental disputes. One of my students responded by noting that disputes could be, and frequently were, solved in the course of conflict. By that, the student didn't mean that he favored murder as a means of settling disputes. Instead, he was merely observing that environmental problems often do create conflicts among people, that conflicts in the U.S. often become resolved in court, that the courts provide a perfectly acceptable means of dispute resolution, and hence that students preparing themselves for a career of resolving environmental problems need to become familiar with the judicial system. The case of Rwanda is again instructive: my student was fundamentally correct about the frequency of resolution by conflict, but the conflict may assume nastier forms than courtroom processes.

In recent decades, Rwanda and neighboring Burundi have become synonymous in our minds with two things: high population, and genocide (Plate 21). They are the two most densely populated countries in Africa, and among the most densely populated in the world: Rwanda's average population density is triple even that of Africa's third most densely populated country (Nigeria), and 10 times that of neighboring Tanzania. Genocide in Rwanda produced the third largest body count among the world's genocides since 1950, topped only by the killings of the 1970s in Cambodia and of 1971 in Bangladesh (at the time East Pakistan). Because Rwanda's total population is 10 times smaller than that of Bangladesh, the scale of Rwanda's genocide, measured in proportion to the total population killed, far exceeds that of Bangladesh and stands second only to Cambodia's. Burundi's genocide was on a smaller scale than Rwanda's, yielding "only" a few hundred thousand victims. That still suffices to place Burundi seventh in the world since 1950 in its number of victims of genocide, and tied for fourth place in proportion of the population killed.

We have come to associate genocide in Rwanda and Burundi with ethnic violence. Before we can understand what else besides ethnic violence was also involved, we need to begin with some background on the genocide's course, the history leading up to it, and their usual interpretation that I shall now sketch, which runs as follows. (I shall mention later some respects in which this usual interpretation is wrong, incomplete, or oversimplified.) The populations of both countries consist of only two major groups, called the Hutu (originally about 85% of the population) and the Tutsi (about 15%). To a considerable degree, the two groups traditionally had filled different economic roles, the Hutu being principally farmers, the Tutsi pastoralists. It is often stated that the two groups look different, Hutu being on the average shorter, stockier, darker, flat-nosed, thick-lipped, and square-jawed, while Tutsi are taller, more slender, paler-skinned, thin-lipped, and narrow-chinned. The Hutu are usually assumed to have settled Rwanda and Burundi first, from the south and west, while the Tutsi are a Nilotic people who are assumed to have arrived later from the north and east and who established themselves as overlords over the Hutu. When German (1897) and then Belgian (1916) colonial governments took over, they found it expedient to govern through Tutsi intermediaries, whom they considered racially superior to Hutu because of the Tutsi's paler skins and supposedly more European or "Hamitic" appearance. In the 1930s the Belgians required everybody to start carrying an identity card classifying themselves as Hutu or Tutsi, thereby markedly increasing the ethnic distinction that had already existed.

Independence came to both countries in 1962. As independence approached, Hutu in both countries began struggling to overthrow Tutsi domination and to replace it with Hutu domination. Small incidents of violence escalated into spirals of killings of Tutsi by Hutu and of Hutu by Tutsi. The outcome in Burundi was that the Tutsi succeeded in retaining their domination, after Hutu rebellions in 1965 and 1970–72 followed by Tutsi killings of a few hundred thousand Hutu. (There is inevitably much uncertainty about this estimated number and many of the following numbers of deaths and exiles.) In Rwanda, however, the Hutu gained the upper hand and killed 20,000 (or perhaps only 10,000?) Tutsi in 1963. Over the course of the next two decades up to a million Rwandans, especially Tutsi, fled into exile in neighboring countries, from which they periodically attempted to invade Rwanda, resulting in further retaliatory killings of Tutsi by Hutu, until in 1973 the Hutu general Habyarimana staged a coup against the previous Hutu-dominated government and decided to leave the Tutsi in peace.

Under Habyarimana, Rwanda prospered for 15 years and became a favorite recipient of foreign aid from overseas donors, who could point to a peaceful country with improving health, education, and economic indicators. Unfortunately, Rwanda's economic improvement became halted by drought and accumulating environmental problems (especially deforestation, soil erosion, and soil fertility losses), capped in 1989 by a steep decline in world prices for Rwanda's principal exports of coffee and tea, austerity measures imposed by the World Bank, and a drought in the south. Habyarimana took yet another attempted Tutsi invasion of northeastern Rwanda from neighboring Uganda in October 1990 as the pretext for rounding up or killing Hutu dissidents and Tutsi all over Rwanda, in order to strengthen his own faction's hold on the country. The civil wars displaced a million Rwandans into settlement camps, from which desperate young men were easily recruited into militias. In 1993 a peace agreement signed at Arusha called for power-sharing and a multi-power government. Still, businessmen close to Habyarimana imported 581,000 machetes for distribution to Hutu for killing Tutsi, because machetes were cheaper than guns.

However, Habyarimana's actions against Tutsi, and his newfound toleration of killings of Tutsi, proved insufficient for Hutu extremists (i.e., Hutu even more extreme than Habyarimana), who feared having their power diluted as a result of the Arusha agreement. They began training their militias, importing weapons, and preparing to exterminate Tutsi. Rwandan Hutu fears of Tutsi grew out of the long history of Tutsi domination of Hutu, the various Tutsi-led invasions of Rwanda, and Tutsi mass killings of Hutu and murder of individual Hutu political leaders in neighboring Burundi. Those Hutu fears increased in 1993, when extremist Tutsi army officers in Burundi murdered Burundi's Hutu president, provoking killings of Burundi Tutsi by Hutu, provoking in turn more extensive killings of Burundi Hutu by Tutsi.

Matters came to a head on the evening of April 6, 1994, when the Rwandan presidential jet plane, carrying Rwanda's President Habyarimana and also (as a last-minute passenger) Burundi's new provisional president back from a meeting in Tanzania, was shot down by two missiles as it came in to land at the airport of Kigali, Rwanda's capital, killing everyone on board. The missiles were fired from immediately outside the airport perimeter. It remains uncertain to this day by whom or why Habyarimana's plane was shot down; several groups had alternative motives for killing him. Whoever

were the perpetrators, Hutu extremists within an hour of the plane's down-
ing began carrying out plans evidently already prepared in detail to kill the
Hutu prime minister and other moderate or at least less extreme members
of the democratic opposition, and Tutsi. Once Hutu opposition had been
eliminated, the extremists took over the government and radio and set out
to exterminate Rwanda's Tutsi, who still numbered about a million even
after all the previous killings and escapes into exile.

The lead in the killings was initially taken by Hutu army extremists,
using guns. They soon turned to efficiently organizing Hutu civilians, distributing weapons, setting up roadblocks, killing Tutsi identified at the
roadblocks, broadcasting radio appeals to every Hutu to kill every "cock-
roach" (as Tutsi were termed), urging Tutsi to gather supposedly for protection at safe places where they could then be killed, and tracking down
surviving Tutsi. When international protests against the killings eventually
began to surface, the government and radio changed the tone of their pro-
paganda, from exhortations to kill cockroaches to urging Rwandans to
practice self-defense and to protect themselves against Rwanda's common
enemies. Moderate Hutu government officials who tried to prevent killings
were intimidated, bypassed, replaced, or killed. The largest massacres, each
of hundreds or thousands of Tutsi at one site, took place when Tutsi took
refuge in churches, schools, hospitals, government offices, or those other
supposed safe places and were then surrounded and hacked or burned
to death. The genocide involved large-scale Hutu civilian participation,
though it is debated whether as many as one-third or just some lesser proportion of Hutu civilians joined in killing Tutsi. After the army's initial
killings with guns in each area, subsequent killings used low-tech means,
mainly machetes or else clubs studded with nails. The killings involved
much savagery, including chopping off arms and legs of intended victims,
chopping breasts off women, throwing children down into wells, and widespread rape.

While the killings were organized by the extremist Hutu government
and largely carried out by Hutu civilians, institutions and outsiders from
whom one might have expected better behavior played an important per-
missive role. In particular, numerous leaders of Rwanda's Catholic Church
either failed to protect Tutsi or else actively assembled them and turned
them over to killers. The United Nations already had a small peacekeeping
force in Rwanda, which it proceeded to order to retreat; the French government sent a peacekeeping force, which sided with the genocidal Hutu gov-

ernment and against invading rebels; and the United States government declined to intervene. In explanation of these policies, the U.N., French government, and U.S. government all referred to "chaos," "a confusing situation," and "tribal conflict," as if this were just one more tribal conflict of a type considered normal and acceptable in Africa, and ignoring evidence for the meticulous orchestration of the killings by the Rwandan government.

Within six weeks, an estimated 800,000 Tutsi, representing about three-quarters of the Tutsi then remaining in Rwanda, or 11% of Rwanda's total population, had been killed. A Tutsi-led rebel army termed the Rwandan Patriotic Front (RPF) began military operations against the government within a day of the start of the genocide. The genocide ended in each part of Rwanda only with the arrival of that RPF army, which declared complete victory on July 18, 1994. It is generally agreed that the RPF army was disciplined and did not enlist civilians to murder, but it did carry out reprisal killings on a much smaller scale than the genocide to which it was responding (estimated number of reprisal victims, "only" 25,000 to 60,000). The RPF set up a new government, emphasized national conciliation and unity, and urged Rwandans to think of themselves as Rwandans rather than as Hutu or Tutsi. About 135,000 Rwandans were eventually imprisoned on suspicion of being guilty of genocide, but few of the prisoners have been tried or convicted. After the RPF victory, about 2,000,000 people (mostly Hutu) fled into exile in neighboring countries (especially the Congo and Tanzania), while about 750,000 former exiles (mostly Tutsi) returned to Rwanda from neighboring countries to which they had fled (Plate 22).

The usual accounts of the genocides in Rwanda and Burundi portray them as the result of pre-existing ethnic hatreds fanned by cynical politicians for their own ends. As summed up in the book *Leave None to Tell the Story: Genocide in Rwanda,* published by the organization Human Rights Watch, "this genocide was not an uncontrollable outburst of rage by a people consumed by 'ancient tribal hatreds.' . . . This genocide resulted from the deliberate choice of a modern elite to foster hatred and fear to keep itself in power. This small, privileged group first set the majority against the minority to counter a growing political opposition within Rwanda. Then, faced with RPF success on the battlefield and at the negotiating table, these few powerholders transformed the strategy of ethnic division into genocide.

They believed that the extermination campaign would restore the solidarity of the Hutu under their leadership and help them win the war . . ." The evidence is overwhelming that this view is correct and accounts in large degree for Rwanda's tragedy.

But there is also evidence that other considerations contributed as well. Rwanda contained a third ethnic group, variously known as the Twa or pygmies, who numbered only 1% of the population, were at the bottom of the social scale and power structure, and did not constitute a threat to anybody—yet most of them, too, were massacred in the 1994 killings. The 1994 explosion was not just Hutu versus Tutsi, but the competing factions were in reality more complex: there were three rival factions composed predominantly or solely of Hutu, one of which may have been the one to trigger the explosion by killing the Hutu president from another faction; and the invading RPF army of exiles, though led by Tutsi, also contained Hutu. The distinction between Hutu and Tutsi is not nearly as sharp as often portrayed. The two groups speak the same language, attended the same churches and schools and bars, lived together in the same village under the same chiefs, and worked together in the same offices. Hutu and Tutsi intermarried, and (before Belgians introduced identity cards) sometimes switched their ethnic identity. While Hutu and Tutsi look different on the average, many individuals are impossible to assign to either of the two groups based on appearance. About one-quarter of all Rwandans have both Hutu and Tutsi among their great-grandparents. (In fact, there is some question whether the traditional account of the Hutu and Tutsi having different origins is correct, or whether instead the two groups just differentiated economically and socially within Rwanda and Burundi out of a common stock.) This intergradation gave rise to tens of thousands of personal tragedies during the 1994 killings, as Hutu tried to protect their Tutsi spouses, relatives, friends, colleagues, and patrons, or tried to buy off would-be killers of those loved ones with money. The two groups were so intertwined in Rwandan society that in 1994 doctors ended up killing their patients and vice versa, teachers killed their students and vice versa, and neighbors and office colleagues killed each other. Individual Hutu killed some Tutsi while protecting other Tutsi. We cannot avoid asking ourselves: how, under those circumstances, were so many Rwandans so readily manipulated by extremist leaders into killing each other with the utmost savagery?

Especially puzzling, if one believes that there was nothing more to the genocide than Hutu-versus-Tutsi ethnic hatred fanned by politicians, are events in northwestern Rwanda. There, in a community where virtually everybody was Hutu and there was only a single Tutsi, mass killings still took place—of Hutu by other Hutu. While the proportional death toll there, estimated as "at least 5% of the population," may have been somewhat lower than that overall in Rwanda (11%), it still takes some explaining why a Hutu community would kill at least 5% of its members in the absence of ethnic motives. Elsewhere in Rwanda, as the 1994 genocide proceeded and as the number of Tutsi declined, Hutu turned to attacking each other.

All these facts illustrate why we need to search for other contributing factors in addition to ethnic hatred.

To begin our search, let's again consider Rwanda's high population density that I mentioned previously. Rwanda (and Burundi) was already densely populated in the 19th century before European arrival, because of its twin advantages of moderate rainfall and an altitude too high for malaria and the tsetse fly. Rwanda's population subsequently grew, albeit with ups and downs, at an average rate of over 3% per year, for essentially the same reasons as in neighboring Kenya and Tanzania (New World crops, public health, medicine, and stable political borders). By 1990, even after the killings and mass exilings of the previous decades, Rwanda's average population density was 760 people per square mile, higher than that of the United Kingdom (610) and approaching that of Holland (950). But the United Kingdom and Holland have highly efficient mechanized agriculture, such that only a few percent of the population working as farmers can produce food for everyone else. Rwandan agriculture is much less efficient and unmechanized; farmers depend on handheld hoes, picks, and machetes; and most people have to remain farmers, producing little or no surplus that could support others.

As Rwanda's population rose after independence, the country carried on with its traditional agricultural methods and failed to modernize, to introduce more productive crop varieties, to expand its agricultural exports, or to institute effective family planning. Instead, the growing population was accommodated just by clearing forests and draining marshes to gain new farmland, shortening fallow periods, and trying to extract two or three consecutive crops from a field within one year. When so many Tutsi fled or were killed in the 1960s and in 1973, the availability of their former lands for redistribution fanned the dream that each Hutu farmer could now, at last, have enough land to feed himself and his family comfortably. By 1985, all arable land outside of national parks was being cultivated. As both population and agricultural production increased, per-capita food production rose from 1966 to 1981 but then dropped back to the level where it had stood in the early 1960s. That, exactly, is the Malthusian dilemma: more food, but also more people, hence no improvement in food per person.

Friends of mine who visited Rwanda in 1984 sensed an ecological disaster in the making. The whole country looked like a garden and banana plantation. Steep hills were being farmed right up to their crests. Even the most elementary measures that could have minimized soil erosion, such as terracing, plowing along contours rather than straight up and down hills, and providing some fallow cover of vegetation rather than leaving fields bare between crops, were not being practiced. As a result, there was much soil erosion, and the rivers carried heavy loads of mud. One Rwandan wrote me, "Farmers can wake up in the morning and find that their entire field (or at least its topsoil and crops) has been washed away overnight, or that their neighbor's field and rocks have now been washed down to cover their own field." Forest clearance led to drying-up of streams, and more irregular rainfall. By the late 1980s famines began to reappear. In 1989 there were more severe food shortages resulting from a drought, brought on by a combination of regional or global climate change plus local effects of deforestation.

The effect of all those environmental and population changes on an area of northwestern Rwanda (Kanama commune) inhabited just by Hutu was studied in detail by two Belgian economists, Catherine André and Jean-Philippe Platteau. André, who was Platteau's student, lived there for a total of 16 months during two visits in 1988 and 1993, while the situation was deteriorating but before the genocide's explosion. She interviewed members of most households in the area. For each household interviewed in each of those two years, she ascertained the number of people living in the household, the total area of land that it owned, and the amount of income that its members earned from jobs off the farm. She also tabulated sales or transfers of land, and disputes requiring mediation. After the genocide of 1994, she tracked down news of survivors and sought to detect any pattern to which particular Hutu ended up being killed by other Hutu. André and Platteau then processed this mass of data together to figure out what it all meant.

Kanama has very fertile volcanic soil, so that its population density is high even by the standards of densely populated Rwanda: 1,740 people per square mile in 1988, rising to 2,040 in 1993. (That's higher even than the value for Bangladesh, the world's most densely populated agricultural nation.) Those high population densities translated into very small farms: a median farm size of only 0.89 acre in 1988, declining to 0.72 acre in 1993. Each farm was divided into (on average) 10 separate parcels, so that farmers were tilling absurdly small parcels averaging only 0.09 acre in 1988 and 0.07 acre in 1993.

Because all land in the commune was already occupied, young people found it difficult to marry, leave home, acquire a farm, and set up their own household. Increasingly, young people postponed marriage and continued to live at home with their parents. For instance, in the 20- to 25-year-old age bracket, the percentage of young women living at home rose between 1988 and 1993 from 39% to 67%, and the percentage of young men rose from 71% to 100%: not a single man in his early 20s lived independently of his parents by 1993. That obviously contributed to the lethal family tensions that exploded in 1994, as I shall explain below. With more young people staying home, the average number of people per farm household increased (between 1988 and 1993) from 4.9 to 5.3, so that the land shortage was even tighter than indicated by the decrease in farm size from 0.89 to 0.72 acre. When one divides decreasing farm area by increasing number of people in the household, one finds that each person was living off of only one-fifth of an acre in 1988, declining to one-seventh of an acre in 1993.

Not surprisingly, it proved impossible for most people in Kanama to feed themselves on so little land. Even when measured against the low calorie intake considered adequate in Rwanda, the average household got only 77% of its calorie needs from its farm. The rest of its food had to be bought with income earned off the farm, at jobs such as carpentry, brick-making, sawing wood, and trade. Two-thirds of households held such jobs, while one-third didn't. The percentage of the population consuming less than 1,600 calories per day (i.e., what is considered below the famine level) was 9% in 1982, rising to 40% in 1990 and some unknown higher percentage thereafter.

All of these numbers that I have quoted so far for Kanama are average numbers, which conceal inequalities. Some people owned larger farms than others, and that inequality increased from 1988 to 1993. Let's define a "very big" farm as larger than 2.5 acres, and a "very small" farm as smaller than 0.6 acre. (Think back to Chapter 1 to appreciate the tragic absurdity of those numbers: I mentioned there that in Montana a 40-acre farm used to be considered necessary to support a family, but even that is now inadequate.) Both the percentage of very big farms and the percentage of very small farms increased between 1988 and 1993, from 5 to 8% and from 36 to 45% respectively. That is, Kanama farm society was becoming increasingly divided between the rich haves and the poor have-nots, with decreasing numbers of people in the middle. Older heads of households tended to be richer and to have larger farms: those in the age ranges 50–59 and 20–29 years old had average farm sizes of 2.05 acres and only 0.37 acre respectively. Of course, family size was larger for the older household heads, so they needed more land, but they still had three times more land per household member than did young household heads.

Paradoxically, off-farm income was earned disproportionately by owners of large farms: the average size of farms that did earn such income was 1.3 acres, compared to only half an acre for farms lacking such income. That difference is paradoxical because the smaller farms are the ones whose household members have less farmland per person to feed themselves, and which thus need more off-farm income. That concentration of off-farm income on the larger farms contributed to the increasing division of Kanama society between haves and have-nots, with the rich becoming richer and the poor becoming poorer. In Rwanda, it's supposedly illegal for owners of small farms to sell any of their land. In fact, it does happen. Investigation of land sales showed that owners of the smallest farms sold land mainly when they needed money for an emergency involving food, health, lawsuit costs, bribes, a baptism, wedding, funeral, or excessive drinking. In contrast, owners of large farms sold for reasons such as to increase farm efficiency (e.g., selling a distant parcel of land in order to buy a parcel nearer to the farmhouse).

The extra off-farm income of larger farms allowed them to buy land from smaller farms, with the result that large farms tended to buy land and become larger, while small farms tended to sell land and become smaller. Almost no large farm sold land without buying any, but 35% of the smallest farms in 1988, and 49% of them in 1993, sold without buying. If one breaks down land sales according to off-farm income, all farms with off-farm income bought land, and none sold land without buying; but only 13% of farms lacking off-farm income bought land, and 65% of them sold land without buying. Again, note the paradox: already-tiny farms, which desperately needed more land, in fact became smaller, by selling land in emergencies to large farms financing their purchases with off-farm income. Remember again that what I term "large farms" are large only by Rwanda standards: "large" means "larger than a mere 1 or 2 acres."

Thus, at Kanama most people were impoverished, hungry, and desperate, but some people were more impoverished, hungry, and desperate than others, and most people were becoming more desperate while a few were becoming less desperate. Not surprisingly, this situation gave rise to frequent serious conflicts that the parties involved could not resolve by themselves, and that they either referred to traditional village conflict mediators or (less often) brought to the courts. Each year, households reported on the average more than one such serious conflict requiring outside resolution. André and Platteau surveyed the causes of 226 such conflicts, as described either by the mediators or by the householders. According to both types of informants, land disputes lay at the root of most serious conflicts: either because the conflict was directly over land (43% of all cases); or because it was a husband/wife, family, or personal dispute often stemming ultimately from a land dispute (I'll give examples in the next two paragraphs); or else because the dispute involved theft by very poor people, known locally as "hunger thieves," who owned almost no land and were without off-farm income and who lived by stealing for lack of other options (7% of all disputes, and 10% of all households).

Those land disputes undermined the cohesion of Rwandan society's traditional fabric. Traditionally, richer landowners were expected to help their poorer relatives. This system was breaking down, because even the landowners who were richer than other landowners were still too poor to be able to spare anything for poorer relatives. That loss of protection especially victimized vulnerable groups in the society: separated or divorced women, widows, orphans, and younger half-siblings. When ex-husbands ceased to provide for their separated or divorced wives, the women would formerly have returned to their natal family for support, but now their own brothers opposed their return, which would make the brothers or the brothers' children even poorer. The women might then seek to return to their natal family only with their daughters, because Rwandan inheritance was traditionally by sons, and the woman's brothers wouldn't see her daughters as competing with their own children. The woman would leave her sons with their father (her divorced husband), but his relatives might then refuse land to her sons, especially if their father died or ceased protecting them. Similarly, a widow would find herself without support from either her husband's family (her brothers-in-law) or from her own brothers, who again saw the widow's children as competing for land with their children. Orphans were traditionally cared for by paternal grandparents; when those grandparents died, the orphans' uncles (the brothers of their deceased father) now sought to disinherit or evict the orphans. Children of polygamous marriages, or of broken marriages in which the man subsequently remarried and had children by a new wife, found themselves disinherited or evicted by their half-brothers.

The most painful and socially disruptive land disputes were those pitting fathers against sons. Traditionally, when a father died, his land all passed to his oldest son, who was expected to manage the land for the whole family and to provide his younger brothers with enough land for their subsistence. As land became scarce, fathers gradually switched to the custom of dividing their land among all sons, in order to reduce the potential for intrafamily conflict after the father's death. But different sons urged on their father different competing proposals for dividing the land. Younger sons became bitter if older brothers, who got married first, received a disproportionately large share—e.g., because the father had had to sell off some land by the time younger sons got married. Younger sons instead demanded strictly equal divisions; they objected to their father giving their older brother a present of land on that brother's marriage. The youngest son, who traditionally was the one expected to care for his parents in their old age, needed or demanded an extra share of land in order to carry out that traditional responsibility. Brothers were suspicious of, and sought to evict, sisters or younger brothers who received from the father any present of land, which the brothers suspected was being given in return for that sister or younger brother agreeing to care for the father in his old age. Sons complained that their father was retaining too much land to support himself in his old age, and they demanded more land now for themselves. Fathers in turn were justifiably terrified of being left with too little land in their old age, and they opposed their sons' demands. All of these types of conflicts ended up before mediators or the courts, with fathers suing sons and vice versa, sisters suing brothers, nephews suing uncles, and so on. These conflicts sabotaged family ties, and turned close relatives into competitors and bitter enemies.

That situation of chronic and escalating conflict forms the background against which the killings of 1994 took place. Even before 1994, Rwanda was experiencing rising levels of violence and theft, perpetrated especially by hungry landless young people without off-farm income. When one compares crime rates for people of age 21–25 among different parts of Rwanda, most of the regional differences prove to be correlated statistically with population density and per-capita availability of calories: high population densities and worse starvation were associated with more crime.

After the explosion of 1994, André tried to track down the fates of Kanama's inhabitants. She found that 5.4% were reported to her as having died as a result of the war. That number is an underestimate of the total casualties, because there were some inhabitants about whose fates she could obtain no information. Hence it remains unknown whether the death rate approached the average value of 11% for Rwanda as a whole. What is clear is that the death rate in an area where the population consisted almost entirely of Hutu was at least half of the death rate in areas where Hutu were killing Tutsi plus other Hutu.

All but one of the known victims at Kanama fell into one of six categories. First, the single Tutsi at Kanama, a widowed woman, was killed. Whether that had much to do with her being Tutsi is unclear, because she furnished so many other motives for killing: she had inherited much land, she had been involved in many land disputes, she was the widow of a polygamous Hutu husband (hence viewed as a competitor of his other wives and their families), and her deceased husband had already been forced off his land by his half-brothers.

Two more categories of victims consisted of Hutu who were large landowners. The majority of them were men over the age of 50, hence at a prime age for father/son disputes over land. The minority were younger people who had aroused jealousy by being able to earn much off-farm income and using it to buy land.

A next category of victims consisted of "troublemakers" known for being involved in all sorts of land disputes and other conflicts.

Still another category was young men and children, particularly ones from impoverished backgrounds, who were driven by desperation to enlist in the warring militias and proceeded to kill each other. This category is especially likely to have been underestimated, because it was dangerous for André to ask too many questions about who had belonged to what militia.

Finally, the largest number of victims were especially malnourished people, or especially poor people with no or very little land and without off-farm income. They evidently died because of starvation, being too weak, or not having money to buy food or to pay the bribes required to buy their survival at roadblocks.

Thus, as André and Platteau note, "The 1994 events provided a unique opportunity to settle scores, or to reshuffle land properties, even among

Hutu villagers. . . . It is not rare, even today, to hear Rwandans argue that a war is necessary to wipe out an excess of population and to bring numbers into line with the available land resources."

That last quote of what Rwandans themselves say about the genocide surprised me. I had thought that it would be exceptional for people to recognize such a direct connection between population pressure and killings. I'm accustomed to thinking of population pressure, human environmental impacts, and drought as ultimate causes, which make people chronically desperate and are like the gunpowder inside the powder keg. One also needs a proximate cause: a match to light the keg. In most areas of Rwanda, that match was ethnic hatred whipped up by politicians cynically concerned with keeping themselves in power. (I say "most areas," because the large-scale killings of Hutu by Hutu at Kanama demonstrate a similar outcome even where everybody belonged to the same ethnic group.) As Gérard Prunier, a French scholar of East Africa, puts it, "The decision to kill was of course made by politicians, for political reasons. But at least part of the reason why it was carried out so thoroughly by the ordinary rank-and-file peasants in their ingo [= family compound] was feeling that there were too many people on too little land, and that with a reduction in their numbers, there would be more for the survivors."

The link that Prunier, and that André and Platteau, see behind population pressure and the Rwandan genocide has not gone unchallenged. In part, the challenges are reactions to oversimplified statements that critics with some justice lampooned as "ecological determinism." For instance, only 10 days after the genocide began, an article in an American newspaper linked Rwanda's dense population to the genocide by saying, "Rwandas [i.e., similar genocides] are endemic, built-in, even, to the world we inhabit." Naturally, that fatalistic oversimplified conclusion provokes negative reactions not only to it, but also to the more complex view that Prunier, André and Platteau, and I present, for three reasons.

First, any "explanation" of why a genocide happened can be misconstrued as "excusing" it. However, regardless of whether we arrive at an oversimplified one-factor explanation or an excessively complex 73-factor explanation for a genocide doesn't alter the personal responsibility of the perpetrators of the Rwandan genocide, as of other evil deeds, for their actions. This is a misunderstanding that arises regularly in discussions of the origins of evil: people recoil at any explanation, because they confuse explanations with excuses. But it *is* important that we understand the origins of the Rwandan genocide—not so that we can exonerate the killers, but so that we can use that knowledge to decrease the risk of such things happening again in Rwanda or elsewhere. Similarly, there are people who have chosen to devote their lives or careers to understanding the origins of the Nazi Holocaust, or to understanding the minds of serial murderers and rapists. They have made that choice not in order to mitigate the responsibility of Hitler, serial murderers, and rapists, but because they want to know how those awful things came to be, and how we can best prevent recurrences.

Second, it is justifiable to reject the simplistic view that population pressure was the single cause of the Rwandan genocide. Other factors did contribute; in this chapter I have introduced ones that seem to me important, and experts on Rwanda have written entire books and articles on the subject, cited in my Further Readings at the back of this book. Just to reiterate: regardless of the order of their importance, those other factors included Rwanda's history of Tutsi domination of Hutu, Tutsi large-scale killings of Hutu in Burundi and small-scale ones in Rwanda, Tutsi invasions of Rwanda, Rwanda's economic crisis and its exacerbation by drought and world factors (especially by falling coffee prices and World Bank austerity measures), hundreds of thousands of desperate young Rwandan men displaced as refugees into settlement camps and ripe for recruitment by militias, and competition among Rwanda's rival political groups willing to stoop to anything to retain power. Population pressure joined with those other factors.

Finally, one should not misconstrue a role of population pressure among the Rwandan genocide's causes to mean that population pressure automatically leads to genocide anywhere around the world. To those who would object that there is not a *necessary* link between Malthusian population pressure and genocide, I would answer, "Of course!" Countries can be overpopulated without descending into genocide, as exemplified by Bangladesh (relatively free of large-scale killings since its genocidal slaughters of 1971) as well as by the Netherlands and multi-ethnic Belgium, despite all three of those countries being more densely populated than Rwanda. Conversely, genocide can arise for ultimate reasons other than overpopulation, as illustrated by Hitler's efforts to exterminate Jews and Gypsies during World War II, or by the genocide of the 1970s in Cambodia, with only one-sixth of Rwanda's population density.

Instead, I conclude that population pressure was *one* of the important factors behind the Rwandan genocide, that Malthus's worst-case scenario may sometimes be realized, and that Rwanda may be a distressing model of that scenario in operation. Severe problems of overpopulation, environmental impact, and climate change cannot persist indefinitely: sooner or later they are likely to resolve themselves, whether in the manner of Rwanda or in some other manner not of our devising, if we don't succeed in solving them by our own actions. In the case of Rwanda's collapse we can put faces and motives on the unpleasant solution; I would guess that similar motives were operating, without our being able to associate them with faces, in the collapses of Easter Island, Mangareva, and the Maya that I described in Part 2 of this book. Similar motives may operate again in the future, in some other countries that, like Rwanda, fail to solve their underlying problems. They may operate again in Rwanda itself, where population today is still increasing at 3% per year, women are giving birth to their first child at age 15, the average family has between five and eight children, and a visitor's sense is of being surrounded by a sea of children.

The term "Malthusian crisis" is impersonal and abstract. It fails to evoke the horrible, savage, numbing details of what millions of Rwandans did, or had done to them. Let us give the last words to one observer, and to one survivor. The observer is, again, Gérard Prunier:

"All these people who were about to be killed had land and at times cows. And somebody had to get these lands and those cows after the owners were dead. In a poor and increasingly overpopulated country this was not a negligible incentive."

The survivor is a Tutsi teacher whom Prunier interviewed, and who survived only because he happened to be away from his house when killers arrived and murdered his wife and four of his five children:

"The people whose children had to walk barefoot to school killed the people who could buy shoes for theirs."

CHAPTER 11

One Island, Two Peoples, Two Histories: The Dominican Republic and Haiti

**Differences ▪ Histories ▪ Causes of divergence ▪
Dominican environmental impacts ▪ Balaguer ▪ The Dominican
environment today ▪ The future ▪**

To anyone interested in understanding the modern world's problems, it's a dramatic challenge to understand the 120-mile-long border between the Dominican Republic and Haiti, the two nations dividing the large Caribbean island of Hispaniola that lies southeast of Florida (map, p. 331). From an airplane flying high overhead, the border looks like a sharp line with bends, cut arbitrarily across the island by a knife, and abruptly dividing a darker and greener landscape east of the line (the Dominican side) from a paler and browner landscape west of the line (the Haitian side). On the ground, one can stand on the border at many places, face east, and look into pine forest, then turn around, face west, and see nothing except fields almost devoid of trees.

That contrast visible at the border exemplifies a difference between the two countries as a whole. Originally, both parts of the island were largely forested: the first European visitors noted as Hispaniola's most striking characteristic the exuberance of its forests, full of trees with valuable wood. Both countries have lost forest cover, but Haiti has lost far more (Plates 23, 24), to the point where it now supports just seven substantial patches of forest, only two of which are protected as national parks, both of them subject to illegal logging. Today, 28% of the Dominican Republic is still forested, but only 1% of Haiti. I was surprised at the extent of woodlands even in the area comprising the Dominican Republic's richest farmland, lying between its two largest cities of Santo Domingo and Santiago. In Haiti and the Dominican Republic just as elsewhere in the world, the consequences of all that deforestation include loss of timber and other forest building materials, soil erosion, loss of soil fertility, sediment loads in the rivers, loss of watershed protection and hence of potential hydroelectric power, and decreased rainfall. All of those problems are more severe in Haiti than in the Dominican Republic. In Haiti, more urgent than any of those just-mentioned consequences is the problem of the loss of wood for making charcoal, Haiti's main fuel for cooking.

The difference in forest cover between the two countries is paralleled by differences in their economies. Both Haiti and the Dominican Republic are poor countries, suffering from the usual disadvantages of most of the world's other tropical countries that were former European colonies: corrupt or weak governments, serious problems of public health, and lower agricultural productivity than in the temperate zones. On all those counts, though, Haiti's difficulties are much more serious than those of the Dominican Republic. It is the poorest country in the New World, and one of the poorest in the world outside of Africa. Its perennially corrupt government offers minimal public services; much or most of the population lives chronically or periodically without public electricity, water, sewage, medical care, and schooling. Haiti is among the most overpopulated countries of the New World, much more so than the Dominican Republic, with barely one-third of Hispaniola's land area but nearly two-thirds of its population (about 10 million), and an average population density approaching 1,000 per square mile. Most of those people are subsistence farmers. The market economy is modest, consisting principally of some coffee and sugar production for export, a mere 20,000 people employed at low wages in free trade zones making clothing and some other export goods, a few vacation enclaves on the coast where foreign tourists can isolate themselves from Haiti's problems, and a large but unquantified trade in drugs being transshipped from Colombia to the U.S. (That's why Haiti is sometimes referred to as a "narcostate.") There is extreme polarization between the masses of poor people living in rural areas or in the slums of the capital of Port-au-Prince, and a tiny population of rich elite in the cooler mountain suburb of Pétionville a half hour drive from the center of Port-au-Prince, enjoying expensive French restaurants with fine wines. Haiti's rate of population growth, and its rates of infection with AIDS, tuberculosis, and malaria, are among the highest in the New World. The question that all visitors to Haiti ask themselves is whether there is any hope for the country, and the usual answer is "no."

The Dominican Republic is also a developing country sharing Haiti's problems, but it is more developed and the problems are less acute. Per-capita income is five times higher, and the population density and population growth rate are lower. For the past 38 years the Dominican Republic

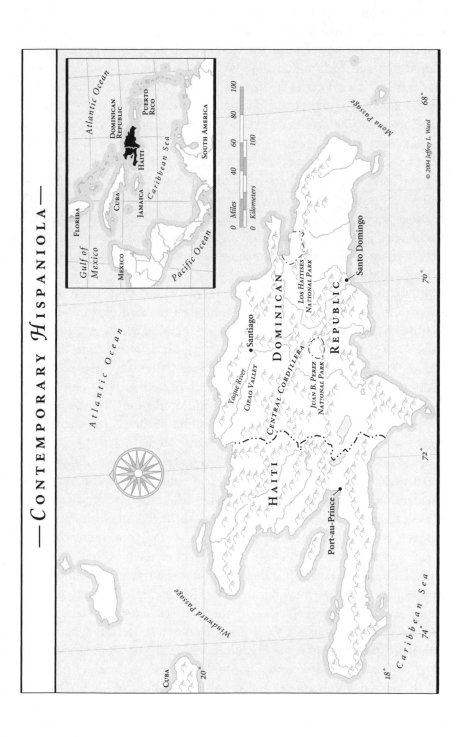

— CONTEMPORARY HISPANIOLA —

Atlantic Ocean

Windward Passage

CUBA

20°

HAITI

Port-au-Prince

Caribbean Sea

74°

18°

Yaque River
CIBAO VALLEY

•Santiago

CENTRAL CORDILLERA

DOMINICAN

JUAN B. PEREZ
NATIONAL PARK

LOS HAITISES
NATIONAL PARK

REPUBLIC

Santo Domingo•

72°

70°

Mona Passage

68°

© 2004 Jeffrey L. Ward

Gulf of
Mexico

MEXICO

FLORIDA

Atlantic Ocean

CUBA

JAMAICA

DOMINICAN
REPUBLIC

HAITI

PUERTO
RICO

Caribbean Sea

SOUTH AMERICA

Pacific Ocean

0 Miles

0 Kilometers

0   20   40   60   80   100

0   20   40   60   80   100

has been at least nominally a democracy without any military coup, and with some presidential elections from 1978 onwards resulting in the defeat of the incumbent and the inauguration of a challenger, along with others marred by fraud and intimidation. Within the booming economy, industries earning foreign exchange include an iron and nickel mine, until recently a gold mine, and formerly a bauxite mine; industrial free trade zones that employ 200,000 workers and export overseas; agricultural exports that include coffee, cacao, tobacco, cigars, fresh flowers, and avocados (the Dominican Republic is the world's third largest exporter of avocados); telecommunications; and a large tourist industry. Several dozen dams generate hydroelectric power. As American sports fans know, the Dominican Republic also produces and exports great baseball players. (I wrote the first draft of this chapter in a state of shock, having just watched the great Dominican pitcher Pedro Martínez, pitching for my favorite team the Boston Red Sox, go down to defeat in extra innings at the hands of their nemesis the New York Yankees in the last game of the 2003 American League Championship Series.) Others on the long list of Dominican baseball players who have gone on to achieve fame in the U.S. include the Alou brothers, Joaquín Andujar, George Bell, Adrian Beltre, Rico Carty, Mariano Duncan, Tony Fernández, Pedro Guerrero, Juan Marichal, José Offerman, Tony Peña, Alex Rodríguez, Juan Samuel, Ozzie Virgil, and of course the "*jonrón* king" Sammy Sosa. As one drives along the Dominican Republic's roads, one cannot go far without seeing a road sign pointing to the nearest stadium for *béisbol,* as the sport is known locally.

The contrasts between the two countries are also reflected in their national park systems. That of Haiti is tiny, consisting of just four parks threatened with encroachment by peasants felling the trees to make charcoal. In contrast, the natural reserve system of the Dominican Republic is relatively the most comprehensive and largest in the Americas, encompassing 32% of the country's land area in 74 parks or reserves, and it incorporates all important types of habitat. Of course the system also suffers from an abundance of problems and a deficiency of funding, but it is nevertheless impressive for a poor country with other problems and priorities. Behind the reserve system stands a vigorous indigenous conservation movement with many non-governmental organizations staffed by Dominicans themselves, rather than foisted on the country by foreign advisors.

All those dissimilarities in forest cover, economy, and natural reserve system arose despite the fact that the two countries share the same island. They also share histories of European colonialism and American occupations, overwhelmingly Catholic religion coexisting with a voodoo pantheon (more notably in Haiti), and mixed African-European ancestry (with a higher proportion of African ancestry in Haiti). For three periods of their history they were joined as a single colony or country.

The differences that exist despite those similarities become even more striking when one reflects that Haiti used to be much richer and more powerful than its neighbor. In the 19th century it launched several major invasions of the Dominican Republic and annexed it for 22 years. Why were the outcomes so different in the two countries, and why was it Haiti rather than the Dominican Republic that went into steep decline? Some environmental differences do exist between the two halves of the island and made some contribution to the outcomes, but that is the smaller part of the explanation. Most of the explanation has instead to do with differences between the two peoples in their histories, attitudes, self-defined identity, and institutions, as well as between their recent leaders of government. For anyone inclined to caricature environmental history as "environmental determinism," the contrasting histories of the Dominican Republic and Haiti provide a useful antidote. Yes, environmental problems do constrain human societies, but the societies' responses also make a difference. So, too, for better or for worse, do the actions and inactions of their leaders.

This chapter will begin by tracing the differing trajectories of political and economic history by which the Dominican Republic and Haiti arrived at their current differences, and the reasons behind those different trajectories. Then I shall discuss the development of Dominican environmental policies, which prove to be a mix of bottom-up and top-down initiatives. The chapter will conclude by examining the current status of environmental problems, the future and hopes of each side of the island, and their effects on each other and on the world.

When Christopher Columbus arrived at Hispaniola during his first transatlantic voyage in the year A.D. 1492, the island had already been settled by Native Americans for about 5,000 years. The occupants in Columbus's time were a group of Arawak Indians called Tainos who lived by farming, were organized into five chiefdoms, and numbered around half a million (the estimates range from 100,000 to 2,000,000). Columbus initially found them peaceful and friendly, until he and his Spaniards began mistreating them.

Unfortunately for the Tainos, they had gold, which the Spanish coveted but didn't want to go to the work of mining themselves. Hence the conquerors divided up the island and its Indian population among individual Spaniards, who put the Indians to work as virtual slaves, accidentally infected them with Eurasian diseases, and murdered them. By the year 1519, 27 years after Columbus's arrival, that original population of half a million had been reduced to about 11,000, most of whom died that year of smallpox to bring the population down to 3,000, and those survivors gradually died out or became assimilated within the next few decades. That forced the Spaniards to look elsewhere for slave laborers.

Around 1520 the Spaniards discovered that Hispaniola was suitable for growing sugar, and so they began importing slaves from Africa. The island's sugar plantations made it a rich colony for much of the 16th century. However, the Spaniards' interest became diverted from Hispaniola for multiple reasons, including their discovery of far more populous and richer Indian societies on the American mainland, particularly in Mexico, Peru, and Bolivia, offering much larger Indian populations to exploit, politically more advanced societies to take over, and rich silver mines in Bolivia. Hence Spain turned its attention elsewhere and devoted little resources to Hispaniola, especially as buying and transporting slaves from Africa were expensive and as Native Americans could be obtained just for the cost of conquering them. In addition, English, French, and Dutch pirates overran the Caribbean and attacked Spanish settlements on Hispaniola and elsewhere. Spain itself gradually went into political and economic decline, to the benefit of the English, French, and Dutch.

Along with those French pirates, French traders and adventurers built up a settlement at the western end of Hispaniola, far from the eastern part where the Spanish were concentrated. France, now much richer and politically stronger than Spain, invested heavily in importing slaves and developing plantations in its western part of the island, to a degree that the Spanish could not afford, and the histories of the two parts of the island began to diverge. During the 1700s the Spanish colony had a low population, few slaves, and a small economy based on raising cattle and selling their hides, while the French colony had a much larger population, more slaves (700,000 in 1785, compared to only 30,000 in the Spanish part), a proportionately much lower non-slave population (only 10% compared to 85%), and an economy based on sugar plantations. French Saint-Domingue, as it was called, became the richest European colony in the New World and contributed one-quarter of France's wealth.

In 1795, Spain finally ceded its no-longer-valuable eastern part of the island to France, so that Hispaniola became briefly unified under France.

After a slave rebellion broke out in French Saint-Domingue in 1791 and 1801, the French sent an army that was defeated by the slave army plus the effects of heavy losses to diseases. In 1804, having sold its North American holdings to the United States as the Louisiana Purchase, France gave up and abandoned Hispaniola. Not surprisingly, French Hispaniola's former slaves, who renamed their country Haiti (the original Taino Indian name for the island), killed many of Haiti's whites, destroyed the plantations and their infrastructure in order to make it impossible to rebuild the plantation slave system, and divided the plantations into small family farms. While that was what the former slaves wanted for themselves as individuals, it proved in the long run disastrous for Haiti's agricultural productivity, exports, and economy when the farmers received little help from subsequent Haitian governments in their efforts to develop cash crops. Haiti also lost human resources with the killing of much of its white population and the emigration of the remainder.

Nevertheless, at the time Haiti achieved independence in 1804, it was still the richer, stronger, and more populous part of the island. In 1805 the Haitians twice invaded the eastern (former Spanish) part of the island, then known as Santo Domingo. Four years later, at their own request, the Spanish settlers reassumed their status as a colony of Spain, which however governed Santo Domingo ineptly and with so little interest that the settlers declared independence in 1821. They were promptly reannexed by the Haitians, who remained until they were expelled in 1844, after which the Haitians continued to launch invasions to conquer the east into the 1850s.

Thus, as of 1850 Haiti in the west controlled less area than its neighbor but had a larger population, a subsistence farming economy with little exporting, and a population composed of a majority of blacks of African descent and a minority of mulattoes (people of mixed ancestry). Although the mulatto elite spoke French and identified themselves closely with France, Haiti's experience and fear of slavery led to the adoption of a constitution forbidding foreigners to own land or to control means of production through investments. The large majority of Haitians spoke a language of their own that had evolved there from French, termed Creole. The Dominicans in the east had a larger area but smaller population, still had an economy based on cattle, welcomed and offered citizenship to immigrants, and spoke Spanish. Over the course of the 19th century, numerically small but economically significant immigrant groups in the Dominican Republic included Curaçao Jews, Canary Islanders, Lebanese, Palestinians, Cubans, Puerto Ricans, Germans, and Italians, to be joined by Austrian Jews,

Japanese, and more Spaniards after 1930. The political aspect in which Haiti and the Dominican Republic most resembled each other was in their political instability. Coups followed on each other frequently, and control passed or alternated between local leaders with their private armies. Out of Haiti's 22 presidents from 1843 to 1915, 21 were assassinated or driven out of office, while the Dominican Republic between 1844 and 1930 had 50 changes of president, including 30 revolutions. In each part of the island the presidents governed in order to enrich themselves and their followers.

Outside powers viewed and treated Haiti and the Dominican Republic differently. To European eyes, the oversimplified image was of the Dominican Republic as a Spanish-speaking, partly European society receptive to European immigrants and trade, while Haiti was seen as a Creole-speaking African society composed of ex-slaves and hostile to foreigners. With the help of invested capital from Europe and later from the U.S., the Dominican Republic began to develop a market export economy, Haiti far less so. That Dominican economy was based on cacao, tobacco, coffee, and (beginning in the 1870s) sugar plantations, which (ironically) had formerly characterized Haiti rather than the Dominican Republic. But both sides of the island continued to be characterized by political instability. A Dominican president towards the end of the 19th century borrowed and failed to repay so much money from European lenders that France, Italy, Belgium, and Germany all sent warships and threatened to occupy the country in order to collect their debts. To forestall that risk of European occupation, the United States took over the Dominican customs service, the sole source of government revenues, and allocated half of the receipts to pay those foreign debts. During World War I, concerned about risks to the Panama Canal posed by political unrest in the Caribbean, the United States imposed a military occupation on both parts of the island, which lasted from 1915 to 1934 in Haiti and from 1916 to 1924 in the Dominican Republic. Thereafter, both parts quickly reverted to their previous political instability and strife between competing would-be presidents.

Instability in both parts was ended, in the Dominican Republic long before Haiti, by the two most evil dictators in Latin America's long history of evil dictators. Rafael Trujillo was the Dominican chief of the national police and then the head of the army that the U.S. military government established and trained. After he took advantage of that position to get himself elected as president in 1930 and to become dictator, he proceeded to remain in power as a result of being very hardworking, a superior administrator, a shrewd judge of people, a clever politician, and absolutely ruthless—and of appearing to act in the broad interests of much of Dominican society. He tortured or killed his possible opponents and imposed an all-intrusive police state.

At the same time, in an effort to modernize the Dominican Republic, Trujillo developed the economy, infrastructure, and industries, mostly running the country as his own private business. He and his family eventually came to own or control most of the country's economy. In particular, either directly or through relatives or allies as front men, Trujillo held national monopolies of beef export, cement, chocolate, cigarettes, coffee, insurance, milk, rice, salt, slaughterhouses, tobacco, and wood. He owned or controlled most forestry operations and sugar production, and owned airlines, banks, hotels, much land, and shipping lines. He took for himself a portion of prostitution earnings and 10% of all public employee salaries. He promoted himself ubiquitously: the capital city was renamed from Santo Domingo to Ciudad Trujillo (Trujillo City), the country's highest mountain was renamed from Pico Duarte to Pico Trujillo, the country's educational system inculcated giving thanks to Trujillo, and signs of thanks posted on every public water faucet proclaimed "Trujillo gives water." To reduce the possibility of a successful rebellion or invasion, the Trujillo government spent half of its budget on a huge army, navy, and air force, the largest in the Caribbean area, larger even than those of Mexico.

In the 1950s, however, several developments conspired to cause Trujillo to begin to lose the former support that he had maintained through his combination of terror methods, economic growth, and distributing land to peasants. The economy deteriorated through a combination of government overspending on a festival to celebrate the 25th anniversary of the Trujillo regime, overspending to buy up privately owned sugar mills and electricity plants, a decline in world prices for coffee and other Dominican exports, and a decision to make a major investment in state sugar production that proved economically unsuccessful. The government responded to an unsuccessful Cuban-backed invasion by Dominican exiles in 1959, and to Cuban radio broadcasts encouraging revolt, by increasing arrests, assassinations, and torture. On May 30, 1961, while traveling in a chauffeur-driven unaccompanied car late at night to visit his mistress, Trujillo was ambushed and assassinated in a dramatic car chase and gun battle by Dominicans, apparently with CIA support.

Throughout most of the Trujillo era in the Dominican Republic, Haiti continued to have an unstable succession of presidents until it too in 1957 passed under the control of its own evil dictator, François "Papa Doc"

Duvalier. While a physician and better educated than Trujillo, he proved to be an equally clever and ruthless politician, equally successful in terrorizing his country by secret police, and ended up killing far more of his country-men than did Trujillo. Papa Doc Duvalier differed from Trujillo in his lack of interest in modernizing his country or in developing an industrial economy for his country or for himself. He died a natural death in 1971, to be succeeded by his son Jean-Claude "Baby Doc" Duvalier, who ruled until forced into exile in 1986.

Since the end of the Duvalier dictatorships, Haiti has resumed its former political instability, and its already weak economy has continued to shrink. It still exports coffee, but the amount exported has remained constant while the population has continued to grow. Its human development index, an in-dex based on a combination of human lifespan and education and standard of living, is the lowest in the world outside Africa. After Trujillo's assassina-tion, the Dominican Republic also remained politically unstable until 1966, including a civil war in 1965 that triggered the arrival again of U.S. marines and the beginning of large-scale Dominican emigration to the U.S. That pe-riod of instability ended with the election of Joaquín Balaguer, former president under Trujillo, to the presidency in 1966, helped by ex-Trujillo army officers who carried out a terrorist campaign against the opposing party. Balaguer, a distinctive person whom we shall consider at more length below, continued to dominate Dominican politics for the next 34 years, rul-ing as president from 1966 to 1978 and again from 1986 until 1996, and ex-ercising much influence even while out of office from 1978 to 1986. His last decisive intervention into Dominican politics, his rescue of the country's natural reserve system, came in the year 2000 at the age of 94, when he was blind, sick, and two years short of his death.

During those post-Trujillo years from 1961 to the present, the Domini-can Republic continued to industrialize and modernize. For a time its export economy depended heavily on sugar, which then yielded in impor-tance to mining, free trade zone industrial exports, and non-sugar agricul-tural exports, as mentioned earlier in this chapter. Also important to the economies of both the Dominican Republic and Haiti has been the export of people. More than a million Haitians and a million Dominicans now liv-ing overseas, especially in the United States, send home earnings that ac-count for a significant fraction of the economies of both countries. The Dominican Republic still rates as a poor country (per-capita income only $2,200 per year), but it exhibits many hallmarks of a growing economy that were obvious during my visit, including a massive construction boom and urban traffic jams.

With that historical background, let's now return to one of those surprising differences with which this chapter began: why did the political, economic, and ecological histories of these two countries sharing the same island unfold so differently?

Part of the answer involves environmental differences. Hispaniola's rains come mainly from the east. Hence the Dominican (eastern) part of the island receives more rain and thus supports higher rates of plant growth. Hispaniola's highest mountains (over 10,000 feet high) are on the Dominican side, and the rivers from those high mountains mainly flow eastwards into the Dominican side. The Dominican side has broad valleys, plains, and plateaus, and much thicker soils; in particular, the Cibao Valley in the north is one of the richest agricultural areas in the world. In contrast, the Haitian side is drier because of that barrier of high mountains blocking rains from the east. Compared to the Dominican Republic, a higher percentage of Haiti's area is mountainous, the area of flat land good for intensive agriculture is much smaller, there is more limestone terrain, and the soils are thinner and less fertile and have a lower capacity for recovery. Note the paradox: the Haitian side of the island was less well endowed environmentally but developed a rich agricultural economy before the Dominican side. The explanation of this paradox is that Haiti's burst of agricultural wealth came at the expense of its environmental capital of forests and soils. This lesson—in effect, that an impressive-looking bank account may conceal a negative cash flow—is a theme to which we shall return in the last chapter.

While those environmental differences did contribute to the different economic trajectories of the two countries, a larger part of the explanation involved social and political differences, of which there were many that eventually penalized the Haitian economy relative to the Dominican economy. In that sense, the differing developments of the two countries were overdetermined: numerous separate factors coincided in tipping the result in the same direction.

One of those social and political differences involved the accident that Haiti was a colony of rich France and became the most valuable colony in France's overseas empire, while the Dominican Republic was a colony of Spain, which by the late 1500s was neglecting Hispaniola and was in economic and political decline itself. Hence France could and chose to invest in developing intensive slave-based plantation agriculture in Haiti, which the Spanish could not or chose not to develop in their side of the island. France imported far more slaves into its colony than did Spain. As a result, Haiti had a population seven times higher than its neighbor during colonial times, and it still has a somewhat larger population today, about 10,000,000 versus 8,800,000. But Haiti's area is only slightly more than half of that of the Dominican Republic, so that Haiti with a larger population and smaller area has double the Republic's population density. The combination of that higher population density and lower rainfall was the main factor behind the more rapid deforestation and loss of soil fertility on the Haitian side. In addition, all of those French ships that brought slaves to Haiti returned to Europe with cargos of Haitian timber, so that Haiti's lowlands and mid-mountain slopes had been largely stripped of timber by the mid-19th century.

A second social and political factor is that the Dominican Republic, with its Spanish-speaking population of predominantly European ancestry, was both more receptive and more attractive to European immigrants and investors than was Haiti with its Creole-speaking population composed overwhelmingly of black former slaves. Hence European immigration and investment were negligible and restricted by the constitution in Haiti after 1804 but eventually became important in the Dominican Republic. Those Dominican immigrants included many middle-class businesspeople and skilled professionals who contributed to the country's development. The people of the Dominican Republic even *chose* to resume their status as a Spanish colony from 1812 to 1821, and its president *chose* to make his country a protectorate of Spain from 1861 to 1865.

Still another social difference contributing to the different economies is that, as a legacy of their country's slave history and slave revolt, most Haitians owned their own land, used it to feed themselves, and received no help from their government in developing cash crops for trade with overseas European countries, while the Dominican Republic eventually did develop an export economy and overseas trade. Haiti's elite identified strongly with France rather than with their own landscape, did not acquire land or develop commercial agriculture, and sought mainly to extract wealth from the peasants.

A recent cause of divergence lies in the differing aspirations of the two dictators: Trujillo sought to develop an industrial economy and modern state (for his own benefit), but Duvalier did not. This might perhaps be

viewed just as an idiosyncratic personal difference between the two dictators, but it may also mirror their different societies.

Finally, Haiti's problems of deforestation and poverty compared to
those of the Dominican Republic have become compounded within the last
40 years. Because the Dominican Republic retained much forest cover and
began to industrialize, the Trujillo regime initially planned, and the regimes
of Balaguer and subsequent presidents constructed, dams to generate hydroelectric power. Balaguer launched a crash program to spare forest use for
fuel by instead importing propane and liquefied natural gas. But Haiti's
poverty forced its people to remain dependent on forest-derived charcoal
from fuel, thereby accelerating the destruction of its last remaining forests.

Thus, there were many reasons why deforestation and other environmental
problems began earlier, developed over a longer time, and proceeded further in Haiti than in the Dominican Republic. The reasons involved four of
the factors in this book's five-factor framework: differences in human environmental impacts, in variously friendly policies or unfriendly policies of
other countries, and in responses by the societies and their leaders. Of the
case studies described in this book, the contrast between Haiti and the Dominican Republic discussed in this chapter, and the contrast between the
fates of the Norse and the Inuit in Greenland discussed in Chapter 8, provide the clearest illustrations that a society's fate lies in its own hands and
depends substantially on its own choices.

What about the Dominican Republic's own environmental problems,
and what about the countermeasures that it adopted? To use the terminology that I introduced in Chapter 9, Dominican measures to protect the
environment began from the bottom up, shifted to top-down control after
1930, and are now a mixture of both. Exploitation of valuable trees in the
Republic increased in the 1860s and 1870s, resulting already then in some
local depletion or extinction of valuable tree species. Rates of deforestation
increased in the late 19th century due to forest clearance for sugar plantations and other cash crops, then continued to increase in the early 20th century as the demand for wood for railroad ties and for incipient urbanization
rose. Soon after 1900 we encounter the first mentions of damage to forest in
low-rainfall areas from harvesting wood for fuel, and of contamination of
streams by agricultural activities along their banks. The first municipal
regulation prohibiting logging and the contamination of streams was passed
in 1901.

Bottom-up environmental protection was launched in a serious way between 1919 and 1930 in the area around Santiago, the Republic's second largest city and the center of its richest and most heavily exploited agricultural area. The lawyer Juan Bautista Pérez Rancier and the physician and surveyor Miguel Canela y Lázaro, struck by the sequence of logging and its associated road network leading to agricultural settlement and watershed damage, lobbied the Santiago Chamber of Commerce to buy land as a forest reserve, and they also sought to raise the necessary funds by public subscription. Success was achieved in 1927, when the Republic's secretary of agriculture contributed additional government funds to make possible the purchase of the first natural reserve, the Vedado del Yaque. The Yaque River is the country's largest river, and a *vedado* is an area of land to which entry is controlled or forbidden.

After 1930, the dictator Trujillo shifted the impetus for environmental management to a top-down approach. His regime expanded the area of the Vedado del Yaque, created other *vedados*, established in 1934 the first national park, set up a corps of forest guards to enforce protection of forests, suppressed the wasteful use of fire to burn forest in order to clear land for agriculture, and banned the cutting of pine trees without his permission in the area around Constanza in the Central Cordillera. Trujillo undertook these measures in the name of environmental protection, but he was probably motivated more strongly by economic considerations, including his own personal economic advantage. In 1937 his regime commissioned a famous Puerto Rican environmental scientist, Dr. Carlos Chardón, to survey the Dominican Republic's natural resources (its agricultural, mineral, and forestry potential). In particular, Chardón calculated the commercial logging potential of the Republic's pine forest, by far the most extensive pine forest in the Caribbean, to be around $40,000,000, a large sum in those days. On the basis of that report, Trujillo himself became involved in logging of pines, and came to own large areas of pine forest and to be the joint owner of the country's main sawmills. In their logging operations, Trujillo's foresters adopted the environmentally sound measure of leaving some mature trees standing as sources of seed for natural reforestation, and those big old trees can still be recognized today in the regenerated forest. Environmental measures under Trujillo in the 1950s included commissioning a Swedish study of the Republic's potential for building dams for hydroelectric power, the planning of such dams, the convening of the country's first environmental congress in 1958, and the establishment of more national parks, at least partly to protect watersheds that would be important for hydroelectric power generation.

Under his dictatorship, Trujillo (as usual, often acting with family members and allies as front men) carried out extensive logging himself, but his dictatorial government prevented others from logging and establishing unauthorized settlements. After Trujillo's death in 1961, that wall against widespread pillaging of the Dominican environment fell. Squatters occupied land and used forest fires to clear woodlands for agriculture; a disorganized large-scale immigration from the countryside into urban barrios sprung up; and four wealthy families of the Santiago area began logging at a rate faster than the rate under Trujillo. Two years after Trujillo's death, the democratically elected President Juan Bosch attempted to persuade loggers to spare the pine forests so that they could remain as watersheds for the planned Yaque and Nizao dams, but the loggers instead joined with other interests to overthrow Bosch. Rates of logging accelerated until the election of Joaquín Balaguer as president in 1966.

Balaguer recognized the country's urgent need for maintaining forested watersheds in order to meet the Republic's energy requirements through hydroelectric power, and to ensure a supply of water sufficient for industrial and domestic needs. Soon after becoming president, he took drastic action by banning all commercial logging in the country, and by closing all of the country's sawmills. That action provoked strong resistance by rich powerful families, who responded by pulling back their logging operations out of public view into more remote areas of forests, and by operating their sawmills at night. Balaguer reacted with the even more drastic step of taking responsibility for enforcing forest protection away from the Department of Agriculture, turning it over to the armed forces, and declaring illegal logging to be a crime against state security. To stop logging, the armed forces initiated a program of survey flights and military operations, which climaxed in 1967 in one of the landmark events of Dominican environmental history, a night raid by the military on a clandestine large logging camp. In the ensuing gunfight a dozen loggers were killed. That strong signal served as a shock to the loggers. While some illegal logging continued, it was met with further raids and shootings of loggers, and it decreased greatly during Balaguer's first period as president (1966 to 1978, comprising three consecutive terms in office).

That was only one of a host of Balaguer's far-reaching environmental measures. Some of the others were as follows. During the eight years when

Balaguer was out of office from 1978 to 1986, other presidents reopened some logging camps and sawmills, and allowed charcoal production from forests to increase. On the first day of his return to the presidency in 1986, Balaguer began issuing executive orders to close logging camps and saw-mills again, and on the next day he deployed military helicopters to detect illegal logging and intrusions into national parks. Military operations re-sumed to capture and imprison loggers, and to remove poor squatters, plus rich agribusinesses and mansions (some of them belonging to Balaguer's own friends), from the parks. The most notorious of those operations took place in 1992 in Los Haitises National Park, 90% of whose forest had been destroyed; the army expelled thousands of squatters. In a further such op-eration two years later, personally directed by Balaguer, the army drove bull-dozers through luxury houses built by wealthy Dominicans within Juan B. Pérez National Park. Balaguer banned the use of fire as an agricultural method, and even passed a law (which proved difficult to enforce) that every fence post should consist of live rooted trees rather than felled timber. As two sets of measures to undermine demand for Dominican tree prod-ucts and to replace them with something else, he opened the market to wood imports from Chile, Honduras, and the U.S. (thereby eliminating most demand for Dominican timber in the country's stores); and he re-duced traditional charcoal production from trees (the curse of Haiti) by contracting for liquefied natural gas imports from Venezuela, building sev-eral terminals to import that gas, subsidizing the cost of gas to the public to outcompete charcoal, and calling for the distribution without cost of propane stoves and cylinders in order to encourage people to shift from charcoal. He greatly expanded the natural reserve system, declared the country's first two coastal national parks, added two submerged banks in the ocean to Dominican territory as humpback whale sanctuaries, pro-tected land within 20 yards of rivers and within 60 yards of the coast, pro-tected wetlands, signed the Rio convention on the environment, and banned hunting for 10 years. He put pressure on industries to treat their wastes, launched with limited success some efforts to control air pollution, and slapped a big tax on mining companies. Among the many environmen-tally damaging proposals that he opposed or blocked were projects for a road to the port of Sanchez through a national park, a north–south road over the Central Cordillera, an international airport at Santiago, a super-port, and a dam at Madrigal. He refused to repair an existing road over the highlands, with the result that it became nearly unusable. In Santa Do-mingo he founded the Aquarium, the Botanical Garden, and the Natural

History Museum and rebuilt the National Zoo, all of which have become major attractions.

As Balaguer's final political act at the age of 94, he teamed up with President-elect Mejia to block President Fernández's plan to reduce and weaken the natural reserve system. Balaguer and Mejia achieved that goal by a clever legislative maneuver in which they amended President Fernández's proposal with a rider that converted the natural reserve system from one existing only by executive order (hence subject to alterations such as those proposed by Fernández), to one established instead by law, in the condition that it had existed in 1996 at the close of Balaguer's last presidency and before Fernández's maneuvers. Thus, Balaguer ended his political career by saving the reserve system to which he had devoted so much attention.

All of those actions by Balaguer climaxed the era of top-down environmental management in the Dominican Republic. In the same era, bottom-up efforts also resumed after vanishing under Trujillo. During the 1970s and 1980s scientists did much inventorying of the country's coastal, marine, and terrestrial natural resources. As Dominicans slowly relearned the methods of private civic participation after decades without it under Trujillo, the 1980s saw the founding of many non-governmental organizations, including several dozen environmental organizations that have become increasingly effective. In contrast to the situation in many developing countries, where environmental efforts are mainly developed by affiliates of international environmental organizations, the bottom-up impetus in the Dominican Republic has come from local NGOs concerned with the environment. Along with universities and with the Dominican Academy of Sciences, these NGOs have now become the leaders of a homegrown Dominican environmental movement.

Why did Balaguer push such a broad range of measures on behalf of the environment? To many of us, it is difficult to reconcile that apparently strong and far-sighted commitment to the environment with his repellent qualities. For 31 years he served under dictator Rafael Trujillo and defended Trujillo's massacres of Haitians in 1937. He ended up as Trujillo's puppet president, but he also served Trujillo in positions where he exercised influence, such as secretary of state. Anyone willing to work with such an evil person as Trujillo immediately becomes suspect and tarnished by association. Balaguer also accumulated his own list of evil deeds after Trujillo's death—deeds that can be blamed only on Balaguer himself. While he won the presidency honestly in the election of 1986, he resorted to fraud, violence, and intimidation to secure his election in 1966 and his reelection in 1970, 1974, 1990, and 1994. He operated his own squads of thugs to assassinate hundreds or perhaps thousands of members of the opposition. He ordered many forced removals of poor people from national parks, and he ordered or tolerated the shooting of illegal loggers. He tolerated widespread corruption. He belonged to Latin America's tradition of political strongmen or *caudillos*. Among the quotes attributed to him is: "The constitution is nothing more than a piece of paper."

Chapters 14 and 15 of this book will discuss the often-complicated reasons why people do or don't pursue environmentalist policies. While I was visiting the Dominican Republic, I was especially interested in learning, from those who had known Balaguer personally or lived through his presidencies, what could have motivated him. I asked every Dominican whom I interviewed their views of him. Among the 20 Dominicans whom I interviewed at length, I got 20 different answers. Many of them were people who had the strongest possible personal motives for loathing Balaguer: they had been imprisoned by him, or had been imprisoned and tortured by the Trujillo government that he served, or had close relatives and friends who had been killed.

Among this divergence of opinion, there were nevertheless numerous points mentioned independently by many of my informants. Balaguer was described as almost uniquely complex and puzzling. He wanted political power, and his pursuit of policies in which he believed was tempered by concern not to do things that would cost him his power (but he still often pushed dangerously close to that limit of losing power through unpopular policies). He was an extremely skilled, cynical, practical politician whose ability nobody else in the last 42 years of Dominican political history has come remotely close to matching, and who exemplified the adjective "Machiavellian." He constantly maintained a delicate balancing act between the military, the masses, and competing scheming groups of elites; he succeeded in forestalling military coups against him by fragmenting the military into competing groups; and he was able to inspire such fear even in military officers abusing forests and national parks that, in the sequel to a famous unplanned confrontation recorded on television in 1994, I was told that an army colonel who had opposed Balaguer's forest protection measures and whom Balaguer angrily summoned ended up urinating in his trousers in terror. In the picturesque words of one historian whom I interviewed, "Balaguer was a snake who shed and changed his skin as needed."

Under Balaguer there was a great deal of corruption that he tolerated, but he himself was not corrupt nor interested in personal wealth, unlike Trujillo. In his own words, "Corruption stops at the door of my office."

Finally, as one Dominican who had been both imprisoned and tortured summed it up for me, "Balaguer was an evil, but a necessary evil at that stage in Dominican history." By that phrase, my informant meant that, at the time Trujillo was assassinated in 1961, there were many Dominicans both overseas and in the country with worthy aspirations, but none of them had a fraction of Balaguer's practical experience in government. Through his actions, he is credited with having consolidated the Dominican middle class, Dominican capitalism, and the country as it exists today, and with having presided over a major improvement in the Dominican economy. Those outcomes inclined many Dominicans to put up with Balaguer's evil qualities.

In response to my question why Balaguer pursued his environmentalist policies, I encountered much more disagreement. Some Dominicans told me that they thought it was just a sham, either to win votes or to polish his international image. One person viewed Balaguer's evictions of squatters from national parks as just part of a broad plot to move peasants out of remote forests where they might hatch a pro-Castro rebellion; to depopulate public lands that could eventually be redeveloped as resorts owned by rich Dominicans, rich overseas resort developers, or military people; and to cement Balaguer's ties with the military.

While there may be some substance to all of those suspected motives, nevertheless the wide range of Balaguer's environmental actions, and the public unpopularity of some of them and public disinterest in others, make it difficult for me to view his policies as just a sham. Some of his environmental actions, especially his use of the military to relocate squatters, made him look very bad, cost him votes (albeit buffered by his rigging of elections), and cost him support of powerful members of the elite and military (although many others of his policies gained him their support). In the case of many of his environmental measures that I listed, I cannot discern a possible connection to wealthy resort developers, counterinsurgency measures, or currying favor with the army. Instead, Balaguer, as an experienced practical politician, seems to have pursued pro-environment policies as vigorously as he could get away with it, without losing too many votes or too many influential supporters or provoking a military coup against him.

Another issue raised by some of the Dominicans whom I interviewed was that Balaguer's environmental policies were selective, sometimes ineffective, and exhibited blind spots. He allowed his supporters to do things destructive to the environment, such as damaging riverbeds by extracting rock, gravel, sand, and other building materials. Some of his laws, such as those against hunting and air pollution and fence poles, didn't work. He sometimes drew back if he encountered opposition to his policies. An especially serious failing of his as an environmentalist was that he neglected to harmonize the needs of rural farmers with environmental concerns, and he could have done much more to foster popular support for the environment. But he still managed to undertake more diverse and more radical pro-environment actions than any other Dominican politician, or indeed than most modern politicians known to me in other countries.

On reflection, it seems to me that the most likely interpretation of Balaguer's policies is that he really did care about the environment, as he claimed. He mentioned it in almost every speech; he said that conserving forests, rivers, and mountains had been his dream since his childhood; and he stressed it in his first speeches on becoming president in 1966 and again in 1986, and in his last (1994) reinaugural speech. When President Fernández asserted that devoting 32% of the country's territory to protected areas was excessive, Balaguer responded that the whole country should be a protected area. But as for how he arrived at his pro-environment views, no two people gave me the same opinion. One person said that Balaguer might have been influenced by exposure to environmentalists during early years in his life that he spent in Europe; one noted that Balaguer was consistently anti-Haitian, and that he may have sought to improve the Dominican Republic's landscape in order to contrast it with Haiti's devastation; another thought that he had been influenced by his sisters, to whom he was close, and who were said to have been horrified by the deforestation and river siltation that they saw resulting from the Trujillo years; and still another person commented that Balaguer was already 60 years old when he ascended to the post-Trujillo presidency and 90 years old when he stepped down from it, so that he might have been motivated by the changes that he saw around him in his country during his long life.

I don't know the answers to these questions about Balaguer. Part of our problem in understanding him may be our own unrealistic expectations. We may subconsciously expect people to be homogeneously "good" or "bad," as if there were a single quality of virtue that should shine through every aspect of a person's behavior. If we find people virtuous or admirable in one respect, it troubles us to find them not so in another respect. It is difficult for us to acknowledge that people are not consistent, but are instead mosaics of traits formed by different sets of experiences that often do not correlate with each other.

We may also be troubled that, if we really acknowledge Balaguer as an environmentalist, his evil traits would unfairly tarnish environmentalism. Yet, as one friend said to me, "Adolf Hitler loved dogs and brushed his teeth, but that doesn't mean that we should hate dogs and stop brushing our teeth." I also have to reflect on my own experiences while working in Indonesia from 1979 to 1996 under its military dictatorship. I loathed and feared that dictatorship because of its policies, and also for personal reasons: especially because of the things that it did to many of my New Guinea friends, and because of its soldiers almost killing me. I was therefore surprised to find that that dictatorship set up a comprehensive and effective national park system in Indonesian New Guinea. I arrived in Indonesian New Guinea after years of experience in the democracy of Papua New Guinea, and I expected to find environmental policies much more advanced under the virtuous democracy than under the evil dictatorship. Instead, I had to acknowledge that the reverse was true.

None of the Dominicans to whom I talked claimed to understand Balaguer. In referring to him, they used phrases such as "full of paradoxes," "controversial," and "enigmatic." One person applied to Balaguer the phrase that Winston Churchill used to describe Russia: "a riddle wrapped in a mystery inside an enigma." The struggle to understand Balaguer reminds me that history, as well as life itself, is complicated; neither life nor history is an enterprise for those who seek simplicity and consistency.

In light of that history of environmental impacts in the Dominican Republic, what is the current status of the country's environmental problems, and of its natural reserve system? The major problems fall into eight of the list of 12 categories of environmental problems that will be summarized in Chapter 16: problems involving forests, marine resources, soil, water, toxic substances, alien species, population growth, and population impact.

Deforestation of the pine forests became locally heavy under Trujillo, and then rampant in the five years immediately following his assassination. Balaguer's ban on logging was relaxed under some other recent presidents. The exodus of Dominicans from rural areas to the cities and overseas has decreased pressure on the forests, but deforestation is continuing especially near the Haitian border, where desperate Haitians cross the border from their almost completely deforested country in order to fell trees for

making charcoal and for clearing land to farm as squatters on the Dominican side. In the year 2000, the enforcement of forest protection reverted
from the armed forces to the Ministry of the Environment, which is weaker
and lacks the necessary funds, so that forest protection is now less effective
than it was from 1967 to 2000.

Along most of the Republic's coastline, marine habitats and coral reefs
have been heavily damaged and overfished.

Soil loss by erosion on deforested land has been massive. There is
concern about that erosion leading to sediment buildup in the reservoirs
behind the dams used to generate the country's hydroelectric power. Salinization has developed in some irrigated areas, such as at the Barahona Sugar
Plantation.

Water quality in the country's rivers is now very poor because of sediment buildup from erosion, as well as toxic pollution and waste disposal.
Rivers that until a few decades ago were clean and safe for swimming
are now brown with sediment and unswimmable. Industries dump their
wastes into streams, as do residents of urban barrios with inadequate or
non-existent public waste disposal. Riverbeds have been heavily damaged
by industrial dredging to extract materials for the construction industry.

Beginning in the 1970s, there have been massive applications of toxic
pesticides, insecticides, and herbicides in rich agricultural areas, such as the
Cibao Valley. The Dominican Republic has continued to use toxins that
were banned in their overseas countries of manufacture long ago. That
toxin use has been tolerated by the government, because Dominican agriculture is so profitable. Workers in rural areas, even children, routinely apply toxic agricultural products without face or hand protection. As a result,
effects of agricultural toxins on human health have now been well documented. I was struck by the near-absence of birds in the Cibao Valley's rich
agricultural areas: if the toxins are so bad for birds, they presumably are also
bad for people. Other toxic problems arise from the large Falconbridge
iron/nickel mine, whose smoke fills the air along parts of the highway between the country's two largest cities (Santo Domingo and Santiago). The
Rosario gold mine has been temporarily closed down because the country
lacks the technology to treat the mine's cyanide and acid effluents. Both
Santo Domingo and Santiago have smog, resulting from mass transit using
obsolete vehicles, increased energy consumption, and the abundance of private generators that people maintain in their homes and businesses because
of the frequent power failures of the public electricity systems. (I experienced several power failures each day that I was in Santo Domingo, and af-

ter my return my Dominican friends wrote me that they were now suffering under 21-hour blackouts.)

As for alien species, in order to reforest logged lands and hurricane-damaged lands in recent decades, the country has resorted to alien tree species that grow more quickly than does the slow-growing native Dominican pine. Among the alien species that I saw in abundance were Honduras pine, casuarinas, several species of acacias, and teak. Some of those alien species have prospered, while others have failed. They raise concern because some of them are prone to diseases to which the native Dominican pine is resistant, so that reforested slopes could lose their cover again if their trees are attacked by disease.

While the country's rate of population increase has decreased, it is estimated as still around 1.6% per year.

More serious than the country's growing population is its rapidly growing per-capita human impact. (By that term, which will recur in the remainder of this book, I mean the average resource consumption and waste production of one person: much higher for modern First World citizens than for modern Third World citizens or for any people in the past. A society's total impact equals its per-capita impact multiplied by its number of people.) Overseas trips by Dominicans, visits to the country by tourists, and television make people well aware of the higher standard of living in Puerto Rico and the United States. Billboards advertising consumer products are everywhere, and I saw street vendors selling cell telephone equipment and CDs at any major intersection in the cities. The country is becoming increasingly dedicated to a consumerism that is not currently supported by the economy and resources of the Dominican Republic itself, and that depends partly on earnings sent home by Dominicans working overseas. All of those people acquiring large amounts of consumer products are putting out correspondingly large amounts of wastes that overwhelm municipal waste disposal systems. One can see the trash accumulating in the streams, along roads, along city streets, and in the countryside. As one Dominican said to me, "The apocalypse here will not take the form of an earthquake or hurricane, but of a world buried in garbage."

The country's natural reserve system of protected areas directly addresses all of these threats except for population growth and consumer impact. The system is a comprehensive one that consists of 74 reserves of various types (national parks, protected marine reserves, and so on) and covers a third of the country's land area. That is an impressive achievement for a densely populated small and poor country whose per-capita income is only one-tenth that of the United States. Equally impressive is that that reserve system was not urged and designed by international environmental organizations but by Dominican NGOs. In my discussions at three of these Dominican organizations—the Academy of Sciences in Santo Domingo, the Fundación Moscoso Puello, and the Santo Domingo branch of The Nature Conservancy (the latter unique among my Dominican contacts in being affiliated with an international organization rather than purely local)—without exception every staff member whom I met was a Dominican. That situation contrasts with the situation to which I have become accustomed in Papua New Guinea, Indonesia, the Solomon Islands, and other developing countries, where scientists from overseas hold key positions and also serve as visiting consultants.

What about the future of the Dominican Republic? Will the reserve system survive under the pressures that it faces? Is there hope for the country?

On these questions I again encountered divergence of opinion among even my Dominican friends. Reasons for environmental pessimism begin with the fact that the reserve system is no longer backed by the iron fist of Joaquín Balaguer. It is underfunded, underpoliced, and has been only weakly supported by recent presidents, some of whom have tried to trim its area or even to sell it. The universities are staffed by few well-trained scientists, so that they in turn cannot educate a cadre of well-trained students. The government provides negligible support for scientific studies. Some of my friends were concerned that the Dominican reserves are turning into parks that exist more on paper than in reality.

On the other hand, a major reason for environmental optimism is the country's growing, well-organized, bottom-up environmental movement that is almost unprecedented in the developing world. It is willing and able to challenge the government; some of my friends in the NGOs were sent to jail for those challenges but won their release and resumed their challenges. The Dominican environmental movement is as determined and effective as in any other country with which I am familiar. Thus, as elsewhere in the world, I see in the Dominican Republic what one friend described as "an exponentially accelerating horse race of unpredictable outcome" between destructive and constructive forces. Both the threats to the environment, and the environmental movement opposing those threats, are gathering strength in the Dominican Republic, and we cannot foresee which will eventually prevail.

Similarly, the prospects of the country's economy and society arouse divergence of opinion. Five of my Dominican friends are now deeply pessimistic, virtually without hope. They feel especially discouraged by the weakness and corruptness of recent governments seemingly interested only in helping the ruling politicians and their friends, and by recent severe setbacks to the Dominican economy. Those setbacks include the virtually complete collapse of the formerly dominant sugar export market, the devaluation of the currency, increasing competition from other countries with lower labor costs for producing free trade zone export products, the collapses of two major banks, and government overborrowing and overspending. Consumerist aspirations are rampant and beyond levels that the country could support. In the opinion of my most pessimistic friends, the Dominican Republic is slipping downhill in the direction of Haiti's grinding desperation, but it is slipping more rapidly than Haiti did: the descent into economic decline that stretched over a century and a half in Haiti will be accomplished within a few decades in the Dominican Republic. According to this view, the Republic's capital city of Santo Domingo will come to rival the misery of Haiti's capital of Port-au-Prince, where most of the population lives below the poverty level in slums lacking public services, while the rich elite sip their French wines in their separate suburb.

That's the worst-case scenario. Others of my Dominican friends responded that they have seen governments come and go over the last 40 years. Yes, they said, the current government is especially weak and corrupt, but it will surely lose the next election, and all of the candidates to become the next president seem preferable to the current president. (In fact, the government did lose the election a few months after that conversation.) Fundamental facts about the Dominican Republic brightening its prospects are that it is a small country in which environmental problems become readily visible to everybody. It is also a "face-to-face society" where concerned and knowledgeable private individuals outside the government have ready access to government ministers, unlike the situation in the United States. Perhaps most important of all, one has to remember that the Dominican Republic is a resilient country that has survived a history of problems far more daunting than its present ones. It survived 22 years of Haitian occupation, then an almost uninterrupted succession of weak or corrupt presidents from 1844 until 1916 and again from 1924 to 1930, and American military occupations from 1916 to 1924 and from 1965 to 1966. It succeeded in rebuilding itself after 31 years under Rafael Trujillo, one of the most evil and destructive dictators in the world's recent history. From the year 1900 to 2000, the Dominican Republic underwent more dramatic socioeconomic change than did almost any other country in the New World.

Because of globalization, what happens to the Dominican Republic affects not only Dominicans but also the rest of the world. It especially affects the United States lying only 600 miles away, and already home to a million Dominicans. New York City now supports the second largest Dominican population of any city in the world, second only to the Republic's own capital of Santo Domingo. There are also large overseas Dominican populations in Canada, the Netherlands, Spain, and Venezuela. The U.S. has already experienced how events in the Caribbean country immediately west of Hispaniola, namely, Cuba, threatened our survival in 1962. Hence the U.S. has a lot at stake in whether the Dominican Republic succeeds in solving its problems.

What about the future of Haiti? Already the poorest and one of the most overcrowded countries in the New World, Haiti is nevertheless continuing to become even poorer and more crowded, with a population growth rate of nearly 3% per year. Haiti is so poor, and so deficient in natural resources and in trained or educated human resources, that it really is difficult to see what might bring about improvement. If one instead looks to the outside world to help through government foreign aid, NGO initiatives, or private efforts, Haiti even lacks the capacity to utilize outside assistance effectively. For instance, the USAID program has put money into Haiti at seven times the rate at which it has put money into the Dominican Republic, but the results in Haiti have still been much more meager, because of the country's deficiency in people and organizations of its own that could utilize the aid. Everyone familiar with Haiti whom I asked about its prospects used the words "no hope" in their answer. Most of them answered simply that they saw no hope. Those who did see hope began by acknowledging that they were in a minority and that most people saw no hope, but they themselves then went on to name some reason why they clung to hope, such as the possibilities of reforestation spreading out from Haiti's existing small forest reserves, the existence of two agricultural areas in Haiti that do produce surplus food for internal export to the capital of Port-au-Prince and the tourist enclaves on the north coast, and Haiti's remarkable achievement in abolishing its army without descending into a constant morass of secession movements and local militias.

Just as the Dominican Republic's future affects others because of globalization, Haiti also affects others through globalization. Just as with Dominicans, that effect of globalization includes the effects of Haitians living overseas—in the United States, Cuba, Mexico, South America, Canada, the Bahamas, the Lesser Antilles, and France. Even more important, though, is the "globalization" of Haiti's problems within the island of Hispaniola, through Haiti's effects on the neighboring Dominican Republic. Near the Dominican border, Haitians commute from their homes to the Dominican side for jobs that at least provide them with meals, and for wood fuel to bring back to their deforested homes. Haitian squatters try to eke out a living as farmers on Dominican land near the border, even on poor-quality land that Dominican farmers scorn. More than a million people of Haitian background live and work in the Dominican Republic, mostly illegally, attracted by the better economic opportunities and greater availability of land in the Dominican Republic, even though the latter itself is a poor country. Hence the exodus of over a million Dominicans overseas has been matched by the arrival of as many Haitians, who now constitute about 12% of the population. Haitians take low-paying and hard jobs that few Dominicans currently want for themselves—especially in the construction industry, as agricultural workers, doing the back-breaking and painful work of cutting sugarcane, in the tourist industry, as watchmen, as domestic workers, and operating bicycle transport (pedaling bicycles while carrying and balancing huge quantities of goods for sale or delivery). The Dominican economy utilizes those Haitians as low-paid laborers, but Dominicans are reluctant in return to provide education, medical care, and housing when they are strapped for funds to provide those public services to themselves. Dominicans and Haitians in the Dominican Republic are divided not only economically but also culturally: they speak different languages, dress differently, eat different foods, and on the average look differently (Haitians tending to be darker-skinned and more African in appearance).

As I listened to my Dominican friends describing the situation of Haitians in the Dominican Republic, I became astonished by the close parallels with the situation of illegal immigrants from Mexico and other Latin American countries in the United States. I heard those sentences about "jobs that Dominicans don't want," "low-paying jobs but still better than what's available for them at home," "those Haitians bring AIDS, TB, and malaria," "they speak a different language and look darker-skinned," and "we have no obligation and can't afford to provide medical care, education, and housing to illegal immigrants." In those sentences, all I had to do was to replace the words "Haitians" and "Dominicans" with "Latin American immigrants" and "American citizens," and the result would be a typical expression of American attitudes towards Latin American immigrants.

At the present rate at which Dominicans are leaving the Dominican Republic for the U.S. and Puerto Rico while Haitians are leaving Haiti for the Dominican Republic, the Republic is becoming a nation with an increasing Haitian minority, just as many parts of the United States are becoming increasingly "Hispanic" (i.e., Latin American). That makes it in the vital interests of the Dominican Republic for Haiti to solve its problems, just as it is in the vital interests of the United States for Latin America to solve its own problems. The Dominican Republic is affected more by Haiti than by any other country in the world.

Might the Dominican Republic play a constructive role in Haiti's future? At first glance, the Republic looks like a very unlikely source of solutions to Haiti's problems. The Republic is poor and has enough problems helping its own citizens. The two countries are separated by that cultural gulf that includes different languages and different self-images. There is a long, deeply rooted tradition of antagonism on both sides, with many Dominicans viewing Haiti as part of Africa and looking down on Haitians, and with many Haitians in turn suspicious of foreign meddling. Haitians and Dominicans cannot forget the history of cruelties that each country inflicted on the other. Dominicans remember Haiti's invasions of the Dominican Republic in the 19th century, including the 22-year occupation (forgetting that occupation's positive aspects, such as its abolition of slavery). Haitians remember Trujillo's worst single atrocity, his ordering the slaughter (by machete) of all 20,000 Haitians living in the northwestern Dominican Republic and parts of the Cibao Valley between October 2 and October 8, 1937. Today, there is little collaboration between the two governments, which tend to view each other warily or with hostility.

But none of these considerations changes two fundamental facts: that the Dominican environment merges continuously into the Haitian environment, and that Haiti is the country with the strongest effect upon the Dominican Republic. Some signs of collaboration between the two are starting to emerge. For example, while I was in the Dominican Republic, for the first time a group of Dominican scientists was about to travel to Haiti for joint meetings with Haitian scientists, and a return visit of the Haitian scientists to Santo Domingo was already scheduled. If the lot of Haiti is to improve at all, I don't see how that could happen without more involvement on the part of the Dominican Republic, even though that is undesired and almost unthinkable to most Dominicans today. Ultimately, though, for the Republic not to be involved with Haiti is even more unthinkable. While the Republic's own resources are scarce, at minimum it could assume a larger role as a bridge, in ways to be explored, between the outside world and Haiti.

Will Dominicans come to share those views? In the past, the Dominican people have accomplished feats much more difficult than becoming constructively engaged with Haiti. Among the many unknowns hanging over the futures of my Dominican friends, I see that as the biggest one.

CHAPTER 12

China, Lurching Giant

China's significance ■ Background ■ Air, water, soil ■ Habitat,
species, megaprojects ■ Consequences ■ Connections ■ The future ■

C hina is the world's most populous country, with about
1,300,000,000 people, or one-fifth of the world's total. In area it is
the third largest country, and in plant species diversity the third
richest. Its economy, already huge, is growing at the fastest rate of any major
country: nearly 10% per year, which is four times the growth rate of First
World economies. It has the world's highest production rate of steel, cement, aquacultured food, and television sets; both the highest production
and the highest consumption of coal, fertilizers, and tobacco; it stands near
the top in production of electricity and (soon) motor vehicles, and in consumption of timber; and it is now building the world's largest dam and
largest water-diversion project.

Marring these superlatives and achievements, China's environmental
problems are among the most severe of any major country, and are getting
worse. The long list ranges from air pollution, biodiversity losses, cropland
losses, desertification, disappearing wetlands, grassland degradation, and
increasing scale and frequency of human-induced natural disasters, to invasive species, overgrazing, river flow cessation, salinization, soil erosion, trash
accumulation, and water pollution and shortages. These and other environmental problems are causing enormous economic losses, social conflicts,
and health problems within China. All these considerations alone would
suffice to make the impact of China's environmental problems on just the
Chinese people a subject of major concern.

But China's large population, economy, and area also guarantee that its
environmental problems will not remain a domestic issue but will spill over
to the rest of the world, which is increasingly affected through sharing the
same planet, oceans, and atmosphere with China, and which in turn affects
China's environment through globalization. China's recent entry into the
World Trade Organization will expand those exchanges with other countries. For instance, China is already the largest contributor of sulfur oxides,

chlorofluorocarbons, other ozone-depleting substances, and (soon) carbon dioxide to the atmosphere; its dust and aerial pollutants are transported eastwards in the atmosphere to neighboring countries and even to North America; and it is one of the two leading importers of tropical rainforest timber, making it a driving force behind tropical deforestation.

Even more important than all those other impacts will be the proportionate increase in total human impact on the world's environments if China, with its large population, succeeds in its goal of achieving First World living standards—which also means catching up to the First World's per-capita environmental impact. As we shall see in this chapter and again in Chapter 16, those differences between First and Third World living standards, and the efforts of China and other developing countries to close that gap, have big consequences that unfortunately are usually ignored. China will also illustrate other themes of this book: the dozen groups of environmental problems facing the modern world, to be detailed in Chapter 16, and all of them serious or extreme in China; the effects of modern globalization on environmental problems; the importance of environmental issues for even the biggest of all modern societies, and not just for the small societies selected as illustrations in most of my book's other chapters; and realistic grounds for hope, despite a barrage of depressing statistics. After setting out some brief background information about China, I shall discuss the types of Chinese environmental impacts, their consequences for the Chinese people and for the rest of the world, and China's responses and future prognosis.

Let's begin with a quick overview of China's geography, population trends, and economy (map, p. 361). The Chinese environment is complex and locally fragile. Its diverse geography includes the world's highest plateau, some of the world's highest mountains, two of the world's longest rivers (the Yangtze and Yellow Rivers), many lakes, a long coastline, and a large continental shelf. Its diverse habitats range from glaciers and deserts to tropical rainforests. Within those ecosystems lie areas fragile for different reasons: for example, northern China has highly variable rainfall, plus simultaneous occurrences of winds and droughts, that make its high-altitude grasslands susceptible to dust storms and soil erosion, while conversely southern China is wet but has heavy rainstorms that cause erosion on slopes.

As for China's population, the two best-known facts about it are that it is the world's largest, and that the Chinese government (uniquely in the

modern world) instituted mandatory fertility control that dramatically decreased the population growth rate to 1.3% per year by the year 2001. That
raises the question whether China's decision will be imitated by other countries, some of which, while recoiling in horror at that solution, may thereby
find themselves drifting into even worse solutions to their population problems.

Less well known, but with significant consequences for China's human
impacts, is that the number of China's households has nevertheless been
growing at 3.5% per year over the last 15 years, more than double the
growth rate of its population during the same period. That's because household size decreased from 4.5 people per house in 1985 to 3.5 in 2000 and is
projected to decrease further to 2.7 by the year 2015. That decreased household size causes China today to have 80 million *more* households than it
would otherwise have had, an increase exceeding the total number of
households in Russia. The household size decrease results from social
changes: especially, population aging, fewer children per couple, an increase
in previously nearly non-existent divorce, and a decline in the former custom of multi-generation households with grandparents, parents, and children living under one roof. At the same time, per-capita floor area per
house increased by nearly three-fold. The net result of those increases in the
number and floor area of households is that China's human impact is increasing despite its low population growth rate.

The remaining feature of China's population trends worth stressing is
rapid urbanization. From 1953 to 2001, while China's total population
"only" doubled, the percentage of its population that is urban tripled from
13 to 38%, hence the urban population increased seven-fold to nearly half a
billion. The number of cities quintupled to almost 700, and existing cities
increased greatly in area.

For China's economy, the simplest short descriptor is "big and fast-
growing." China is the world's largest producer and consumer of coal, accounting for one-quarter of the world's total. It is also the world's largest
producer and consumer of fertilizer, accounting for 20% of world use, and
for 90% of the global increase in fertilizer use since 1981, thanks to a quin-
tupling of its own fertilizer use, now three times the world average per acre.
As the second largest producer and consumer of pesticides, China accounts
for 14% of the world total and has become a net exporter of pesticides. On
top of that, China is the largest producer of steel, the largest user of agricultural films for mulching, the second largest producer of electricity and
chemical textiles, and the third largest oil consumer. In the last two decades,

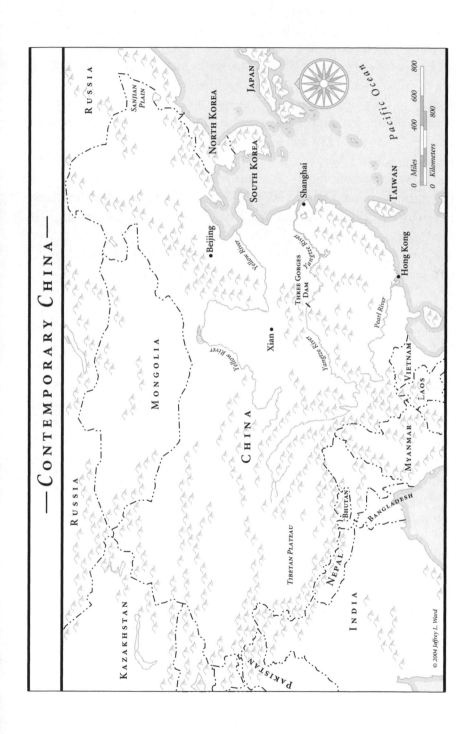

CONTEMPORARY CHINA

RUSSIA

SANJIAN PLAIN

NORTH KOREA

JAPAN

SOUTH KOREA

Shanghai

Beijing

Yellow River

Pacific Ocean

TAIWAN

Hong Kong

Three Gorges Dam

Yangtze River

Pearl River

Xian

Yangtze River

Yellow River

MONGOLIA

CHINA

RUSSIA

KAZAKHSTAN

VIETNAM

LAOS

MYANMAR

BANGLADESH

BHUTAN

NEPAL

TIBETAN PLATEAU

INDIA

PAKISTAN

0   200   400   600   800
Miles

0   200   400   600   800
Kilometers

© 2004 Jeffrey L. Ward

while its production of steel, steel products, cement, plastics, and chemical fiber were increasing 5-, 7, 10-, 19-, and 30-fold respectively, its washing machine output increased 34,000 times.

Pork used to be overwhelmingly the main meat in China. With increasing affluence, demand for beef, lamb, and chicken products has increased rapidly, to the point where per-capita egg consumption now equals that of the First World. Per-capita consumption of meat, eggs, and milk increased four-fold between 1978 and 2001. That means much more agricultural waste, because it takes 10 or 20 pounds of plants to produce one pound of meat. The annual output of animal droppings on land is already three times the output of industrial solid wastes, to which should be added the increase in fish droppings and fish food and fertilizer for aquaculture, tending to increase terrestrial and aquatic pollution respectively.

China's transportation network and vehicle fleet have grown explosively. Between 1952 and 1997 the length of railroads, motor roads, and airline routes increased 2.5-, 10-, and 108-fold. The number of motor vehicles (mostly trucks and buses) increased 15-fold between 1980 and 2001, cars 130-fold. In 1994, after the number of motor vehicles had increased 9 times, China decided to make car production one of its four so-called pillar industries, with the goal of increasing production (now especially of cars) by another factor of 4 by the year 2010. That would make China the world's third largest vehicle manufacturing country, after the U.S. and Japan. Considering how bad the air quality already is in Beijing and other cities, due mostly to motor vehicles, it will be interesting to see what urban air quality is like in 2010. The planned increase in motor vehicles will also impact the environment by requiring more land conversion into roads and parking lots.

Behind those impressive statistics on the scale and growth of China's economy lurks the fact that much of it is based on outdated, inefficient, or polluting technology. China's energy efficiency in industrial production is only half that of the First World; its paper production consumes more than twice as much water as in the First World; and its irrigation relies on inefficient surface methods responsible for water wastage, soil nutrient losses, eutrophication, and river sediment loads. Three-quarters of China's energy consumption depends on coal, the main cause of its air pollution and acid rain and a significant cause of inefficiency. For instance, China's coal-based production of ammonia, required for fertilizer and textile manufacture, consumes 42 times more water than natural-gas-based ammonia production in the First World.

Another distinctive inefficient feature of China's economy is its rapidly

expanding small-scale rural economy: its so-called township and village en-
terprises, or TVEs, with an average of only six employees per enterprise, and
especially involved in construction and in producing paper, pesticides, and
fertilizer. They account for one-third of China's production and half of its
exports but contribute disproportionately to pollution in the form of sulfur
dioxide, waste water, and solid wastes. Hence in 1995 the government declared an emergency and banned or closed 15 of the worst-polluting types
of small-scale TVEs.

China's history of environmental impacts has gone through phases. Even already by several thousand years ago, there was large-scale deforestation. After the end of World War II and the Chinese Civil War, the return of peace
in 1949 brought more deforestation, overgrazing, and soil erosion. The
years of the Great Leap Forward, from 1958 to 1965, saw a chaotic increase
in the number of factories (a four-fold increase in the two-year period
1957–1959 alone!), accompanied by still more deforestation (to obtain the
fuel needed for inefficient backyard steel production) and pollution. During
the Cultural Revolution of 1966–1976, pollution spread still further, as
many factories were relocated to deep valleys and high mountains from
coastal areas considered vulnerable in case of war. Since economic reform
began in 1978, environmental degradation has continued to increase or accelerate. China's environmental problems can be summarized under six
main headings: air, water, soil, habitat destruction, biodiversity losses, and
megaprojects.

To begin with China's most notorious pollution problem, its air quality
is dreadful, symbolized by now-familiar photographs of people having to
wear face masks on the streets of many Chinese cities (Plate 25). Air pollution in some cities is the worst in the world, with pollutant levels several
times higher than levels considered safe for people's health. Pollutants such
as nitrogen oxides and carbon dioxide are rising due to the increasing numbers of motor vehicles and the coal-dominated energy generation. Acid
rain, confined in the 1980s to just a few areas in the southwest and south,
has spread over much of the country and is now experienced in one-quarter
of Chinese cities for more than half of the rainy days each year.

Similarly, water quality in most Chinese rivers and groundwater sources
is poor and declining, due to industrial and municipal waste water discharges, and agricultural and aquacultural runoffs of fertilizers, pesticides,
and manure causing widespread eutrophication. (That term refers to

growth of excessive algal concentrations as a result of all that nutrient runoff.) About 75% of Chinese lakes, and almost all coastal seas, are polluted. Red tides in China's seas—blooms of plankton whose toxins are poisonous to fish and other ocean animals—have increased to nearly 100 per year, from only one in every five years in the 1960s. The famous Guanting Reservoir in Beijing was declared unsuitable for drinking in 1997. Only 20% of domestic waste water is treated, as compared to 80% in the First World.

Those water problems are exacerbated by shortages and waste. By world standards, China is poor in fresh water, with a quantity per person only one-quarter of the world average value. Making matters worse, even that little water is unevenly distributed, with North China having only one-fifth the per-capita water supply of South China. That underlying water shortage, plus wasteful use, causes over 100 cities to suffer from severe water shortages and occasionally even halts industrial production. Of the water required for cities and for irrigation, two-thirds depends on groundwater pumped from wells tapping aquifers. However, those aquifers are becoming depleted, permitting seawater to enter them in most coastal areas, and causing land to sink under some cities as the aquifers are becoming emptied. China also already has the world's worst problem of cessation of river flows, and that problem is becoming much worse because water continues to be drawn from rivers for use. For instance, between 1972 and 1997 there were flow stoppages on the lower Yellow River (China's second longest river) in 20 out of the 25 years, and the number of days without any flow increased from 10 days in 1988 to the astonishing total of 230 days in 1997. Even on the Yangtze and Pearl Rivers in wetter South China, flow cessation happens during the dry season and impedes ship navigation.

China's soil problems start with its being one of the world's countries most severely damaged by erosion (Plate 26), now affecting 19% of its land area and resulting in soil loss at 5 billion tons per year. Erosion is especially devastating on the Loess Plateau (the middle stretch of the Yellow River, about 70% of the plateau eroded), and increasingly on the Yangtze River, whose sediment discharge from erosion exceeds the confined discharges of the Nile and Amazon, the world's two longest rivers. By filling up China's rivers (as well as its reservoirs and lakes), sediment has shortened China's navigable river channels by 50% and restricted the size of ships that can use them. Soil quality and fertility as well as soil quantity have declined, partly because of long-term fertilizer use plus pesticide-related drastic declines in soil-renewing earthworms, thereby causing a 50% decrease in the area of cropland considered to be of high quality. Salinization, whose causes will be discussed in detail in the next chapter (Chapter 13) on Australia, has affected 9% of China's lands, mainly due to poor design and management of irrigation systems in dry areas. (This is one environmental problem that government programs have made good progress in combating and starting to reverse.) Desertification, due to overgrazing and land reclamation for agriculture, has affected more than one-quarter of China, destroying about 15% of North China's area remaining for agriculture and pastoralism within the last decade.

All of these soil problems—erosion, fertility losses, salinization, and desertification—have joined urbanization and land appropriation for mining, forestry, and aquaculture in reducing China's area of cropland. That poses a big problem for China's food security, because at the same time as its cropland has been declining, its population and per-capita food consumption have been increasing, and its area of potentially cultivatable land is limited. Cropland per person is now only one hectare, barely half of the world average, and nearly as low as the value for Northwest Rwanda discussed in Chapter 10. In addition, because China recycles very little trash, huge quantities of industrial and domestic trash are dumped into open fields, polluting soil and taking over or damaging cropland. More than two-thirds of China's cities are now surrounded by trash whose composition has changed dramatically from vegetable leftovers, dust, and coal residues to plastics, glass, metal, and wrapping paper. As my Dominican friends envisioned for their country's future (Chapter 11), a world buried in garbage will figure prominently in China's future as well.

Discussions of habitat destruction in China begin with deforestation. China is one of the world's most forest-poor countries, with only 0.3 acres of forest per person compared to a world average of 1.6, and with forests covering only 16% of China's land area (compared to 74% of Japan's). While government efforts have increased the area of single-species tree plantations and thereby slightly increased the total area considered forested, natural forests, especially old-growth forests, have been shrinking. That deforestation is a major contributor to China's soil erosion and floods. After the great floods of 1996 had caused $25 billion in damages, the even bigger 1998 floods that affected 240 million people (one-fifth of China's population) shocked the government into action, including the banning of any further logging of natural forests. Along with climate change, deforestation has probably contributed to China's increasing frequency of droughts, which now affect 30% of its cropland each year.

The other two most serious forms of habitat destruction in China besides deforestation are destruction or degradation of grasslands and wetlands. China is second only to Australia in the extent of its natural grasslands, which cover 40% of its area, mainly in the drier north. However, because of China's large population, that translates into a per-capita grassland area less than half of the world average. China's grasslands have been subject to severe damage by overgrazing, climate change, and mining and other types of development, so that 90% of China's grasslands are now considered degraded. Grass production per hectare has decreased by about 40% since the 1950s, and weeds and poisonous grass species have spread at the expense of high-quality grass species. All that degradation of grassland has implications extending beyond the mere usefulness to China of grassland for food production, because China's grasslands of the Tibetan Plateau (the world's largest high-altitude plateau) are the headwaters for major rivers of India, Pakistan, Bangladesh, Thailand, Laos, Cambodia, and Vietnam as well as of China. For example, grassland degradation has increased the frequency and severity of floods on China's Yellow and Yangtze Rivers, and has also increased the frequency and severity of dust storms in eastern China (notably in Beijing, as seen by television viewers around the world).

Wetlands have been decreasing in area, their water level has been fluctuating greatly, their capacity to mitigate floods and to store water has decreased, and wetland species have become endangered or extinct. For example, 60% of the swamps in the Sanjian Plain in the northeast, the area with China's largest freshwater swamps, have already been converted to farmland, and at the present ongoing rate of drainage the 8,000 square miles remaining of those swamps will disappear within 20 years.

Other biodiversity losses with big economic consequences include the severe degradation of both freshwater and coastal marine fisheries by overfishing and pollution, because fish consumption is rising with growing affluence. Per-capita consumption increased nearly five-fold in the past 25 years, and to that domestic consumption must be added China's growing exports of fish, molluscs, and other aquatic species. As a result, the white sturgeon has been pushed to the brink of extinction, the formerly robust Bohai prawn harvest declined 90%, formerly abundant fish species like the yellow croaker and hairtail must now be imported, the annual take of wild fish in the Yangtze River has declined 75%, and that river had to be closed to fishing for the first time ever in 2003. More generally, China's biodiversity is very high, with over 10% of the world's plant and terrestrial vertebrate species. However, about one-fifth of China's native species (including its best-known one, the Giant Panda) are now endangered, and many other distinctive rare ones (such as Chinese Alligators and ginkgos) are already at risk of extinction.

The flip side of these declines in native species has been a rise in invasive species. China has had a long history of intentionally introducing species considered beneficial. Now, with the recent 60-fold increase in international trade, those intentional introductions are being joined by accidental intro- ductions of many species that no one would consider beneficial. For exam- ple, in Shanghai Harbor alone between 1986 and 1990, examination of imported materials carried by 349 ships from 30 countries revealed as con- taminants almost 200 species of foreign weeds. Some of those invasive plants, insects, and fish have gone on to establish themselves as pests and weeds causing huge economic damage to Chinese agriculture, aquaculture, forestry, and livestock production.

If all that were not enough, under way in China are the world's largest development projects, all expected to cause severe environmental problems. The Three Gorges Dam of the Yangtze River—the world's largest dam, started in 1993 and projected for completion in 2009—aims to provide electricity, flood control, and improved navigation at a financial cost of $30 billion, social costs of uprooting millions of people, and environmental costs associated with soil erosion and the disruption of a major ecosystem (that of the world's third longest river). Still more expensive is the South-to- North Water Diversion Project, which began in 2002, is not scheduled for completion until around 2050, and is projected to cost $59 billion, to spread pollution, and to cause water imbalance in China's longest river. Even that project will be exceeded by the projected development of currently under- developed western China, making up over half of the country's land area and viewed by China's leaders as the key to national development.

Let's now pause to distinguish, as elsewhere in this book, between conse- quences for animals and plants by themselves, and consequences for people. Recent developments in China are clearly bad news for Chinese earthworms and yellow croakers, but how much difference does it all make for Chinese people? The consequences for them can be partitioned into economic costs, health costs, and exposure to natural disasters. Here are some estimates or examples for each of those three categories.

As examples of economic costs, let's start with small ones and proceed to larger ones. A small cost is the mere $72 million per year being spent to curb the spread of a single weed, the alligator weed that was introduced from Brazil as pig forage and escaped to infest gardens, sweet potato fields, and citrus groves. Also a bargain is the annual loss of just $250 million arising from factory closures due to water shortages in a single city, Xian. Sandstorms inflict damage of about $540 million per year, and losses of crops and forests due to acid rain amount to about $730 million per year. More serious are the $6 billion costs of the "green wall" of trees being built to shield Beijing against sand and dust, and the $7 billion per year of losses created by pest species other than alligator weed. We enter the zone of impressive numbers when we consider the onetime cost of the 1996 floods ($27 billion, but still cheaper than the 1998 floods), the annual direct losses due to desertification ($42 billion), and the annual losses due to water and air pollution ($54 billion). The combination of the latter two items alone costs China the equivalent of 14% of its gross domestic product each year.

Three items may be selected to give an indication of health consequences. Average blood lead levels in Chinese city-dwellers are nearly double the levels considered elsewhere in the world to be dangerously high and to put at risk the mental development of children. About 300,000 deaths per year, and $54 billion of health costs (8% of the gross national product), are attributed to air pollution. Smoking deaths amount to about 730,000 per year and are rising, because China is the world's largest consumer and producer of tobacco and is home to the most smokers (320 million of them, one-quarter of the world's total, smoking an average of 1,800 cigarettes per year per person).

China is noted for the frequency, number, extent, and damage of its natural disasters. Some of these—especially dust storms, landslides, droughts, and floods—are closely related to human environmental impacts and have become more frequent as those impacts have increased. For instance, dust storms have increased in frequency and severity as more land has been laid bare by deforestation, overgrazing, erosion, and partly human-caused droughts. From A.D. 300 to 1950 dust storms used to afflict northwestern China on the average once every 31 years; from 1950 to 1990, once every 20 months; and since 1990, almost every year. The huge dust storm of May 5, 1993, killed about a hundred people. Droughts have increased because of deforestation interrupting the rain-producing natural hydro-logical cycle, and perhaps also because of the draining and overuse of lakes and wetlands and hence the decrease in water surfaces for evaporation. The area of cropland damaged each year by droughts is now about 60,000 square miles, double the annual area damaged in the 1950s. Flooding has greatly increased because of deforestation; the 1996 and 1998 floods were the worst in recent memory. The alternating occurrence of droughts and floods has also become more frequent and is more damaging than ei-ther disaster alone, because droughts first destroy vegetation cover, then floods on bare ground cause worse erosion than would have been the case otherwise.

Even if China's people had no connection through trade and travel with people elsewhere, China's large territory and population would guarantee effects on other peoples merely because China is releasing its wastes and gases into the same ocean and atmosphere. But China's connections to the rest of the world through trade, investment, and foreign aid have been ac-celerating almost exponentially in the last two decades, although trade (now $621 billion per year) was negligible before 1980 and foreign investment in China still negligible as recently as 1991. Among other consequences, the development of export trade has been a driving force behind increased pol-lution in China, because the highly polluting and inefficient little rural in-dustries (the TVEs) that produce half of China's exports in effect ship their finished products abroad but leave behind their pollutants in China. In 1991 China became the country annually receiving the second highest amount of foreign investment behind the U.S., and in 2002 China moved into first place by receiving record investments of $53 billion. Foreign aid between 1981 and 2000 included $100 million from international NGOs, a large sum as measured by NGO budgets but a paltry amount compared to China's other sources: half a billion dollars from the United Nations Devel-opment program, $10 billion from Japan's International Development Agency, $11 billion from the Asian Development Bank, and $24 billion from the World Bank.

All of those transfers of money contribute to fueling China's rapid eco-nomic growth and environmental degradation. Let's now consider other ways in which the rest of the world influences China, then how China influ-ences the rest of the world. These reciprocal influences are aspects of the modern buzzword "globalization," which is important for the purposes of this book. The interconnectedness of societies in today's world causes some of the most important differences (to be explored in Chapter 16) between how environmental problems played out in the past on Easter Island or among the Maya and Anasazi, and how they play out today.

Among the bad things that China receives from the rest of the world, I already mentioned economically damaging invasive species. Another large-scale import that will surprise readers is garbage (Plate 27). Some First World countries reduce their mountains of garbage by paying China to accept untreated garbage, including wastes containing toxic chemicals. In addition, China's expanding manufacturing economy and industries accept garbage/scrap that could serve as cheap sources of recoverable raw materials. Just to take one item as an example, in September 2002 a Chinese customs office in Zhejiang Province recorded a 400-ton shipment of "electronic garbage" originating from the U.S., and consisting of scrap electronic equipment and parts such as broken or obsolete color TV sets, computer monitors, photocopiers, and keyboards. While statistics on the amount of such garbage imported are inevitably incomplete, available numbers show an increase from one million to 11 million tons from 1990 to 1997, and an increase in First World garbage transshipped to China via Hong Kong from 2.3 to over 3 million tons per year from 1998 to 2002. This represents direct transfer of pollution from the First World to China.

Even worse than garbage, while many foreign companies have helped China's environment by transferring advanced technology to China, others have hurt it by transferring pollution-intensive industries (PIIs), including technologies now illegal in the country of origin. Some of these technologies are then in turn transferred from China to still less developed countries. As one example, in 1992 the technology for producing Fuyaman, a pesticide against aphids banned in Japan 17 years earlier, was sold to a Sino-Japanese joint company in Fujian Province, where it proceeded to poison and kill many people and to cause serious environmental pollution. In Guangdong Province alone the amount of ozone-destroying chlorofluorocarbons imported by foreign investors reached 1,800 tons in 1996, thereby making it more difficult for China to eliminate its contribution to world ozone destruction. As of 1995, China was home to an estimated 16,998 PII firms with a combined industrial product of about $50 billion.

Turning now from China's imports to its exports in a broad sense, China's high native biodiversity means that China gives back to other countries many invasive species that were already well adapted to competing in China's species-rich environment. For instance, the three best-known pests that have wiped out numerous North American tree populations—the chestnut blight, the misnamed "Dutch" elm disease, and the Asian long-horned beetle—all originated in China or else somewhere nearby in East Asia. Chestnut blight already wiped out native chestnut trees in the U.S.; Dutch elm disease has been eliminating the elm trees that used to be a hallmark of New England towns while I was growing up there over 60 years ago; and the Asian long-horned beetle, first discovered in the U.S. in 1996 attacking maple and ash trees, has the potential for causing U.S. tree losses of up to $41 billion, more than those due to the other two of those pests combined. Another recent arrival, China's grass carp, is now established in rivers and lakes of 45 U.S. states, where it competes with native fish species and causes large changes in aquatic plant, plankton, and invertebrate communities. Still another species of which China has an abundant population, which has large ecological and economic impacts, and which China is exporting in increasing numbers is *Homo sapiens.* For instance, China has now moved into third place as a source of legal immigration into Australia (Chapter 13), and significant numbers of illegal as well as legal immigrants crossing the Pacific Ocean reach even the U.S.

While inadvertently or intentionally exported Chinese insects, freshwater fish, and people reach overseas countries by ship and plane, other inadvertent exports arrive in the atmosphere. China became the world's largest producer and consumer of gaseous ozone-depleting substances, such as chlorofluorocarbons, after First World countries phased them out in 1995. China also now contributes to the atmosphere 12% of the world's carbon dioxide emissions that play a major role in global warming. If current trends continue—emissions rising in China, steady in the U.S., declining elsewhere—China will become the world's leader in carbon dioxide emissions, accounting for 40% of the world's total, by the year 2050. China already leads the world in production of sulfur oxides, with an output double that of the U.S. Propelled eastwards by winds, the pollutant-laden dust, sand, and soil originating from China's deserts, degraded pastures, and fallow farmland get blown to Korea, Japan, Pacific islands, and across the Pacific within a week to the U.S. and Canada. Those aerial particles are the result of China's coal-burning economy, deforestation, overgrazing, erosion, and destructive agricultural methods.

The next exchange between China and other countries involves an import doubling as an export: imported timber, hence exported deforestation. China ranks third in the world in timber consumption, because wood provides 40% of the nation's rural energy in the form of firewood, and provides almost all the raw material for the paper and pulp industry and also the panels and lumber for the construction industry. But a growing gap has been developing between China's increasing demand for wood products and its declining domestic supply, especially since the national logging ban went into effect after the floods of 1998. Hence China's wood imports have increased six-fold since the ban. As an importer of tropical lumber from countries on all three continents that span the tropics (especially from Malaysia, Gabon, Papua New Guinea, and Brazil), China now stands second only to Japan, which it is rapidly overtaking. It also imports timber from the temperate zone, especially from Russia, New Zealand, the U.S., Germany, and Australia. With China's entrance into the World Trade Organization, those timber imports are expected to increase even more, because tariffs on wood products are about to be reduced from a rate of 15–20% to 2–3%. In effect, this means that China, like Japan, will be conserving its own forests, but only by exporting deforestation to other countries, several of which (including Malaysia, Papua New Guinea, and Australia) have already reached or are on the road to catastrophic deforestation.

Potentially more important than all of these other impacts is a rarely discussed consequence of the aspirations of China's people, like other people in developing countries, to a First World lifestyle. That abstract phrase means many specific things to an individual Third World citizen: acquiring a house, appliances, utensils, clothes, and consumer products manufactured commercially by energy-consuming processes, not made at home or locally by hand; having access to manufactured modern medicines, and to doctors and dentists educated and equipped at much expense; eating abundant food grown at high production rates with synthetic fertilizers, not with animal manure or plant mulches; eating some industrially processed food; traveling by motor vehicle (preferably one's own car), not by walking or bicycle; and having access to other products manufactured elsewhere and arriving by motor vehicle transport, not just to local products carried to consumers. All Third World peoples of whom I am aware—even those trying to retain or re-create some of their traditional lifestyle—also value at least some elements of this First World lifestyle.

The global consequences of everybody aspiring to the lifestyle currently enjoyed by First World citizens are well illustrated by China, because it combines the world's largest population with the fastest-growing economy. Total productions or consumptions are products of population sizes times per-capita production or consumption rates. For China, those total productions are already high because of its huge population, and despite its per-

capita rates still being very low: for instance, only 9% of per-capita consumption rates of the leading industrial countries in the case of four major
industrial metals (steel, aluminum, copper, and lead). But China is progressing rapidly towards its goal of achieving a First World economy. If
China's per-capita consumption rates do rise to First World levels, and
even if nothing else about the world changed—e.g., even if population and
production/consumption rates everywhere else remained unchanged—
then that production/consumption rate increase alone would translate (as
multiplied by China's population) into an increase in total *world* production or consumption of 94% in that same case of industrial metals. In other
words, China's achievement of First World standards will approximately
double the entire world's human resource use and environmental impact.
But it is doubtful whether even the world's current human resource use and
impact can be sustained. Something has to give way. That is the strongest
reason why China's problems automatically become the world's problems.

China's leaders used to believe that humans can and should conquer Nature, that environmental damage was a problem affecting only capitalist
societies, and that socialist societies were immune to it. Now, facing overwhelming signs of China's own severe environmental problems, they know
better. The shift in thinking began as early as 1972, when China sent a dele-
gation to the First United Nations Conference on the Human Environment.
The year 1973 saw the establishment of the government's so-called Leading
Group for Environmental Protection, which morphed in 1998 (the year of
the great floods) into the State Environmental Protection Administration.
In 1983 environmental protection was declared a basic national principle—
in theory. In reality, although much effort has been made to control environmental degradation, economic development still takes priority and
remains the chief criterion for evaluating government officials' performance. Many environmental protection laws and policies that have been
adopted on paper are not effectively implemented or enforced.

What does the future hold for China? Of course, the same question
arises everywhere in the world: the development of environmental problems is accelerating, the development of attempted solutions is also accelerating, which horse will win the race? In China this question has special
urgency, not only because of China's already-discussed scale and impact on
the world, but also because of a feature of Chinese history that may be
termed "lurching." (I use this term in its neutral strict sense of "swaying

suddenly from side to side," not in its pejorative sense of the gait of a drunk person.) By this metaphor, I am thinking of what seems to me the most distinctive feature of Chinese history, which I discussed in my earlier book *Guns, Germs, and Steel*. Because of geographic factors—such as China's relatively smooth coastline, its lack of major peninsulas as large as Italy and Spain/Portugal, its lack of major islands as large as Britain and Ireland, and its parallel-flowing major rivers—China's geographic core was unified already in 221 B.C. and has remained unified for most of the time since then, whereas geographically fragmented Europe has never been unified politically. That unity enabled China's rulers to command changes over a larger area than any European ruler could ever command—both changes for the better, and changes for the worse, often in rapid alternation (hence "lurching"). China's unity and decisions by emperors may contribute to explaining why China at the time of Renaissance Europe developed the world's best and largest ships, sent fleets to India and Africa, and then dismantled those fleets and left overseas colonization to much smaller European states; and why China began, and then did not pursue, its own incipient industrial revolution.

The strengths and risks of China's unity have persisted into recent times, as China continues to lurch on major policies affecting its environment and its population. On the one hand, China's leaders have been able to solve problems on a scale scarcely possible for European and American leaders: for instance, by mandating a one-child policy to reduce population growth, and by ending logging nationally in 1998. On the other hand, China's leaders have also succeeded in creating messes on a scale scarcely possible for European and American leaders: for instance, by the chaotic transition of the Great Leap Forward, by dismantling the national educational system in the Cultural Revolution, and (some would say) by the emerging environmental impacts of the three megaprojects.

As for the outcome of China's current environmental problems, all one can say for sure is that things will get worse before they get better, because of time lags and the momentum of damage already under way. One big factor acting both for the worse and for the better is the anticipated increase in China's international trade as a result of its joining the World Trade Organization (WTO), thereby lowering or abolishing tariffs and increasing exports and imports of cars, textiles, agricultural products, and many other commodities. Already, China's export industries tend to send manufactured finished products overseas and to leave in China the pollutants involved in their manufacture; there will presumably now be more of that. Some of

China's imports, such as garbage and cars, have already been bad for the environment; there may be more of that too. On the other hand, some countries belonging to the WTO adhere to environmental standards much stricter than China's, and that will force China to adopt those international standards as a condition of its exports being admitted by those countries. More agricultural imports may permit China to decrease its use of fertilizers, pesticides, and low-productivity cropland, while importation of oil and natural gas will let China decrease pollution from its burning of coals. A two-edged consequence of WTO membership may be that, by increasing imports and thereby decreasing Chinese domestic production, it will merely enable China to transfer environmental damage from China itself to overseas, as has already happened in the shift from domestic logging to imported timber (thereby in effect paying countries other than China to suffer the harmful consequences of deforestation).

A pessimist will note many dangers and bad harbingers already operating in China. Among generalized dangers, economic growth rather than environmental protection or sustainability is still China's priority. Public environmental awareness is low, in part because of China's low investment in education, less than half that of First World countries as a proportion of gross national production. With 20% of the world's population, China accounts for only 1% of the world's outlay on education. A college or university education for children is beyond the means of most Chinese parents, because one year's tuition would consume the average salary of one city worker or three rural workers. China's existing environmental laws were largely written piecemeal, lack effective implementation and evaluation of long-term consequences, and are in need of a systems approach: for instance, there is no overall framework for protection of China's rapidly vanishing wetlands, despite individual laws affecting them. Local officials of China's State Environmental Protection Administration (SEPA) are appointed by local governments rather than by upper-level officials of the SEPA itself, so that local governments often block enforcement of national environmental laws and regulations. Prices for important environmental resources are set so low as to encourage waste: e.g., a ton of Yellow River water for use in irrigation costs only between $1/10$ and $1/100$ of a small bottle of spring water, thereby removing any financial incentive for irrigation farmers to conserve water. Land is owned by the government and is leased by farmers, but may be leased to a series of different farmers within a short time span, so that farmers lack incentive to make long-term investments in their land or to take good care of it.

The Chinese environment also faces more specific dangers. Already under way are a big increase in the number of cars, the three megaprojects, and the rapid disappearance of wetlands, whose harmful consequences will continue to accumulate in the future. The projected decrease in Chinese household size to 2.7 people by the year 2015 will add 126 million new households (more than the total number of U.S. households), even if China's population size itself remains constant. With growing affluence and hence growing meat and fish consumption, environmental problems from meat production and aquaculture, such as pollution from all the animal and fish droppings and eutrophication from uneaten feed for fish, will increase. Already, China is the world's largest producer of aquaculture-grown food, and is the sole country in which more fish and aquatic foods are obtained from aquaculture than from wild fisheries. The world consequences of China's catching up to First World levels of meat consumption exemplify the broader issue, which I already illustrated by metal consumption, of the current gap between per-capita First World and Third World consumption and production rates. China will of course not tolerate being told not to aspire to First World levels. But the world cannot sustain China and other Third World countries and current First World countries all operating at First World levels.

Offsetting all of those dangers and discouraging signs, there are also important promising signs. Both WTO membership and the impending 2008 Olympic Games in China have spurred the Chinese government to pay more attention to environmental problems. For instance, a $6 billion "green wall" or tree belt is now under development around Beijing to protect the city against dust and sandstorms. To reduce air pollution in Beijing, its city government ordered that motor vehicles be converted to permit the use of natural gas and liquefied petroleum gas. China phased out lead in gasoline in little more than a year, something that Europe and the U.S. took many years to achieve. It recently decided to establish fuel efficiency minima for automobiles, including even SUVs. New cars are required to meet exacting emission standards prevailing in Europe.

China is already making a big effort to protect its outstanding biodiversity with 1,757 nature reserves covering 13% of its land area, not to mention all of its zoos, botanical gardens, wildlife breeding centers, museums, and gene and cell banks. China uses some distinctive, environmentally friendly, traditional technologies on a large scale, such as the common South Chinese practice of raising fish in irrigated rice fields. That recycles the fish droppings as natural fertilizer, increases rice production, uses fish to control

insect pests and weeds, decreases herbicide and pesticide and synthetic fertilizer use, and yields more dietary protein and carbohydrate without increasing environmental damage. Encouraging signs in reafforestation are
the initiation of major tree plantations in 1978, and in 1998 the national
ban on logging and the start of the Natural Forest Conservation Program to
reduce the risk of further destructive flooding. Since 1990, China has combatted desertification on 15,000 square miles of land by reafforestation and
fixation of sand dunes. The Grain-to-Green program, begun in 2000, gives
grain subsidies to farmers who convert cropland to forest or grassland, and
is thereby reducing the use of environmentally sensitive steep hillsides for
agriculture.

How will it all end up? Like the rest of the world, China is lurching between accelerating environmental damage and accelerating environmental
protection. China's large population and large growing economy, and its
current and historic centralization, mean that China's lurches involve more
momentum than those of any other country. The outcome will affect not
just China, but the whole world as well. While I was writing this chapter, I
found my own feelings lurching between despair at the mind-numbing
litany of depressing details, and hope inspired by the drastic and rapidly implemented measures of environmental protection that China has already
adopted. Because of China's size and its unique form of government, top-
down decision-making has operated on a far larger scale there than anywhere else, utterly dwarfing the impacts of the Dominican Republic's
President Balaguer. My best-case scenario for the future is that China's government will recognize that its environmental problems pose an even graver
threat that did its problem of population growth. It may then conclude that
China's interests require environmental policies as bold, and as effectively
carried out, as its family planning policies.

CHAPTER 13

"Mining" Australia

Australia's significance ■ Soils ■ Water ■ Distance ■ Early history ■
Imported values ■ Trade and immigration ■ Land degradation ■
Other environmental problems ■ Signs of hope and change ■

Mining in the literal sense—i.e., the mining of coal, iron, and so on—
is a key to Australia's economy today, providing the largest share of
its export earnings. In a metaphorical sense, however, mining is
also a key to Australia's environmental history and to its current predicament. That's because the essence of mining is to exploit resources that do
not renew themselves with time, and hence to deplete those resources. Since
gold in the ground doesn't breed more gold and one thus has no need to
take account of gold renewal rates, miners extract gold from a gold lode as
rapidly as is economically feasible, until the lode is exhausted. Mining minerals may thus be contrasted with exploiting renewable resources—such as
forests, fish, and topsoil—that do regenerate themselves by biological reproduction or by soil formation. Renewable resources can be exploited indefinitely, provided that one removes them at a rate less than the rate at which
they regenerate. If however one exploits forests, fish, or topsoil at rates exceeding their renewal rates, they too will eventually be depleted to extinction, like the gold in a gold mine.

Australia has been and still is "mining" its renewable resources as if they
were mined minerals. That is, they are being overexploited at rates faster
than their renewal rates, with the result that they are declining. At present
rates, Australia's forests and fisheries will disappear long before its coal and
iron reserves, which is ironic in view of the fact that the former are renewable but the latter aren't.

While many other countries today besides Australia are mining their environments, Australia is an especially suitable choice for this final case study
of past and present societies, for several reasons. It is a First World country,
unlike Rwanda, Haiti, the Dominican Republic, and China, but like the
countries in which most of the likely readers of this book live. Among First
World countries, its population and economy are much smaller and less

complex than are those of the U.S., Europe, or Japan, so that the Australian situation is more easily grasped. Ecologically, the Australian environment is exceptionally fragile, the most fragile of any First World country except perhaps Iceland. As a consequence, many problems that could eventually become crippling in other First World countries and already are so in some Third World countries—such as overgrazing, salinization, soil erosion, introduced species, water shortages, and man-made droughts—have already become severe in Australia. That is, while Australia shows no prospects of collapsing like Rwanda and Haiti, it instead gives us a foretaste of problems that actually will arise elsewhere in the First World if present trends continue. Yet Australia's prospects for solving those problems give me hope and are not depressing. Then, too, Australia has a well educated populace, a high standard of living, and relatively honest political and economic institutions by world standards. Hence Australia's environmental problems cannot be dismissed as products of ecological mismanagement by an uneducated, desperately impoverished populace and grossly corrupt government and businesses, as one might perhaps be inclined to explain away environmental problems in some other countries.

Still another virtue of Australia as the subject of this chapter is that it illustrates strongly the five factors whose interplay I have identified throughout this book as useful for understanding possible ecological declines or collapses of societies. Humans have had obvious massive impacts on the Australian environment. Climate change is exacerbating those impacts today. Australia's friendly relations with Britain as a trade partner and model society have shaped Australian environmental and population policies. While modern Australia has not been invaded by outside enemies—bombed, yes, but not invaded—Australian perception of actual and potential overseas enemies has also shaped Australian environmental and population policies. Australia also displays the importance of cultural values, including some imported ones that could be viewed as inappropriate to the Australian landscape, for understanding environmental impacts. Perhaps more than any other First World citizens known to me, Australians are beginning to think radically about the central question: which of our traditional core values can we retain, and which ones instead no longer serve us well in today's world?

A final reason for my choosing Australia for this chapter is that it's a country that I love, of which I have long experience, and which I can describe both from firsthand knowledge and sympathetically. I first visited Australia in 1964, en route to New Guinea. Since then I have returned dozens of times, including for a sabbatical at Australian National University in Australia's capital city of Canberra. During that sabbatical I bonded to and imprinted on Australia's beautiful eucalyptus woodlands, which continue to fill me with a sense of peace and wonder as do just two other of the world's habitats, Montana coniferous forest and New Guinea rainforest. Australia and Britain are the only countries to which I have seriously considered emigrating. Thus, after beginning this book's series of case studies with the Montana environment that I learned to love as a teenager, I wanted to close the series with another that I came to love later in my life.

For purposes of understanding modern human impacts on the Australian environment, three features of that environment are particularly important: Australian soils, especially their nutrient and salt levels; availability of freshwater; and distances, both within Australia and also between Australia and its overseas trading partners and potential enemies.

When one starts to think of Australian environmental problems, the first thing that comes to mind is water shortage and deserts. In fact, Australia's soils have caused even bigger problems than has its water availability. Australia is the most unproductive continent: the one whose soils have on the average the lowest nutrient levels, the lowest plant growth rates, and the lowest productivity. That's because Australian soils are mostly so old that they have become leached of their nutrients by rain over the course of billions of years. The oldest surviving rocks in the Earth's crust, nearly four billion years old, are in the Murchison Range of Western Australia.

Soils that have been leached of nutrients can have their nutrient levels renewed by three major processes, all of which have been deficient in Australia compared to other continents. First, nutrients can be renewed by volcanic eruptions spewing fresh material from within the Earth onto the Earth's surface. While this has been a major factor in creating fertile soils in many countries, such as Java, Japan, and Hawaii, only a few small areas of eastern Australia have had volcanic activity within the last hundred million years. Second, advances and retreats of glaciers strip, dig up, grind up, and redeposit the Earth's crust, and those soils redeposited by glaciers (or else blown by the wind from glacial redeposits) tend to be fertile. Almost half of North America's area, about 7 million square miles, has been glaciated within the last million years, but less than 1% of the Australian mainland: just about 20 square miles in the southeastern Alps, plus a thousand square miles of the Australian offshore island of Tasmania. Finally, slow uplift of crust also brings up new soils and has contributed to the fertility of large parts of North America, India, and Europe. However, again only a few small areas of Australia have been uplifted within the last hundred million years, mainly in the Great Dividing Range of southeastern Australia and in the area of South Australia around Adelaide (map, p. 386). As we shall see, those small fractions of the Australian landscape that have recently had their soils renewed by volcanism, glaciation, or uplift are exceptions to Australia's otherwise prevalent pattern of unproductive soils, and contribute disproportionately today to modern Australia's agricultural productivity.

The low average productivity of Australian soils has had major economic consequences for Australian agriculture, forestry, and fisheries. Such nutrients as were present in arable soils at the onset of European agriculture quickly became exhausted. In effect, Australia's first farmers were inadvertently mining their soils for nutrients. Thereafter, nutrients have had to be supplied artificially in the form of fertilizer, thus increasing agricultural production costs compared to those in more fertile soils overseas. Low soil productivity means low growth rates and low average yields of crops. Hence a larger area of land has to be cultivated in Australia than elsewhere to obtain equivalent crop yields, so that fuel costs for agricultural machinery such as tractors and sowers and harvesters (approximately proportional to the area of land that must be covered by the machines) also tend to be relatively high. An extreme case of infertile soils occurs in southwestern Australia, Australia's so-called wheat belt and one of its most valuable agricultural areas, where wheat is grown on sandy soils leached of nutrients and essentially all nutrients must be added artificially as fertilizer. In effect, the Australian wheat belt is a gigantic flowerpot in which (just as in a real flowerpot) the sand provides nothing more than the physical substrate, and where the nutrients have to be supplied.

As a result of the extra expenses for Australian agriculture due to disproportionately high fertilizer and fuel costs, Australian farmers selling to local Australian markets sometimes cannot compete against overseas growers who ship the same crops across the ocean to Australia, despite the added costs of that overseas transport. For example, with modern globalization, it is cheaper to grow oranges in Brazil and ship the resulting orange juice concentrate 8,000 miles to Australia than to buy orange juice produced from Australian citrus trees. The same is true of Canadian pork and bacon compared to their Australian equivalents. Conversely, only in some specialized "niche markets"—i.e., crops and animal products with high added value beyond ordinary growing costs, such as wine—can Australian farmers compete successfully in overseas markets.

A second economic consequence of low Australian soil productivity involves agroforestry, or tree agriculture, as discussed for Japan in Chapter 9. In Australian forests most of the nutrients are actually in the trees themselves, not in the soils. Hence when the native forests that the first European settlers encountered had been cut down, and when modern Australians had either logged the regrowing natural forests or invested in agroforestry by establishing tree plantations, tree growth rates have been low in Australia compared to those in other timber-producing countries. Ironically, Australia's leading native timber tree (the blue gum of Tasmania) is now being grown more cheaply in many overseas countries than in Australia itself.

The third consequence surprised me and may surprise many readers. One doesn't immediately think of fisheries as dependent on soil productivity: after all, fish live in rivers and in the ocean, not in soils. However, all of the nutrients in rivers, and at least some of those in oceans near the coastline, come from the soils drained by the rivers and then carried out into the ocean. Hence Australia's rivers and coastal waters are also relatively unproductive, with the result that Australia's fisheries have been quickly mined and overexploited like its farmlands and its forests. One Australian marine fishery after another has been overfished to the point of becoming uneconomic, often within just a few years of the fishery's discovery. Today, out of the nearly 200 countries in the world, Australia has the third-largest exclusive marine zone surrounding it, but it ranks only 55th among the world's countries in the value of its marine fisheries, while the value of its freshwater fisheries is now negligible.

A further feature of Australia's low soil productivity is that the problem was not perceptible to the first European settlers. Instead, when they encountered magnificent extensive woodlands that included what may have been the tallest trees in the modern world (the blue gums of Victoria's Gippsland, up to 400 feet tall), they were deceived by appearances into thinking that the land was highly productive. But after loggers had removed the first standing crop of trees, and after sheep had grazed the standing crop of grass, the settlers were surprised to discover that trees and grass grew back very slowly, that the land was agriculturally uneconomic, and that in many areas it had to be abandoned after farmers and pastoralists had made big capital investments in building homes, fences, and buildings and making other agricultural improvements. From early colonial times continuing until today, Australian land use has gone through many such cycles of land clearance, investment, bankruptcy, and abandonment.

All those economic problems of Australian agriculture, forestry, fisheries, and failed land development are consequences of the low productivity of Australian soils. The other big problem of Australia's soils is that in many areas they are not only low in nutrients but also high in salt, from three causes. In southwestern Australia's wheat belt the salt in the ground arises from its having been carried inland over the course of millions of years by sea breezes off the adjacent Indian Ocean. In southeastern Australia, Australia's other area of most productive farmland rivaling the wheat belt, the basin of Australia's largest river system, the Murray and Darling Rivers, lies at low elevations and has been repeatedly inundated by the sea and then drained again, leaving much of the salt behind. Still another low-lying basin in Australia's inland was formerly filled by a freshwater lake that did not drain to the sea, became salty by evaporation (like Utah's Great Salt Lake and Israel's and Jordan's Dead Sea), and eventually dried out, leaving behind salt deposits that became carried by winds to other parts of eastern Australia. Some Australian soils contain more than 200 pounds of salt per square yard of surface area. We shall discuss later the consequences of all that salt in the soil: briefly, they include the problem that the salt is easily brought to the surface by land clearance and irrigation agriculture, resulting in salty topsoils in which no crop can grow (Plate 28). Just as Australia's first farmers, without modern analyses of soil chemistry, could not be aware of the nutrient poverty of Australian soils, they similarly could not be aware of all that salt in the ground. They could no more anticipate the problem of salinization than of nutrient depletion resulting from agriculture.

Whereas the infertility and salinity of Australia's soils were invisible to the first farmers and are not well known outside Australia among the lay public today, Australia's water problems are obvious and familiar, such that "desert" is the first association of most people overseas to mention of the Australian environment. That reputation is justified: a disproportionately large fraction of Australia's area has low rainfall or is extreme desert where agriculture would be impossible without irrigation. Much of Australia's area remains useless today for any form of agriculture or pastoralism. In those areas where food production is nevertheless possible, the usual pattern is that rainfall is higher near the coast than inland, so that as one proceeds inland one first encounters farmland for growing crops, plus half of

Autralia's cattle maintained at high stocking rates; farther inland, sheep stations; still farther inland, cattle stations (the other half of Australia's cattle, maintained at very low stocking rates), because it remains economic to raise cattle in areas with lower rainfall than sheep; and finally, still farther inland, the desert where there is no food production of any sort.

A more subtle problem with Australia's rainfall than its low average values is its unpredictability. In many parts of the world supporting agriculture, the season in which rain falls is predictable from year to year: for example, in Southern California where I live, one can be virtually certain that whatever rain falls will be concentrated in the winter, and that there will be little or no rain in the summer. In many of those productive overseas agriculture areas, not only rain's seasonality but also its occurrence is relatively reliable from year to year: major droughts are infrequent, and a farmer can go to the effort and expense of plowing and planting each year with the expectation that there will be enough rain for that crop to mature.

Over most of Australia, however, rainfall depends upon the so-called ENSO (the El Niño Southern Oscillation), which means that rain is unpredictable from year to year within a decade, and is even more unpredictable from decade to decade. The first European farmers and herders to settle in Australia had no way of knowing about Australia's ENSO-driven climate, because the phenomenon is difficult to detect in Europe, and it is only within recent decades that it has become recognized even by professional climatologists. In many areas of Australia the first farmers and herders had the misfortune to arrive during a string of wet years. Hence they were deceived into misjudging the Australian climate, and they commenced raising crops or sheep in the expectation that the favorable conditions greeting their eyes were the norm. In fact, in most of Australia's farmlands the rainfall is sufficient to raise crops to maturity in only a fraction of all years: not more than half of all years at most locations, and in some agricultural areas only in two years out of 10. That contributes to making Australian agriculture expensive and uneconomic: the farmer goes to the expense of plowing and sowing, and then in half or more of years there is no resulting crop. An additional unfortunate consequence is that, when the farmer plows the ground and plows underground whatever cover of weeds has sprung up since the last harvest, bare soil becomes exposed. If the crops that the farmer then sows do not mature, the soil is left bare, not even covered by weeds, and thus exposed to erosion. Thus, the unpredictability of Australia's rainfall makes growing crops more expensive in the short run, and increases erosion in the long run.

The principal exception to Australia's ENSO-driven pattern of unpredictable rain is the wheat belt of its southwest, where (at least until recently) the winter rains came reliably from year to year, and where a farmer could count on a successful wheat crop almost every year. That reliability propelled wheat within recent decades to overtake both wool and meat as Australia's most valuable agricultural export. As already mentioned, that wheat belt also happens to be the area with particularly extreme problems of low soil fertility and high salinity. But global climate change in recent years has been undermining even that compensating advantage of predictable winter rains: they have declined dramatically in the wheat belt since 1973, while increasingly frequent summer rains there fall on harvested bare ground and cause increased salinization. Thus, as I mentioned for Montana in Chapter 1, global climate change is producing both winners and losers, and Australia will be a loser even more than will Montana.

Australia lies largely within the temperate zones, but it lies thousands of miles overseas from other temperate-zone countries that are potential export markets for Australian products. Hence Australian historians speak of the "tyranny of distance" as an important factor in Australia's development. That expression refers to the long overseas ship journeys making transport costs per pound or per unit of volume for Australian exports higher than for exports from the New World to Europe, so that only products with low bulk and high value could be exported economically from Australia. Originally in the 19th century, minerals and wool were the main such exports. Around 1900, when refrigeration of ship cargo became economic, Australia also began to export meat overseas, particularly to England. (I recall an Australian friend who disliked the British, and who worked in a meat-processing factory, telling me that he and his mates occasionally dropped a gallbladder or two into boxes of frozen liver marked for export to Britain, and that his factory defined "lamb" as a sheep under six months old if it was destined for local consumption, but defined it as any sheep up to 18 months old if it was destined for export to Britain.) Today, Australia's principal exports remain low-bulk, high-value items, including steel, minerals, wool, and wheat; increasingly within the last few decades, wine and macadamia nuts as well; and also some specialty crops that are bulky but that have high

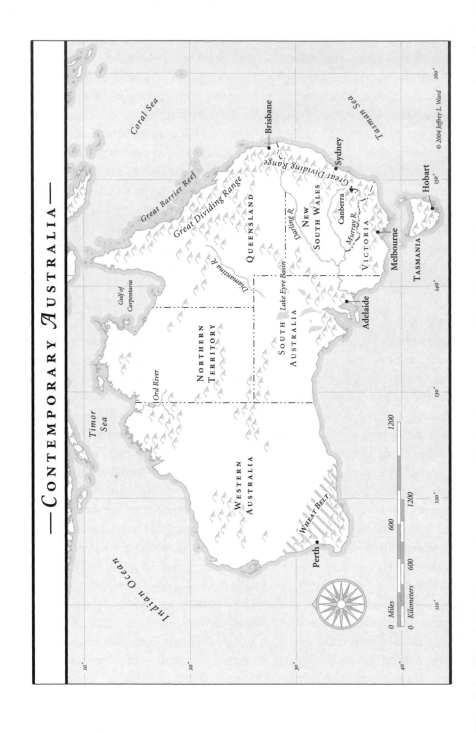

─ CONTEMPORARY AUSTRALIA ─

Indian Ocean

Timor Sea

Coral Sea

Great Barrier Reef

Gulf of Carpentaria

Ord River

WESTERN AUSTRALIA

NORTHERN TERRITORY

Great Dividing Range

Diamantina R.

QUEENSLAND

Brisbane

Great Dividing Range

Darling R.

NEW SOUTH WALES

Lake Eyre Basin

SOUTH AUSTRALIA

Sydney

Canberra

Murray R.

VICTORIA

Melbourne

Adelaide

WHEAT BELT

Perth

Tasman Sea

TASMANIA

Hobart

© 2004 Jeffrey L. Ward

10°   20°   30°   40°

110°   120°   130°   140°   150°   160°

0   600   1200   Miles
0   600   1200   Kilometers

value because Australia produces unique crops aimed at specialty niche markets for which some consumers are willing to pay a premium, such as durum wheat and other special wheat varieties, and wheat and beef raised without pesticides or other chemicals.

But there is an additional tyranny of distance, one within Australia itself. Australia's productive or settled areas are few and scattered: the country has a population only $1/14$ that of the U.S., scattered over an area equal to that of the U.S.'s lower 48 states. The resulting high costs of transportation within Australia make it expensive to sustain a First World civilization there. For example, the Australian government pays for telephone connection to the national phone grid for any Australian home or business at any location within Australia, even for outback stations hundreds of miles from the nearest such station. Today, Australia is the most urbanized country in the world, with 58% of its population concentrated in just five large cities (Sydney with 4.0 million people, Melbourne 3.4 million, Brisbane 1.6 million, Perth 1.4 million, and Adelaide 1.1 million as of 1999). Among those five cities, Perth is the world's most isolated large city, lying farther than any other from the next large city (Adelaide, 1,300 miles to the east). It is no accident that two of Australia's largest companies, its national airline Qantas and its telecommunications company Telstra, are based on bridging those distances.

Australia's internal tyranny of distance, in combination with its droughts, is also responsible for the fact that banks and other businesses are closing their branches in Australia's isolated towns, because those branches have become uneconomic. Doctors are leaving those towns for the same reason. As a result, whereas the U.S. and Europe have a continuous distribution of settlement sizes—large cities, medium-sized towns, and small villages—Australia is increasingly without medium-sized towns. Instead, most Australians today live either in a few large cities with all the amenities of the modern First World, or in smaller villages or else outback stations without banks, doctors, or other amenities. Australia's small villages of a few hundred people can survive a five-year drought, such as arises often in Australia's unpredictable climate, because the village has so little economic activity anyway. Big cities can also survive a five-year drought, because they integrate the economy over a huge catchment area. But a five-year drought tends to wipe out medium-sized towns, whose existence depends on their ability to provide enough business branches and services to compete with more distant cities, but which aren't big enough to integrate over a huge catchment. Increasingly, most Australians don't depend on or really live in the Australian environment: they live instead in those five big cities, which are connected to the outside world rather than to the Australian landscape.

Europe claimed most of its overseas colonies in hopes of financial gain or supposed strategic advantages. Locations of those colonies to which many Europeans actually emigrated—i.e., excluding trading stations where only relatively few Europeans settled in order to trade with the local population— were chosen on the basis of the land's perceived suitability for the successful founding of an economically prosperous or at least self-supporting society. The unique exception was Australia, whose immigrants for many decades arrived not to seek their fortunes but because they were compelled to go there.

Britian's principal motive for settling Australia was to relieve its festering problem of large numbers of jailed poor people, and to forestall a rebellion that might otherwise break out if they could not somehow be disposed of. In the 18th century British law prescribed the death penalty for stealing 40 shillings or more, so judges preferred to find thieves guilty of stealing 39 shillings in order to avoid imposing the death penalty. That resulted in prisons and moored ship hulks filling with people convicted of petty crimes such as theft and debt. Until 1783, that pressure on the available jail space was relieved by sending convicts as indentured servants to North America, which was also being settled by voluntary emigrants seeking improvement of their economic lot or else religious freedom.

But the American Revolution cut off that escape valve, forcing Britain to seek some other place to dump its convicts. Initially, the two leading candidate locations under consideration were either 400 miles up the Gambia River in tropical West Africa, or else in desert at the mouth of the Orange River on the boundary between modern South Africa and Namibia. It was the impossibility of both of those proposals, evident on sober reflection, that led to the fallback choice of Australia's Botany Bay near the site of modern Sydney, known at the time only from Captain Cook's visit in 1770. That was how the First Fleet brought to Australia in 1788 its first European settlers, consisting of convicts plus soldiers to guard them. Convict shipments went on until 1868, and through the 1840s they comprised most of Australia's European settlers.

With time, four other scattered Australian coastal sites besides Sydney, near the sites of the modern cities of Melbourne, Brisbane, Perth, and Hobart, were chosen as locations of other convict dumps. Those settlements became the nucleus of five colonies, governed separately by Britain, that eventually became five of the six states of modern Australia: New South Wales, Victoria, Queensland, Western Australia, and Tasmania, respectively. All five of those initial settlements were at locations chosen for advantages of their harbors or locations on rivers, rather than for any agricultural advantages. In fact, all proved to be sites poor for agriculture and incapable of becoming self-supporting in food production. Instead, Britain had to send out food subsidies to the colonies in order to feed the convicts and their guards and governors. That was not the case, however, for the area around Adelaide that became the nucleus of the remaining modern Australian state, South Australia. There, good soil resulting from geological uplift, plus fairly reliable winter rains, attracted German farmers as the sole early group of emigrants not from Britain. Melbourne also has good soils west of the city that became the site of a successful agricultural settlement in 1835, after a convict dump founded in 1803 in poor soils east of the city quickly failed.

The first economic payoff from British settlement of Australia came from sealing and whaling. The next payoff came from sheep, when a route across the Blue Mountains 60 miles west of Sydney was finally discovered in 1813, giving access to productive pasture land beyond. However, Australia did not become self-supporting, and Britain's food subsidies did not cease, until the 1840s, just before Australia's first gold rush of 1851 at last brought some prosperity.

When that European settlement of Australia began in 1788, Australia had of course been settled for over 40,000 years by Aborigines, who had worked out successful sustainable solutions to the continent's daunting environmental problems. At the sites of initial European occupation (the convict dumps) and in subsequently settled areas suitable for farming, Australian whites had even less use for Aborigines than white Americans had for Indians: the Indians in the eastern United States were at least farmers and provided crops critical for survival of European settlers during the first years, until Europeans began to grow their own crops. Thereafter, Indian farmers were merely competition for American farmers and were killed or driven out. Aboriginal Australians, however, did not farm, hence could not provide food for settlements, and were killed or driven out of the initial white settled areas. That remained Australian policy as whites expanded into areas suitable for farming. However, when whites reached areas too dry for farming but suitable for pastoralism, they found Aborigines useful as stockmen to look after sheep: unlike Iceland and New Zealand, two sheep-raising countries that have no native predators on sheep, Australia had dingos which do prey on sheep, so that Australian sheep farmers needed shepherds and employed Aborigines because of the shortage of white labor in Australia. Some Aborigines also worked with whalers, sealers, fishermen, and coastal traders.

Just as the Norse settlers of Iceland and Greenland brought over the cultural values of their Norwegian homeland (Chapters 6–8), so too did the British settlers of Australia carry British cultural values. Just as was the case in Iceland and Greenland, in Australia as well some of those imported cultural values proved inappropriate to the Australian environment, and some of those inappropriate values continue to have legacies today. Five sets of cultural values were particularly important: those involving sheep, rabbits and foxes, native Australian vegetation, land values, and British identity.

In the 18th century Britain produced little wool itself but instead imported it from Spain and Saxony. Those continental sources of wool were cut off during the Napoleonic Wars, raging during the first decades of British settlement in Australia. Britain's King George III was particularly interested in this problem, and with his support the British succeeded in smuggling merino sheep from Spain into Britain and then sending some to Australia to become the founders of Australia's wool flock. Australia evolved into Britain's main source of wool. Conversely, wool was Australia's main export from about 1820 to 1950, because its low bulk and high value overcame the tyranny-of-distance problem preventing bulkier potential Australian exports from competing in overseas markets.

Today, a significant fraction of all food-producing land in Australia is still used for sheep. Sheep farming is ingrained into Australia's cultural identity, and rural voters whose livelihood depends on sheep are disproportionately influential in Australian politics. But the appropriateness of Australian land for sheep is deceptive: while it initially supported lush grass, or could be cleared to support lush grass, its soil productivity was (as already mentioned) very low, so the sheep farmers were in effect mining the land's fertility. Many sheep properties had to be quickly abandoned; Australia's existing sheep industry is a money-losing proposition (to be discussed below); and its legacy is ruinous land degradation through overgrazing (Plate 29).

In recent years there have been suggestions that, instead of raising sheep, Australia should be raising kangaroos, which (unlike sheep) are native Australian species that are adapted to Australian plants and climates. It is claimed that the soft paws of kangaroos are less damaging to soil than are the hard hooves of sheep. Kangaroo meat is lean, healthy, and (in my opinion) absolutely delicious. In addition to their meat, kangaroos yield valuable hides. All of those points are cited as arguments to support replacing sheep herding with kangaroo ranching.

However, that proposal faces real obstacles, both biological and cultural ones. Unlike sheep, kangaroos are not herd animals that will docilely obey one shepherd and a dog, or that can be rounded up and marched obediently up ramps into trucks for shipment to the slaughterhouse. Instead, would-be kangaroo ranchers have to hire hunters to chase down and shoot their kangaroos one by one. Further strikes against kangaroos are their mobility and fence-jumping prowess: if you invest in promoting growth of a kangaroo population on your property, and if your kangaroos perceive some inducement to move (such as rain falling somewhere else), your valuable crop of kangaroos may end up 30 miles away on somebody else's property. While kangaroo meat is accepted in Germany and some is exported there, sales of kangaroo meat face cultural obstacles elsewhere. Australians think of kangaroos as vermin holding little appeal for displacing good old British mutton and beef from the dinner plate. Many Australian animal welfare advocates oppose kangaroo harvesting, overlooking the facts that living conditions and slaughter methods are much crueler for domestic sheep and cattle than for wild kangaroos. The U.S. explicitly forbids the importation of kangaroo meat because we find the beasts cute, and because a congressman's wife heard that kangaroos are endangered. Some kangaroo species are indeed endangered, but ironically the species actually harvested for meat are abundant pest animals in Australia. The Australian government strictly regulates their harvest and sets a quota.

Whereas introduced sheep have undoubtedly been of great economic benefit (as well as harm) to Australia, introduced rabbits and foxes have been unmitigated disasters. British colonists found Australia's environment, plants, and animals alien and wanted to be surrounded by familiar European plants and animals. Hence they attempted to introduce many European bird species, only two of which, the House Sparrow and Starling, became widespread, while others (the Blackbird, Song Thrush, Tree Sparrow, Goldfinch, and Greenfinch) became established only locally. At least, those introduced bird species have not done much harm, while Australia's rabbits in plague numbers cause enormous economic damage and land degradation by consuming about half of the pasture vegetation that would otherwise have been available to sheep and cattle (Plate 30). Along with habitat changes through sheep grazing and suppression of Aboriginal land burning, the combination of introduced rabbits and introduced foxes has been a major cause of the extinctions or population crashes of most species of small native Australian mammals: foxes prey on them, and rabbits compete with native herbivorous mammals for food.

European rabbits and foxes were introduced to Australia almost simultaneously. It is unclear whether foxes were introduced first to permit traditional British fox hunting, then rabbits introduced later to provide additional food for the foxes, or whether rabbits were introduced first for hunting or to make the countryside look more like Britain and then foxes introduced later to control the rabbits. In any case, both have been such expensive disasters that it now seems incredible that they were introduced for such trivial reasons. Even more incredible are the efforts to which Australians went to establish rabbits: the first four attempts failed (because the rabbits released were tame white rabbits that died), and not until wild Spanish rabbits were used for the fifth attempt did success follow.

Ever since those rabbits and foxes did become established and Australians realized the consequences, they have been trying to eliminate or reduce their populations. The war against foxes involves poisoning or trapping them. One method in the war against rabbits, memorable to all non-Australians who saw the recent film *Rabbit Proof Fence,* is to divide up the landscape by long fences and attempt to eliminate rabbits from one side of the fence. Farmer Bill McIntosh told me how he makes a map of his property to mark the locations of every one of its thousands of rabbit burrows, which he destroys individually with a bulldozer. He then returns to a burrow later, and if it shows any fresh sign of rabbit activity, he drops dynamite down the burrow to kill the rabbits and then seals up the burrow. In this laborious way he has destroyed 3,000 rabbit burrows. Such expensive measures led Australians several decades ago to place great hopes in introducing a rabbit disease called myxomatosis, which initially did reduce the population by over 90% until rabbits became resistant and rebounded. Current efforts to control rabbits are using another microbe called the calicivirus.

Just as British colonists preferred their familiar rabbits and blackbirds and felt uncomfortable amidst Australia's strange-looking kangaroos and friarbirds, they also felt uncomfortable among Australia's eucalyptus and acacia trees, so different in appearance, color, and leaves from British woodland trees. Settlers cleared the land of vegetation partly because they didn't like its appearance, but also for agriculture. Until about 20 years ago, the

Australian government not only subsidized land clearance but actually required it of lease holders. (Much agricultural land in Australia is not owned outright by farmers, as in the U.S., but is owned by the government and leased to farmers.) Leaseholders were given tax deductions for agricultural machinery and labor involved in land clearance, were assigned quotas of land to clear as a condition of retaining their lease, and forfeited the lease if they did not fulfill those quotas. Farmers and businesses were able to make a profit just by buying or leasing land covered with native vegetation and unsuitable for sustained agriculture, clearing that vegetation, planting one or two wheat crops that exhausted the soil, and then abandoning the property. Today, when Australian plant communities are recognized as unique and endangered, and when land clearance is regarded as one of the two major causes of land degradation by salinization, it is sad to recall that the government until recently paid and required farmers to destroy native vegetation. The ecological economist Mike Young, whose job for the Australian government now includes the task of figuring out how much land has been rendered worthless by land clearance, told me of his childhood memories of clearing land with his father on their family farm. Mike and his father would each drive a tractor, the two tractors advancing in parallel and connected by a chain, with the chain dragging over the ground to remove native vegetation and replace it with crops, in return for which his father received a big tax deduction. Without that deduction provided by the government as an incentive, much of the land would never have been cleared.

As settlers arrived in Australia and began buying or leasing land from each other or from the government, land prices were set according to values prevailing back home in England, and justified there by the returns that could be obtained from England's productive soils. In Australia that has meant that land is "overcapitalized": that is, it sells or leases for more than can be justified by the financial returns from agricultural use of the land. When a farmer then buys or leases land and takes out a mortgage, the need to pay the interest on that high mortgage resulting from land overcapitalization pressures the farmer to try to extract more profit from the land than it could sustainably yield. That practice, termed "flogging the land," has meant stocking too many sheep per acre, or planting too much land in wheat. Land overcapitalization resulting from British cultural values (monetary values and belief systems) has been a major contributor to the Australian practice of overstocking, which has led to overgrazing, soil erosion, and farmer bankruptcies and abandonments.

More generally, high valuation on land has translated into Australians' embracing rural agricultural values justified by their British background but not justified by Australia's low agricultural productivity. Those rural values continue to pose an obstacle to solving one of modern Australia's built-in political problems: the Australian constitution gives a disproportionate vote to rural areas. In the Australian mystique even more than in Europe and the U.S., rural people are considered honest, and city-dwellers are considered dishonest. If a farmer goes bankrupt, it's assumed to be the misfortune of a virtuous person overcome by forces beyond his control (such as a drought), while a city-dweller who goes bankrupt is assumed to have brought it on himself through dishonesty. This rural hagiography and disproportionately strong rural vote ignore the already-mentioned reality that Australia is the most highly urbanized nation. They have contributed to the government's long-continued perverse support for measures mining rather than sustaining the environment, such as land clearance and indirect subsidies of uneconomic rural areas.

Until 50 years ago, emigration to Australia was overwhelmingly from Britain and Ireland. Many Australians today still feel strongly connected to their British heritage and would indignantly reject any suggestion that they treasure it inordinately. Yet that heritage has led Australians to do things that they consider admirable but that would strike a dispassionate outsider as inappropriate and not necessarily in Australia's best interest. In both World War I and World War II Australia declared war upon Germany as soon as Britain and Germany declared war on each other, though Australia's own interests were never affected in World War I (except for giving Australians an excuse to conquer Germany's New Guinea colony) and did not become affected in World War II until the outbreak of war with Japan, more than two years after the outbreak of war between Britain and Germany. The major national holiday of Australia (and also of New Zealand) is Anzac Day, April 25, commemorating a disastrous slaughter of Australian and New Zealand troops on Turkey's remote Gallipoli Peninsula on that date in 1915, as a result of incompetent British leadership of those troops who were joining British forces in an unsuccessful attempt to attack Turkey. The bloodbath at Gallipoli became for Australians a symbol of their country's "coming of age," supporting its British motherland, and assuming its place among nations as a united federation rather than as half-a-dozen colonies with separate governor-generals. For Americans of my generation, the closest parallel to Gallipoli's meaning to Australians is the meaning to us of the disastrous Japanese attack of December 7, 1941, on our Pearl Harbor base, which overnight unified Americans and pulled us out of our foreign policy based on isolation. Yet people other than Australians cannot escape the irony of Australia's national holiday being associated with the Gallipoli Peninsula, situated one-third of the way around the world and on the opposite side of the equator: no other geographic location could be more irrelevant to Australia's interests.

Those emotional ties to Britain continue today. When I first visited Australia in 1964, having lived previously in Britain for four years, I found Australia more British than modern Britain itself in its architecture and attitudes. Until 1973, the Australian government still submitted to Britain each year a list of Australians to be knighted, and those honors were considered the highest possible ones for an Australian. Britain still appoints a governor general for Australia, with the power to fire the Australian prime minister, and the governor general actually did so in 1975. Until the early 1970s, Australia maintained a "White Australia policy" and virtually banned immigration from its Asian neighbors, a policy that understandably angered them. Only within the last 25 years has Australia belatedly become engaged with its Asian neighbors, come to recognize its place as being in Asia, accepted Asian immigrants, and cultivated Asian trade partners. Britain has now fallen to a ranking in eighth place among Australia's export markets, behind Japan, China, Korea, Singapore, and Taiwan.

That discussion of Australia's self-image as a British country or as an Asian country raises an issue that has recurred throughout this book: the importance of friends and enemies to a society's stability. What countries has Australia perceived as its friends, its trade partners, and its enemies, and what has been the influence of those perceptions? Let's start with trade and then proceed to immigration.

For over a century until 1950, agricultural products, especially wool, were Australia's main exports, followed by minerals. Today Australia is still the world's largest wool producer, but Australian production and overseas demand are both decreasing because of increasing competition from synthetic fibers to fill wool's former uses. Australia's number of sheep peaked in 1970 at 180 million (representing an average of 14 sheep for every Australian then) and has been declining steadily ever since. Almost all of Australia's wool production is exported, especially to China and Hong Kong. Other important agricultural exports include wheat (sold especially to Russia, China, and India), specialty durum wheat, wine, and chemical-free beef. At present, Australia produces more food than it consumes and is a net food exporter, but Australia's domestic food consumption is increasing as its population grows. If that trend continues, Australia could become a net importer rather than exporter of food.

Wool and other agricultural products now rank only in third place among Australia's earners of foreign exchange, behind tourism (number two) and minerals (number one). The minerals highest in export value are coal, gold, iron, and aluminum in that sequence. Australia is the world's leading exporter of coal. It has the world's largest reserves of uranium, lead, silver, zinc, titanium, and tantalum and is among the world's top six countries in its reserves of coal, iron, aluminum, copper, nickel, and diamonds. Especially its reserves of coal and iron are huge and not expected to run out in the foreseeable future. While Australia's largest export customers for its minerals used to be Britain and other European countries, Asian countries now import nearly five times more minerals from Australia than do European countries. The top three customers are presently Japan, South Korea, and Taiwan in that order: for instance, Japan buys nearly half of Australia's exported coal, iron, and aluminum.

In short, over the last half century Australia's exports have shifted from predominantly agricultural products to minerals, while its trade partners have shifted from Europe to Asia. The U.S. remains Australia's largest source of imports and (after Japan) its second largest export customer.

Those shifts in trade patterns have been accompanied by shifts in immigration. With an area similar to that of the U.S., Australia has a much smaller population (currently about 20 million), for the obvious good reason that the Australian environment is far less productive and can support far fewer people. Nevertheless, in the 1950s many Australians, including government leaders, looked fearfully at Australia's much more populous Asian neighbors, especially Indonesia with its 200 million people. Australians were also strongly influenced by their World War II experience of being menaced and bombed by populous but more distant Japan. Many Australians concluded that their country suffered from a dangerous problem of being greatly underpopulated compared to those Asian neighbors, and that it would become a tempting target for Indonesian expansion unless it quickly filled all that empty space. Hence the 1950s and 1960s brought a crash program to attract immigrants as a matter of public policy.

That program involved abandoning the country's former White Australia Policy, under which (as one of the first acts of the Australian Commonwealth formed in 1901) immigration was not only virtually restricted to people of European origin but even predominantly to people from

Britain and Ireland. In the words of the official government yearbook, there was concern that "non-Anglo-Celtic background people would not be able to adjust." The perceived population shortage led the government first to accept, and then actively to recruit, immigrants from other European countries—especially Italy, Greece, and Germany, then the Netherlands and the former Yugoslavia. Not until the 1970s did the desire to attract more immigrants than could be recruited from Europe, combined with growing recognition of Australia's Pacific rather than just British identity, induce the government to remove legal obstacles to Asian immigration. While Britain, Ireland, and New Zealand are still Australia's major sources of immigrants, one-quarter of all immigrants now come from Asian countries, with Vietnam, the Philippines, Hong Kong, and (currently) China variously predominating in recent years. Immigration reached its all-time peak in the late 1980s, with the result that nearly one-quarter of all Australians today are immigrants born overseas, as compared to only 12% of Americans and 3% of Dutch.

The fallacy behind this policy of "filling up" Australia is that there are compelling environmental reasons why, even after more than two centuries of European settlement, Australia has not "filled itself up" to the population density of the U.S. Given Australia's limited supplies of water and limited potential for food production, it lacks the capacity to support a significantly larger population. An increase in population would also dilute its earnings from mineral exports on a per-capita basis. Australia has recently been receiving immigrants only at the net rate of about 100,000 per year, which yields an annual population growth by immigration of only 0.5%.

Nevertheless, many influential Australians, including the recent Prime Minister Malcolm Fraser, the leaders of both major political parties, and the Australian Business Council, still argue that Australia should try to increase its population to 50 million people. The reasoning invokes a combination of continued fear of the "Yellow Peril" from overpopulated Asian countries, the aspiration for Australia to become a major world power, and the belief that that goal could not be achieved if Australia had only 20 million people. But those aspirations of a few decades ago have receded to the point where Australians today no longer expect to become a major world power. Even if they did have that expectation, Israel, Sweden, Denmark, Finland, and Singapore provide examples of countries with populations far less than that of Australia (only a few million each) that nevertheless are major economic powers and make big contributions to world technological innovation and culture. Contrary to their government and business leaders, 70% of

Australians say that they want less rather than more immigration. In the long run it is doubtful that Australia can even support its present population: the best estimate of a population sustainable at the present standard of living is 8 million people, less than half of the present population.

Driving inland from the state capital of Adelaide in South Australia, the only Australian state to have originated as a self-supporting colony because of its soils' decent productivity (high by Australian standards, modest by standards outside Australia), I saw in this prime farmland of Australia one ruin after another of abandoned farms. I was able to visit one of those ruins preserved as a tourist attraction: Kanyaka, a large manor developed as a sheep farm at considerable expense by English nobility in the 1850s, only to fail in 1869, to become abandoned, and never to be reoccupied. Much of that area of inland South Australia was developed for sheep farming during the wet years of the 1850s and early 1860s, when the land was covered with grass and looked lush. With droughts beginning in 1864, the overgrazed landscape became littered with the bodies of dead sheep, and those sheep farms were abandoned. That disaster stimulated the government to send the surveyor-general G. W. Goyder to identify how far inland from the coast the area with rainfall sufficiently reliable to justify farming extended. He defined a line that became known as the Goyder Line, north of which the likelihood of drought made attempts at farming imprudent. Unfortunately, a series of wet years in the 1870s encouraged the government to resell at high prices the abandoned sheep farms of the 1860s, as small overcapitalized wheat farms. Towns sprang up beyond the Goyder Line, railways expanded, and those wheat farms in turn succeeded for a few years of abnormally high rainfall until they too failed and became consolidated into larger holdings that reverted to being large sheep farms in the late 1870s. With the return of drought, many of those sheep farms subsequently failed once again, and those that still survive today cannot support themselves based on sheep: their farmer/owners require second jobs, tourism, or outside investments to make a living.

There have been more or less similar histories in most other food-producing areas of Australia. What made so many initially profitable food-producing properties become less profitable? The reason is Australia's number-one environmental problem, land degradation, resulting from a set of nine types of damaging environmental impacts: clearance of native vegetation, overgrazing by sheep, rabbits, soil nutrient exhaustion, soil erosion,

man-made droughts, weeds, misguided government policies, and salinization. All of these damaging phenomena operate elsewhere in the world, in
some cases with even greater individual impact than in Australia. Briefly,
these impacts are as follows:

I mentioned above that the Australian government formerly required
tenants leasing government land to clear native vegetation. While that requirement has now been dropped, Australia still clears more native vegetation per year than any other First World country, and its clearance rates are
exceeded in the world only by Brazil, Indonesia, the Congo, and Bolivia.
Most of Australia's current land clearance is going on in the state of
Queensland for the purpose of creating pasture land for beef cattle. The
Queensland government has announced that it will phase out large-scale
clearing—but not until 2006. The resulting damage to Australia includes
land degradation through dryland salinization and soil erosion, impairment of water quality by runoff of salt and sediment, loss of agricultural
productivity and land values, and damage to the Great Barrier Reef (see below). Rotting and burning of the bulldozed vegetation contribute to Australia's annual greenhouse gas admissions a gas quantity approximately
equal to the country's total motor vehicle emissions.

A second major cause of land degradation is overstocking of sheep in
numbers that graze down the vegetation faster than it can regrow. In some
areas such as in parts of the Murchison District of Western Australia, overgrazing was ruinous and irreversible because it led to loss of the soil. Today,
now that overgrazing's effects are recognized, the Australian government
imposes *maximum* stocking rates for sheep: i.e., farmers are *forbidden* to
stock more than a certain number of sheep per acre on leased land. Formerly, however, the government imposed *minimum* stocking rates: farmers
were *obliged* to stock a certain minimum number of sheep per acre as a condition of holding the lease. When sheep stocking rates first became well
documented in the late 19th century, they were three times higher than the
rates considered sustainable today, and before documentation began in the
1890s sheep stocking rates were apparently up to 10 times higher than sustainable rates. That is, the first settlers mined the standing crop of grass,
rather than treating it as a potentially renewable resource. Just as was true
for land clearance, the government thus required farmers to damage the
land and cancelled leases of farmers who failed to damage the land.

Three other causes of land degradation have already been mentioned.
Rabbits remove vegetation as do sheep, cost farmers by reducing the pasturage available to sheep and cattle, and also cost farmers through the

expense of the bulldozers, dynamite, fences, and virus release measures that farms adopt to control rabbit populations. Nutrient exhaustion of soils often develops within the first few years of agriculture, because of the low initial nutrient content of Australian soils. Erosion of topsoil by water and wind increases after its cover of vegetation has been thinned or cleared. The resulting runoff of soil via rivers into the sea, by making coastal waters turbid, is now damaging and killing the Great Barrier Reef, one of Australia's major tourist attractions (not to mention its biological value in its own right and as a nursery of fish).

The term "man-made drought" refers to a form of land degradation secondary to land clearance, sheep overgrazing, and rabbits. When the cover of vegetation is removed by any of these means, land that the vegetation had previously shaded now becomes directly exposed to the sun, thereby making the soil hotter and drier. That is, the secondary effects creating hot and dry soil conditions impede plant growth in much the same way as does a natural drought.

Weeds, discussed in Chapter 1 in connection with Montana, are defined as plants of low value to farmers, either because they are less palatable (or totally unpalatable) to sheep and cattle than preferred pasture plants, or because they compete with useful crops. Some weeds are plant species unintentionally introduced from overseas; about 15% were intentionally but misguidedly introduced for use in agriculture; one-third escaped into the wild from gardens where they had been intentionally introduced as ornamentals; and other weed species are Australian native plants. Because grazing animals prefer to eat certain plants, the action of grazing animals tends to increase the abundance of weeds and to convert pasture cover to plant species that are less utilized or unutilizable (in some cases, poisonous to animals). Weeds vary in the ease with which they can be combatted: some weed species are easy to remove and to replace with palatable species or crops, but other weed species are very expensive or prohibitively difficult to eliminate once they have become established.

About 3,000 plant species are considered weeds in Australia today and cause economic losses of about $2 billion per year. One of the worst is Mimosa, which threatens an especially valuable area, the Kakadu National Park and the World Heritage Area. It is prickly, grows up to 20 feet tall, and produces so many seeds that it can double the area that it covers within a year. Even worse is rubber vine, introduced in the 1870s as an ornamental shrub from Madagascar to make Queensland mining towns prettier. It escaped to become a plant monster of a type depicted in science fiction:

besides being poisonous to livestock, smothering other vegetation, and growing into impenetrable thickets, it drops pods that disperse far by floating down rivers, and that eventually pop open to release 300 seeds carried far by the wind. The seeds within one pod suffice to cover two-and-a-half acres with new rubber vines.

To the misguided government policies of land clearance and sheep overstocking previously mentioned may be added the policies of the government's Wheat Board. It has tended to make rosy predictions of higher world wheat prices, thereby encouraging farmers to incur debt for capital investments in machinery to plant wheat on land marginal for wheat growing. Many farmers then discovered, to their misfortune after investing much money, that the land could support wheat for only a few years, and that wheat prices dropped.

The remaining cause of land degradation in Australia, salinization, is the most complex and requires the most explanation. I mentioned previously that large areas of Australia contain much salt in the soil, as legacies of salty sea breezes, former ocean basins, or dried-out lakes. While a few plants can tolerate salty soils, most plants, including almost all of our crops, cannot. If the salt below the root zone just stayed there, it wouldn't be a problem. But two processes can bring it up towards the surface and start causing problems: irrigation salinization and dryland salinization.

Irrigation salinization has the potential for arising in dry areas where rainfall is too low or too unreliable for agriculture, and where irrigation is necessary instead, as in parts of southeastern Australia. If a farmer "drip-irrigates," i.e., installs a small irrigation water fixture at the base of each fruit tree or crop row and allows just enough water to drip out as the tree's or crop's roots can absorb, then little water is wasted, and there is no problem. But if the farmer instead follows the commoner practice of "broadcast irrigation," i.e., flooding the land or else using a sprinkler to distribute the water over a large area, then the ground gets saturated with more water than the roots can absorb. The unabsorbed excess water percolates down to that deeper layer of salty soil, thereby establishing a continuous column of wetted soil through which the deep-lying salt can percolate either up to the shallow root zone and the surface, where it will inhibit or prevent growth of plants other than salt-tolerant species, or else down to the groundwater table and from there into a river. In that sense, the water problems of Australia, which we think of as (and which is) a dry continent, are not problems of too little water but of too much water: water is still sufficiently cheap and available to permit its use in some areas for broadcast irrigation. More exactly, parts of Australia have enough water to permit broadcast irrigation, but not enough water to flush out all the resulting mobilized salt. In principle, problems of irrigation salinization can be partly mitigated by going to the expense of installing drip irrigation instead of broadcast irrigation.

The other process responsible for salinization, besides irrigation salinization, is dryland salinization, potentially operating in areas where rainfall suffices for agriculture. That's true especially in the areas of Western Australia and parts of South Australia with reliable (or formerly reliable) winter rains. As long as ground in such areas is still covered with its natural vegetation, which is present all year, the plants' roots take up most of the rain falling, and little rainwater remains to percolate down through the soil to establish contact with the deeper salt layers. But suppose a farmer clears the natural vegetation and replaces it with crops, which are planted seasonally and then harvested, leaving the ground bare for part of the year. Rain soaking the ground when it is bare does percolate down to the deep-lying salt, permitting it to diffuse up to the surface. Unlike irrigation salinization, dryland salinization is difficult, expensive, or essentially impossible to reverse once the natural vegetation has been cleared.

One can think of salt mobilized by either irrigation or dryland salinization into soil water as like a salty underground river, which in some parts of Australia has salt concentrations three times those of the ocean. That underground river flows downhill just as does a normal above-ground river, but much more slowly. Eventually, it may seep out into a downhill depression, creating hypersaline ponds that I saw in South Australia. If a farmer on a hilltop adopts bad land management practices that cause his land to become salinized, the salt may slowly flow through the ground to the land of farms lying downhill, even if those farms are well managed. In Australia there is no mechanism whereby the owner of a downhill farm that has been thus ruined can collect compensation from the owner of an uphill farm responsible for his ruin. Some of the underground river doesn't emerge in downhill depressions but instead flows down into above-ground rivers, including Australia's largest river system, the Murray/Darling.

Salinization inflicts heavy financial losses on the Australian economy, in three ways. First, it is rendering much farmland, including some of the most valuable land in Australia, less productive or useless to grow crops and raise livestock. Second, some of the salt is carried into city drinking water supplies. For instance, the Murray/Darling River provides between 40% and 90% of the drinking water of Adelaide, South Australia's capital, but the river's rising salt levels could eventually make it unsuitable for human consumption or crop irrigation without the added expense of desalination. Even more expensive than either of those two problems are the damages caused by salt corroding infrastructure, including roads, railroads, airfields, bridges, buildings, water pipes, hot water systems, rainwater systems, sewers, household and industrial appliances, power and telecommunication lines, and water treatment plants. Overall, it is estimated that only about a third of Australia's economic losses arising from salinization are the direct costs to Australian agriculture; the losses "beyond the farm gate" and downstream, to Australia's water supplies and infrastructure, cost twice as much.

As for the extent of salinization, it already affects about 9% of all cleared land in Australia, and that percentage is projected under present trends to rise to about 25%. Salinization is currently especially serious in the states of Western Australia and South Australia; the former state's wheat belt is considered one of the worst examples of dryland salinization in the world. Of its original native vegetation, 90% has now been cleared, mostly between 1920 and 1980, culminating in the "Million Acres a Year" program pushed by the Western Australia state government in the 1960s. No other equally large area of land in the world was cleared of its natural vegetation so quickly. The proportion of the wheat belt sterilized by salinization is expected to reach one-third within the next two decades.

The total area in Australia to which salinization has the potential for spreading is more than 6 times the current extent and includes a 4-fold increase in Western Australia, 7-fold increase in Queensland, 10-fold increase in Victoria, and 60-fold increase in New South Wales. In addition to the wheat belt, another major problem area is the basin of the Murray/Darling River, which accounts for nearly half of Australia's agricultural production but which now gets progressively saltier downstream towards Adelaide because of more salty underground water entering and more water being extracted for irrigation by humans along its length. (In some years so much water is extracted that no water is left in the river to enter the ocean.) That salt input into the Murray/Darling arises not just from irrigation practices along the river's lower reaches but also from the impact of increasingly extensive industrial-scale cotton farming along its headwaters in Queensland and New South Wales. Those cotton operations are considered Australia's biggest single dilemma of land and water management, because on the one hand cotton by itself is Australia's most valuable crop after wheat, but on the other hand the mobilized salt and applied pesticides associated with cotton-growing damage other types of agriculture downstream in the Murray/Darling Basin.

Once salinization has been initiated, it is often either poorly reversible (especially in the case of dryland salinization), or prohibitively expensive to solve, or solutions take a prohibitively long time. Underground rivers flow very slowly, such that once one has mobilized salt through bad land management, it may take 500 years to flush that mobilized salt out of the ground even if one switches overnight to drip irrigation and stops mobilizing further salt.

While land degradation resulting from all those causes is Australia's most expensive environmental problem, five other sets of serious problems deserve briefer mention: those involving forestry, marine fisheries, freshwater fisheries, freshwater itself, and alien species.

Apart from Antarctica, Australia is the continent with proportionately the least area covered by forests: only about 20% of the continent's total area. They used to include possibly the world's tallest trees, now-felled Victorian Blue Gums, rivaling or topping California Coast Redwoods in height. Of Australia's forests standing at the time of European settlement in 1788, 40% have already been cleared, 35% have been partly logged, and only 25% remain intact. Nevertheless, logging of that small area of remaining old-growth forests is continuing and constitutes yet another instance of mining the Australian landscape.

The export uses (in addition to domestic consumption) to which timber logged from Australia's remnant forests is being put are remarkable. Of forest product exports, half are not in the form of logs or finished materials but are turned into wood chips and sent mostly to Japan, where they are used to produce paper and its products and make up one-quarter of the material in Japanese paper. While the price that Japan pays to Australia for those wood chips has dropped to $7 per ton, the resulting paper sells in Japan for $1,000 per ton, so that almost all of the value added to the timber after it is cut accrues to Japan rather than to Australia. At the same time as it exports wood chips, Australia imports nearly three times more forest products than it exports, with more than half of those imports being in the form of paper and paperboard products.

Thus, the Australian forest products trade involves a double irony. On the one hand, Australia, one of the First World countries with the least forest, is still logging those shrinking forests to export their products to Japan, the First World country with the highest percentage of its land under forest (74%) and with that percentage still growing. Second, Australia's forest products trade in effect consists of exporting raw material at a low price, to be converted in another country into finished material at a high price and with high added value, and then importing finished materials. One expects to encounter that particular type of asymmetry not in the trade relations between two First World countries, but instead when an economically backward, non-industrialized Third World colony unsophisticated at negotiations deals with a First World country sophisticated at exploiting Third World countries, buying their raw materials cheaply, adding value to the materials at home, and exporting expensive manufactured goods to the colony. (Japan's major exports to Australia include cars, telecommunications equipment, and computing equipment, while coal and minerals are Australia's other major exports to Japan.) That is, it would appear that Australia is squandering a valuable resource and receiving little money for it.

The continued logging of old-growth forests is giving rise to one of the most passionate environmental debates in Australia today. Most of the logging and the fiercest debate are going on in the state of Tasmania, where Tasmania Blue Gums, at up to 305 feet tall some of the world's tallest remaining trees outside of California, are now being logged faster than ever. Both of Australia's major political parties, at both the state and federal levels, favor continued logging of Tasmanian old-growth forests. A possible reason is suggested by the fact that, after the National Party announced its strong support for Tasmanian logging in 1995, it became known that the party's three biggest financial contributors were logging companies.

In addition to mining its old-growth forests, Australia has also planted agroforestry plantations, both of native and of non-native tree species. For all the reasons mentioned previously—low soil nutrient levels, low and unpredictable rainfall, and resulting low growth rates of trees—agroforestry is much less profitable and faces higher costs in Australia than in 12 out of the 13 countries that are among its principal competitors. Even Australia's most valuable commercially surviving timber tree species, that Tasmanian Blue Gum, grows faster and more profitably in overseas plantations where it has been planted (in Brazil, Chile, Portugal, South Africa, Spain, and Vietnam) than in Tasmania itself.

The mining of Australia's marine fisheries resembles that of its forests. Basically, Australia's tall trees and lush grass deceived the first European settlers into overrating Australia's potential for food production on land: in technical terms used by ecologists, the land supported large standing crops but low productivity. The same is true of Australia's oceans, whose productivity is low because it depends on nutrient runoff from that same unproductive land, and because Australian coastal waters lack nutrient-rich upwellings comparable to the Humboldt current off the west coast of South America. Australia's marine populations tend to have low growth rates, so that they are easily overfished. For example, within the last two decades there has been a worldwide boom in a fish called Orange Roughy, caught in Australian and New Zealand waters and providing the basis of a fishery that has been profitable in the short term. Unfortunately, closer studies showed that Orange Roughy are very slow-growing, they do not start to breed until they are about 40 years old, and the fish caught and eaten are often 100 years old. Hence Orange Roughy populations cannot possibly breed fast enough to replace the adults being removed by fishermen, and that fishery is now in decline.

Australia has exhibited a history of marine overfishing: mining one stock until it is depleted to uneconomically low levels, then discovering a new fishery and switching to it until it too collapses within a short time, like a gold rush. After a new fishery opens, a scientific study by marine biologists may be initiated to determine the maximal sustainable harvesting rates, but the fishery is at risk of collapsing before recommendations from the study become available. Australian victims of such overfishing, besides Orange Roughy, include Coral Trout, Eastern Gemfish, Exmouth Gulf Tiger Prawns, School Sharks, Southern Bluefin Tuna, and Tiger Flathead. The only Australian marine fishery for which there are well-supported claims of sustainable harvesting involves the Western Australian rock lobster population, which is currently Australia's most valuable seafood export and whose healthy status has been evaluated independently by the Marine Stewardship Council (to be discussed in Chapter 15).

Like its marine fisheries, Australia's freshwater fisheries as well are limited by low productivity because of low nutrient runoff from the unproductive land. Also like the marine fisheries, the freshwater fisheries have deceptively large standing crops but low production. For example, Australia's largest freshwater fish species is the Murray Cod, up to three feet long and confined to the Murray/Darling river system. It is good eating, highly valued, and formerly so abundant that it used to be caught and shipped to markets by the truckload. Now, the Murray Cod fishery has been closed because of the decline and collapse of the catch. Among the causes of that collapse are the overharvesting of a slow-growing fish species, as in the case of Orange Roughy; effects of introduced carp, which increase water turbidity; and several consequences of dams built on the Murray River in the 1930s, which interrupted fish spawning movements, decreased river water temperature (because dam managers released cold bottom water too cold for the fish's reproduction, rather than warmer surface water), and converted a river formerly receiving periodic nutrient inputs from floods into permanent bodies of water with little nutrient renewal.

Today, the financial yield from Australia's freshwater fisheries is trivial. For instance, all freshwater fisheries in the state of South Australia generate only $450,000 per year, divided among 30 people who fish only as a part-time occupation. A properly managed sustainable fishery for Murray Cod and Golden Perch, the Murray/Darling's other economically valuable fish species, could surely yield far more money than that, but it is unknown whether damage to Murray/Darling fisheries is now irreversible.

As for freshwater itself, Australia is the continent with the least of it. Most of that little freshwater that is readily accessible to populated areas is already utilized for drinking or agriculture. Even the country's largest river, the Murray/Darling, has two-thirds of its total water flow drawn off by humans in an average year, and in some years virtually all of its water. Australia's freshwater sources that remain unutilized consist mainly of rivers in remote northern areas, far from human settlements or agricultural lands where they could be put to use. As Australia's population grows, and as its unutilized supplies of freshwater dwindle, some settled areas may be forced to turn to more expensive desalinization for their freshwater. There is already a desalinization plant on Kangaroo Island, and one may be needed soon on the Eyre Peninsula.

Several major projects in the past to modify unutilized Australian rivers have turned out to be costly failures. For instance, in the 1930s it was proposed to build several dozen dams along the Murray River in order to permit freight traffic by ship, and about half of those planned dams were built by the U.S. Army Corps of Engineers before the plan was abandoned. There is now no commercial freight traffic on the Murray River, but the dams did contribute to the already-mentioned collapse of the Murray Cod fishery. One of the most expensive failures was the Ord River Scheme, which involved damming a river in a remote and sparsely populated area of northwestern Australia in order to irrigate land for growing barley, corn, cotton, safflower, soybeans, and wheat. Eventually, only cotton among all those crops was grown on a small scale and failed after 10 years. Sugar and melons are now being produced there, but the value of their yield does not come close to matching the project's great expense.

In addition to those problems of water quantity, accessibility, and use, there are also issues of water quality. Utilized rivers contain toxins, pesticides, or salts from upstream that reach urban drinking areas and agricultural irrigation areas downstream. Examples that I already mentioned are the salt and agricultural chemicals from the Murray River, which furnishes much of Adelaide's drinking water, and the pesticides from New South Wales and Queensland cotton fields, which jeopardize the marketability of downstream attempts to grow chemical-free wheat and beef.

In part because Australia itself has fewer native animal species than the other continents, it has been especially vulnerable to exotic species from overseas becoming intentionally or accidentally established, and then depleting or exterminating populations of native animals and plants without evolved defenses against such alien species. Notorious examples that I already mentioned are rabbits, which consume about half of the pasturage that could otherwise be consumed by sheep and cattle; foxes, which have preyed on and exterminated many native mammal species; several thousand species of plant weeds, which have transformed habitats, crowded out native plants, degraded pasture quality, and occasionally poisoned livestock; and carp, which have damaged water quality in the Murray/Darling River.

A few other horror stories involving introduced pests deserve briefer mention. Domestic buffalo, camels, donkeys, goats, and horses that have gone feral trample, browse, and otherwise damage large areas of habitat. Hundreds of species of insect pests have established themselves more easily in Australia than in temperate-zone countries with cold winters. Among them, blowflies, mites, and ticks have been especially damaging to livestock and pastures, while caterpillars, fruit flies, and many others are damaging to crops. Cane Toads, introduced in 1935 to control two insect pests of sugarcane, failed to do that but did spread over an area of 100,000 square miles, assisted by the fact that they can live for up to 20 years and that females annually lay 30,000 eggs. The toads are poisonous, inedible to all native Australian animals, and rate as one of the worst mistakes ever committed in the name of pest control.

Finally, Australia's isolation by the oceans, and hence its heavy reliance on ship transport from overseas, has resulted in many marine pests arriving in discharged ballast water and dry ballast of ships, on ship hulls, and in materials imported for aquaculture. Among those marine pests are comb jellies, crabs, toxic dinoflagellates, shellfish, worms, and a Japanese starfish that depleted the Spotted Handfish native only to southeastern Australia. Many of these pests are enormously expensive in the damage that they cause and in the annual control costs that they necessitate every year: e.g., a few hundred million dollars per year for rabbits, $600 million for flies and ticks of livestock, $200 million for a pasture mite, $2.5 billion for other insect pests, over $3 billion for weeds, and so on.

Thus, Australia has an exceptionally fragile environment, damaged in a multitude of ways incurring enormous economic costs. Some of those costs stem from past damage that is now irreversible, such as some forms of land degradation and the extinctions of native species (relatively more species in recent times in Australia than on any other continent). Most of the types of damage are still ongoing today, or even increasing or accelerating as in the case of old-growth forest logging in Tasmania. Some of the damaging processes are virtually impossible to halt now because of long built-in time delays, such as the effects of slow underground downhill flows of already-mobilized saline groundwater that will continue to spread for centuries. Many Australian cultural attitudes, as well as government policies, remain the ones that caused damage in the past and are still continuing to cause it. For instance, among the political obstacles to a reform of water policies are obstacles arising from a market for "water licenses" (rights to extract water for irrigation). The purchasers of those licenses understandably feel that they actually own the water that they have paid dearly to extract, even though full exercise of the licenses is impossible because the total amount of water for which licenses have been issued may exceed the amount of water available in a normal year.

To those of us inclined to pessimism or even just to realistic sober thinking, all those facts give us reason to wonder whether Australians are doomed to a declining standard of living in a steadily deteriorating environment. That is an entirely realistic scenario for Australia's future—much more likely than either a plunge into an Easter Island–like population crash and political collapse as prophesized by doomsday advocates, or a continuation of current consumption rates and population growth as blithely assumed by many of Australia's current politicians and business leaders. The implausibility of the latter two scenarios, and the realistic prospects of the first scenario, apply to the rest of the First World as well, with the sole difference that Australia could end up in the first scenario sooner.

Fortunately, there are signs of hope. They involve changing attitudes, rethinking by Australia's farmers, private initiatives, and the beginnings of radical governmental initiatives. All that rethinking illustrates a theme that we already encountered in connection with the Greenland Norse (Chapter 8), and to which we shall return in Chapters 14 and 16: the challenge of deciding which of a society's deeply held core values are compatible with the society's survival, and which ones instead have to be given up.

When I first visited Australia 40 years ago, many Australian landowners responded to criticism that they were damaging their land for future generations or producing damage for other people by responding, "It's my land, and I can bloody well do with it whatever I bloody please." While one still hears such attitudes today, they are becoming less frequent and less publicly acceptable. Whereas the government until a few decades ago faced little resistance to its enforcing environmentally destructive regulations (e.g., *requiring* land clearance) and putting through environmentally destructive schemes (e.g., the Murray River dams and the Ord River Scheme), the Australian public today, like the public in Europe, North America, and other areas, is increasingly vocal on environmental matters. Public opposition has been especially loud to land clearance, river development, and old-growth logging. At the moment that I write these lines, those public attitudes have just resulted in the South Australian state government's instituting a new tax (thereby breaking an election promise) to raise $300 million to undo damage to the Murray River; the Western Australian state government's proceeding with the phasing-out of old-growth logging; the New South Wales state government and its farmers' reaching agreement on a $406 million plan to streamline resource management and end large-scale land clearing; and the state government in Queensland, historically the most conservative Australian state, announcing a joint proposal with the national (Commonwealth) government to end large-scale clearing of mature bushland by the year 2006. All of these measures were unimaginable 40 years ago.

These signs of hope include changed attitudes of the voting public as a whole, resulting in changed governmental policies. Another sign of hope involves changed attitudes of farmers in particular, who are increasingly realizing that the farming methods of the past cannot be sustained and wouldn't permit them to pass on their farms in good condition to their children. That prospect hurts Australian farmers, because (like the Montana farmers whom I interviewed for Chapter 1) it's love for the farming lifestyle, rather than farming's meager financial rewards, that motivates them to carry on with the hard work of being farmers. Symbolic of those changed attitudes was a conversation that I had with sheep farmer Bill McIntosh, the one whom I mentioned as having mapped, bulldozed, and dynamited the rabbit warrens on his farm, which had belonged to his family since 1879. He showed me photos of the same hill, taken in 1937 and in 1999, and illustrating dramatically the sparse vegetation in 1937 due to sheep overstocking and the vegetation's subsequent recovery. Among his own measures to keep his farm sustainable, he is stocking sheep at levels below those considered as an acceptable maximum by the government, and is thinking about switching to wool-less sheep kept just for meat production (because they require less attention and less land). As one method of coping with the weed problem and preventing less palatable plant species from taking over pasture, he has adopted a practice termed "cell grazing," under which sheep are not permitted to eat just the most palatable plants and then moved to the next pasture, but are instead left in the same pasture until they have been forced to consume its less palatable as well as its more palatable plants. Astonishingly to me, he keeps costs down and manages the entire farm without any full-time employee besides himself, by herding his several thousand sheep while riding on his motorbike, carrying binoculars and a radio and accompanied by his dog. Simultaneously, he somehow makes time for trying to develop other sources of business income, such as bed-and-breakfast tourism, because he recognizes that his farm alone would be marginal in the long run.

Farmer peer pressure, in combination with recently changed government policies, is reducing stocking rates and improving pasture conditions. In inland parts of South Australia where the government owns land fit for pastoralism and leases it to farmers on 42-year leases, an agency called the Pastoral Board assesses the land's condition every 14 years, reduces the permissible stocking rate if the vegetation's condition is not improving, and revokes the lease if it decides that the farmer/tenant was managing the property unsatisfactorily. Closer to the coast, land tends to be owned outright (as freehold) or under perpetual lease, so that such direct governmental control is not possible, but there is still indirect control enforced in two ways. By law, landowners or leaseholders still bear a "duty-of-care" obligation to prevent land degradation. The first stage of enforcement involves local farmer boards that monitor degradation and apply peer pressure to try to achieve compliance. The second stage depends on soil conservators who can intervene if the local board is not effective. Bill McIntosh related to me four cases in which local boards or soil conservators in his area ordered farmers to reduce sheep stocking rates, or actually confiscated the property when the farmer did not obey.

Among Australia's many innovative private initiatives to address environmental problems are several that I encountered while visiting a former sheep and farm property of nearly 1,000 square miles near the Murray River, called Calperum Station. First leased for grazing in 1851, it fell victim to the usual panoply of Australian environmental problems: deforestation, foxes, land clearance by chaining and burning, overirrigation, overstocking, rabbits, salinization, weeds, wind erosion, and so on. In 1993 it was bought by the Australian Commonwealth Government and the Chicago Zoological Society, the latter (despite being U.S.-based) already attracted by Australia's pioneering efforts in developing ecologically sustainable land practices. For some years after that purchase, government managers applied top-down control and gave orders to local community volunteers, who became increasingly frustrated, until in 1998 control was turned over to the private Australian Landscape Trust mobilizing 400 local volunteers for bottom-up community management. The trust is funded in large degree by Australia's largest private philanthropic organization, The Potter Foundation, which is expressly concerned with reversing the degradation of Australia's farmland.

Under the trust's management, local volunteers at Calperum threw themselves into whatever projects appealed to each volunteer's own interest. By thus enlisting volunteers, this private initiative has been able to accomplish far more than would have been possible with the limited available government funds alone. Volunteers trained at Calperum have then gone on to use those skills to undertake other conservation projects elsewhere. Among the projects that I saw, one volunteer was devoting herself to a small endangered kangaroo species whose population she was trying to restore; another volunteer preferred to poison foxes, one of the area's most damaging introduced pest species; and still other volunteers were attacking the ubiquitous problem of rabbits, seeking ways to control introduced carp in the Murray River, perfecting a strategy for non-chemical control of insect pests of citrus trees, restoring lakes that had become sterile, revegetating overgrazed land, and developing markets for growing and selling local wildflowers and plants controlling erosion. These efforts deserve a prize for imagination and enthusiasm. Literally tens of thousands of other such private initiatives are operating around Australia: for instance, another organization that also grew in part out of The Potter Foundation's Potter Farmland Plan, called Landcare, is helping 15,000 individual farmers wanting to help themselves to pass on their farms in decent condition to their children.

Complementing these imaginative private initiatives are government initiatives that include a radical rethinking of Australian agriculture, in response to growing awareness of the seriousness of Australia's problems. It is too early to guess whether any of these radical plans will be adopted, but the fact that salaried government employees are being permitted and even paid to develop them is remarkable. The proposals are not coming from idealistic bird-loving environmentalists but from hard-nosed economists, who are asking themselves: would Australia be better off economically without much of its present agricultural enterprise?

The background to this rethinking is the realization that only tiny areas of Australian land currently being used for agriculture are productive and suitable for sustained agricultural operations. While 60% of Australia's land area and 80% of its human water use are dedicated to agriculture, the value of agriculture relative to other sectors of the Australian economy has been shrinking to the point where it now contributes less than 3% of the gross national product. That's a huge allocation of land and scarce water to an enterprise of such low value. Furthermore, it is astonishing to realize that over 99% of that agricultural land makes little or no positive contribution to Australia's economy. It turns out that about 80% of Australia's agricultural profits are derived from less than 0.8% of its agricultural land, virtually all of it in the southwestern corner, on the south coast around Adelaide, in the southeastern corner, and in eastern Queensland. Those are the few areas favored by volcanic or recently uplifted soils, reliable winter rains, or both. Most of Australia's remaining agriculture is in effect a mining operation that does not add to Australia's wealth but merely converts environmental capital of soil and native vegetation irreversibly into cash, with the help of indirect government subsidies in the forms of below-cost water, tax concessions, and free telephone linkups and other infrastructure. Is it a good use of Australian taxpayers' money to subsidize so much unprofitable or destructive land use?

Even from the narrowest point of view, some Australian agriculture is uneconomic to the individual consumer, who can buy its products (such as orange juice concentrate and pork) more cheaply as imports from overseas than as domestic produce. Much agriculture is also uneconomic to the individual farmer, as measured by what is termed "profit at full equity." That is, if one counts among a farm's expenses not only its cash expenditures but also the value of the farmer's labor, two-thirds of Australia's agricultural land (mainly land used for raising sheep and beef cattle) operates at a net loss to the farmer.

For instance, consider Australian pastoralists raising sheep for their wool. On the average, pastoralists' farm income is lower than the national minimum wage, and they are accumulating debts. The farm's capital plant of its buildings and fences is running down because the farm doesn't yield enough money to maintain the plant in good condition. Nor does wool yield enough profit to pay the interest costs on the farm's mortgage. The means by which the average wool-grower survives economically are through non-farm income, earned by holding a second job as a nurse or in a store, operating a bed-and-breakfast, or other ways. In effect, those second jobs, plus the farmers' willingness to work on their farms for little or no pay, are subsidizing their own money-losing farm operations. Many in the current generation of farmers pursue the profession because they grew up to admire the rural life, even though they could earn more money doing something else. In Australia as in Montana, the children of the current generation of farmers are unlikely to make that same choice when they will be facing the decision whether they want to take over the family farm from their parents. Only 29% of current Australian farmers expect that their children will run the farm.

That's the economic value of much Australian farming to the individual consumer and the individual farmer. What about its value to Australia as a whole? For any given piece of the farming enterprise, one has to take into account a broadened view of its costs to the entire economy, as well as its benefits. One big piece of those broadened costs is government support to farmers through means such as tax subsidies and expenditures for drought assistance, research, advising, and agricultural extension services. Those government expenditures eat up about one-third of Australian agriculture's nominal net profits. Another big piece of those broadened costs is the losses that agriculture imposes on other segments of the Australian economy. In effect, agricultural uses of land compete with other potential uses of the same land, and using one piece of land for agriculture may damage the value of another piece of land for tourism, forestry, fisheries, recreation, or even for agriculture itself. For instance, soil runoff caused by land clearance for agriculture is damaging and locally killing the Great Barrier Reef, one of Australia's major tourist attractions, but tourism is already more important to Australia than agriculture as a source of foreign-exchange earnings. Or suppose one wheat farmer on uphill land can make a profit for a few years by growing irrigated wheat that causes massive salinization of larger properties lying downhill, ruining those properties in perpetuity. In those cases the farmer clearing land in the reef's watershed, or operating the uphill farm, may show a profit to himself as a result of his activities, but Australia as a whole shows a loss.

Another case that has come in for much recent discussion involves industrial-scale cotton-growing in southern Queensland and in northern New South Wales, on the upper reaches of tributaries of the Darling River (flowing down through agricultural districts of southern New South Wales and South Australia) and of the Diamantina River (flowing down into the Lake Eyre Basin). In a narrow sense, cotton is Australia's second most profitable agricultural export, after wheat. But cotton-growing depends on irrigation water provided at low cost or no cost by the government. In addition, all major cotton-growing areas pollute the water with their heavy applications of pesticides, herbicides, defoliants, and high-phosphorus and high-nitrogen fertilizers (causing algal blooms). Those pollutants even include DDT and its metabolites, last used about 25 years ago but still persisting in the environment because they resist breakdown. In the downstream reaches of those polluted rivers are wheat and cattle growers who appeal to a high-value niche market by raising wheat and beef without adding their own chemicals. They have been protesting vigorously, because their ability to sell their supposedly chemical-free produce is being undermined by those side effects of the cotton industry. Thus, while growing cotton unquestionably brings profits to the owners of the cotton agribusinesses, one would have to calculate indirect costs, such as those of subsidized water and damage to other agricultural sectors, if one wanted to evaluate whether cotton produces a gain or a loss to Australia as a whole.

The remaining example considers Australia's agricultural production of the greenhouse gases carbon dioxide and methane. That's an especially serious problem for Australia, because global warming (thought to result in large degree from greenhouse gases) is breaking down the pattern of reliable winter rains that turned wheat grown in southwestern Australia's wheat belt into Australia's single most valuable agricultural export. The carbon dioxide emissions from Australian agriculture exceed those produced by motor vehicles and all the rest of the transport industry. Even worse are cows, whose digestion produces methane, 20 times more potent than carbon dioxide in causing global warming. The simplest way for Australia to fulfill its stated commitment to reduce its greenhouse gas emissions would be to eliminate its cattle!

While that and other radical suggestions have been put forward, there are currently no signs of their being adopted soon. It would be a "first" for the modern world if a government voluntarily decided to phase out much of its agricultural enterprise, in anticipation of future problems, before being forced in desperation to do so. Nevertheless, even the mere existence of these suggestions raises a larger point. Australia illustrates in extreme form the exponentially accelerating horse race in which the world now finds itself. ("Accelerating" means going faster and faster; "exponentially accelerating" means accelerating in the manner of a nuclear chain reaction, twice as fast and then 4, 8, 16, 32 . . . times faster after equal time intervals.) On the one hand, the development of environmental problems in Australia, as in the whole world, is accelerating exponentially. On the other hand, the development of public environmental concern, and of private and governmental countermeasures, is also accelerating exponentially. Which horse will win the race? Many readers of this book are young enough, and will live long enough, to see the outcome.

PART FOUR

PRACTICAL LESSONS

■ ■ ■

CHAPTER 14

Why Do Some Societies
Make Disastrous Decisions?

Road map for success ■ Failure to anticipate ■ Failure to perceive ■
Rational bad behavior ■ Disastrous values ■ Other irrational failures ■
Unsuccessful solutions ■ Signs of hope ■

Education is a process involving two sets of participants who supposedly play different roles: teachers who impart knowledge to students,
and students who absorb knowledge from teachers. In fact, as every
open-minded teacher discovers, education is also about students imparting
knowledge to their teachers, by challenging the teachers' assumptions and
by asking questions that the teachers hadn't previously thought of. I recently repeated that discovery when I taught a course, on how societies cope
with environmental problems, to highly motivated undergraduates at my
institution, the University of California at Los Angeles (UCLA). In effect,
the course was a trial run-through of this book's material, at a time when I
had drafted some chapters, was planning other chapters, and could still
make extensive changes.

My first lecture after the class's introductory meeting was on the collapse
of Easter Island society, the subject of this book's Chapter 2. In the class discussion after I had finished my presentation, the apparently simple question
that most puzzled my students was one whose actual complexity hadn't
sunk into me before: how on earth could a society make such an obviously
disastrous decision as to cut down all the trees on which it depended? One
of the students asked what I thought the islander who cut down the last
palm tree said as he was doing it. For every other society that I treated in
subsequent lectures, my students raised essentially the same question. They
also asked the related question: how often did people wreak ecological damage intentionally, or at least while aware of the likely consequences? How
often did people instead do it without meaning to, or out of ignorance? My
students wondered whether—if there are still people left alive a hundred
years from now—those people of the next century will be as astonished

about our blindness today as we are about the blindness of the Easter Islanders.

This question of why societies end up destroying themselves through disastrous decisions astonishes not only my UCLA undergraduates but also professional historians and archaeologists. For example, perhaps the most cited book on societal collapses is *The Collapse of Complex Societies,* by the archaeologist Joseph Tainter. In assessing competing explanations for ancient collapses, Tainter remained skeptical of even the possibility that they might have been due to depletion of environmental resources, because that outcome seemed a priori so unlikely to him. Here is his reasoning: "One supposition of this view must be that these societies sit by and watch the encroaching weakness without taking corrective actions. Here is a major difficulty. Complex societies are characterized by centralized decision-making, high information flow, great coordination of parts, formal channels of command, and pooling of resources. Much of this structure seems to have the capability, if not the designed purpose, of countering fluctuations and deficiencies in productivity. With their administrative structure, and capacity to allocate both labor and resources, dealing with adverse environmental conditions may be one of the things that complex societies do best (see, for example, Isbell [1978]). It is curious that they would collapse when faced with precisely those conditions they are equipped to circumvent. . . . As it becomes apparent to the members or administrators of a complex society that a resource base is deteriorating, it seems most reasonable to assume that some rational steps are taken toward a resolution. The alternative assumption— of idleness in the face of disaster—requires a leap of faith at which we may rightly hesitate."

That is, Tainter's reasoning suggested to him that complex societies are not likely to allow themselves to collapse through failure to manage their environmental resources. Yet it is clear from all the cases discussed in this book that precisely such a failure has happened repeatedly. How did so many societies make such bad mistakes?

My UCLA undergraduates, and Joseph Tainter as well, have identified a baffling phenomenon: namely, failures of group decision-making on the part of whole societies or other groups. That problem is of course related to the problem of failures of individual decision-making. Individuals, too, make bad decisions: they enter bad marriages, they make bad investments and career choices, their businesses fail, and so on. But some additional factors enter into failures of group decision-making, such as conflicts of interest among members of the group, and group dynamics. This is obviously a complex subject to which there would not be a single answer fitting all situations.

What I'm going to propose instead is a road map of factors contributing to failures of group decision-making. I'll divide the factors into a fuzzily delineated sequence of four categories. First of all, a group may fail to anticipate a problem before the problem actually arrives. Second, when the problem does arrive, the group may fail to perceive it. Then, after they perceive it, they may fail even to try to solve it. Finally, they may try to solve it but may not succeed. While all this discussion of reasons for failure and societal collapses may seem depressing, the flip side is a heartening subject: namely, successful decision-making. Perhaps if we understood the reasons why groups often make bad decisions, we could use that knowledge as a checklist to guide groups to make good decisions.

The first stop on my road map is that groups may do disastrous things because they failed to anticipate a problem before it arrived, for any of several reasons. One is that they may have had no prior experience of such problems, and so may not have been sensitized to the possibility.

A prime example is the mess that British colonists created for themselves when they introduced foxes and rabbits from Britain into Australia in the 1800s. Today these rate as two of the most disastrous examples of impacts of alien species on an environment to which they were not native (see Chapter 13 for details). These introductions are all the more tragic because they were carried out intentionally at much effort, rather than resulting inadvertently from tiny seeds overlooked in transported hay, as in so many cases of establishment of noxious weeds. Foxes have proceeded to prey on and exterminate many species of native Australian mammals without evolutionary experience of foxes, while rabbits consume much of the plant fodder intended for sheep and cattle, outcompete native herbivorous mammals, and undermine the ground by their burrows.

With the gift of hindsight, we now view it as incredibly stupid that colonists would intentionally release into Australia two alien mammals that have caused billions of dollars in damages and expenditures to control them. We recognize today, from many other such examples, that introductions often prove disastrous in unexpected ways. That's why, when you go to Australia or the U.S. as a visitor or returning resident, one of the first questions you are now asked by immigration officers is whether you are carrying any plants, seeds, or animals—to reduce the risk of their escaping and becoming established. From abundant prior experience we have now learned (often but not always) to anticipate at least the potential dangers of introducing species. But it's still difficult even for professional ecologists to predict which introductions will actually become established, which established successful introductions will prove disastrous, and why the same species establishes itself at certain sites of introduction and not at others. Hence we really shouldn't be surprised that 19th century Australians, lacking the 20th century's experience of disastrous introductions, failed to anticipate the effects of rabbits and foxes.

In this book we have encountered other examples of societies understandably failing to anticipate a problem of which they lacked prior experience. In investing heavily in walrus hunting in order to export walrus ivory to Europe, the Greenland Norse could hardly have anticipated that the Crusades would eliminate the market for walrus ivory by reopening Europe's access to Asian and African elephant ivory, or that increasing sea ice would impede ship traffic to Europe. Again, not being soil scientists, the Maya at Copán could not foresee that deforestation of the hill slopes would trigger soil erosion from the slopes into the valley bottoms.

Even prior experience is not a guarantee that a society will anticipate a problem, if the experience happened so long ago as to have been forgotten. That's especially a problem for non-literate societies, which have less capacity than literate societies to preserve detailed memories of events long in the past, because of the limitations of oral transmission of information compared to writing. For instance, we saw in Chapter 4 that Chaco Canyon Anasazi society survived several droughts before succumbing to a big drought in the 12th century A.D. But the earlier droughts had occurred long before the birth of any Anasazi affected by the big drought, which would thus have been unanticipated because the Anasazi lacked writing. Similarly, the Classic Lowland Maya succumbed to a drought in the 9th century, despite their area having been affected by drought centuries earlier (Chapter 5). In that case, although the Maya did have writing, it recorded kings' deeds and astronomical events rather than weather reports, so that the drought of the 3rd century did not help the Maya anticipate the drought of the 9th century.

In modern literate societies whose writing does discuss subjects besides kings and planets, that doesn't necessarily mean that we draw on prior experience committed to writing. We, too, tend to forget things. For a year or two after the gas shortages of the 1973 Gulf oil crisis, we Americans shied away from gas-guzzling cars, but then we forgot that experience and are now embracing SUVs, despite volumes of print spilled over the 1973 events. When the city of Tucson in Arizona went through a severe drought in the 1950s, its alarmed citizens swore that they would manage their water better, but soon returned to their water-guzzling ways of building golf courses and watering their gardens.

Another reason why a society may fail to anticipate a problem involves reasoning by false analogy. When we are in an unfamiliar situation, we fall back on drawing analogies with old familiar situations. That's a good way to proceed if the old and new situations are truly analogies, but it can be dangerous if they are only superficially similar. For instance, Vikings who immigrated to Iceland beginning around the year A.D. 870 arrived from Norway and Britain, which have heavy clay soils ground up by glaciers. Even if the vegetation covering those soils is cleared, the soils themselves are too heavy to be blown away. When the Viking colonists encountered in Iceland many of the same tree species already familiar to them from Norway and Britain, they were deceived by the apparent similarity of the landscape (Chapter 6). Unfortunately, Iceland's soils arose not through glacial grinding but through winds carrying light ash blown out in volcanic eruptions. Once the Vikings had cleared Iceland's forests to create pastures for their livestock, the light soil became exposed for the wind to blow out again, and much of Iceland's topsoil soon eroded away.

A tragic and famous modern example of reasoning by false analogy involves French military preparations from World War II. After the horrible bloodbath of World War I, France recognized its vital need to protect itself against the possibility of another German invasion. Unfortunately, the French army staff assumed that a next war would be fought similarly to World War I, in which the Western Front between France and Germany had remained locked in static trench warfare for four years. Defensive infantry forces manning elaborate fortified trenches had been usually able to repel infantry attacks, while offensive forces had deployed the newly invented tanks only individually and just in support of attacking infantry. Hence France constructed an even more elaborate and expensive system of fortifications, the Maginot Line, to guard its eastern frontier against Germany. But the German army staff, having been defeated in World War I, recognized the need for a different strategy. It used tanks rather than infantry to spearhead its attacks, massed the tanks into separate armored divisions, bypassed the Maginot Line through forested terrain previously considered unsuitable for tanks, and thereby defeated France within a mere six weeks. In reasoning by false analogy after World War I, French generals made a common mistake: generals often plan for a coming war as if it will be like the previous war, especially if that previous war was one in which their side was victorious.

The second stop on my road map, after a society has or hasn't anticipated a problem before it arrives, involves its perceiving or failing to perceive a problem that has actually arrived. There are at least three reasons for such failures, all of them common in the business world and in academia.

First, the origins of some problems are literally imperceptible. For example, the nutrients responsible for soil fertility are invisible to the eye, and only in modern times did they become measurable by chemical analysis. In Australia, Mangareva, parts of the U.S. Southwest, and many other locations, most of the nutrients had already been leached out of the soil by rain before human settlement. When people arrived and began growing crops, those crops quickly exhausted the remaining nutrients, with the result that agriculture failed. Yet such nutrient-poor soils often bear lush-appearing vegetation; it's just that most of the nutrients in the ecosystem are contained in the vegetation rather than in the soil, and are removed if one cuts down the vegetation. There was no way for the first colonists of Australia and Mangareva to perceive that problem of soil nutrient exhaustion—nor for farmers in areas with salt deep in the ground (like eastern Montana and parts of Australia and Mesopotamia) to perceive incipient salinization— nor for miners of sulfide ores to perceive the toxic copper and acid dissolved in mine runoff water.

Another frequent reason for failure to perceive a problem after it has arrived is distant managers, a potential issue in any large society or business. For example, the largest private landowner and timber company in Montana today is based not within that state but 400 miles away in Seattle, Washington. Not being on the scene, company executives may not realize that they have a big weed problem on their forest properties. Well-run companies avoid such surprises by periodically sending managers "into the field" to observe what is actually going on, while a tall friend of mine who was a college president regularly practiced with his school's undergraduates on their basketball courts in order to keep abreast of student thinking. The opposite of failure due to distant managers is success due to on-the-spot managers. Part of the reason why Tikopians on their tiny island, and New Guinea highlanders in their valleys, have successfully managed their resources for more than a thousand years is that everyone on the island or in the valley is familiar with the entire territory on which their society depends.

Perhaps the commonest circumstance under which societies fail to perceive a problem is when it takes the form of a slow trend concealed by wide up-and-down fluctuations. The prime example in modern times is global warming. We now realize that temperatures around the world have been slowly rising in recent decades, due in large part to atmospheric changes caused by humans. However, it is not the case that the climate each year has been exactly 0.01 degree warmer than in the previous year. Instead, as we all know, climate fluctuates up and down erratically from year to year: three degrees warmer in one summer than in the previous one, then two degrees warmer the next summer, down four degrees the following summer, down another degree the next one, then up five degrees, etc. With such large and unpredictable fluctuations, it has taken a long time to discern the average upwards trend of 0.01 degree per year within that noisy signal. That's why it was only a few years ago that most professional climatologists previously skeptical of the reality of global warming became convinced. As of the time that I write these lines, President Bush of the U.S. is still not convinced of its reality, and he thinks that we need more research. The medieval Greenlanders had similar difficulties in recognizing that their climate was gradually becoming colder, and the Maya and Anasazi had trouble discerning that theirs was becoming drier.

Politicians use the term "creeping normalcy" to refer to such slow trends concealed within noisy fluctuations. If the economy, schools, traffic congestion, or anything else is deteriorating only slowly, it's difficult to recognize that each successive year is on the average slightly worse than the year before, so one's baseline standard for what constitutes "normalcy" shifts gradually and imperceptibly. It may take a few decades of a long sequence of such slight year-to-year changes before people realize, with a jolt, that conditions used to be much better several decades ago, and that what is accepted as normalcy has crept downwards.

Another term related to creeping normalcy is "landscape amnesia": forgetting how different the surrounding landscape looked 50 years ago, because the change from year to year has been so gradual. An example involves the melting of Montana's glaciers and snowfields caused by global warming (Chapter 1). After spending the summers of 1953 and 1956 in Montana's Big Hole Basin as a teenager, I did not return until 42 years later, in 1998, when I began visiting every year. Among my vivid teenaged memories of the Big Hole were the snow covering the distant mountaintops even in mid-summer, my resulting sense that a white band low in the sky encircled the basin, and my recollection of a weekend camping trip when two friends and I clambered up to that magical band of snow. Not having lived through the fluctuations and gradual dwindling of summer snow during the intervening 42 years, I was stunned and saddened on my return to the Big Hole in 1998 to find the band almost gone, and in 2001 and 2003 actually all melted off. When I asked my Montana resident friends about the change, they were less aware of it: they unconsciously compared each year's band (or lack thereof) with the previous few years. Creeping normalcy or landscape amnesia made it harder for them than for me to remember what conditions had been like in the 1950s. Such experiences are a major reason why people may fail to notice a developing problem, until it is too late.

I suspect that landscape amnesia provided part of the answer to my UCLA students' question, "What did the Easter Islander who cut down the last palm tree say as he was doing it?" We unconsciously imagine a sudden change: one year, the island still covered with a forest of tall palm trees being used to produce wine, fruit, and timber to transport and erect statues; the next year, just a single tree left, which an islander proceeds to fell in an act of incredibly self-damaging stupidity. Much more likely, though, the changes in forest cover from year to year would have been almost undetectable: yes, this year we cut down a few trees over there, but saplings are starting to grow back again here on this abandoned garden site. Only the oldest islanders, thinking back to their childhoods decades earlier, could have recognized a difference. Their children could no more have comprehended their parents' tales of a tall forest than my 17-year-old sons today can comprehend my wife's and my tales of what Los Angeles used to be like 40 years ago. Gradually, Easter Island's trees became fewer, smaller, and less important. At the time that the last fruit-bearing adult palm tree was cut, the species had long ago ceased to be of any economic significance. That left only smaller and smaller palm saplings to clear each year, along with other bushes and treelets. No one would have noticed the falling of the last little palm sapling. By then, the memory of the valuable palm forest of centuries earlier had succumbed to landscape amnesia. Conversely, the speed with which deforestation spread over early Tokugawa Japan made it easier for its shoguns to recognize the landscape changes and the need for preemptive action.

■ ■ ■

The third stop on the road map of failure is the most frequent, the most surprising, and requires the longest discussion because it assumes such a wide variety of forms. Contrary to what Joseph Tainter and almost anyone else would have expected, it turns out that societies often fail even to attempt to solve a problem once it has been perceived.

Many of the reasons for such failure fall under the heading of what economists and other social scientists term "rational behavior," arising from clashes of interest between people. That is, some people may reason correctly that they can advance their own interests by behavior harmful to other people. Scientists term such behavior "rational" precisely because it employs correct reasoning, even though it may be morally reprehensible. The perpetrators know that they will often get away with their bad behavior, especially if there is no law against it or if the law isn't effectively enforced. They feel safe because the perpetrators are typically concentrated (few in number) and highly motivated by the prospect of reaping big, certain, and immediate profits, while the losses are spread over large numbers of individuals. That gives the losers little motivation to go to the hassle of fighting back, because each loser loses only a little and would receive only small, uncertain, distant profits even from successfully undoing the minority's grab. Examples include so-called perverse subsidies: the large sums of money that governments pay to support industries that might be uneconomic without the subsidies, such as many fisheries, sugar-growing in the U.S., and cotton-growing in Australia (subsidized indirectly through the government's bearing the cost of water for irrigation). The relatively few fishermen and growers lobby tenaciously for the subsidies that represent much of their income, while the losers (all the taxpayers) are less vocal because the subsidy is funded by just a small amount of money concealed in each citizen's tax bill. Measures benefiting a small minority at the expense of a large majority are especially likely to arise in certain types of democracies that bestow "swing power" on some small groups: e.g., senators from small states in the U.S. Senate, or small religious parties often holding the balance of power in Israel to a degree scarcely possible under the Dutch parliamentary system.

A frequent type of rational bad behavior is "good for me, bad for you and for everybody else"—to put it bluntly, "selfish." As a simple example, most Montana fishermen fish for trout. A few fishermen who prefer to fish for a pike, a larger fish-eating fish not native to western Montana, surreptitiously and illegally introduced pike to some western Montana lakes and rivers, where they proceeded to destroy trout fishing by eating out the trout. That was good for the few pike fishermen and bad for the far greater number of trout fishermen.

An example producing more losers and higher dollar losses is that, until 1971, mining companies in Montana on closing down a mine just left it with its copper, arsenic, and acid leaking out into rivers, because the state of Montana had no law requiring companies to clean up after mine closure. In 1971 the state of Montana did pass such a law, but companies discovered that they could extract the valuable ore and then just declare bankruptcy before going to the expense of cleaning up. The result has been about $500,000,000 of cleanup costs to be borne by the citizens of Montana and the U.S. Mining company CEOs had correctly perceived that the law permitted them to save money for their companies, and to advance their own interests through bonuses and high salaries, by making messes and leaving the burden to society. Innumerable other examples of such behavior in the business world could be cited, but it is not as universal as some cynics suspect. In the next chapter we shall examine how that range of outcomes results from the imperative for businesses to make money to the extent that government regulations, laws, and public attitudes permit.

One particular form of clashes of interest has become well known under the name "tragedy of the commons," in turn closely related to the conflicts termed "the prisoner's dilemma" and "the logic of collective action." Consider a situation in which many consumers are harvesting a communally owned resource, such as fishermen catching fish in an area of ocean, or herders grazing their sheep on a communal pasture. If everybody overharvests the resource, it will become depleted by overfishing or overgrazing and thus decline or even disappear, and all of the consumers will suffer. It would therefore be in the common interests of all consumers to exercise restraint and not overharvest. But as long as there is no effective regulation of how much resource each consumer can harvest, then each consumer would be correct to reason, "If I don't catch that fish or let my sheep graze that grass, some other fisherman or herder will anyway, so it makes no sense for me to refrain from overfishing or overharvesting." The correct rational behavior is then to harvest before the next consumer can, even though the eventual result may be the destruction of the commons and thus harm for all consumers.

In reality, while this logic has led to many commons resources becoming overharvested and destroyed, others have been preserved in the face of harvesting for hundreds or even thousands of years. Unhappy outcomes include the overexploitation and collapse of most major marine fisheries, and the extermination of much of the megafauna (large mammals, birds, and reptiles) on every oceanic island or continent settled by humans for the first time within the last 50,000 years. Happy outcomes include the maintenance of many local fisheries, forests, and water sources, such as the Montana trout fisheries and irrigation systems that I described in Chapter 1. Behind these happy outcomes lie three alternative arrangements that have evolved to preserve a commons resource while still permitting a sustainable harvest.

One obvious solution is for the government or some other outside force to step in, with or without the invitation of the consumers, and to enforce quotas, as the shogun and daimyo in Tokugawa Japan, Inca emperors in the Andes, and princes and wealthy landowners in 16th-century Germany did for logging. However, that is impractical in some situations (e.g., the open ocean) and involves excessive administrative and policing costs in other situations. A second solution is to privatize the resource, i.e., to divide it into individually owned tracts that each owner will be motivated to manage prudently in his/her own interests. That practice was applied to some village-owned forests in Tokugawa Japan. Again, though, some resources (such as migratory animals and fish) are impossible to subdivide, and the individual owners may find it even harder than a government's coast guard or police to exclude intruders.

The remaining solution to the tragedy of the commons is for the consumers to recognize their common interests and to design, obey, and enforce prudent harvesting quotas themselves. That is likely to happen only if a whole series of conditions is met: the consumers form a homogeneous group; they have learned to trust and communicate with each other; they expect to share a common future and to pass on the resource to their heirs; they are capable of and permitted to organize and police themselves; and the boundaries of the resource and of its pool of consumers are well-defined. A good example is the case, discussed in Chapter 1, of Montana water rights for irrigation. While the allocation of those rights has been written into law, nowadays the ranchers mostly obey the water commissioner whom they themselves elect, and they no longer take their disputes to court for resolution. Other such examples of homogeneous groups prudently managing resources that they expect to pass to their children are the Tikopia Islanders, New Guinea highlanders, members of Indian castes, and other groups discussed in Chapter 9. Those small groups, along with the Icelanders (Chapter 6) and the Tokugawa Japanese constituting larger groups, were further motivated to reach agreement by their effective isolation: it was obvious to the whole group that they would have to survive just on their resources for the foreseeable future. Such groups knew that they could not make the frequently heard "ISEP" excuse that is a recipe for mismanagement: "It's not my problem, it's someone else's problem."

Clashes of interest involving rational behavior are also prone to arise when the principal consumer has no long-term stake in preserving the resource but society as a whole does. For example, much commercial harvesting of tropical rainforests today is carried out by international logging companies, which typically take out short-term leases on land in one country, cut down the rainforest on all their leased land in that country, and then move on to the next country. The loggers have correctly perceived that, once they have paid for their lease, their interests are best served by cutting its forest as quickly as possible, reneging on any agreements to replant, and leaving. In that way, loggers destroyed most of the lowland forests of the Malay Peninsula, then of Borneo, then of the Solomon Islands and Sumatra, now of the Philippines, and coming up soon of New Guinea, the Amazon, and the Congo Basin. What is thus good for the loggers is bad for the local people, who lose their source of forest products and suffer consequences of soil erosion and stream sedimentation. It's also bad for the host country as a whole, which loses some of its biodiversity and its foundations for sustainable forestry. The outcome of this clash of interests involving short-term leased land contrasts with a frequent outcome when the logging company owns the land, anticipates repeated harvests, and may find a long-term perspective to be in its interests (as well as in the interests of local people and the country). Chinese peasants in the 1920s recognized a similar contrast when they compared the disadvantages of being exploited by two types of warlords. It was hard to be exploited by a "stationary bandit," i.e., a locally entrenched warlord, who would at least leave peasants with enough resources to generate more plunder for that warlord in future years. Worse was to be exploited by a "roving bandit," a warlord who like a logging company with short-term leases would leave nothing for a region's peasants and just move on to plunder another region's peasants.

A further conflict of interest involving rational behavior arises when the interests of the decision-making elite in power clash with the interests of the rest of society. Especially if the elite can insulate themselves from the consequences of their actions, they are likely to do things that profit themselves, regardless of whether those actions hurt everybody else. Such clashes, flagrantly personified by the dictator Trujillo in the Dominican Republic and the governing elite in Haiti, are becoming increasingly frequent in the modern U.S., where rich people tend to live within their gated compounds (Plate 36) and to drink bottled water. For example, Enron's executives correctly calculated that they could gain huge sums of money for themselves by looting the company coffers and thereby harming all the stockholders, and that they were likely to get away with their gamble.

Throughout recorded history, actions or inactions by self-absorbed kings, chiefs, and politicians have been a regular cause of societal collapses, including those of the Maya kings, Greenland Norse chiefs, and modern Rwandan politicians discussed in this book. Barbara Tuchman devoted her book *The March of Folly* to famous historical examples of disastrous decisions, ranging from the Trojans bringing the Trojan horse within their walls, and the Renaissance popes provoking the Protestant succession, to the German decision to adopt unrestricted submarine warfare in World War I (thereby triggering America's declaration of war), and Japan's Pearl Harbor attack that similarly triggered America's declaration of war in 1941. As Tuchman put it succinctly, "Chief among the forces affecting political folly is lust for power, named by Tacitus as 'the most flagrant of all passions.' " As a result of lust for power, Easter Island chiefs and Maya kings acted so as to accelerate deforestation rather than to prevent it: their status depended on their putting up bigger statues and monuments than their rivals. They were trapped in a competitive spiral, such that any chief or king who put up smaller statues or monuments to spare the forests would have been scorned and lost his job. That's a regular problem with competitions for prestige, which are judged on a short time frame.

Conversely, failures to solve perceived problems because of conflicts of interest between the elite and the masses are much less likely in societies where the elite cannot insulate themselves from the consequences of their actions. We shall see in the final chapter that the high environmental awareness of the Dutch (including their politicians) goes back to the fact that much of the population—both the politicians and the masses—lives on land lying below sea level, where only dikes stand between them and drowning, so that foolish land planning by politicians would be at their own personal peril. Similarly, New Guinea highlands big-men live in the same type of huts as everyone else, scrounge for firewood and timber in the same places as everyone else, and were thereby highly motivated to solve their society's need for sustainable forestry (Chapter 9).

■   ■   ■

All of these examples in the preceding several pages illustrate situations in which a society fails to try to solve perceived problems because the maintenance of the problem is good for some people. In contrast to that so-called rational behavior, other failures to attempt to solve perceived problems involve what social scientists consider "irrational behavior": i.e., behavior that is harmful for everybody. Such irrational behavior often arises when each of us individually is torn by clashes of values: we may ignore a bad status quo because it is favored by some deeply held value to which we cling. "Persistence in error," "wooden-headedness, "refusal to draw inference from negative signs," and "mental standstill or stagnation" are among the phrases that Barbara Tuchman applies to this common human trait. Psychologists use the term "sunk-cost effect" for a related trait: we feel reluctant to abandon a policy (or to sell a stock) in which we have already invested heavily.

Religious values tend to be especially deeply held and hence frequent causes of disastrous behavior. For example, much of the deforestation of Easter Island had a religious motivation: to obtain logs to transport and erect the giant stone statues that were the object of veneration. At the same time, but 9,000 miles away and in the opposite hemisphere, the Greenland Norse were pursuing their own religious values as Christians. Those values, their European identity, their conservative lifestyle in a harsh environment where most innovations would in fact fail, and their tightly communal and mutually supportive society allowed them to survive for centuries. But those admirable (and, for a long time, successful) traits also prevented them from making the drastic lifestyle changes and selective adoptions of Inuit technology that might have helped them survive for longer.

The modern world provides us with abundant secular examples of admirable values to which we cling under conditions where those values no longer make sense. Australians brought from Britain a tradition of raising sheep for wool, high land values, and an identification with Britain, and thereby accomplished the feat of building a First World democracy remote from any other (except New Zealand), but are now beginning to appreciate that those values also have downsides. In modern times a reason why Montanans have been so reluctant to solve their problems caused by mining, logging, and ranching is that those three industries used to be the pillars of the Montana economy, and that they became bound up with Montana's pioneer spirit and identity. Montanans' pioneer commitment to individual freedom and self-sufficiency has similarly made them reluctant to accept their new need for government planning and for curbing individual rights. Communist China's determination not to repeat the errors of capitalism led it to scorn environmental concerns as just one more capitalist error, and thereby to saddle China with enormous environmental problems. Rwandans' ideal of large families was appropriate in traditional times of high childhood mortality, but has led to a disastrous population explosion today. It appears to me that much of the rigid opposition to environmental concerns in the First World nowadays involves values acquired early in life and never again reexamined: "the maintenance intact by rulers and policy-makers of the ideas they started with," to quote Barbara Tuchman once again.

It is painfully difficult to decide whether to abandon some of one's core values when they seem to be becoming incompatible with survival. At what point do we as individuals prefer to die than to compromise and live? Millions of people in modern times have indeed faced the decision whether, to save their own life, they would be willing to betray friends or relatives, acquiesce in a vile dictatorship, live as virtual slaves, or flee their country. Nations and societies sometimes have to make similar decisions collectively.

All such decisions involve gambles, because one often can't be certain that clinging to core values will be fatal, or (conversely) that abandoning them will ensure survival. In trying to carry on as Christian farmers, the Greenland Norse in effect were deciding that they were prepared to die as Christian farmers rather than live as Inuit; they lost that gamble. Among five small Eastern European countries faced with the overwhelming might of Russian armies, the Estonians and Latvians and Lithuanians surrendered their independence in 1939 without a fight, the Finns fought in 1939–40 and preserved their independence, and Hungarians fought in 1956 and lost their independence. Who among us is to say which country was wiser, and who could have predicted in advance that only the Finns would win their gamble?

Perhaps a crux of success or failure as a society is to know which core values to hold on to, and which ones to discard and replace with new values, when times change. In the last 60 years the world's most powerful countries have given up long-held cherished values previously central to their national image, while holding on to other values. Britain and France abandoned their centuries-old role as independently acting world powers; Japan abandoned its military tradition and armed forces; and Russia abandoned its long experiment with communism. The United States has retreated substantially (but hardly completely) from its former values of legalized racial discrimination, legalized homophobia, a subordinate role of women, and sexual repression. Australia is now reevaluating its status as a rural farming society with British identity. Societies and individuals that succeed may be those that have the courage to take those difficult decisions, and that have the luck to win their gambles. The world as a whole today faces similar decisions about its environmental problems that we shall consider in the final chapter.

Those are examples of how irrational behavior associated with clashes of values does or doesn't prevent a society from trying to solve perceived problems. Common further irrational motives for failure to address problems include that the public may widely dislike those who first perceive and complain about the problem—such as Tasmania's Green Party that first protested foxes' introduction into Tasmania. The public may dismiss warnings because of previous warnings that proved to be false alarms, as illustrated by Aesop's fable about the eventual fate of the shepherd boy who had repeatedly cried "Wolf!" and whose cries for help were then ignored when a wolf did appear. The public may shirk its responsibility by invoking ISEP (p. 430: "It's someone else's problem").

Partly irrational failures to try to solve perceived problems often arise from clashes between short-term and long-term motives of the same individual. Rwandan and Haitian peasants, and billions of other people in the world today, are desperately poor and think only of food for the next day. Poor fishermen in tropical reef areas use dynamite and cyanide to kill coral reef fish (and incidentally to kill the reefs as well) in order to feed their children today, in the full knowledge that they are thereby destroying their future livelihood. Governments, too, regularly operate on a short-term focus: they feel overwhelmed by imminent disasters and pay attention only to problems that are on the verge of explosion. For example, a friend of mine who is closely connected to the current federal administration in Washington, D.C., told me that, when he visited Washington for the first time after the 2000 national elections, he found that our government's new leaders had what he termed a "90-day focus": they talked only about those problems with the potential to cause a disaster within the next 90 days. Economists rationally attempt to justify these irrational focuses on short-term profits by "discounting" future profits. That is, they argue that it may be better to harvest a resource today than to leave some of the resource intact for harvesting tomorrow, on the grounds that the profits from today's harvest could be invested, and that the investment interest thereby accumulated between now and some alternative future harvest time would tend to make to-day's harvest more valuable than the future harvest. In that case, the bad consequences are born by the next generation, but that generation cannot vote or complain today.

Some other possible reasons for irrational refusal to try to solve a perceived problem are more speculative. One is a well-recognized phenomenon in short-term decision-making termed "crowd psychology." Individuals who find themselves members of a large coherent group or crowd, especially one that is emotionally excited, may become swept along to support the group's decision, even though the same individuals might have rejected the decision if allowed to reflect on it alone at leisure. As the German dramatist Schiller wrote, "Anyone taken as an individual is tolerably sensible and reasonable—as a member of a crowd, he at once becomes a blockhead." Historical examples of crowd psychology in operation include late medieval Europe's enthusiasm for the Crusades, accelerating overinvestment in fancy tulips in Holland peaking between 1634 and 1636 ("Tulipomania"), periodic outbursts of witch-hunting like the Salem witch trials of 1692, and the crowds whipped up into frenzies by skillful Nazi propagandists in the 1930s.

A calmer small-scale analog of crowd psychology that may emerge in groups of decision-makers has been termed "groupthink" by Irving Janis. Especially when a small cohesive group (such as President Kennedy's advisors during the Bay of Pigs crisis, or President Johnson's advisors during the escalation of the Vietnam War) is trying to reach a decision under stressful circumstances, the stress and the need for mutual support and approval may lead to suppression of doubts and critical thinking, sharing of illusions, a premature consensus, and ultimately a disastrous decision. Both crowd psychology and groupthink may operate over periods of not just a few hours but also up to a few years: what remains uncertain is their contribution to disastrous decisions about environmental problems unfolding over the course of decades or centuries.

The final speculative reason that I shall mention for irrational failure to try to solve a perceived problem is psychological denial. This is a technical term with a precisely defined meaning in individual psychology, and it has been taken over into the pop culture. If something that you perceive arouses in you a painful emotion, you may subconsciously suppress or deny your perception in order to avoid the unbearable pain, even though the practical results of ignoring your perception may prove ultimately disastrous. The emotions most often responsible are terror, anxiety, and grief. Typical examples include blocking the memory of a frightening experience, or refusing to think about the likelihood that your husband, wife, child, or best friend is dying because the thought is so painfully sad.

For example, consider a narrow river valley below a high dam, such that if the dam burst, the resulting flood of water would drown people for a considerable distance downstream. When attitude pollsters ask people downstream of the dam how concerned they are about the dam's bursting, it's not surprising that fear of a dam burst is lowest far downstream, and increases among residents increasingly close to the dam. Surprisingly, though, after you get to just a few miles below the dam, where fear of the dam's breaking is found to be highest, the concern then falls off to zero as you approach closer to the dam! That is, the people living immediately under the dam, the ones most certain to be drowned in a dam burst, profess unconcern. That's because of psychological denial: the only way of preserving one's sanity while looking up every day at the dam is to deny the possibility that it could burst. Although psychological denial is a phenomenon well established in individual psychology, it seems likely to apply to group psychology as well.

Finally, even after a society has anticipated, perceived, or tried to solve a problem, it may still fail for obvious possible reasons: the problem may be beyond our present capacities to solve, a solution may exist but be prohibitively expensive, or our efforts may be too little and too late. Some attempted solutions backfire and make the problem worse, such as the Cane Toad's introduction into Australia to control insect pests, or forest fire suppression in the American West. Many past societies (such as medieval Iceland) lacked the detailed ecological knowledge that now permits us to cope better with the problems that they faced. Others of those problems continue to resist solution today.

For instance, please think back to Chapter 8 on the ultimate failure of the Greenland Norse to survive after four centuries. The cruel reality is that, for the last 5,000 years, Greenland's cold climate and its limited, unpredictably variable resources have posed an insuperably difficult challenge to human efforts to establish a long-lasting sustainable economy. Four successive waves of Native American hunter-gatherers tried and ultimately failed before the Norse failed. The Inuit came closest to success by maintaining a self-sufficient lifestyle in Greenland for 700 years, but it was a hard life with frequent deaths from starvation. Modern Inuit are no longer willing to subsist traditionally with stone tools, dogsleds, and hand-held harpooning of whales from skin boats, without imported technology and food. Modern Greenland's government has not yet developed a self-supporting economy independent of foreign aid. The government has experimented again with livestock as did the Norse, eventually gave up on cattle, and still subsidizes sheep farmers who cannot make a profit by themselves. All that history makes the ultimate failure of the Greenland Norse unsurprising. Similarly, the Anasazi ultimate "failure" in the U.S. Southwest has to be seen in the perspective of many other ultimately "failed" attempts to establish long-lasting farming societies in that environment so hostile for farming.

Among the most recalcitrant problems today are those posed by introduced pest species, which often prove impossible to eradicate or control once they have become established. For example, the state of Montana continues to spend over a hundred million dollars per year on combatting Leafy Spurge and other introduced weed species. That's not because Montanans don't try to eradicate them, but simply because the weeds are impossible to eradicate at present. Leafy Spurge has roots 20 feet deep, too long to pull up by hand, and specific weed-controlled chemicals cost up to $800 per gallon. Australia has tried fences, foxes, shooting, bulldozers, myxomatosis virus, and calicivirus in its ongoing efforts to control rabbits, which have survived all such efforts so far.

The problem of catastrophic forest fires in dry parts of the U.S. Intermontane West could probably be brought under control by management techniques to reduce the fuel load, such as by mechanically thinning out new growth in the understory and removing fallen dead timber. Unfortunately, carrying out that solution on a large scale is considered prohibitively expensive. The fate of Florida's Dusky Seaside Sparrow similarly illustrates failure due to expense, as well as due to the usual penalty for procrastination ("too little, too late"). As the sparrow's habitat dwindled, action was postponed because of arguments over whether its habitat really was becoming critically small. By the time the U.S. Fish and Wildlife Service agreed in the late 1980s to buy its remaining habitat at the high cost of $5,000,000, that habitat had become so degraded that its sparrows died out. An argument then raged over whether to breed the last sparrows in captivity to the closely related Scott's Seaside Sparrow, and then reestablish purer Dusky Seaside Sparrows by back-crossing the resulting hybrids. By the time that permission was finally granted, those last Dusky captives had become infertile through old age. Both the habitat preservation effort and the captive breeding effort would have been cheaper and more likely to succeed if they had been begun earlier.

■   ■   ■

Thus, human societies and smaller groups may make disastrous decisions for a whole sequence of reasons: failure to anticipate a problem, failure to perceive it once it has arisen, failure to attempt to solve it after it has been perceived, and failure to succeed in attempts to solve it. This chapter began with my relating the incredulity of my students, and of Joseph Tainter, that societies could allow environmental problems to overwhelm them. Now, at the end of this chapter, we seem to have moved towards the opposite extreme: we have identified an abundance of reasons why societies might fail. For each of those reasons, each of us can draw on our own life experiences to think of groups known to us that failed at some task for that particular reason.

But it's also obvious that societies don't regularly fail to solve their problems. If that were true, all of us would now be dead or else living again under the Stone Age conditions of 13,000 years ago. Instead, the cases of failure are sufficiently noteworthy to warrant writing this book about them—a book of finite length, about only certain societies, and not an encyclopedia of every society in history. In Chapter 9 we specifically discussed some examples drawn from the majority of societies that succeeded.

Why, then, do some societies succeed and others fail, in the various ways discussed in this chapter? Part of the reason, of course, involves differences among environments rather than among societies: some environments pose much more difficult problems than do others. For instance, cold isolated Greenland was more challenging than was southern Norway, whence many of Greenland's colonists originated. Similarly, dry, isolated, high-latitude, low-elevation Easter Island was more challenging than was wet, less isolated, equatorial, high Tahiti where ancestors of the Easter Islanders may have lived at one stage. But that's only half of the story. If I were to claim that such environmental differences were the sole reason behind different societal outcomes of success or failure, it would indeed be fair to charge me with "environmental determinism," a view unpopular among social scientists. In fact, while environmental conditions certainly make it more difficult to support human societies in some environments than in others, that still leaves much scope for a society to save or doom itself by its own actions.

It's a large subject why some groups (or individual leaders) followed one of the paths to failure discussed in this chapter, while others didn't. For instance, why did the Inca Empire succeed in reafforesting its dry cool environment, while the Easter Islanders and Greenland Norse didn't? The answer partly depends on idiosyncrasies of particular individuals and will defy prediction. But I still hope that better understanding of the potential causes of failure discussed in this chapter may help planners to become aware of those causes, and to avoid them.

A striking example of such understanding being put to good use is provided by the contrast between the deliberations over two consecutive crises involving Cuba and the U.S., by President Kennedy and his advisors. In early 1961 they fell into poor group decision-making practices that led to their disastrous decision to launch the Bay of Pigs invasion, which failed ignominiously, leading to the much more dangerous Cuban Missile Crisis. As Irving Janis pointed out in his book *Groupthink*, the Bay of Pigs deliberations exhibited numerous characteristics that tend to lead to bad decisions, such as a premature sense of ostensible unanimity, suppression of personal doubts and of expression of contrary views, and the group leader (Kennedy) guiding the discussion in such a way as to minimize disagreement. The subsequent Cuban Missile Crisis deliberations, again involving Kennedy and many of the same advisors, avoided those characteristics and instead proceeded along lines associated with productive decision-making, such as Kennedy ordering participants to think skeptically, allowing discussion to be freewheeling, having subgroups meet separately, and occasionally leaving the room to avoid his overly influencing the discussion himself.

Why did decision-making in these two Cuban crises unfold so differently? Much of the reason is that Kennedy himself thought hard after the 1961 Bay of Pigs fiasco, and he charged his advisors to think hard, about what had gone wrong with their decision-making. Based on that thinking, he purposely changed how he operated the advisory discussions in 1962.

In this book that has dwelt on Easter Island chiefs, Maya kings, modern Rwandan politicians, and other leaders too self-absorbed in their own pursuit of power to attend to their society's underlying problems, it is worth preserving balance by reminding ourselves of other successful leaders besides Kennedy. To solve an explosive crisis, as Kennedy did so courageously, commands our admiration. Yet it calls for a leader with a different type of courage to anticipate a growing problem or just a potential one, and to take bold steps to solve it before it becomes an explosive crisis. Such leaders expose themselves to criticism or ridicule for acting before it becomes obvious to everyone that some action is necessary. But there have been many such courageous, insightful, strong leaders who deserve our admiration. They include the early Tokugawa shoguns, who curbed deforestation in Japan long before it reached the stage of Easter Island; Joaquín Balaguer, who (for whatever motives) strongly backed environmental safeguards on the eastern Dominican side of Hispaniola while his counterparts on the western Haitian side didn't; the Tikopian chiefs who presided over the decision to exterminate their island's destructive pigs, despite the high status of pigs in Melanesia; and China's leaders who mandated family planning long before overpopulation in China could reach Rwandan levels. Those admirable leaders also include the German chancellor Konrad Adenauer and other Western European leaders, who decided after World War II to sacrifice separate national interests and to launch Europe's integration in the European Economic Community, with a major motive being to minimize the risk of another such European war. We should admire not only those courageous leaders, but also those courageous peoples—the Finns, Hungarians, British, French, Japanese, Russians, Americans, Australians, and others—who decided which of their core values were worth fighting for, and which no longer made sense.

Those examples of courageous leaders and courageous peoples give me hope. They make me believe that this book on a seemingly pessimistic subject is really an optimistic book. By reflecting deeply on causes of past failures, we too, like President Kennedy in 1961 and 1962, may be able to mend our ways and increase our chances for future success (Plate 32).

CHAPTER 15

Big Businesses and the Environment: Different Conditions, Different Outcomes

Resource extraction ■ Two oil fields ■ Oil company motives ■
Hardrock mining operations ■ Mining company motives ■
Differences among mining companies ■ The logging industry ■
Forest Stewardship Council ■ The seafood industry ■
Businesses and the public ■

All modern societies depend on extracting natural resources, both non-renewable resources (like oil and metals) and renewable ones (like wood and fish). We get most of our energy from oil, gas, and coal. Virtually all of our tools, containers, machines, vehicles, and buildings are made of metal, wood, or petrochemical-derived plastics and other synthetics. We write and print on wood-derived paper. Our principal wild sources of food are fish and other seafoods. The economies of dozens of countries depend heavily on extractive industries: for instance, of the three countries where I've done most of my fieldwork, the main props of the economy are logging followed by mining in Indonesia, logging and fishing in the Solomon Islands, and oil, gas, mining, and (increasingly) logging in Papua New Guinea. Thus, our societies are committed to extracting those resources: the only questions involve where, in what amounts, and by what means we choose to do so.

Because a resource extraction project usually requires large capital inputs up front, most of the extraction is done by big businesses. Familiar controversies exist between environmentalists and big businesses, which tend to view each other as enemies. Environmentalists blame businesses for harming people by damaging the environment, and routinely putting the business's financial interests above the public good. Yes, those accusations are often true. Conversely, businesses blame environmentalists for routinely being ignorant of and uninterested in business realities, ignoring the desires of local people and host governments for jobs and development, placing the welfare of birds above that of people, and failing to praise businesses when they do practice good environmental policies. Yes, those accusations too are often true.

In this chapter I shall argue that the interests of big businesses, environmentalists, and society as a whole coincide more often than you might guess from all the mutual blaming. In many other cases, however, there really is a conflict of interest: what makes money for a business, at least in the short run, may be harmful for society as a whole. Under those circumstances, the behavior of businesses becomes a large-scale example of rational behavior on the part of one group (a business in this case) translating into disastrous decision-making by a society, as discussed in the preceding chapter. This chapter will use examples from four extractive industries, of which I have firsthand experience, to explore some of the reasons why different companies perceive it as being in their interests to adopt different policies, either harming or sparing the environment. My motivation is the practical one of identifying what changes would be most effective in inducing companies that currently harm the environment to spare it instead. The industries that I shall discuss are oil, hardrock mining and coal, logging, and marine fishing.

My experience of the oil industry in the New Guinea region has involved two oil fields at opposite ends of the spectrum of harmful versus beneficial environmental impacts. I found these experiences instructive, because I had previously assumed that oil industry impacts were overwhelmingly harmful. Like much of the public, I loved to hate the oil industry, and I deeply suspected the credibility of anyone who dared to report anything positive about the industry's performance or its contribution to society. My observations forced me to think about factors that might encourage more companies to set positive examples.

My first experience of an oil field was on Salawati Island off the coast of Indonesian New Guinea. The purpose of my visit there had nothing to do with oil but was part of a survey of birds on islands of the New Guinea region; it merely happened that much of Salawati had been leased for oil exploration to the Indonesian national oil company, Pertamina. I visited Salawati in 1986 with the permission and as a guest of Pertamina, whose vice president and public relations officer kindly provided me with a vehicle to drive along company roads.

In view of that kindness, I am sorry to report on the conditions that I encountered. From a long distance, the field's location could be recognized by a flame shooting out of a high tower, where natural gas obtained as a by-product of oil extraction was being burned off, there being nothing else to do with it. (Facilities to liquefy and transport it for sale were lacking.) To construct access roads through Salawati's forests, swathes 100 yards wide had been cleared, much too wide for many species of New Guinea rainforest mammals, birds, frogs, and reptiles to cross. There were numerous oil spills on the ground. I encountered only three species of large fruit pigeons, of which 14 have been recorded elsewhere on Salawati and which are among the prime targets of hunters in the New Guinea region because they are large, meaty, and good to eat. A Pertamina employee described to me the location of two pigeon breeding colonies, where he said that he hunted them with his shotgun. I assume that their numbers within the field had been depleted by hunting.

My second experience was of the Kutubu oil field that a subsidiary of the large international oil company Chevron Corporation operated in the Kikori River watershed of Papua New Guinea. (I shall refer to the operator for short as "Chevron" in the present tense, but the actual operator was Chevron Niugini Pty. Ltd., a wholly owned subsidiary of Chevron Corporation; the field was a joint venture of six oil companies, including Chevron Niugini Pty. Ltd.; the parent company Chevron Corporation merged in 2001 with Texaco to become ChevronTexaco; and in 2003 ChevronTexaco sold its interests in the joint venture, whose operator then became another one of the partners, Oil Search Limited.) The environment in the Kikori River watershed is sensitive and difficult to work in because of frequent landslides, much limestone karst terrain, and one of the highest recorded rainfalls in the world (on the average, 430 inches per year, and up to 14 inches per day). In 1993 Chevron engaged World Wildlife Fund (WWF) to prepare a large-scale integrated conservation and development project for the whole watershed. Chevron's expectation was that WWF would be effective at minimizing environmental damage, lobbying the Papua New Guinea government for environmental protection, serving as a credible partner in the eyes of environmental activist groups, benefiting local communities economically, and attracting World Bank funding for local community projects. From 1998 to 2003 I made four visits of one month each to the oil fields and watershed as a consultant to WWF. I was allowed freedom to travel throughout the area in a WWF vehicle and to interview Chevron employees privately.

As my airplane flight from Papua New Guinea's capital of Port Moresby droned on towards the field's main airstrip at Moro and was approaching its scheduled arrival time, I looked out the airplane window for some signs of the oil field infrastructure that I expected to see looming up. I became increasingly puzzled still to be seeing only an uninterrupted expanse of rainforest stretching between the horizons. Finally, I spotted a road, but it was only a thin cleared line about 10 yards broad through the rainforest, in many places overhung with trees growing on either side—a birdwatcher's dream. The main practical difficulty in rainforest bird studies is that it's hard to see birds inside the forest itself, and the best opportunities to observe them are from narrow trails where one can watch the forest from the side. Here was such a trail over 100 miles long, from the highest oil field at an altitude of nearly 6,000 feet on Mt. Moran down to the coast. On the following day, when I began walking along that pencil line of a road during my surveys, I found birds routinely flying across it, and mammals, lizards, snakes, and frogs hopping, running, or crawling across it. It turned out that the road had been designed to be just broad enough for two vehicles to pass safely in opposite directions. Initially, the seismic exploration platforms and exploration oil wells had been put in without construction of any access roads at all, and had been serviced instead just by helicopter and on foot.

My next surprise came when my plane landed at Chevron's Moro airstrip, and again later when I flew out. Although I had already gone through baggage inspection by the Papua New Guinea Customs Department upon my arrival in the country, on both arrival and departure at Chevron's airstrip I had to open all my bags for further inspections more thorough than on any other occasion I had experienced except when I flew to Israel's Tel Aviv airport. What were those inspectors looking for? On the flight in, the articles absolutely forbidden were firearms or hunting equipment of any sort, drugs, and alcohol; on the flight out, animals or plants or their feathers or parts that might be smuggled. Violation of those rules results in immediate automatic expulsion from company premises, as a WWF secretary innocently but foolishly carrying a package for someone else discovered to her misfortune (because the package turned out to contain drugs).

A further surprise came the next morning, after I had walked out on the road before dawn to bird-watch and returned a few hours later. The camp safety representative summoned me to his office and told me that I had already been reported for two violations of Chevron regulations, which I was not to repeat. First, I had been noticed stepping several feet out into the roadway to observe a bird. That posed the hazard that a vehicle might hit me, or that in swerving to avoid hitting me it might crash into an oil pipeline at the side of the road and cause an oil spill. From now on, I should please stay off the road while bird-watching. Second, I had been seen bird-watching while not wearing a protective helmet, but this whole area was a hardhat area; at this point the officer gave me a hardhat, which I should henceforth please wear for my own safety while bird-watching, e.g., in case a tree fell.

That was an introduction to Chevron's extreme concern, constantly instilled in its employees, about safety and environmental protection. I have never observed an oil spill on any of my four visits, but I do read the reports posted each month on Chevron bulletin boards about incidents and near-incidents, which are the concern of the safety representative who travels around by plane or truck to investigate each. Out of interest, I recorded the full list of 14 incidents from March 2003. The most serious near-incidents requiring scrutiny and review of safety procedures in that month were that a truck backed into a stop sign, another truck was reported with its emergency brake improperly set, a package of chemicals lacked the correct paperwork, and gas was found leaking from a compressor needle valve.

My remaining surprise came in the course of bird-watching. New Guinea has many bird and mammal species whose presence and abundance are sensitive indicators of human disturbance, because they are either large and hunted for their meat, hunted for their spectacular plumage, or else confined to the interior of undisturbed forests and absent from modified secondary habitats. They include tree kangaroos (New Guinea's largest native mammals); cassowaries, hornbills, and large pigeons (New Guinea's largest birds); birds of paradise, and Pesquet's Parrot and other colorful parrots (valued for their beautiful plumage); and hundreds of species of the forest interior. When I began bird-watching in the Kutubu area, I anticipated that my main goal would be to determine how much less numerous these species were inside the area of Chevron's oil fields, facilities, and pipeline than outside it.

Instead, I discovered to my astonishment that these species are much *more* numerous inside the Chevron area than anywhere else that I have visited on the island of New Guinea except for a few remote uninhabited areas. The only place that I have seen tree kangaroos in the wild in Papua New Guinea, in my 40 years there, is within a few miles of Chevron camps; elsewhere, they are the first mammal to become shot out by hunters, and those few surviving learn to be active only at night, but I saw them active during the day in the Kutubu area. Pesquet's Parrot, the New Guinea Harpy Eagle, birds of paradise, hornbills, and large pigeons are common in the immediate vicinity of the oil camps, and I have seen Pesquet's Parrots perching on the camp communications towers. That's because there is an absolute prohibition against Chevron employees and contractors hunting any animal or fishing by any means in the project area, and because the forest is intact. The birds and animals sense that and become tame. In effect, the Kutubu oil field functions as by far the largest and most rigorously controlled national park in Papua New Guinea.

For months, I was greatly puzzled by these conditions in the Kutubu oil field. After all, Chevron is neither a non-profit environmental organization, nor a National Park Service. Instead, it is a for-profit oil company, owned by its shareholders. If Chevron were to spend money on environmental policies that ultimately decreased its profits from its oil operations, its shareholders would and should sue it. The company evidently decided that those policies would ultimately help it make more money from its oil operations. How do they help?

Chevron company publications refer to concern for the environment itself as a motivating factor. That is undoubtedly true. However, in conversations over the last six years with dozens of lower-level as well as senior Chevron employees, employees of other oil companies, and people outside the oil industry, I have come to realize that many other factors as well have contributed to these environmental policies.

One such factor is the importance of avoiding very expensive environmental disasters. When I asked a Chevron safety representative who happened to be a bird-watcher what had prompted these policies, his short answer was: "*Exxon Valdez*, Piper Alpha, and Bhopal." He was referring to the huge oil spill from the running aground off Alaska of Exxon's oil tanker the *Exxon Valdez* in 1989, the 1988 fire on Occidental Petroleum's Piper Alpha oil platform in the North Sea that killed 167 people (Plate 33), and the 1984 escape of chemicals at Union Carbide's Bhopal chemical plant in India that killed 4,000 people and injured 200,000 (Plate 34). These were three of the most notorious, best-publicized, and most expensive industrial accidents of recent times. Each of them cost the company responsible billions of dollars, and the Bhopal accident ultimately cost Union Carbide its existence as an independent company. My informant could also have mentioned the blowout and catastrophic oil spill at Union Oil's Platform A in the Santa Barbara Channel off Los Angeles in 1969, serving already then as a wake-up call for the oil industry. Chevron and some of the other large international oil companies thereby realized that, by spending each year an extra few million dollars on a project, or even a few tens of millions of dollars, they would save money in the long run by minimizing the risk of losing billions of dollars in such an accident, or of having an entire project closed down and losing its whole investment. One Chevron manager explained to me that he had learned the economic value of clean environmental policies when he was responsible for cleaning up oil pits in a Texas oil field and found that the cleanup cost for even a small pit averaged $100,000. That is, cleaning up pollution is usually far more expensive than preventing pollution, just as doctors usually find it far more expensive and less effective to try to cure already sick patients than to prevent diseases in the first place by cheap, simple public health measures.

In prospecting for oil and then building an oil field, an oil company makes a large initial investment in a field that remains a producing asset for between 20 and 50 years. If your environmental and safety policies reduced your risk of a big oil spill to "only" once every decade on the average, that would not be nearly good enough, because you would then have to expect between two and five big oil spills in your 20 to 50 years of operations. It's essential to be more rigorous. I first encountered this long-range outlook of oil companies when I was contacted by the director of a London office of Royal Dutch Shell Oil Company. That office's job is to try to predict likely alternative scenarios for the state of the world 30 years from now. The director explained to me that Shell operates that office because it expects a typical oil field to be operated for several decades, and it needs to understand the likely shape of the world several decades in the future if it is to be able to invest intelligently.

A related factor is public expectations. Unlike the toxic mine runoffs to be discussed below, oil spills tend to be highly visible, and often their occurrences are sudden and obvious (as when a pipeline, platform, or tanker breaks or blows out). The impact of the spill is also usually obvious, for instance in the form of oil-coated dead birds whose pictures saturate television screens and newspapers. Hence the public can be expected to howl at the kind of big environmental mistake most likely for an oil company.

Those considerations of public expectations and minimizing environmental damage were especially important in Papua New Guinea, a decentralized democracy with a relatively weak central government, weak police force and army, and strong voice of local communities. Because local landowners at the Kutubu oil fields relied on gardens, forests, and rivers for their subsistence, an oil spill there would impact their lives much more seriously than oil-coated seabirds impact the lives of American television viewers. As one Chevron employee explained it to me, "We recognized that in Papua New Guinea no natural resource project could be successful in the long run without the support of the local landowners and villagers. They would disrupt the project and shut it down, as they did in Bougainville [see below for explanation], if they perceived environmental harm affecting their land and food sources. The central government lacked the ability to prevent disruptions by landowners, so we needed to take prudent steps to minimize harm and maintain a good relationship with the local people." Another Chevron employee expressed a similar idea in different words: "We were adamant at the outset that the success of the Kutubu project would depend on our ability to work with the local landowner communities, to the extent that they would believe they are better off with us there than they would be if we were gone."

A minor aspect of that constant scrutiny of Chevron's operations by local New Guineans is that they understand the money that can be made by pressuring entities with deep pockets, like big oil companies. They count the number of trees cut down during construction of a road, placing particular value on trees in which birds of paradise display, and then they present a bill for damages. In one case of which I was told, when New Guinean landowners learned that Chevron was contemplating constructing a road to an oil site, they rushed out and planted coffee trees along the proposed route, so that they could claim damages for each coffee tree uprooted. That's an argument for keeping forest clearance to a minimum by making roads as narrow as possible, and by accessing drill sites by helicopter whenever possible. But the much bigger risk was that landowners angry at damage to their land might shut down the entire oil project. My informant's mention of Bougainville refers to what had been Papua New Guinea's biggest investment and development project, its Bougainville copper mine, which was shut down by landowners angry at environmental damage in 1989, and which has never reopened despite the efforts of the country's minuscule police force and army that provoked a civil war. The fate of the Bougainville mine warned Chevron of the likely fate of the Kutubu oil field if it too caused environmental damage.

Another warning sign for Chevron was the Point Arguello oil field, discovered by Chevron off the coast of California in 1981, which was estimated to be the largest oil find in the U.S. since the discovery of the Prudhoe Bay field. As a result of public disenchantment with oil companies, local community opposition, and layer after onerous layer of government regulatory delays, oil production could not begin until 10 years later, and Chevron ended up with a large write-down on its investment. The Kutubu oil field gave Chevron the opportunity to refute that disenchantment by showing that it would take excellent care of the environment without being prodded by overly stringent government regulation.

In that respect the Kutubu project illustrates the value of anticipating increasingly rigorous government environmental standards. The trend throughout the world (with obvious exceptions) is for governments, as the years pass, to demand more rather than less rigorous environmental precautions. Even developing countries from which one might not at first have expected environmental concerns are becoming more and more demanding. For example, one Chevron employee working in Bahrain told me that, when he recently drilled another offshore well there, the Bahrain government for the first time required a detailed expensive environmental impact plan that provided for environmental monitoring during drilling, assessment of impacts after drilling, and minimizing effects on dugongs and on a breeding colony of cormorants. Oil companies have learned that it is far cheaper to build a clean facility incorporating environmental precautions at the outset, than to retrofit that facility later when government standards become tightened. The companies have come to expect that, if a country in which they are operating is not environmentally aware now, it is likely to become so within the lifetime of the facility.

Still a further advantage to Chevron's environmentally clean practices is that the reputation it has thereby gained sometimes gives it a competitive advantage in obtaining contracts. For example, recently the government of Norway, a country whose people and government today are very concerned about environmental issues, solicited bids for development of an oil/gas field in the North Sea. Chevron was among the firms bidding, and it succeeded in winning the contract, probably in part because of its good environmental reputation. If that was indeed the case, then some friends within Chevron suggested to me that the Norwegian contract might have been the biggest single financial benefit to the company from its rigid environmental safeguards in the Kutubu oil fields.

A company's audience includes not only the public, governments, and local landowners, but also its employees. An oil field poses especially complicated technological, construction, and management problems, and a large fraction of oil company employees have higher education and advanced degrees. They tend to be environmentally aware. It is expensive to train them, and their salaries are high. While most employees of the Kutubu project are resident citizens of Papua New Guinea, others are Americans or Australians who are flown out to Papua New Guinea to work there for five weeks, then are flown back home to spend five weeks with their family, and those airplane fares are also expensive. All those employees see for themselves the state of the environment in the oil fields, and they see the company's commitment to clean environmental policies. Many Chevron employees told me that that issue of employee morale and environmental views was both a benefit of their company's visibly clean environmental policies and also a driving force behind the adoption of those policies in the first place.

In particular, environmental concern has been one criterion used to select company executives, and Chevron's two most recent CEOs, first Ken Derr and then David O'Reilly, have both been personally concerned about environmental issues. Chevron employees in several countries told me independently that every month they and every other Chevron employee around the world receive from the CEO an e-mail about the state of affairs in the company. The e-mails often talk about environment and safety issues and speak of them as being number-one priorities, and as making good economic sense for the company. Thus, employees see that environmental matters are taken seriously, and are not just window-dressing that is for public display but that is ignored within the company itself. This observation corresponds to a conclusion that Thomas Peters and Robert Waterman Jr. drew in their best-selling book on business management *In Search of Excellence: Lessons from America's Best-Run Companies.* The authors found that if managers want their employees to behave in a certain way, the most effective motivation is for the employees to see the managers themselves behaving in that way.

Finally, new technology has made it easier for oil companies to operate more cleanly now than in the past. For instance, several horizontal or diagonal wells can now be drilled from a single surface location, whereas formerly each well had to be drilled vertically from a separate surface location, each causing environmental impacts. The rock debris (the so-called cuttings) that is ground up as a well is drilled can now be pumped into an isolated underground formation containing no producible oil, instead of (as before) dumping the rocks into a pit or into the ocean. Natural gas obtained as a by-product of oil extraction is now either reinjected into an underground reservoir (the procedure used in the Kutubu Project), or (in some other oil fields) shipped out by pipeline or else liquefied for storage and transport by ship and then sold, instead of burning it off ("flaring" it). In many oil fields, as in much of the Kutubu fields, it is now routine to operate exploration drill sites by means of helicopters rather than by putting in roads; helicopter use is of course expensive, but road construction and impacts are often even more expensive.

These, then, are reasons why Chevron and the handful of other big international oil companies have been taking environmental issues seriously. What it all adds up to is that clean environmental practices help them make money and gain long-term access to new oil and gas fields. But I should reiterate that I am not thereby claiming that the oil industry is now uniformly clean, responsible, and admirable in its behavior. Among the most widely publicized persisting and serious problems are recent large spills at sea from wrecks of poorly maintained and poorly operated single-hulled tankers (such as the sinking of the 26-year-old tanker *Prestige* off Spain in 2002), belonging to shipowners other than the large oil companies, which have mostly switched to double-hulled tankers. Other major problems include legacies of old, environmentally dirty facilities, constructed before the more recent availability of cleaner technologies and difficult or expensive to retrofit (e.g., in Nigeria and Ecuador); and operations under the auspices of corrupt and abusive governments, such as those of Nigeria and Indonesia. Instead, the case of Chevron Niugini illustrates how it is possible for an oil company to operate in a way that delivers environmental benefits to an area of operations and to the people there—especially compared to alternative proposed uses of the same area for logging, or even just for subsistence hunting and farming. The case also illustrates the factors combining to produce that outcome in the Kutubu oil fields but not in many other large industrial projects, and the potential role of the public in influencing outcomes.

In particular, the question remains why I observed indifference to environmental problems in the Salawati oil field of the Indonesian oil company Pertamina in 1986, but clean practices in Chevron's Kutubu field when I began visiting there in 1998. There are several differences between Pertamina's situation as a national oil company in Indonesia in 1986, and Chevron's situation as an international company operating in Papua New Guinea in 1998, that may account for the differing outcomes. The Indonesian public, government, and judiciary are less interested in, and expect less from, the behavior of oil companies than do their European and American counterparts encompassing Chevron's major customers. Pertamina's Indonesian employees have had less exposure to environmental concerns than have Chevron's American and Australian employees. Papua New Guinea is a democracy whose citizens enjoy the freedom to obstruct proposed development projects, but Indonesia in 1986 was a military dictatorship whose citizens enjoyed no such freedom. Beyond that, the Indonesian government was dominated by people from its most populous island (Java), looked on its New Guinea province as a source of income and a place to resettle Java's surplus population, and was less concerned with the opinions of New Guineans than is the government of Papua New Guinea, which owns the eastern half of the same island. Pertamina did not face rising environmental standards from the Indonesian government, such as those that international oil companies face. Pertamina is largely a national oil company within Indonesia, competing for fewer overseas contracts than do the big international companies, so that Pertamina does not derive an international competitive advantage from clean environmental policies. Pertamina has not had CEOs who send out monthly newsletters stressing the environment as the highest priority. Finally, my visit to Pertamina's Salawati oil field was in 1986; I don't know whether Pertamina policies have changed since then.

Let's now turn from the oil and gas industry to the hardrock mining industry. (That term refers to mines that excavate ores from which to extract metals, as opposed to mines that excavate coal.) The industry is currently the leading toxic polluter in the U.S., responsible for nearly half of reported industrial pollution. Of western U.S. rivers, nearly half have sections of their headwaters polluted by mining. In most of the U.S. the hardrock mining industry is now declining towards extinction, largely because of its own misdeeds. Environmental groups have for the most part not taken the trouble to learn essential facts about the hardrock mining industry, and declined to participate in an initially promising international initiative that the industry commenced in 1998 to change its behavior.

These and other features of the hardrock mining industry's current status are initially puzzling, because the industry seems superficially so like the oil and gas industry that we just discussed, and also like the coal industry. Don't all three industries involve extracting non-renewable resources from the ground? Yes, they do, but they have nevertheless unfolded differently, for three reasons: different economics and technology, different attitudes within the industry itself, and different attitudes of the public and government towards the industry.

The environmental problems caused by hardrock mining are of several types. One involves disturbance of land surface by digging it up. This problem especially affects surface mines and open-pit mines, where the ore lies near the surface and is reached by scraping away the earth over it. In contrast, no one now extracts oil by digging the surface off of an entire oil formation; instead, oil companies typically disturb only a small surface area sufficient to drill a well to tap down into the oil formation. Similarly, there are some mines at which the ore body does not lie near the surface but deep underground, and at which tunnels and waste piles disturbing only a small surface area are dug down to the ore body.

Further environmental problems caused by hardrock mining involve water pollution by metals themselves, processing chemicals, acid drainage, and sediment. Metals and metal-like elements in the ore itself—especially copper, cadmium, lead, mercury, zinc, arsenic, antimony, and selenium—are toxic and prone to cause trouble by ending up in nearby streams and water tables as a result of mining operations. A notorious example was a wave of cases of bone disease caused by cadmium discharged into Japan's Jinzu River from a lead and zinc mine. Quite a few of the chemicals used in mining—such as cyanide, mercury, sulfuric acid, and nitrate produced from dynamite—are also toxic. More recently, it has become appreciated that acid draining out of sulfide-containing ores exposed to water and air through mining causes serious water pollution and leaches out metals. Sediment transported out of mines in runoff water may be harmful to aquatic life, for instance by covering up fish spawning beds. In addition to those types of pollution, the mere consumption of water by many mines is high enough to be significant.

The remaining environmental problem concerns where to dump all the dirt and wastes dug up in the course of mining, consisting of four components: the "overburden" (dirt scraped away to get down to the ore); waste rock found to contain too little mineral to be of economic value; tailings, the ground-up residue of ore after its minerals have been extracted; and the residues of heap-leach pads after mineral extraction. The latter two types of residue are generally left in the tailings impoundment or pad respectively, while the overburden and waste rock are left in dumps. Depending on the laws in the particular country where the mine is located, the methods of disposing of tailings (a slurry of water and solids) involve either dumping them into a river or ocean, piling them up on land, or (most often) piling them up behind a dam. Unfortunately, tailings dams fail in a surprisingly high percentage of cases: they are often designed with insufficient strength (to save money), they are often constructed cheaply from wastes themselves instead of from concrete, and they are built over extended periods so that their condition must be monitored constantly and can't be subjected to a final inspection declaring them completed and safe. On the average around the world each year, there is one big accident involving a tailings dam. The largest such accident in the U.S. was West Virginia's Buffalo Creek disaster of 1972, which killed 125 people.

Several of these environmental problems are illustrated by the status of the four most valuable mines on New Guinea and neighboring islands, where I do my fieldwork. The copper mine at Panguna on Papua New Guinea's Bougainville Island was formerly the country's largest enterprise and biggest earner of foreign exchange, and one of the largest copper mines in the world. It dumped its tailings directly into a tributary of the Jaba River, thereby creating monumental environmental impacts. When the government failed to resolve that situation and associated political and social problems, Bougainville's inhabitants revolted, triggering a civil war that cost thousands of lives and nearly tore apart the nation of Papua New Guinea. Fifteen years after the war's outbreak, peace has still not been fully restored on Bougainville. The Panguna mine was of course closed down, has no prospect of reopening, and the owners and lenders (including the Bank of America, U.S. Export-Import Bank, and Australian and Japanese subscribers and lenders) lost their investment. That history provided a reason why Chevron worked so closely with local landowners at the Kutubu oil fields to gain their acceptance.

The gold mine on Lihir Island dumps its tailings into the ocean via a deep pipe (a method viewed by environmentalists as highly damaging), and the owners claim that this is not harmful. Whatever the effects of that one mine on marine life around Lihir Island, the world would have a major problem if many other mines similarly dumped their tailings into the ocean. The Ok Tedi copper mine on the mainland of New Guinea did construct a tailings dam, but experts who reviewed its design before construction warned that the dam would fail soon. It did fail within a few months, so that 200,000 tons of mine tailings and wastes are now discharged each day into the Ok Tedi River and have destroyed its fishery. From the Ok Tedi the water flows directly into New Guinea's largest river with its most valuable fishery, the Fly River, where suspended sediment concentrations have now increased five-fold, resulting in flooding, deposition of mine wastes on the river's floodplain, and killing of floodplain vegetation over an area of 200 square miles so far. In addition, a barge carrying barrels of cyanide for the mine up the Fly River sank, and the barrels have gradually been corroding and releasing their cyanide into the river. In 2001 BHP, the world's fourth largest mining company, which operated the Ok Tedi mine, sought to close it, explaining, "Ok Tedi is not compatible with our environmental values, and the company should never have been involved." However, because the mine accounts for 20% of Papua New Guinea's total exports, the government arranged for the mine to be kept open while permitting BHP to withdraw. Finally, the Grasberg-Ertsberg copper and gold mine of Indonesian New Guinea, a huge open-pit operation that is Indonesia's most valuable mine, dumps its tailings directly into the Mimika River, whence they reach the shallow Arafura Sea between New Guinea and Australia. Along with the Ok Tedi mine and another gold mine in New Guinea, the Grasberg-Ertsberg mine is one of only three large mines in the world that is currently being operated by an international company and that disposes of its wastes into a river.

The prevalent policy of mining companies towards environmental damage is to clean up and restore the mined area only after the mine has shut down, rather than follow the coal mining industry's practice of reclaiming the area as mining proceeds; the hardrock mining industry opposes that strategy. Companies assume that what is called "walkaway" restoration will be adequate: i.e., that cleanup and restoration will incur minimal costs, will go on for only 2 to 12 years after mine closure (whereupon the company can walk away from the site with no further obligations), and will involve nothing more than resloping of disturbed areas to prevent erosion, applying a growth medium like salvaged topsoil to stimulate revegetation, and treating water flowing out of the mine site for a few years. In reality, this inexpensive walkaway strategy has never sufficed for any major modern mine and regularly leaves water quality standards violated. It is instead necessary to cover and revegetate all areas that could be sources of acid drainage, and to capture and treat polluted groundwater and surface water flowing out of the site for as long as the water remains polluted, which often means forever. The actual direct and indirect costs of cleanup and restoration have typically proved to be 1.5 to 2 times mining industry walkaway estimates for mines without acid drainage, and 10 times those estimates for mines with acid drainage. The biggest uncertainty in those costs is whether the mine will produce acid drainage, a problem recognized only recently at copper mines though appreciated earlier at other mines, and almost never predicted accurately in advance.

Hardrock mining companies facing cleanup costs frequently avoid those costs by declaring bankruptcy and transferring their assets to other corporations controlled by the same individuals. One such example is Montana's

Zortman-Landusky gold mine mentioned already in Chapter 1 and developed by Pegasus Gold Inc., a Canadian company. When opened in 1979, it was the first large-scale open-pit cyanide heap-leach gold mine in the U.S., and the largest gold mine in Montana. The mine proceeded to cause a long series of cyanide leaks, spills, and acid drainage, abetted by the fact that neither the federal government nor the Montana state government required the company to test for acid drainage. By 1992, state inspectors had established that the mine was contaminating streams with heavy metals and acid. In 1995 Pegasus Gold agreed to pay $36 million to settle all lawsuits by the federal government, state of Montana, and local Indian tribes. Finally, in 1998, at a time when less than 15% of the mine site had undergone any surface reclamation, Pegasus Gold's board of directors voted themselves more than $5 million in bonuses, transferred Pegasus's remaining profitable assets to the new company of Apollo Gold that they created, and thereupon declared Pegasus Gold bankrupt. (Like most mine directors, those of Pegasus Gold did not live in the downstream watershed of the Zortman-Landusky mine, and they thus exemplified elites insulated from the consequences of their actions as discussed in Chapter 14.) The state and federal governments then adopted a plan of surface reclamation to cost $52 million, of which $30 million would come from the $36 million payment by Pegasus while $22 million would be paid by U.S. taxpayers. However, that surface reclamation plan still does not include the expense of water treatment in perpetuity, which will cost taxpayers much more. It turns out that five out of the 13 recent major hardrock mines in Montana, four of them (including the Zortman-Landusky mine) open-pit heap-leach cyanide mines, were owned by the bankrupt Pegasus Gold Inc., and that 10 of the major mines will require water treatment forever, thereby increasing their closure and reclamation costs by up to 100 times previous estimates.

A bankruptcy more expensive to taxpayers was that of another Canadian-owned heap-leach gold mine in the U.S., Galactic Resources' Summitville Mine in a mountainous area of Colorado receiving over 32 feet of snow annually. In 1992, eight years after the state of Colorado had issued an operating permit to Galactic Resources, the company declared bankruptcy and closed the mine on less than a week's notice, leaving a large local tax bill unpaid, laying off its employees, stopping essential environmental maintenance, and abandoning the site. A few months later, after the start of the winter snowfalls, the heap-leach system overflowed, sterilizing an 18-mile stretch of the Alamosa River with cyanide. It was then discovered that the state of Colorado had required a financial guarantee of only $4,500,000 from Galactic Resources as a condition for issuing the operating permit, but that the cleanup would cost $180,000,000. After the government had extracted another $28,000,000 as part of the bankruptcy settlement, taxpayers were left to pay $147,500,000 through the Environmental Protection Agency.

As a result of such experiences, American states and the federal government eventually began to require hardrock mining companies to guarantee in advance some form of financial assurance that enough money would be available for cleanup and restoration, in case the mining company itself refused or proved financially unable to pay for the cleanup. Unfortunately, those assurance costs are typically based on a cleanup cost estimate made by the mining company itself, because government regulatory bodies lack the time, knowledge, and detailed mine engineering plans necessary to make such an estimate for themselves. In the many cases where mining companies have not cleaned up and the government has been forced to fall back on that assurance, the actual cleanup costs have proved to be up to 100 times the mining company estimate. That's not surprising, because the estimate was provided by the company, which regularly underestimates because it has no financial incentive or government regulatory pressure to estimate the amount fully. The assurance is provided in one of three forms: cash equivalents or a letter of credit, the safest form; a bond that the mining company obtains from an insurance company in return for an annual premium; and a "self-guarantee," meaning that the mining company pledges in good faith that it will clean up and that its assets stand behind its pledge. However, frequent breaking of such pledges has shown self-guarantees to be meaningless, and they are now no longer accepted for mines on federal land, but they still account for most assurance in Arizona and Nevada, the American states most friendly to the mining industry.

U.S. taxpayers currently face a liability of up to $12 billion to clean up and restore hardrock mines. Why is our liability so large, when governments have supposedly been requiring financial assurance of cleanup costs? Parts of the difficulty are the just-mentioned ones of assurance costs being underestimated by the mining companies, and the two states with the biggest taxpayer liabilities (Arizona and Nevada) accepting company self-guarantees and not requiring insurance bonds. Even when an underfunded but real insurance company bond exists, taxpayers face further costs for reasons that will be familiar to any of us who have tried to collect from our insurance company for a large loss in a home fire. The insurance company regularly reduces the amount of the bond payoff by what are euphemistically termed "negotiations": i.e., "If you don't like our reduced offer, you may go to the expense of hiring lawyers and waiting five years for the courts to resolve the case." (A friend of mine who suffered a house fire has just been going through a year of hell over such negotiations.) Then the insurance company pays out the bonded or negotiated amount only over the years as cleanup and restoration are carried out, but the bond contains no clause for inevitable cost escalations with time. Then, too, not only mining companies but sometimes also insurance companies faced with large liabilities file for bankruptcy. Of the mines posing the 10 biggest taxpayer liabilities in the U.S. (adding up to about half of the total of up to $12 billion), two are owned by a mining company on the verge of bankruptcy (ASARCO, accounting for about $1 billion), six others are owned by companies that have proved especially recalcitrant at meeting their obligations, only two are owned by less recalcitrant companies, and all 10 may be acid-generating and may require water treatment for a long time or forever.

Not surprisingly, as a result of taxpayers' being left to foot bills, there has been a backlash of anti-mining public sentiment in Montana and some other states. The future of hardrock mining in the U.S. is bleak, except for gold mines in underregulated Nevada and platinum/palladium mines in Montana (a special case about which I shall say more below). Only one-quarter as many American college undergraduates (a mere 578 students in the whole U.S.) are preparing for careers in mining as in 1938, despite the explosive growth of the total college population in the intervening years. Since 1995, public opposition in the U.S. has been increasingly successful in blocking mine proposals, and the mining industry can no longer count on lobbyists and friendly legislators to do its bidding. The hardrock mining industry is the prime example of a business whose short-term favoring of its own interests over those of the public proved in the long term self-defeating and have been driving the industry into extinction.

This sad outcome is initially surprising. Like the oil industry, the hardrock mining industry too stands to benefit from clean environmental policies, through lower labor costs (less turnover and absenteeism) resulting from higher job satisfaction, lower health costs, cheaper bank loans and insurance policies, community acceptance, less risk of the public blocking projects, and the relative cheapness of installing state-of-the-art clean technology at a project's outset as compared to having to retrofit old technology as environmental standards become more stringent. How could the hardrock mining industry have adopted such self-defeating behavior, especially when the oil industry and the coal mining industry facing apparently similar problems have not driven themselves towards extinction? The answer has to do with the three sets of factors that I mentioned earlier: economics, mining industry attitudes, and society's attitudes.

Economic factors that make environmental cleanup costs less bearable to the hardrock mining industry than to the oil industry (or even the coal industry) include lower profit margins, more unpredictable profits, higher cleanup costs, more insidious and long-lasting pollution problems, less ability to pass on those costs to consumers, less capital with which to absorb those costs, and a different labor force. To begin with, while some mining companies are more profitable than other mining companies, the industry as a whole operates at such low profit margins that its average rate of return over the last 25 years hasn't even met the cost of its capital. That is, if a mining company CEO with $1,000 to spare had invested it in 1979, then by the year 2000 the investment would have grown to only $2,220 if invested in steel industry stock; to only $1,530 if invested in metal stocks other than iron and steel; to only $590, representing a net loss even without considering inflation, if invested in gold mine stock; but to $9,320 if invested in an average mutual fund. If you're a miner, it doesn't pay you to invest in your own industry!

Even those mediocre profits are unpredictable, at the level both of the individual mine and of the industry as a whole. While an individual oil well within a proven oil field may turn out to be dry, the reserves and oil grade of a whole oil field are often relatively predictable in advance. But the grade (i.e., the metal content, and hence the profitability) of a metal ore often changes unpredictably as one digs one's way through an ore deposit. Half of all mines that are developed prove unprofitable. The average profits of the whole mining industry are also unpredictable, because metals prices are notoriously volatile and fluctuate with world commodity prices to a much greater degree than do oil and coal prices. The reasons for that volatility are complex and include the lower bulk and smaller amounts consumed of metals than of oil or coal (making metals easier to stockpile); our perception that we always need oil and coal but that gold and silver are dispensable luxuries during a recession; and the fact that gold price fluctuations are driven by factors having nothing to do with the supply of gold and the industrial demand for gold—namely, speculators, investors buying gold when they grow nervous about the stock market, and governments selling off their gold reserves.

Hardrock mines create far more wastes, requiring much more expensive cleanup costs, than do oil wells. The wastes that are pumped up from an oil well and that have to be disposed of are mostly just water, typically in a waste-to-oil ratio of only around one or not much higher. If it weren't for the access roads and the occasional oil spill, oil and gas extraction would have little environmental impact. In contrast, metals constitute only a small fraction of a metal-bearing ore, which in turn constitutes only a small fraction of the dirt that has to be dug up to extract the ore. Hence the ratio of waste dirt to metal is typically 400 for a copper mine, and 5,000,000 for a gold mine. That's a huge amount of dirt for mining companies to clean up.

Pollution problems are more insidious and much more long-lasting for the mining industry than for the oil industry. Oil pollution problems arise mainly from quick and visible spills, many of which it has been possible to avoid by careful maintenance and inspections and by improved engineering design (such as double-hulled rather than single-hulled tankers), so that the oil spills that still occur today are mainly ones due to human error (such as the *Exxon Valdez* tanker accident), which can in turn be minimized by rigorous training procedures. Oil spills can generally be cleaned up within a few years or less, and oil degrades naturally. While mine pollution problems also occasionally appear as a quick visible pulse that suddenly kills lots of fish or birds (like the fish-killing cyanide overflow from the Summitville mine), more often they take the form of a chronic leak of toxic but invisible metals and acid that don't degrade naturally, continue to leak for centuries, and leave slowly weakened people rather than a sudden pile of carcasses. Tailings dams and other engineered safeguards against mine spills continue to suffer from a high rate of failure.

Like coal, oil is a bulk material that we see. The gas pump gauge tells us how many gallons we just bought. We know what it is used for, we consider it essential, we have experienced and been inconvenienced by oil shortages, we are frightened of their possible recurrence, we are grateful to be able to get gas for our cars at all, and we don't balk too much at paying higher prices. Hence the oil and coal industries may have been able to pass on their costs of environmental cleanup to consumers. But metals other than iron (in the form of steel) are mostly used for invisible little parts inside our cars, phones, and other equipment. (Tell me quickly without looking up the answer in an encyclopedia: where are you using copper and palladium, and how many ounces of each were in the things that you bought last year?) If increased environmental costs of copper and palladium mining tend to increase the cost of your car, you don't say to yourself, "Sure, I'm willing to pay another dollar per ounce for copper and palladium, just as long as I can still buy a car this year." Instead, you shop around for a better deal on a car. The copper and palladium middlemen and car manufacturers know how you feel, and they pressure the mining companies into keeping their prices down. That makes it hard for a mining company to pass on its cleanup costs.

Mining companies have much less capital to absorb their cleanup costs than do oil companies. Both the oil industry and the hardrock mining industry face so-called legacy problems, which mean the burden of costs from a century of environmentally damaging practices before the recent growth of environmental awareness. To pay those costs, as of the year 2001 the total capitalization of the entire mining industry was only $250 billion, and its three largest companies (Alcoa, BHP, and Rio Tinto) were capitalized with only $25 billion each. But the leading individual companies in other industries—Wal-Mart Stores, Microsoft, Cisco, Pfizer, Citigroup, Exxon-Mobil, and others—had capitalizations of $250 billion each, while General Electric alone had $470 billion (almost double the value of the entire mining industry). Hence those legacy problems are relatively a much heavier burden on the hardrock mining industry than on the oil industry. For example, Phelps-Dodge, the largest surviving U.S. mining company, faces U.S. mine reclamation and closure liabilities of about $2 billion, equal to its entire market capitalization. All of the company's assets amount to only about $8 billion, and most of those assets are in Chile and cannot be used to pay North American costs. In contrast, the oil company ARCO, which inherited the responsibility of $1 billion or more for Butte copper mines when it bought Anaconda Copper Mining Company, had North American assets of over $20 billion. That cruel economic factor alone goes a long way towards explaining why Phelps-Dodge has been much more recalcitrant about mine cleanup than has ARCO.

Thus, there are many economic reasons why it is more burdensome for mining companies than for oil companies to pay cleanup costs. In the short run, it's cheaper for a mining company just to pay lobbyists to press for weak regulatory laws. Given society's attitudes and existing laws and regulations, that strategy has worked—until recently.

Those economic disincentives are exacerbated by the attitudes and corporate culture that have become traditional within the hardrock mining industry. In the history of the U.S., and analogously also in South Africa and Australia, the government promoted mining as a tool to encourage settlement of the West. Hence the mining industry evolved in the U.S. with an inflated sense of entitlement, a belief that it is above the rules, and a view of itself as the West's salvation—thereby illustrating the problem of values that have outlived their usefulness, as discussed in the preceding chapter. Mine executives respond to environmental criticism with homilies on how civilization would be impossible without mining, and how more regulation would mean less mining and hence less civilization. Civilization as we know it would also be impossible without oil, farm food, wood, or books, but oil executives, farmers, loggers, and book publishers nevertheless don't cling to that quasi-religious fundamentalism of mine executives: "God put those metals there for the benefit of mankind, to be mined." The CEO and most officers of one of the major American mining companies are members of a church that teaches that God will soon arrive on Earth, hence if we can just postpone land reclamation for another 5 or 10 years it will then be irrelevant anyway. My friends within the mining industry have used many colorful phrases to characterize prevailing attitudes: "a rape-and-run attitude"; "robber-baron mentality"; "a rough-and-tumble heroic struggle of one man against nature"; "the most conservative businesspeople I've ever met"; and "a speculative attitude that a mine is there to let its executives roll the dice and get personally rich by striking the mother lode, rather than the oil company motto of increasing asset value for the shareholders." To claims of toxic problems at mines, the mining industry routinely responds with denial. No one in the oil industry today would deny that spilled oil is harmful, but mine executives do deny the harm of spilled metals and acid.

The third factor underlying mining industry environmental practices, besides economics and corporate attitudes, is the attitudes of our government and society, which permit the industry to continue with its own attitudes. The basic federal law governing mining in the U.S. is still the General Mining Act passed in 1872. It provides massive subsidies to mining companies, such as a billion dollars per year of royalty-free minerals from publicly owned lands, unlimited use of public lands for dumping mine wastes in some cases, and other subsidies costing taxpayers a quarter of a billion dollars per year. The detailed rules adopted by the federal government in 1980, termed the "3809 rules," did not require mining companies to provide financial assurance of cleanup costs, and did not adequately define reclamation and closure. In the year 2000 the outgoing Clinton administration proposed mining regulations that achieved both of those goals while also eliminating corporate self-guarantees of financial assurance. But in October 2001 a proposal by the incoming Bush administration eliminated almost all of those proposals except for continuing to require financial assurance, a requirement that would in any case be meaningless without a definition of the reclamation and cleanup costs to be covered by financial assurance.

It is rare that our society has effectively held the mining industry responsible for damages. Laws, regulatory policies, and the political will to chase mining scofflaws have been absent. For a long time the Montana state government was notorious for its deference to mining lobbyists, and the Arizona and Nevada state governments still are. For example, the state of New Mexico estimated reclamation costs for the Chino copper mine of Phelps-Dodge Corporation at $780 million, but then decreased that estimate to $391 million under political pressure from Phelps-Dodge. When our American public and governments demand so little of the mining industry, why should we be surprised that the industry itself volunteers little?

My account of hardrock mining so far may have given the false impression that the industry is monolithically uniform in its attitudes. Of course, this is not true, and it's instructive to examine the reasons why some hardrock miners or related industries have adopted or considered cleaner policies. I'll briefly mention half a dozen such cases: coal mining, the current status of Anaconda Copper Company's Montana properties, Montana platinum and palladium mines, the recent MMSD initiative, Rio Tinto, and DuPont.

Coal mining is superficially even more similar to hardrock mining than is the oil industry, in that its operations inevitably create heavy environmental impacts. Coal mines tend to make even bigger messes than do hardrock mines, because the quantity of coal extracted per year is relatively enormous: more than triple the combined mass of all the metals extracted from hardrock mines. Thus, coal mines usually disturb more area, and in some cases they strip the soil down to bedrock and dump mountaintops into rivers. On the other hand, coal occurs in pure seams up to 10 feet thick stretching for miles, so that the ratio of dumped wastes to product extracted is only about one for a coal mine, far less than the already-mentioned figures of 400 for a copper mine and 5,000,000 for a gold mine.

The lethal Buffalo Creek disaster at a U.S. coal mine in 1972 served as a wake-up call for the coal industry, much as the *Exxon Valdez* and North Sea oil rig disasters did for the oil industry. While the hardrock mining industry has had its share of disasters in the Third World, those have occurred too far from the eyes of the First World public to have served as a comparable wake-up call. Stimulated by Buffalo Creek, the U.S. federal government in the 1970s and 1980s instituted tighter regulation, and required stricter operating plans and financial assurance, for coal mining than for hardrock mining.

The initial response of the coal industry to those government initiatives was to prophesy disaster for the industry, but 20 years later that has been forgotten, and the coal industry has learned to live with the new regulations. (Of course that doesn't mean that the industry is consistently virtuous, just that it is more regulated than 20 years ago.) One reason is that many (but certainly not all) coal mines are not in beautiful Montana mountains but in flatland not highly valued for other reasons, so that restoration is economically feasible. Unlike the hardrock mining industry, the coal industry now often restores mined areas within a year or two of ceasing operations. Another reason may be that coal (like oil but unlike gold) is perceived as a necessity for our society, and we all know how we use coal and oil but few of us know how we use copper, so the coal industry may have been able to pass on its increased environmental costs to consumers.

Still another factor behind the response of the coal industry is that it typically has short transparent supply chains, in which coal is shipped directly or else via just one intermediate supplier to the electric generating plants, steel plants, and other main consumers of coal. That makes it easy for the public to figure out whether any particular consumer of coal is obtaining it from a cleanly or dirtily operated coal mining company. Oil has a supply chain that is even shorter in number of business entities, even if sometimes long in geographic distances: big oil companies like Chevron-Texaco, ExxonMobil, Shell, and BP sell their fuel to consumers at gas stations, thereby permitting consumers enraged by the *Exxon Valdez* disaster to boycott gas stations selling Exxon fuel. But gold passes from the mine to the consumer via a long supply chain that includes refiners, warehouses, jewelry manufacturers in India, and European wholesalers before arriving at a retail jewelry store. Take a look at your gold wedding ring: you don't have the faintest idea where the gold came from, whether it was mined last year or stockpiled for the last 20 years, what company mined it, and what their environmental practices were. For copper the situation is even more obscure: there is an extra intermediate step of a smelter, and you don't even realize that you are buying some copper when you buy a car or phone. That long supply chain prevents copper and gold mining companies from counting on consumer willingness to pay for cleaner mines.

Among Montana mines with a historical legacy of environmental damage, the ones that have come furthest towards paying their cleanup costs are the former properties of Anaconda Copper Mining Company around and downstream of Butte. The reason is simple: Anaconda was bought by the big oil company ARCO, which in turn was bought by the even bigger British oil company BP (British Petroleum). The result illustrates more clearly than could anything else the differing approaches to environmental messes in the hardrock mining industry and in the oil industry: same mining properties, different owners. When they discovered the mess that they had inherited, ARCO and then BP eventually decided that their own interests would be better served by trying to get the problems behind them than by denying all responsibility. That is not to say that ARCO and BP have shown any enthusiasm for spending the hundreds of millions of dollars to which they were obligated. They have tried the usual resistive strategies, such as denying the reality of toxic effects, funding local citizens' support groups to state their case, proposing cheaper solutions than those proposed by the government, and so on. But at least they have spent large sums of money, they are evidently resigned to spending more, they are much too large to declare bankruptcy over just their Montana mines, and they are interested in bringing matters to a resolution rather than delaying indefinitely.

The other somewhat bright spot in the Montana mining picture is two platinum and palladium mines owned by Stillwater Mining Company, which entered into good-neighbor agreements with local environmental groups (the sole such agreements reached by any mining company in the U.S.), gave money to those groups, allows the groups free access to their mining area, actually requested the environmental organization Trout Unlimited (to the latter's astonishment) to monitor effects of their mines on local trout populations in the Boulder River, and reached long-term agreements with the surrounding communities regarding labor, electricity, schools, and city services—in return for environmentalists and local citizens' not opposing Stillwater. It seems obvious that this peace treaty between Stillwater, environmentalists, and the community benefits everybody concerned. How can we explain the surprising fact that, among Montana mining companies, only Stillwater reached this conclusion?

Several factors contributed. Stillwater owns a uniquely valuable deposit: the sole primary deposit of platinum and palladium (much used in the automobile and chemical industries) outside of South Africa. The deposit is so deep that it is expected to last for at least a century and probably much longer; that encourages a long-term perspective rather than the usual rape-and-run attitude. The mine is underground, hence it presents fewer problems of surface impact than an open-pit mine. Its ores are relatively low in sulfide, and most of that sulfide is extracted with the product, so that problems of acid sulfide drainage are minimized and environmental impact mitigation is less expensive than at Montana copper and gold mines. In 1999 the company brought in a new CEO, Bill Nettles, who came from the auto industry (the biggest user of the mine's products) rather than from a traditional mining background, did not inherit the usual mining attitudes, recognized the mining industry's awful public relations problems, and was interested in finding fresh long-term solutions. Finally, at the time that Stillwater officers reached some of the above-mentioned agreements in the year 2000, they were afraid that the U.S. presidential election would be won by the pro-environment candidate Al Gore, that the Montana gubernatorial election would be won by an anti-business candidate, and that good-neighbor agreements offered Stillwater its best chance to buy itself a stable future. In other words, Stillwater's executives pursued their own perception of their company's best interests by negotiating good-neighbor agreements, whereas most other large American mining companies have pursued their own differing vision of their company's interests by denying responsibility, hiring lobbyists to oppose governmental regulation, and in the last resort filing bankruptcy.

In 1998 top executives of some of the world's largest international mining companies nevertheless became concerned that their industry around the world was "losing its social license to operate," as the expression goes. They formed an initiative termed the Mining Minerals and Sustainable Development (MMSD) project, launched a series of studies on sustainable mining, enlisted a well-known environmentalist (the president of the National Wildlife Federation) as director of the initiative, and attempted without success to involve the broader environmental community, which refused because of its historical disgust with mining companies. In the year 2002 the study arrived at a series of recommendations, but then most of the mining companies involved unfortunately declined to implement the recommendations.

The exception is the British mining giant Rio Tinto, which decided to move ahead on some of the recommendations on its own, under pressure from its strongly supportive CEO and from British stockholders, and burned by the memory of having owned Bougainville's Panguna Copper Mine, whose environmental messes had proved so disastrously expensive to the company. Just as Chevron Oil Company found in negotiating with the Norwegian government, Rio Tinto foresaw business advantages to being seen as an industry leader in social responsibility. Its borax mine in California's Death Valley is now perhaps the most cleanly operated mine in the U.S.

One payoff that Rio Tinto has already reaped is that when Tiffany & Co., eager to fend off the risk of environmental protestors marching in front of its jewelry stores with posters about the cyanide releases and dead fish caused by gold mining, decided to stress environmental considerations in selecting a mining company to which to award a contract as gold supplier, Tiffany chose Rio Tinto because of the latter's increasingly clean reputation. Tiffany's further motives included some of the exact same considerations that I already mentioned as having motivated ChevronTexaco: establishing a good reputation for their brand name, maintaining a motivated and high-caliber workforce, and the philosophy of company executives.

The remaining instructive example involves U.S.-based DuPont Company, the world's leading buyer of titanium metal and titanium compounds used in paints, jet engines, high-speed planes and space vehicles, and for other purposes. Much titanium is extracted from Australian beach sands rich in rutile, a mineral that consists of almost pure titanium dioxide. DuPont is a manufacturing company, not a mining company, and so it buys the rutile from Australian mining companies. However, DuPont puts its name on all its products, including its titanium-based house paints, and it does not want all its products to get a bad reputation just because its titanium suppliers arouse consumer wrath through dirty practices. Hence DuPont, in collaboration with public interest groups, has worked out buyers' agreements and suppliers' codes of responsibility that it enforces on all of its Australian titanium suppliers.

These two examples involving Tiffany and DuPont illustrate an important point. Individual consumers collectively hold some clout over oil companies and (to a lesser extent) coal mining companies, because the public buys fuel directly from the oil companies and buys electricity from the energy generating companies that buy coal. Hence consumers know whom to embarrass or boycott in the event of an oil spill or coal mine accident. However, individual consumers are eight steps removed from the hardrock mining companies that extract minerals, making a direct boycott of a dirty mining company virtually impossible. In the case of copper, not even an indirect boycott of copper-containing products would be feasible, because most consumers don't know which of their purchases are the ones containing small amounts of copper. But consumers do have leverage over Tiffany, DuPont, and other retailers that buy metals and that have the technical ability to distinguish clean from dirty mines. We shall see that consumer leverage over retail buyers has already begun to be an effective means for consumers to influence the timber and seafood industries. Environmental groups are just beginning to apply this same tactic to the hardrock mining industry, by confronting metal buyers rather than confronting metal miners themselves.

At least in the short run, environmental safeguards, cleanup, and restoration incur costs for mining companies adopting them, regardless of whether government regulations or public attitudes ensure that the safeguards save the companies money in the long run. Who should pay for those costs? When the cleanup is of messes that mining companies made legally in the past because of weak government regulation, the public has no choice except to pay the costs itself through government tax revenues, even though it galls us to pay for messes made by companies whose directors voted themselves bonuses just before declaring bankruptcy. Instead, the practical question is: who should pay for the environmental costs of mining being carried out now or to be carried out in the future?

The reality is that the mining industry is on the average so unprofitable that consumers could not point to excessive company profits from which costs should be met. The reason why we want mining companies to clean up is that we, the public, are the ones who suffer from mining-related messes: unusable mined land surfaces, unsafe drinking water, and polluted air. Even the cleanest methods for mining coal and copper create messes. If we want coal and copper, we have to recognize the environmental costs of extracting them as a legitimate necessary cost of hardrock mining, as legitimate as the costs of the bulldozer that digs the pit or the smelter that smelts the ore. The environmental costs should be factored into metals prices and passed on to consumers, just as oil and coal companies already do. Only the long and opaque supply chain from mineral mines to the public, and the historically bad behavior of most mining companies, has obscured this simple conclusion to date.

The remaining two resource extraction industries that I shall discuss are the logging industry and the fishing industry. They differ from the oil industry, and from the hardrock mining and coal industries, in two basic ways. First, trees and fish are renewable resources that reproduce themselves. Hence if you harvest them at a rate no higher than the rate at which they reproduce, your harvest can be sustained indefinitely. In contrast, oil, metals, and coal are not renewable; they don't reproduce, sprout, or have sex to produce baby oil droplets or coal nuggets. Even if you pump or mine them slowly, that doesn't let them reproduce and maintain the field's oil, metal, or coal reserves at constant levels. (Strictly speaking, oil and coal do become formed over long geological times of millions of years, but that is much too slow to balance our pumping or extraction rates.) Second, in the logging and fishing industries the things that you are removing—the trees and the fish—are valuable parts of the environment. Hence any logging or fishing, almost by definition, may cause environmental damage. However, oil, metals, and coal play little or no role in ecosystems. If you can find some way of extracting them without damaging the rest of the ecosystem, then you have not removed anything ecologically valuable, although their subsequent use or burning may still cause damage. I shall first discuss forestry, and then (more briefly) fisheries.

For humans, forests represent much value that becomes jeopardized by cutting them down. Most obviously, they are our principal source of timber products, among which are firewood, office paper, newspaper, paper for books, toilet paper, construction timber, plywood, and wood for furniture. For Third World people, who constitute a substantial fraction of the world's population, they are also the principal source of non-timber products such as natural rope and roofing materials, birds and mammals hunted for food, fruits and nuts and other edible plant parts, and plant-derived medicines. For First World people, forests offer popular recreational sites. They function as the world's major air filter removing carbon monoxide and other air pollutants, and forests and their soils are a major sink for carbon, with the result that deforestation is an important driving force behind global warming by decreasing that carbon sink. Water transpiration from trees returns water to the atmosphere, so that deforestation tends to cause diminished rainfall and increased desertification. Trees retain water in the soil and keep it moist. They protect the land surface against landslides, erosion, and sediment runoff into streams. Some forests, notably some tropical rainforests, hold the major portion of an ecosystem's nutrients, so that logging and carting the logs away tends to leave the cleared land infertile. Finally, forests provide the habitat for most other living things on the land: for instance, tropical forests cover 6% of the world's land surface but hold between 50% and 80% of the world's terrestrial species of plants and animals.

Given all these values of forests, loggers have developed many ways of minimizing the potentially negative environmental impacts of logging. These ways include removing individuals of valuable tree species selectively and leaving the rest of the forest, rather than clear-cutting an entire forest; logging at a sustainable rate, so that the rate of tree regrowth equals the rate of tree removal; cutting small rather than large patches of forest, so that the cut area remains surrounded by trees producing seeds to start regrowth of the logged area; individually replanting trees; and removing individual big trees by helicopter if the trees are sufficiently valuable (as is true in many dipterocarp and araucaria forests), instead of removing trees by trucks and access roads that damage the rest of the forest. Depending on the circumstances, these environmental safeguards may end up either losing money or gaining money for the logging company. I shall now illustrate these opposite outcomes by two examples: the recent experiences of my friend Aloysius, and the operations of the Forest Stewardship Council.

Aloysius is not his real name but one that I have made up for him, for reasons that will become obvious. He is a citizen of one of the Asian/Pacific countries where I have done fieldwork. When I met him six years ago, he quickly struck me as the most extroverted, curious, happy, humorous, confident, independent, and smart person in his office. He courageously and single-handedly faced down and pacified a group of mutinying workers. He repeatedly ran (yes, literally ran) up and down a steep mountain trail at night, to coordinate work at two campsites. Having heard that I had written a book on human sexuality, within 15 minutes of meeting me he broke out into a laugh and said that it was now time for me to tell him what I knew about sex rather than about birds.

We saw each other while jointly involved in several subsequent projects, and then two years passed before I returned to his country. When I saw Aloysius next, it was obvious that something had changed. He was now speaking nervously, and his eyes darted around as if he were afraid of something. That surprised me, because the venue for our conversation was an auditorium in the national capital where I was giving a public lecture in the presence of government ministers, and I could detect absolutely no signs of danger. After we had reminisced about the mutiny, mountain camps, and sex, I asked how he had been, and out came the story:

Aloysius now had a new job, working for a non-governmental organization concerned with tropical deforestation. In the tropics of Southeast Asia and the Pacific islands, large-scale logging is carried out mainly by international logging companies whose subsidiaries are in many countries but whose home offices are mainly in Malaysia, and also in Taiwan and South Korea. They operate by leasing logging rights on land still owned by local people, exporting unfinished logs, and not replanting. Much or most of the value of a log is added on by cutting up and processing it after it has been felled: that is, the finished timber sells for far more than the log from which it was cut. Hence exporting unfinished logs deprives local people and the national government of most of the potential value of their resource. The companies frequently obtain the required government logging permit by bribing government officials, and then proceeding to build roads and cut logs beyond the boundaries of the area actually leased. Alternatively, the companies merely send in a logging ship, quickly negotiate permission with local people, carry out the logging, and dispense with a government permit. For example, about 70% of all wood cut in Indonesia comes from illegal operations that cost the Indonesian government nearly a billion dollars a year in lost taxes, royalties, and lease payments. Local permission is obtained by wooing village leaders who may or may not have the power to sign away logging rights, and by taking those leaders to the national capital or else overseas to Hong Kong, where they are plied with luxury hotel accommodations, food, drink, and prostitutes until they sign. This sounds like an expensive way to do business, until one realizes that a single big rainforest tree is worth thousands of dollars. Acquiescence of the ordinary village population is bought by paying them an amount of cash that seems to them enormous but that they will actually spend on food and other consumables within a year. In addition, the company also obtains local acquiescence by making promises that will not be carried out, such as a promise to replant the forest and build hospitals. In some well-publicized cases in Indonesian Borneo, the Solomon Islands, and elsewhere, when loggers have arrived at a forest with a permit from the central government and started logging, local people who realized that this would be a bad deal for them attempted to stop the logging by blocking roads or burning sawmills, whereupon the logging company enlisted the police or army to enforce their rights. I had heard that logging companies also intimidate opponents by threatening to kill them.

Aloysius was such an opponent. The loggers did threaten to kill him, but he persisted because he was confident that he could take care of himself. They then threatened to kill his wife and children, who he knew could not take care of themselves, and whom he would not be in a position to protect whenever he was away at work. To save their lives, he moved them overseas to another country and became more vigilant about possible murder attempts on himself. That explained his new nervousness and the loss of his former happy, confident manner.

With such logging companies, as with the mining companies that we already discussed, we have to ask ourselves why they behave in a way that is morally reprehensible. The answer, again, is that their behavior is profitable to them because of the same three factors motivating mining companies:

economics, the industry's corporate culture, and attitudes of society and government. Tropical hardwood logs are so valuable and in demand that rape-and-run logging of leased tropical forest land is immensely profitable. Acquiescence of local people can frequently be obtained, because the local people are desperate for cash and have never seen the disastrous consequences that clear-cutting tropical rainforest brings to local landowners. (One of the most cost-effective ways by which organizations opposed to tropical rainforest logging have induced landowners to refuse permission is by taking them to already-logged areas to talk with regretful landowners and to see for themselves.) Officials in the government forestry department can often be bribed, lack the international perspective and financial resources of the logging companies, and may not realize the high value of finished timber. Under those circumstances, rape-and-run will continue to be good business until the companies start to run out of unlogged countries, and until national governments and local landowners are prepared to refuse permission and to muster superior force in order to resist unpermitted logging backed by force.

In other countries, notably western Europe and the United States, rape-and-run logging has become increasingly unprofitable. In contrast to the situation in much of the tropics, western European and American virgin forests have already been cut or are in steep decline. Large logging companies operate on land that they own or else hold by long-term lease rather than short-term lease, thereby giving them under some circumstances an economic incentive for sustainability. Many consumers are sufficiently aware environmentally to care whether the wood products that they are purchasing have been harvested in destructive non-sustainable ways. Government regulation is sometimes serious and restrictive, and government officials are not readily bribed.

The result is that some logging companies operating in western Europe and the United States have become increasingly concerned not only about their ability to compete against Third World producers with lower costs, but also about their own survival, or (to use mining and oil industry terminology) their "social license to operate." Some logging companies have adopted sound practices and have attempted to convince the public of that, but they found that their claims on their own behalf lacked credibility in the eyes of the public. For instance, many wood and paper products that are offered to consumers for sale carry labels making pro-environmental claims such as "for every tree felled, at least two are planted." However, a survey of 80 such claims found that 77 could not be substantiated at all, 3 could be only partially substantiated, and almost all were withdrawn when challenged. Understandably, the public has learned to dismiss such claims made by companies themselves.

Adding to the timber companies' concern about their social license and credibility was their concern about the impending extinction of forests, the basis of their business. More than half of the world's original forests have been cut down or heavily damaged in the last 8,000 years. Yet our consumption of forest products is accelerating, with the result that more than half of those losses have occurred within the past 50 years—for instance, because of forest clearance for agriculture, and because world consumption of paper has increased five-fold since 1950. Logging is often just the first step in a chain reaction: after loggers build access roads into a forested area, poachers follow those roads to hunt animals, and squatters follow them to settle. Only 12% of the world's forests lie within protected areas. In a worst-case scenario, all of the world's readily accessible remaining forests outside those protected areas would be destroyed by unsustainable harvesting within the next several decades, although in a best-case scenario the world could meet its timber needs sustainably from a small area (20% or less) of those forests if they were well managed.

Those concerns about the long-term future of their own industry impelled some timber industry representatives and foresters in the early 1990s to launch discussions with environmental and social organizations and associations of indigenous peoples. In 1993 those discussions resulted in the formation of an international non-profit organization called the Forest Stewardship Council (FSC), which is headquartered in Germany and funded by several businesses, governments, foundations, and environmental organizations. The council is run by an elected board, and ultimately by the FSC's membership, which includes representatives of the timber industry and of environmental and social interests. The FSC's original tasks were three-fold: to draw up a list of criteria of sound forest management; then, to set up a mechanism for certifying whether any particular forest satisfied those criteria; and, finally, to set up another mechanism for tracing products from such a certified forest through the complex supplier chain all the way to the consumers, so that a consumer could know whether the paper, chair, or board that he or she was buying in a store, and that carried the FSC logo, actually came from a soundly managed forest.

The first of those tasks resulted in the formulation of 10 detailed criteria of sound and sustainable forest management. Those include: harvesting trees only at a rate that can be sustained indefinitely, with growth of new trees adequate to replace felled trees; sparing of forests of special conservation value, such as old-growth forests, which should not be converted into homogenous tree plantations; long-term preservation of biodiversity, nutrient recycling, soil integrity, and other forest ecosystem functions; protection of watersheds, and maintenance of adequately wide riparian zones along streams and lakes; a long-term management plan; acceptable off-site disposal of chemicals and waste; obedience of prevailing laws; and acknowledgment of the rights of local indigenous communities and forest workers.

The next task was to establish a process for ascertaining whether the management of a given forest does meet those criteria. The FSC does not certify forests itself: instead, it accredits forest certification organizations that actually visit a forest and spend up to two weeks inspecting it. There are a dozen such organizations around the world, all of them accredited to operate internationally; the two that do most of the inspections in the U.S. are called SmartWood and Scientific Certification Systems, headquartered in Vermont and in California, respectively. An owner or manager of a forest contracts with a certification organization for an inspection, and pays for the audit, without any advance guarantee of a favorable outcome. The certifier's response after the inspection is often to impose a list of pre-conditions that must be met before approval, or just to grant provisional approval based on a list of conditions that must be met before use of the FSC label will be permitted.

It should be emphasized that the initiative in getting a forest certified must always be taken by the owner or manager; the certifiers do not go around inspecting forests uninvited. Of course, that raises the question why any forest owner or manager would choose to pay in order to be inspected. The answer is that increasing numbers of owners and managers decide that it will be in their financial interest, because the certification fee will be earned back as a result of access to more markets and consumers through the improved image and credibility gained through independent third-party certification. The essence of FSC certification is that consumers can believe it, because it is not an unsubstantiated boast by the company itself but the result of an examination, against internationally accepted standards of best practice, by trained and experienced auditors who don't hesitate to say no or to impose conditions.

The remaining step was to document what is called the "chain of custody," or paper trail by which wood from a tree cut in Oregon ends up as a board offered for sale in a store in Miami. Even if a forest itself is certified, the forest's owners may sell its timber to a sawmill that also saws uncertified timber, then the sawmill may sell its cut wood to a manufacturer that also buys uncertified cut wood, and so on. The web of interrelationships between producers, suppliers, manufacturers, wholesalers, and retail stores is so complex that even companies themselves rarely know where their wood ultimately comes from or goes to, except for knowing their immediate suppliers and customers. For the ultimate consumer in Miami to be able to have confidence that the board she is buying really came from a tree in a certified forest, intermediate suppliers must keep certified and non-certified material separate, and auditors must certify that every intermediate supplier is actually doing that. That constitutes "certifying the chain of custody": tracking certified materials through the whole supply chain. The end result is that only about 17% of the products from certified forests end up bearing the FSC's logo in a retail store; the other 83% get commingled with non-certified products along the chain. Certifying the chain of custody sounds like, and really is, a big pain in the neck. But it is an essential pain in the neck, because otherwise the consumer could not be confident of the ultimate origins of that board in the Miami store.

Do enough members of the public really care about environmental issues for FSC certification to help sell wood products? When asked in surveys, 80% of consumers claim that they would prefer to buy products of environmentally clean provenance if given the choice. But are those just empty words, or do people really pay attention to FSC labels when they are in a store? And would they be willing to pay a little more for an FSC-labeled product?

These issues are crucial to companies pondering whether to apply and pay for certification. The questions were put to the test in an experiment carried out at two Home Depot stores in Oregon. Each store set up two nearby bins containing plywood pieces of the same size, and similar except that the plywood in one bin carried the FSC label and the plywood in the other bin didn't. The experiment was run twice: either with the plywood in the two bins costing the same, or else with the FSC-labeled plywood costing 2% more than the unlabeled plywood. It turned out that, when the cost was the same, FSC-labeled plywood outsold unlabeled plywood by more than 2 to 1. (At one of the stores in a "liberal," environmentally aware university town, the factor was 6 to 1, but even at the store in the more "conservative" town the labeled plywood still outsold unlabeled plywood by 19%.) When the labeled plywood cost 2% more than the unlabeled plywood, of course most customers preferred the cheaper product, but nevertheless a large minority (37%) still proceeded to buy the labeled product. Thus, much of the public really does weigh environmental values in its purchasing decisions, and a significant fraction of the public is willing to pay more for those values.

When FSC certification was first introduced, there was much fear that certified products would indeed end up costing more, either because of the expense of the certification audit or of the forestry practices necessary for certification. Much subsequent experience has shown that certification usually does not add to a wood product's inherent cost. In cases where markets did price certified products higher than comparable non-certified ones, that turned out to be due just to the laws of supply and demand rather than inherent costs: retailers selling a certified product available only in short supply, for which there was high demand, found that they could get away with raising the price.

The list of big businesses that participated in the initial formation of the FSC, joined the board of directors, or committed themselves more recently to FSC goals includes some of the world's largest producers and sellers of timber products. Among U.S.-based companies are Home Depot, the world's largest retailer of lumber; Lowe's, second only to Home Depot in the U.S. home improvement industry; Columbia Forest Products, one of the largest forest product companies in the U.S.; Kinko's (now merged with FedEx), the world's largest provider of business services and document copying; Collins Pine and Kane Hardwoods, one of the U.S.'s largest producers of cherry; Gibson Guitars, one of the world's leading guitar manufacturers; Seven Islands Land Company, which manages a million acres of forest in the state of Maine; and Andersen Corporation, the world's largest manufacturer of doors and windows. Major participants outside the U.S. include Tembec and Domtar, two of Canada's largest forest managers; B & Q, the United Kingdom's largest do-it-yourself-in-the-home business, analogous to Home Depot in the U.S.; Sainsbury's, the second largest United Kingdom supermarket chain; Swedish-based IKEA, the world's largest retailer of ready-to-assemble home furnishings; and SCA and Svea Skog (formerly Asi Domain), two of Sweden's largest forestry companies. These and other businesses all embraced the FSC because they saw it as advancing their economic interests, but they reached that conclusion through varying combinations of "push" and "pull." The "push" is that some of these firms were targets of campaigns by environmental groups dissatisfied with company practices such as dealing in old-growth timber: for instance, Home Depot was pressured by the Rainforest Action Network. As for the "pull" factor, companies recognized many opportunities for maintaining or increasing their sales to an increasingly discerning public. In defense of Home Depot and other companies whose motivation included some "pushing," they understandably had to move cautiously while making changes in the network of suppliers that they had built up over many years. They then proceeded to learn quickly, to the point where Home Depot itself is now pressuring its suppliers in Chile and South Africa to adopt FSC standards.

In connection with the mining industry, I mentioned that the most effective pressure on mining companies to change their practices has come not from individual consumers picketing mine sites, but from big companies that buy metals (like DuPont and Tiffany) and that sell to individual consumers. A similar phenomenon has unfolded in the timber industry. While the largest consumption of wood is for home construction, most homeowners don't know, select, or control the choice of forestry companies producing the wood used in their house. Instead, the customers of forestry companies are big forest products companies, like Home Depot and IKEA, and big institutional buyers, like the City of New York and the University of Wisconsin. The role of such companies and institutions in the successful campaign to end apartheid in South Africa demonstrated their ability to command the attention of even such powerful, rich, determined, well-armed, and apparently rigid entities as the apartheid-era South African government. Many retail and industrial companies in the forest products chain have increased their clout by organizing themselves into what are termed "buyers' groups" that commit themselves over a specified time frame to increase their sales of certified products, with preference for FSC-labeled products. Around the world today, there are more than a dozen such groups, of which the largest is in the United Kingdom and includes some of the largest U.K. retailers. Buyers' groups are also increasingly strong in the Netherlands and other western European countries, the U.S., Brazil, and Japan.

Besides these buyers' groups, another potent force behind the spread of FSC-labeled products in the U.S. is the "green building standard" known as LEED (Leadership in Energy and Environmental Design). This code rates the environmental design and use of materials in the construction industry. An increasing number of American state governments and cities give tax credits to companies adopting high LEED standards, and many American government building projects require companies involved to follow LEED standards. This has turned out to be a significant consideration for builders, contractors, and architectural firms that don't deal directly with the public and are not very visible to consumers, but that nevertheless choose to buy FSC-labeled products because they benefit from decreased taxes and increased access to bidding on projects. I should make clear, in connection both with LEED standards and with buyers' groups, that both are driven ultimately by environmental concerns of individual consumers, and by the desire of companies to have their corporate brand become associated with environmental responsibility by consumers. What LEED standards and buyers' groups do is to provide a mechanism whereby individual consumers can influence the behavior of companies that would otherwise not be directly responsive to individual consumers.

The forest certification movement has spread rapidly around the world since the FSC's launching in 1993, to the point where at present there are certified forests and chains of custody in about 64 countries. The area of certified forests now totals 156,000 square miles, of which 33,000 are in North America. Nine countries each contain at least 4,000 square miles of certified forests, led by Sweden with 38,000 square miles (representing more than half of that country's total forested area), and followed in descending order by Poland, the U.S., Canada, Croatia, Latvia, Brazil, the United Kingdom, and Russia. The countries in which the highest percentages of forest products sold are FSC-labeled are the United Kingdom, where about 20% of all wood sold is FSC-certified, and the Netherlands. Sixteen countries have individual certified forests exceeding 400 square miles in area, of which the largest in North America is the 7,800-square-mile Gordon Cosens Forest in Ontario, managed by the Canadian timber and paper giant Tembec. By the near future, Tembec intends to certify all of the 50,000 square miles of forest that it manages in Canada. Certified forests include both publicly and privately owned ones: for instance, the largest single owner of certified forest in the U.S. is the State of Pennsylvania, with about 3,000 square miles.

Initially after the formation of the FSC, the area of forests certified was doubling each year. More recently, the rate of growth has slowed to "only" 40% per year. That's because the first forest companies and managers that became certified were ones that had already espoused FSC standards. The companies whose forests have become accredited more recently tend to be ones that must change their operations in order to achieve FSC standards. That is, the FSC initially served mainly to recognize companies with environmentally sound practices, and is now increasingly serving to change the practices of other companies that were initially less sound environmentally.

The effectiveness of the Forest Stewardship Council has received the ultimate compliment from logging companies opposed to it: they have set up their own competing certification organizations with weaker standards. These include the Sustainable Forestry Initiative in the U.S., set up by the American Forest and Paper Association; the Canadian Standards Association; and the Pan-European Forest Council. The effect (and presumably the purpose) is to confuse the public with competing claims: for instance, the Sustainable Forestry Initiative initially proposed six different labels making six different claims. All of these "knockoffs" differ from the FSC in that they do not require independent third-party certification, but they permit companies to certify themselves (I'm not joking). They do not ask companies to judge themselves by uniform standards and quantifiable results (e.g., "width of the strips of riparian vegetation flanking streams"), but instead by unquantifiable processes ("we have a policy," "our managers participate in discussions"). They lack chain-of-custody certification, so that any product of a sawmill that receives both certified and uncertified timber becomes certified. The Pan-European Forest Council practices regional automatic certification, by which for instance the entire country of Austria became certified quickly. It remains to be seen whether, in the future, these competing industry attempts at self-certification will be outcompeted by the FSC through losing credibility in the eyes of consumers, or will instead converge on FSC standards in order to gain credibility.

The last industry that I shall discuss is the seafood industry (marine fisheries), which faces the same fundamental problem as do the oil, mining, and timber industries: rising world population and affluence leading to increasing demand for decreasing supplies. While seafood consumption is high and rising in the First World, it is even higher and rising faster elsewhere, e.g., having doubled in China within the last decade. Fish now account for 40% of all protein (of both plant and animal origin) consumed in the Third World and are the main animal protein source for over a billion Asians. Worldwide population shifts from the interior towards the coast within countries will increase the demand for seafood, because three-quarters of the world's population will be living within 50 miles of the seacoast by the year 2010. As a result of our dependence on seafood, the sea provides jobs and income for 200,000,000 people around the world, and fishing is the most important basis of the economies of Iceland, Chile, and some other countries.

While any renewable biological resource poses difficult management problems, marine fisheries are especially hard to manage. Even fisheries confined to waters controlled by a single nation pose difficulties, but fisheries extending over water controlled by multiple nations pose greater problems and have tended to be the earliest to collapse, because no single nation can impose its will. Fisheries in the open ocean outside the 200-mile marine limit lie beyond the control of any national government. Studies suggest that, with proper management, the world's seafood catch could be sustained at a level even higher than its present level. Sadly, though, the majority of the world's commercially important marine fisheries have already either collapsed to the point of being commercially extinct, have been severely depleted, are currently overfished or fished to the limit, are recovering only slowly from past overfishing, or are otherwise in urgent need of management. Among the most important fisheries that have already collapsed are Atlantic halibut, Atlantic bluefin tuna, Atlantic swordfish, North Sea herring, Grand Banks cod, Argentinian hake, and Australian Murray River cod. In overfished areas of the Atlantic and Pacific Oceans, peak catches were attained in the year 1989 and have declined since then. The main reasons behind all these failures are the tragedy of the commons, discussed in the preceding chapter, which makes it difficult for consumers exploiting a shared renewable resource to reach agreement despite their shared interest in doing so; the widespread lack of effective management and regulation; and so-called perverse subsidies, i.e., the economically senseless subsidies that many governments pay for political reasons to support fishing fleets that are too large in relation to their fish stocks, that lead almost inevitably to overfishing, and that yield too low profits to survive without the subsidies.

The damage caused by overfishing extends beyond the future prospects of all of us to eat seafood, and beyond the survival of the particular fish or seafood stocks that we harvest. Most seafood is captured by netting and other methods that result in our hauling in unwanted animals besides those actually sought. Those other animals, referred to as by-catch, constitute a proportion varying between one-quarter and two-thirds of the total catch. In most cases the by-catch dies and is thrown back overboard. Included in the by-catch are unwanted fish species, juveniles of the targeted fish species, seals, dolphins and whales, sharks, and sea turtles. Yet by-catch mortality is not inevitable: for example, recent changes in fishing gear and practices reduced dolphin mortality in the eastern Pacific tuna fishery by a factor of 50. There is also heavy damage to marine habitats, notably to the seabed by trawlers and to coral reefs by dynamite and cyanide fishing. Finally, overfishing damages fishermen, by ultimately eliminating the basis of their livelihood and costing them their jobs.

All of these problems troubled not only economists and environmentalists but also some leaders of the seafood industry itself. Among the latter were executives of Unilever, one of the world's largest buyers of frozen fish, whose products were familiar to consumers under the brand names of Gorton in the U.S. (subsequently sold by Unilever), Birdseye Walls and Iglo in Britain, and Findus and Frudsa in Europe. The executives became concerned that fish, the commodities that they bought and sold, were in steep decline throughout the world, just as the timber company executives who launched the Forest Stewardship Council became concerned about the steep decline of forest. Hence in 1997, four years after the establishment of the FSC, Unilever teamed up with World Wildlife Fund to found a similar organization termed the Marine Stewardship Council (MSC). Its goal was to offer credible eco-labeling to consumers, and to encourage fishermen to solve their own tragedies of the commons by the positive incentive of market appeal rather than the negative incentive of threatened boycotts. Other companies and foundations, plus international agencies, have now joined Unilever and World Wildlife Fund in funding the MSC.

In Britain the companies besides Unilever that support the MSC or buy its certified seafood products include Young's Bluecrest Seafood Company, Britain's largest seafood company; Sainsbury's, Britain's largest fresh food supplier; the supermarket chains Marks and Spencer, and Safeway; and the Boyd Line, which operates a fleet of fishing trawlers. U.S. supporters include Whole Foods, the world's largest retailer of natural and organic foods, plus Shaw's supermarkets and Trader Joe's markets. Among supporters elsewhere are Migros, which is Switzerland's largest food retailer, and Kailis and France Foods, a large operator of fishing boats, factories, markets, and exports in Australia.

The criteria that the MSC applies to fisheries were developed in consultation between fishermen, fisheries managers, seafood processors, retailers, fishery scientists, and environmental groups. The principal criteria are that the fishery should maintain its fish stock's health (including the stock's sex and age distribution and genetic diversity) for the indefinite future, should yield a sustainable harvest, should maintain ecosystem integrity, should minimize impacts on marine habitats and on non-targeted species (the bycatch), should have rules and procedures for managing stocks and minimizing impacts, and should comply with prevailing laws.

Seafood companies bombard the consuming public with widely differing

claims, some of them deceptive or confusing, about the supposed environmental benignness of their fishing practices. Hence the essence of the MSC,
as of the FSC, is independent third-party certification. Again as with the
FSC, the MSC accredits several certifying organizations, rather than carrying out certifying audits itself. Application for certification is completely
voluntary: it's up to a company to decide if it thinks that the benefits of certification would warrant the cost. For the smaller fisheries seeking assessment, a foundation called the David and Lucille Packard Foundation now
contributes to paying those costs through the Sustainable Fisheries Fund.
The process begins with a confidential pre-assessment of the applying company by the certifying organization, then (if the company still wants to be
audited) comes a full assessment typically requiring one or two years (up to
three years for big complicated fisheries) and specifying issues that must be
addressed. If the audit is favorable and the specified issues are resolved, the
company receives certification for five years but is subject each year to an
audit without prior notification. Those annual audit results are posted on a
public website and get scrutinized and often challenged by interested parties. Experience shows that most companies, once they have received MSC
certification, are anxious not to lose it and want to do whatever is required
to pass the annual audit. As with the FSC, there are also chain-of-custody
audits to trace fish caught by a certified fishery from the fishing boat to the
dock where the catch is landed, then to wholesale markets, processors
(freezers and canners), wholesale dealers, and distributors, to the retail market. Only products of a certified fishery that can be traced through this
whole chain are permitted to carry the MSC logo when offered for sale to a
consumer in a shop or restaurant.

What gets certified is a fishery or a fish stock, *and* the fishing method,
practice, or gear used to harvest that stock. The entities seeking certification
are collectives of fishermen, government fisheries departments acting on
behalf of a national or local fishery, and intermediate processors and distributors. Applications are considered from "fisheries" not only of fish, but
also of molluscs and crustacea. Of the seven fisheries certified to date, the
largest is the wild salmon fishery of the U.S. state of Alaska, represented by
the Alaska Department of Fish and Game. The next largest are Western Australian rock lobster (Australia's most valuable single-species fishery, accounting for 20% of the value of all Australian fisheries) and New Zealand
hoki (New Zealand's most valuable export fishery). The other four fisheries
already certified are smaller ones in Britain: Thames herring, Cornwall
mackerel caught by handline, Burry Inlet cockles, and Loch Torridon

Nephrops. Pending accreditation are Alaska pollock, the largest fishery in the U.S., accounting for half of the U.S. catch; U.S. West Coast halibut, Dungeness crab, and spotted prawn; U.S. East Coast striped bass; and Baja California lobster. Plans are also under way to extend certification from wild-caught fish to aquaculture operations (which pose their own big problems mentioned in the next chapter), beginning with shrimp and proceeding to 10 other species, including perhaps salmon. It appears at present that the most difficult problems of certification for the world's major fisheries will arise with wild-caught shrimp (because it is caught mostly by bottom-trawling producing a large by-catch), and with fisheries extending beyond the jurisdiction of a single nation.

Overall, certification has been proving more difficult and slower for fisheries than for forests. Nevertheless, I find myself pleasantly surprised by the progress in fisheries certification achieved in the last five years: I had expected it to be even more difficult and slower than it actually has been.

In brief, environmental practices of big businesses are shaped by a fundamental fact that for many of us offends our sense of justice. Depending on the circumstances, a business really may maximize its profits, at least in the short term, by damaging the environment and hurting people. That is still the case today for fishermen in an unmanaged fishery without quotas, and for international logging companies with short-term leases on tropical rainforest land in countries with corrupt government officials and unsophisticated landowners. It was also the case for oil companies before the Santa Barbara Channel oil spill disaster of 1969, and for Montana mining companies before recent cleanup laws. When government regulation is effective, and when the public is environmentally aware, environmentally clean big businesses may outcompete dirty ones, but the reverse is likely to be true if government regulation is ineffective and if the public doesn't care.

It is easy and cheap for the rest of us to blame a business for helping itself by hurting other people. But that blaming alone is unlikely to produce change. It ignores the fact that businesses are not non-profit charities but profit-making companies, and that publicly owned companies with shareholders are under obligation to those shareholders to maximize profits, provided that they do so by legal means. Our laws make a company's directors legally liable for something termed "breach of fiduciary responsibility" if they knowingly manage a company in a way that reduces profits. The car manufacturer Henry Ford was in fact successfully sued by stockholders in

1919 for raising the minimum wage of his workers to $5 per day: the courts declared that, while Ford's humanitarian sentiments about his employees were nice, his business existed to make profits for its stockholders.

Our blaming of businesses also ignores the ultimate responsibility of the public for creating the conditions that let a business profit through hurting the public: e.g., for not requiring mining companies to clean up, or for continuing to buy wood products from non-sustainable logging operations. In the long run, it is the public, either directly or through its politicians, that has the power to make destructive environmental policies unprofitable and illegal, and to make sustainable environmental policies profitable. The public can do that by suing businesses for harming them, as happened after the *Exxon Valdez*, Piper Alpha, and Bhopal disasters; by preferring to buy sustainably harvested products, a preference that caught the attention of Home Depot and Unilever; by making employees of companies with poor track records feel ashamed of their company and complain to their own management; by preferring their governments to award valuable contracts to businesses with a good environmental track record, as the Norwegian government did to Chevron; and by pressing their governments to pass and enforce laws and regulations requiring good environmental practices, such as the U.S. government's new regulations for the coal industry in the 1970s and 1980s. In turn, big businesses can exert powerful pressure on their suppliers that might ignore public or government pressure. For instance, after the U.S. public became concerned about the spread of mad cow disease, and after the U.S. government's Food and Drug Administration introduced rules demanding that the meat industry abandon practices associated with the risk of spread, meat packers resisted for five years, claiming that the rules would be too expensive to obey. But when McDonald's Corporation then made the same demands after customer purchases of its hamburgers plummeted, the meat industry complied within weeks: "because we have the world's biggest shopping cart," as a McDonald's representative explained. The public's task is to identify which links in the supply chain are sensitive to public pressure: for instance, McDonald's, Home Depot, and Tiffany, but not meat packers, loggers, or gold miners.

Some readers may be disappointed or outraged that I place the ultimate responsibility, for business practices harming the public, on the public itself. I also assign to the public the added costs, if any, of sound environmental practices, which I regard as normal costs of doing business, like any others. My views may seem to ignore a moral imperative that businesses should follow virtuous principles, whether or not it is most profitable for them to do so. I instead prefer to recognize that, throughout human history, in all politically complex human societies in which people encounter other individuals with whom they have no ties of family or clan relationship, government regulation has arisen precisely because it was found to be necessary for the enforcement of moral principles. Invocation of moral principles is a necessary first step for eliciting virtuous behavior, but that alone is not a sufficient step.

To me, the conclusion that the public has the ultimate responsibility for the behavior of even the biggest businesses is empowering and hopeful, rather than disappointing. My conclusion is not a moralistic one about who is right or wrong, admirable or selfish, a good guy or a bad guy. My conclusion is instead a prediction, based on what I have seen happening in the past. Businesses have changed when the public came to expect and require different behavior, to reward businesses for behavior that the public wanted, and to make things difficult for businesses practicing behaviors that the public didn't want. I predict that in the future, just as in the past, changes in public attitudes will be essential for changes in businesses' environmental practices.

The World as a Polder:
What Does It All Mean to Us Today?

Introduction ∎ **The most serious problems** ∎ **If we don't solve
them . . .** ∎ **Life in Los Angeles** ∎ **One-liner objections** ∎
The past and the present ∎ **Reasons for hope** ∎

The chapters of this book have discussed why past or present societies
succeed or fail at solving their environmental problems. Now, this final chapter considers the book's practical relevance: what does it all
mean to us today?

I shall begin by explaining the major sets of environmental problems
facing modern societies, and the time scale on which they pose threats. As a
specific example of how these problems play out, I examine the area where I
have spent most of the last 39 years of my life, Southern California. I then
consider the objections most often raised to dismiss the significance of environmental problems today. Since half of this book was devoted to ancient
societies because of the lessons that they might hold for modern societies, I
look at differences between the ancient and the modern worlds that affect
what lessons we can draw from the past. Finally, for anyone who asks,
"What can I do as an individual?" I offer suggestions in the Further Readings section.

It seems to me that the most serious environmental problems facing past
and present societies fall into a dozen groups. Eight of the 12 were significant already in the past, while four (numbers 5, 7, 8, and 10: energy, the
photosynthetic ceiling, toxic chemicals, and atmospheric changes) became
serious only recently. The first four of the 12 consist of destruction or losses
of natural resources; the next three involve ceilings on natural resources; the
three after that consist of harmful things that we produce or move around;
and the last two are population issues. Let's begin with the natural resources

that we are destroying or losing: natural habitats, wild food sources, biological diversity, and soil.

1. At an accelerating rate, we are destroying natural habitats or else converting them to human-made habitats, such as cities and villages, farmlands and pastures, roads, and golf courses. The natural habitats whose losses have provoked the most discussion are forests, wetlands, coral reefs, and the ocean bottom. As I mentioned in the preceding chapter, more than half of the world's original area of forest has already been converted to other uses, and at present conversion rates one-quarter of the forests that remain will become converted within the next half-century. Those losses of forests represent losses for us humans, especially because forests provide us with timber and other raw materials, and because they provide us with so-called ecosystem services such as protecting our watersheds, protecting soil against erosion, constituting essential steps in the water cycle that generates much of our rainfall, and providing habitat for most terrestrial plant and animal species. Deforestation was a or *the* major factor in all the collapses of past societies described in this book. In addition, as discussed in Chapter 1 in connection with Montana, issues of concern to us are not only forest destruction and conversion, but also changes in the structure of wooded habitats that do remain. Among other things, that changed structure results in changed fire regimes that put forests, chaparral woodlands, and savannahs at greater risk of infrequent but catastrophic fires.

Other valuable natural habitats besides forests are also being destroyed. An even larger fraction of the world's original wetlands than of its forests has already been destroyed, damaged, or converted. Consequences for us arise from wetlands' importance in maintaining the quality of our water supplies and the existence of commercially important freshwater fisheries, while even ocean fisheries depend on mangrove wetlands to provide habitat for the juvenile phase of many fish species. About one-third of the world's coral reefs—the oceanic equivalent of tropical rainforests, because they are home to a disproportionate fraction of the ocean's species—have already been severely damaged. If current trends continue, about half of the remaining reefs would be lost by the year 2030. That damage and destruction result from the growing use of dynamite as a fishing method, reef overgrowth by algae ("seaweeds") when the large herbivorous fish that normally graze on the algae become fished out, effects of sediment runoff and pollutants from adjacent lands cleared or converted to agriculture, and coral bleaching due to rising ocean water temperatures. It has recently become appreciated that fishing by trawling is destroying much or most of the shallow ocean bottom and the species dependent on it.

2. Wild foods, especially fish and to a lesser extent shellfish, contribute a large fraction of the protein consumed by humans. In effect, this is protein that we obtain for free (other than the cost of catching and transporting the fish), and that reduces our needs for animal protein that we have to grow ourselves in the form of domestic livestock. About two billion people, most of them poor, depend on the oceans for protein. If wild fish stocks were managed appropriately, the stock levels could be maintained, and they could be harvested perpetually. Unfortunately, the problem known as the tragedy of the commons (Chapter 14) has regularly undone efforts to manage fisheries sustainably, and the great majority of valuable fisheries already either have collapsed or are in steep decline (Chapter 15). Past societies that overfished included Easter Island, Mangareva, and Henderson.

Increasingly, fish and shrimp are being grown by aquaculture, which in principle has a promising future as the cheapest way to produce animal protein. In several respects, though, aquaculture as commonly practiced today is making the problem of declining wild fisheries worse rather than better. Fish grown by aquaculture are mostly fed wild-caught fish and thereby usually consume more wild fish meat (up to 20 times more) than they yield in meat of their own They contain higher toxin levels than do wild-caught fish. Cultured fish regularly escape, interbreed with wild fish, and thereby harm wild fish stocks genetically, because cultured fish strains have been selected for rapid growth at the expense of poor survival in the wild (50 times worse survival for cultured salmon than for wild salmon). Aquaculture runoff causes pollution and eutrophication. The lower costs of aquaculture than of fishing, by driving down fish prices, initially drive fishermen to exploit wild fish stocks even more heavily in order to maintain their incomes constant when they are receiving less money per pound of fish.

3. A significant fraction of wild species, populations, and genetic diversity has already been lost, and at present rates a large fraction of what remains will be lost within the next half-century. Some species, such as big edible animals, or plants with edible fruits or good timber, are of obvious value to us. Among the many past societies that harmed themselves by exterminating such species were the Easter and Henderson Islanders whom we have discussed.

But biodiversity losses of small inedible species often provoke the response, "Who cares? Do you really care less for humans than for some lousy useless little fish or weed, like the snail darter or Furbish lousewort?" This response misses the point that the entire natural world is made up of wild species providing us for free with services that can be very expensive, and in many cases impossible, for us to supply ourselves. Elimination of lots of lousy little species regularly causes big harmful consequences for humans, just as does randomly knocking out many of the lousy little rivets holding together an airplane. The literally innumerable examples include: the role of earthworms in regenerating soil and maintaining its texture (one of the reasons that oxygen levels dropped inside the Biosphere 2 enclosure, harming its human inhabitants and crippling a colleague of mine, was a lack of appropriate earthworms, contributing to altered soil/atmosphere gas exchange); soil bacteria that fix the essential crop nutrient nitrogen, which otherwise we have to spend money to supply in fertilizers; bees and other insect pollinators (they pollinate our crops for free, whereas it's expensive for us to pollinate every crop flower by hand); birds and mammals that disperse wild fruits (foresters still haven't figured out how to grow from seed the most important commercial tree species of the Solomon Islands, whose seeds are naturally dispersed by fruit bats, which are becoming hunted out); elimination of whales, sharks, bears, wolves, and other top predators in the seas and on the land, changing the whole food chain beneath them; and wild plants and animals that decompose wastes and recycle nutrients, ultimately providing us with clean water and air.

4. Soils of farmlands used for growing crops are being carried away by water and wind erosion at rates between 10 and 40 times the rates of soil formation, and between 500 and 10,000 times soil erosion rates on forested land. Because those soil erosion rates are so much higher than soil formation rates, that means a net loss of soil. For instance, about half of the topsoil of Iowa, the state whose agriculture productivity is among the highest in the U.S., has been eroded in the last 150 years. On my most recent visit to Iowa, my hosts showed me a churchyard offering a dramatically visible example of those soil losses. A church was built there in the middle of farmland during the 19th century and has been maintained continuously as a church ever since, while the land around it was being farmed. As a result of soil being eroded much more rapidly from fields than from the churchyard, the yard now stands like a little island raised 10 feet above the surrounding sea of farmland.

Other types of soil damage caused by human agricultural practices include salinization, as discussed for Montana, China, and Australia in Chapters 1, 12, and 13; losses of soil fertility, because farming removes nutrients much more rapidly than they are restored by weathering of the underlying rock; and soil acidification in some areas, or its converse, alkalinization, in other areas. All of these types of harmful impacts have resulted in a fraction of the world's farmland variously estimated at between 20% and 80% having become severely damaged, during an era in which increasing human population has caused us to need more farmland rather than less farmland. Like deforestation, soil problems contributed to the collapses of all past societies discussed in this book.

The next three problems involve ceilings—on energy, freshwater, and photosynthetic capacity. In each case the ceiling is not hard and fixed but soft: we can obtain more of the needed resource, but at increasing costs.

5. The world's major energy sources, especially for industrial societies, are fossil fuels: oil, natural gas, and coal. While there has been much discussion about how many big oil and gas fields remain to be discovered, and while coal reserves are believed to be large, the prevalent view is that known and likely reserves of readily accessible oil and natural gas will last for a few more decades. This view should not be misinterpreted to mean that all of the oil and natural gas within the Earth will have been used up by then. Instead, further reserves will be deeper underground, dirtier, increasingly expensive to extract or process, or will involve higher environmental costs. Of course, fossil fuels are not our sole energy sources, and I shall consider problems raised by the alternatives below.

6. Most of the world's freshwater in rivers and lakes is already being utilized for irrigation, domestic and industrial water, and in situ uses such as boat transportation corridors, fisheries, and recreation. Rivers and lakes that are not already utilized are mostly far from major population centers and likely users, such as in Northwestern Australia, Siberia, and Iceland. Throughout the world, freshwater underground aquifers are being depleted at rates faster than they are being naturally replenished, so that they will eventually dwindle. Of course, freshwater can be made by desalinization of seawater, but that costs money and energy, as does pumping the resulting desalinized water inland for use. Hence desalinization, while it is useful locally, is too expensive to solve most of the world's water shortages. The Anasazi and Maya were among the past societies to be undone by water problems, while today over a billion people lack access to reliable safe drinking water.

7. It might at first seem that the supply of sunlight is infinite, so one might reason that the Earth's capacity to grow crops and wild plants is also infinite. Within the last 20 years, it has been appreciated that that is not the case, and that's not only because plants grow poorly in the world's Arctic regions and deserts unless one goes to the expense of supplying heat or water. More generally, the amount of solar energy fixed per acre by plant photosynthesis, hence plant growth per acre, depends on temperature and rainfall. At any given temperature and rainfall the plant growth that can be supported by the sunlight falling on an acre is limited by the geometry and biochemistry of plants, even if they take up the sunlight so efficiently that not a single photon of light passes through the plants unabsorbed to reach the ground. The first calculation of this photosynthetic ceiling, carried out in 1986, estimated that humans then already used (e.g., for crops, tree plantations, and golf courses) or diverted or wasted (e.g., light falling on concrete roads and buildings) about half of the Earth's photosynthetic capacity. Given the rate of increase of human population, and especially of population impact (see point 12 below), since 1986, we are projected to be utilizing most of the world's terrestrial photosynthetic capacity by the middle of this century. That is, most energy fixed from sunlight will be used for human purposes, and little will be left over to support the growth of natural plant communities, such as natural forests.

The next three problems involve harmful things that we generate or move around: toxic chemicals, alien species, and atmospheric gases.

8. The chemical industry and many other industries manufacture or release into the air, soil, oceans, lakes, and rivers many toxic chemicals, some of them "unnatural" and synthesized only by humans, others present naturally in tiny concentrations (e.g., mercury) or else synthesized by living things but synthesized and released by humans in quantities much larger than natural ones (e.g., hormones). The first of these toxic chemicals to achieve wide notice were insecticides, pesticides, and herbicides, whose effects on birds, fish, and other animals were publicized by Rachel Carson's 1962 book *Silent Spring*. Since then, it has been appreciated that the toxic effects of even greater significance for us humans are those on ourselves. The culprits include not only insecticides, pesticides, and herbicides, but also mercury and other metals, fire-retardant chemicals, refrigerator coolants, detergents, and components of plastics. We swallow them in our food and water, breathe them in our air, and absorb them through our skin. Often in very low concentrations, they variously cause birth defects, mental retardation, and temporary or permanent damage to our immune and re-productive systems. Some of them act as endocrine disruptors, i.e., they in-terfere with our reproductive systems by mimicking or blocking effects of our own sex hormones. They probably make the major contribution to the steep decline in sperm count in many human populations over the last sev-eral decades, and to the apparently increasing frequency with which couples are unable to conceive, even when one takes into account the increasing av-erage age of marriage in many societies. In addition, deaths in the U.S. from air pollution alone (without considering soil and water pollution) are con-servatively estimated at over 130,000 per year.

Many of these toxic chemicals are broken down in the environment only slowly (e.g., DDT and PCBs) or not at all (mercury), and they persist in the environment for long times before being washed out. Thus, cleanup costs of many polluted sites in the U.S. are measured in the billions of dollars (e.g., Love Canal, the Hudson River, Chesapeake Bay, the *Exxon Valdez* oil spill, and Montana copper mines). But pollution at those worst sites in the U.S. is mild compared to that in the former Soviet Union, China, and many Third World mines, whose cleanup costs no one even dares to think about.

9. The term "alien species" refers to species that we transfer, intentionally or inadvertently, from a place where they are native to another place where they are not native. Some alien species are obviously valuable to us as crops, domestic animals, and landscaping. But others devastate populations of na-tive species with which they come in contact, either by preying on, para-sitizing, infecting, or outcompeting them. The aliens cause these big effects because the native species with which they come in contact had no previous evolutionary experience of them and are unable to resist them (like human populations newly exposed to smallpox or AIDS). There are by now literally hundreds of cases in which alien species have caused one-time or annually recurring damages of hundreds of millions of dollars or even billions of dollars. Modern examples include Australia's rabbits and foxes, agricultural weeds like Spotted Knapweed and Leafy Spurge (Chapter 1), pests and pathogens of trees and crops and livestock (like the blights that wiped out American chestnut trees and devasted American elms), the water hyacinth that chokes waterways, the zebra mussels that choke power plants, and the lampreys that devastated the former commercial fisheries of the North American Great Lakes (Plates 30, 31). Ancient examples include the intro-duced rats that contributed to the extinction of Easter Island's palm tree by gnawing its nuts, and that ate the eggs and chicks of nesting birds on Easter, Henderson, and all other Pacific islands previously without rats.

10. Human activities produce gases that escape into the atmosphere, where they either damage the protective ozone layer (as do formerly widespread refrigerator coolants) or else act as greenhouse gases that absorb sunlight and thereby lead to global warming. The gases contributing to global warming include carbon dioxide from combustion and respiration, and methane from fermentation in the intestines of ruminant animals. Of course, there have always been natural fires and animal respiration producing carbon dioxide, and wild ruminant animals producing methane, but our burning of firewood and of fossil fuels has greatly increased the former, and our herds of cattle and of sheep have greatly increased the latter.

For many years, scientists debated the reality, cause, and extent of global warming: are world temperatures really historically high now, and, if so, by how much, and are humans the leading cause? Most knowledgeable scientists now agree that, despite year-to-year ups and downs of temperature that necessitate complicated analyses to extract warming trends, the atmosphere really has been undergoing an unusually rapid rise in temperature recently, and that human activities are the or a major cause. The remaining uncertainties mainly concern the future expected magnitude of the effect: e.g., whether average global temperatures will increase by "just" 1.5 degrees Centigrade or by 5 degrees Centigrade over the next century. Those numbers may not sound like a big deal, until one reflects that average global temperatures were "only" 5 degrees cooler at the height of the last Ice Age.

While one might at first think that we should welcome global warming on the grounds that warmer temperatures mean faster plant growth, it turns out that global warming will produce both winners and losers. Crop yields in cool areas with temperatures marginal for agriculture may indeed increase, while crop yields in already warm or dry areas may decrease. In Montana, California, and many other dry climates, the disappearance of mountain snowpacks will decrease the water available for domestic uses, and for irrigation that actually limits crop yields in those areas. The rise in global sea levels as a result of snow and ice melting poses dangers of flooding and coastal erosion for densely populated low-lying coastal plains and river deltas already barely above or even below sea level. The areas thereby threatened include much of the Netherlands, Bangladesh, and the seaboard of the eastern U.S., many low-lying Pacific islands, the deltas of the Nile and Mekong Rivers, and coastal and riverbank cities of the United Kingdom (e.g., London), India, Japan, and the Philippines. Global warming will also produce big secondary effects that are difficult to predict exactly in advance and that are likely to cause huge problems, such as further climate changes resulting from changes in ocean circulation resulting in turn from melting of the Arctic ice cap.

The remaining two problems involve the increase in human population:

11. The world's human population is growing. More people require more food, space, water, energy, and other resources. Rates and even the direction of human population change vary greatly around the world, with the highest rates of population growth (4% per year or higher) in some Third World countries, low rates of growth (1% per year or less) in some First World countries such as Italy and Japan, and negative rates of growth (i.e., decreasing populations) in countries facing major public health crises, such as Russia and AIDS-affected African countries. Everybody agrees that the world population is increasing, but that its annual percentage rate of increase is not as high as it was a decade or two ago. However, there is still disagreement about whether the world's population will stabilize at some value above its present level (double the present population?), and (if so) how many years (30 years? 50 years?) it will take for population to reach that level, or whether population will continue to grow.

There is long built-in momentum to human population growth because of what is termed the "demographic bulge" or "population momentum," i.e., a disproportionate number of children and young reproductive-age people in today's population, as a result of recent population growth. That is, suppose that every couple in the world decided tonight to limit themselves to two children, approximately the correct number of children to yield an unchanging population in the long run by exactly replacing their two parents who will eventually die (actually, 2.1 children when one considers childless couples and children who won't marry). The world's population would nevertheless continue to increase for about 70 years, because more people today are of reproductive age or entering reproductive age than are old and post-reproductive. The problem of human population growth has received much attention in recent decades and has given rise to movements such as Zero Population Growth, which aim to slow or halt the increase in the world's population.

12. What really counts is not the number of people alone, but their impact on the environment. If most of the world's 6 billion people today were in cryogenic storage and neither eating, breathing, nor metabolizing, that large population would cause no environmental problems. Instead, our numbers pose problems insofar as we consume resources and generate wastes. That per-capita impact—the resources consumed, and the wastes put out, by each person—varies greatly around the world, being highest in the First World and lowest in the Third World. On the average, each citizen of the U.S., western Europe, and Japan consumes 32 times more resources such as fossil fuels, and puts out 32 times more wastes, than do inhabitants of the Third World (Plate 35).

But low-impact people are becoming high-impact people for two reasons: rises in living standards in Third World countries whose inhabitants see and covet First World lifestyles; and immigration, both legal and illegal, of individual Third World inhabitants into the First World, driven by political, economic, and social problems at home. Immigration from low-impact countries is now the main contributor to the increasing populations of the U.S. and Europe. By the same token, the overwhelmingly most important human population problem for the world as a whole is not the high rate of population increase in Kenya, Rwanda, and some other poor Third World countries, although that certainly does pose a problem for Kenya and Rwanda themselves, and although that is the population problem most discussed. Instead, the biggest problem is the increase in total human impact, as the result of rising Third World living standards, and of Third World individuals moving to the First World and adopting First World living standards.

There are many "optimists" who argue that the world could support double its human population, and who consider only the increase in human numbers and not the average increase in per-capita impact. But I have not met anyone who seriously argues that the world could support 12 times its current impact, although an increase of that factor would result from all Third World inhabitants adopting First World living standards. (That factor of 12 is less than the factor of 32 that I mentioned in the preceding paragraph, because there are already First World inhabitants with high-impact lifestyles, although they are greatly outnumbered by Third World inhabitants.) Even if the people of China alone achieved a First World living standard while everyone else's living standard remained constant, that would double our human impact on the world (Chapter 12).

People in the Third World aspire to First World living standards. They develop that aspiration through watching television, seeing advertisements for First World consumer products sold in their countries, and observing First World visitors to their countries. Even in the most remote villages and refugee camps today, people know about the outside world. Third World citizens are encouraged in that aspiration by First World and United

Nations development agencies, which hold out to them the prospect of achieving their dream if they will only adopt the right policies, like balancing their national budgets, investing in education and infrastructure, and so on.

But no one at the U.N. or in First World governments is willing to acknowledge the dream's impossibility: the unsustainability of a world in which the Third World's large population were to reach and maintain current First World living standards. It is impossible for the First World to resolve that dilemma by blocking the Third World's efforts to catch up: South Korea, Malaysia, Singapore, Hong Kong, Taiwan, and Mauritius have already succeeded or are close to success; China and India are progressing rapidly by their own efforts; and the 15 rich Western European countries making up the European Union have just extended Union membership to 10 poorer countries of Eastern Europe, in effect thereby pledging to help those 10 countries catch up. Even if the human populations of the Third World did not exist, it would be impossible for the First World alone to maintain its present course, because it is not in a steady state but is depleting its own resources as well as those imported from the Third World. At present, it is untenable politically for First World leaders to propose to their own citizens that they lower their living standards, as measured by lower resource consumption and waste production rates. What will happen when it finally dawns on all those people in the Third World that current First World standards are unreachable for them, and that the First World refuses to abandon those standards for itself? Life is full of agonizing choices based on trade-offs, but that's the cruelest trade-off that we shall have to resolve: encouraging and helping all people to achieve a higher standard of living, without thereby undermining that standard through overstressing global resources.

I have described these 12 sets of problems as separate from each other. In fact, they are linked: one problem exacerbates another or makes its solution more difficult. For example, human population growth affects all 11 other problems: more people means more deforestation, more toxic chemicals, more demand for wild fish, etc. The energy problem is linked to other problems because use of fossil fuels for energy contributes heavily to greenhouse gases, the combating of soil fertility losses by using synthetic fertilizers requires energy to make the fertilizers, fossil fuel scarcity increases our interest in nuclear energy which poses potentially the biggest "toxic" problem of all in case of an accident, and fossil fuel scarcity also makes it more expensive to solve our freshwater problems by using energy to desalinize ocean

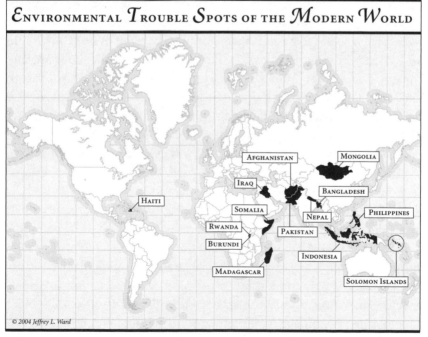

POLITICAL TROUBLE SPOTS OF THE MODERN WORLD

AFGHANISTAN
MONGOLIA
IRAQ
BANGLADESH
HAITI
SOMALIA
PHILIPPINES
NEPAL
RWANDA
PAKISTAN
BURUNDI
INDONESIA
MADAGASCAR
SOLOMON ISLANDS

© 2004 Jeffrey L. Ward

ENVIRONMENTAL TROUBLE SPOTS OF THE MODERN WORLD

AFGHANISTAN
MONGOLIA
IRAQ
BANGLADESH
HAITI
SOMALIA
PHILIPPINES
NEPAL
RWANDA
PAKISTAN
BURUNDI
INDONESIA
MADAGASCAR
SOLOMON ISLANDS

© 2004 Jeffrey L. Ward

water. Depletion of fisheries and other wild food sources puts more pressure on livestock, crops, and aquaculture to replace them, thereby leading to more topsoil losses and more eutrophication from agriculture and aquaculture. Problems of deforestation, water shortage, and soil degradation in the Third World foster wars there and drive legal asylum seekers and illegal emigrants to the First World from the Third World.

Our world society is presently on a non-sustainable course, and any of our 12 problems of non-sustainability that we have just summarized would suffice to limit our lifestyle within the next several decades. They are like time bombs with fuses of less than 50 years. For example, destruction of accessible lowland tropical rainforest outside national parks is already virtually complete in Peninsular Malaysia, will be complete at current rates within less than a decade in the Solomon Islands, the Philippines, on Sumatra, and on Sulawesi, and will be complete around the world except perhaps for parts of the Amazon Basin and Congo Basin within 25 years. At current rates, we shall have depleted or destroyed most of the world's remaining marine fisheries, depleted clean or cheap or readily accessible reserves of oil and natural gas, and approached the photosynthetic ceiling within a few decades. Global warming is projected to have reached a degree Centigrade or more, and a substantial fraction of the world's wild animal and plant species are projected to be endangered or past the point of no return, within half a century. People often ask, "What is the single most important environmental/population problem facing the world today?" A flip answer would be, "The single most important problem is our misguided focus on identifying the single most important problem!" That flip answer is essentially correct, because any of the dozen problems if unsolved would do us grave harm, and because they all interact with each other. If we solved 11 of the problems, but not the 12th, we would still be in trouble, whichever was the problem that remained unsolved. We have to solve them all.

Thus, because we are rapidly advancing along this non-sustainable course, the world's environmental problems *will* get resolved, in one way or another, within the lifetimes of the children and young adults alive today. The only question is whether they will become resolved in pleasant ways of our own choice, or in unpleasant ways not of our choice, such as warfare, genocide, starvation, disease epidemics, and collapses of societies. While all of those grim phenomena have been endemic to humanity throughout our history, their frequency increases with environmental degradation, population pressure, and the resulting poverty and political instability.

Examples of those unpleasant solutions to environmental and population problems abound in both the modern world and the ancient world. The examples include the recent genocides in Rwanda, Burundi, and the former Yugoslavia; war, civil war, or guerrilla war in the modern Sudan, Philippines, and Nepal, and in the ancient Maya homeland; cannibalism on prehistoric Easter Island and Mangareva and among the ancient Anasazi; starvation in many modern African countries and on prehistoric Easter Island; the AIDS epidemic already in Africa, and incipiently elsewhere; and the collapse of state government in modern Somalia, the Solomon Islands, and Haiti, and among the ancient Maya. An outcome less drastic than a worldwide collapse might "merely" be the spread of Rwanda-like or Haiti-like conditions to many more developing countries, while we First World inhabitants retain many of our First World amenities but face a future with which we are unhappy, beset by more chronic terrorism, wars, and disease outbreaks. But it is doubtful that the First World could retain its separate lifestyle in the face of desperate waves of immigrants fleeing from collapsing Third World countries, in numbers much larger than the current unstoppable influx. I'm reminded again of how I picture the end of Gardar Cathedral Farm and its splendid cattle barn on Greenland, overwhelmed by the influx of Norse from poorer farms where all the livestock had died or been eaten.

But before we let ourselves give way to this one-sidedly pessimistic scenario, let's examine further the problems facing us, and their complexities. This will bring us, I feel, to a position of cautious optimism.

To make the preceding discussion less abstract, I shall now illustrate how those dozen environmental problems affect lifestyles in the part of the world with which I am most familiar: the city of Los Angeles in Southern California, where I live. After growing up on the East Coast of the United States and living for several years in Europe, I first visited California in 1964. It immediately appealed to me, and I moved here in 1966.

Thus, I have seen how Southern California has changed over the last 39 years, mostly in ways that make it less appealing. By world standards, Southern California's environmental problems are relatively mild. Jokes of East Coast Americans to the contrary, this is not an area at imminent risk of a societal collapse. By world standards and even by U.S. standards, its human population is exceptionally rich and environmentally educated. Los Angeles is well known for some problems, especially its smog, but most of its environmental and population problems are modest or typical compared to those of other leading First World cities. How do those problems affect the lives of my fellow Angelenos and me?

The complaints voiced by virtually everybody in Los Angeles are those directly related to our growing and already high population: our incurable traffic jams; the very high price of housing (Plate 36), as a result of millions of people working in a few centers of employment, and only limited residential space near those centers; and, as a consequence, the long distances, of up to two hours and 60 miles one way, over which people commute daily in their cars between home and work. Los Angeles became the U.S. city with the worst traffic in 1987 and has remained so every year since then. Everyone recognizes that these problems have gotten worse within the last decade. They are now the biggest single factor hurting the ability of Los Angeles employers to attract and retain employees, and they affect our willingness to drive to events and to visit friends. For the 12-mile trip from my home to downtown Los Angeles or its airport, I now allow an hour and 15 minutes. The average Angeleno spends 368 hours per year, or the equivalent of fifteen 24-hour days, commuting to and from work, without considering time spent driving for other purposes (Plate 37).

No cure is even under serious discussion for these problems, which will only get worse. Such highway construction as is now proposed or under way aims only at smoothing a few of the tightest points of congestion and will be overwhelmed by the increasing number of cars. There is no end in sight to how much worse Los Angeles's problems of congestion will become, because millions of people put up with far worse traffic in other cities. For example, my friends in Bangkok, the capital of Thailand, now carry a portable small chemical toilet in their car because travel can be so prolonged and slow; they once set off to go out of town on a holiday weekend but gave up and returned home after 17 hours, when they had advanced only three miles through the traffic jam. While there are optimists who explain in the abstract why increased population will be good and how the world can accommodate it, I have never met an Angeleno (and very few people anywhere in the world) who personally expressed a desire for increased population in the area where he or she personally lived.

The contribution of Southern California to the ongoing increase in the world's average per-capita human impact, as a result of transfers of people from the Third World to the First World, has for years been the most explosive issue in California politics. California's population growth is accelerating, due almost entirely to immigration and to the large average family sizes of the immigrants after their arrival. The border between California and

Mexico is long and impossible to patrol effectively against people from Central America seeking to immigrate here illegally in search of jobs and personal safety. Every month, one reads of would-be immigrants dying in the desert or being robbed or shot, but that does not deter them. Other illegal immigrants come from as far away as China and Central Asia, in ships that unload them just off the coast. California residents are of two minds about all those Third World immigrants seeking to come here to attain the First World lifestyle. On the one hand, our economy is utterly dependent on them to fill jobs in the service and construction industries and on farms. On the other hand, California residents complain that the immigrants compete with unemployed residents for many jobs, depress wages, and burden our already overcrowded hospitals and public education system. A measure (Proposition 187) on the 1994 state election ballot, overwhelmingly approved by voters but then gutted by the courts on constitutional grounds, would have deprived illegal immigrants of most state-funded benefits. No California resident or elected official has suggested a practical solution to the long-standing contradiction, reminiscent of Dominicans' attitude towards Haitians, between needing immigrants as workers and otherwise resenting their presence and their own needs.

Southern California is a leading contributor to the energy crisis. Our city's former network of electric streetcars collapsed in bankruptcies in the 1920s and 1930s, and the rights of way were bought up by automobile manufacturers and subdivided so as to make it impossible to rebuild the network (which competed with automobiles). Angelenos' preference for living in houses rather than in high-rise apartments, and the long distances and diverse routes over which employees working in any given district commute, have made it impossible to design systems of public transportation that would satisfy the needs of most residents. Hence Los Angelenos are dependent on motorcars.

Our high gas consumption, the mountains ringing much of the Los Angeles basin, and prevailing wind directions generate the smog problem that is our city's most notorious drawback (Plate 38). Despite progress in combating smog in recent decades, and despite seasonal variation (smog worst in the late summer and early autumn) and local variation (smog generally worse as one precedes inland), Los Angeles on the average continues to rank near the bottom of American cities for air quality. After years of improvement, our air quality has again been deteriorating in recent years. Another toxic problem that affects lifestyle and health is the spread of the disease-causing organism giardia in California's rivers and lakes over the last several decades. When I first moved here in the 1960s and went hiking in the mountains, it was safe to drink water from streams; today the guaranteed result would be giardia infection.

The problem of habitat management of which we are most conscious is the fire risk in Southern California's two predominant habitats, chaparral (a scrub woodland similar to the *macchia* of the Mediterranean) and oak woodland. Under natural conditions both habitats experienced occasional fires from lightning strikes, like the situation in Montana forests that I discussed in Chapter 1. Now that people are living in and next to those highly flammable habitats, Angelenos demand that fires be suppressed immediately. Each year, the late summer and early fall, which are the hottest and driest and windiest time of year in Southern California, are the fire season, when somewhere or other hundreds of homes will go up in flames. The canyon in which I live has not had a fire get out of control since 1961, when there was a big fire that burned 600 houses. A theoretical solution to this problem, as in Montana forests, might be frequent controlled small-scale fires to reduce the fuel load, but such fires would be absurdly dangerous in this densely populated urban area, and the public would not stand for it.

Introduced alien species are a big threat and economic burden to California agriculture, the current leading threat being the Mediterranean fruit fly. Non-agricultural threats are introduced pathogens threatening to kill our oak trees and pine trees. Because one of my two sons became interested as a child in amphibians (frogs and salamanders), I have learned that most species of native amphibians have been exterminated from two-thirds of the streams in Los Angeles County, as the result of the spread of three alien predators on amphibians (a crayfish, bullfrog, and mosquitofish) against which Southern California amphibians are helpless because they never evolved to avoid those threats.

The major soil problem affecting California agriculture is salinization as a result of irrigation agriculture, ruining expanses of agricultural land in California's Central Valley, the richest farmland in the United States.

Because rainfall is low in Southern California, Los Angeles depends for its water on long aqueducts, principally from the Sierra Nevada mountain range and adjacent valleys of Northern California, and from the Colorado River on the eastern border of our state. With the growth of California's population, there has been increasing competition for those water supplies among farmers and cities. With global warming, the Sierra snowpack that provides most of our water will decrease, just as in Montana, increasing the likelihood of water shortages in Los Angeles.

As for collapses of fisheries, the sardine fishery of Northern California collapsed early in the 20th century, the abalone industry of Southern California collapsed a few decades ago soon after my arrival, and the rockfish fishery of Southern California is now collapsing and has become subject to severe restrictions or closure within the last year. Fish prices in Los Angeles supermarkets have increased by a factor of 4 since I moved here.

Finally, losses of biodiversity have affected Southern California's most distinctive species. The symbol of the state of California, and of my university (the University of California), is the California Golden Bear, but it is now extinct. (What dreadful symbolism for one's state and university!) Southern California's population of sea otters was exterminated in the last century, and the outcome of recent attempts at reintroduction is uncertain. Within the time that I've lived in Los Angeles, populations of two of our most characteristic bird species, the Roadrunner and the California Quail, have crashed. Southern California amphibians whose numbers have plummeted are the California Newt and the California Tree Frog.

Thus, environmental and population problems have been undermining the economy and the quality of life in Southern California. They are in large measure ultimately responsible for our water shortages, power shortages, garbage accumulation, school crowding, housing shortages and price rises, and traffic congestion. In most of these respects except for our especially bad traffic jams and air quality, we are no worse off than many other areas of the United States.

Most environmental problems involve detailed uncertainties that are legitimate subjects for debate. In addition, however, there are many reasons that are commonly advanced to dismiss the importance of environmental problems, and that are in my opinion not well informed. These objections are often posed in the form of simplistic "one-liners." Here are a dozen of the commonest ones:

"The environment has to be balanced against the economy." This quote portrays environmental concerns as a luxury, views measures to solve environmental problems as incurring a net cost, and considers leaving environmental problems unsolved to be a money-saving device. This one-liner puts the truth exactly backwards. Environmental messes cost us huge sums of money both in the short run and in the long run; cleaning up or preventing those messes saves us huge sums in the long run, and often in the short run as well. In caring for the health of our surroundings, just as of our bodies, it

is cheaper and preferable to avoid getting sick than to try to cure illnesses after they have developed. Just think of the damage caused by agricultural weeds and pests, non-agricultural pests like water hyacinths and zebra mussels, the recurrent annual costs of combating those pests, the value of lost time when we are stuck in traffic, the financial costs resulting from people getting sick or dying from environmental toxins, cleanup costs for toxic chemicals, the steep increase in fish prices due to depletion of fish stocks, and the value of farmland damaged or ruined by erosion and salinization. It adds up to a few hundred million dollars per year here, tens of billions of dollars there, another billion dollars over here, and so on for hundreds of different problems. For instance, the value of "one statistical life" in the U.S.—i.e., the cost to the U.S. economy resulting from the death of an average American whom society has gone to the expense of rearing and educating but who dies before a lifetime of contributing to the national economy—is usually estimated at around $5 million. Even if one takes the conservative estimate of annual U.S. deaths due to air pollution as 130,000, then deaths due to air pollution cost us about $650 billion per year. That illustrates why the U.S. Clean Air Act of 1970, although its cleanup measures do cost money, has yielded estimated net health savings (benefits in excess of costs) of about $1 trillion per year, due to saved lives and reduced health costs.

"Technology will solve our problems." This is an expression of faith about the future, and therefore based on a supposed track record of technology having solved more problems than it created in the recent past. Underlying this expression of faith is the implicit assumption that, from tomorrow onwards, technology will function primarily to solve existing problems and will cease to create new problems. Those with such faith also assume that the new technologies now under discussion will succeed, and that they will do so quickly enough to make a big difference soon. In extended conversations that I had with two of America's most successful and best-known businessmen and financiers, both of them eloquently described to me emerging technologies and financial instruments that differ fundamentally from those of the past and that, they confidently predicted, would solve our environmental problems.

But actual experience is the opposite of this assumed track record. Some dreamed-of new technologies succeed, while others don't. Those that do succeed typically take a few decades to develop and phase in widely: think of gas heating, electric lighting, cars and airplanes, television, computers, and so on. New technologies, whether or not they succeed in solving the problem that they were designed to solve, regularly create unanticipated new problems. Technological solutions to environmental problems are routinely far more expensive than preventive measures to avoid creating the problem in the first place: for example, the billions of dollars of damages and cleanup costs associated with major oil spills, compared to the modest cost of safety measures effective at minimizing the risks of a major oil spill.

Most of all, advances in technology just increase our ability to do things, which may be either for the better or for the worse. All of our current problems are unintended negative consequences of our existing technology. The rapid advances in technology during the 20th century have been creating difficult new problems faster than they have been solving old problems: that's why we're in the situation in which we now find ourselves. What makes you think that, as of January 1, 2006, for the first time in human history, technology will miraculously stop causing new unanticipated problems while it just solves the problems that it previously produced?

From thousands of examples of unforeseen harmful side effects of new technological solutions, two must suffice: CFCs (chlorofluorocarbons) and motor vehicles. The coolant gases formerly used in refrigerators and air conditioners were toxic ones (like ammonia) that could prove fatal if those appliances leaked while the homeowner was asleep at night. Hence it was hailed as a great advance when CFCs (alias freons) were developed as synthetic refrigerant gases. They are odorless, non-toxic, and highly stable under ordinary conditions at the Earth's surface, so that initially no bad side effects were observed or expected. Within a short time they became viewed as miracle substances and adopted throughout the world as refrigerator and air-conditioner coolants, foam-blowing agents, solvents, and propellants in aerosol cans. But in 1974 it was discovered that in the stratosphere they are broken down by intense ultraviolet radiation to yield highly reactive chlorine atoms that destroy a significant fraction of the ozone layer protecting us and all other living things against lethal ultraviolet effects. That discovery provoked vigorous denial by some corporate interests, fueled not only by the $200 billion value of CFC-based industrial efforts but also by genuine doubts because of scientific complications involved. Hence the phasing-out of CFCs has taken a long time: not until 1988 did the DuPont Company (the largest manufacturer of CFCs) decide to stop manufacturing them, in 1992 industrialized countries agreed to cease CFC production by 1995, and China and some other developing countries are still producing them.

Unfortunately, the amounts of CFCs already in the atmosphere are sufficiently large, and their breakdown sufficiently slow, that they will continue to be present for many decades after the eventual end of all CFC production.

The other example involves the introduction of the motor vehicle. When I was a child in the 1940s, some of my teachers were old enough to remember the first decades of the 20th century, when motor vehicles were in the process of replacing horse-drawn carriages and trams on city streets of the United States. The two biggest immediate consequences experienced by urban Americans, my teachers recall, were that American cities became wonderfully cleaner and quieter. No longer were streets constantly polluted with horse manure and urine, and no longer was there the constant din of horse hoofs clicking on the pavement. Today, after a century's experience of cars and buses, it strikes us as ludicrous or inconceivable that anyone could praise them for being non-polluting and quiet. While no one is advocating a return to the horse as a solution to smog from engine emissions, the example does serve to illustrate the unanticipated negative side effects even of technologies that (unlike CFCs) we choose to retain.

"If we exhaust one resource, we can always switch to some other resource meeting the same need." Optimists who make such claims ignore the unforeseen difficulties and long transition times regularly involved. For instance, one area in which switching based on not-yet-perfected new technologies has repeatedly been touted as promising to solve a major environmental problem is automobiles. The current hope for breakthrough involves hydrogen cars and fuel cells, which are technologically in their infancy as applied to motor transport. Thus, there is not a track record justifying faith in the hydrogen-car solution to our fossil fuel problem. However, we do have a track record of a long series of other proposed new car technologies touted as breakthroughs, such as rotary engines and (most recently) electric cars, that aroused much discussion and even sales of production models, only to decline or disappear because of unforeseen problems.

Equally instructive is the automobile industry's recent development of fuel-efficient hybrid gas/electric cars, which have been enjoying increasing sales. However, it would be unfair for a believer in switching to mention hybrid cars without also mentioning the automobile industry's simultaneous development of SUVs, which have been outselling hybrids by a big margin and more than offsetting their fuel savings. The net result of these two technological breakthroughs has been that the fuel consumption and exhaust production of our national car fleet has been going up rather than down.

Nobody has figured out a method to ensure that technology will yield only increasingly environment-friendly effects and products (e.g., hybrid cars), without also yielding environment-unfriendly effects and products (e.g., SUVs).

Another example of faith in switching and substitution is the hope that renewable energy sources, such as wind and solar energy, may solve the energy crisis. These technologies do indeed exist; many Californians now use solar energy to heat their swimming pools, and wind generators are already supplying about one-sixth of Denmark's energy needs. However, wind and solar energy have limited applicability because they can be used only at locations with reliable winds or sunlight. In addition, the recent history of technology shows that conversion times for adoption of major switches— e.g., from candles to oil lamps to gas lamps to electric lights for lighting, or from wood to coal to petroleum for energy—require several decades, because so many institutions and secondary technologies associated with the former technology have to be changed. It is indeed likely that energy sources other than fossil fuels will make increasing contributions to our motor transport and energy generation, but this is a long-term prospect. We'll also need to solve our fuel and energy problems for the next several decades, before new technologies become widespread. All too often, a focus by politicians or industries on the promise of hydrogen cars and wind energy for the distant future distracts attention from all the obvious measures needed right now to decrease driving and fuel consumption by existing cars, and to decrease consumption by fossil fuel generating plants.

"There really isn't a world food problem; there is already enough food; we only need to solve the transportation problem of distributing that food to places that need it." (The same thing could be said for energy.) Or else: *"The world's food problem is already being solved by the Green Revolution, with its new high-yield varieties of rice and other crops, or else it will be solved by genetically modified crops."* This argument notes two things: that First World citizens enjoy on the average greater per-capita food consumption than do Third World citizens; and that some First World countries, such as the United States, do or can produce more food than their citizens consume. If food consumption could be equalized over the world, or if surplus First World food could be exported to the Third World, might that alleviate Third World starvation?

The obvious flaw in the first half of this argument is that First World citizens show no interest in eating less, in order that Third World citizens could eat more. The flaw in the second half of the argument is that, while

First World countries are willing occasionally to export food to mitigate starvation occasioned by some crisis (such as a drought or war) in certain Third World countries, First World citizens have shown no interest in paying on a regular basis (via their tax dollars that support foreign aid and subsidies to farmers) to feed billions of Third World citizens on a chronic basis. If that did happen but without effective overseas family planning programs, which the U.S. government currently opposes on principle, the result would just be Malthus's dilemma, i.e., an increase in population proportional to an increase in available food. Population increase and Malthus's dilemma also contribute to explaining why, after decades of hope and money invested in the Green Revolution and high-yield varieties, starvation is still widespread in the world. All of these considerations mean that genetically modified (GM) food varieties by themselves are equally unlikely to solve the world's food problems (while world population supposedly remains stationary?). In addition, virtually all GM crop production at present is of just four crops (soybeans, corn, canola, and cotton) not eaten directly by humans but used for animal fodder, oil, or clothing, and grown in six temperate-zone countries or regions. Reasons are the strong consumer resistance to eating GM foods; and the cruel fact that companies developing GM crops can make money by selling their products to rich farmers in mostly affluent temperate-zone countries, but not by selling to poor farmers in developing tropical countries. Hence the companies have no interest in investing heavily to develop GM cassava, millet, or sorghum for Third World farmers.

"As measured by commonsense indicators such as human lifespan, health, and wealth (in economists' terms, per-capita gross national product or GNP), conditions have actually been getting better for many decades." Or: *"Just look around you: the grass is still green, there is plenty of food in the supermarkets, clean water still flows from the taps, and there is absolutely no sign of imminent collapse."* For affluent First World citizens, conditions have indeed been getting better, and public health measures have on the average lengthened lifespans in the Third World as well. But lifespan alone is not a sufficient indicator: billions of Third World citizens, constituting about 80% of the world's population, still live in poverty, near or below the starvation level. Even in the United States, an increasing fraction of the population is at the poverty level and lacks affordable medical care, and all proposals to change this situation (e.g., "Just provide everyone with health insurance paid by the government") have been politically unacceptable.

In addition, all of us know as individuals that we don't measure our economic well-being just by the present *size* of our bank accounts: we also look at our *direction* of cash flow. When you look at your bank statement and you see a positive $5,000 balance, you don't smile if you then realize that you have been experiencing a net cash drain of $200 per month for the last several years, and at that rate you have just two years and one month left before you have to file for bankruptcy. The same principle holds for our national economy, and for environmental and population trends. The prosperity that the First World enjoys at present is based on spending down its environmental capital in the bank (its capital non-renewable energy sources, fish stocks, topsoil, forests, etc.). Spending capital should not be misrepresented as making money. It makes no sense to be content with our present comfort when it is clear that we are currently on a non-sustainable course.

In fact, one of the main lessons to be learned from the collapses of the Maya, Anasazi, Easter Islanders, and those other past societies (as well as from the recent collapse of the Soviet Union) is that a society's steep decline may begin only a decade or two after the society reaches its peak numbers, wealth, and power. In that respect, the trajectories of the societies that we have discussed are unlike the usual courses of individual human lives, which decline in a prolonged senescence. The reason is simple: maximum population, wealth, resource consumption, and waste production mean maximum environmental impact, approaching the limit where impact outstrips resources. On reflection, it's no surprise that declines of societies tend to follow swiftly on their peaks.

"Look at how many times in the past the gloom-and-doom predictions of fearmongering environmentalists have proved wrong. Why should we believe them this time?" Yes, some predictions by environmentalists have proved incorrect, favorite examples of critics being a prediction made in 1980 by Paul Ehrlich, John Harte, and John Holdren about rises in prices of five metals, and predictions made in the Club of Rome forecast of 1972. But it is misleading to look selectively for environmentalist predictions that proved wrong, and not also to look for environmentalist predictions that proved right, or anti-environmentalist predictions that proved wrong. There is an abundance of errors of the latter sort: e.g., overly optimistic predictions that the Green Revolution would already have solved the world's hunger problems; the prediction of the economist Julian Simon that we could feed the world's population as it continues to grow for the next 7 billion years; and Simon's prediction "Copper can be made from other elements" and thus there is no risk of a copper shortage. As regards the first of Simon's two predictions, continuation of our current population growth rate would yield

10 people per square yard of land in 774 years, a mass of people equal to the Earth's mass in slightly under 2,000 years, and a mass of people equal to the universe's mass in 6,000 years, long before Simon's forecast of 7 billion years without such problems. As regards his second prediction, we learn in our first course of chemistry that copper is an element, which means that by definition it cannot be made from other elements. My impression is that pessimistic predictions that have proved incorrect, such as Ehrlich's, Harte's, and Holdren's about metal prices or the Club of Rome's about future food supplies, have on the average been much more realistic possibilities at the time that they were made than were Simon's two predictions.

Basically, the one-liner about some environmentalist predictions proving wrong boils down to a complaint about false alarms. In other spheres of our lives, such as fires, we adopt a commonsense attitude towards false alarms. Our local governments maintain expensive firefighting forces, even though in some small towns they are rarely called on to put out fires. Of the fire alarms phoned in to fire departments, many prove to be false alarms, and many others involve small fires that the property owner himself then succeeds in putting out before the fire engines arrive. We comfortably accept a certain frequency of such false alarms and extinguished fires, because we understand that fire risks are uncertain and hard to judge when a fire has just started, and that a fire that does rage out of control may exact high costs in property and human lives. No sensible person would dream of abolishing the town fire department, whether manned by full-time professionals or volunteers, just because a few years went by without a big fire. Nor would anyone blame a homeowner for calling the fire department on detecting a small fire, only to succeed in quenching the fire before the fire truck's arrival. Only if false alarms become an inordinately high proportion of all fire alarms do we feel that something is wrong. In effect, the proportion of false alarms that we tolerate is based on subconsciously comparing the frequency and destructive costs of big fires with the frequency and wasted-services costs of false alarms. A very low frequency of false alarms proves that too many homeowners are being too cautious, waiting too long to call the fire department, and consequently losing their homes.

By the same reasoning, we must expect some environmentalist warnings to turn out to be false alarms, otherwise we would know that our environmental warning systems were much too conservative. The multibillion-dollar costs of many environmental problems justify a moderate frequency of false alarms. In addition, the reason that alarms proved false is often that they convinced us to adopt successful countermeasures. For example, it's true that our air quality here in Los Angeles today is not as bad as some gloom-and-doom predictions of 50 years ago. However, that's entirely because Los Angeles and the state of California were thereby aroused to adopt many countermeasures (such as vehicle emission standards, smog certificates, and lead-free gas), not because initial predictions of the problem were exaggerated.

"The population crisis is already solving itself, because the rate of increase of the world's population is decreasing, such that world population will level off at less than double its present level." While the prediction that world population will level off at less than double its present level may or may not prove true, it is at present a realistic possibility. However, we can take no comfort in this possibility, for two reasons: by many criteria, even the world's present population is living at a non-sustainable level; and, as explained earlier in this chapter, the larger danger that we face is not just of a two-fold increase in population, but of a much larger increase in human impact if the Third World's population succeeds in attaining a First World living standard. It is surprising to hear some First World citizens nonchalantly mentioning the world's adding "only" 2½ billion more people (the lowest estimate that anyone would forecast) as if that were acceptable, when the world already holds that many people who are malnourished and living on less than $3 per day.

"The world can accommodate human population growth indefinitely. The more people, the better, because more people mean more inventions and ultimately more wealth." Both of these ideas are associated especially with Julian Simon but have been espoused by many others, especially by economists. The statement about our ability to absorb current rates of population growth indefinitely is not to be taken seriously, because we have already seen that that would mean 10 people per square yard in the year 2779. Data on national wealth demonstrate that the claim that more people mean more wealth is the opposite of correct. The 10 countries with the most people (over 100 million each) are, in descending order of population, China, India, the U.S., Indonesia, Brazil, Pakistan, Russia, Japan, Bangladesh, and Nigeria. The 10 countries with the highest affluence (per-capita real GDP) are, in descending order, Luxembourg, Norway, the U.S., Switzerland, Denmark, Iceland, Austria, Canada, Ireland, and the Netherlands. The only country on both lists is the U.S.

Actually, the countries with large populations are disproportionately poor: eight of the 10 have per-capita GDP under $8,000, and five of them under $3,000. The affluent countries have disproportionately few people: seven of the 10 have populations below 9,000,000, and two of them under

500,000. Instead, what does distinguish the two lists is population growth rates: all 10 of the affluent countries have very low relative population growth rates (1% per year or less), while eight of the 10 most populous countries have higher relative population growth rates than any of the most affluent countries, except for two large countries that achieved low population growth in unpleasant ways: China, by government order and enforced abortion, and Russia, whose population is actually decreasing because of catastrophic health problems. Thus, as an empirical fact, more people and a higher population growth rate mean more poverty, not more wealth.

"Environmental concerns are a luxury affordable just by affluent First World yuppies, who have no business telling desperate Third World citizens what they should be doing." This view is one that I have heard mainly from affluent First World yuppies lacking experience of the Third World. In all my experience of Indonesia, Papua New Guinea, East Africa, Peru, and other Third World countries with growing environmental problems and populations, I have been impressed that their people know very well how they are being harmed by population growth, deforestation, overfishing, and other problems. They know it because they immediately pay the penalty, in forms such as loss of free timber for their houses, massive soil erosion, and (the tragic complaint that I hear incessantly) their inability to afford clothes, books, and school fees for their children. The reason why the forest behind their village is nevertheless being logged is usually either that a corrupt government has ordered it logged over their often-violent protest, or else that they signed a logging lease with great reluctance because they saw no other way to get the money needed next year for their children. My best friends in the Third World, with families of 4 to 8 children, lament that they have heard of the benign forms of contraception widespread in the First World, and they want those measures desperately for themselves, but they can't afford or obtain them, due in part to the refusal of the U.S. government to fund family planning in its foreign aid programs.

Another view that is widespread among affluent First World people, but which they will rarely express openly, is that they themselves are managing just fine at carrying on with their lifestyles despite all those environmental problems, which really don't concern them because the problems fall mainly on Third World people (though it is not politically correct to be so blunt). Actually, the rich are not immune to environmental problems. CEOs of big First World companies eat food, drink water, breathe air, and have (or try to conceive) children, like the rest of us. While they can usually avoid problems of water quality by drinking bottled water, they find it much more difficult to avoid being exposed to the same problems of food and air quality as the rest of us. Living disproportionately high on the food chain, at levels at which toxic substances become concentrated, they are at more rather than less risk of reproductive impairment due to ingestion of or exposure to toxic materials, possibly contributing to their higher infertility rates and the increasing frequency with which they require medical assistance in conceiving. In addition, one of the conclusions that we saw emerging from our discussion of Maya kings, Greenland Norse chieftains, and Easter Island chiefs is that, in the long run, rich people do not secure their own interests and those of their children if they rule over a collapsing society and merely buy themselves the privilege of being the last to starve or die. As for First World society as a whole, its resource consumption accounts for most of the world's total consumption that has given rise to the impacts described at the beginning of this chapter. Our totally unsustainable consumption means that the First World could not continue for long on its present course, even if the Third World didn't exist and weren't trying to catch up to us.

"If those environmental problems become desperate, it will be at some time far off in the future, after I die, and I can't take them seriously." In fact, at current rates most or all of the dozen major sets of environmental problems discussed at the beginning of this chapter will become acute within the lifetime of young adults now alive. Most of us who have children consider the securing of our children's future as the highest priority to which to devote our time and our money. We pay for their education and food and clothes, make wills for them, and buy life insurance for them, all with the goal of helping them to enjoy good lives 50 years from now. It makes no sense for us to do these things for our individual children, while simultaneously doing things undermining the world in which our children will be living 50 years from now.

This paradoxical behavior is one of which I personally was guilty, because I was born in the year 1937, hence before the birth of my children I too could not take seriously any event (like global warming or the end of the tropical rainforests) projected for the year 2037. I shall surely be dead before that year, and even the date 2037 struck me as unreal. However, when my twin sons were born in 1987, and when my wife and I then started going through the usual parental obsessions about schools, life insurance, and wills, I realized with a jolt: 2037 is the year in which my kids will be my own age of 50 (then)! It's not an imaginary year! What's the point of willing our property to our kids if the world will be in a mess then anyway?

Having lived for five years in Europe shortly after World War II, and then having married into a Polish family with a Japanese branch, I saw at first hand what can happen when parents take good care of their individual children but not of their children's future world. The parents of my Polish, German, Japanese, Russian, British, and Yugoslav friends also bought life insurance, made wills, and obsessed about the schooling of their children, as my wife and I have been doing more recently. Some of them were rich and would have had valuable property to will to their children. But they did not take good care of their children's world, and they blundered into the disaster of World War II. As a result, most of my European and Japanese friends born in the same year as I had their lives blighted in various ways, such as being orphaned, separated from one or both parents during their childhood, bombed out of their houses, deprived of schooling opportunities, deprived of their family estates, or raised by parents burdened with memories of war and concentration camps. The worst-case scenarios that today's children face if we too blunder about their world are different, but equally unpleasant.

This leaves us with two other common one-liners that we have not considered: *"There are big differences between modern societies and those past societies of Easter Islanders, Maya, and Anasazi who collapsed, so that we can't straightforwardly apply lessons from the past."* And: *"What can I, as an individual, do, when the world is really being shaped by unstoppable powerful juggernauts of governments and big businesses?"* In contrast to the previous one-liners, which upon examination can be quickly dismissed, these two concerns are valid and cannot be dismissed. I shall devote the remainder of this chapter to the former question, and a section of the Further Readings (pp. 555–59) to the latter question.

Are the parallels between the past and present sufficiently close that the collapses of the Easter Islanders, Henderson Islanders, Anasazi, Maya, and Greenland Norse could offer any lessons for the modern world? At first, a critic, noting the obvious differences, might be tempted to object, "It's ridiculous to suppose that the collapses of all those ancient peoples could have broad relevance today, especially to the modern U.S. Those ancients didn't enjoy the wonders of modern technology, which benefits us and which lets us solve problems by inventing new environment-friendly technologies. Those ancients had the misfortune to suffer from effects of climate change. They behaved stupidly and ruined their own environment by

doing obviously dumb things, like cutting down their forests, overharvesting wild animal sources of their protein, watching their topsoil erode away,
and building cities in dry areas likely to run short of water. They had foolish
leaders who didn't have books and so couldn't learn from history, and who
embroiled them in expensive and destabilizing wars, cared only about staying in power, and didn't pay attention to problems at home. They got overwhelmed by desperate starving immigrants, as one society after another
collapsed, sending floods of economic refugees to tax the resources of the
societies that weren't collapsing. In all those respects, we moderns are fundamentally different from those primitive ancients, and there is nothing
that we could learn from them. Especially we in the U.S., the richest and
most powerful country in the world today, with the most productive environment and wise leaders and strong loyal allies and only weak insignificant
enemies—none of those bad things could possibly apply to us."

Yes, it's true that there are big differences between the situations of those
past societies and our modern situation today. The most obvious difference
is that there are far more people alive today, packing far more potent technology that impacts the environment, than in the past. Today we have over
6 billion people equipped with heavy metal machinery such as bulldozers
and nuclear power, whereas the Easter Islanders had at most a few tens of
thousands of people with stone chisels and human muscle power. Yet the
Easter Islanders still managed to devastate their environment and bring
their society to the point of collapse. That difference greatly increases,
rather than decreases, the risks for us today.

A second big difference stems from globalization. Leaving out of this
discussion for the moment the question of environmental problems within
the First World itself, let's just ask whether the lessons from past collapses
might apply anywhere in the Third World today. First ask some ivory-tower
academic ecologist, who knows a lot about the environment but never reads
a newspaper and has no interest in politics, to name the overseas countries
facing some of the worst problems of environmental stress, overpopulation,
or both. The ecologist would answer: "That's a no-brainer, it's obvious. Your
list of environmentally stressed or overpopulated countries should surely
include Afghanistan, Bangladesh, Burundi, Haiti, Indonesia, Iraq, Madagascar, Mongolia, Nepal, Pakistan, the Philippines, Rwanda, the Solomon Islands, and Somalia, plus others" (map, p. 497).

Then go ask a First World politician, who knows nothing and cares less
about the environment and population problems, to name the world's
worst trouble spots: countries where state government has already been

overwhelmed and has collapsed, or is now at risk of collapsing, or has been
wracked by recent civil wars; and countries that, as a result of those problems of their own, are also creating problems for us rich First World countries, which may end up having to provide foreign aid for them, or may face
illegal immigrants from them, or may decide to provide them with military
assistance to deal with rebellions and terrorists, or may even have to send in
our own troops. The politician would answer, "That's a no-brainer, it's obvious. Your list of political trouble spots should surely include Afghanistan,
Bangladesh, Burundi, Haiti, Indonesia, Iraq, Madagascar, Mongolia, Nepal,
Pakistan, the Philippines, Rwanda, the Solomon Islands, and Somalia, plus
others."

Surprise, surprise: the two lists are very similar. The connection between
the two lists is transparent: it's the problems of the ancient Maya, Anasazi,
and Easter Islanders playing out in the modern world. Today, just as in the
past, countries that are environmentally stressed, overpopulated, or both
become at risk of getting politically stressed, and of their governments collapsing. When people are desperate, undernourished, and without hope,
they blame their governments, which they see as responsible for or unable
to solve their problems. They try to emigrate at any cost. They fight each
other over land. They kill each other. They start civil wars. They figure that
they have nothing to lose, so they become terrorists, or they support or tolerate terrorism.

The results of these transparent connections are genocides such as
the ones that already exploded in Bangladesh, Burundi, Indonesia, and
Rwanda; civil wars or revolutions, as in most of the countries on the lists;
calls for the dispatch of First World troops, as to Afghanistan, Haiti, Indonesia, Iraq, the Philippines, Rwanda, the Solomon Islands, and Somalia; the
collapse of central government, as has already happened in Somalia and the
Solomon Islands; and overwhelming poverty, as in all of the countries on
these lists. Hence the best predictors of modern "state failures"—i.e., revolutions, violent regime change, collapse of authority, and genocide—prove
to be measures of environmental and population pressure, such as high infant mortality, rapid population growth, a high percentage of the population in their late teens and 20s, and hordes of unemployed young men
without job prospects and ripe for recruitment into militias. Those pressures create conflicts over shortages of land (as in Rwanda), water, forests,
fish, oil, and minerals. They create not only chronic internal conflict, but
also emigration of political and economic refugees, and wars between coun-

tries arising when authoritarian regimes attack neighboring nations in order to divert popular attention from internal stresses.

In short, it is not a question open for debate whether the collapses of past societies have modern parallels and offer any lessons to us. That question is settled, because such collapses have actually been happening recently, and others appear to be imminent. Instead, the real question is how many more countries will undergo them.

As for terrorists, you might object that many of the political murderers, suicide bombers, and 9/11 terrorists were educated and moneyed rather than uneducated and desperate. That's true, but they still depended on a desperate society for support and toleration. Any society has its murderous fanatics; the U.S. produced its own Timothy McVeigh and its Harvard-educated Theodore Kaczinski. But well-nourished societies offering good job prospects, like the U.S., Finland, and South Korea, don't offer broad support to their fanatics.

The problems of all these environmentally devastated, overpopulated, distant countries become our own problems because of globalization. We are accustomed to thinking of globalization in terms of us rich advanced First Worlders sending our good things, such as the Internet and Coca-Cola, to those poor backward Third Worlders. But globalization means nothing more than improved worldwide communications, which can convey many things in either direction; globalization is not restricted to good things carried only from the First to the Third World.

Among bad things transported from the First World to developing countries, we already mentioned the millions of tons of electronic garbage intentionally transported each year from industrialized nations to China. To grasp the worldwide scale of unintentional garbage transport, consider the garbage collected on the beaches of tiny Oeno and Ducie Atolls in the Southeast Pacific Ocean (see map on p. 122): uninhabited atolls, without freshwater, rarely visited even by yachts, and among the world's most remote bits of land, each over a hundred miles even from remote uninhabited Henderson Island. Surveys there detected, for each linear yard of beach, on the average one piece of garbage, which must have drifted from ships or else from Asian and American countries on the Pacific Rim thousands of miles distant. The commonest items proved to be plastic bags, buoys, glass and plastic bottles (especially Suntory whiskey bottles from Japan), rope, shoes, and lightbulbs, along with oddities such as footballs, toy soldiers and airplanes, bike pedals, and screwdrivers.

A more sinister example of bad things transported from the First World to developing countries is that the highest blood levels of toxic industrial chemicals and pesticides reported for any people in the world are for Eastern Greenland's and Siberia's Inuit people (Eskimos), who are also among the most remote from sites of chemical manufacture or heavy use. Their blood mercury levels are nevertheless in the range associated with acute mercury poisoning, while the levels of toxic PCBs (polychlorinated biphenyls) in Inuit mothers' breast milk fall in a range high enough to classify the milk as "hazardous waste." Effects on the women's babies include hearing loss, altered brain development, and suppressed immune function, hence high rates of ear and respiratory infections.

Why should levels of these poisonous chemicals from remote industrial nations of the Americas and Europe be higher in the Inuit than even in urban Americans and Europeans? It's because staples of the Inuit diet are whales, seals, and seabirds that eat fish, molluscs, and shrimp, and the chemicals become concentrated at each step as they pass up this food chain. All of us in the First World who occasionally consume seafood are also ingesting these chemicals, but in smaller amounts. (However, that doesn't mean that you will be safe if you stop eating seafood, because you now can't avoid ingesting such chemicals no matter what you eat.)

Still other bad impacts of the First World on the Third World include deforestation, Japan's imports of wood products currently being a leading cause of deforestation in the tropical Third World; and overfishing, due to fishing fleets of Japan, Korea, Taiwan and the heavily subsidized fleets of the European Union scouring the world's oceans. Conversely, people in the Third World can now, intentionally or unintentionally, send us their own bad things: their diseases like AIDS, SARS, cholera, and West Nile fever, carried inadvertently by passengers on transcontinental airplanes; unstoppable numbers of legal and illegal immigrants arriving by boat, truck, train, plane, and on foot; terrorists; and other consequences of their Third World problems. We in the U.S. are no longer the isolated Fortress America to which some of us aspired in the 1930s; instead, we are tightly and irreversibly connected to overseas countries. The U.S. is the world's leading importer nation: we import many necessities (especially oil and some rare metals) and many consumer products (cars and consumer electronics), as well as being the world's leading importer of investment capital. We are also the world's leading exporter, particularly of food and of our own manufactured products. Our own society opted long ago to become interlocked with the rest of the world.

That's why political instability anywhere in the world now affects us, our trade routes, and our overseas markets and suppliers. We are so dependent on the rest of the world that if, 30 years ago, you had asked a politician to name the countries most geopolitically irrelevant to our interests because of their being so remote, poor, and weak, the list would surely have begun with Afghanistan and Somalia, yet they subsequently became recognized as important enough to warrant our dispatching U.S. troops. Today the world no longer faces just the circumscribed risk of an Easter Island society or Maya homeland collapsing in isolation, without affecting the rest of the world. Instead, societies today are so interconnected that the risk we face is of a worldwide decline. That conclusion is familiar to any investor in stock markets: instability of the U.S. stock market, or the post-9/11 economic downturn in the U.S., affects overseas stock markets and economies as well, and vice versa. We in the U.S. (or else just affluent people in the U.S.) can no longer get away with advancing our own self-interests, at the expense of the interests of others.

A good example of a society minimizing such clashes of interest is the Netherlands, whose citizens have perhaps the world's highest level of environmental awareness and of membership in environmental organizations. I never understood why, until on a recent trip to the Netherlands I posed the question to three of my Dutch friends while driving through their countryside (Plates 39, 40). Their answer was one that I shall never forget:

"Just look around you here. All of this farmland that you see lies below sea level. One-fifth of the total area of the Netherlands is below sea level, as much as 22 feet below, because it used to be shallow bays, and we reclaimed it from the sea by surrounding the bays with dikes and then gradually pumping out the water. We have a saying, 'God created the Earth, but we Dutch created the Netherlands.' These reclaimed lands are called 'polders.' We began draining them nearly a thousand years ago. Today, we still have to keep pumping out the water that gradually seeps in. That's what our windmills used to be for, to drive the pumps to pump out the polders. Now we use steam, diesel, and electric pumps instead. In each polder there are lines of pumps, starting with those farthest from the sea, pumping the water in sequence until the last pump finally pumps it out into a river or the ocean. In the Netherlands, we have another expression, 'You have to be able to get along with your enemy, because he may be the person operating the neighboring pump in your polder.' And we're all down in the polders together. It's not the case that rich people live safely up on tops of the dikes while poor people live down in the polder bottoms below sea level. If the dikes and pumps fail, we'll all drown together. When a big storm and high tides swept inland over Zeeland Province on February 1, 1953, nearly 2,000 Dutch people, both rich and poor, drowned. We swore that we would never let that happen again, and the whole country paid for an extremely expensive set of tide barriers. If global warming causes polar ice melting and a world rise in sea level, the consequences will be more severe for the Netherlands than for any other country in the world, because so much of our land is already under sea level. That's why we Dutch are so aware of our environment. We've learned through our history that we're all living in the same polder, and that our survival depends on each other's survival."

That acknowledged interdependence of all segments of Dutch society contrasts with current trends in the United States, where wealthy people increasingly seek to insulate themselves from the rest of society, aspire to create their own separate virtual polders, use their own money to buy services for themselves privately, and vote against taxes that would extend those amenities as public services to everyone else. Those private amenities include living inside gated walled communities (Plate 36), relying on private security guards rather than on the police, sending one's children to well-funded private schools with small classes rather than to the underfunded crowded public schools, purchasing private health insurance or medical care, drinking bottled water instead of municipal water, and (in Southern California) paying to drive on toll roads competing with the jammed public freeways. Underlying such privatization is a misguided belief that the elite can remain unaffected by the problems of society around them: the attitude of those Greenland Norse chiefs who found that they had merely bought themselves the privilege of being the last to starve.

Throughout human history, most peoples have been connected to some other peoples, living together in small virtual polders. The Easter Islanders comprised a dozen clans, dividing their island polder into a dozen territories, and isolated from all other islands, but sharing among clans the Rano Raraku statue quarry, the Puna Pau pukao quarry, and a few obsidian quarries. As Easter Island society disintegrated, all the clans disintegrated together, but nobody else in the world knew about it, nor was anybody else affected. Southeast Polynesia's polder consisted of three interdependent islands, such that the decline of Mangareva's society was disastrous also for the Pitcairn and Henderson Islanders but for no one else. To the ancient Maya, their polder consisted at most of the Yucatán Peninsula and neighboring areas. When the Classic Maya cities collapsed in the southern Yucatán, refugees may have reached the northern Yucatán, but certainly not

Florida. In contrast today our whole world has become one polder, such that events anywhere affect Americans. When distant Somalia collapsed, in went American troops; when the former Yugoslavia and Soviet Union collapsed, out went streams of refugees over all of Europe and the rest of the world; and when changed conditions of society, settlement, and lifestyle spread new diseases in Africa and Asia, those diseases moved over the globe. The whole world today is a self-contained and isolated unit, as Tikopia Island and Tokugawa Japan used to be. We need to realize, as did the Tikopians and Japanese, that there is no other island/other planet to which we can turn for help, or to which we can export our problems. Instead, we need to learn, as they did, to live within our means.

I introduced this section by acknowledging that there are important differences between the ancient world and the modern world. The differences that I then went on to mention—today's larger population and more potent destructive technology, and today's interconnectedness posing the risk of a global rather than a local collapse—may seem to suggest a pessimistic outlook. If the Easter Islanders couldn't solve their milder local problems in the past, how can the modern world hope to solve its big global problems?

People who get depressed at such thoughts often then ask me, "Jared, are you optimistic or pessimistic about the world's future?" I answer, "I'm a cautious optimist." By that, I mean that, on the one hand, I acknowledge the seriousness of the problems facing us. If we don't make a determined effort to solve them, and if we don't succeed at that effort, the world as a whole within the next few decades will face a declining standard of living, or perhaps something worse. That's the reason why I decided to devote most of my career efforts at this stage of my life to convincing people that our problems have to be taken seriously and won't go away otherwise. On the other hand, we shall be able to solve our problems—if we choose to do so. That's why my wife and I did decide to have children 17 years ago: because we did see grounds for hope.

One basis for hope is that, realistically, we are not beset by insoluble problems. While we do face big risks, the most serious ones are not ones beyond our control, like a possible collision with an asteroid of a size that hits the Earth every hundred million years or so. Instead, they are ones that we are generating ourselves. Because we are the cause of our environmental problems, we are the ones in control of them, and we can choose or not choose to stop causing them and start solving them. The future is up for grabs, lying in our own hands. We don't need new technologies to solve our problems; while new technologies can make some contribution, for the most part we "just" need the political will to apply solutions already available. Of course, that's a big "just." But many societies did find the necessary political will in the past. Our modern societies have already found the will to solve some of our problems, and to achieve partial solutions to others.

Another basis for hope is the increasing diffusion of environmental thinking among the public around the world. While such thinking has been with us for a long time, its spread has accelerated, especially since the 1962 publication of *Silent Spring*. The environmental movement has been gaining adherents at an increasing rate, and they act through a growing diversity of increasingly effective organizations, not only in the United States and Europe but also in the Dominican Republic and other developing countries. At the same time as the environmental movement is gaining strength at an increasing rate, so too are the threats to our environment. That's why I referred earlier in this book to our situation as that of being in an exponentially accelerating horse race of unknown outcome. It's neither impossible, nor is it assured, that our preferred horse will win the race.

What are the choices that we must make if we are now to succeed, and not to fail? There are many specific choices, of which I discuss examples in the Further Readings section, that any of us can make as individuals. For our society as a whole, the past societies that we have examined in this book suggest broader lessons. Two types of choices seem to me to have been crucial in tipping their outcomes towards success or failure: long-term planning, and willingness to reconsider core values. On reflection, we can also recognize the crucial role of these same two choices for the outcomes of our individual lives.

One of those choices has depended on the courage to practice long-term thinking, and to make bold, courageous, anticipatory decisions at a time when problems have become perceptible but before they have reached crisis proportions. This type of decision-making is the opposite of the short-term reactive decision-making that too often characterizes our elected politicians—the thinking that my politically well-connected friend decried as "90-day thinking," i.e., focusing only on issues likely to blow up in a crisis within the next 90 days. Set against the many depressing bad examples of such short-term decision-making are the encouraging examples of courageous long-term thinking in the past, and in the contemporary world of NGOs, business, and government. Among past societies faced with the prospect of ruinous deforestation, Easter Island and Mangareva chiefs succumbed to their immediate concerns, but Tokugawa shoguns, Inca emperors, New Guinea highlanders, and 16th-century German landowners adopted a long view and reafforested. China's leaders similarly promoted reafforestation in recent decades and banned logging of native forests in 1998. Today, many NGOs exist specifically for the purpose of promoting sane long-term environmental policies. In the business world the American corporations that remain successful for long times (e.g., Procter and Gamble) are ones that don't wait for a crisis to force them to reexamine their policies, but that instead look for problems on the horizon and act before there is a crisis. I already mentioned Royal Dutch Shell Oil Company as having an office devoted just to envisioning scenarios decades off in the future.

Courageous, successful, long-term planning also characterizes some governments and some political leaders, some of the time. Over the last 30 years a sustained effort by the U.S. government has reduced levels of the six major air pollutants nationally by 25%, even though our energy consumption and population increased by 40% and our vehicle miles driven increased by 150% during those same decades. The governments of Malaysia, Singapore, Taiwan, and Mauritius all recognized that their long-term economic well-being required big investments in public health to prevent tropical diseases from sapping their economies; those investments proved to be a key to those countries' spectacular recent economic growth. Of the former two halves of the overpopulated nation of Pakistan, the eastern half (independent since 1971 as Bangladesh) adopted effective family planning measures to reduce its rate of population growth, while the western half (still known as Pakistan) did not and is now the world's sixth most populous country. Indonesia's former environmental minister Emil Salim, and the Dominican Republic's former president Joaquín Balaguer, exemplify government leaders whose concern about chronic environmental dangers made a big impact on their countries. All of these examples of courageous long-term thinking in both the public sector and the private sector contribute to my hope.

The other crucial choice illuminated by the past involves the courage to make painful decisions about values. Which of the values that formerly served a society well can continue to be maintained under new changed circumstances? Which of those treasured values must instead be jettisoned and replaced with different approaches? The Greenland Norse refused to jettison part of their identity as a European, Christian, pastoral society, and they died as a result. In contrast, Tikopia Islanders did have the courage to eliminate their ecologically destructive pigs, even though pigs are the sole large domestic animal and a principal status symbol of Melanesian societies. Australia is now in the process of reappraising its identity as a British agricultural society. The Icelanders and many traditional caste societies of India in the past, and Montana ranchers dependent on irrigation in recent times, did reach agreement to subordinate their individual rights to group interests. They thereby succeeded in managing shared resources and avoiding the tragedy of the commons that has befallen so many other groups. The government of China restricted the traditional freedom of individual reproductive choice, rather than let population problems spiral out of control. The people of Finland, faced with an ultimatum by their vastly more powerful Russian neighbor in 1939, chose to value their freedom over their lives, fought with a courage that astonished the world, and won their gamble, even while losing the war. While I was living in Britain from 1958 to 1962, the British people were coming to terms with the outdatedness of cherished long-held values based on Britain's former role as the world's dominant political, economic, and naval power. The French, Germans, and other European countries have advanced even further in subordinating to the European Union their national sovereignties for which they used to fight so dearly.

All of these past and recent reappraisals of values that I have just mentioned were achieved despite being agonizingly difficult. Hence they also contribute to my hope. They may inspire modern First World citizens with the courage to make the most fundamental reappraisal now facing us: how much of our traditional consumer values and First World living standard can we afford to retain? I already mentioned the seeming political impossibility of inducing First World citizens to lower their impact on the world. But the alternative, of continuing our current impact, is more impossible. This dilemma reminds me of Winston Churchill's response to criticisms of democracy: "It has been said that Democracy is the worst form of government except all those other forms that have been tried from time to time." In that spirit, a lower-impact society is the most impossible scenario for our future—except for all other conceivable scenarios.

Actually, while it won't be easier to reduce our impact, it won't be impossible either. Remember that impact is the product of two factors: population, multiplied times impact per person. As for the first of those two factors, population growth has recently declined drastically in all First World countries, and in many Third World countries as well—including China, Indonesia, and Bangladesh, with the world's largest, fourth largest, and ninth largest populations respectively. Intrinsic population growth in

Japan and Italy is already below the replacement rate, such that their existing populations (i.e., not counting immigrants) will soon begin shrinking. As for impact per person, the world would not even have to decrease its current consumption rates of timber products or of seafood: those rates could be sustained or even increased, if the world's forests and fisheries were properly managed.

My remaining cause for hope is another consequence of the globalized modern world's interconnectedness. Past societies lacked archaeologists and television. While the Easter Islanders were busy deforesting the highlands of their overpopulated island for agricultural plantations in the 1400s, they had no way of knowing that, thousands of miles to the east and west at the same time, Greenland Norse society and the Khmer Empire were simultaneously in terminal decline, while the Anasazi had collapsed a few centuries earlier, Classic Maya society a few more centuries before that, and Mycenean Greece 2,000 years before that. Today, though, we turn on our television sets or radios or pick up our newspapers, and we see, hear, or read about what happened in Somalia or Afghanistan a few hours earlier. Our television documentaries and books show us in graphic detail why the Easter Islanders, Classic Maya, and other past societies collapsed. Thus, we have the opportunity to learn from the mistakes of distant peoples and past peoples. That's an opportunity that no past society enjoyed to such a degree. My hope in writing this book has been that enough people will choose to profit from that opportunity to make a difference.

ACKNOWLEDGMENTS

I acknowledge with gratitude the big debts that I owe to many people for their contributions to this book. With these friends and colleagues, I shared the pleasure and excitement of exploring the ideas presented here.

A special badge of heroism was earned by six friends who read and critiqued the entire manuscript: Julio Betancourt, Stewart Brand, my wife Marie Cohen, Paul Ehrlich, Alan Grinnell, and Charles Redman. That same badge of heroism, and more, are due to my editors Wendy Wolf at Penguin Group (New York) and Stefan McGrath and Jon Turney at Viking Penguin (London), and to my agents John Brockman and Katinka Matson, who besides reading the whole manuscript helped in myriad ways to shape this book from its initial conception through all stages of production. Gretchen Daily, Larry Linden, Ivan Barkhorn, and Bob Waterman similarly read and critiqued the concluding chapters on the modern world.

Michelle Fisher-Casey typed the whole manuscript, many times. Boratha Yeang tracked down books and articles, Ruth Mandel tracked down photographs, and Jeffrey Ward prepared the maps.

I presented much of the material of this book to two successive classes of undergraduates at the University of California at Los Angeles, where I teach in the Geography Department. I also offered a mini-course as a visitor to a graduate seminar in the Department of Anthropological Sciences at Stanford University. As willing guinea pigs, those students and colleagues contributed fresh and stimulating outlooks.

Earlier versions of some material of seven chapters appeared as articles in *Discover* magazine, the *New York Review of Books, Harper's* magazine, and *Nature.* In particular, Chapter 12 (on China) is an expanded version of a joint article that Jianguo (Jack) Liu and I wrote, that Jack drafted, and for which he gathered the information.

I also thank other friends and other colleagues in connection with each chapter. They variously arranged my visits to countries where they lived or conducted research, guided me in the field, patiently shared their experience with me, sent me articles and references, critiqued my chapter draft, or did several or all of these things. They generously gave me many days or weeks of their time. My debt to them is enormous. They include the following people, listed by chapter:

Chapter 1. Allen Bjergo, Marshall and Tonia and Seth Bloom, Diane Boyd, John and Pat Cook, John Day, Gary Decker, John and Jill Eliel, Emil Erhardt, Stan Falkow, Bruce Farling, Roxa French, Hank Goetz, Pam Gouse, Roy Grant, Josette Hackett, Dick and Jack Hirschy, Tim and Trudy Huls, Bob Jirsa, Rick and Frankie Laible, Jack Losensky, Land Lindbergh, Joyce McDowell, Chris Miller, Chip Pigman, Harry Poett, Steve Powell, Jack Ward Thomas, Lucy Tompkins, Pat Vaughn, Marilyn Wildee, and Vern and Maria Woolsey.

Chapter 2. Jo Anne Van Tilburg, Barry Rolett, Claudio Cristino, Sonia Haoa, Chris Stevenson, Edmundo Edwards, Catherine Orliac, and Patricia Vargas.

Chapter 3. Marshall Weisler.

Chapter 4. Julio Betancourt, Jeff Dean, Eric Force, Gwinn Vivian, and Steven LeBlanc.

Chapter 5. David Webster, Michael Coe, Bill Turner, Mark Brenner, Richardson Gill, and Richard Hansen.

Chapter 6. Gunnar Karlsson, Orri Vésteinsson, Jesse Byock, Christian Keller, Thomas McGovern, Paul Buckland, Anthony Newton, and Ian Simpson.

Chapters 7 and 8. Christian Keller, Thomas McGovern, Jette Arneborg, Georg Nygaard, and Richard Alley.

Chapter 9. Simon Haberle, Patrick Kirch, and Conrad Totman.

Chapter 10. René Lemarchand, David Newbury, Jean-Philippe Platteau, James Robinson, Vincent Smith.

Chapter 11. Andres Ferrer Benzo, Walter Cordero, Richard Turits, Neici Zeller, Luis Arambilet, Mario Bonetti, Luis Carvajal, Roberto and Angel Cassá, Carlos Garcia, Raimondo Gonzalez, Roberto Rodríguez Mansfield, Eleuterio Martinez, Nestor Sanchez Sr., Nestor Sanchez Jr., Ciprian Soler, Rafael Emilio Yunén, Steve Latta, James Robinson, and John Terborgh.

Chapter 12. Jianguo (Jack) Liu.

Chapter 13. Tim Flannery, Alex Baynes, Patricia Feilman, Bill McIntosh, Pamela Parker, Harry Recher, Mike Young, Michael Archer, K. David Bishop, Graham Broughton, Senator Bob Brown, Judy Clark, Peter Copley, George Ganf, Peter Gell, Stefan Hajkowicz, Bob Hill, Nalini Klopf, David Paton, Marilyn Renfrew, Prue Tucker, and Keith Walker.

Chapter 14. Elinor Ostrom, Marco Janssen, Monique Borgerhoff Mulder, Jim Dewar, and Michael Intrilligator.

Chapter 15. Jim Kuipers, Bruce Farling, Scott Burns, Bruce Cabarle, Jason Clay, Ned Daly, Katherine Bostick, Ford Denison, Stephen D'Esposito, Francis Grant-Suttie, Toby Kiers, Katie Miller, Michael Ross, and many people in the business world.

Chapter 16. Rudy Drent, Kathryn Fuller, Terry Garcia, Francis Lanting, Richard Mott, Theunis Piersma, William Reilly, and Russell Train.

Support for these studies was generously provided by the W. Alton Jones Foundation, Jon Kannegaard, Michael Korney, the Eve and Harvey Masonek and Samuel F. Heyman and Eve Gruber Heyman 1981 Trust Undergraduate Research Scholars Fund, Sandra McPeak, the Alfred P. Sloan Foundation, the Summit Foundation, the Weeden Foundation, and the Winslow Foundation.

FURTHER READINGS

These suggestions of some selected references are for those interested in reading further. Rather than devote space to extensive bibliographies, I have favored citing recent publications that do provide comprehensive listings of the earlier literature. In addition, I cite some key books and articles. A journal title (in italics) is followed by the volume number, followed after a colon by the first and last page numbers, and then by the year of publication in parentheses.

Prologue

Influential comparative studies of collapses of ancient advanced societies around the world include Joseph Tainter, *The Collapse of Complex Societies* (Cambridge: Cambridge University Press, 1988), and Norman Yoffee and George Cowgill, eds., *The Collapse of Ancient States and Civilizations* (Tucson: University of Arizona Press, 1988). Books focusing specifically on environmental impacts of past societies, or on the role of such impacts in collapses, include Clive Ponting, *A Green History of the World: The Environment and the Collapse of Great Civilizations* (New York: Penguin, 1991); Charles Redman, *Human Impact on Ancient Environments* (Tucson: University of Arizona Press, 1999); D. M. Kammen, K. R. Smith, K. T. Rambo, and M.A.K. Khalil, eds., *Preindustrial Human Environmental Impacts: Are There Lessons for Global Change Science and Policy?* (an issue of the journal *Chemosphere,* volume 29, no. 5, September 1994); and Charles Redman, Steven James, Paul Fish, and J. Daniel Rogers, eds., *The Archaeology of Global Change: The Impact of Humans on Their Environment* (Washington, D.C.: Smithsonian Books, 2004). Among books discussing the role of climate change in the context of comparative studies of past societies are three by Brian Fagan: *Floods, Famines, and Emperors: El Niño and the Fate of Civilizations* (New York: Basic Books, 1999); *The Little Ice Age* (New York: Basic Books, 2001); and *The Long Summer: How Climate Changed Civilization* (New York: Basic Books, 2004).

Comparative studies of relations between the rises and the falls of states include Peter Turchin, *Historical Dynamics: Why States Rise and Fall* (Princeton, N.J.: Princeton University Press, 2003), and Jack Goldstone, *Revolution and Rebellion in the Early Modern World* (Berkeley: University of California Press, 1991).

Chapter 1

Histories of the state of Montana include Joseph Howard, *Montana: High, Wide, and Handsome* (New Haven: Yale University Press, 1943); K. Ross Toole, *Montana: An Uncommon Land* (Norman: University of Oklahoma Press, 1959); K. Ross Toole,

20th-Century Montana: A State of Extremes (Norman: University of Oklahoma Press, 1972); and Michael Malone, Richard Roeder, and William Lang, *Montana: A History of Two Centuries,* revised edition (Seattle: University of Washington Press, 1991). Russ Lawrence offered an illustrated book on the Bitterroot Valley, *Montana's Bitterroot Valley* (Stevensville, Mont.: Stoneydale Press, 1991). Bertha Francis, *The Land of Big Snows* (Butte, Mont.: Caxton Printers, 1955) gives an account of the history of the Big Hole Basin. Thomas Power, *Lost Landscapes and Failed Economies: The Search for Value of Place* (Washington, D.C.: Island Press, 1996), and Thomas Power and Richard Barrett, *Post-Cowboy Economics: Pay and Prosperity in the New American West* (Washington, D.C.: Island Press, 2001), discuss the economic problems of Montana and the U.S. Mountain West. Two books on the history and impacts of mining in Montana are David Stiller, *Wounding the West: Montana, Mining, and the Environment* (Lincoln: University of Nebraska Press, 2000) and Michael Malone, *The Battle for Butte: Mining and Politics on the Northern Frontier, 1864–1906* (Helena, Mont.: Montana Historical Society Press, 1981). Stephen Pyne's books on forest fires include *Fire in America: A Cultural History of Wildland and Rural Fire* (Princeton, N.J.: Princeton University Press, 1982) and *Year of the Fires: The Story of the Great Fires of 1910* (New York: Viking Penguin, 2001). An account of fires focused on the western United States by two authors, one of them a resident of the Bitterroot Valley, is Stephen Arno and Steven Allison-Bunnell, *Flames in our Forests: Disaster or Renewal?* (Washington, D.C.: Island Press, 2002). Harsh Bais et al., "Allelopathy and exotic plant invasion: from molecules and genes to species interactions" (*Science* 301:1377–1380 (2003)) show that the means by which Spotted Knapweed displaces native plants include secreting from its roots a toxin to which the weed itself is impervious. Impacts of ranching on the U.S. West in general, including Montana, are discussed by Lynn Jacobs, *Waste of the West: Public Lands Ranching* (Tucson: Lynn Jacobs, 1991).

Current information on some Montana problems discussed in my chapter can be obtained from Web sites and e-mail addresses of organizations concerned with these problems. Some of these organizations, and their addresses, are as follows: Bitterroot Land Trust: www.BitterRootLandTrust.org. Bitterroot Valley Chamber of Commerce: www.bvchamber.com. Bitterroot Water Forum: brwaterforum@bitterroot.mt. Friends of the Bitterroot: www.FriendsoftheBitterroot.org. Montana Weed Control Association: www.mtweed.org. Plum Creek Timber: www.plumcreek.com. Trout Unlimited's Missoula office: montrout@montana.com. Whirling Disease Foundation: www.whirling-disease.org. Sonoran Institute: www.sonoran.org/programs/si_se. Center for the Rocky Mountain West: www.crmw.org/read. Montana Department of Labor and Industry: http://rad.dli.state.mt.us/pubs/profile.asp. Northwest Income Indicators Project: http://niip.wsu.edu/.

Chapter 2

The general reader seeking an overview of Easter Island should begin with three books: John Flenley and Paul Bahn, *The Enigmas of Easter Island* (New York: Oxford University Press, 2003, updating Paul Bahn and John Flenley, *Easter Island, Earth Island* (London: Thames and Hudson, 1992); Jo Anne Van Tilburg, *Easter Island: Archaeology, Ecology, and Culture* (Washington, D.C.: Smithsonian Institution Press, 1994); and Jo Anne Van Tilburg, *Among Stone Giants* (New York: Scribner, 2003). The last-mentioned book is a biography of Katherine Routledge, a remarkable English archaeologist whose 1914–15 visit enabled her to interview islanders with personal memories of the last Orongo ceremonies, and whose life was as colorful as a fantastic novel.

Two other recent books are Catherine and Michel Orliac, *The Silent Gods: Mysteries of Easter Island* (London: Thames and Hudson, 1995), a short illustrated overview; and John Loret and John Tancredi, eds., *Easter Island: Scientific Exploration into the World's Environmental Problems in Microcosm* (New York: Kluwer/Plenum, 2003), 13 chapters on results of recent expeditions. Anyone who becomes seriously interested in Easter Island will want to read two classic earlier books: Katherine Routledge's own account, *The Mystery of Easter Island* (London: Sifton Praed, 1919, reprinted by Adventure Unlimited Press, Kempton, Ill., 1998), and Alfred Métraux, *Ethnology of Easter Island* (Honolulu: Bishop Museum Bulletin 160, 1940, reprinted 1971). Eric Kjellgren, ed., *Splendid Isolation: Art of Easter Island* (New York: Metropolitan Museum of Art, 2001) assembles dozens of photos, many in color, of petroglyphs, rongo-rongo boards, moai kavakava, barkcloth figures, and a red feather headdress of a type that may have inspired the red stone pukao.

Articles by Jo Anne Van Tilburg include "Easter Island (Rapa Nui) archaeology since 1955: some thoughts on progress, problems and potential," pp. 555–577 in J. M. Davidson et al., eds., *Oceanic Culture History: Essays in Honour of Roger Green* (New Zealand Journal of Archaeology Special Publication, 1996); Jo Anne Van Tilburg and Cristián Arévalo Pakarati, "The Rapanui carvers' perspective: notes and observations on the experimental replication of monolithic sculpture (moai)," pp. 280–290 in A. Herle et al., eds., *Pacific Art: Persistence, Change and Meaning* (Bathurst, Australia: Crawford House, 2002); and Jo Anne Van Tilburg and Ted Ralston, "Megaliths and mariners: experimental archaeology on Easter Island (Rapa Nui)," in press in K. L. Johnson, ed., *Onward and Upward! Papers in Honor of Clement W. Meighan* (University Press of America). The latter two of those three articles describe experimental studies aimed at understanding how many people were required to carve and transport statues, and how long it would have taken.

Many good books accessible to the general reader describe the settlement of Polynesia or the Pacific as a whole. They include Patrick Kirch, *On the Road of the Winds: An Archaeological History of the Pacific Islands Before European Contact* (Berkeley: University of California Press, 2000), *The Lapita Peoples: Ancestors of the Oceanic World* (Oxford: Blackwell, 1997), and *The Evolution of the Polynesian Chief-*

doms (Cambridge: Cambridge University Press, 1984); Peter Bellwood, *The Polynesians: Prehistory of an Island People,* revised edition (London: Thames and Hudson, 1987); and Geoffrey Irwin, *The Prehistoric Exploration and Colonisation of the Pacific* (Cambridge: Cambridge University Press, 1992). David Lewis, *We, the Navigators* (Honolulu: University Press of Hawaii, 1972) is a unique account of traditional Pacific navigational techniques, by a modern sailor who studied those techniques by embarking on long voyages with surviving traditional navigators. Patrick Kirch and Terry Hunt, eds., *Historical Ecology in the Pacific Islands: Prehistoric Environmental and Landscape Change* (New Haven, Conn.: Yale University Press, 1997) consists of papers about human environmental impacts on Pacific Islands other than Easter.

Two books by Thor Heyerdahl that inspired my interest and that of many others in Easter Island are *The Kon-Tiki Expedition* (London: Allen & Unwin, 1950) and *Aku-Aku: The Secret of Easter Island* (London: Allen & Unwin, 1958). A rather different interpretation emerges from the excavations of the archaeologists whom Heyerdahl brought to Easter Island, as described in Thor Heyerdahl and E. Ferdon, Jr., eds., *Reports of the Norwegian Archaeological Expedition to Easter Island and the East Pacific, vol. 1: The Archaeology of Easter Island* (London: Allen & Unwin, 1961). Steven Fischer, *Glyph Breaker* (New York: Copernicus, 1997) and *Rongorongo: The Easter Island Script* (Oxford: Oxford University Press, 1997) describe Fischer's efforts at deciphering the Rongorongo text. Andrew Sharp, ed., *The Journal of Jacob Roggeveen* (London: Oxford University Press, 1970) reprints on pp. 89–106 the first European eyewitness description of Easter Island.

An archaeological mapping of Easter Island is summarized in Claudio Cristino, Patricia Vargas, and R. Izaurieta, *Atlas Arqueológico de Isla de Pascua* (Santiago: University of Chile, 1981). Detailed articles about Easter Island are published regularly in the *Rapa Nui Journal* by the Easter Island Foundation, which also publishes occasional conferences about the island. Important collections of papers are Claudio Cristino, Patricia Vargas et al., eds., *First International Congress, Easter Island and East Polynesia, vol. 1 Archaeology* (Santiago: University of Chile, 1988); Patricia Vargas Casanova, ed., *Easter Island and East Polynesia Prehistory* (Santiago: University of Chile, 1998); and Christopher Stevenson and William Ayres, eds., *Easter Island Archaeology: Research on Early Rapanui Culture* (Los Osos, Calif.: Easter Island Foundation, 2000). A summary of the history of cultural contacts is to be found in Claudio Cristino et al. *Isla de Pascua: Procesos, Alcances y Efectos de la Aculturación* (Easter Island: University of Chile, 1984).

David Steadman reports his identification of bird bones and other remains excavated at Anakena Beach in three papers: "Extinctions of birds in Eastern Polynesia: a review of the record, and comparisons with other Pacific Island groups" (*Journal of Archaeological Science* 16:177–205 (1989)), and "Stratigraphy, chronology, and cultural context of an early faunal assemblage from Easter Island" (*Asian Perspectives* 33:79–96 (1994)), both with Patricia Vargas and Claudio Cristino; and

"Prehistoric extinctions of Pacific Island birds: biodiversity meets zooarchaeology" (*Science* 267:1123–1131 (1995)). William Ayres, "Easter Island subsistence" (*Journal de la Société des Océanistes* 80:103–124 (1985)) provides further archaeological evidence of foods consumed. For solution of the mystery of the Easter Island palm and other insights from pollen in sediment cores, see J. R. Flenley and Sarah King, "Late Quaternary pollen records from Easter Island" (*Nature* 307:47–50 (1984)), J. Dransfield et al., "A recently extinct palm from Easter Island" (*Nature* 312:750–752 (1984)), and J. R. Flenley et al., "The Late Quaternary vegetational and climatic history of Easter Island" (*Journal of Quaternary Science* 6:85–115 (1991)). Catherine Orliac's identifications are reported in a paper in the above-cited edited volume by Stevenson and Ayres, and in "Données nouvelles sur la composition de la flore de l'Île de Pâques" (*Journal de la Société des Océanistes* 2:23–31 (1998)). Among the papers resulting from the archaeological surveys by Claudio Cristino and his colleagues are Christopher Stevenson and Claudio Cristino, "Residential settlement history of the Rapa Nui coastal plain (*Journal of New World Archaeology* 7:29–38 (1986)); Daris Swindler, Andrea Drusini, and Claudio Cristino, "Variation and frequency of three-rooted first permanent molars in precontact Easter Islanders: anthropological significance (*Journal of the Polynesian Society* 106:175–183 (1997)); and Claudio Cristino and Patricia Vargas, "Ahu Tongariki, Easter Island: chronological and sociopolitical significance" (*Rapa Nui Journal* 13:67–69 (1999)).

Christopher Stevenson's papers on intensive agriculture and lithic mulches include *Archaeological Investigations on Easter Island; Maunga Tari: An Upland Agriculture Complex* (Los Osos, Calif.: Easter Island Foundation, 1995), (with Joan Wozniak and Sonia Haoa) "Prehistoric agriculture production on Easter Island (Rapa Nui), Chile" (*Antiquity* 73:801–812 (1999)), and (with Thegn Ladefoged and Sonia Haoa) "Productive strategies in an uncertain environment: prehistoric agriculture on Easter Island" (*Rapa Nui Journal* 16:17–22 (2002)). Christopher Stevenson, "Territorial divisions on Easter Island in the 16th century: evidence from the distribution of ceremonial architecture," pp. 213–229 in T. Ladefoged and M. Graves, eds., *Pacific Landscapes* (Los Osos, Calif.: Easter Island Foundation, 2002) reconstructs the boundaries of Easter's 11 traditional clans.

Dale Lightfoot, "Morphology and ecology of lithic-mulch agriculture" (*Geographical Review* 84:172–185 (1994)) and Carleton White et al., "Water conservation through an Anasazi gardening technique" (*New Mexico Journal of Science* 38:251–278 (1998)) provide evidence for the function of lithic mulches elsewhere in the world. Andreas Mieth and Hans-Rudolf Bork "Diminution and degradation of environmental resources by prehistoric land use on Poike Peninsula, Easter Island (Rapa Nui)" (*Rapa Nui Journal* 17:34–41 (2003)) discuss deforestation and erosion on the Poike Peninsula. Karsten Haase et al., "The petrogenetic evolution of lavas from Easter Island and neighboring seamounts, near-ridge hotspot volcanoes in the S.E. Pacific" (*Journal of Petrology* 38:785–813 (1997)) analyze the dates and chemical compositions of Easter's volcanoes. Erika Hagelberg et al., "DNA from ancient Easter Islanders" (*Nature* 369:25–26 (1994)) analyze DNA extracted from 12 Easter Island skeletons. James Brander and M. Scott Taylor, "The simple economics of Easter Island: a Ricardo-Malthus model of renewable resource use" (*American Economic Review* 38:119–138 (1998)) give an economist's view of overexploitation on Easter.

Chapter 3

The settlement of Southeast Polynesia is covered in the sources for the settlement of Polynesia as a whole that I provided under the Further Readings for Chapter 2. *The Pitcairn Islands: Biogeography, Ecology, and Prehistory* (London: Academic Press, 1995), edited by Tim Benton and Tom Spencer, is the product of a 1991–92 expedition to Pitcairn, Henderson, and the coral atolls Oeno and Ducie. The volume consists of 27 chapters on the islands' geology, vegetation, birds (including Henderson's extinct birds), fishes, terrestrial and marine invertebrates, and human impacts.

Most of our information about the Polynesian settlement and abandonment of Pitcairn and Henderson comes from the studies of Marshall Weisler and various colleagues. Weisler provides an overall account of his research in a chapter, "Henderson Island prehistory: colonization and extinction on a remote Polynesian island," on pp. 377–404 of the above-cited volume by Benton and Spencer. Two other overview papers by Weisler are "The settlement of marginal Polynesia: new evidence from Henderson Island" (*Journal of Field Archaeology* 21:83–102 (1994)) and "An archaeological survey of Mangareva: implications for regional settlement models and interaction studies" (*Man and Culture and Oceania* 12:61–85 (1996)). Four papers by Weisler explain how chemical analysis of basalt adzes can identify on what island the basalt was quarried, and thus can help trace out trade routes: "Provenance studies of Polynesian basalt adzes material: a review and suggestions for improving regional databases" (*Asian Perspectives* 32:61–83 (1993)); "Basalt pb isotope analysis and the prehistoric settlement of Polynesia," coauthored with Jon D. Whitehead (*Proceedings of the National Academy of Sciences, USA* 92:1881–1885 (1995)); "Interisland and interarchipelago transfer of stone tools in prehistoric Polynesia," coauthored with Patrick V. Kirch (*Proceedings of the National Academy of Sciences, USA* 93:1381–1385 (1996)); and "Hard evidence for prehistoric interaction in Polynesia" (*Current Anthropology* 39:521–532 (1998)). Three papers describe the East and Southeast Polynesia trade network: Marshall Weisler and R. C. Green, "Holistic approaches to interaction studies: a Polynesian example," pp. 413–453 in Martin Jones and Peter Sheppard, eds., *Australasian Connections and New Directions* (Auckland, N.Z.: Department of Anthropology, University of Auckland, 2001); R. C. Green and Marshall Weisler, "The Mangarevan sequence and dating of the geographic expansion into Southeast Polynesia" (*Asian Perspectives* 41:213–241 (2002)); and Marshall Weisler, "Centrality and the collapse of long-distance voyaging in East Polynesia," pp. 257–273 in Michael D. Glascock, ed., *Geochemical Evidence for Long-Distance Exchange* (London: Bergin and Garvey, 2002). Three papers on Henderson Island crops and skeletons are Jon G. Hather and Marshall Weisler, "Prehistoric giant swamp taro *(Cyrtosperma chamissonis)* from Henderson Island, Southeast Polynesia" *(Pacific Science* 54:149–156 (2000)); Sara Collins and Marshall Weisler, "Human dental and skeletal remains from Henderson Island, Southeast Polynesia" *(People and Culture in Oceania* 16:67–85 (2000)); and Vincent Stefan, Sara Collins, and Marshall Weisler, "Henderson Island crania and their implication for southeastern Polynesian prehistory" *(Journal of the Polynesian Society* 111:371–383 (2002)).

No one interested in Pitcairn and Henderson, and no one who loves a great story, should miss the novel *Pitcairn's Island* by Charles Nordhoff and James Norman Hall (Boston: Little, Brown, 1934)—a realistically re-created account of the lives and mutual murders of the H.M.S. *Bounty* mutineers and their Polynesian companions on Pitcairn Island, after they had seized the *Bounty* and cast Captain Bligh and his supporters adrift. Caroline Alexander, *The Bounty* (New York: Viking, 2003) offers the most thorough effort to understand what really did happen.

Chapter 4

The prehistory of the U.S. Southwest is well served by books written for the general public and well illustrated, often in color. Those books include Robert Lister and Florence Lister, *Chaco Canyon* (Albuquerque: University of New Mexico Press, 1981); Stephen Lekson, *Great Pueblo Architecture of Chaco Canyon, New Mexico* (Albuquerque: University of New Mexico Press, 1986); William Ferguson and Arthur Rohn, *Anasazi Ruins of the Southwest in Color* (Albuquerque: University of New Mexico Press, 1987); Linda Cordell, *Ancient Pueblo Peoples* (Montreal: St. Remy Press, 1994); Stephen Plog, *Ancient Peoples of the American Southwest* (New York: Thames and Hudson, 1997); Linda Cordell, *Archaeology of the Southwest,* 2nd ed. (San Diego: Academic Press, 1997); and David Stuart, *Anasazi America* (Albuquerque: University of New Mexico Press, 2000).

Not to be missed are three illustrated books on the glorious painted pottery of the Mimbres people: J. J. Brody, *Mimbres Painted Pottery* (Santa Fe: School of American Research, 1997); Steven LeBlanc, *The Mimbres People: Ancient Pueblo Painters of the American Southwest* (London: Thames and Hudson, 1983); and Tony Berlant, Steven LeBlanc, Catherine Scott, and J. J. Brody, *Mimbres Pottery: Ancient Art of the American Southwest* (New York: Hudson Hills Press, 1983).

Three detailed accounts of warfare and violence among the Anasazi and their neighbors are Christy Turner II and Jacqueline Turner, *Man Corn: Cannibalism and Violence in the Prehistoric American Southwest* (Salt Lake City: University of Utah Press, 1999); Steven LeBlanc, *Prehistoric Warfare in the American Southwest* (Salt

Lake City: University of Utah Press, 1999); and Jonathan Haas and Winifred Creamer, *Stress and Warfare Among the Kayenta Anasazi of the Thirteenth Century* A.D. (Chicago: Field Museum of Natural History, 1993).

Monographs or scholarly books on specific problems or peoples in the Southwest include Paul Minnis, *Social Adaptation to Food Stress: A Prehistoric Southwestern Example* (Chicago: University of Chicago Press, 1985); W. H. Wills, *Early Prehistoric Agriculture in the American Southwest* (Santa Fe: School of American Research, 1988); R. Gwinn Vivian, *The Chacoan Prehistory of the San Juan Basin* (San Diego: Academic Press, 1990); Lynne Sebastian, *The Chaco Anasazi: Sociopolitical Evolution and the Prehistoric Southwest* (Cambridge: Cambridge University Press, 1992); and Charles Redman, *People of the Tonto Rim: Archaeological Discovery in Prehistoric Arizona* (Washington, D.C.: Smithsonian Institution Press, 1993). Eric Force, R. Gwinn Vivian, Thomas Windes, and Jeffrey Dean reevaluated the incised arroyo channels that lowered Chaco Canyon's water table in their monograph *Relation of "Bonito" Paleo-channel and Base-level Variations to Anasazi Occupation, Chaco Canyon, New Mexico* (Tuscon: Arizona State Museum, University of Arizona, 2002). Everything that you might want to know about *Packrat Middens* is described in the book with that title by Julio Betancourt, Thomas Van Devender, and Paul Martin (Tucson: University of Arizona Press, 1990).

The Southwest has also been well served by edited multiauthored volumes collecting chapters by numerous scholars. Among them are David Grant Nobel, ed., *New Light on Chaco Canyon* (Santa Fe: School of American Research, 1984); George Gumerman, ed., *The Anasazi in a Changing Environment* (Cambridge: Cambridge University Press, 1988); Patricia Crown and W. James Judge, eds., *Chaco and Hohokam: Prehistoric Regional Systems in the American Southwest* (Santa Fe: School of American Research, 1991); David Doyel, ed., *Anasazi Regional Organization and the Chaco System* (Albuquerque: Maxwell Museum of Anthropology, 1992); Michael Adler, ed., *The Prehistoric Pueblo World* A.D. *1150–1350* (Tucson: University of Arizona Press, 1996); Jill Neitzel, ed., *Great Towns and Regional Polities in the Prehistoric American Southwest and Southeast* (Dragoon, Ariz.: Amerind Foundation, 1999); Michelle Hegmon, ed., *The Archaeology of Regional Interaction: Religion, Warfare, and Exchange Across the American Southwest and Beyond* (Boulder: University Press of Colorado, 2000); and Michael Diehl and Steven LeBlanc, *Early Pithouse Villages of the Mimbres Valley and Beyond* (Cambridge, Mass.: Peabody Museum of Archaeology and Ethnology, Harvard University, 2001).

The bibliographies of the books that I have cited will provide signposts to the literature of scholarly articles on the Southwest. A few articles particularly relevant to this chapter will now be mentioned separately. Papers by Julio Betancourt and his colleagues on what can be learned from historical reconstructions of the vegetation at Chaco Canyon include Julio Betancourt and Thomas Van Devender, "Holocene vegetation in Chaco Canyon, New Mexico" (*Science* 214:656–658

(1981)); Michael Samuels and Julio Betancourt, "Modeling the long-term effects of fuelwood harvests on pinyon-juniper woodlands" (*Environmental Management* 6:505–515 (1982)); and Julio Betancourt, Jeffrey Dean, and Herbert Hull, "Prehistoric long-distance transport of construction beams, Chaco Canyon, New Mexico" (*American Antiquity* 51:370–375 (1986)). Two papers on changes in Anasazi wood use through time are Timothy Kohler and Meredith Matthews, "Long-term Anasazi land use and forest production: a case study of Southwest Colorado" (*American Antiquity* 53:537–564 (1988)), and Thomas Windes and Dabney Ford, "The Chaco wood project: the chronometric reappraisal of Pueblo Bonito" (*American Antiquity* 61:295–310 (1996)). William Bull provides a good review of the complex origins of arroyo cutting in his paper "Discontinuous ephemeral streams" (*Geomorphology* 19:227–276 (1997)). Strontium isotopes were used to identify the local origins of Chaco timber and maize by the authors of two papers: for timber, Nathan English, Julio Betancourt, Jeffrey Dean, and Jay Quade, "Strontium isotopes reveal distant sources of architectural timber in Chaco Canyon, New Mexico" (*Proceedings of the National Academy of Sciences, USA* 98:11891–11896 (2001)); and, for maize, Larry Benson et al., "Ancient maize from Chacoan great houses: where was it grown?" (*Proceedings of the National Academy of Sciences, USA* 100:13111–13115 (2003)). R. L. Axtell et al. provide a detailed reconstruction of population size and agricultural potential for the Kayenta Anasazi of Long House Valley in their paper "Population growth and collapse in a multiagent model of the Kayenta Anasazi in Long House Valley" (*Proceedings of the National Academy of Sciences, USA* 99:7275–7279 (2002)).

Chapter 5

Three recent books presenting different views of the Maya collapse are David Webster, *The Fall of the Ancient Maya* (New York: Thames and Hudson, 2002), Richardson Gill, *The Great Maya Droughts* (Albuquerque: University of New Mexico Press, 2000), and Arthur Demerest, Prudence Rice, and Don Rice, eds., *The Terminal Classic in the Maya Lowlands* (Boulder: University Press of Colorado, 2004). Webster provides an overview of Maya society and history and interprets the collapse in terms of a mismatch between population and resources, while Gill focuses on climate and interprets the collapse in terms of drought, and Demerest et al. emphasize complex variation among sites and deemphasize uniform ecological interpretations. Earlier, multiauthored edited volumes setting out diverse interpretations are T. Patrick Culbert, ed., *The Classic Maya Collapse* (Albuquerque: University of New Mexico Press, 1973), and T. Patrick Culbert and D. S. Rice, eds., *Precolumbian Population History in the Maya Lowlands* (Albuquerque: University of New Mexico Press, 1990). David Lentz, ed., *Imperfect Balance: Landscape Transformation in the Precolumbian Americas* (New York: Columbia University Press, 2000) contains several chapters relevant to the Maya, plus chapters on other relevant societies mentioned elsewhere in this book, including Hohokam, Andean, and Mississippian societies.

Books summarizing the rises and falls of specific cities include David Webster, AnnCorinne Freter, and Nancy Gonlin, *Copán: The Rise and Fall of an Ancient Maya Kingdom* (Fort Worth: Harcourt Brace, 2000); Peter Harrison, *The Lords of Tikal* (New York: Thames and Hudson, 1999); Stephen Houston, *Hieroglyphs and History at Dos Pilas* (Austin: University of Texas Press, 1993); and M. P. Dunning, *Lords of the Hills: Ancient Maya Settlement in the Puuc Region, Yucatán, Mexico* (Madison, Wis.: Prehistory Press, 1992). For books about Maya history and society not focusing specifically on the collapse, see especially Michael Coe, *The Maya,* 6th ed. (New York: Thames and Hudson, 1999); also, Simon Martin and Nikolai Grube, *Chronicle of the Maya Kings and Queens* (New York: Thames and Hudson, 2000); Robert Sharer, *The Ancient Maya* (Stanford, Calif.: Stanford University Press, 1994); Linda Schele and David Freidel, *A Forest of Kings* (New York: William Morrow, 1990); and Linda Schele and Mary Miller, *The Blood of Kings* (New York: Braziller, 1986).

The two classic books by John Stephens describing his rediscoveries are *Incidents of Travel in Central America, Chiapas and Yucatan* (New York: Harper, 1841) and *Incidents of Travel in Yucatan* (New York: Harper, 1843); both have been reprinted by Dover Publications. Victor Wolfgang von Hagen, *Maya Explorer* (Norman: University of Oklahoma Press, 1948) combines a biography of John Stephens with an account of his discoveries.

Numerous papers and books by B. L. Turner II discuss aspects of Maya agricultural intensification and population. They include B. L. Turner II, "Prehistoric intensive agriculture in the Mayan lowlands" (*Science* 185:118–124 (1974)); B. L. Turner II and Peter Harrison, "Prehistoric raised-field agriculture in the Maya lowlands" (*Science* 213:399–405 (1981)); B. L. Turner II and Peter Harrison, *Pulltrouser Swamp: Ancient Maya Habitat, Agriculture, and Settlement in Northern Belize* (Austin: University of Texas Press, 1983); Thomas Whitmore and B. L. Turner II, "Landscapes of cultivation in Mesoamerica on the eve of the conquest" (*Annals of the Association of American Geographers* 82:402–425 (1992)); and B. L. Turner II and K. W. Butzer "The Columbian encounter and land-use change" (*Environment* 43:16–20 and 37–44 (1992)).

Recent articles describing in detail the studies of lake cores that provide evidence for links between droughts and Maya collapses include Mark Brenner et al., "Paleolimnology of the Maya lowlands: long-term perspectives on interactions among climate, environment, and humans" (*Ancient Mesoamerica* 13:141–157 (2002)) (see also other articles on pp. 79–170 and 265–345 of the same volume); David Hodell et al., "Solar forcing of drought frequency in the Maya lowlands" (*Science* 292:1367–1370 (2001)); Jason Curtis et al., "Climate variability of the Yucatán Peninsula (Mexico) during the past 3500 years, and implications for Maya cultural evolution" (*Quaternary Research* 46:37–47 (1996)); and David Hodell et al., "Possible role of climate in the collapse of Classic Maya civilization" (*Nature* 375: 391–394 (1995)). Two articles by the same group of scientists discussing drought inferences from lake cores specifically for the Petén region are: Michael Rosenmeier, "A 4,000-year lacustrine record of environmental change in the southern Maya lowlands, Petén, Guatemala" (*Quaternary Research* 57:183–190 (2002)); and Jason Curtis et al., "A multi-proxy study of Holocene environmental change in the Maya lowlands of Peten, Guatemala" (*Journal of Paleolimnology* 19:139–159 (1998)). Supplementing these studies of lake sediments, Gerald Haug et al., "Climate and the collapse of Maya civilization" (*Science* 299:1731–1735 (2003)) extract year-to-year rainfall changes by analyzing sediments washed by rivers into the ocean.

No one interested in the Maya should miss Mary Ellen Miller, *The Murals of Bonampak* (Princeton, N.J.: Princeton University Press, 1986), with its beautiful color as well as black-and-white reproductions of the murals and their grisly torture scenes; nor Justin Kerr's series of volumes reproducing Maya pottery, *The Maya Vase Book* (New York: Kerr Associates, various dates). The fascinating story of how Maya writing was deciphered is related by Michael Coe, *Breaking the Maya Code*, 2nd ed. (New York: Thames and Hudson, 1999), and Stephen Houston, Oswaldo Chinchilla Mazareigos, and David Stuart, *The Decipherment of Ancient Maya Writing* (Norman: University of Oklahoma, 2001). The reservoirs of Tikal are described by Vernon Scarborough and Gari Gallopin, "A water storage adaptation in the Maya lowlands" (*Science* 251:658–662 (1991)). Lisa Lucero's article "The collapse of the Classic Maya: a case for the role of water control" (*American Anthropologist* 104:814–826 (2002)) explains why differing local water problems might have contributed to the non-uniformity of the Classic collapse, with different cities meeting differing fates at different dates. Arturo Gómez-Pompa, José Salvador Flores, and Victoria Sosa, "The 'pet kot': a man-made tropical forest of the Maya" (*Interciencia* 12:10–15 (1987)) describe Maya cultivation of forest patches with useful trees. Timothy Beach, "Soil catenas, tropical deforestation, and ancient and contemporary soil erosion in the Petén, Guatemala" (*Physical Geography* 19:378–405 (1998)) shows that the Maya in some areas but not in others were able to reduce soil erosion by terracing. Richard Hansen et al., "Climatic and environmental variability in the rise of Maya civilization: a preliminary perspective from northern Petén" (*Ancient Mesoamerica* 13:273–295 (2002)) presents a multidisciplinary study of an area densely populated already in pre-Classic times, and yielding evidence for plaster production as a driving force behind deforestation there.

Chapters 6–8

Vikings: The North Atlanta Saga, edited by William Fitzhugh and Elisabeth Ward (Washington, D.C.: Smithsonian Institution Press, 2000), is a multiauthored volume, beautifully illustrated in color, whose 31 chapters cover in detail the Vikings' society, their expansion over Europe, and their North Atlantic colonies. Shorter, single-authored overviews of the Vikings include Eric Christiansen, *The Norsemen in the Viking Age* (Oxford: Blackwell, 2002), F. Donald Logan, *The Vikings in History,* 2nd ed. (New York: Routledge, 1991), and Else Roestahl, *The Vikings* (New York: Penguin, 1987). Gwyn Jones, *Vikings: The North Atlantic Saga,* 2nd ed. (Oxford: Oxford University Press, 1986) and G. J. Marcus, *The Conquest of the North Atlantic* (New York: Oxford University Press, 1981) are instead concerned specifically with the Vikings' three remote North Atlantic colonies of Iceland, Greenland, and Vinland. A useful additional feature of Jones's book is that among its appendices are translations of the most relevant saga source documents, including the Book of the Icelanders, both of the Vinland sagas, and the Story of Einar Sokkason.

Two recent books summarizing Iceland's history are Jesse Byock, *Viking Age Iceland* (New York: Penguin Putnam, 2001), which takes the story up to the end of the Icelandic Commonwealth in 1262–1264, and which builds on the same author's earlier *Medieval Iceland: Society, Sagas, and Present* (Berkeley: University of California Press, 1988); and Gunnar Karlsson, *Iceland's 1100 Years: The History of a Marginal Society* (London: Hurst, 2000), which covers not only the medieval but also the modern era. *Environmental Change in Iceland: Past and Present* (Dordrecht: Kluwer, 1991), edited by Judith Maizels and Chris Caseldine, is a more technical, multiauthored account of Iceland's environmental history. Kirsten Hastrup, *Island of Anthropology: Studies in Past and Present Iceland* (Viborg: Odense University Press, 1990) collects the author's anthropological papers on Iceland. *The Sagas of Icelanders: A Selection* (New York: Penguin, 1997) offers translations of 17 of the sagas (including the two Vinland sagas), drawn from a five-volume *The Complete Sagas of Icelanders* (Reykjavík: Leifur Eiriksson, 1997).

Two related papers on landscape change in Iceland are Andrew Dugmore et al., "Tephrochronology, environmental change and the Norse settlement of Iceland" (*Environmental Archaeology* 5:21–34 (2000)), and Ian Simpson et al., "Crossing the thresholds: human ecology and historical patterns of landscape degradation" (*Catena* 42:175–192 (2001)). Because each insect species has specific habitat and climate requirements, Paul Buckland and his colleagues have been able to use insects preserved at archaeological sites as environmental indicators. Their papers include Gudrún Sveinbjarnardóttir et al. "Landscape change in Eyjafjallasveit, Southern Iceland" (*Norsk Geog. Tidsskr* 36:75–88 (1982)); Paul Buckland et al., "Late Holocene palaeoecology at Ketilsstadir in Myrdalur, South Iceland" (*Jökull* 36:41–55 (1986)); Paul Buckland et al., "Holt in Eyjafjallasveit, Iceland: a paleoecological study of the impact of Landnám" (*Acta Archaeologica* 61:252–271 (1991)); Gudrún Sveinbjarnardóttir et al., "Shielings in Iceland: an archaeological and historical survey" (*Acta Archaeologica* 61:74–96 (1991)); Paul Buckland et al., "Palaeoecological investigations at Reykholt, Western Iceland," pp. 149–168 in C. D. Morris and D. J. Rackhan, eds., *Norse and Later Settlement and Subsistence in the North Atlantic* (Glasgow: Glasgow University Press, 1992); and Paul Buckland et al., "An insect's eye-view of the Norse farm," pp. 518–528 in Colleen Batey et al., eds., *The Viking Age in Caithness, Orkney and the North Atlantic* (Edinburgh: Edinburgh University Press, 1993). The same insect-based approach to understanding environmental change in the Faeroe Islands is used by Kevin Edwards et al., "Landscapes at landnám: palynological and palaeoentomological evidence from Toftanes, Faroe Islands" (*Fródskaparrit* 46:177–192 (1998)).

Two books assemble in detail the available information on Norse Greenland: Kirsten Seaver, *The Frozen Echo: Greenland and Exploration of North America ca. A.D. 1000–1500* (Stanford, Calif.: Stanford University Press, 1996), and Finn Gad, *The History of Greenland, vol. I: Earliest Times to 1700* (Montreal: McGill-Queen's University Press, 1971). A subsequent book by Finn Gad, *The History of Greenland, vol. II: 1700–1782* (Montreal: McGill-Queen's University Press, 1973), continues the story through the period of Greenland's "rediscovery" and Danish colonization. Niels Lynnerup reported on his analysis of the available Norse skeletons from Greenland in his monograph *The Greenland Norse: A Biologic-Anthropological Study* (Copenhagen: Commission for Scientific Research in Greenland, 1998). Two multiauthored monographs with many papers on the Inuit and their Native American predecessors in Greenland are Martin Appelt and Hans Christian Gullóv, eds., *Late Dorset in High Arctic Greenland* (Copenhagen: Danish Polar Center, 1999), and Martin Appelt et al., eds., *Identities and Cultural Contacts in the Arctic* (Copenhagen: Danish Polar Center, 2000). An intimately personal insight into the lives of Greenland Inuit was gained from the discovery of six women, a child, and an infant who died and were buried around 1475, and whose bodies and clothing remained well preserved because of the cold dry climate. Those mummies are described and illustrated in Jens Peder Hart Hansen et al., eds., *The Greenland Mummies* (London: British Museum Press, 1991); the book's cover is a haunting, unforgettable photograph of the face of the six-month-old infant.

The two most important series of archaeological studies of the Greenland Norse within the last 20 years have been by Thomas McGovern and by Jette Arneborg and their colleagues. Among McGovern's papers are Thomas McGovern, "The Vinland adventure: a North Atlantic perspective" (*North American Archaeologist* 2:285–308 (1981)); Thomas McGovern, "Contributions to the paleoeconomy of Norse Greenland" (*Acta Archaeologica* 54:73–122 (1985)); Thomas McGovern et al., "Northern islands, human era, and environmental degradation: a view of social and ecological change in the medieval North Atlantic" (*Human Ecology* 16:225–270 (1988)); Thomas McGovern, "Climate, correlation, and causation in Norse Greenland" (*Arctic Anthropology* 28:77–100 (1991)); Thomas McGovern et al., "A vertebrate zooarchaeology of Sandnes V51: economic change at a chieftain's farm in West Greenland" (*Arctic Anthropology* 33:94–121 (1996)); Thomas Amorosi et al., "Raiding the landscape: human impact from the Scandinavian North Atlantic" (*Human Ecology* 25:491–518 (1997)); and Tom Amorosi et al., "They did not live by grass alone: the politics and paleoecology of animal fodder in the North Atlantic region" (*Environmental Archaeology* 1:41–54 (1998)). Arneborg's papers include Jette Arneborg, "The Roman church in Norse Greenland" (*Acta Archaeologica* 61:142–150 (1990)); Jette Arneborg, "Contact between Eskimos and Norsemen in Greenland: a review of the evidence," pp. 23–35 in *Tvaerfaglige Vikingesymposium* (Aarhus, Denmark: Aarhus University, 1993); Jette Arneborg, "Burgundian caps, Basques and dead Norsemen at Herjolfsnaes, Greenland," pp. 75–83 in *Nationalmuseets Arbejdsmark* (Copenhagen: Nationalmuseet, 1996); and Jette Arneborg et al., "Change of diet of the Greenland Vikings determined from stable carbon isotope analysis and ^{14}C dating of their bones" (*Radiocarbon* 41:157–168 (1999)). Among the Greenland sites that Arneborg and her colleagues excavated was the remarkable "Farm beneath the sand," a large Norse farm sealed under a thick layer of sand at Western Settlement; that site and several other Greenland sites are described in a monograph edited by Jette Arneborg and Hans Christian Gullóv, *Man, Culture and Environment in Ancient Greenland* (Copenhagen: Danish Polar Center, 1998). C. L. Vebaek described his excavations from 1945 to 1962 in three monographs: respectively numbers 14, 17, and 18 (1991, 1992, and 1993) in the series *Meddelelser om Grónland,* Man and Society, Copenhagen: *The Church Topography of the Eastern Settlement and the Excavation of the Benedictine Convent at Narsarsuaq in the Uunartoq Fjord; Vatnahverfi: An Inland District of the Eastern Settlement in Greenland;* and *Narsaq: A Norse Landnáma Farm.*

Among important individual papers on Norse Greenland are Robert McGhee, "Contact between Native North Americans and the medieval Norse: a review of the evidence" (*American Antiquity* 49:4–26 (1984)); Joel Berglund, "The decline of the Norse settlements in Greenland" (*Arctic Anthropology* 23:109–135 (1986)); Svend Albrethsen and Christian Keller, "The use of the saeter in medieval Norse farming in Greenland" (*Arctic Anthropology* 23:91–107 (1986)); Christian Keller, "Vikings in the West Atlantic: a model of Norse Greenlandic medieval society" (*Acta Archaeologica* 61:126–141 (1990)); Bent Fredskild, "Agriculture in a marginal area: South Greenland from the Norse landnam (1985 A.D.) to the present 1985 A.D.," pp. 381–393 in Hilary Birks et al., eds., *The Cultural Landscape: Past, Present and Future* (Cambridge: Cambridge University Press, 1988); Bent Fredskild, "Erosion and vegetational changes in South Greenland caused by agriculture" (*Geografisk Tidsskrift* 92:14–21 (1992)); and Bjarne Jakobsen "Soil resources and soil erosion in the Norse Settlement area of Østerbygden in southern Greenland" (*Acta Borealia* 1:56–68 (1991)).

Chapter 9

Three books, excellent in different ways, that portray New Guinea highland societies are: a historical account by Gavin Souter, *New Guinea: The Last Unknown* (Sydney: Angus and Robertson, 1964); Bob Connolly and Robin Anderson, *First*

Contact (New York: Viking, 1987), a moving account of the first encounters of high-land New Guineans with Europeans; and Tim Flannery, *Throwim Way Leg* (New York: Atlantic Monthly Press, 1998), a zoologist's experiences with highlanders. Two papers by R. Michael Bourke discuss casuarina agroforestry and other agricultural practices maintaining soil fertility in the New Guinea highlands: "Indigenous conservation farming practices," *Report of the Joint ASOCON/Commonwealth Workshop,* pp. 67–71 (Jakarta: Asia Soil Conservation Network, 1991), and "Management of fallow species composition with tree planting in Papua New Guinea," *Resource Management in Asia/Pacific Working Paper* 1997/5 (Canberra: Research School of Pacific and Asian Studies, Australia National University, 1997). Three papers by Simon Haberle summarize the paleobotanical evidence for reconstructing the history of casuarina agroforestry: "Paleoenvironmental changes in the eastern highlands of Papua New Guinea" (*Archaeology in Oceania* 31:1–11 (1996)); "Dating the evidence for agricultural change in the Highlands of New Guinea: the last 2000 years" (*Australian Archaeology* no. 47:1–19 (1998)); and S. G. Haberle, G. S. Hope, and Y. de Fretes, "Environmental change in the Baliem Valley, montane Irian Jaya, Republic of Indonesia" (*Journal of Biogeography* 18:25–40 (1991)).

Patrick Kirch and Douglas Yen described their fieldwork on Tikopia in the monograph *Tikopia: The Prehistory and Ecology of a Polynesia Outlier* (Honolulu: Bishop Museum Bulletin 238, 1982). Subsequent accounts of Tikopia by Kirch include "Exchange systems and inter-island contact in the transformation of an island society: the Tikopia case," pp. 33–41 in Patrick Kirch, ed., *Island Societies: Archaeological Approaches to Evolution and Transformation* (Cambridge: Cambridge University Press, 1986); Chapter 12 of his book *The Wet and the Dry* (Chicago: University of Chicago Press, 1994); "Tikopia social space revisited," pp. 257–274 in J. M. Davidson et al., eds., *Oceanic Culture History: Essays in Honour of Roger Green* (New Zealand Journal of Archaeology Special Publication, 1996); and "Microcosmic histories: island perspectives on 'global' change" (*American Anthropologist* 99:30–42 (1997)). Raymond Firth's series of books on Tikopia began with *We, the Tikopia* (London: George Allen and Unwin, 1936) and *Primitive Polynesian Economy* (London: George Routledge and Sons, 1939). The extirpations of bird populations during the earliest phase of Tikopian settlement are described by David Steadman, Dominique Pahlavin, and Patrick Kirch, "Extinction, biogeography, and human exploitation of birds on Tikopia and Anuta, Polynesian outliers in the Solomon Islands" (*Bishop Museum Occasional Papers* 30:118–153 (1990)). For an account of population changes and population regulation on Tikopia, see W. D. Borrie, Raymond Firth, and James Spillius, "The population of Tikopia, 1929 and 1952" (*Population Studies* 10:229–252 (1957)).

My account of forest policy in Tokugawa Japan is based on three books by Conrad Totman: *The Green Archipelago: Forestry in Preindustrial Japan* (Berkeley: University of California Press, 1989); *Early Modern Japan* (Berkeley: University of California Press, 1993); and *The Lumber Industry in Early Modern Japan* (Honolulu: University of Hawaii Press, 1995). Chapter 5 of John Richards, *The Unending Frontier: An Environmental History of the Early Modern World* (Berkeley: University of California Press, 2003) draws on Totman's books and other sources to discuss Japanese forestry in the comparative context of other modern environmental case studies. Luke Roberts, *Mercantilism in a Japanese Domain: The Merchant Origins of Economic Nationalism in 18th-Century Tosa* (Cambridge: Cambridge University Press, 1998) discusses the economy of one daimyo domain that depended heavily on its forest. The formation and early history of Tokugawa Japan is covered in vol. 4 of the *Cambridge History of Japan,* John Whitney Hall, ed., *Early Modern Japan* (Cambridge: Cambridge University Press, 1991).

The switch from deforestation to reforestation in Denmark, Switzerland, and France is explained by Alexander Mather, "The transition from deforestation to re-forestation in Europe" pp. 35–52 in A. Angelsen and D. Kaimowitz, eds., *Agriculture Technologies and Tropical Deforestation* (New York: CABI Publishing, 2001). For an account of reforestation in the Andes under the Incas, see Alex Chepstow-Lusty and Mark Winfield, "Inca agroforestry: lessons from the past" (*Ambio* 29:322–328 (1998)).

Accounts of self-sustaining small-scale modern rural societies include: for the Swiss Alps, Robert Netting, "Of men and meadows: strategies of alpine land use" (*Anthropological Quarterly* 45:132–144 (1972)); "What alpine peasants have in common: observations on communal tenure in a Swiss village" (*Human Ecology* 4:135–146 (1976)), and *Balancing on an Alp* (Cambridge: Cambridge University Press, 1981); for Spanish irrigation systems, T. F. Glick, *Irrigation and Society in Medieval Valencia* (Cambridge, Mass.: Harvard University Press, 1970) and A. Maass and R. L. Anderson, *And the Desert Shall Rejoice: Conflict, Growth and Justice in Arid Environments* (Malabar, Fla.: Krieger, 1986); and, for Philippine irrigation systems, R. Y. Siy Jr., *Community Resource Management: Lessons from the Zanjera* (Quezon City: University of Philippines Press, 1982). Those Swiss, Spanish, and Philippine studies are compared in Chapter 3 of Elinor Ostrom's book *Governing the Commons* (Cambridge: Cambridge University Press, 1990).

Accounts of ecological specialization within the Indian caste system include Madhav Gadgil and Ramachandra Guha, *This Fissured Land: An Ecological History of India* (Delhi: Oxford University Press, 1992). Two papers that may serve as examples of prudent resource management by ecologically specialized Indian castes include Madhav Gadgil and K. C. Malhotra, "Adaptive significance of the Indian castes system: an ecological perspective" (*Annals of Human Biology* 10:465–478 (1983)), and Madhav Gadgil and Prema Iyer, "On the diversification of common-property resource use by Indian society," pp. 240–255 in F. Berkes, ed., *Common Property Resources: Ecology and Community-based Sustainable Development* (London: Belhaven, 1989).

■ ■ ■

Before leaving these examples of success or failure in the past, let us mention some more examples of failure. I have discussed five failures in detail, because they seem to me to be the best understood cases. However, there are many other past societies, some of them well known, that may also have overexploited their resources, sometimes to the point of decline or collapse. I do not discuss them at length in this book, because they are subject to more uncertainties and debate than the cases that I do discuss in detail. However, just to make the record more complete, I shall now briefly mention nine of them, proceeding geographically through the New and then the Old World:

Native Americans of the California Channel Islands off Los Angeles overexploited different species of shellfish in succession, as shown by shells in their middens. The oldest middens contain mostly the shells of the largest species that lives closest to shore and would have been easiest to bring up by diving. With time in the archaeological record, the middens show that the individuals harvested of that species became smaller and smaller, until people switched to harvesting the next-smaller species that lived farther offshore in deeper water. Again, the individuals harvested of that species decreased in size with time. Thus, each species in turn was overharvested until it became uneconomic to exploit, whereupon people fell back upon the next species, which was less desirable and more difficult to harvest. See Terry Jones, ed., *Essays on the Prehistory of Maritime California* (Davis, Calif.: Center for Archaeological Research, 1992); and L. Mark Raab, "An optimal foraging analysis of prehistoric shellfish collecting on San Clemente Island, California" (*Journal of Ethnobiology* 12:63–80 (1992)). Another food source presumably overharvested by Native Americans on the same islands was a flightless species of sea duck called *Chendytes lawesi,* which must have been easy to kill because it was flightless, and which was eventually exterminated after human settlement of the Channel Islands. The abalone industry in modern Southern California met a similar fate: when I first moved to Los Angeles in 1966, one could still buy abalone in the supermarkets and harvest it on the coast, but abalone disappeared from Los Angeles menus during my lifetime here because of overharvesting.

The largest Native American city in North America was Cahokia, which arose outside St. Louis and some of whose enormous mounds have survived as tourist attractions. With the arrival in the Mississippi Valley of a productive new variety of corn, the Mississippian Mound Builder culture arose there and in the U.S. Southeast. Cahokia reached its peak in the 1200s and then collapsed long before the arrival of Europeans. The cause of Cahokia's collapse is debated, but deforestation, resulting in erosion and the filling up of oxbow lakes with sediment, may have played a role. See Neal Lopinot and William Woods, "Wood exploitation and the collapse of Cahokia," pp. 206–231 in C. Margaret Scarry, ed., *Foraging and Farming in the Eastern Woodlands* (Gainesville: University Press of Florida, 1993); Timothy Pauketat and Thomas Emerson, eds., *Cahokia: Domination and Ideology in the Mis-*

sissippian World (Lincoln: University of Nebraska Press, 1997); and George Milner, *The Cahokia Chiefdom: The Archaeology of a Mississippian Society* (Washington, D.C.: Smithsonian Institution, 1998). In the remainder of the U.S. Southeast, chiefdoms of Mound Builder societies rose and fell; exhaustion of soil nutrients may have played a role.

The first state-level society on the coast of Peru was that of the Moche, famous for their realistic pottery, especially their portrait vessels. Moche society collapsed by around A.D. 800, apparently because of some combination of El Niño events, destruction of irrigation works by flooding, and drought (see Brian Fagan's 1999 book, cited under Further Readings for the Prologue, for discussion and references).

One of the empires or cultural horizons of the Andean Highlands that preceded the Incas was the Tiwanaku Empire, in whose collapse drought may have played a role. See Alan Kolata, *Tiwanaku* (Oxford: Blackwell, 1993); Alan Kolata, ed., *Tiwanaku and Its Hinterland: Archaeology and Paleoecology of an Andean Civilization* (Washington, D.C.: Smithsonian Institution, 1996); and Michael Binford et al., "Climate variation and the rise and fall of an Andean civilization" (*Quaternary Research* 47:235–248 (1997)).

Ancient Greece went through cycles of environmental problems and recovery, at intervals of about 400 years. In each cycle, human population built up, forests were cut down, hillsides were terraced to reduce erosion, and dams were built to minimize siltation in the valley bottoms. Eventually in each cycle, the terraces and dams became overwhelmed, and the region had to be abandoned or suffered a drastic decrease in population and in societal complexity, until the landscape had recovered sufficiently to permit a further population buildup. One of those collapses coincided with the fall of Mycenaean Greece, the Greek society that was celebrated by Homer and that fought the Trojan War. Mycenaean Greece possessed writing (the Linear B script), but with the collapse of Mycenaean society that writing disappeared, and Greece became non-literate until the return of literacy (now based on the alphabet) around 800 B.C. (see Charles Redman's 1999 book, cited under Further Readings for the Prologue, for discussion and references).

What we think of as civilization began around 10,000 years ago in the part of Southwest Asia known as the Fertile Crescent, and encompassing parts of modern Iran, Iraq, Syria, southeastern Turkey, Lebanon, Jordan, and Israel/Palestine. The Fertile Crescent was where the world's oldest agriculture arose, and where metallurgy, writing, and state societies first developed. Thus, peoples of the Fertile Crescent enjoyed their head start of thousands of years over the rest of the world. Why, after leading the world for so long, did the Fertile Crescent decline, to the point where today it is poor except for its oil reserves and the name "Fertile Crescent" is a cruel joke? Iraq is now anything but the leader in world agriculture. Much of the explanation has to do with deforestation in the low-rainfall environment of the Fertile Crescent, and salinization that permanently ruined some of the world's oldest farmlands (see the two books written or edited by Charles Redman, and cited under Further Readings for the Prologue, for discussion and references).

The most famous monumental ruins in Africa south of the equator are those of Great Zimbabwe, consisting of a center with large stone structures in what is now the country of Zimbabwe. Great Zimbabwe thrived in the 11th to 15th centuries, controlling trade between Africa's interior and its east coast. Its decline may have involved a combination of deforestation and a shift of trade routes. See David Phillipson, *African Archaeology*, 2nd ed. (Cambridge: Cambridge University Press, 1993); Christopher Ehret, *The Civilizations of Africa: A History to 1800* (Charlottesville: University Press of Virginia, 2002).

The earliest cities and large states of the Indian subcontinent arose in the third millennium B.C. in the Indus Valley of what is now Pakistan. Those Indus Valley cities belong to what is known as Harappan civilization, whose writing remains undeciphered. It used to be thought that Harappan civilization was terminated by invasions of Indo-European-speaking Aryans from the northwest, but it now appears that the cities were in decline before those invasions (Plate 41). Droughts, and shifts of the course of the Indus River, may have played a role. See Gregory Possehl, *Harappan Civilization* (Warminster, England: Aris and Phillips, 1982); Michael Jansen, Maire Mulloy, and Günter Urban, eds., *Forgotten Cities of the Indus* (Mainz, Germany: Philipp von Zabern, 1991); and Jonathan Kenoyer, *Ancient Cities of the Indus Valley Civilization* (Karachi, Pakistan: Oxford University Press, 1998).

Finally, the enormous temple complexes and reservoirs of Angkor Wat, former capital of the Khmer Empire, constitute the most famous ruins and archaeological "mystery" of Southeast Asia, within modern Cambodia (Plate 42). The Khmer decline may have involved the silting up of reservoirs that supplied water for intensive irrigated rice agriculture. As the Khmer Empire grew weak, it proved unable to hold off its chronic enemies the Thais, whom the Khmer Empire had been able to resist while at full strength. See Michael Coe, *Angkor and the Khmer Civilization* (London: Thames and Hudson, 2003), and the papers and books by Bernard-Philippe Groslier cited by Coe.

Chapter 10

If you decide to consult these primary sources on the Rwandan genocide and its antecedents, brace yourself for some painful reading.

Catharine Newbury, *The Cohesion of Oppression: Clientship and Ethnicity in Rwanda, 1860–1960* (New York: Columbia University Press, 1988) describes how Rwandan society became transformed, and how the roles of the Hutu and the Tutsi became polarized, from precolonial times to the eve of independence.

Human Rights Watch, *Leave None to Tell the Story: Genocide in Rwanda* (New York: Human Rights Watch, 1999) presents in mind-numbing detail the immediate background to the events of 1994, then a 414-page account of the killings themselves, and finally their aftermath.

Philip Gourevitch, *We Wish to Inform You That Tomorrow We Will Be Killed with Our Families* (New York: Farrar, Straus and Giroux, 1998) is an account of the genocide by a journalist who interviewed many survivors, and who depicts as well the failure of other countries and of the United Nations to prevent the killings.

My chapter includes several quotations from Gérard Prunier, *The Rwanda Crisis: History of Genocide* (New York: Columbia University Press, 1995), a book by a French specialist on East Africa who wrote in the immediate aftermath of the genocide, and who vividly reconstructs the motives of participants and of the French government's intervention. My account of the Hutu-versus-Hutu killings in Kanama commune is based on the analysis in Catherine André and Jean-Philippe Platteau's paper "Land relations under unbearable stress: Rwanda caught in the Malthusian trap" (*Journal of Economic Behavior and Organization* 34:1–47 (1998)).

Chapter 11

Two books comparing the histories of the two countries sharing the island of Hispaniola are a lively account in English by Michele Wecker, *Why the Cocks Fight: Dominicans, Haitians, and the Struggle for Hispaniola* (New York: Hill and Wang, 1999), and a geographic and social comparison in Spanish by Rafael Emilio Yunén Z., *La Isla Como Es* (Santiago, República Dominicana: Universidad Católica Madre y Maestra, 1985).

Three books by Mats Lundahl will serve as an introduction into the literature on Haiti: *Peasants and Poverty: A Study of Haiti* (London: Croom Helm, 1979); *The Haitian Economy: Man, Land, and Markets* (London: Croom Helm, 1983); and *Politics or Markets? Essays on Haitian Underdevelopment* (London: Routledge, 1992). The classic study of the Haitian revolution of 1781–1803 is C.L.R. James, *The Black Jacobins*, 2nd ed. (London: Vintage, 1963).

The standard English-language history of the Dominican Republic is Frank Moya Pons, *The Dominican Republic: A National History* (Princeton, N.J.: Markus Wiener, 1998). The same author wrote a different text in Spanish: *Manual de Historia Dominicana*, 9th ed. (Santiago, República Dominicana, 1999). Also in Spanish is a two-volume history by Roberto Cassá, *Historia Social y Económica de la República Dominicana* (Santo Domingo: Editora Alfa y Omega, 1998 and 2001). Marlin Clausner's history focuses on rural areas: *Rural Santo Domingo: Settled, Unsettled, Resettled* (Philadelphia: Temple University Press, 1973). Harry Hoetink, *The Dominican People, 1850–1900: Notes for a Historical Sociology* (Baltimore: Johns Hopkins University Press, 1982) deals with the late 19th century. Claudio Vedovato, *Politics, Foreign Trade and Economic Development: A Study of the Dominican Republic* (London: Croom Helm, 1986) focuses on the Trujillo and post-Trujillo eras. Two books providing an entry into the Trujillo era are Howard Wiarda, *Dictatorship and*

Development: The Methods of Control in Trujillo's Dominican Republic (Gainesville, University of Florida Press, 1968) and the more recent Richard Lee Turits, *Foundations of Despotism: Peasants, the Trujillo Regime, and Modernity in Dominican History* (Palo Alto, Calif.: Stanford University Press, 2002).

A manuscript tracing the history of environmental policies in the Dominican Republic, hence especially relevant to this chapter, is Walter Cordero, "Introducción: bibliografía sobre medio ambiente y recursos naturales en la República Dominicana" (2003).

Chapter 12

Most of the up-to-date primary literature on China's environmental and population issues is in Chinese, or on the Web, or both. References will be found in an article by Jianguo Liu and me, "China's environment in a globalizing world" (in preparation). As for English-language sources in books or journals, the Woodrow Wilson Center in Washington, D.C. (e-mail address chinaenv@erols.com), publishes a series of annual volumes entitled the China Environment Series. World Bank publications include *China: Air, Land, and Water* (Washington, D.C.: The World Bank, 2001), available either as a book or as a CD-ROM. Some other books are L. R. Brown, *Who Will Feed China?* (New York: Norton, 1995); M. B. McElroy, C. P. Nielson, and P. Lydon, eds., *Energizing China: Reconciling Environmental Protection and Economic Growth* (Cambridge, Mass.: Harvard University Press, 1998); J. Shapiro, *Mao's War Against Nature* (Cambridge: Cambridge University Press, 2001); D. Zweig, *Internationalizing China: Domestic Interests and Global Linkages* (Ithaca, N.Y.: Cornell University Press, 2002); and Mark Elvin, *The Retreat of the Elephants: An Environmental History of China* (New Haven: Yale University Press, 2004). For an English-language translation of a book originally published in Chinese, see Qu Geping and Li Jinchang, *Population and Environment in China* (Boulder, Colo.: Lynne Rienner, 1994).

Chapter 13

A deservedly acclaimed account of the early history of the British colonies in Australia from their origins in 1788 into the 19th century is Robert Hughes, *The Fatal Shore: The Epic of Australia's Founding* (New York: Knopf, 1987). Tim Flannery, *The Future Eaters: An Ecological History of the Australasian Lands and People* (Chatsworth, New South Wales: Reed, 1994) begins instead with the arrival of Aborigines over 40,000 years ago and traces their impact and that of Europeans on the Australian environment. David Horton, *The Pure State of Nature: Sacred Cows, Destructive Myths and the Environment* (St. Leonards, New South Wales: Allen & Unwin, 2000) offers a perspective different from Flannery's.

Three government sources provide encyclopedic accounts of Australia's environment, economy, and society: Australian State of the Environment Committee 2001, *Australia: State of the Environment 2001* (Canberra: Department of Environment and Heritage, 2001), supplemented by reports on the website http://www. ea.gov.au/soe/; its predecessor State of the Environment Advisory Committee 1996, *Australia: State of the Environment 1996* (Melbourne: CSIRO Publishing, 1996); and Dennis Trewin, *2001 Year Book Australia* (Canberra: Australian Bureau of Statistics, 2001), a Centenary of Australia's Federation celebratory edition of a yearbook published annually since 1908.

Two well-illustrated books by Mary E. White provide overviews of Australian environmental problems: *Listen . . . Our Land Is Crying* (East Roseville, New South Wales: Kangaroo Press, 1997) and *Running Down: Water in a Changing Land* (East Roseville, New South Wales: Kangaroo Press, 2000). Tim Flannery's "Beautiful lies: population and environment in Australia" (*Quarterly Essay* no. 9, 2003) is a provocative shorter overview. Salinization's history and impacts in Australia are covered by Quentin Beresford, Hugo Bekle, Harry Phillips, and Jane Mulcock, *The Salinity Crisis: Landscapes, Communities and Politics* (Crawley, Western Australia: University of Western Australia Press, 2001). Andrew Campbell, *Landcare: Communities Shaping the Land and the Future* (St. Leonards, New South Wales: Allen & Unwin, 1994) describes an important grassroots movement to improve land management in rural Australia.

Chapter 14

Along with questions by my UCLA students, Joseph Tainter's book *The Collapses of Complex Societies* (Cambridge: Cambridge University Press, 1988) provided a starting point for this chapter, by stating clearly why a society's failure to solve its environmental problems poses a puzzle crying out for explanation. Thomas McGovern et al. "Northern islands, human error, and environmental degradation: a view of social and ecological change in the medieval North Atlantic" (*Human Ecology* 16:225–270 (1988)) traces a sequence of reasons why the Greenland Norse failed to perceive or solve their own environmental problems. The sequence of reasons that I propose in this chapter overlaps partly with that of McGovern et al., whose model should be consulted by anyone interested in pursuing this puzzle.

Elinor Ostrom and her colleagues have studied the tragedy of the commons (alias common-pool resources), using both comparative surveys and experimental games to identify the conditions under which consumers are most likely to recognize their common interests and to implement an effective quota system themselves. Ostrom's books include Elinor Ostrom, *Governing the Commons: The Evolution of Institutions for Collective Action* (Cambridge: Cambridge University Press, 1990) and Elinor Ostrom, Roy Gardner, and James Walker, *Rules, Games, and Common-Pool Resources* (Ann Arbor: University of Michigan Press, 1994). Her more recent articles include Elinor Ostrom, "Coping with tragedies of the commons" *Annual Reviews of Political Science* 2: 493–535 (1999); Elinor Ostrom et al., "Revisiting the commons: local lessons, global challenges" *Science* 284:278–282 (1999); and Thomas Dietz, Elinor Ostrom, and Paul Stern, "The struggle to govern the commons" *Science* 302:1907–1912 (2003).

Barbara Tuchman, *The March of Folly: From Troy to Vietnam* (New York: Ballantine Books, 1984) covers disastrous decisions over exactly the time span that she names in the book's title, also reflecting en route from Troy to Vietnam on the follies of the Aztec emperor Montezuma, the fall of Christian Spain to the Moslems, England's provocation of the American Revolution, and other such self-destructive acts. Charles Mackay, *Extraordinary Popular Delusions and the Madness of Crowds* (New York: Barnes and Noble, 1993, reprint of the original 1852 edition) covers an even wider range of follies than does Tuchman, including (just to name a few) the South Sea bubble in 18th-century England, tulip madness in 17th-century Holland, prophecies of the Last Judgment, the Crusades, witch hunting, belief in ghosts and sacred relics, dueling, and kings' decrees about hair length, beards, and mustaches. Irving Janis, *Groupthink* (Boston: Houghton Mifflin, 1983, revised 2nd ed.) explores the subtle group dynamics that contributed to the success or failure of deliberations involving recent American presidents and their advisors. Janis's case studies are of the 1961 Bay of Pigs invasion, the American army's crossing of the 38th parallel in Korea in 1950, American's non-preparation for Japan's 1941 Pearl Harbor attack, America's escalation of the Vietnam War from 1964 to 1967, the Cuban Missile Crisis of 1962, and America's adoption of the Marshall Plan in 1947.

Garrett Hardin's classic and often-cited article "The tragedy of the commons" appeared in *Science* 162:1243–1248 (1968). Mancur Olson applies the metaphor of stationary bandits and roving bandits to Chinese warlords and other extractive agents in "Dictatorship, democracy, and development" (*American Political Science Review* 87:567–576 (1993)). Sunk-cost effects are explained by Hal Arkes and Peter Ayton, "The sunk cost and Concorde effects: are humans less rational than lower animals?" (*Psychological Bulletin* 125:591–600 (1999)), and by Marco Janssen et al., "Sunk-cost effects and vulnerability to collapse in ancient societies" (*Current Anthropology* 44:722–728 (2003)).

Chapter 15

Two books on the oil industry's history and on scenarios for its future are: Kenneth Deffeyes, *Hubbert's Peak: The Impending World Oil Shortage* (Princeton, N.J.: Princeton University Press, 2001); and Paul Roberts, *The End of Oil* (Boston: Houghton Mifflin, 2004). For a perspective within the industry, a place to start would be the websites of the major international oil companies, such as that of ChevronTexaco: www.chevrontexaco.com.

Fact-filled publications on the state of the mining industry were produced by an initiative termed "Mining, Minerals, and Sustainable Development," resulting from a partnership supported by major mining companies. Two of these publications are: *Breaking New Ground: Mining, Minerals and Sustainable Development* (London: Earthscan, 2002); and Alistair MacDonald, *Industry in Transition: A Profile of the North American Mining Sector* (Winnipeg: International Institute for Sustainable Development, 2002). Other fact-filled sources are the publications of the Mineral Policy Center in Washington, D.C., recently renamed Earthworks (Web site www.mineralpolicy.org). Some books on environmental issues raised by mining are: Duane Smith, *Mining America: The Industry and the Environment, 1800–1980* (Boulder: University Press of Colorado, 1993); Thomas Power, *Lost Landscapes and Failed Economies: The Search for a Value of Place* (Washington, D.C.: Island Press, 1996); Jerrold Marcus, ed., *Mining Environmental Handbook: Effects of Mining on the Environment and American Environmental Controls on Mining* (London: Imperial College Press, 1997); and Al Gedicks, *Resource Rebels: Native Challenges to Mining and Oil Corporations* (Cambridge, Mass.: South End Press, 2001). Two books describing the collapse of copper mining on the island of Bougainville, triggered in part by environmental impacts, are: M. O'Callaghan, *Enemies Within: Papua New Guinea, Australia, and the Sandline Crisis: The Inside Story* (Sydney: Doubleday, 1999); and Donald Denoon, *Getting Under the Skin: The Bougainville Copper Agreement and Creation of the Panguna Mine* (Melbourne: Melbourne University Press, 2000).

Information about forest certification may be obtained from the website of the Forest Stewardship Council: www.fscus.org. For a comparison of forest certification by the FSC with other forest certification schemes, see Saskia Ozinga, *Behind the Logs: An Environmental and Social Assessment of Forest Certification Schemes* (Moreton-in-Marsh, UK: Fern, 2001). Two books on the history of deforestation are John Perlin, *A Forest Journey: The Role of Wood in the Development of Civilization* (New York: Norton, 1989); and Michael Williams, *Deforesting the Earth: From Prehistory to Global Crisis* (Chicago: University of Chicago Press, 2003).

Information about fisheries certification may be obtained from the Web site of the Marine Stewardschip Council: www.msc.org. Howard M. Johnson (Web site www.hmj.com) produces a series called *Annual Report on the United States Seafood Industry* (Jacksonville, Ore.: Howard Johnson, annually). Aquaculture of shrimp and salmon is treated in two chapters of Jason Clay, *World Agriculture and the Environment: A Commodity-by-Commodity Guide to Impacts and Practices* (Washington, D.C.: Island Press, 2004). Four books on overfishing of fish in general or of specific fish species are: Mark Kurlansky, *Cod: A Biography of the Fish That Changed the World* (New York: Walker, 1997); Suzanne Ludicello, Michael Weber, and Robert Wreland, *Fish, Markets, and Fishermen: The Economics of Overfishing* (Washington, D.C.: Island Press, 1999); David Montgomery, *King of Fish: The Thousand-Year Run of Salmon* (New York: Westview, 2003); and Daniel Pauly and Jay Maclean, *In a Perfect Ocean* (Washington, D.C.: Island Press, 2003). An example of an article on overfishing is: Jeremy Jackson et al., "Historical overfishing and the recent collapse of coastal ecosystems" (*Science* 293:629–638 (2001)). The discovery that aquacultured salmon contain higher concentrations of toxic contaminates than do wild salmon was reported by Ronald Hits et al., "Global assessment of organic contaminates in farmed salmon" (*Science* 303:226–229: 2004).

It would be impossible to understand environmental practices of big businesses without first understanding the realities of what companies must do to survive in an intensely competitive business world. Three widely read books on this subject are: Thomas Peters and Robert Waterman Jr., *In Search of Excellence: Lessons from America's Best-Run Companies* (New York: HarperCollins, 1982, republished in 2004); Robert Waterman Jr., *The Renewal Factor: How the Best Get and Keep the Competitive Edge* (Toronto: Bantam Books, 1987); and Robert Waterman Jr., *Adhocracy: The Power to Change* (New York: Norton, 1990).

Books that discuss the circumstances under which businesses may be environmentally constructive rather than destructive include Tedd Saunders and Loretta McGovern, *The Bottom Line of Green Is Black: Strategies for Creating Profitable and Environmentally Sound Businesses* (San Francisco: HarperSanFrancisco, 1993); and Jem Bendell, ed., *Terms for Endearment: Business NGOs and Sustainable Development* (Sheffield, UK: Greenleaf, 2000).

Chapter 16

Some books, published since 2001, that provide an overview of current environmental problems and an introduction to the large literature on this subject include: Stuart Pimm, *The World According to Pimm: A Scientist Audits the Earth* (New York: McGraw-Hill, 2001); Lester Brown's three books *Eco-economy: Building an Economy for the Earth* (New York: Norton, 2001), *Plan B: Rescuing a Planet Under Stress and Civilization in Trouble* (New York: Norton, 2003), and *State of the World* (New York: Norton, published annually since 1984); Edward Wilson, *The Future of Life* (New York: Knopf, 2002); Gretchen Daily and Katherine Ellison, *The New Economy of Nature: The Quest to Make Conservation Profitable* (Washington, D.C.: Island Press, 2002); David Lorey, ed., *Global Environmental Challenges of the Twenty-first Century: Resources, Consumption, and Sustainable Solutions* (Wilmington, Del.: Scholarly Resources, 2003); Paul Ehrlich and Anne Ehrlich, *One with Nineveh: Politics, Consumption, and the Human Future* (Washington, D.C.: Island Press, 2004); and James Speth, *Red Sky at Morning: America and the Crisis of the Global Environment* (New Haven: Yale University Press, 2004).

The Further Readings for Chapter 15 provided references for problems of deforestation, overfishing, and oil. Vaclav Smil, *Energy at the Crossroads: Global Perspectives and Uncertainties* (Cambridge, Mass.: MIT Press, 2003) offers an account not only of oil, coal, and gas but also of other forms of energy production. The biodiversity crisis and habitat destruction are discussed by John Terborgh, *Where Have*

All the Birds Gone? (Princeton, N.J.: Princeton University Press, 1989) and *Requiem for Nature* (Washington, D.C.: Island Press, 1999); David Quammen, *Song of the Dodo* (New York: Scribner, 1997); and Marjorie Reaka-Kudla et al., eds., *Biodiversity 2: Understanding and Protecting Our Biological Resources* (Washington, D.C.: Joseph Henry Press, 1997).

Some recent papers on coral reef destruction are: T. P. Hughes, "Climate change, human impacts, and the resilience of coral reefs" (*Science* 301:929–933 (2003)); J. M. Pandolfi et al., "Global trajectories of the long-term decline of coral reef ecosystems" (*Science* 301:955–958 (2003)); and D. R. Bellwood et al., "Confronting the coral reef crisis" (*Nature* 429:827–833 (2004)).

Books on soil problems include the classic Vernon Gill Carter and Tom Dale, *Topsoil and Civilization,* revised ed. (Norman: University of Okalahoma Press, 1974), and Keith Wiebe, ed., *Land Quality, Agricultural Productivity, and Food Security: Biophysical Processes and Economic Choices at Local, Regional, and Global Levels* (Cheltenham, UK: Edward Elgar, 2003). Articles offering different perspectives on soil problems are David Pimentel et al., "Environmental and economic costs of soil erosion and conservation benefits" (*Science* 267:1117–1123 (1995)); Stanley Trimble and Pierre Crosson, "U.S. soil erosion rates—myth and reality" (*Science* 289:248–250 (2000)); and a set of eight articles by various authors, published in *Science* 304:1613–1637 (2004).

For issues concerning the world's water supplies, see the reports authored by Peter Gleick and published every two years: e.g., Peter Gleick, *The World's Water, 1998–1999: The Biennial Report on Freshwater Resources* (Washington, D.C.: Island Press, 2000). Vernon Scarborough, *The Flow of Power: Ancient Water Systems and Landscapes* (Santa Fe: School of American Research, 2003) compares solutions to water problems in ancient societies around the world.

A global accounting of the fraction of solar energy utilized by plant photosynthesis (termed "net primary production") was offered by Peter Vitousek et al., "Human domination of Earth's ecosystems" (*Science* 277:494–499 (1997)), and updated and broken down by region by Mark Imhoff et al. "Global patterns in human consumption of net primary production" (*Nature* 429:870–873 (2004)).

Effects of toxic chemicals on living things, including humans, are summarized by Theo Colborn, Dianne Dumanoski, and John Peterson Myers, *Our Stolen Future* (New York: Plume, 1997). One specific example of the high economic costs of toxic and other impacts on an entire ecosystem is an account for Chesapeake Bay: Tom Horton and William Eichbaum, *Turning the Tide: Saving the Chesapeake Bay* (Washington, D.C.: Island Press, 1991).

Among books offering good accounts of global warming and climate change are Steven Schneider, *Laboratory Earth: The Planetary Gamble We Can't Afford to Lose* (New York: Basic Books, 1997); Michael Glantz, *Currents of Change: Impacts of El Niño and La Niña on Climate and Society,* 2nd ed. (Cambridge: Cambridge University Press, 2001); and Spencer Weart, *The Discovery of Global Warming* (Cambridge, Mass.: Harvard University Press, 2003).

Three classics in the large literature on human population are Paul Ehrlich, *The Population Bomb* (New York: Ballantine Books, 1968); Paul Ehrlich and Anne Ehrlich, *The Population Explosion* (New York: Simon & Schuster, 1990); and Joel Cohen, *How Many People Can the Earth Support?* (New York: Norton, 1995).

To place my assessment of the environmental and population problems of my city of Los Angeles in a wider context, see a book-length corresponding effort for the whole United States: The Heinz Center, *The State of the Nation's Ecosystems: Measuring the Lands, Waters, and Living Resources of the United States* (New York: Cambridge University Press, 2002).

Readers interested in more detailed statements of the dismissals of environmentalists' concerns that I list as one-liners may consult Bjórn Lomborg, *The Skeptical Environmentalist* (Cambridge: Cambridge University Press, 2001). For more extended responses to the one-liners, see Paul Ehrlich and Anne Ehrlich, *Betrayal of Science and Reason* (Washington, D.C.: Island Press, 1996). The Club of Rome study discussed in that section of my chapter is Donella Meadows et al., *The Limits to Growth* (New York: Universe Books, 1972), updated by Donella Meadows, Jorgen Randers, and Dennis Meadows, *The Limits to Growth: The 30-Year Update* (White River Junction, Vt.: Chelsea Green, 2004). For the issue of how to decide whether there are too few or too many false alarms, see S. W. Pacala et al., "False alarm over environmental false alarms" (*Science* 301:1187–1188 (2003)).

Some entries to the literature on the connections between environmental and population problems on the one hand, and political instability on the other hand, include: the website of Population Action International, www.population action.org; Richard Cincotta, Robert Engelman, and Daniele Anastasion, *The Security Demographic: Population and Civil Conflict after the Cold War* (Washington, D.C.: Population Action International, 2004); the annual journal *The Environmental Change and Security Project Report,* published by the Woodrow Wilson Center (website www.wilson.org/ecsp); and Thomas Homer-Dixon, "Environmental scarcities and violent conflict: evidence from cases" (*International Security* 19:5–40 (1994)).

Finally, readers curious about what other garbage besides dozens of Suntory whiskey bottles drifted onto the beaches of remote Oeno and Ducie atolls in the Southeast Pacific Ocean should consult the three tables in T. G. Benton, "From castaways to throwaways: marine litter in the Pitcairn Islands" (*Biological Journal of the Linnean Society* 56:415–422 (1995)).

For all of the 12 major sets of environmental problems that I summarized at the beginning of Chapter 16, there already exist many excellent books discussing how governments and organizations could address them. But there still remains the question that many people ask themselves: what can *I* do, as an individual, that might make a difference? If you are wealthy, you can obviously do a lot: for example, Bill and Melinda Gates have decided to devote billions of dollars to urgent public health problems around the world. If you are in a position of power, you can use that position to advance your agenda: for example, President George W. Bush of the U.S., and President Joaquín Balaguer of the Dominican Republic, used their positions to influence decisively, albeit in different ways, the environmental agendas of their respective countries. However, the vast majority of us who lack that wealth and power tend to feel helpless and hopeless in the face of the overwhelming power of governments and big businesses. Is there anything that a poor individual who is neither a CEO nor a political leader can do to make a difference?

Yes, there are half-a-dozen types of actions that often prove effective. But it needs to be said at the outset that an individual should not expect to make a difference through a single action, or even through a series of actions that will be completed within three weeks. Instead, if you do want to make a difference, plan to commit yourself to a consistent policy of actions over the duration of your life.

In a democracy, the simplest and cheapest action is to vote. Some elections, contested by candidates with very different environmental agendas, are settled by ridiculously small numbers of votes. An example was the year 2000 U.S. presidential election, decided by a few hundred votes in the state of Florida. Besides voting, find out the addresses of your elected representatives, and take some time each month to let them know your views on specific current environmental issues. If representatives don't hear from voters, they will conclude that voters aren't interested in the environment.

Next, you can reconsider what you, as a consumer, do or don't buy. Big businesses aim to make money. They are likely to discontinue products that the public doesn't buy, and to manufacture and promote products that the public does buy. The reason that increasing numbers of logging companies are adopting sustainable logging practices is that consumer demand for wood products certified by the Forest Stewardship Council exceeds supply. Of course, it is easiest to influence companies in your own country, but in today's globalized world the consumer has increasing ability to influence overseas companies and policy-makers as well. A prime example is the collapse of white-minority government and apartheid policies in South Africa between 1989 and 1994, as the result of the economic boycott of South Africa by individual consumers and investors overseas, leading to an unprecedented economic divestiture by overseas corporations, public pension funds, and governments. During my several visits to South Africa in the 1980s, the South African state seemed to me so irrevocably committed to apartheid that I never imagined it would back down, but it did.

Another way in which consumers can influence policies of big companies, besides buying or refusing to buy their products, is by drawing public attention to the company's policies and products. One set of examples is the campaigns against animal cruelty that led major fashion houses, such as Bill Blass, Calvin Klein, and Oleg Cassini, to publicly renounce their use of fur. Another example involves the public activists who helped convince the world's largest wood products company, Home Depot, to commit to ending its purchases of wood from endangered forest regions and to give preference to certified forest products. Home Depot's policy shift greatly surprised me: I had supposed consumer activists to be hopelessly outgunned in trying to influence such a powerful company.

Most examples of consumer activism have involved trying to embarrass a company for doing bad things, and that one-sidedness is unfortunate, because it has given environmentalists a reputation for being monotonously shrill, depressing, boring, and negative. Consumer activists could also be influential by taking the initiative to praise companies whose policies they do like. In Chapter 15 I mentioned big businesses that are indeed doing things sought by environmentalist consumers, but those companies have received much less praise for their good deeds than blame for their bad deeds. Most of us are familiar with Aesop's fable concerning the competition between the wind and the sun to persuade a man to take off his coat: after the wind blew hard and failed, the sun then shone brightly and succeeded. Consumers could make much more use of the lesson of that fable, because big businesses adopting environmentalist policies know that they are unlikely to be believed if they praise their own policies to a cynical public; the businesses need outside help in becoming recognized for their efforts. Among the many big companies that have benefited recently from favorable public comment are Chevron-Texaco and Boise Cascade, praised for their environmental management of their Kutubu oil field and for their decision to phase out products of unsustainably managed forests, respectively. In addition to activists castigating "the dirty dozen," they could also praise "the terrific ten."

Consumers who wish to influence big businesses by either buying or refusing to buy their products, or by embarrassing or praising them, need to go to the trouble of learning which links in a business chain are most sensitive to public influence, and also which links are in the strongest position to influence other links. Businesses that sell directly to the consumer, or whose brands are on sale to the consumer, are much more sensitive than businesses that sell only to other businesses and whose products reach the public without a label of origin. Retail businesses that, by themselves or as part of a large buyers' group, buy much or all of the output of some particular producing business are in a much stronger position to influence that producer than is a member of the public. I mentioned several examples in Chapter 15, and many other examples can be added.

For instance, if you do or don't approve of how some big international oil company manages its oil fields, it does make sense to buy at, boycott, praise, or picket that company's gas stations. If you admire Australian titanium mining practices and dislike Lihir Island gold mining practices, don't waste your time fantasizing that you could have any influence on those mining companies yourself; turn your attention instead to DuPont, and to Tiffany and Wal-Mart, which are major retailers of titanium-based paints and of gold jewelry, respectively. Don't praise or blame logging companies without readily traceable retail products; leave it instead to Home Depot, Lowe's, B and Q, and the other retail giants to influence the loggers. Similarly, seafood retailers like Unilever (through its various brands) and Whole Foods are the ones who care whether you buy seafood from them; they, not you, can influence the fishing industry itself. Wal-Mart is the world's largest grocery retailer; they and other such retailers can virtually dictate agricultural practices to farmers; you can't dictate to farmers, but you do have clout with Wal-Mart. If you want to know where in the business chain you as a consumer have influence, there are now organizations such as the Mineral Policy Center/Earthworks, the Forest Stewardship Council, and the Marine Stewardship Council that can tell you the answer for many business sectors. (For their website addresses, see the Further Readings to Chapter 15.)

Of course, you as a single voter or consumer won't swing an election's outcome or impress Wal-Mart. But any individual can multiply his or her power by talking to other people who also vote and buy. You can start with your parents, children, and friends. That was a significant factor in the international oil companies beginning to reverse direction from environmental indifference to adopting stringent environmental safeguards. Too many valuable employees were complaining or taking other jobs because friends, casual acquaintances, and their own children and spouses made them feel ashamed of themselves for their employer's practices. Most CEOs, including Bill Gates, have children and a spouse, and I have learned of many CEOs who changed their company's environmental policies as a result of pressure from their children or spouse, in turn influenced by the latter's friends. While few of us are personally acquainted with Bill Gates or George Bush, a surprising number of us discover that our own children's classmates and our friends include children, friends, and relatives of influential people, who may be sensitive to how they are viewed by their children, friends, and relatives. An example is that pressure from his sisters may have strengthened President Joaquín Balaguer's concern for the Dominican Republic's environment. The 2000 U.S. presidential election was actually decided by a single vote in the U.S. Supreme Court's 5-to-4 decision on the Florida vote challenge, but all nine Supreme Court justices had children, spouses, relatives, or friends who helped form their outlook.

Those of us who are religious can further multiply our power by developing support within our church, synagogue, or mosque. It was churches that led the civil rights movement, and some religious leaders have also been outspoken on the environment, but not many so far. Yet there is much potential for building religious support, because people more readily follow the suggestions of their religious leaders than the suggestions of historians and scientists, and because there are strong religious reasons to take the environment seriously. Members of congregations can remind fellow members and their leaders (their priests, ministers, rabbis, etc.) of the sanctity of the created order, of biblical metaphors for keeping Nature fertile and productive, and of the implications of the concept of stewardship that all religions acknowledge.

An individual who wants to benefit directly from his or her actions can consider investing time and effort in improving one's own local environment. The example most familiar to me from firsthand experience at my family's summer vacation site in Montana's Bitterroot Valley is the Teller Wildlife Refuge, a small private non-profit organization devoted to habitat preservation and restoration along the Bitterroot River. While the organization's founder, Otto Teller, was rich, his friends who sensitized him to environmental issues were not rich, nor are most of the people who volunteer to help the Teller Refuge today. As a benefit to themselves (actually, to anyone living in or visiting the Bitterroot Valley), they continue to enjoy gorgeous scenery and good fishing, which would otherwise by now have been eliminated for land development. Such examples can be multiplied indefinitely: almost every local area has its own neighborhood group, landowners' association, or other such organizations.

Working to fix your local environment has another benefit besides making your own life more pleasant. It also sets an example to others, both in your own country and overseas. Local environmental organizations tend to be in frequent contact with each other, exchanging ideas and drawing inspiration. When I was scheduling interviews with Montana residents associated with the Teller Wildlife Refuge and the Blackfoot Initiative, one of the constraints on their schedules arose from trips that they were making to advise other such local initiatives in Montana and neighboring states. Also, when Americans tell people in China or other countries what the Chinese should (in the opinion of the Americans) be doing for the good of themselves and the rest of the world, our message tends to fall on unreceptive ears because of our own well-known environmental misdeeds. We would be more effective in persuading people overseas to adopt environmental policies good for the rest of humanity (including for us) if we ourselves were seen to be pursuing such policies in more cases.

Finally, any of you who have some discretionary money can multiply your impact by making a donation to an organization promoting policies of your choice. There is an enormous range of organizations to fit anyone's interests: Ducks Unlimited for those interested in ducks, Trout Unlimited for those into fishing, Zero Population Growth for those concerned with population problems, Seacology for those interested in islands, and so on. All such environmental organizations operate on low budgets, and many operate cost-effectively, so that small additional sums of money make big differences. That's true even of the largest and richest environmental organizations. For example, World Wildlife Fund is one of the three largest and best-funded environmental organizations operating around the world, and it is active in more countries than any other. The annual budget of WWF's largest affiliate, its U.S. branch, averages about $100 million per year, which sounds like a lot of money—until one realizes that that money has to fund its programs in over 100 countries, covering all plant and animal species and all marine and terrestrial habitats. That budget also has to cover not only mega-scale projects (such as a $400-million, 10-year program to triple the area of habitat protected in the Amazon Basin), but also a multitude of small-scale projects on individual species. Lest you think that your small donation is meaningless to such a big organization, consider that a gift of just a few hundred dollars suffices to support a trained park ranger, outfitted with global positioning software, to survey Congo Basin primate populations whose conservation status would otherwise be unknown. Consider also that some environmental organizations are highly leveraged and use private gifts to attract further funds from the World Bank, governments, and aid agencies on a dollar-for-dollar basis. For instance, WWF's Amazon Basin project is leveraged by a factor of more than 6-to-1, so that your $300 gift actually ends up putting almost $2,000 into the project.

Of course, I mention these numbers for WWF merely because it's the organization with whose budget I happen to be most familiar, and not in order to recommend it over many other equally worthy environmental organizations with different goals. Such examples of how efforts by individuals make a difference can be multiplied indefinitely.

INDEX

ILLUSTRATION CREDITS